Visual Basic And Databases

A Computer Programming Tutorial

Visual Studio 2019 Edition

16th Edition

By
Philip Conrod & Lou Tylee

©2019 Kidware Software LLC

PO Box 701
Maple Valley, WA 98038
http://www.kidwaresoftware.com

Copyright © 2019 Kidware Software LLC.   All rights reserved

Kidware Software LLC
PO Box 701
Maple Valley, Washington 98038
1.425.413.1185
www.kidwaresoftware.com

All Rights Reserved. No part of the contents of this book may be reproduced or transmitted in any form or by any means without the written permission of the publisher.

Printed in the United States of America

ISBN-13: 978-1-951077-13-6 (Electronic Edition)
ISBN-13: 978-1-951077-12-9 (Printed Edition)

Cover Design by Neil Sauvageau
Cover Image by Enot Poloskun

This copy of "Visual Basic and Databases" and the associated software is licensed to a single user. Copies of the course are not to be distributed or provided to any other user. Multiple copy licenses are available for educational institutions. Please contact Kidware Software for school site license information.

This guide was developed for the course, "Visual Basic and Databases," produced by Kidware Software, Maple Valley, Washington. It is not intended to be a complete reference to the Visual Basic language. Please consult the Microsoft website for detailed reference information.

This guide refers to several software and hardware products by their trade names. These references are for informational purposes only and all trademarks are the property of their respective companies and owners. Microsoft, Visual Studio, Small Basic, Visual Basic, Visual J#, and Visual C#, IntelliSense, Word, Excel, MSDN, and Windows are all trademark products of the Microsoft Corporation.   Java is a trademark product of the Oracle Corporation.

The example companies, organizations, products, domain names, e-mail addresses, logos, people, places, and events depicted are fictitious. No association with any real company, organization, product, domain name, e-mail address, logo, person, place, or event is intended or should be inferred.

This book expresses the author's views and opinions. The information in this book is distributed on an "as is" basis, without and expresses, statutory, or implied warranties.

Neither the author(s) nor Kidware Software LLC shall have any liability to any person or entity with respect to any loss nor damage caused or alleged to be caused directly or indirectly by the information contained in this book.

About The Authors

Philip Conrod has authored, co-authored and edited over two dozen computer programming books over the past thirty years. Philip holds a Bachelor's Degree in Computer Information Systems and a Master's certificate in the Essentials of Business Development from Regis University. Philip has served in various Information Technology leadership roles in companies like Sundstrand Aerospace, Safeco Insurance, FamilyLife, Kenworth Truck Company, and PACCAR. Philip last served as the Chief Information Officer (CIO) for Darigold for over a decade before returning to teaching and writing full-time. Today, Philip serves as the President & Publisher of Kidware Software LLC which is based in Maple Valley, Washington.

Lou Tylee holds BS and MS degrees in Mechanical Engineering and a PhD in Electrical Engineering. Lou has been programming computers since 1969 when he took his first Fortran course in college. He has written software to control suspensions for high speed ground vehicles, monitor nuclear power plants, lower noise levels in commercial jetliners, compute takeoff speeds for jetliners, locate and identify air and ground traffic and to let kids count bunnies, learn how to spell and do math problems. He has written several on-line texts teaching Visual Basic, Visual C# and Java to thousands of people. He taught computer programming courses for over 15 years at the University of Washington and currently teaches math and engineering courses at the Oregon Institute of Technology. Lou also works as a research engineer at a major Seattle aerospace firm. He is the proud father of five children, has six grandchildren and is married to an amazing woman. Lou and his family live in Seattle, Washington.

Acknowledgements

I want to thank my three wonderful daughters - Stephanie, Jessica and Chloe, who helped with various aspects of the book publishing process including software testing, book editing, creative design and many other more tedious tasks like finding errors and typos. I could not have accomplished this without all your hard work, love and support. I want to also thank my best friend Jesus, who has always been there by my side giving me wisdom and guidance. Without you, this book would have never been printed or published.

I also want to thank my multi-talented co-author, Lou Tylee, for doing all the real hard work necessary to develop, test, debug, and keep current all the 'beginner-friendly' applications, games and base tutorial text found in this book. Lou has tirelessly poured his heart and soul into so many previous versions of this tutorial and there are so many beginners who have benefited from his work over the years. Lou is by far one of the best application developers and tutorial writers I have ever worked with. Thank you Lou for collaborating with me on this book project.

Praise for Previous Editions of this Textbook

Philip Conrod & Lou Tylee's programming and database books for Visual Basic and C# are exceptional. The content starts with the basics and graduates in small and clear but functional increments. It makes database programming much easier to teach and learn. These books are much better and far less expensive than other books. It is with absolute confidence that I recommend Mr. Conrod's Visual Basic and C# Database programming books for 2015. - David Taylor, The VB Professor

"As someone who has always struggled trying to use Visual Basic with databases - this book is my savior! I LOVE the fact that it gives COMPLETE code examples for both Access and Sequel Server. I am also trying to learn how to build good databases and am currently using Access 2013 as my tool, so the Access examples are a huge plus for me. Visual Studio Data Wizard? Never again! You will never learn how to program with databases, strictly relying on the wizard to do the work for you. This is where I went completely wrong - looking for the easy way. Fortunately, the authors explain everything you need to know to do the coding yourself - and everything is explained at a level that is extremely easy to understand. Queries, reporting, database management, design, distribution, and more - it's ALL there! So, as a beginner programmer who could never grasp the fundamentals to actually writing the code for database programming, I can honestly say that, for me, this book was worth every penny!" - Paul

"Visual Basic and Databases was well organized and the various projects that I had to create in order to learn the material was exhaustive and intensive (which is good!). The course was fun, entertaining and rewarding." - Ray Torres, Developer, Miami, FL

"The Visual Basic & Databases Tutorial was the best tutorial and samples I found to use Visual Basic". - Lester Torres Rivera, Teacher, Puerto Rico, USA

"I really enjoyed the Visual Basic & Databases tutorial, the database connection examples really helped me." - Bruce Chin, Amateur Developer, Toronto, Ontario

"I have to congratulate you on your excellent and very professionally written tutorial. It is very clear, concise and to the point. Well done – it is money well spent." - TM, Brisbane, Australia.

"Your notes have helped me tremendously in figuring out Visual Basic 2005. I was able to find a lot of the information that I wasn't able to find elsewhere. I had spent hours searching for information, trying something out, cussing when it didn't work, and then repeating the cycle. That alone was worth the price of the course." - TS, Bloomington, Illinois.

"Working with my daughter, she is having fun grasping this stuff. Your documents are written in plain speak and are straightforward. She is an accelerated reader and I have been translating the technical stuff. Kids are sponges." - PT, Orland Park, Illinois.

"There are many tutorials on the internet, but those by KidwareSoftware.com are easy to follow. There is no confusing technobabble, but clear explanations. These are high quality and you come away with new skills and better understanding." - RM, Espanola, New Mexico.

"I really love these courses. They keep me going when I'm housebound." - CO, London, England.

"I want to commend you on the quality of these materials. I have recommended the course to several of my friends." - SM, Reno, Nevada.

"I have both your VB6 and VB6 database courses and they have both been excellent tools for learning." - GO, Otaki, New Zealand.

"I thought your VISUAL BASIC AND DATABASES was great. I've learned more from your book than my college text book. Clear, concise and it works!" - MC, Tampa, Florida.

"After buying over 15 books, I think this is probably the best. It is a fabulous product, and I have referred back to it even after studying the "deeper" texts I've purchased." - JM, Oradell, New Jersey.

"I wish to thank you for providing a straight forward guide to what can be a complex subject." - IS, Somersby, Australia.

"I really appreciate your wonderful resource. You are a fantastic company." - DW, Albany, New York.

"I love this course. The way you go about teaching is great." - RW, Prescott Valley, Arizona.

"Your notes and lessons are more meaningful than the professional looking books by Microsoft experts." - BT, Gladstone, Missouri.

"I am writing to inform you that not only was the tutorial most satisfactory, but helped me finish my project at work." - SJ, Tamworth, United Kingdom.

"May I thank you for your great work in this course. I am enjoying reading it." - ML, Cairo, Egypt.

"Your tutorial VISUAL BASIC AND DATABASES is quite good. It's to the point and the no-nonsense explanations are a breath of fresh air. Thank you! " - KM, Connellsville, Pennsylvania.

"I have learned more in the last 5 days from your tutorial than reading other books for a month. It is well-written and easy to follow. " - WZ, Toronto, Ontario, Canada.

"I am pleased to find a product that does not have errors in it like other books I have used. You should publish it as a book. " - JR, Oamaru, New Zealand.

"After having purchased several volumes of training materials, I downloaded your VISUAL BASIC AND DATABASES and have learned more than from all the others, at a fraction of the cost. " - DG, Morris, Oklahoma.

"It is very clear and the style is learner-centered. It is very kind to the reader." - JM, Roxas City, Philipines.

"The most intelligently written training I've seen. Concise with an element of common sense." - JR, La Grange Park, Illinois.

"VISUAL BASIC AND DATABASES is exactly what I was looking for and provided me with a thorough grounding in database applications." - AR, New York, New York.

"This is an excellent tutorial on the subject of databases, probably the best." - WB, Midland, Texas.

"I learned more in two hours with VISUAL BASIC AND DATABASES than with any of the several hundreds of dollars worth of books I have purchased. " - TB, Southaven, Mississippi.

"I was impressed by the clarity, simplicity and fluency with which you are able to approach so delicate topic. " - OB, Havana, Cuba.

"VISUAL BASIC AND DATABASES is more thorough and understandable than the other books. We will use this as a part of our curriculum. " - DT, Newtown, Connecticut.

"Your book VISUAL BASIC AND DATABASES is great! " - VV, Buenos Aires, Argentina.

"Many thanks for your VISUAL BASIC AND DATABASES. I love it! " - SK, Melbourne, Australia.

"I've begun VISUAL BASIC AND DATABASES and just want to say - Nice Job! " - DR, Kenosha, Wisconsin.

"Excellent work! Your presentation is one of the best I have seen. I loved reading your tutorial. " - RV, Brussels, Belgium.

"VISUAL BASIC AND DATABASES is very good!" - MG, London, England.

"At last - someone has explained database management in understandable terms. Thanks for a great piece of work!" - GS, Seattle, Washington.

"I just want to thank you for the many tutorials that I have ordered from your company over the past decade. Your tutorials have been instrumental in allowing me, a secondary school teacher in Ontario, to learn what I need to know in order to conduct my own High School Computer Science Classes in Visual Basic and Visual C#. I thank you, and urge you to keep up the excellent work. It has been instrumental in helping me learn and grow as a teacher." - Alan Payne, TA, Blakelock High School, Oakville, ON

Table of Contents

Course Description xv
Course Prerequisites xv
How To Take the Course xv
Installing and Using the Downloadable Solution Files xvi
Installing Visual Basic and Databases xvi
System Requirements xvii
A Note on Visual Basic Naming Conventions xviii
Foreword by David B. Taylor, Former College Professor & Dept. Chair ... xxi

1. Introducing Visual Basic and Databases

Preview 1-1
Course Objectives 1-2
Course Requirements 1-3
What is a Database? 1-4
Where Does Visual Basic Fit In? 1-6
Building a Visual Basic Application 1-8
    Structure of a Visual Basic Application 1-9
    Steps in Developing Application 1-10
    Drawing the User Interface and Setting Properties 1-11
    Setting Properties of Controls at Design Time 1-17
    Setting Properties at Run-Time 1-19
    How Names are Used in Object Events 1-20
Writing Code 1-21
    Review of Variables 1-22
    Visual Basic Data Types 1-23
    Variable Declaration 1-24
Example 1-1. Mailing List Application 1-27
Summary 1-36

2. Introduction to Databases

Review and Preview.. 2-1
Database Structure and Terminology 2-2
Relational Databases... 2-4
Using SQL Server Databases.. 2-6
Sample Relational Database 2-7
Sample Database Structure 2-11
Virtual Database Tables 2-13
Creating a Database... 2-16
Summary... 2-17

3. Database Connection

Review and Preview.. 3-1
Data Object Preview 3-2
Connection Object 3-3
Connection Object – Access Database 3-4
Access Databases and 64 Bit Operating Systems 3-5
Connection Object – SQL Server Database 3-7
Example 3-1. Accessing the Books Database 3-8
Command Object 3-14
Command Object – Access Database... 3-15
Command Object – SQL Server Database...................................... 3-15
Example 3-1 (Command Object). Books Database 3-16
DataAdapter Object... 3-19
DataAdapter Object – Access Database 3-20
DataAdapter Object – SQL Server Database 3-21
DataSet Object... 3-22
DataTable Object... 3-23
DataRow Object 3-24
Example 3-1 (Data Table). Books Database.................................. 3-25
Data Bound Controls 3-28
Example 3-1 (Data Binding). Books Database 3-30
CurrencyManager Object 3-36
Example 3-1 (Final Version). Books Database 3-38
Data Wizards 3-45
Example 3-2 (Access Database). Books Database with Wizards........... 3-46
Example 3-2 (SQL Server Database). Books Database with Wizards 3-58
Summary 3-72
Example 3-3. Northwinds Trader Database 3-73

4. Database Queries with SQL

Review and Preview	4-1
SQL Background	4-2
Basics of SQL	4-3
Where Does SQL Fit In Visual Basic?	4-5
Example 4-1. SQL Tester	4-6
SELECT/FROM SQL Statement	4-14
ORDER BY Clause	4-18
WHERE Clause	4-20
Single Table WHERE Clause	4-21
Multiple Table WHERE Clause	4-27
INNER JOIN Clause	4-32
OUTER JOIN Clause	4-36
Functions with SQL (Access Database)	4-38
Functions with SQL (SQL Server Database)	4-40
SQL Aggregate Functions	4-42
SQL Construction Tools	4-45
SQL Statements with Access	4-46
SQL Statements with the Data Wizard	4-48
Building SQL Commands in Code	4-55
Example 4-2. Searching the Books Database	4-56
Summary	4-66
Example 4-3. Northwind Traders Database	4-67

5. Visual Basic Interface Design

Review and Preview 5-1
Interface Design Philosophy 5-2
Example 5-1. Mailing List Revisited 5-4
Visual Basic Standard Controls 5-6
    Form Control 5-7
    Button Control 5-9
    Label Control 5-10
    TextBox Control 5-12
    CheckBox Control 5-14
    RadioButton Control 5-16
    GroupBox Control 5-18
    Panel Control 5-19
    PictureBox Control 5-20
Example 5-2. Authors Table Input Form 5-21
MessageBox Object 5-29
Example 5-3. Authors Table Input Form (Message Box) 5-34
Application State 5-36
Example 5-4. Authors Table Input Form (Application State) 5-38
Entry Validation 5-43
Key Trapping 5-44
Example 5-5. Authors Table Input Form (Entry Validation) 5-46
Input Validation 5-47
Example 5-6. Authors Table Input Form (Input Validation) 5-49
Error Trapping and Handling 5-53
Example 5-7. Authors Table Input Form (Error Trapping) 5-56
On-Line Help Systems 5-61
    Creating a Help File 5-63
    Starting the HTML Help Workshop 5-64
    Creating Topic Files 5-66
    Creating Table of Contents File 5-69
    Compiling the Help File 5-74
HelpProvider Control 5-79
Example 5-8. Authors Table Input Form (On-Line Help) 5-81
Application Testing 5-85
Other Controls 5-86
    MaskedTextBox Control 5-87
    NumericUpDown Control 5-89
    TabControl Control 5-91
    Toolstrip (Toolbar) Control 5-94
    ListBox Control 5-98
    ComboBox Control 5-102
    DataGridView Control 5-103
    MonthCalendar Control 5-105
    DateTimePicker Control 5-107

OpenFileDialog Control 5-108
SaveFileDialog Control 5-111
Summary 5-114
Example 5-9. Publisher Table Input Form 5-115
Build Interface 5-116
Add Message Box(es) 5-125
Code Application State 5-126
Perform Entry Validation 5-129
Perform Input Validation 5-130
Add Error Trapping and Handling 5-131
Add On-Line Help System 5-132
Application Testing... 5-135

6. Database Management

Review and Preview	6-1
Database Management Tasks	6-2
Editing Database Records	6-3
Phone Contact Database	6-5
Example 6-1. Editing Database Records	6-6
Adding Database Records	6-22
Example 6-2. Adding Database Records	6-24
Deleting Database Records	6-30
Example 6-3. Deleting Database Records	6-31
Finding Records in a Database	6-33
Example 6-4. Finding Database Records	6-36
Modifying Records in Code	6-37
Example 6-5. Modifying Records in Code	6-39
Stopping a Database Application	6-41
Example 6-6. Stopping a Database Application	6-43
Example 6-7. Authors Table Input Form	6-47
Additional Navigation Capabilities	6-48
Editing Records	6-50
Adding Records	6-53
Deleting Records	6-55
Stopping the Application	6-57
Example 6-8. Publishers Table Input Form	6-59
Additional Navigation Capabilities	6-60
Editing Records	6-63
Adding Records	6-66
Deleting Records	6-68
Stopping the Application	6-70
Multiple Table Database Management	6-72
Database Keys	6-73
Database Modifications	6-74
Final Application	6-75
Example 6-9. Books Database Management System	6-76
Basic Book Titles Input Form	6-77
Finding Records	6-93
Navigation Information	6-97
Adding Publisher Name	6-98
Adding Publisher Editing	6-108
Modify Publishers Input Form	6-113
Modify Authors Input Form	6-118
Adding Author Names	6-123
Example 6-10. Database Detective – Author Search	6-124
Viewing Author Selections	6-129
Viewing Author Names	6-140
Saving Author Names	6-145

    Adding Author Editing..6-149
    Input Control Navigation 6-153
    Entry and Input Validation 6-156
    Titles Form On-Line Help..6-163
Summary..6-167

7. Database Reports

Review and Preview 7-1
PrintDocument Object 7-2
Printing Document Pages 7-5
Pen Object 7-7
Brush Object 7-8
Graphics Methods 7-9
PageSetupDialog Control 7-12
PrintDialog Control 7-15
PrintPreviewDialog Control 7-17
PrintDocument Object with Databases 7-19
Example 7-1. Database Report 7-21
Example 7-2. Titles Listing 7-28
Example 7-3. Book Publishers Listing 7-34
    User Interface 7-35
    Database Connection and Printing 7-38
Other Approaches to Database Reports 7-47
Summary 7-48

8. Distributing a Database Application

Review and Preview.. 8-1
Accessing Database Files in Code 8-2
Database File in Application Path... 8-3
Example 8-1. Opening Database Files in Application Directory............ 8-4
Database File Location with OpenFile Dialog Control...................... 8-11
Example 8-2. Opening Database Files with OpenFile Dialog Control 8-13
Distribution of a Visual Basic Database Application 8-20
Applications Icons 8-24
Custom Icons 8-26
Example 8-3. Visual Basic Setup Wizard 8-29
    Step 1. Welcome to the Setup Project Wizard.......................... 8-33
    Step 2. Choose a project type... 8-34
    Step 3. Choose project outputs to include 8-35
    Step 4. Choose files to include 8-37
    Step 5. Create project.. 8-38
Building the Setup Program... 8-42
Installing a Visual Basic Application 8-43
Summary.. 8-45

9. Database Design Considerations

Review and Preview... 9-1
Database Design 9-2
Database Modeling 9-3
Information Requirements 9-4
Table Requirements.. 9-6
Field Requirements... 9-10
Field Types 9-12
Null Values... 9-14
Database Design Implementation 9-15
Building Databases with Microsoft Access 9-16
Example 9-1. KWSALES Database with Microsoft Access................. 9-17
    Getting Started 9-18
    Customers Table... 9-20
    Orders Table 9-24
    Purchases Table 9-25
    Products Table 9-27
    Define Relationships 9-28
Building SQL Server Databases with Server Explorer 9-31
Example 9-2. KWSALES Database with Server Explorer 9-32
    Getting Started 9-33
    Customers Table... 9-35
    Orders Table 9-41
    Purchases Table 9-43
    Products Table 9-45
    Define Relationships 9-47
Building Access Databases with ADOX Objects................................ 9-51
Example 9-3. KWSALES Access Database with ADOX 9-52
    Adding Reference to ADOX Library.. 9-53
    Create a Database.. 9-54
    Create a Table 9-57
    Add Fields to Table.. 9-59
    Define Table Primary Key 9-63
    Define Table Indexes... 9-65
    Define Table Relationships... 9-70
Example 9-4. SQL Server Database with Visual Basic 9-73
Design Refinement 9-78
Summary 9-79

10. Sample Database Projects

Review and Preview 10-1
Overview of Database Projects 10-2
Example 10-1. Sales Order Form Project 10-3
    Preliminaries 10-4
    Order Information 10-5
    Existing Customer Information 10-11
    Adding a New Customer 10-21
    Product Selection 10-34
    Submitting an Order 10-45
    Printing an Invoice 10-54
    Suggested Improvements 10-57
Example 10-2. Home Inventory Project 10-58
    Home Inventory Database 10-59
    Preliminaries 10-62
    Home Inventory Interface 10-63
    Database Connection 10-67
    Display Photo 10-72
    Database Navigation 10-74
    Editing Records 10-77
    Load Photo 10-82
    Adding Records 10-85
    Deleting Records 10-91
    Entry Validation 10-93
    Input Validation 10-97
    Inventory Report 10-99
    Stopping the Application 10-105
    Suggested Improvements 10-109
Example 10-3. Weather Monitor Project 10-110
    Weather Monitor Interface 10-111
    Record Weather Data Tab 10-113
    Weather Monitor Database (Access) 10-117
    Weather Monitor Database (SQL Server) 10-122
    Adding Date Values and Editing Features 10-125
    Opening Database Files 10-135
    Date Display Coordination 10-137
    View Temperature Data Tab 10-139
    Temperature Summary Statistics 10-145
    Temperature Plot 10-151
    View Precipitation Data Tab 10-153
    Precipitation Summary Statistics 10-157
    Precipitation Plot 10-161
    Weather Monitor Printed Reports 10-163
    Weather Data Report 10-165
    Temperature Data Report 10-168

Contents

    Precipitation Data Report 10-170
    Weather Monitor Help System 10-172
    Weather Monitor Icon 10-175
    Weather Monitor Distribution Package 10-176
    Suggested Improvements 10-177
Summary 10-178

11. Other Database Topics

Review and Preview 11-1
Exporting Database Data 11-2
    Opening a Sequential File for Output 11-3
    Writing Data to a Sequential File 11-4
    Saving a Sequential File 11-5
    Example 11-1. Exporting Database Data 11-6
Importing Database Data 11-10
    Opening a Sequential File for Input 11-11
    Reading Data from a Sequential File 11-12
    Closing a Sequential File 11-14
    Example 11-2. Importing Database Data 11-15
Other Database Types 11-21
    ODBC Data Objects 11-22
    Oracle Data Objects 11-23
Multi-User Considerations 11-24
Database Web Applications 11-25
Starting a New Web Application 11-26
Web Form Controls 11-31
Building a Web Application 11-38
Example 11-3. Viewing Weather Data 11-40
Summary 11-45
Example 11-4. The Last Database Project 11-46

Contents

Course Description:

Visual Basic and Databases is a tutorial that provides a detailed introduction to using Visual Basic for accessing and maintaining databases. Topics covered include: database structure, database design, Visual Basic project building, ADO .NET data objects, data bound controls, proper interface design, structured query language (SQL), and database reports.

Visual Basic and Databases is presented using a combination of over 850 pages of course notes and actual Visual Basic examples. No previous experience working with databases is presumed. It is assumed, however, that users of the course are familiar with the Visual Basic environment and the steps involved in building a Visual Basic application.

Course Prerequisites:

To grasp the concepts presented in ***Visual Basic and Databases***, you should possess a working knowledge of Windows 10. No previous experience working with databases is presumed. It is assumed, however, that users of the course are familiar with the Visual Basic environment and the steps involved in building a Visual Basic application (such background can be gained from our ***Learn Visual Basic*** course). You will also need the ability to view and print documents saved in Adobe Acrobat format. Finally, and most obvious, you need to have Microsoft Visual Studio Community Edition (contains Visual Basic). This is a download available free of charge from Microsoft.

https://www.visualstudio.com/free-developer-offers/

How To Take the Course:

Visual Basic and Databases is a self-paced course. Each chapter will require a different amount of time. The suggested approach is to decide how much time you can spend each week working through the notes. Print out the notes one chapter at a time. Then, work through the notes at your own pace. Try to do each example as it is encountered in the notes. Work through the projects. If you need any help, all completed projects are included in the **Access** and **SQL Server** folders.

Installing and Using the Downloadable Solution Files

If you purchased this directly from our website you received an email with a special and individualized internet download link where you could download the compressed Program Solution Files. If you purchased this book through a 3rd Party Book Store like Amazon.com, the solutions files for this tutorial are included in a compressed ZIP file that is available for download directly from our website (after registration) at:

http://www.kidwaresoftware.com/vbdb2019-solutions.htm

Complete the online web form at the webpage above with your name, shipping address, email address, the exact title of this book, date of purchase, online or physical store name, and your order confirmation number from that store. We also ask you to include the last 4 digits of your credit card so we can match it to the credit card that was used to purchase this tutorial. After we receive all this information, we will email you a download link for the Source Code Solution Files associated with this book.

Warning: If you purchased this book "used" or "second hand" you are not licensed or entitled to download the Program Solution Files. However, you can purchase the Digital Download Version of this book at a highly discounted price which allows you access to the digital source code solutions files required for completing this tutorial.

Installing Visual Basic and Databases:

The course notes and code for Visual Basic and Databases are included in one single ZIP file. Use your favorite 'unzipping' application to write all files to your computer. The course is included in the folder entitled VBDB. This folder contains five other folders: Notes, General, Access, SQL Server, and Databases (includes all needed databases).

The **General** folder contains information not dependent on the particular database type used. The **Access** folder includes all the Visual Basic projects developed during the course using Access databases. The **SQL Server** folder includes the same projects developed using SQL Server databases. Each of these folders is further divided into **Class** folders. Each class folder contains the **Visual Basic and Database** project folders. As an example, to open the Access project named Example 3-1 discussed in Class 3, you would go to this directory:

C:\VBDB\Access\Class 3\Example 3-1

System Requirements

Visual Studio 2019 will install and run on the following operating systems:

- Windows 10 version 1507 or higher: Home, Professional, Education, and Enterprise (LTSB is not supported)
- Windows Server 2016: Standard and Datacenter
- Windows 8.1 (with Update 2919355): Basic, Professional, and Enterprise
- Windows Server 2012 R2 (with Update 2919355): Essentials, Standard, Datacenter
- Windows 7 SP1 (with latest Windows Updates): Home Premium, Professional, Enterprise, Ultimate

Hardware

- 1.8 GHz or faster processor. Dual-core or better recommended
- 2 GB of RAM; 4 GB of RAM recommended (2.5 GB minimum if running on a virtual machine)
- Hard disk space: 1GB to 40GB, depending on features installed
- Video card that supports a minimum display resolution of 720p (1280 by 720); Visual Studio will work best at a resolution of WXGA (1366 by 768) or higher

A Note on Visual Basic Naming Conventions

Controls

The accepted standard for naming controls is to assign a three letter (lower case) prefix (identifying the type of control) followed by a descriptive name you assign. Some of the prefixes are:

Control	Prefix	Example
Form	frm	frmWatch
Button	btn	btnExit, btnStart
Label	lbl	lblStart, lblEnd
Text Box	txt	txtTime, txtName
Menu	mnu	mnuExit, mnuSave
Check Box	chk	chkChoice

Event Procedures

Once a control is named, the standard for naming an event procedure associated with a control is

Private Sub ControlName_Event (**Arguments**) **Handles** ControlName.Event
    .
    .
End Sub

So, for a button control name **btnExample**, the event procedure for the **Click** event would be named **btnExample_Click**. And, since the earliest days of Visual Studio, if you double-click on a button control named **btnExample**, the event procedure appearing in the code window was:

```
Private Sub btnExample_Click(sender As Object, e As
EventArgs) Handles btnExample.Click

End Sub
```

This has changed with Visual Studio 2019.

In Visual Studio 2019, if you double-click on a button control named **btnExample**, the event procedure appearing in the code window is:

```
Private Sub BtnExample_Click(sender As Object, e As
EventArgs) Handles btnExample.Click

End Sub
```

Note that the first letter of the control name is automatically capitalized. The folks at Microsoft have decided that the first letter of every procedure in Visual Basic should be upper case (and there doesn't appear to be any way to turn off this "feature"). This creates a mismatch between the assigned control name (**btnExample**) and the name used in the event procedure (**BtnExample**). For our Visual Basic tutorials, we needed to decide what to do about this new convention.

Our Naming Conventions

The mismatch between control name and event procedure name would quickly go away if we simply choose to apply a new control naming convention where the first letter of every control name is an upper case letter. We did not take this route – it would require a massive paradigm shift. And, it would require extensive rewriting of all legacy code written using the standard convention. We decided to continue use of the time-tested control naming convention, a three letter lower case prefix, followed by a describing name with mixed upper and lower case letters. This standard has been around forever and will probably remain so. With this decision, we had to choose what to do about event procedure names.

First, realize that the name of the event procedure associated with a control is completely arbitrary. You can give the procedure any name you want as long as it's properly connected to the correct event procedure using the Visual Studio properties window. So, we could continue to use our old standard of naming event procedures, starting with a lower case letter. For a button control named **btnExample**, the **Click** event procedure would be

```
Private Sub btnExample_Click(sender As Object, e As
EventArgs) Handles btnExample.Click

End Sub
```

Such a convention will work in Visual Studio 2019, but comes with problems. The first problem in using the 'old standard' is that Visual Studio will flag each so named event procedure with an error message saying: 'Naming rule violation: These words must begin with upper case characters: btnExample_Click'. Again, the code will still work, but there will be all these annoying messages.

The second problem in using the 'old standard' in Visual Studio 2019 is that when building a project, if you double-click on a control to establish an event procedure, the first letter will be automatically capitalized. Then, you have to remember to change the case of that letter for every event procedure established. This would be a headache.

We have decided to live with this new naming convention where the first letter of every event procedure is capitalized, realizing there is a mismatch between the control names and associated event procedures. So, in our tutorials, when we refer to the **Click** event procedure for a control named **btnExample**, that procedure's name in code will be **BtnExample_Click**. We recognize this is a change for programmers, but hopefully is something you can get used to. In our experience, it just took a few examples for the new convention to seem 'normal'.

Foreword By David B. Taylor, Former College Professor & Department Chair

Most computer programs in use today require some interaction with information stored in a database so learning to program with databases increases the marketability of a developer exponentially.

This book is structured as a self-study guide, but it is easily adapted to classroom lectures and discussion. The content of the book is excellent. It starts with the basics and graduates in small and clear but functional increments. It makes database programming much easier to teach and learn.

"Visual Basic and Databases" provides a complete, thorough, and easy to understand explanation of database program development from two people who came up through the ranks as software developers. Their examples reflect real-world applications that will help new developers quickly master database software development. Students can easily convert and expand the examples for their own applications. For example, the Books Database in Chapter 4 could easily be modified to search a similar database of cars, bikes, or passwords, etc. Examples are created using Microsoft's Access database management system (DBMS) and SQL Server. This makes it easy for the student to compare their capabilities and syntax.

I have sincerely enjoyed reading and working through the examples in, "Visual Basic and Databases". The examples are clear and easy to follow. If I had any questions or if my code did not work, I could simply peek at the author's completed code examples to get back on track.

Throughout the book the authors bring attention to the importance of user interface (UI) design. This is more important than may be obvious at first but developers tend to focus on the code and forget about the UI but eventually someone needs to use this program so a functional and attractive presentation of the program can be the difference between success and failure of the end product.

A major plus for this text is how the authors include additional and very useful parallel topics such as the On-Line Help system created in HTML in Chapter 5 and the Graphics Methods in Chapter 7. The book is not about HTML or graphics but the coincidental inclusion gives the student a valuable glimpse at other topics of importance. These are just two examples that didn't have to be included but they are added as part of other chapters and will ultimately benefit the student. This took a lot of forethought by the authors and demonstrates the real value of the book.

As a programmer, a long-time college professor, and as the former head of the Computer, Engineering, and Business Department, I have reviewed countless programming books for most of the popular programming languages. "Visual Basic and Databases" by Conrod and Tylee is my favorite text for helping developers make the leap into the rewarding field of database development. I highly recommend this book for anyone who is serious about becoming a professional software developer/engineer.

David B. Taylor, B.S.E.T., M.A.Ed., Ed.S.
Former Professor and Department Chair
Computer, Engineering, and Business
Seminole State College
Sanford, Florida

1

Introducing Visual Basic and Databases

Preview

In this first chapter, we will do a quick overview of what the course entails. We will discuss what you need to complete the course.

We'll take a brief look at what databases are, where they are used, and how Visual Basic is used with databases. And, we'll review the Visual Basic development environment and the steps followed to build an application in Visual Basic.

Course Objectives

⇒ Understand the benefits of using Microsoft Visual Basic to build a 'front-end' interface as a database programming tool
⇒ Learn database structure, terminology, and proper database design
⇒ Learn how to connect to a database using Visual Basic data objects
⇒ Learn the use of Visual Basic data bound controls
⇒ Learn to make database queries using SQL (structured query language)
⇒ Understand proper database search techniques
⇒ Learn how to ADOX (Active Data Object Extended) technology to create a database
⇒ Learn database management techniques
⇒ Learn to create and produce database reports
⇒ Learn how to distribute a Visual Basic database application
⇒ Understand connection to different types of databases and remote databases
⇒ Introduce other advanced database concepts

Course Requirements

An obvious requirement is a Windows-based computer with Windows 10 installed, as well as Visual Studio Community Edition. The student should be familiar with the basics of using the Windows operating system.

No knowledge of databases or how to work with databases is presumed. Adequate introductory material is presented. Even if you've worked with databases before, it is suggested you read through this introductory information to become acquainted with the nomenclature used by the author for databases and their component parts.

This course does **not** teach you how to build a Visual Basic application. It is assumed that the reader has a basic understanding of the Visual Basic development environment and knows the steps involved in building a Visual Basic application. You should feel quite comfortable with building the example application at the end of this first chapter. If not, our company, KIDware, offers several tutorials that teach this information. Please visit our web site or contact us for more information.

What is a Database?

A **database** is a collection of **information**. This information is stored in a very structured manner. By exploiting this known structure, we can access and modify the information quickly and correctly.

In this information age, databases are everywhere:

- ⇒ When you go to the library and look up a book on their computer, you are accessing the library's book **database**.
- ⇒ When you go on-line and purchase some product, you are accessing the web merchant's product **database**.
- ⇒ Your friendly bank keeps all your financial records on their **database**. When you receive your monthly statement, the bank generates a **database report**.
- ⇒ When you call to make a doctor appointment, the receptionist looks into their **database** for available times.
- ⇒ When you go to your car dealer for repairs, the technician calls up your past work record on the garage **database**.
- ⇒ At the grocery store, when the checker scans each product, the price is found in the store's **database**, where inventory control is also performed.
- ⇒ When you are watching a baseball game on television and the announcer tells you that "the batter is hitting .328 against left-handed pitchers whose mother was born in Kentucky on a Tuesday morning," that useless information is pulled from the team's **database** (apologies to our foreign readers who don't understand the American game of baseball!).

You can surely think of many more places that databases enter your life. The idea is that they are everywhere. And, each database requires some way for a user to interact with the information within. Such interaction is performed by a **database management system (DBMS)**.

Introducing Visual Basic and Databases 1-5

The tasks of a **DBMS** are really quite simple. In concept, there are only a few things you can do with a database:

1. View the data
2. Find some data of interest
3. Modify the data
4. Add some data
5. Delete some data

There are many commercial database management systems that perform these tasks. Programs like Access (a Microsoft product) and Oracle are used worldwide. In this course, we look at using **Visual Basic** as a **DBMS**.

Examples where you might use Visual Basic as a DBMS:

⇒ Implementing a new application that requires management of a database
⇒ Connecting to an existing database
⇒ Interacting with a database via a server or the internet

In a DBMS, the database may be available **locally** on your (or the user's) computer, available on a **LAN** (local area network) shared by multiple users, or only available on a **web server** via the Internet. In this course, we spend most of our time looking at local databases, but access with remote databases is addressed.

We will look at databases in more depth in the next chapter. You will see that databases have their own vocabulary. Now, let's take a look at how Visual Basic fits into the database management system.

Where Does Visual Basic Fit In?

For database management, we say our Visual Basic application acts as a **front-end** to the database. This means the Visual Basic application provides the **interface** between the user and the database. This interface allows the user to tell the database what he or she needs and allows the database to respond to the request displaying the requested information in some manner.

A Visual Basic application cannot directly interact with a database. There is a set of intermediate components between the application and the database known as **ADO** (ActiveX Data Object) **.NET data objects**:

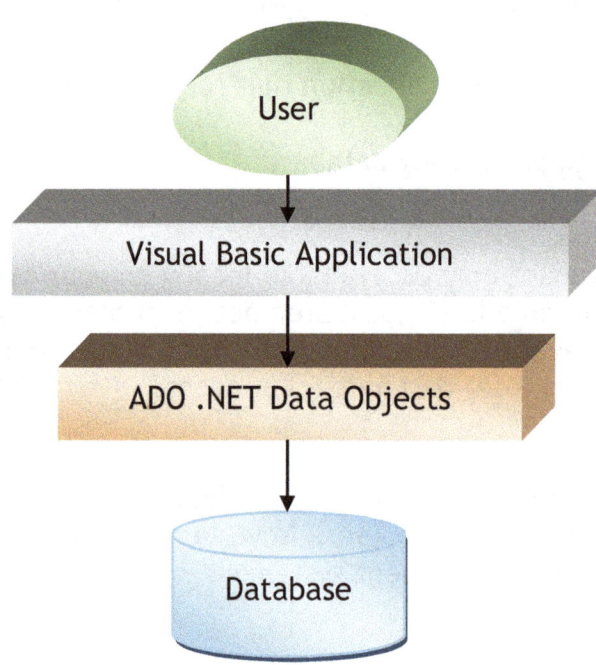

The **data objects** are Visual Basic components that allow connection to the database, creation of data sets from the database and management of the database contents. These objects are the conduit between the application and the database, passing information back and forth between the two.

Introducing Visual Basic and Databases 1-7

As mentioned earlier, there are many commercial products (Access, SQL Server, Oracle) that do database management tasks. You may be asking why use Visual Basic as a database management system (DBMS) when these commercial products are available? There are two primary advantages to using Visual Basic as a DBMS instead of Access:

1. Your users don't need to have any commercial product installed on their computers or know how to use such products. This saves the users money.

2. By building a custom front-end, you limit what your user can do with the information within the database. Under normal operation, commercial DBMS provide no such limits.

So, in this course, we will look at how to build Visual Basic applications that operate as front-ends to databases. Research has shown that over half of all Visual Basic applications involve working with databases. We will look at how to make our applications into complete database management systems, being able to view, search, modify, add, and/or delete database information.

Before going any further, let's review the steps in building a Visual Basic application and then build a simple application for practice.

Building a Visual Basic Application

In the remainder of this chapter, we will provide an overview of a Visual Basic application and how the Visual Basic development environment is used to develop an application. This should provide you with some idea of what knowledge you need to possess to proceed in this course and introduce the terminology used by the author to describe a Visual Basic application.

Structure of a Visual Basic Windows Application

Project

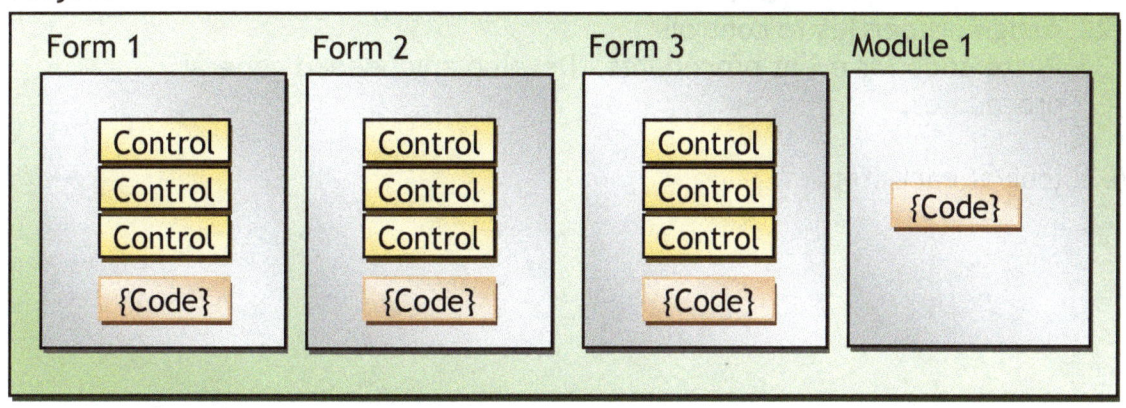

Form 1	Form 2	Form 3	Module 1
Control Control Control {Code}	Control Control Control {Code}	Control Control Control {Code}	{Code}

Application (Project) is made up of:

- **Forms** - Windows that you create for user interface
- **Controls** - Graphical features drawn on forms to allow user interaction (text boxes, labels, scroll bars, buttons, etc.) Forms and Controls are **objects**.
- **Properties** - Every characteristic of a form or control is specified by a property. Example properties include names, Texts, size, color, position, and contents. Visual Basic applies default properties. You can change properties when designing the application or even when an application is executing.
- **Methods** - Built-in procedures that can be invoked to impart some action to a particular object.
- **Event Procedures** - **Code** related to some object or control. This is the code that is executed when a certain event occurs. In our applications, this code will be written in the BASIC language.
- **General Procedures** - **Code** not related to objects. This code must be invoked or called in the application.
- **Modules** - Collection of general procedures, variable declarations, and constant definitions used by an application.

Steps in Developing Application

There are three primary steps involved in building a Visual Basic application:

1. **Draw** the user **interface**
2. **Assign properties** to controls
3. **Write code** for event procedures. Develop any needed general procedures.

We'll look at each step.

Drawing the User Interface and Setting Properties

Visual Basic operates in three modes.

⇒ **Design** mode - used to build application
⇒ **Running** mode - used to run the application
⇒ **Debugging** mode - application halted and debugger is available

We focus here on the **design** mode.

Several windows should appear when you start Visual Basic. If any of these windows do not appear, they may be accessed using the main window menu **View** item.

⇒ The **Main Window** consists of the title bar, menu bar, and toolbar. The title bar indicates the project name. The menu bar has drop-down menus from which you control the operation of the Visual Basic environment. The toolbar has buttons that provide shortcuts to some of the menu options (ToolTips indicate their function).

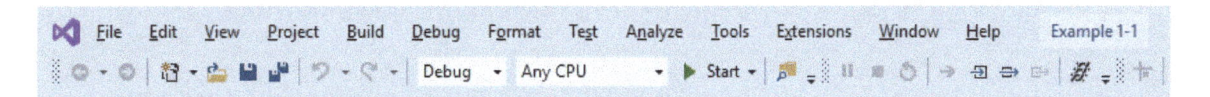

⇒ The **Form Window** is central to developing Visual Basic applications. It is where you draw your application.

Introducing Visual Basic and Databases 1-13

⇒ The **Toolbox** is the selection menu for controls (objects) used in your application.

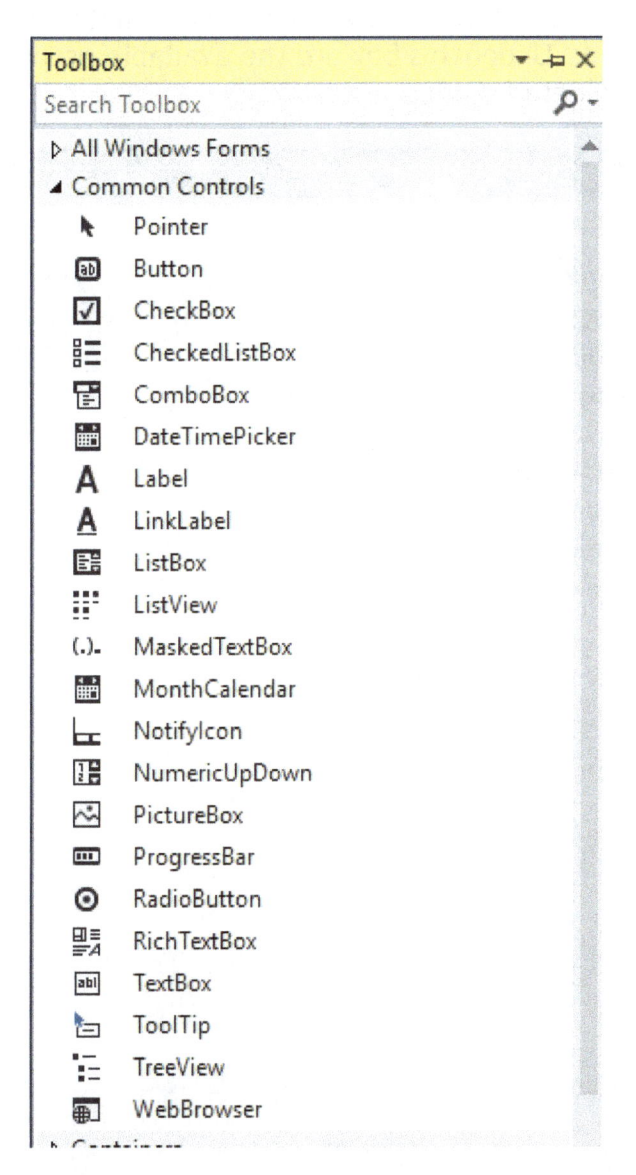

```
Toolbox
Search Toolbox
▷ All Windows Forms
▲ Common Controls
    Pointer
    Button
    CheckBox
    CheckedListBox
    ComboBox
    DateTimePicker
    Label
    LinkLabel
    ListBox
    ListView
    MaskedTextBox
    MonthCalendar
    NotifyIcon
    NumericUpDown
    PictureBox
    ProgressBar
    RadioButton
    RichTextBox
    TextBox
    ToolTip
    TreeView
    WebBrowser
```

⇒ The **Properties Window** is used to establish initial property values for objects. The drop-down box at the top of the window lists all objects in the current form. Two views are available: **Alphabetic** and **Categorized**. Under this box are the available properties for the currently selected object.

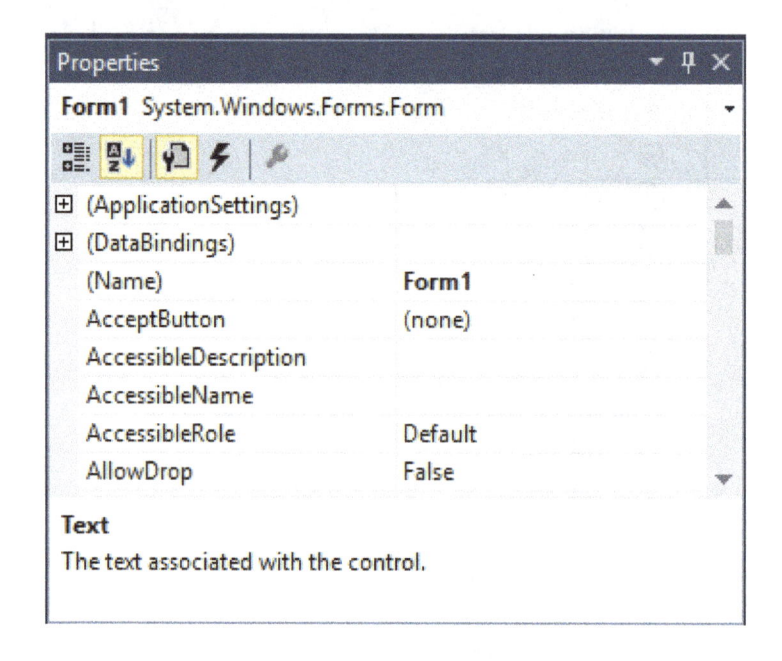

Properties	
Form1 System.Windows.Forms.Form	
⊞ (ApplicationSettings)	
⊞ (DataBindings)	
(Name)	**Form1**
AcceptButton	(none)
AccessibleDescription	
AccessibleName	
AccessibleRole	Default
AllowDrop	False

Text
The text associated with the control.

Introducing Visual Basic and Databases   1-15

⇒ The **Solution Explorer Window** displays a list of all forms, modules and other files making up your application

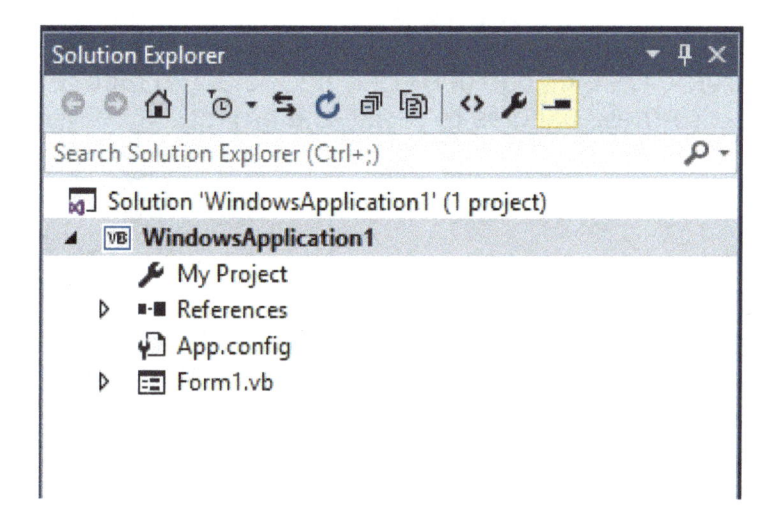

As mentioned, the user interface is 'drawn' in the form window. There are four ways to place controls on a form:

1. Click the tool in the toolbox and hold the mouse button down. Drag the selected tool over the form. When the cursor pointer is at the desired upper left corner, release the mouse button and the default size control will appear. This is the classic "drag and drop" operation.
2. Double-click the tool in the toolbox and it is created with a default size on the form. You can then move it or resize it.
3. Click the tool in the toolbox, then move the mouse pointer to the form window. The cursor changes to a crosshair. Place the crosshair at the upper left corner of where you want the control to be and click the left mouse button. The control will appear at the clicked point.
4. Click the tool in the toolbox, then move the mouse pointer to the form window. The cursor changes to a crosshair. Place the crosshair at the upper left corner of where you want the control to be, press the left mouse button and hold it down while dragging the cursor toward the lower right corner. A rectangle will be drawn. When you release the mouse button, the control is drawn in the rectangle.

1-16 **Visual Basic and Databases**

To **move** a control you have drawn, click the object in the form (a cross with arrows will appear). Now, drag the control to the new location. Release the mouse button.

To **resize** a control, click the control so that it is selected (active) and sizing handles appear. Use these handles to resize the object.

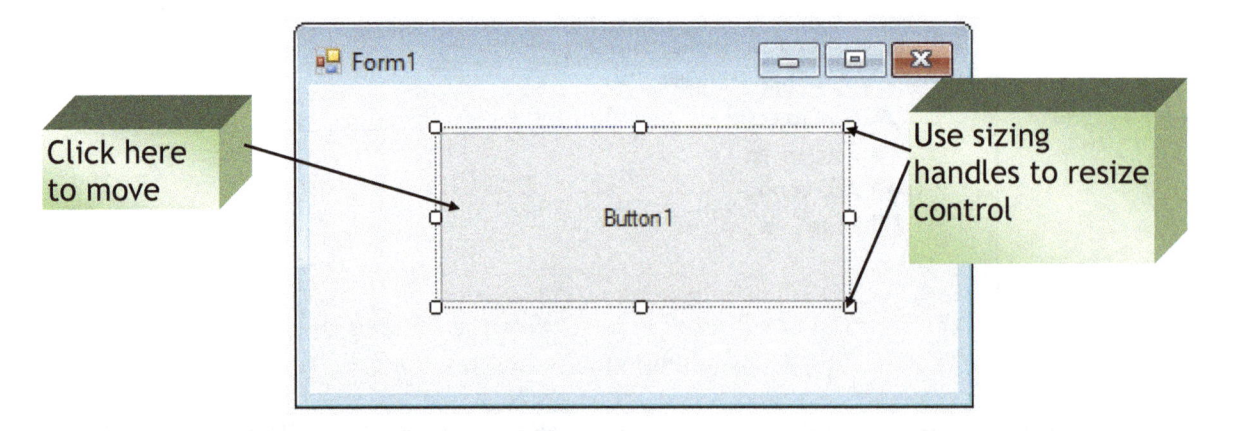

To delete a control, select that control so it is active (sizing handles will appear). Then, press **<Delete>** on the keyboard. Or, right-click the control. A menu will appear. Choose the **Delete** option. You can change your mind immediately after deleting a control by choosing the **Undo** option under the **Edit** menu.

Setting Properties of Controls at Design Time

Each form and control has **properties** assigned to it by default when you start up a new project. There are two ways to display the properties of an object. The first way is to click on the object (form or control) in the form window. Sizing handles will appear on that control. When a control has sizing handles, we say it is the **active** control. Now, click on the Properties window or the Properties window button in the tool bar. The second way is to first click on the Properties window. Then, select the object from the drop-down box at the top of the Properties window. When you do this, the selected object (control) will now be active (have sizing handles). Shown is the Properties window for the **Form** object:

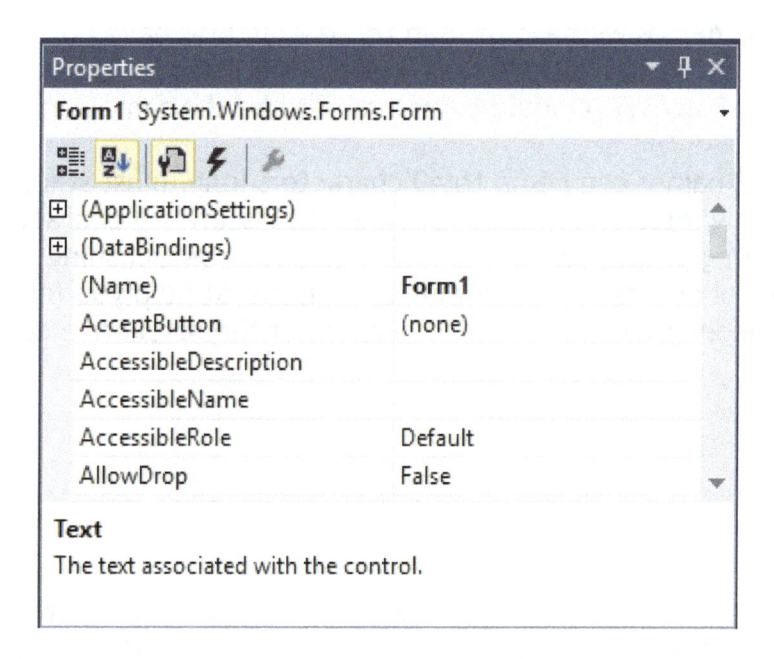

```
Properties                               ▼ ╄ ×
Form1  System.Windows.Forms.Form              ▼
⊞ (ApplicationSettings)
⊞ (DataBindings)
  (Name)                    Form1
  AcceptButton              (none)
  AccessibleDescription
  AccessibleName
  AccessibleRole            Default
  AllowDrop                 False

Text
The text associated with the control.
```

The drop-down box at the top of the Properties Window is the **Object** box. It displays the name of each object in the application as well as its type. This display shows the **Form** object. The **Properties** list is directly below this box. In this list, you can scroll through the list of properties for the selected object. You select a property by clicking on it. Properties can be changed by typing a new value or choosing from a list of predefined settings (available as a drop down list). Properties can be viewed in two ways: **Alphabetic** and **Categorized** (selected using the menu bar under the Object box). At the bottom of the Properties window is a short description of the selected property (a kind of dynamic help system).

A very important property for each control is its **Name**. The name is used by Visual Basic to refer to a particular object or control in code. A convention has been established for naming Visual Basic controls. This convention is to use a three letter (lower case) prefix (identifying the type of control) followed by a name you assign. A few of the prefixes are (we'll see more as we progress in the notes):

Control	Prefix	Example
Form	frm	frmWatch
Button	btn	btnExit, btnStart
Label	lbl	lblStart, lblEnd
Text Box	txt	txtTime, txtName
Menu	mnu	mnuExit, mnuSave
Check box	chk	chkChoice

Even though the names we have used in these examples have both lower and upper case letters, Visual Basic is **case-insensitive**. Hence, the names **frmWatch** and **FRMWATCH** would be assumed to be the same name.

Control (object) names can be up to 40 characters long, must start with a letter, must contain only letters, numbers, and the underscore (_) character. Names are used in setting properties at run-time and also in establishing procedure names for control events. Use meaningful names that help you (or another programmer) understand the type and purpose of the respective controls.

Setting Properties at Run Time

In addition to setting properties at design time, you can set or modify properties while your application is running. To do this, you must write some code. The code format is:

   ObjectName.PropertyName = NewValue

Such a format is referred to as dot notation. For example, to change the **BackColor** property of a button named **btnStart**, we'd type:

```
btnStart.BackColor = Color.Blue
```

Good naming conventions make it easy to understand what's going on here. The button named **btnStart** will now have a blue background.

How Names are Used in Control Events

The names you assign to controls are also used by Visual Basic to set up a framework of event-driven procedures for you to add code to. Hence, proper naming makes these procedures easier to understand.

The format for each of these procedures, or subroutines (all event procedures in Visual Basic are subroutines), is:

Private Sub ControlName_Event (**Arguments**) **Handles** ControlName.Event
   .
   .
End Sub

where **Arguments** provides information needed by the procedure to do its work.

Visual Basic provides the **Sub** line with its arguments and the **End Sub** statement. You provide any needed code. Notice that with proper naming convention, it is easy to identify what tasks are associated with a particular event of a particular control.

Writing Code

The last step in building a Visual Basic application is to write code using the **BASIC** language. This is the most time consuming task in any Visual Basic application. It is also the most fun and most rewarding task. As controls are added to a form, Visual Basic automatically builds a framework of all event procedures. We simply add code to the event procedures we want our application to respond to. And, if needed, we write general procedures.

Code is placed in the **Code Window**. At the top of the code window are two boxes, the **object** (or control) **list** and the **procedure list**. Select an object and the corresponding event procedure. A blank procedure will appear in the window where you write BASIC code.

Review of Variables

Variables are used by Visual Basic to hold information needed by your application. Rules used in naming variables:

⇒ No more than 40 characters
⇒ They may include letters, numbers, and underscore (_)
⇒ The first character must be a letter
⇒ You cannot use a reserved word (word needed by Visual Basic)

Visual Basic Data Types

⇒ **Boolean** (True or False)
⇒ **Short, Integer, Long** (Whole numbers)
⇒ **Single, Double** (Floating point numbers)
⇒ **Date**
⇒ **Object** (yes, objects can be variables!)
⇒ **String** (Used for many control properties)
⇒ **Char** (single character string variables)

Variable Declaration

Once we have decided on a variable name and the type of variable, we must tell our Visual Basic application what that name and type are. We say, we must **explicitly declare** the variable.

It is possible to use Visual Basic without declaring variables, but this is a dangerous practice. There are many advantages to **explicitly** typing variables. Primarily, we insure all computations are properly done, mistyped variable names are easily spotted, and Visual Basic will take care of insuring consistency in variable names. Because of these advantages, and because it is good programming practice, we will always explicitly type variables.

To **explicitly** type a variable, you must first determine its **scope**. There are four levels of scope:

- ⇒ Procedure level
- ⇒ Procedure level, static
- ⇒ Form and module level
- ⇒ Global level

Within a procedure, variables are declared using the **Dim** statement:

```
Dim MyInt As Integer
Dim MyDouble As Double
Dim MyString As String, YourString As String
```

Procedure level variables declared in this manner do not retain their value once a procedure terminates.

To make a procedure level variable retain its value upon exiting the procedure, replace the Dim keyword with **Static**:

```
Static MyInt As Integer
Static MyDouble As Double
```

Form (module) level variables retain their value and are available to all procedures within that form (module). Form (module) level variables are declared immediately following the header line in the code window. The **Dim** keyword is used:

```
Dim MyInt As Integer
Dim MyDate As Date
```

Global level variables retain their value and are available to all procedures within an application. Module level variables are declared after the header line of a module's code window. (It is advisable to keep all global variables in one module.) Use the **Public** keyword:

```
Public MyInt As Integer
Public MyDate As Date
```

What happens if you declare a variable with the same name in two or more places? More local variables **shadow** (are accessed in preference to) less local variables. For example, if a variable MyInt is defined as global in a module and declared local in a routine MyRoutine, while in MyRoutine, the local value of MyInt is accessed. Outside MyRoutine, the global value of MyInt is accessed.

Example of Variable Scope:

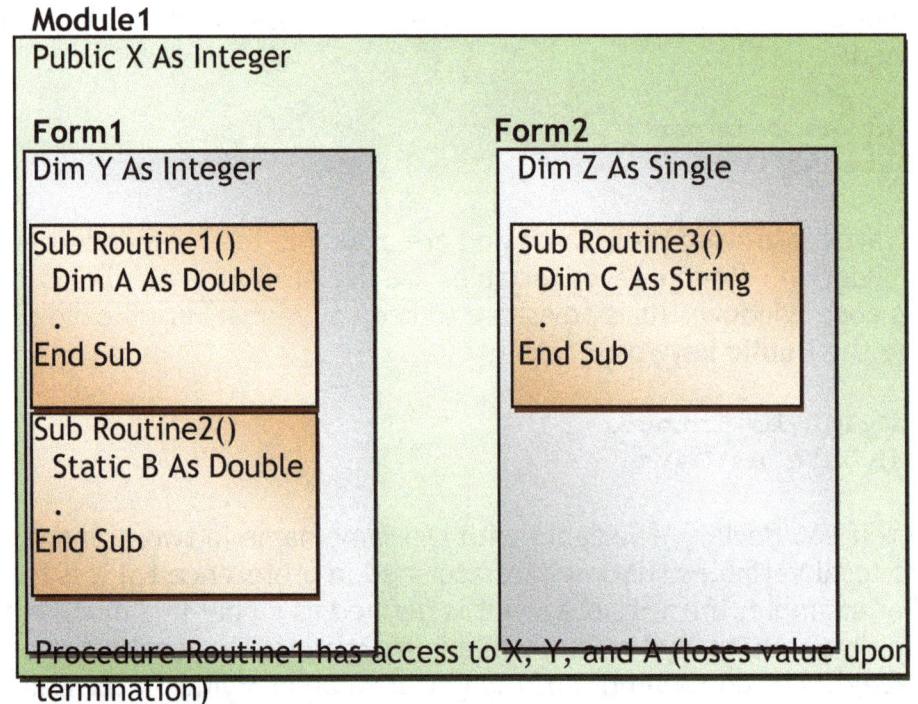

Module1
Public X As Integer

Form1
Dim Y As Integer

Sub Routine1()
  Dim A As Double
  .
End Sub

Sub Routine2()
  Static B As Double
  .
End Sub

Form2
Dim Z As Single

Sub Routine3()
  Dim C As String
  .
End Sub

Procedure Routine1 has access to X, Y, and A (loses value upon termination)
Procedure Routine2 has access to X, Y, and B (retains value)
Procedure Routine3 has access to X, Z, and C (loses value)

Example 1-1

Mailing List Application

In this example, we will build a Visual Basic application that could function as a database interface. The application allows the entry of information (names and addresses) to build a mailing list. An added feature is a timer that keeps track of the time spent entering addresses. After each entry, rather than write the information to a database (as we would normally do), the input information is simply displayed in a Visual Basic message box. We present this example to illustrate the steps in building an application. If you feel comfortable building this application and understanding the corresponding code, you probably possess the Visual Basic skills needed to proceed with this course.

1. Start a new project. Place two group boxes on the form (one for entry of address information and one for the timing function). In the first group box, place five labels, five text boxes, and two buttons. In the second group box, place a text box and three buttons. Add a timer control. Resize and position controls so your form resembles this:

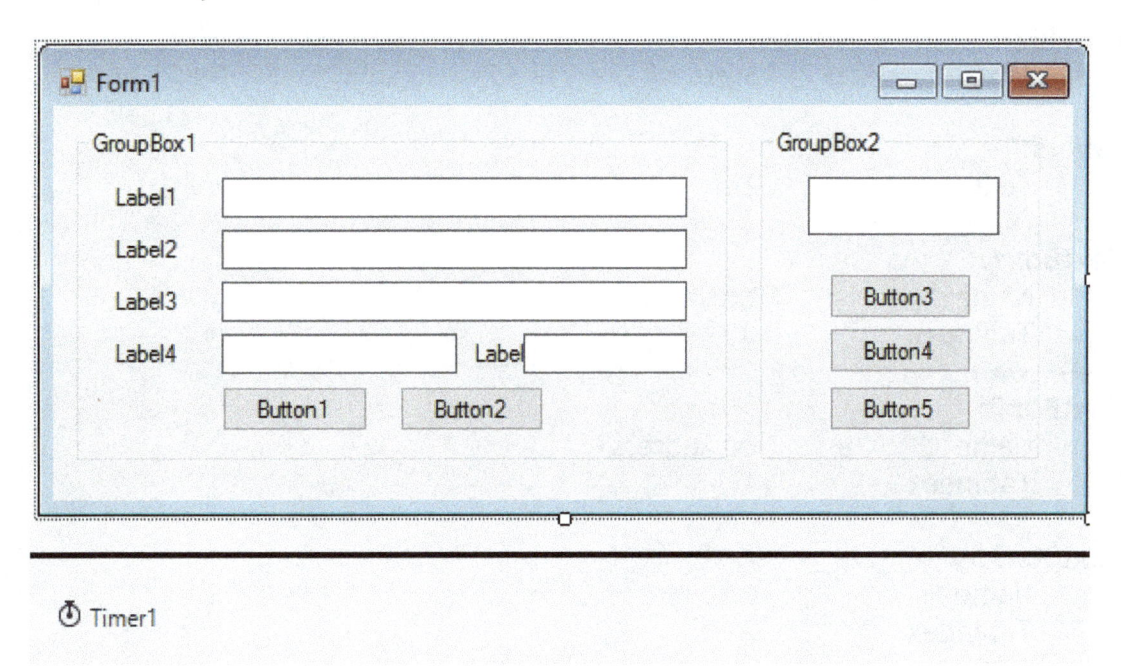

2. Set properties for the form and controls (these are just suggestions – make any changes you might like):

Form1:
    Name   frmMailingList
    FormBorderStyle   Fixed Single
    Text   Mailing List Application

GroupBox1:
    Name   grpMail
    Text   Address Information
    Enabled   False

Label1:
    Text   Name

Label2:
    Text   Address

Label3:
    Text   City

Label4:
    Text   State

Label5:
    Text   Zip

TextBox1:
    Name   txtName
    TabIndex   0

TextBox2:
    Name   txtAddress
    TabIndex   1

TextBox3:
    Name   txtCity
    TabIndex   2

TextBox4:
    Name   txtState
    TabIndex   3

TextBox5:
    Name   txtZip
    TabIndex   4

Button1:
    Name   btnAccept
    Text   &Accept
    TabIndex   5

Button2:
    Name   btnClear
    Text   &Clear

GroupBox2:
    Name   grpTime
    Text   Elapsed Time

TextBox6:
    Name   txtElapsedTime
    Font   Bold, Size 14
    TabStop   False
    Text   00:00:00
    TextAlign   Center

Button3:
    Name   btnStart
    Text   &Start

Button4:
    Name   btnPause
    Text   &Pause
    Enabled   False

Button5:
    Name   btnExit
    Text   E&xit

Timer1:
    Name   timSeconds
    Enabled   False
    Interval   1000

When done, the form should appear something like this:

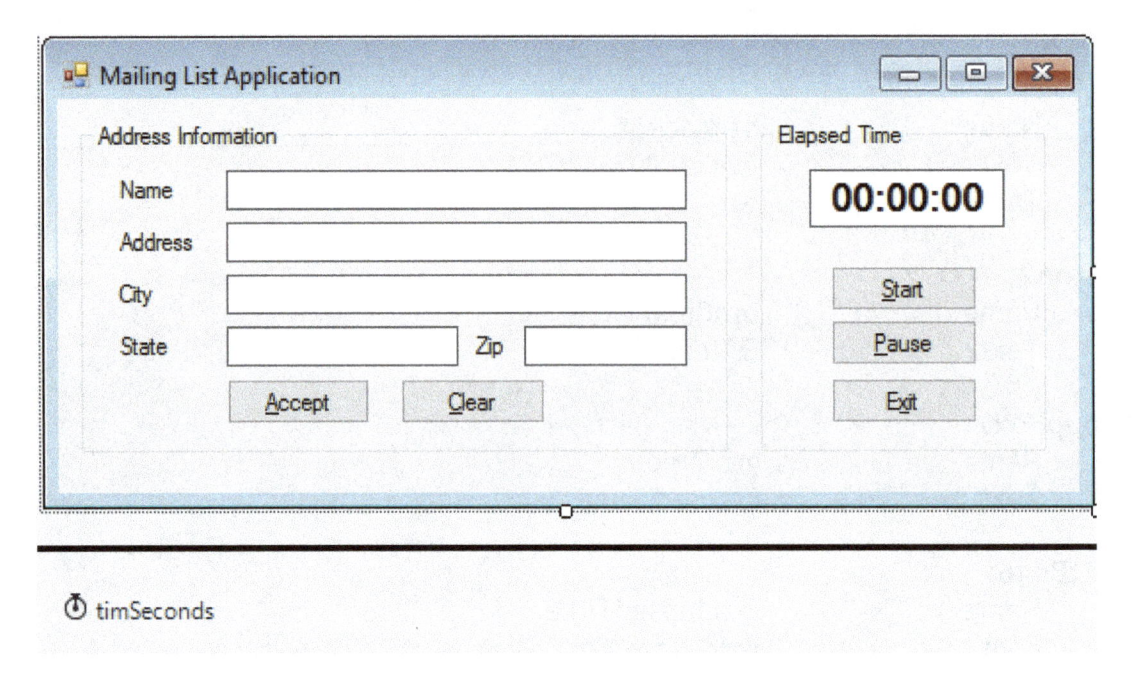

3. Form level variable declarations:

```
Dim ElapsedTime As Integer = 0
Dim LastNow As Date
```

Introducing Visual Basic and Databases   1-31

4. Put this code in the **btnStart_Click** event procedure:

```
Private Sub BtnStart_Click(ByVal sender As System.Object, ByVal e As System.EventArgs) Handles btnStart.Click
    'Start button clicked
    'Disable start and exit buttons
    'Enabled pause button
    btnStart.Enabled = False
    btnExit.Enabled = False
    btnPause.Enabled = True
    'Establish start time and start timer control
    LastNow = Now
    timSeconds.Enabled = True
    'Enable mailing list frame
    grpMail.Enabled = True
    txtName.Focus()
End Sub
```

5. Put this code in the **btnPause_Click** event procedure:

```
Private Sub BtnPause_Click(ByVal sender As System.Object, ByVal e As System.EventArgs) Handles btnPause.Click
    'Pause button clicked
    'Disable pause button
    'Enabled start and exit buttons
    btnPause.Enabled = False
    btnStart.Enabled = True
    btnExit.Enabled = True
    'Stop timer
    timSeconds.Enabled = False
    'Disable editing frame
    grpMail.Enabled = False
End Sub
```

6. Put this code in the **btnExit_Click** event procedure:

```
Private Sub btnExit_Click(ByVal sender As System.Object, ByVal e As System.EventArgs) Handles btnExit.Click
    Me.Close()
End Sub
```

7. Put this code in the **timSeconds_Timer** event procedure:

```
Private Sub TimSeconds_Tick(ByVal sender As System.Object, ByVal e As System.EventArgs) Handles timSeconds.Tick
    'Compute elapsed time and display
    ElapsedTime += DateDiff(DateInterval.Second, LastNow, Now)
    txtElapsedTime.Text = HMS(ElapsedTime)
    LastNow = Now
End Sub
```

which uses the **HMS** general function to format the time:

```
Private Function HMS(ByVal T As Integer) As String
  Dim H As Integer, M As Integer, S As Integer
  'Break time down into hours, minutes, and seconds
  H = T \ 3600 ' note integer division
  M = (T - H * 3600) \ 60 ' again integer division
  S = T - H * 3600 - M * 60
  Return (Format(H, "00") & ":" & Format(M, "00") & ":" & Format(S, "00"))
End Function
```

Note a couple of lines in the code above are so long that the word processor wraps them around at the margin. Type each as one long line, not two separate lines or review the use of the Visual Basic line continuation character (_). Be aware this happens quite often in these notes when actual code is being presented.

Introducing Visual Basic and Databases 1-33

8. Put this code in the **txtInput_KeyPress** event procedure (handles the KeyPress event for all input text boxes):

```
Private Sub TxtInput_KeyPress(ByVal sender As
System.Object, ByVal e As
System.Windows.Forms.KeyPressEventArgs) Handles
txtName.KeyPress, txtZip.KeyPress, txtState.KeyPress,
txtCity.KeyPress, txtAddress.KeyPress
    Dim WhichTextBox As TextBox
    WhichTextBox = CType(sender, TextBox)
    'Check for return key
    If e.KeyChar = ControlChars.Cr Then
      Select Case WhichTextBox.Name
        Case "txtName"
          txtAddress.Focus()
        Case "txtAddress"
          txtCity.Focus()
        Case "txtCity"
          txtState.Focus()
        Case "txtState"
          txtZip.Focus()
        Case "txtZip"
          btnAccept.Focus()
      End Select
    End If
    'In Zip text box, make sure only numbers or backspace pressed
    If WhichTextBox.Name.Equals("txtZip") Then
      If (e.KeyChar >= CChar("0") And e.KeyChar <= CChar("9")) Or e.KeyChar = ControlChars.Back Then
        e.Handled = False
      Else
        e.Handled = True
      End If
    End If
  End Sub
```

9. Put this code in the **btnAccept_Click** event procedure:

```vb
Private Sub BtnAccept_Click(ByVal sender As System.Object, ByVal e As System.EventArgs) Handles btnAccept.Click
    Dim S As String
    'Accept button clicked - form label and output in message box
    'Make sure each text box has entry
    If txtName.Text = "" Or txtAddress.Text = "" Or txtCity.Text = "" Or txtState.Text = "" Or txtZip.Text = "" Then
        MessageBox.Show("Each box must have an entry!", "Error", MessageBoxButtons.OK, MessageBoxIcon.Information)
        txtName.Focus()
        Exit Sub
    End If
    S = txtName.Text + ControlChars.CrLf + txtAddress.Text + ControlChars.CrLf
    S += txtCity.Text + ", " + txtState.Text + " " + txtZip.Text
    MessageBox.Show(S, "Mailing Label", MessageBoxButtons.OK)
    btnClear.PerformClick()
End Sub
```

10. Put this code in the **btnClear_Click** event procedure:

```vb
Private Sub BtnClear_Click(ByVal sender As System.Object, ByVal e As System.EventArgs) Handles btnClear.Click
    txtName.Text = ""
    txtAddress.Text = ""
    txtCity.Text = ""
    txtState.Text = ""
    txtZip.Text = ""
    txtName.Focus()
End Sub
```

Introducing Visual Basic and Databases   1-35

11. Save the application (saved in the **Example 1-1** folder in **VBDB\General\Class 1** folder). Run the application. Make sure it functions as designed. Here's the running program.

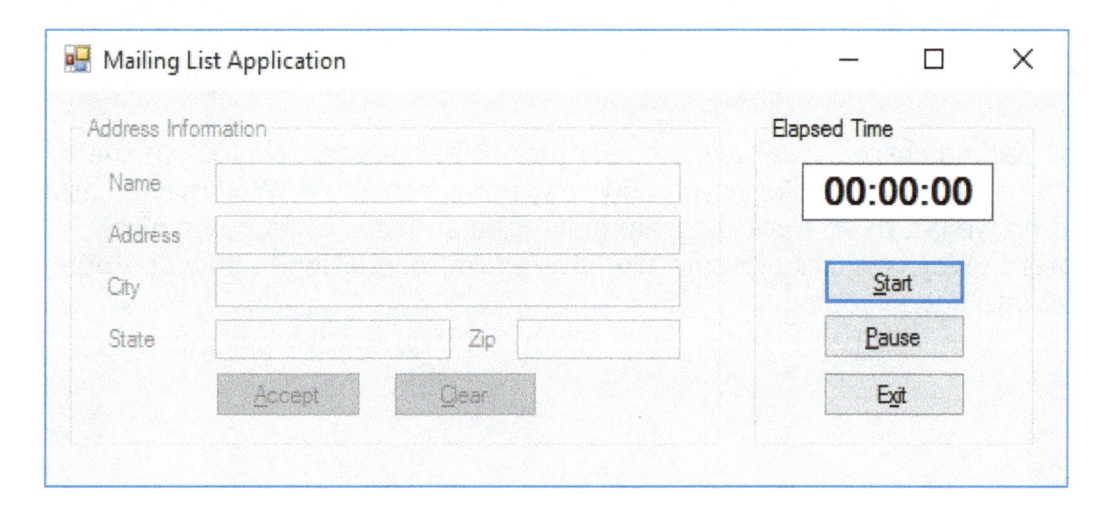

Note that you cannot enter mailing list information unless the timer is running. Here's the program after I entered some information:

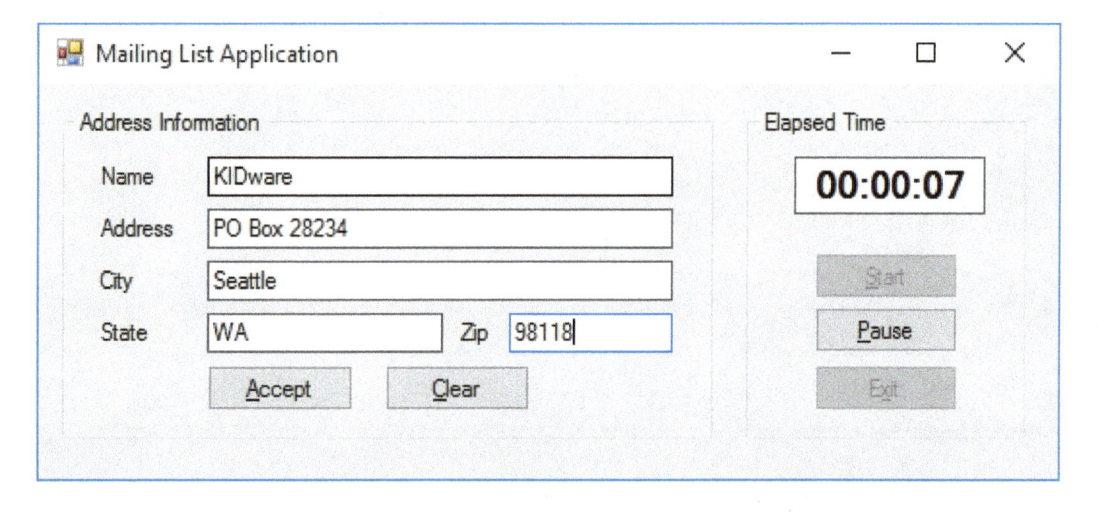

and here's what I see when I click **Accept**:

Summary

In this chapter, we introduced databases in general terms and how Visual Basic can be used to develop a front-end application to interact with the database. And, we reviewed the steps involved in building a Visual Basic application.

In the second chapter, we take a closer look at databases. We look at their structure, their terminology, and how they are constructed. You may be asking - when do we get to do some programming? The answer - in a couple more chapters. We want to make sure we have a firm foundation in place before diving into actual coding.

2
Introduction to Databases

Review and Preview

In the last chapter, we looked at a database in very general terms. We learned that the central parts of a Visual Basic database application are the ADO .NET data objects.

In this chapter, we provide more details into the structure of databases and how they are created. We will use a sample database to illustrate the concepts presented.

Database Structure and Terminology

In simplest terms, a **database** is a collection of information. This collection is stored in one or more well-defined **tables**, or matrices.

The **rows** in a database table are used to describe similar items. The rows are referred to as database **records**. In general, no two rows in a database table will be alike.

The **columns** in a database table provide characteristics of the records. These characteristics are called database **fields**. Each field contains one specific piece of information. In defining a database field, you specify the data type, assign a length, and describe other attributes. Some field types include Binary, Boolean, Counter, Double, Single, Long, Integer, etc.

Here is a simple database example:

ID_No	Name	Date_of_Birth	Height	Weight
1	Bob Jones	01/04/58	72	170
2	Mary Rodgers	11/22/61	65	125
3	Sue Williams	06/11/57	68	130

In this database **table**, each **record** represents a single individual. The **fields** (descriptors of the individuals) include an identification number (ID_No), Name, Date_of_Birth, Height, and Weight.

Most databases use **indexes** to allow faster access to the information in the database. Indexes are sorted lists that point to a particular row in a table. We can create an index for any field we might want to perform a search on. The neat thing about an index is that the Visual Basic data objects handle all the details. We simply flag a field as an index and the code does the work.

Introduction to Databases 2-3

A database using a single table is called a **flat database**. Early database software worked only with flat databases. And, for simple applications, flat databases may be adequate. For large amounts of data, however, flat databases are cumbersome and become very large, very quickly.

Relational Databases

Most databases are made up of many tables stored in a single file. Each table contains a logical grouping of information with its own records and fields. When using multiple tables within a database, the tables must have some common fields to allow cross-referencing of the tables. The referral of one table to another via a common field is called a **relation**. Such groupings of tables are called **relational databases**.

Relational databases allow us to store vast amounts of data with far simpler maintenance and smaller storage requirements than the equivalent flat database. As an example, say we had a flat database listing products stocked by a grocery store with several fields describing each product's manufacturer (manufacturer name, address, phone, ...). If you have 1,000 products made by the same manufacturer, there is much repetition of information in the flat database. And, if the manufacturer changed their phone number, you would have to make that change in 1,000 places! In a relational database, you could use two tables, one for products, one for manufacturers. In the product table, you would simply have a manufacturer ID that would correspond with an ID in the manufacturer table (a **relation**), which would have that manufacturer's information. Then, if the phone number changed, you would only have to change one field in the manufacturer table - quite a savings in work! When you break down database tables into simpler tables, the process is known as **database normalization**.

Relations among tables in a relational database are established using **keys**. A **primary key** is a field that uniquely identifies a record so it can be referenced from a related table. A **foreign key** is a field that holds identification values to relate records stored in other tables.

When one record in one table is linked to only one record in another table, we say there is a **one-to-one** relation. When one record in one table links to many records in another table, we say there is a **one-to-many** relation. And, when many records in one table are linked to many records in another table, we say there is a **many-to-many** relation.

Introduction to Databases 2-5

In the first few chapters in this course, we will use a sample database. This relational database (**BooksDB.accdb**) is found in the **VBDB\Databases** folder installed with these notes. This database is a classic, used by generations of Visual Basic programmers to understand database programming. You will become very familiar with this database. It is a database of books about computer programming (and databases). Let's look at its relational structure to illustrate the many new concepts being introduced.

To make sure this database works with Visual Studio, you need a proper driver. Download and install the driver from

[Download Driver](#)

Using SQL Server Databases

You may notice that the sample used here (**BooksDB.accdb**) is a Microsoft Access database. These notes were originally developed using Access databases. If you prefer to use SQL Server databases, the notes have been modified to allow this capability. In each example developed, look for sections named **Access Database** and **SQL Server Database** for particular modifications.

To use SQL Server databases, it is assumed you have installed SQL Server on your computer. We use **SQL Server Express** available as a free download from Microsoft:

> https://www.microsoft.com/en-us/sql-server/sql-server-editions-express

The website gives full installation instructions. Click on Download Now.

Also, you use SQL Server versions of the Access databases included with these notes. The SQL Server databases are distinguished by an **mdf** file extension. If interested, these conversions were created with another free Microsoft Product named **SQL Server Migration Assistant for Access**. Information about this product can be found at:

> https://docs.microsoft.com/en-us/sql/ssma/sql-server-migration-assistant?view=sql-server-2017

The remainder of the information in this chapter is independent of which database product you choose to use.

Sample Relational Database

The books (**BooksDB.accdb**) database is made up of four tables:

Authors (6,246 records)
Publishers (727 records)
Titles (8,569 records)
Title_Author (16,056 records)

As you look at each table, pay attention to how the tables are logical groupings of information. Examine the record and field structures. In particular, note each field with an 'ID' in the name acts as a key to relate one table to another.

The **Authors** table contains information about the authors of the books in the database. The table has three (3) fields: Au_ID, Name, and Year_Born:

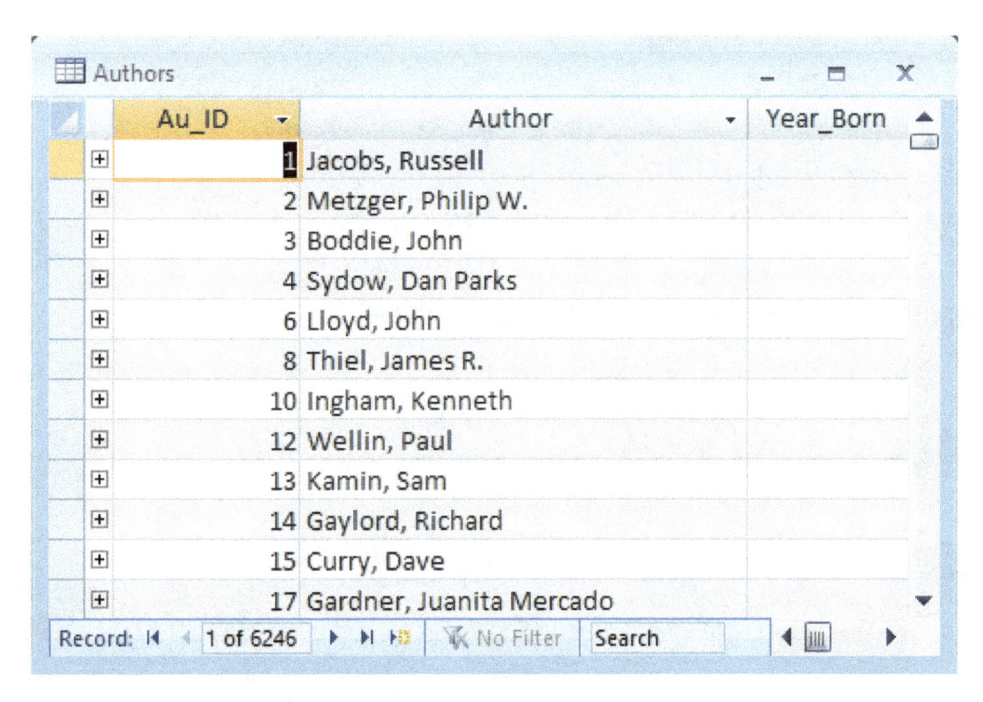

Au_ID	Author	Year_Born
1	Jacobs, Russell	
2	Metzger, Philip W.	
3	Boddie, John	
4	Sydow, Dan Parks	
6	Lloyd, John	
8	Thiel, James R.	
10	Ingham, Kenneth	
12	Wellin, Paul	
13	Kamin, Sam	
14	Gaylord, Richard	
15	Curry, Dave	
17	Gardner, Juanita Mercado	

There are 6,246 different authors in the database.

The **Publishers** table contains information about the publishers in the book database. The table has ten (10) fields: PubID, Name, Company_Name, Address, City, State, Zip, Telephone, Fax, and Comments:

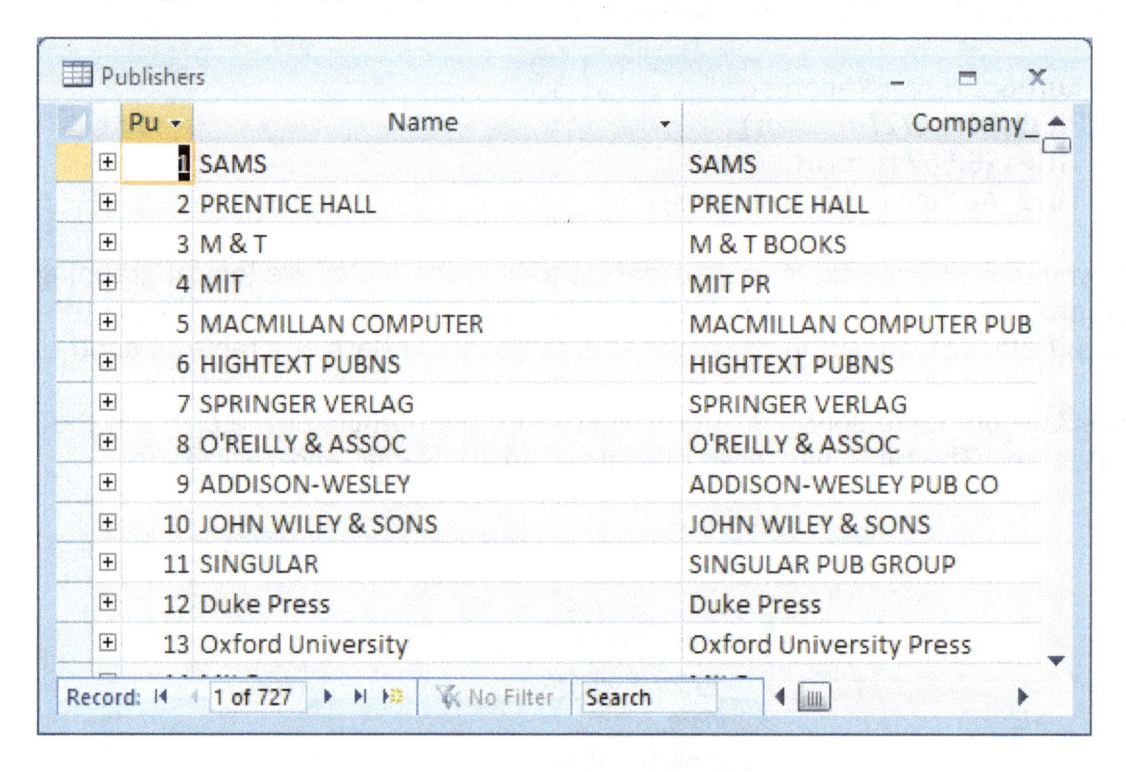

Pu	Name	Company_
1	SAMS	SAMS
2	PRENTICE HALL	PRENTICE HALL
3	M & T	M & T BOOKS
4	MIT	MIT PR
5	MACMILLAN COMPUTER	MACMILLAN COMPUTER PUB
6	HIGHTEXT PUBNS	HIGHTEXT PUBNS
7	SPRINGER VERLAG	SPRINGER VERLAG
8	O'REILLY & ASSOC	O'REILLY & ASSOC
9	ADDISON-WESLEY	ADDISON-WESLEY PUB CO
10	JOHN WILEY & SONS	JOHN WILEY & SONS
11	SINGULAR	SINGULAR PUB GROUP
12	Duke Press	Duke Press
13	Oxford University	Oxford University Press

There are 727 different publishers in the database.

Introduction to Databases

The **Titles** table contains information about each book title in the database. The table has eight (8) fields: Title, Year_Published, ISBN, PubID, Description, Notes, Subject, and Comments:

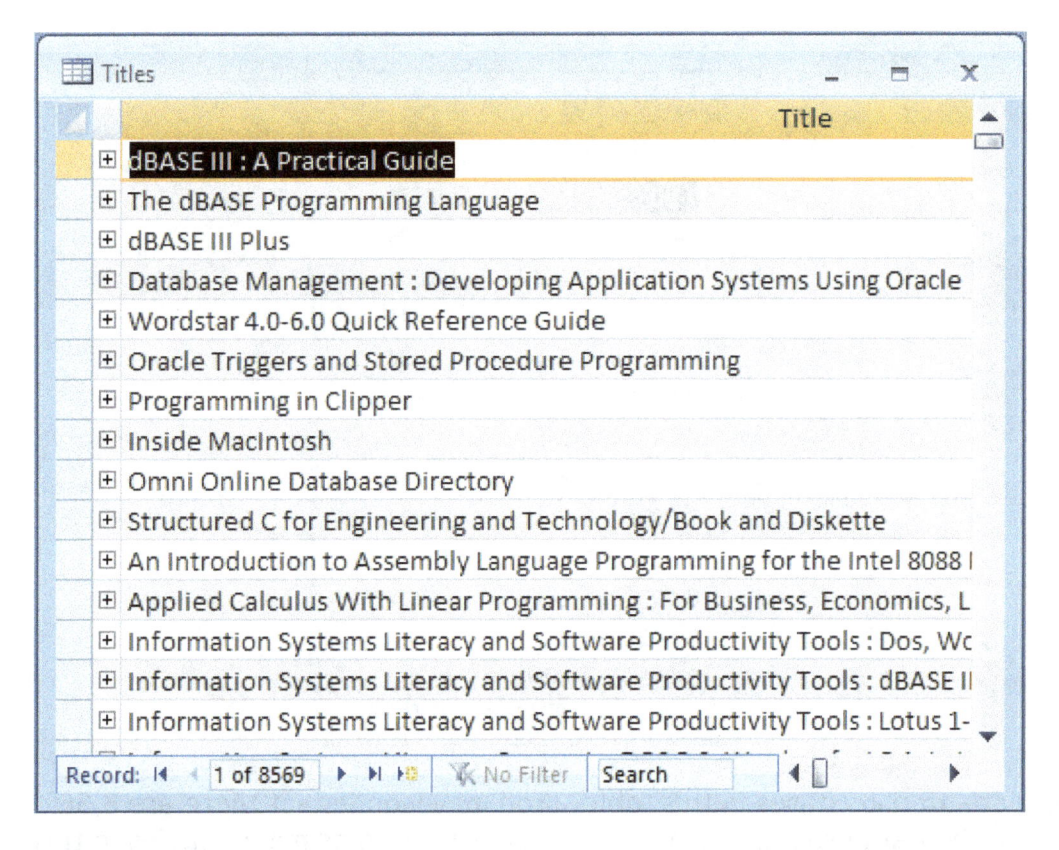

Title
dBASE III : A Practical Guide
The dBASE Programming Language
dBASE III Plus
Database Management : Developing Application Systems Using Oracle
Wordstar 4.0-6.0 Quick Reference Guide
Oracle Triggers and Stored Procedure Programming
Programming in Clipper
Inside MacIntosh
Omni Online Database Directory
Structured C for Engineering and Technology/Book and Diskette
An Introduction to Assembly Language Programming for the Intel 8088
Applied Calculus With Linear Programming : For Business, Economics, L
Information Systems Literacy and Software Productivity Tools : Dos, Wc
Information Systems Literacy and Software Productivity Tools : dBASE I
Information Systems Literacy and Software Productivity Tools : Lotus 1-

Record: 1 of 8569

There are 8,569 distinct book titles in the database.

The **Title_Author** table contains information relating book titles to authors within the database. It has just two fields: ISBN (International Standard Book Number, a number used by bookstores and libraries to reference books) and Au_ID:

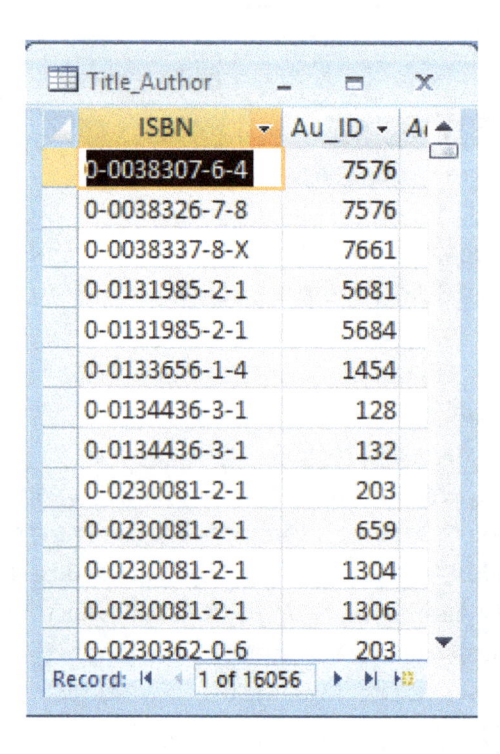

ISBN	Au_ID
0-0038307-6-4	7576
0-0038326-7-8	7576
0-0038337-8-X	7661
0-0131985-2-1	5681
0-0131985-2-1	5684
0-0133656-1-4	1454
0-0134436-3-1	128
0-0134436-3-1	132
0-0230081-2-1	203
0-0230081-2-1	659
0-0230081-2-1	1304
0-0230081-2-1	1306
0-0230362-0-6	203

Record: 1 of 16056

There are 16,056 entries in this table. You may wonder - if there are 8,569 titles in the database, how can there be nearly twice as many entries in this table. The answer is that many books have more than one author and this table lists all the authors for each title.

There is obviously a lot of information in the books database! This example, though, is very useful and shows the kind of database we can work with using Visual Basic. It is a well-designed database we can learn from. We will discuss database design in a later chapter, so much of what is discussed here will be very useful information later on. You may be wondering – where did these views of the database tables come from? They were obtained using Microsoft Access. In a couple of more chapters, you will be able to obtain such views using Visual Basic.

Sample Database Structure

Let's examine the books database a little closer. To help, we'll use this block diagram (obtained using Access) that illustrates the database structure:

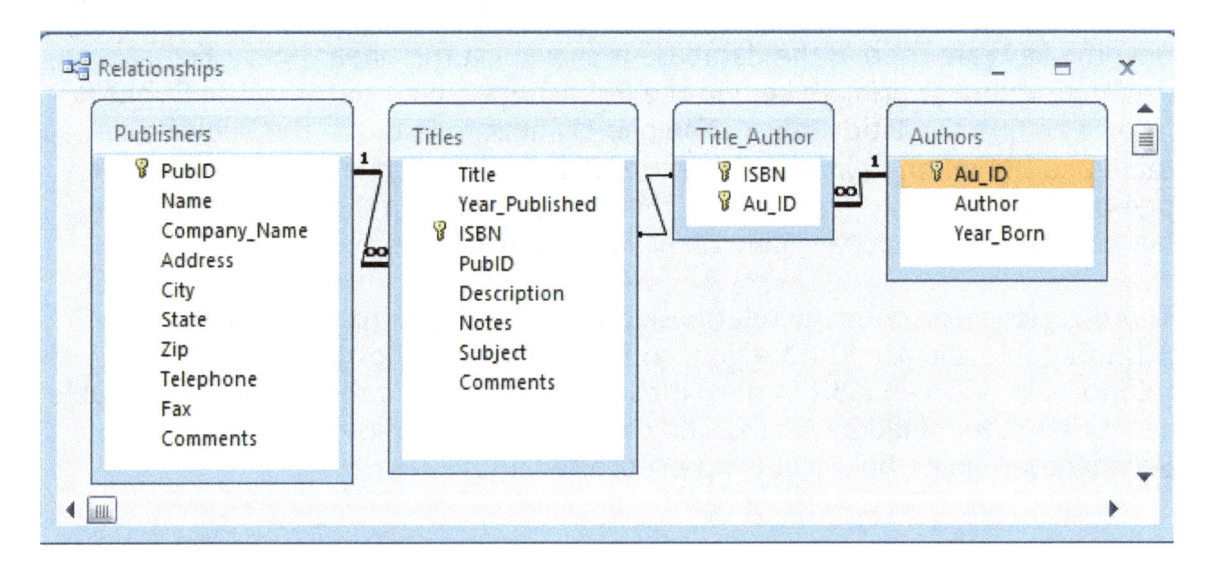

[Relationships diagram showing four tables:

Publishers: PubID (key), Name, Company_Name, Address, City, State, Zip, Telephone, Fax, Comments

Titles: Title, Year_Published, ISBN (key), PubID, Description, Notes, Subject, Comments

Title_Author: ISBN (key), Au_ID (key)

Authors: Au_ID (key), Author, Year_Born

Relationships: Publishers (1) — (∞) Titles; Title_Author (∞) — (1) Authors]

This diagram shows each table as a separate window listing the corresponding fields. Relations between tables are illustrated via linear links.

Look at the books database tables. Note each table is a logical grouping of information. Book publishers are in a single table (**Publishers**), book titles are in a single table (**Titles**), and book authors are in a single table (**Authors**). A well-designed database has such well-defined tables. Well-defined tables make database management a far simpler task.

Note each table has two types of information: **source** data and **relational** data. Source data is actual information, such as names, phone numbers, and addresses. Relational data are references to data in other tables via **keys**, such as **PubID**, **ISBN**, and **Au_ID**.

A **primary** key defines a unique record. **PubID** in the **Publishers** table, **ISBN** in the **Titles** Table, and **Au_ID** in the **Authors** table are primary keys. They identify a unique entry in their respective table.

A **foreign** key is a piece of relational information in one table that links to information in another table. In the **Titles** table, **PubID** is a foreign key. Using a PubID from this table in conjunction with the PubID primary key in the **Publishers** table will provide us with complete information about a particular publisher. In the **Title_Author** table, **ISBN** and **Au_ID** are foreign keys.

How the keys are used in the database is shown via the linear links. For example, **PubID** (a primary key) in the **Publishers** table relates to the **PubID** (a foreign key) in the **Titles** table. The one (**1**) next to PubID in the Publishers table and the infinity symbol (∞) next to PubID in the Titles table show this is a **one-to-many** relationship. That is, there is one PubID in the Publishers table, but this value may appear many times in the Titles table.

There is also a one-to-many relationship between **Au_ID** (primary key) in the **Authors** table and **Au_ID** (foreign key) in the **Title_Author** table. The exact relationship between **ISBN** in the **Titles** table and **ISBN** in the **Title_Author** table cannot be determined by Access (indicated by no markings on the linear link). Such indeterminate links will happen occasionally.

Virtual Database Tables

The primary purpose of the books database (**BooksDB.accdb**) is to track information about book titles. Note each table gives us a piece of information about a particular book, but to get all the information about a book, we need all four tables.

Using the relational data in the four tables, we should be able to obtain a complete description of any book in the database. Let's look at one example. Here's an entry (a record) from the **Titles** table:

Title	1-2-3 Database Techniques
Year_Published	1990
ISBN	0-8802234-6-4
PubID	45
Description	29.95
Notes	650.0285536920
Subject	[Blank]
Comments	HF5548.4.L67A52 1989

Taking the **ISBN** into the **Title_Author** table will provide us with these **Au_ID** values:

Au_ID	2467, 5265, 5266

Note the book has three authors. Using these **Au_ID** values in the **Authors** table reveals author information:

<u>Au_ID=2467</u>
Author						Stern, Nancy
Year_Born					[Blank]

<u>Au_ID=5265</u>
Author						Weil, Bill
Year_Born					[Blank]

<u>Au_ID=5266</u>
Author						Anderson, Dick
Year_Born					[Blank]

A last relational move of using the **PubID** in the **Publishers** table will give us complete details about the book publisher:

Name						QUE CORP
Company_Name				QUE CORP
Address						11711 N College Ave, Suite 140
City						Carmel
State						IN
Zip							46032
Telephone					[Blank]
Fax							[Blank]
Comments					[Blank]

Once done, we know everything there is to know about this one particular book "1-2-3 Database Techniques." What we essentially have done is formed one huge table with a single record and many, many fields. This new view of the data in the database is called a **virtual database table**. It is virtual because it doesn't exist as a native table in the **BooksDB.accdb** database – it was formed using the native four tables.

Making a **query** of the database created a virtual table above. We asked the database to tell us everything it knew about the book "1-2-3 Database Techniques." The database responded (well, we really did the work) with all information from its four tables. This is a very common task in database management systems and one we will be doing often in this course, **querying the database**. With each query of the database, we form a virtual table that contains the results of our query. Our queries will not be as comprehensive as the one made here (show me everything!). Usually, the query will ask for all records that meet some particular criteria. As an example, we might like to query the books database to show us all books published by a specific company. The results of this query would be returned in a virtual table.

Database queries are made with a specific language named **SQL** (structured query language). We will study SQL in a later chapter. For now, be aware that SQL can be used to form virtual tables from a database. These tables show us information of interest from the database. And, with Visual Basic as the front-end, doing a query with SQL is simple. We form the query, pass it on to the data objects and these objects do all the work for us, returning all records that our query requested. It's like magic! In the first few chapters, we will be doing just that – opening the books database and forming virtual tables we can view.

Creating a Database

Before leaving this database introduction, you may be asking yourself - how are databases like the books database created? How are tables defined? How are fields defined? How are records created?

Databases are created using commercial applications like Access, dBase, FoxPro, Oracle, SQL Server and others. Each of these products has a design mode where you define a table and the fields that are part of the table. You can also enter records into the table using these applications. The books database was built with Access. In the first part of this course, we will work with existing databases and will not be concerned with creating a database.

Later chapters discuss proper database design and creation of databases. If you have a commercial database product and know how to use it, you could use that when the time for creating a database arises. We will address other possibilities later in the course, including using Visual Basic to create a database.

Summary

In this chapter, we looked at our first database – the books database (**BooksDB.accdb**) that is included with these course notes. We studied the structure of a relational database, discussing tables, records, and fields. Relationships using primary and foreign keys were illustrated.

The concept of a virtual table was introduced. Making a query of the database forms virtual tables. In the next chapter, we begin learning how to use Visual Basic to connect to a database and process queries to form such virtual tables.

3

Database Connection

Review and Preview

At this point, we have looked at databases and how they are structured. We have seen that data objects work between the database and the Visual Basic 'front-end' to manage the database. In this chapter, for the first time, we use Visual Basic to connect to a database.

This connection is made with the data objects we have been referring to. Using data bound controls, in conjunction with the data objects, will allow us to view information in the database.

Data Object Overview

Visual Basic provides several objects that allow interaction with databases. These objects fall in one of five categories:

⇒ **Connections** allow a program to connect to a database
⇒ **Data containers** hold data after it has been loaded from a database.
⇒ **Data adapters** move data between databases and containers
⇒ **Command objects** allow manipulation of the data
⇒ **Navigation objects** allow a user to move through (and also modify) data

Some objects (data containers, data adapters, navigation objects) are generic in nature and work with any type of database.

Connection objects and command objects are specific to the type of database being used. Visual Basic provides objects that work with Object Linking and Embedding Databases (OLE DB), SQL Server, including the Microsoft Data Engine (MSDE), Open Database Connectivity (ODBC) and Oracle databases. Don't worry if you don't understand all this, right now. In these notes, we will work with Access databases (OLE DB) and SQL Server databases. In the final chapter, we'll look at connecting to other databases.

We will look at each data object in detail. As we progress through our discussion of these objects, we will gradually open and view items from the books database using Visual Basic.

Connection Object

The **connection object** establishes a connection between your application and the database.

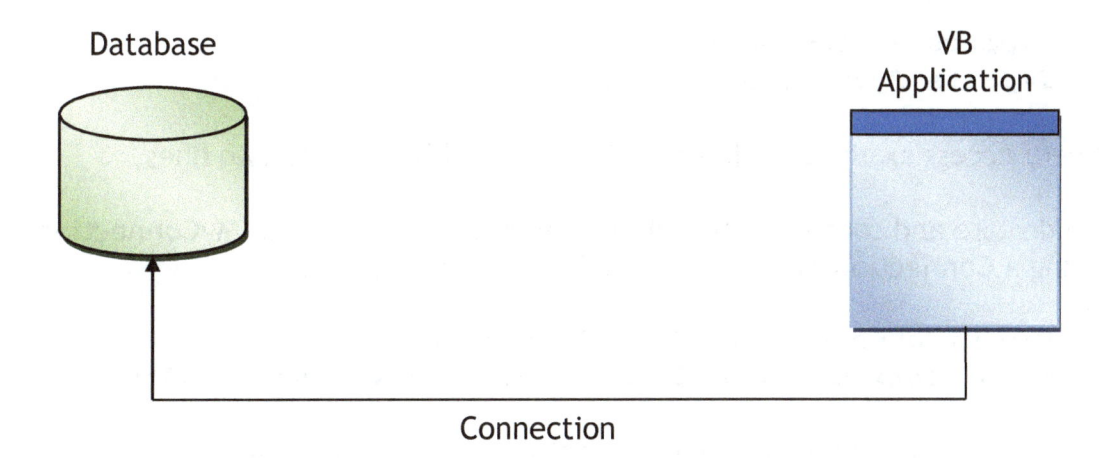

As mentioned, Visual Basic supports several databases types. Hence, it offers several different connection objects: **OleDbConnection**, **SqlConnection**, **OdbcConnection**, **OracleConnection**.

Connection object **properties**:

ConnectionString	Contains the information used to establish a connection to a database.
Database	Name of the current database.
DataSource	Name of the current database file.
State	Current connection state (Closed, Connecting, Open, Executing, Fetching, Broken)

Connection object **methods**:

Open	Open the connection.
Close	Close the connection.
Dispose	Dispose of the connection object.

Connection Object - Access Database

To use the **OleDbConnection** object and other OLE database objects, an application must have these two lines at the top of the corresponding code listing:

```
Imports System.Data
Imports System.Data.OleDb
```

Every Access example we build in this class will have these two lines.

To declare and construct an **OleDbConnection** object named **MyConnection**, using a **ConnectionString** named **MyConnectionString**, use:

```
Dim MyConnection As OleDbConnection
MyConnection = New OleDbConnection(MyConnectionString)
```

The **ConnectionString** for an Access database is the following string:

```
Provider=Microsoft.ACE.OLEDB.12.0; Data Source =
DatabaseName
```

where **DatabaseName** is a complete path to the database.

We're about to start looking at the books database (**BooksDB.accdb**) discussed in Chapter 2. This database is found in the **VBDB\Databases** directory. Make a copy of the database and place it in a working directory (you decide on a name – we will use **VBDB\Working**). We do this to insure there is always a valid copy of **BooksDB.accdb** on your computer. You will see that the power of the Visual Basic opens up the possibility of doing damage to a database (we, of course, will try to minimize this possibility). So, we are just living by the adage, "Better safe, than sorry."

Access Databases and 64-Bit Operating Systems

The Access databases used in these notes only work with 32-bit operating systems. If you are using a 64-bit version of Visual Studio, you need to make one change to each project you build.

Follow these steps:

- Once your project is built, choose the **Project** menu item, and select your project's **Properties** entry.
- In the window that appears, choose the **Compile** tab.
- Under **Target CPU**, make sure the selection is **x86**, not **AnyCPU**. The changed window should look like this:

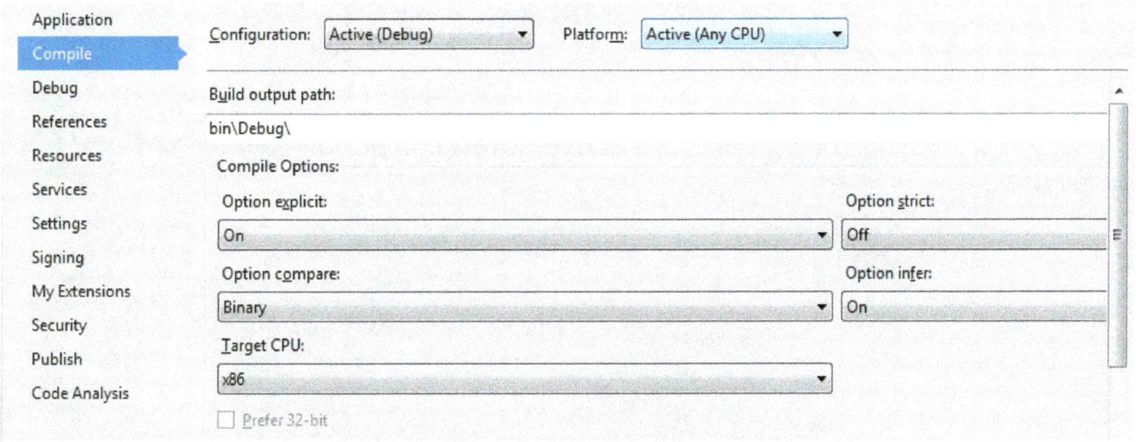

- Close the window to finalize the change.

3-6 Visual Basic and Databases

How will you know if you have an operating system problem? The first symptom is that your application will have no data displayed, indicating the database did not open correctly. Secondly, the **Immediate Window** will have this error message:

`An unhandled exception of type 'System.InvalidOperationException' occurred in System.Data.dll`

Or, when opening the database, you may see a window similar to this:

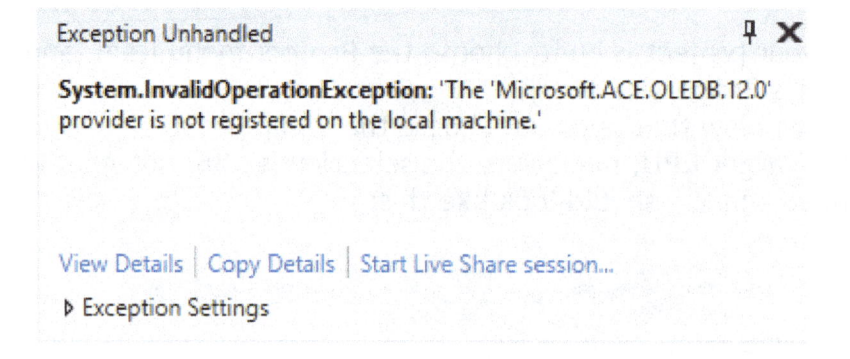

> **Exception Unhandled**
>
> **System.InvalidOperationException:** 'The 'Microsoft.ACE.OLEDB.12.0' provider is not registered on the local machine.'
>
> View Details | Copy Details | Start Live Share session...
> ▷ Exception Settings

If you see such symptoms, make the above noted correction to your project's properties.

Connection Object - SQL Server Database

To use the **SqlConnection** object, an application must have these two lines at the top of the corresponding code listing:

```
Imports System.Data
Imports System.Data.SqlClient
```

Every SQL Server example we build in this class will have these two lines.

To declare and construct an **SqlConnection** object named **MyConnection**, using a **ConnectionString** named **MyConnectionString**, use:

```
Dim MyConnection As SqlConnection
MyConnection = New SqlConnection(MyConnectionString)
```

The **ConnectionString** for an SQL Server database is the following string:

```
Data Source=SQLInstanceName;
AttachDbFilename=DatabaseName; Integrated Security=True;
Connect Timeout=30; User Instance=True
```

where **SQLInstanceName** is the name of your SQL Server instance (set when installed; if using default SQL Server Express settings, name is **.\SQLEXPRESS**) and **DatabaseName** is a complete path to the database.

We're about to start looking at the books database (**SQLBooks.mdf**), SQL Server version of **BooksDB.accdb**). Make a copy of the database and place it in a working directory (you decide on a name - we will use **VBDB\Working**).

Example 3-1

Books Database

After copying the database (**BooksDB.accdb** or **SQLBooksDB.mdf**) to your working directory, start a new application. Our end goal with this application is to develop a form where we can look through the **Titles** table in the books database. We start by simply opening the database using a connection object.

1. Place a single label control on the form.

2. Set the following properties:

Form1:
    Name   frmTitles
    FormBorderStyle FixedSingle
    StartPosition   CenterScreen
    Text   Titles Database

Label1:
    Name   lblState
    AutoSize   False
    BackColor   White
    BorderStyle   Fixed3D
    Text   [blank]

Database Connection 3-9

When done, the form will look something like this:

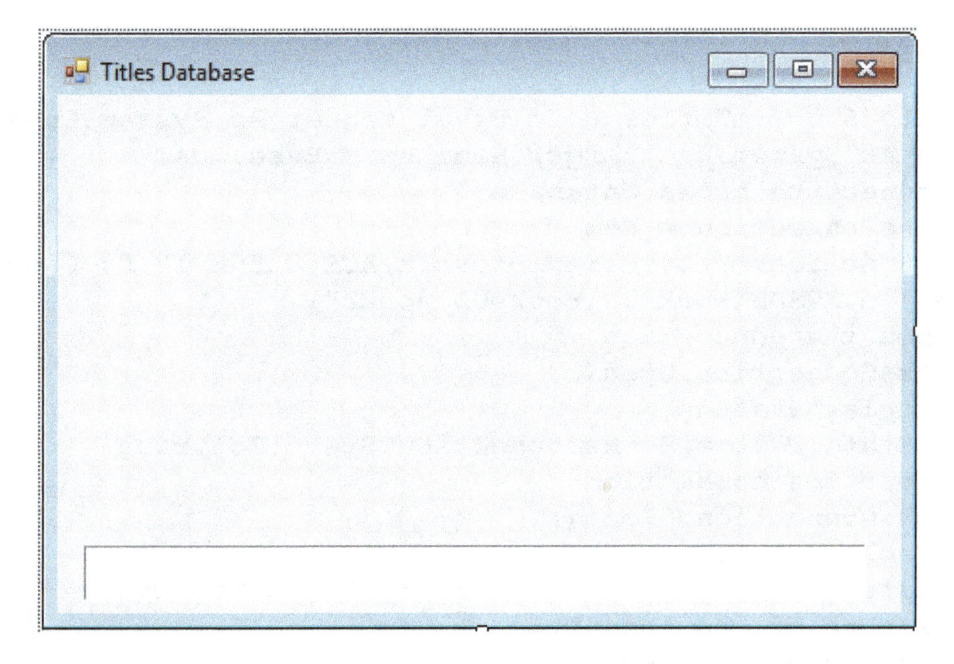

All the extra space will be used as we continue building this application.

3. Open the code window and place these two lines at the top:

Access Database:

    Imports System.Data
    Imports System.Data.OleDb

SQL Server Database:

    Imports System.Data
    Imports System.Data.SqlClient

4. Use this form level declaration to declare the connection:

Access Database:

    Dim BooksConnection As OleDbConnection

SQL Server Database:

    Dim BooksConnection As SqlConnection

3-10 Visual Basic and Databases

5. Add this code to the **frmTitles Load** procedure:

Access Database:

```
  Private Sub FrmTitles_Load(ByVal sender As System.Object, ByVal e As System.EventArgs) Handles MyBase.Load
    'connect to books database
    BooksConnection = New OleDbConnection("Provider=Microsoft.ACE.OLEDB.12.0; Data Source = c:\VBDB\Working\BooksDB.accdb")
    'open the connection
    BooksConnection.Open()
    'display state
    lblState.Text = BooksConnection.State.ToString
    'close the connection
    BooksConnection.Close()
    'display state
    lblState.Text += BooksConnection.State.ToString
    'dispose of the connection object
    BooksConnection.Dispose()
  End Sub
```

SQL Server Database:

```
  Private Sub FrmTitles_Load(ByVal sender As System.Object, ByVal e As System.EventArgs) Handles MyBase.Load
    'connect to books database
    BooksConnection = New SqlConnection("Data Source=.\SQLEXPRESS;AttachDbFilename=C:\VBDB\Working\SQLBooksDB.mdf; Integrated Security=True; Connect Timeout=30; User Instance=True")
    'open the connection
    BooksConnection.Open()
    'display state
    lblState.Text = BooksConnection.State.ToString
    'close the connection
    BooksConnection.Close()
    'display state
    lblState.Text += BooksConnection.State.ToString
    'dispose of the connection object
    BooksConnection.Dispose()
  End Sub
```

Database Connection

In this code we construct the connection using the proper connection string. Notice the connection string assumes the database is in the **c:\VBDB\Working** folder. You will have to change this if your working copy of the database is located elsewhere. Then, we simply open, close and dispose of the connection. The status is displayed in the **lblState** control.

The finished code should be:

Access Database:

```
Imports System.Data
Imports System.Data.OleDb
Public Class frmTitles
   Dim BooksConnection As OleDbConnection
   Private Sub FrmTitles_Load(ByVal sender As System.Object, ByVal e As System.EventArgs) Handles MyBase.Load
     'connect to books database
     BooksConnection = New OleDbConnection("Provider=Microsoft.ACE.OLEDB.12.0; Data Source = c:\VBDB\Working\BooksDB.accdb")
     'open the connection
     BooksConnection.Open()
     'display state
     lblState.Text = BooksConnection.State.ToString
     'close the connection
     BooksConnection.Close()
     'display state
     lblState.Text += BooksConnection.State.ToString
     'dispose of the object(s)
     BooksConnection.Dispose()
   End Sub
End Class
```

SQL Server Database:

```
Imports System.Data
Imports System.Data.SqlClient
Public Class frmTitles
  Dim BooksConnection As SqlConnection
  Private Sub FrmTitles_Load(ByVal sender As System.Object, ByVal e As System.EventArgs) Handles MyBase.Load
    'connect to books database
    BooksConnection = New SqlConnection("Data Source=.\SQLEXPRESS; AttachDbFilename=C:\VBDB\Working\SQLBooksDB.mdf; Integrated Security=True; Connect Timeout=30; User Instance=True")
    'open the connection
    BooksConnection.Open()
    'display state
    lblState.Text = BooksConnection.State.ToString
    'close the connection
    BooksConnection.Close()
    'display state
    lblState.Text += BooksConnection.State.ToString
    'dispose of the object(s)
    BooksConnection.Dispose()
  End Sub
End Class
```

6. Save the application. Run the application. You should see:

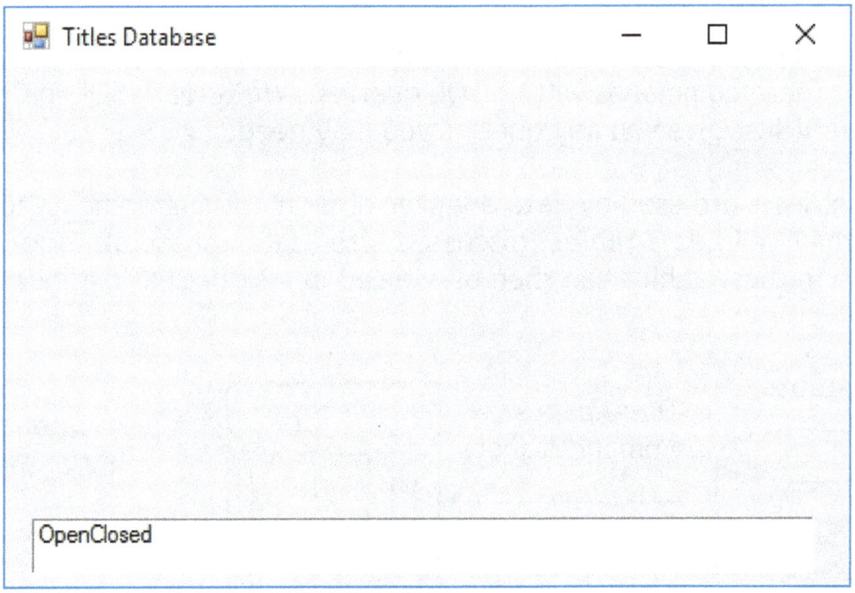
Titles Database
OpenClosed

This shows that the connection was opened and then closed. If you do not see this or you get an error message, make sure your connection string is correct and the books database is really located where you (and your connection string) think it is.

If you get an error message similar to this

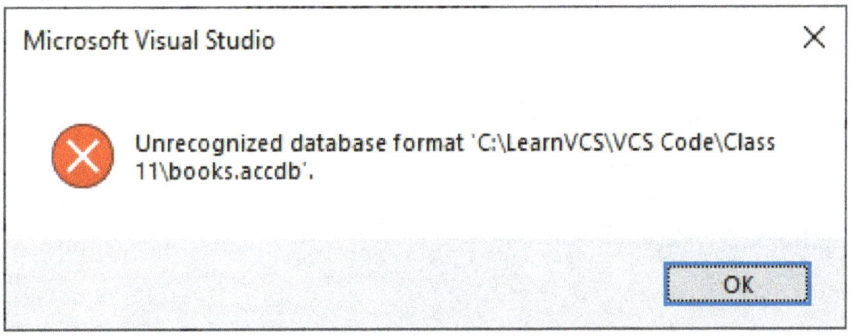
Microsoft Visual Studio
Unrecognized database format 'C:\LearnVCS\VCS Code\Class 11\books.accdb'.
OK

This indicates you are missing the proper driver for the Access Database. See the proper download instructions in Class 2.

Command Object

The **command object** is used to define commands to send to the database. In this course, these commands will be SQL queries. We'll learn SQL in Chapter 4. For now, we'll just give you any queries you may need.

Command objects are used by **data adapter** objects (discussed next) to create **datasets** which hold **data tables** (discussed after data adapters). The information in these tables can then be viewed in a Visual Basic application:

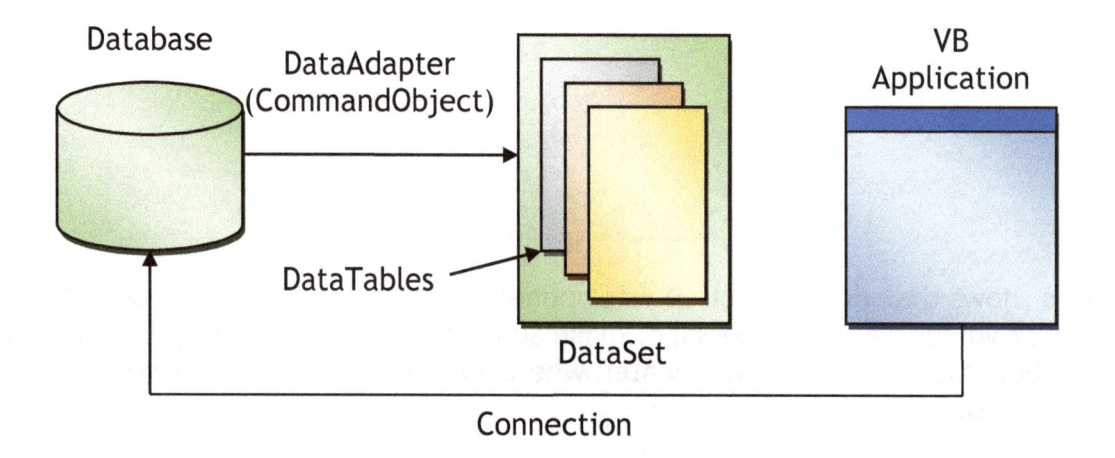

Command Object - Access Database

To declare and construct an **OleDbCommand** object named **MyCommand** using a SQL query named **MyQuery** for a connection object named **MyConnection**, use:

```
Dim MyCommand As OleDbCommand
MyCommand = New OleDbCommand(MyQuery, MyConnection)
```

After a quick example, we see how to use such an object with a data adapter to create a data table.

Command Object - SQL Server Database

To declare and construct an **SqlCommand** object named **MyCommand** using a SQL query named **MyQuery** for a connection object named **MyConnection**, use:

```
Dim MyCommand As SqlCommand
MyCommand = New SqlCommand(MyQuery, MyConnection)
```

After a quick example, we see how to use such an object with a data adapter to create a data table.

Example 3-1 (Command Object)

Books Database

We add a command object to our example. We need a SQL query to retrieve data from the **Titles** table of the books database. The query that does this is:

Select * From Titles

This says select all fields (* is a wildcard) from the **Titles** table.

1. Add this form level declaration:

Access Database:

```
Dim TitlesCommand As OleDbCommand
```

SQL Server Database:

```
Dim TitlesCommand As SqlCommand
```

Database Connection 3-17

2. Add the shaded code to the **frmTitles Load** procedure:

Access Database:

```
Private Sub FrmTitles_Load(ByVal sender As System.Object, ByVal e As System.EventArgs) Handles MyBase.Load
    'connect to books database
    BooksConnection = New OleDbConnection("Provider=Microsoft.ACE.OLEDB.12.0; Data Source = c:\VBDB\Working\BooksDB.accdb")
    'open the connection
    BooksConnection.Open()
    'display state
    lblState.Text = BooksConnection.State.ToString
    'establish command object
    TitlesCommand = New OleDbCommand("Select * from Titles", BooksConnection)
    'close the connection
    BooksConnection.Close()
    'display state
    lblState.Text += BooksConnection.State.ToString
    'dispose of the connection object(s)
    BooksConnection.Dispose()
    TitlesCommand.Dispose()
End Sub
```

Visual Basic and Databases

SQL Server Database:

```
Private Sub FrmTitles_Load(ByVal sender As System.Object, ByVal e As System.EventArgs) Handles MyBase.Load
    'connect to books database
    BooksConnection = New SqlConnection("Data Source=.\SQLEXPRESS; AttachDbFilename=C:\VBDB\Working\SQLBooksDB.mdf; Integrated Security=True; Connect Timeout=30; User Instance=True")
    'open the connection
    BooksConnection.Open()
    'display state
    lblState.Text = BooksConnection.State.ToString
    'establish command object
    TitlesCommand = New SqlCommand("Select * from Titles", BooksConnection)
    'close the connection
    BooksConnection.Close()
    'display state
    lblState.Text += BooksConnection.State.ToString
    'dispose of the object(s)
    BooksConnection.Dispose()
    TitlesCommand.Dispose()
  End Sub
```

This code creates the command object for the books connection object.

3. Resave and rerun the application, making sure you get no errors.

DataAdapter Object

As just seen, a **data adapter** object uses a **command object** to transfer data between a **connection object** and a **dataset** containing one or more **data table(s)**. For our initial work, we will use a data adapter to directly form a data table (discussed next), without using a dataset. In general, you need one data adapter object for each table of data you want to view.

Data adapter **properties**:

DeleteCommand	Command object that allows the adapter to delete rows from a data table.
InsertCommand	Command object that allows the adapter to insert rows into a data table.
SelectCommand	Command object that the adapter uses to select rows for a data table.
UpdateCommand	Command object that the adapter uses to update rows in a data table.

Data adapter **methods**:

Fill	Fills the data adapter with a given data table.
Update	Updates the data table held by the data adapter.

DataAdapter Object - Access Database

To declare and construct an **OleDbDataAdapter** named **MyAdapter**, use:

```
Dim MyAdapter As OleDbDataAdapter
MyAdapter = New OleDbDataAdapter()
```

We specify the **SelectCommand** (**MyCommand**, a command object) with a SQL query to select the rows that will make up the corresponding data table.

```
MyAdapter.SelectCommand = MyCommand
```

Once the **SelectCommand** is specified, the other command objects (**DeleteCommand**, **InsertCommand**, **UpdateCommand**) are built using a **command builder** object. The statement that accomplishes this task for our example adapter (**MyAdapter**) is:

```
Dim MyCommandBuilder As New OleDbCommandBuilder(MyAdapter)
```

Once this line is executed, the three command objects can be viewed (if desired) by examining:

```
MyCommandBuilder.GetDeleteCommand.CommandText
MyCommandBuilder.GetInsertCommand.CommandText
MyCommandBuilder.GetUpdateCommand.CommandText
```

We really don't ever look at these command objects - they are used by the **Update** method of the data adapter. We look at that method in Chapter 5 when we start our study of database management tasks.

Believe it or not, we're getting close to seeing some actual data! The data adapter's **Fill** method accomplishes this task, but first we need to look at datasets and data tables.

DataAdapter Object - SQL Server Database

To declare and construct an **SqlDataAdapter** named **MyAdapter**, use:

```
Dim MyAdapter As SqlDataAdapter
MyAdapter = New SqlDataAdapter()
```

We specify the **SelectCommand** (**MyCommand**, a command object) with a SQL query to select the rows that will make up the corresponding data table.

```
MyAdapter.SelectCommand = MyCommand
```

Once the **SelectCommand** is specified, the other command objects (**DeleteCommand, InsertCommand, UpdateCommand**) are built using a **command builder** object. The statement that accomplishes this task for our example adapter (**MyAdapter**) is:

```
Dim MyCommandBuilder As New SqlCommandBuilder(MyAdapter)
```

Once this line is executed, the three command objects can be viewed (if desired) by examining:

```
MyCommandBuilder.GetDeleteCommand.CommandText
MyCommandBuilder.GetInsertCommand.CommandText
MyCommandBuilder.GetUpdateCommand.CommandText
```

We really don't ever look at these command objects - they are used by the **Update** method of the data adapter. We look at that method in Chapter 5 when we start our study of database management tasks.

Believe it or not, we're getting close to seeing some actual data! The data adapter's **Fill** method accomplishes this task, but first we need to look at datasets and data tables.

DataSet Object

A **dataset** object provides all the features you need to build, load, store, manipulate and save data in a relational database. It is a 'container' for multiple data table objects.

Dataset **properties**:

DataSetName	Name assigned to dataset.
Tables	A collection of data tables stored in the dataset.

To declare and construct a **DataSet** named **MyDataSet**, use:

```
Dim MyDataSet As DataSet
MyDataSet = New DataSet()
```

To add a data table (**MyTable**) to a dataset, use:

```
MyDataSet.Tables.Add(MyTable)
```

We don't use data set objects a lot in this course. We prefer to work directly with data tables.

DataTable Object

A **data table** object represents the data contained in one table of a **dataset** object.

Data table **properties**:

Columns	Collection of **DataColumn** objects that define information in the columns of the table.
DataSet	The **DataSet** object (if any) that contains this **DataTable**.
DefaultView	A **DataView** representing the **DataTable** contents.
Rows	Collection of **DataRow** objects that define each table row.
TableName	Name of data table.

Data table **methods**:

Clear	Removes all rows from data table.
Copy	Makes a copy of the data table.
ImportRow	Copies a **DataRow** object into the data table.
NewRow	Creates a new **DataRow** object for the data table.

To declare and construct a data table named **MyTable**, use:

```
Dim MyTable As DataTable
MyTable = New DataTable()
```

Once the table is created, it is filled with data using the **Fill** method for a corresponding data adapter control. If that adapter is **MyAdapter**, the syntax is:

```
MyAdapter.Fill(MyTable)
```

At this point, we have a data table (formed using by sending a SQL query to the database) we can view in a Visual Basic application.

DataRow Object

A **data row** object represents the information in one record of a data table. It is very useful for retrieving and/or modifying individual fields in a record.

Data row **properties**:

Item	Gets or sets one of the row's fields. The parameter can be the column index or the field name.
Table	Reference to data table containing the row.

Data row **methods**:

BeginEdit	Puts data row in edit mode.
CancelEdit	Cancels the current edit on the data row.
Delete	Deletes the row from the data table.

We will look at data rows in more detail later in the course, especially in the example projects in Chapter 10.

Database Connection 3-25

Example 3-1 (Data Table)

Books Database

We add a data adapter object and a data table object to our example. The data table associated with the data adapter will have the **Titles** table from the books database.

1. Add these form level declarations:

Access Database:

```
Dim TitlesAdapter As OleDbDataAdapter
Dim TitlesTable As DataTable
```

SQL Server Database:

```
Dim TitlesAdapter As SqlDataAdapter
Dim TitlesTable As DataTable
```

2. Add the shaded code to the **frmTitles Load** procedure:

Access Database:

```
Private Sub FrmTitles_Load(ByVal sender As System.Object, ByVal e As System.EventArgs) Handles MyBase.Load
    'connect to books database
    BooksConnection = New OleDbConnection("Provider=Microsoft.ACE.OLEDB.12.0; Data Source = c:\VBDB\Working\BooksDB.accdb")
    'open the connection
    BooksConnection.Open()
    'display state
    lblState.Text = BooksConnection.State.ToString
    'establish command object
    TitlesCommand = New OleDbCommand("Select * from Titles",
```

```
BooksConnection)
    'establish data adapter/data table
    TitlesAdapter = New OleDbDataAdapter()
    TitlesAdapter.SelectCommand = TitlesCommand
    TitlesTable = New DataTable()
    TitlesAdapter.Fill(TitlesTable)
    'close the connection
    BooksConnection.Close()
    'display state
    lblState.Text += BooksConnection.State.ToString
    'dispose of the object(s)
    BooksConnection.Dispose()
    TitlesCommand.Dispose()
    TitlesAdapter.Dispose()
    TitlesTable.Dispose()
  End Sub
```

SQL Server Database:

```
  Private Sub FrmTitles_Load(ByVal sender As System.Object, ByVal e As System.EventArgs) Handles MyBase.Load
    'connect to books database
    BooksConnection = New SqlConnection("Data Source=.\SQLEXPRESS; AttachDbFilename=C:\VBDB\Working\SQLBooksDB.mdf; Integrated Security=True; Connect Timeout=30; User Instance=True")
    'open the connection
    BooksConnection.Open()
    'display state
    lblState.Text = BooksConnection.State.ToString
    'establish command object
    TitlesCommand = New SqlCommand("Select * from Titles", BooksConnection)
    'establish data adapter/data table
    TitlesAdapter = New SqlDataAdapter()
    TitlesAdapter.SelectCommand = TitlesCommand
    TitlesTable = New DataTable()
    TitlesAdapter.Fill(TitlesTable)
    'close the connection
    BooksConnection.Close()
    'display state
    lblState.Text += BooksConnection.State.ToString
    'dispose of the object(s)
    BooksConnection.Dispose()
    TitlesCommand.Dispose()
    TitlesAdapter.Dispose()
    TitlesTable.Dispose()
  End Sub
```

Database Connection 3-27

This new code creates the data adapter and loads it with data from the **Titles** table.

3. Resave and rerun the application. Again, make sure there are no errors. If no errors occur, you have successfully created a data table. Next, we look at how to view information from this table in a Visual Basic application.

Data Bound Controls

We have seen that the ADO .NET data objects allow us to connect to a database and form a data table. Yet, these objects do not provide us with any way to view the information in a database. To view the information, we use **data bound controls** that are special controls with properties established by database fields. A data bound control is needed for each field (column) in the database table you need to view. Most of the standard Visual Basic tools can be used as **data bound** controls.

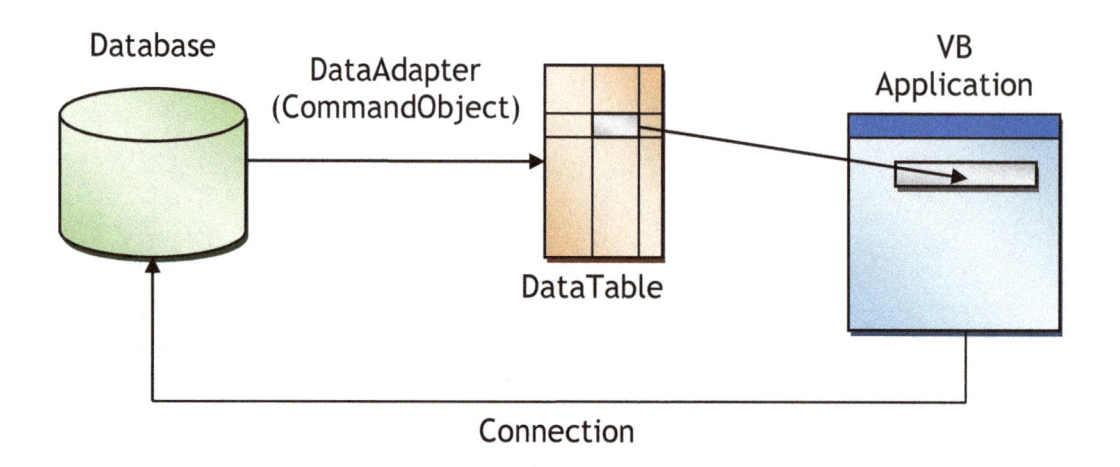

Some data bound data controls (using simple binding) are:

Label   Can be used to provide display-only access to a specified text data field. The label **Text** property is usually bound.

Text Box   Can be used to provide read/write access to a specified text data field. Probably, the most widely used data bound tool. **Text** property is usually bound.

Check Box Used to provide read/write access to a Boolean field. **Value** property is data bound.

Picture Box Used to display a graphical image from a bitmap, icon, gif, jpeg, or metafile file. Provides read/write access to a image/binary data field. **Image** property is data bound.

Other controls using complex binding (look at in further detail later in this course):

- **List Box**   Can be used to display all values of a particular field in a database.
- **Combo Box**   Can be used to display all values of a particular field in a database.
- **Data Grid View** Can be used to display an entire database table.

To bind a particular property (**MyProperty**) of a control (**MyControl**) to a particular field (**MyField**) of a data table object (**MyTable**), the syntax is:

```
MyControl.DataBindings.Add(MyProperty, MyTable, MyField)
```

So, every control that is to be bound to a database field needs a statement like this. The bindings are usually done in the initial form's **Load** procedure.

To clear a previously defined data binding, the syntax is:

```
MyControl.DataBindings.Clear()
```

Example 3-1 (Data Binding)

Books Database

We now add some controls that are bound to fields in the **Titles** database table so we can view some data.

1. Remove the label control used to display state (we know things are working okay by now).

2. Add four label controls and four text box controls, so the form looks like this:

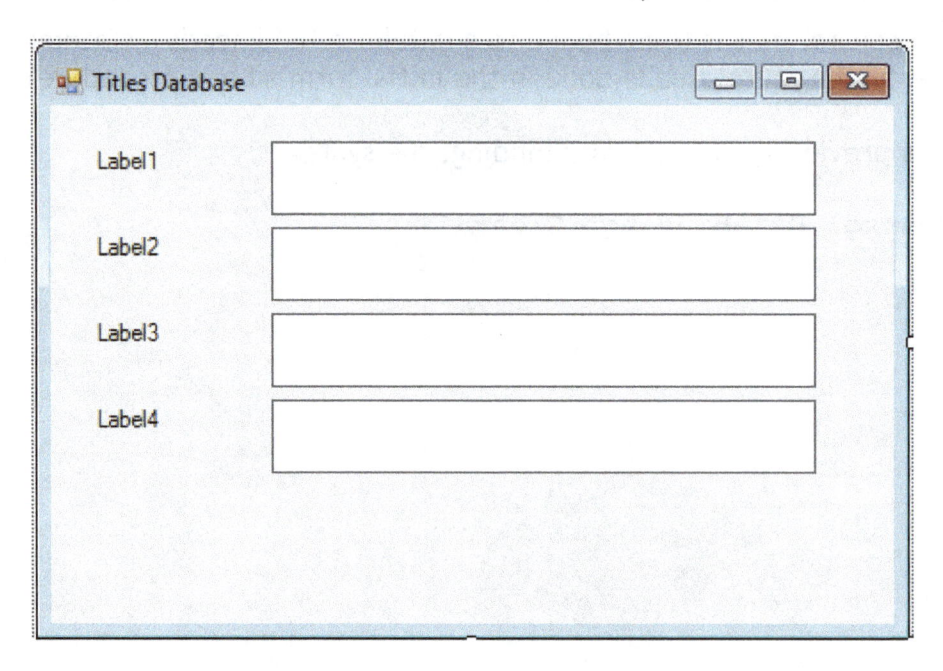

3. Set the following properties:

Label1:
    Text   Title

Label2:
    Text   Year Published

Label3:
    Text   ISBN

Label4:
    Text   Publisher ID

TextBox1:
    Name   txtTitle
    BackColor   White
    ReadOnly   True
    MultiLine   True

TextBox2:
    Name   txtYearPublished
    BackColor   White
    ReadOnly   True
    MultiLine   True

TextBox3:
    Name   txtISBN
    BackColor   White
    ReadOnly   True
    MultiLine   True

TextBox4:
    Name   txtPubID
    BackColor   White
    ReadOnly   True
    MultiLine   True

Visual Basic and Databases

The finished form should appear as:

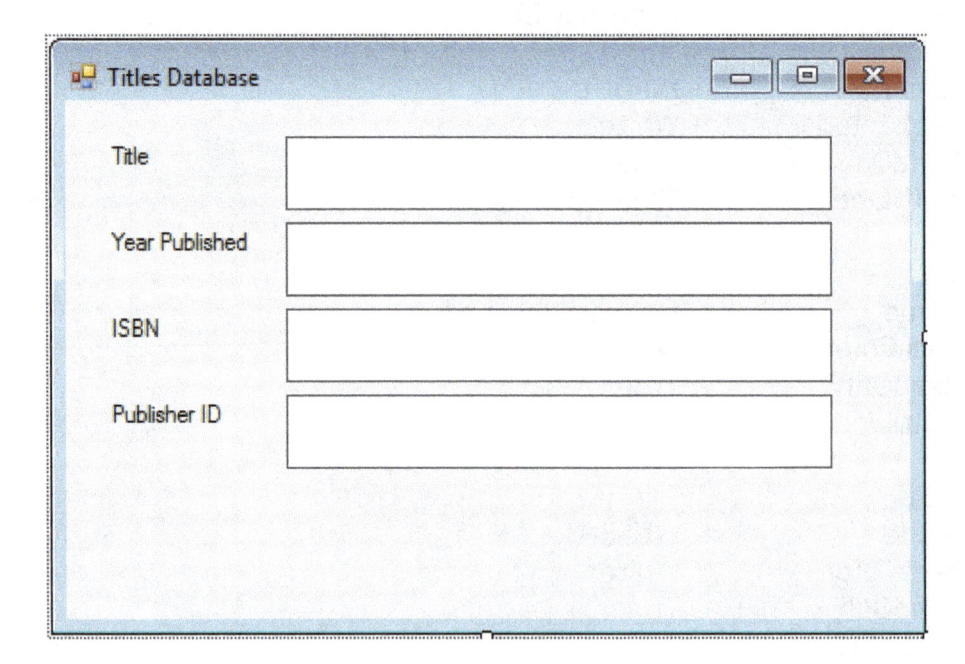

Database Connection 3-33

4. Add the shaded lines to the **frmTitles Load** procedure. These lines bind the four text boxes to their respective fields in the **Titles** table. Remove the lines referring to **lblState** (we removed that control).

Access Database:

```
  Private Sub FrmTitles_Load(ByVal sender As System.Object,
ByVal e As System.EventArgs) Handles MyBase.Load
    'connect to books database
    BooksConnection = New
OleDbConnection("Provider=Microsoft.ACE.OLEDB.12.0; Data
Source = c:\VBDB\Working\BooksDB.accdb")
    'open the connection
    BooksConnection.Open()
    'establish command object
    TitlesCommand = New OleDbCommand("Select * from Titles",
BooksConnection)
    'establish data adapter/data table
    TitlesAdapter = New OleDbDataAdapter()
    TitlesAdapter.SelectCommand = TitlesCommand
    TitlesTable = New DataTable()
    TitlesAdapter.Fill(TitlesTable)
    'bind controls to data table
    txtTitle.DataBindings.Add("Text", TitlesTable, "Title")
    txtYearPublished.DataBindings.Add("Text", TitlesTable,
"Year_Published")
    txtISBN.DataBindings.Add("Text", TitlesTable, "ISBN")
    txtPubID.DataBindings.Add("Text", TitlesTable, "PubID")
    'close the connection
    BooksConnection.Close()
    'dispose of the connection object
    BooksConnection.Dispose()
    TitlesCommand.Dispose()
    TitlesAdapter.Dispose()
    TitlesTable.Dispose()
  End Sub
```

SQL Server Database:

```
  Private Sub FrmTitles_Load(ByVal sender As System.Object, ByVal e As System.EventArgs) Handles MyBase.Load
    'connect to books database
    BooksConnection = New SqlConnection("Data Source=.\SQLEXPRESS; AttachDbFilename=C:\VBDB\Working\SQLBooksDB.mdf; Integrated Security=True; Connect Timeout=30; User Instance=True")
    'open the connection
    BooksConnection.Open()
    'establish command object
    TitlesCommand = New SqlCommand("Select * from Titles", BooksConnection)
    'establish data adapter/data table
    TitlesAdapter = New SqlDataAdapter()
    TitlesAdapter.SelectCommand = TitlesCommand
    TitlesTable = New DataTable()
    TitlesAdapter.Fill(TitlesTable)
    'bind controls to data table
    txtTitle.DataBindings.Add("Text", TitlesTable, "Title")
    txtYearPublished.DataBindings.Add("Text", TitlesTable, "Year_Published")
    txtISBN.DataBindings.Add("Text", TitlesTable, "ISBN")
    txtPubID.DataBindings.Add("Text", TitlesTable, "PubID")
    'close the connection
    BooksConnection.Close()
    'dispose of the object(s)
    BooksConnection.Dispose()
    TitlesCommand.Dispose()
    TitlesAdapter.Dispose()
    TitlesTable.Dispose()
  End Sub
```

Database Connection 3-35

5. Resave and rerun the application. You should see:

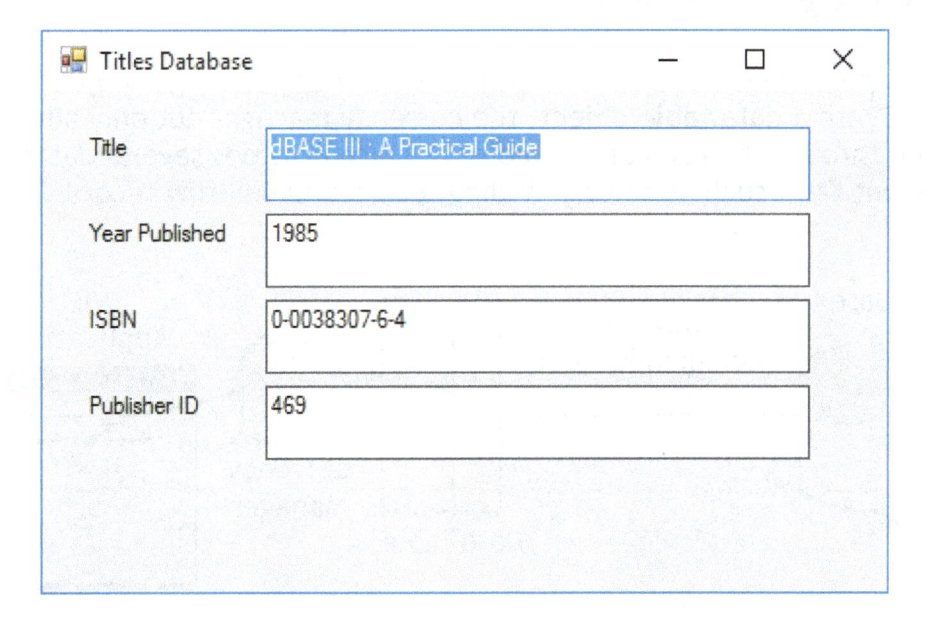

Titles Database	
Title	dBASE III : A Practical Guide
Year Published	1985
ISBN	0-0038307-6-4
Publisher ID	469

At long last, we see some data in our Visual Basic application. The first record in the **Titles** table is being displayed. We still have no way of navigating through the table. We add that capability next with a very powerful data object, the **CurrencyManager** object.

CurrencyManager Object

A final component we need to view data is a **currency manager** object. Once associated with a **data table** object, the currency manager not only allows navigation through the rows of the table, but also provides several database management tasks such as editing, adding record and deleting records.

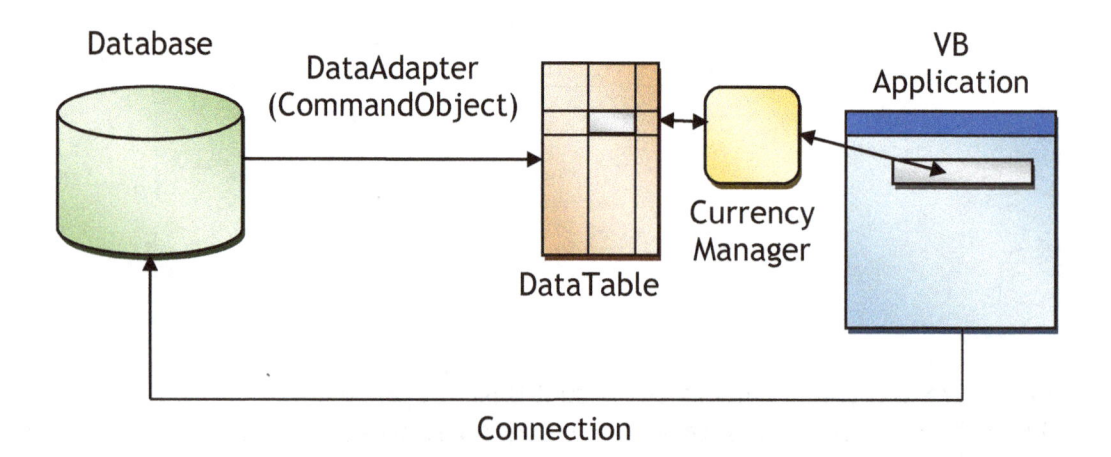

Currency manager object **properties**:

Bindings	Collection of controls bound to this manager.
Count	Number of rows in table associated with manager.
Position	Gets or sets the current row in the data table (ranges from 0 to Count - 1).

Currency manager **methods**:

AddNew	Add a new row to the data source.
CancelCurrentEdit	Cancels the current editing operation.
EndCurrentEdit	Ends the current editing operation, accepting any changes.
Refresh	Refreshes the bound controls.
RemoveAt	Removes the indicated data row.

Database Connection

For now, we look specifically at the navigational abilities of the currency manager object. First, declare a currency manager object (**MyManager**) using:

```
Dim MyManager As CurrencyManager
```

We use the **BindingContext** of the associated data table to establish a reference for the currency manager. For a table named **MyTable**, we use this syntax:

```
MyManager = DirectCast(Me.BindingContext(MyTable), CurrencyManager)
```

This simply converts the binding context information of the table into a currency manager object.

Once the currency manager object is established, basic navigation among the **Count** rows in the data table is accomplished via a simple modification of the **Position** property. Look at the final incarnation of Example 3-1 to see its use in such a manner.

Example 3-1 (Final Version)

Books Database

Lastly, we add some controls that allow navigation through the rows of the **Titles** database table

1. Add four button controls so the form looks like this:

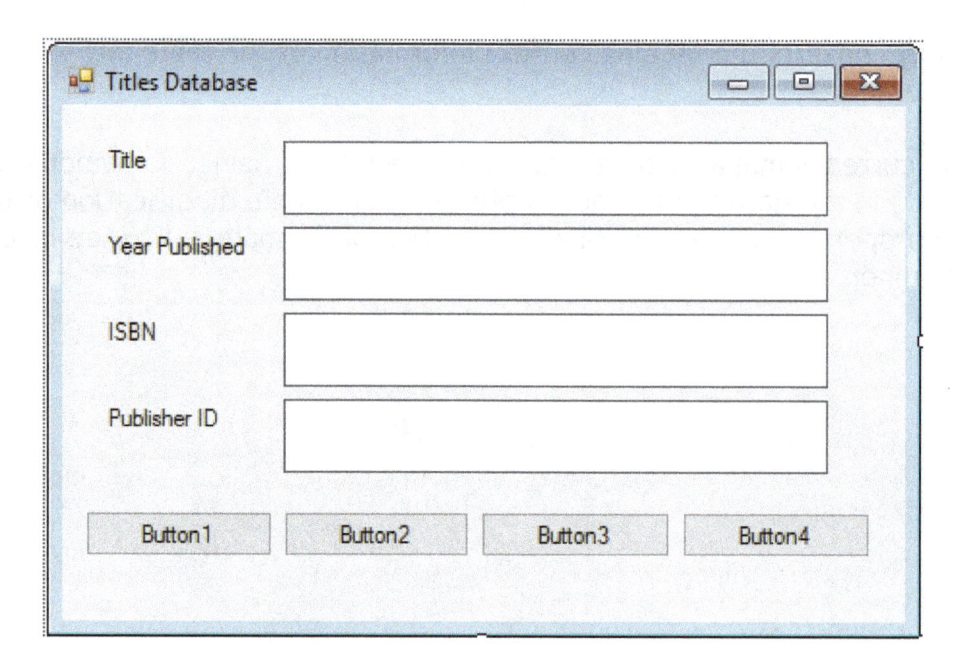

Database Connection

2. Set the following properties:

Button1:
- Name   btnFirst
- Text   &First

Button2:
- Name   btnPrevious
- Text   &Previous

Button3:
- Name   btnNext
- Text   &Next

Button4:
- Name   btnLast
- Text   &Last

The finished form is:

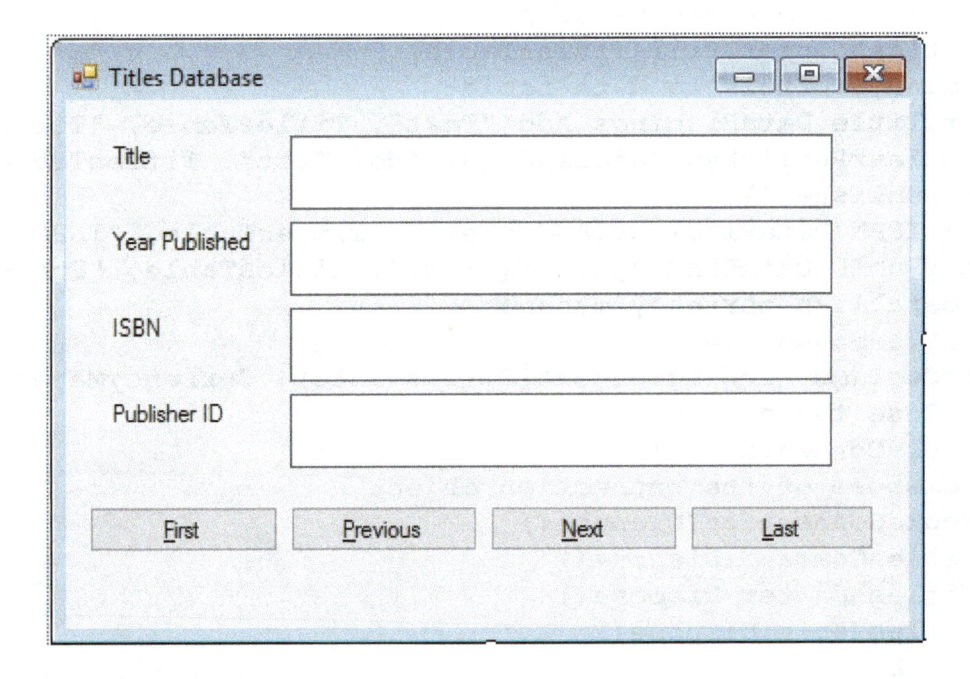

3. Add this form level declaration:

```
Dim TitlesManager As CurrencyManager
```

3-40   Visual Basic and Databases

4. Add the shaded lines to the **frmTitles Load** procedure. These lines set up the currency manager reference to the **Titles** table.

Access Database:

```
Private Sub FrmTitles_Load(ByVal sender As System.Object, ByVal e As System.EventArgs) Handles MyBase.Load
    'connect to books database
    BooksConnection = New OleDbConnection("Provider=Microsoft.ACE.OLEDB.12.0; Data Source = c:\VBDB\Working\BooksDB.accdb")
    'open the connection
    BooksConnection.Open()
    'establish command object
    TitlesCommand = New OleDbCommand("Select * from Titles", BooksConnection)
    'establish data adapter/data table
    TitlesAdapter = New OleDbDataAdapter()
    TitlesAdapter.SelectCommand = TitlesCommand
    TitlesTable = New DataTable()
    TitlesAdapter.Fill(TitlesTable)
    'bind controls to data table
    txtTitle.DataBindings.Add("Text", TitlesTable, "Title")
    txtYearPublished.DataBindings.Add("Text", TitlesTable, "Year_Published")
    txtISBN.DataBindings.Add("Text", TitlesTable, "ISBN")
    txtPubID.DataBindings.Add("Text", TitlesTable, "PubID")
    'establish currency manager
    TitlesManager = DirectCast(Me.BindingContext(TitlesTable), CurrencyManager)
    'close the connection
    BooksConnection.Close()
    'dispose of the connection object
    BooksConnection.Dispose()
    TitlesCommand.Dispose()
    TitlesAdapter.Dispose()
    TitlesTable.Dispose()
End Sub
```

Database Connection 3-41

SQL Server Database:

```vb
    Private Sub FrmTitles_Load(ByVal sender As System.Object, ByVal e As System.EventArgs) Handles MyBase.Load
        'connect to books database
        BooksConnection = New SqlConnection("Data Source=.\SQLEXPRESS;AttachDbFilename=C:\VBDB\Working\SQLBooksDB.mdf;Integrated Security=True;Connect Timeout=30;User Instance=True")
        'open the connection
        BooksConnection.Open()
        'establish command object
        TitlesCommand = New SqlCommand("Select * from Titles", BooksConnection)
        'establish data adapter/data table
        TitlesAdapter = New SqlDataAdapter()
        TitlesAdapter.SelectCommand = TitlesCommand
        TitlesTable = New DataTable()
        TitlesAdapter.Fill(TitlesTable)
        'bind controls to data table
        txtTitle.DataBindings.Add("Text", TitlesTable, "Title")
        txtYearPublished.DataBindings.Add("Text", TitlesTable, "Year_Published")
        txtISBN.DataBindings.Add("Text", TitlesTable, "ISBN")
        txtPubID.DataBindings.Add("Text", TitlesTable, "PubID")
        'establish currency manager
        TitlesManager = DirectCast(Me.BindingContext(TitlesTable), CurrencyManager)
        'close the connection
        BooksConnection.Close()
        'dispose of the object(s)
        BooksConnection.Dispose()
        TitlesCommand.Dispose()
        TitlesAdapter.Dispose()
        TitlesTable.Dispose()
    End Sub
```

5. Add these four **Click** procedures for the navigation buttons; each procedure simply modifies the **Position** property accordingly:

```
Private Sub BtnFirst_Click(ByVal sender As System.Object, ByVal e As System.EventArgs) Handles btnFirst.Click
    TitlesManager.Position = 0
End Sub

Private Sub BtnPrevious_Click(ByVal sender As System.Object, ByVal e As System.EventArgs) Handles btnPrevious.Click
    TitlesManager.Position -= 1
End Sub

Private Sub BtnNext_Click(ByVal sender As System.Object, ByVal e As System.EventArgs) Handles btnNext.Click
    TitlesManager.Position += 1
End Sub

Private Sub BtnLast_Click(ByVal sender As System.Object, ByVal e As System.EventArgs) Handles btnLast.Click
    TitlesManager.Position = TitlesManager.Count - 1
End Sub
```

Database Connection 3-43

6. Save the application one last time (Access version saved in the **Example 3-1** folder in **VBDB\Access\Class 3** folder; SQL Server version saved in the **Example 3-1** folder in **VBDB\SQL Server\Class 3** folder). Run the application. Try out the navigation buttons. Notice how all the fields update with each click of a button. Here's the second record (I clicked **Next** once).

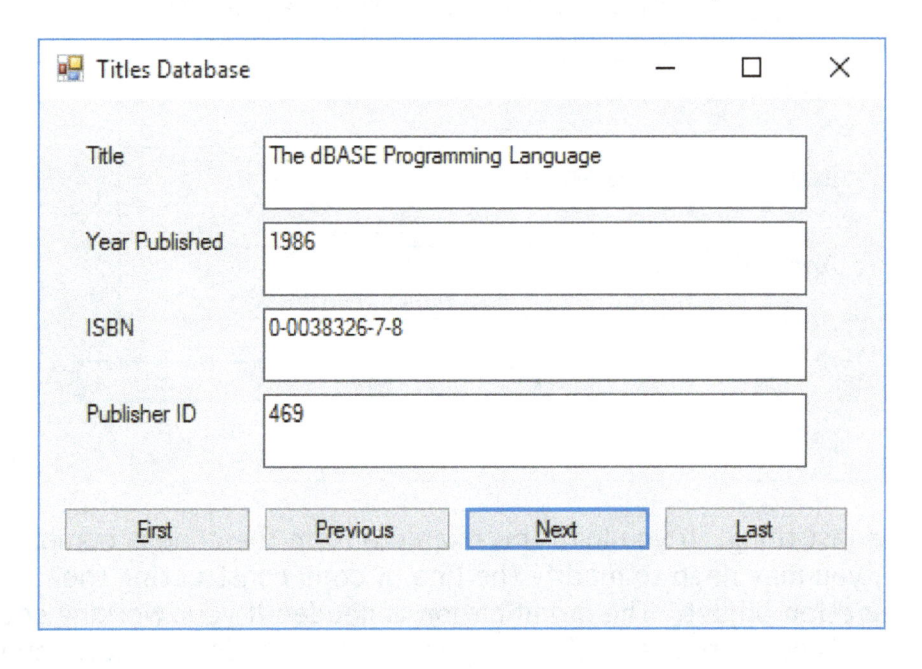

Titles Database	
Title	The dBASE Programming Language
Year Published	1986
ISBN	0-0038326-7-8
Publisher ID	469

[First] [Previous] [Next] [Last]

Here's the last record:

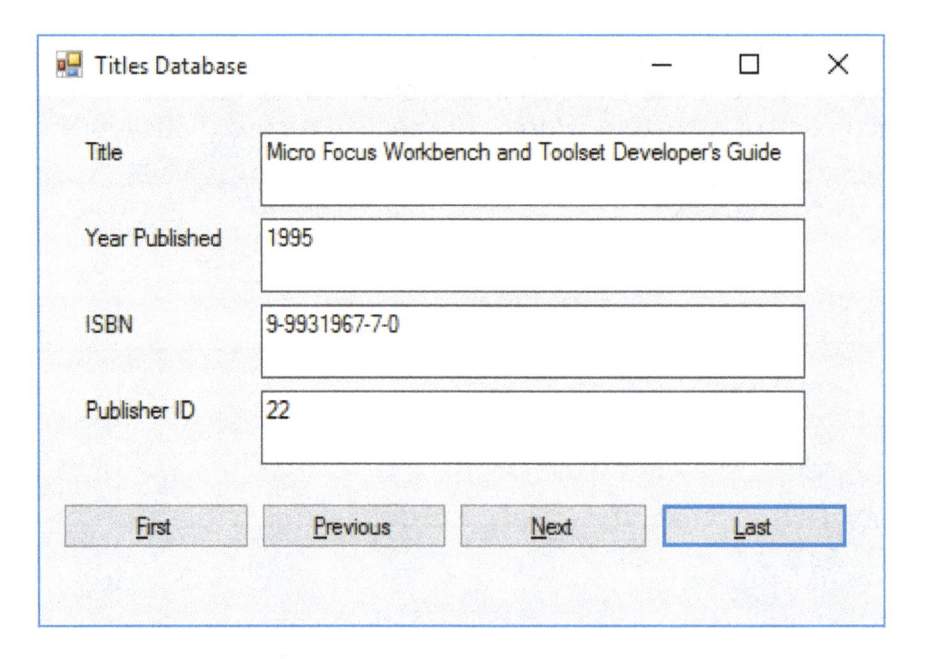

Titles Database

Title	Micro Focus Workbench and Toolset Developer's Guide
Year Published	1995
ISBN	9-9931967-7-0
Publisher ID	22

[First] [Previous] [Next] [Last]

There's one last thing. If you load this example from the code accompanying the course, you may need to modify the line of code constructing the **BooksConnection** object. The modification is needed if your working copy of the database is not in the same directory indicated in code. In fact, you will have to do this anytime you use the examples provided with the course.

Data Wizards

When learning new material, many times you are taught the "hard way" to do something before learning the "easy way." We're going to show you an easier way to build the application we just built by using Visual Basic's **data wizards**. Wizards are just that - tools that make your life easier. You will see Example 3-1 can be rebuilt without writing a single line of code!

Even though wizards are easy to use, they have their drawbacks. That's why you haven't seen wizards yet - we will always use the "hard way" (data objects) to connect to databases. Wizards provide quick results, but their results are many times inflexible. For databases, the big drawback is that connection information is hard-coded into your programs, making distribution to others very difficult.

Look through Example 3-2 if you like. It steps you through use of data wizards to rebuild Example 3-1. You'll see that wizards are pretty cool! I still use them for quickly building applications for personal use. And they're great for quick testing of database application concepts. You decide if you like them or not. As mentioned, they will not be used in this course.

Example 3-2 (Access Database)

Books Database with Wizards

We will rebuild Example 3-1 using data wizards – an application where we can look at a few fields in the **Titles** table of the books database (**BooksDB.accdb**).

1. Start a new application with just a form. Set the following properties:

Form1:
    Name   frmTitles
    FormBorderStyle   FixedSingle
    StartPosition   CenterScreen
    Text   Titles Database

The form should look something like this:

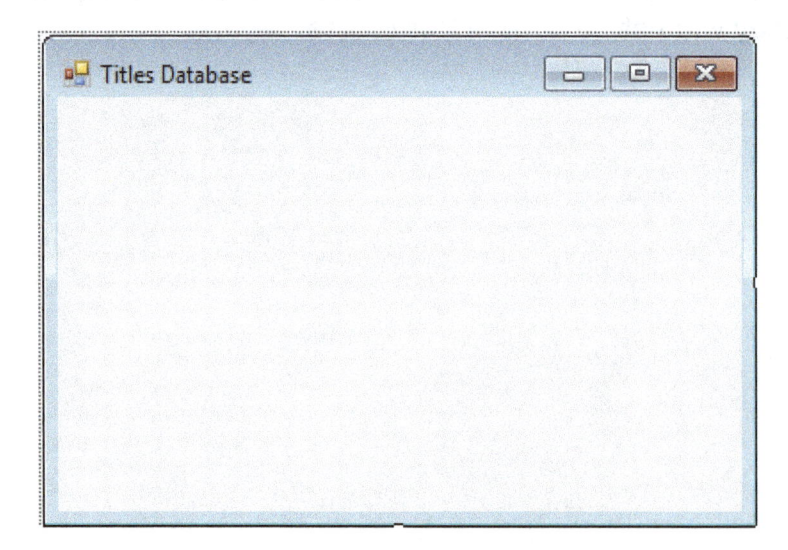

Database Connection 3-47

2. We now connect to the database. There are many steps. Select the **Project** menu option and choose **Add New Data Source**. This window will appear:

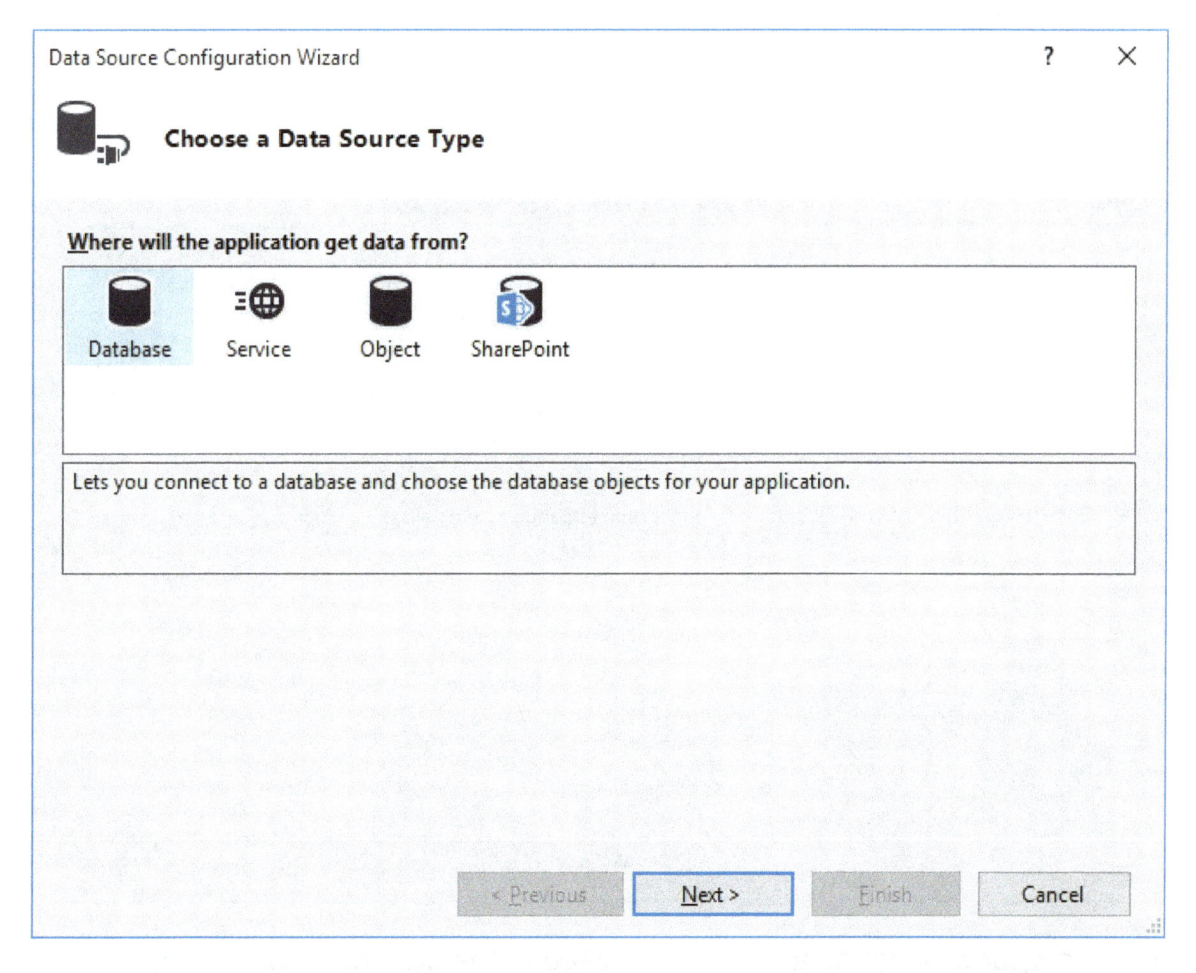

Choose the **Database** icon and click **Next**. You will see a screen asking what **database model** you want to use. Choose **Dataset** and click **Next**.

3-48　　　　　　　　　Visual Basic and Databases

You next specify where the database is located:

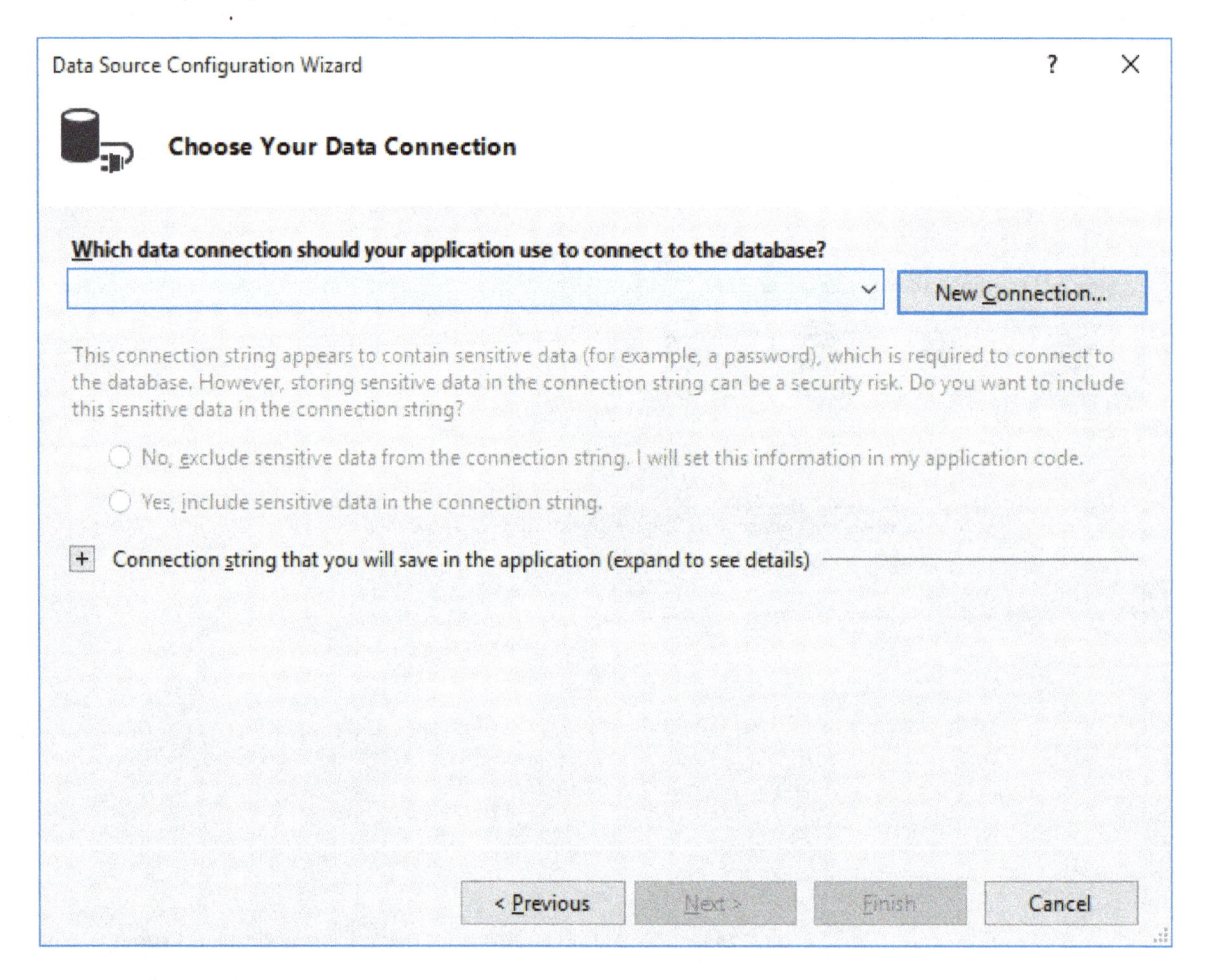

There may or may not be a connection listed in the drop down box. Here is where we will form a needed **Connection string** to connect to the database. Click **New Connection**.

Database Connection

In the next screen, you will see:

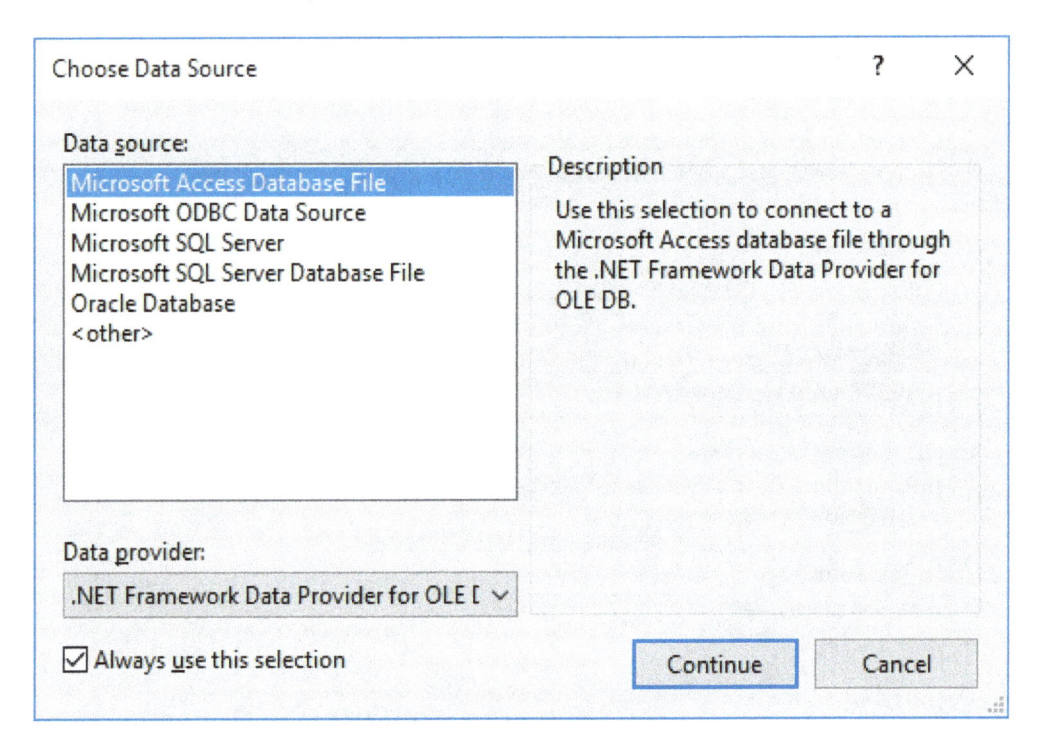

[Choose Data Source dialog: "Microsoft Access Database File" is selected in the Data source list (other options: Microsoft ODBC Data Source, Microsoft SQL Server, Microsoft SQL Server Database File, Oracle Database, <other>). Description: "Use this selection to connect to a Microsoft Access database file through the .NET Framework Data Provider for OLE DB." Data provider: .NET Framework Data Provider for OLE D. "Always use this selection" is checked. Buttons: Continue, Cancel.]

As shown, choose **Microsoft Access Database File**. This is the proper choice for a Microsoft Access database. Click **Continue**.

You are shown to the **Add Connection** window:

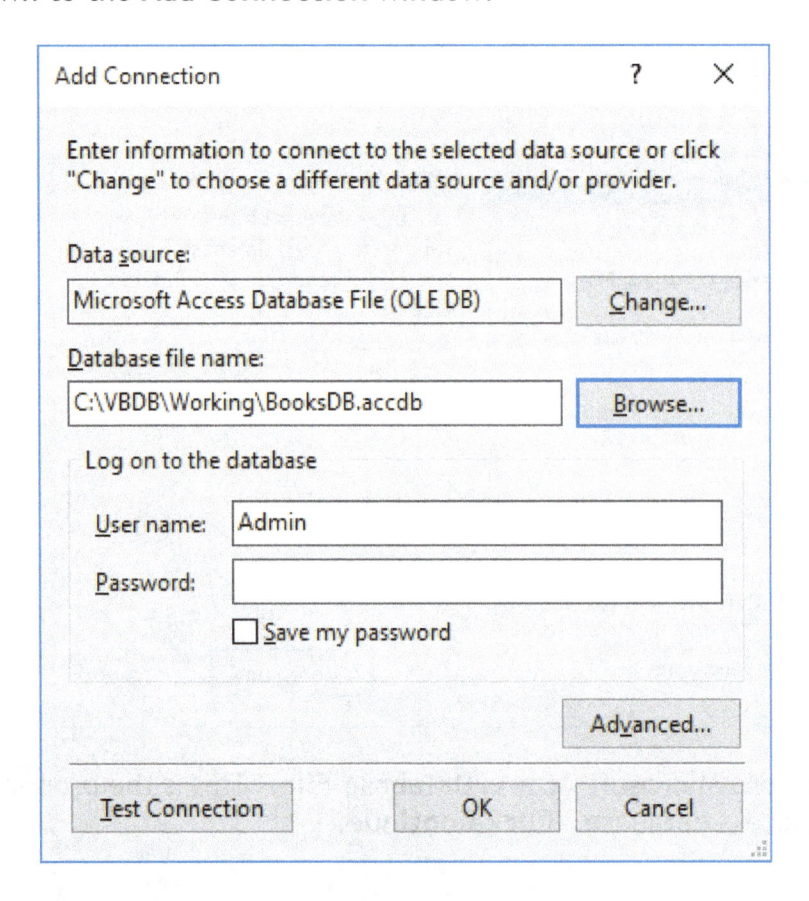

[Add Connection dialog window showing Data source: Microsoft Access Database File (OLE DB), Database file name: C:\VBDB\Working\BooksDB.accdb, User name: Admin, with Test Connection, OK, and Cancel buttons]

Click the **Browse** button and point to the **BooksDB.accdb** database in your working folder - here it is **VBDB\Working**). Once selected, click **Test Connection** to insure a proper connection.

Database Connection 3-51

Once the connection is verified, click **OK** and you will be returned to the **Data Source Configuration Wizard** main screen. Click **Next** and you may be asked if you want to copy the database to your project:

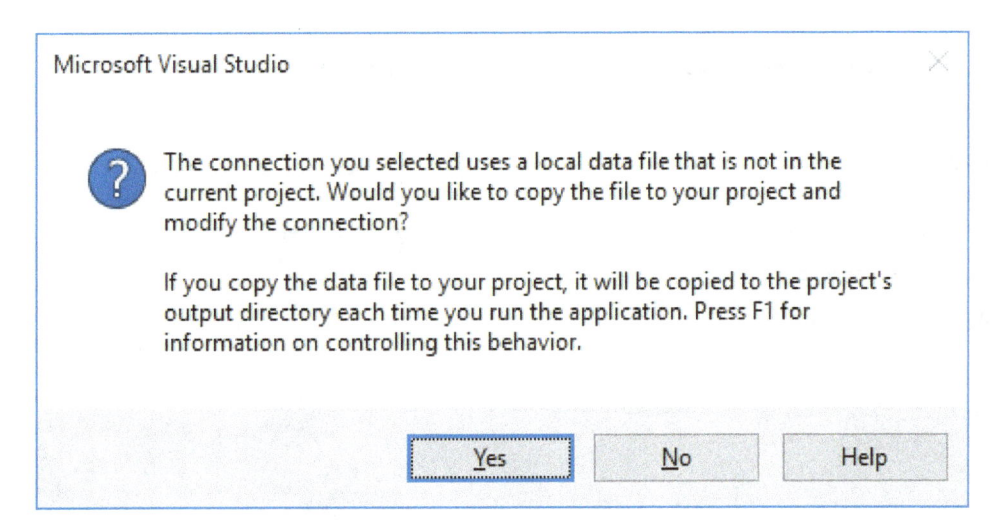

For our example, answer **No.**

Visual Basic and Databases

The next screen shows:

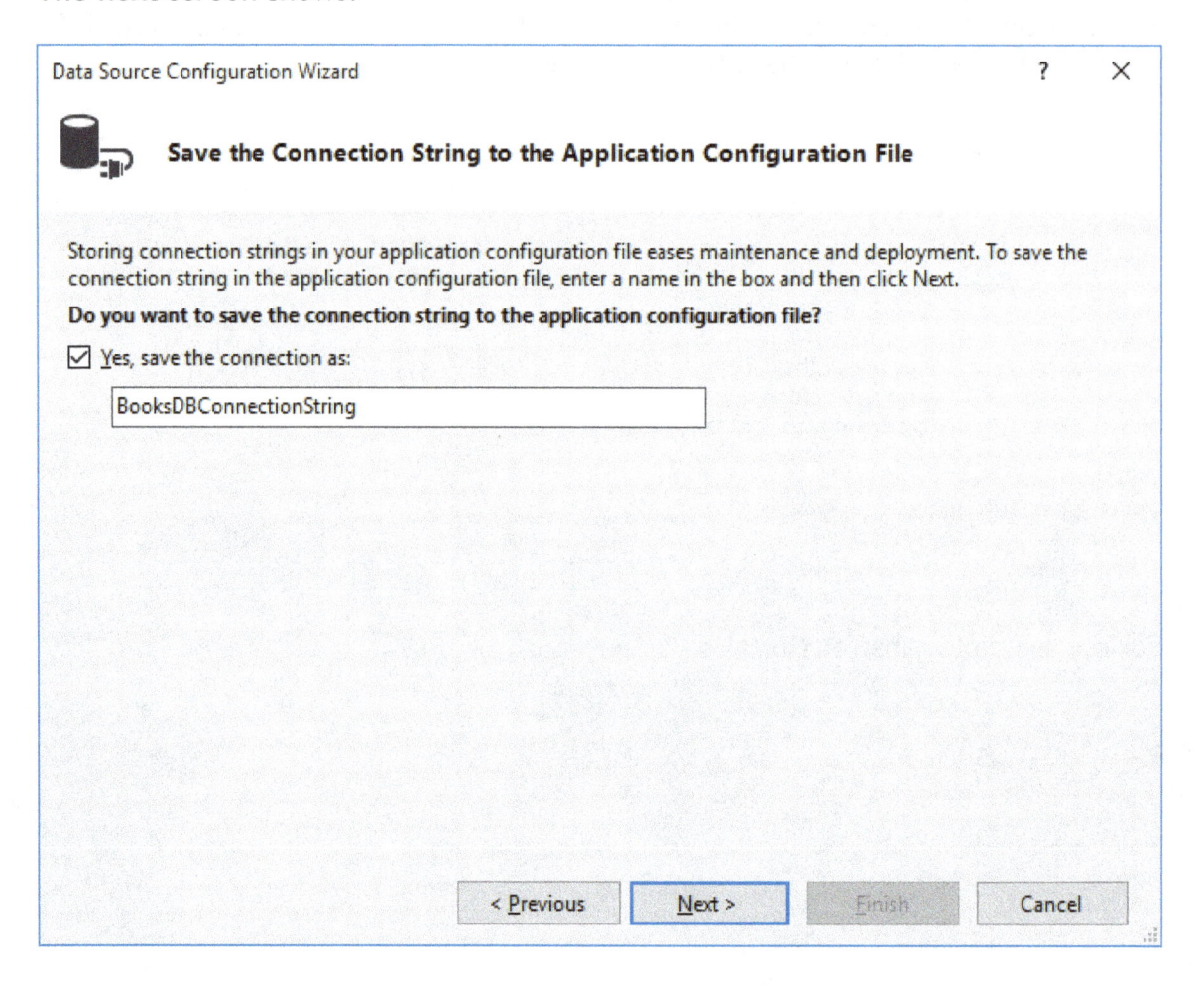

Data Source Configuration Wizard

Save the Connection String to the Application Configuration File

Storing connection strings in your application configuration file eases maintenance and deployment. To save the connection string in the application configuration file, enter a name in the box and then click Next.

Do you want to save the connection string to the application configuration file?

☑ Yes, save the connection as:

BooksDBConnectionString

[< Previous]   [Next >]   [Finish]   [Cancel]

The **connection string** specifies what database fields are used to form the dataset. Choose the default connection string and click **Next**. The database connection is finally complete.

Database Connection 3-53

3. We now need to specify the **DataSet** or table of data we want to generate. We want to choose the **Title**, **Year_Published**, **ISBN** and **PubID** fields in the **Titles** table. Expand the **Tables** object, then choose the **Titles** table and place checks next to the desired fields:

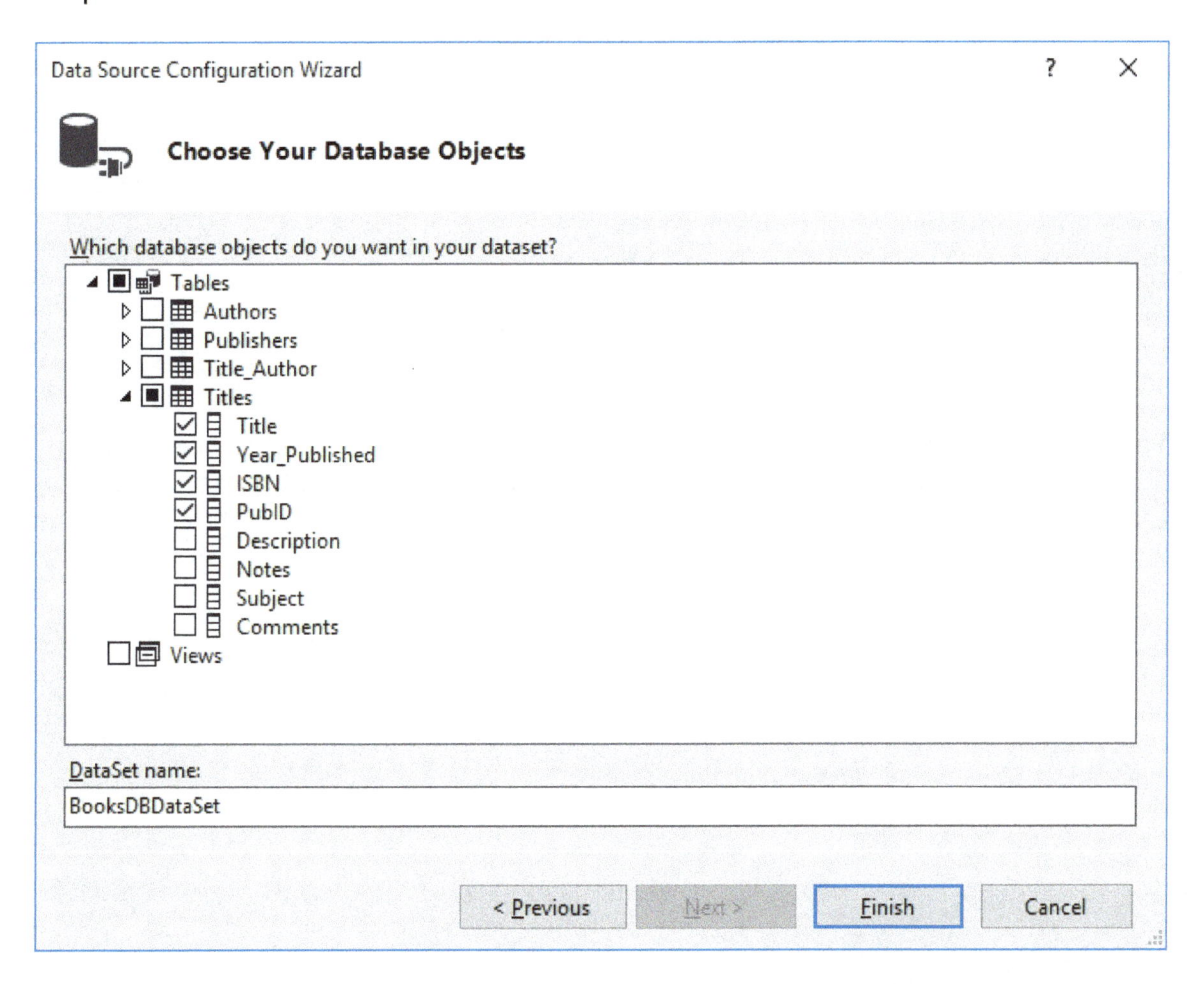

Data Source Configuration Wizard

Choose Your Database Objects

Which database objects do you want in your dataset?

- ▲ ☑ Tables
  - ▷ ☐ Authors
  - ▷ ☐ Publishers
  - ▷ ☐ Title_Author
  - ▲ ☑ Titles
    - ☑ Title
    - ☑ Year_Published
    - ☑ ISBN
    - ☑ PubID
    - ☐ Description
    - ☐ Notes
    - ☐ Subject
    - ☐ Comments
- ☐ Views

DataSet name:
BooksDBDataSet

[< Previous] [Next >] [**Finish**] [Cancel]

Once these selections are done, click **Finish** to complete specification of the **DataSet**.

4. Choose the **View** menu option, then **Other Windows** and click **Data Sources**. Pin this window to the IDE. Look in the **Data Sources** window in your project and you should see the newly created **DataSet** object (**BooksDBDataSet**). The dataset contains one table (**Titles**):

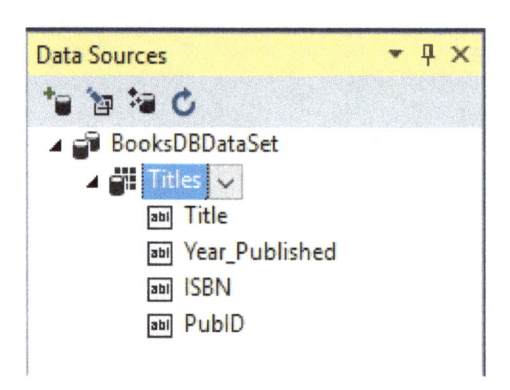

To form this **DataTable**, Visual Basic 'queried' the database (generating its own SQL statement) to pull the **Title**, **Year_Published**, **ISBN** and **PubID** fields out of the database.

5. Here's where the magic begins. Click the **Title** field in the **Data Sources** window, then drag and drop it onto the form. You will see:

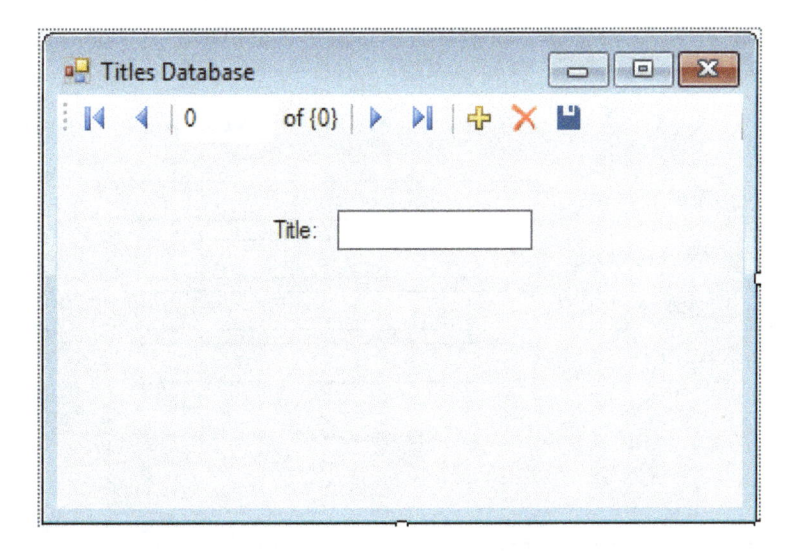

The wizard has created a label and a data bound text box for the **Title** field. It has also added a navigation tool at the top (you should recognize buttons to move to the first, previous, next and last records, respectively). Below the form are:

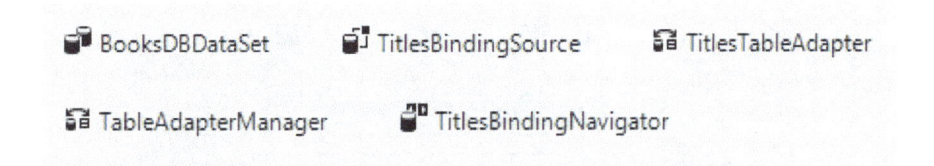

We recognize the **BooksDBDataSet** object. The **TitlesTableAdapter** object is a **DataAdapter** that controls communication between the books database and the dataset. The **TitlesBindingSource** and **TitlesBindingNavigator** controls navigation through the dataset. The wizard has essentially done all the steps of doing a connection, establishing a command object, creating a data adapter, a data table and a navigation object. These are all steps we did with code in Example 3-1.

6. Drag and drop the three other fields (**Year_Published**, **ISBN**, **PubID**) from the data source window onto the form. Resize things until it resembles this:

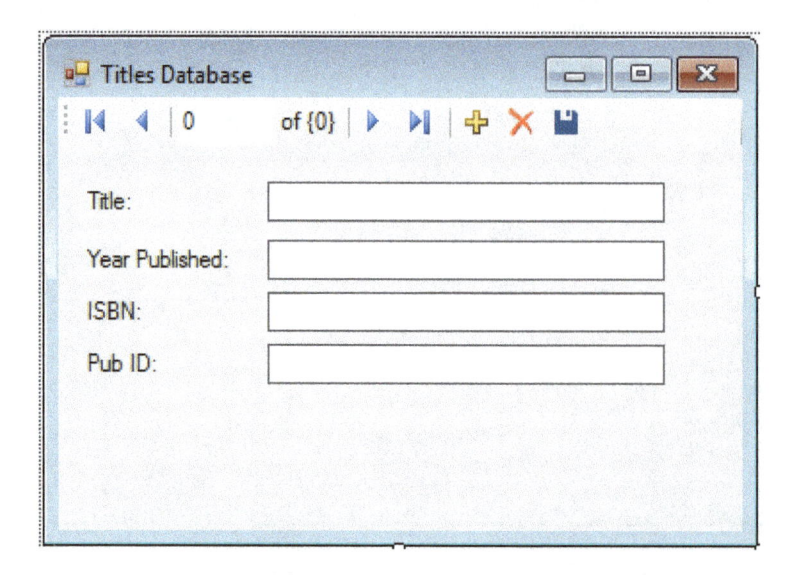

7. Save the application (saved in the **Example 3-2** folder in **VBDB\Access\Class 3** folder). Run the application. Try out the navigation buttons. Notice how all the fields update with each click of a button. Here's the first record:

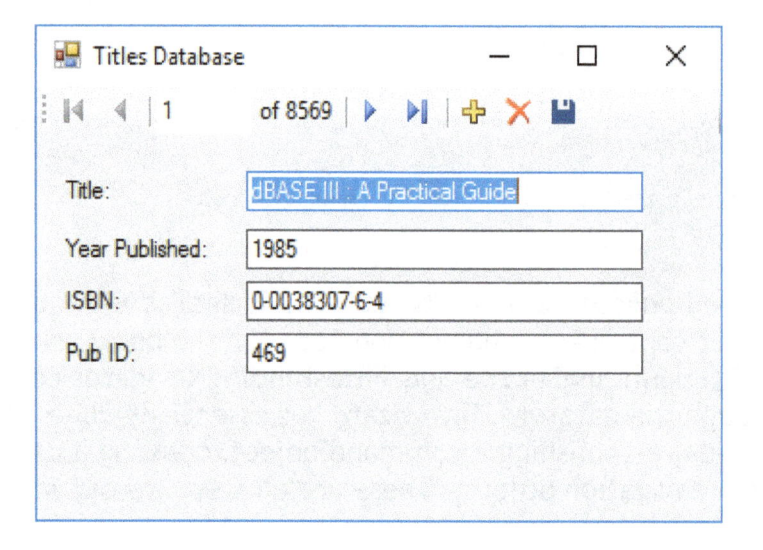

Here's the last record:

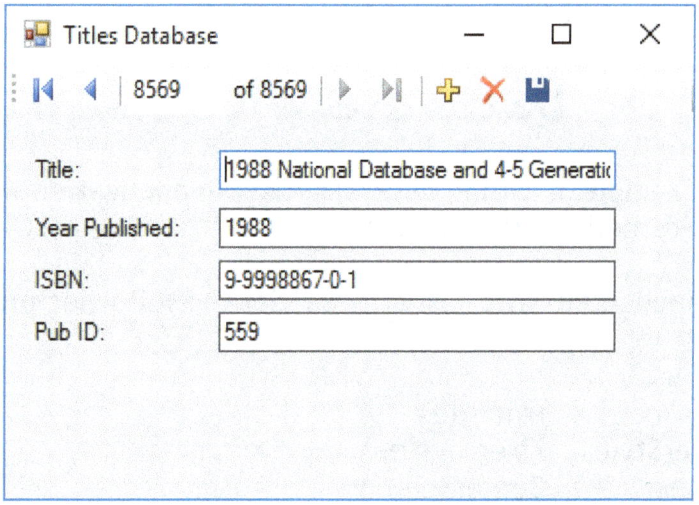
Titles Database
8569
of 8569
Title:
1988 National Database and 4-5 Generati
Year Published:
1988
ISBN:
9-9998867-0-1
Pub ID:
559

There's lots of power with this data wizard. A tool to view the **Titles** table was built without writing a line of code. The power of the wizard is its downfall, however. If you don't like the appearance of the navigation tool, you can't use the wizard. All of the information used to build the database connection and other objects is hard-coded into the application. So, if the **BooksDB.accdb** database is not in the specific folder designated when building the connection, the application will not work.

You decide where data wizards fit within your arsenal of database programming tools. I use them for quick personal applications and to test various database management tasks.

Example 3-2 (SQL Server Database)

Books Database with Wizards

We will rebuild Example 3-1 using data wizards – an application where we can look at a few fields in the **Titles** table of the books database (**SQLBooksDB.mdf**).

1. Start a new application with just a form. Set the following properties:

Form1:
    Name   frmTitles
    FormBorderStyle   FixedSingle
    StartPosition   CenterScreen
    Text   Titles Database

The form should look something like this:

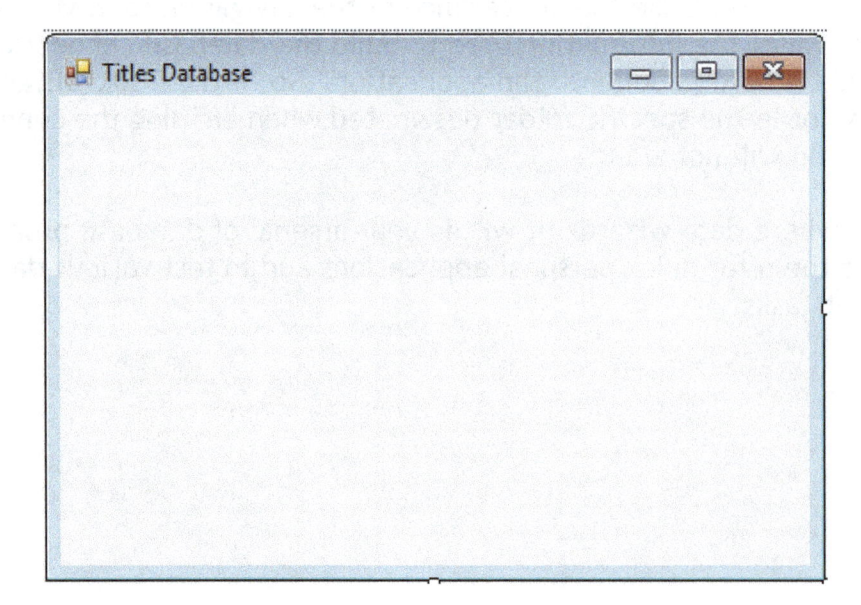

Database Connection 3-59

2. We now connect to the database. There are many steps. Select the **Project** menu option and choose **Add New Data Source**. This window will appear:

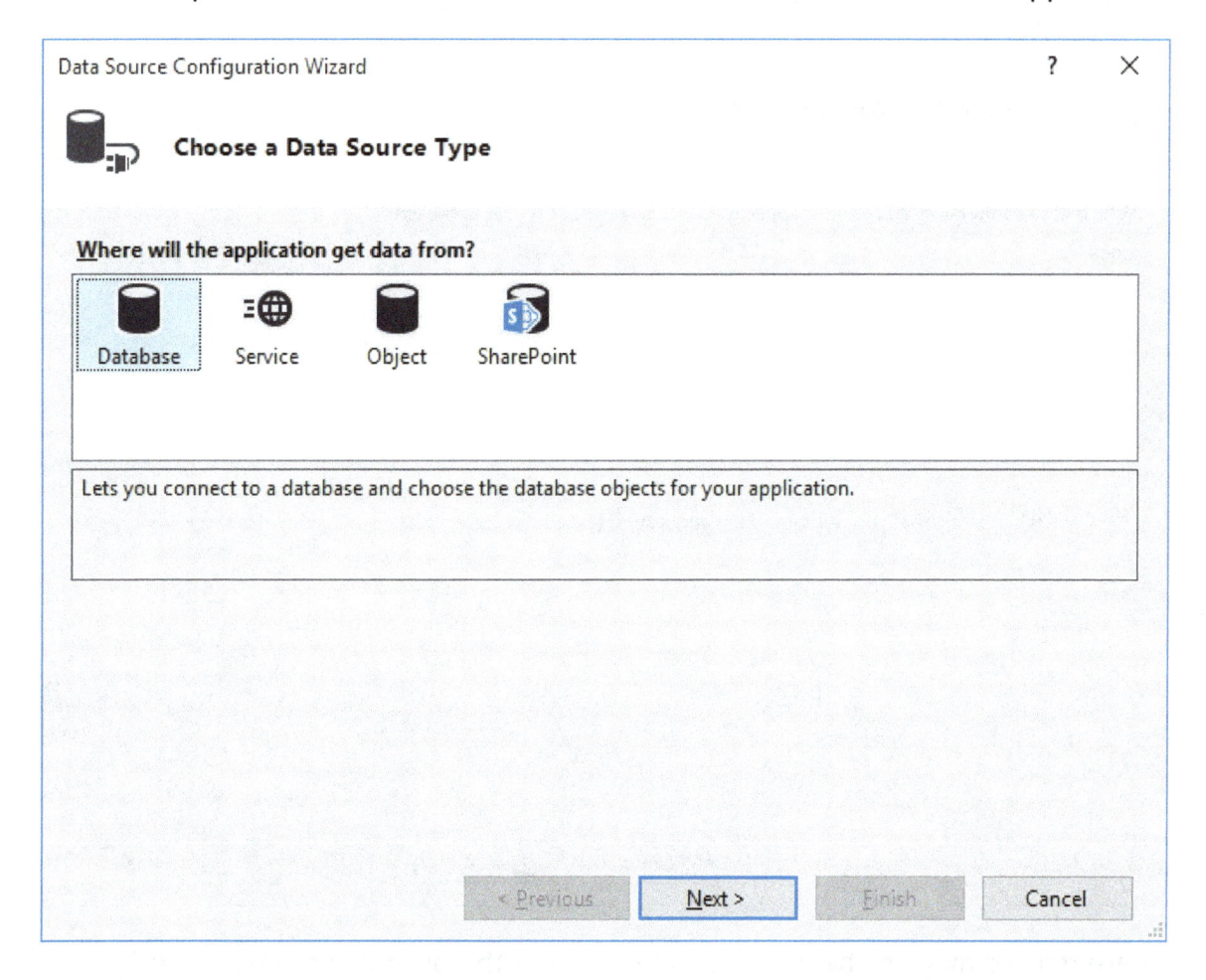

```
Data Source Configuration Wizard                                    ?   X

    Choose a Data Source Type

Where will the application get data from?

   [Database]   [Service]   [Object]   [SharePoint]

Lets you connect to a database and choose the database objects for your application.




                           < Previous   Next >   Finish    Cancel
```

Choose the **Database** icon and click **Next**. You will see a screen asking what **database model** you want to use. Choose **Dataset** and click **Next**.

3-60 Visual Basic and Databases

You next specify where the database is located:

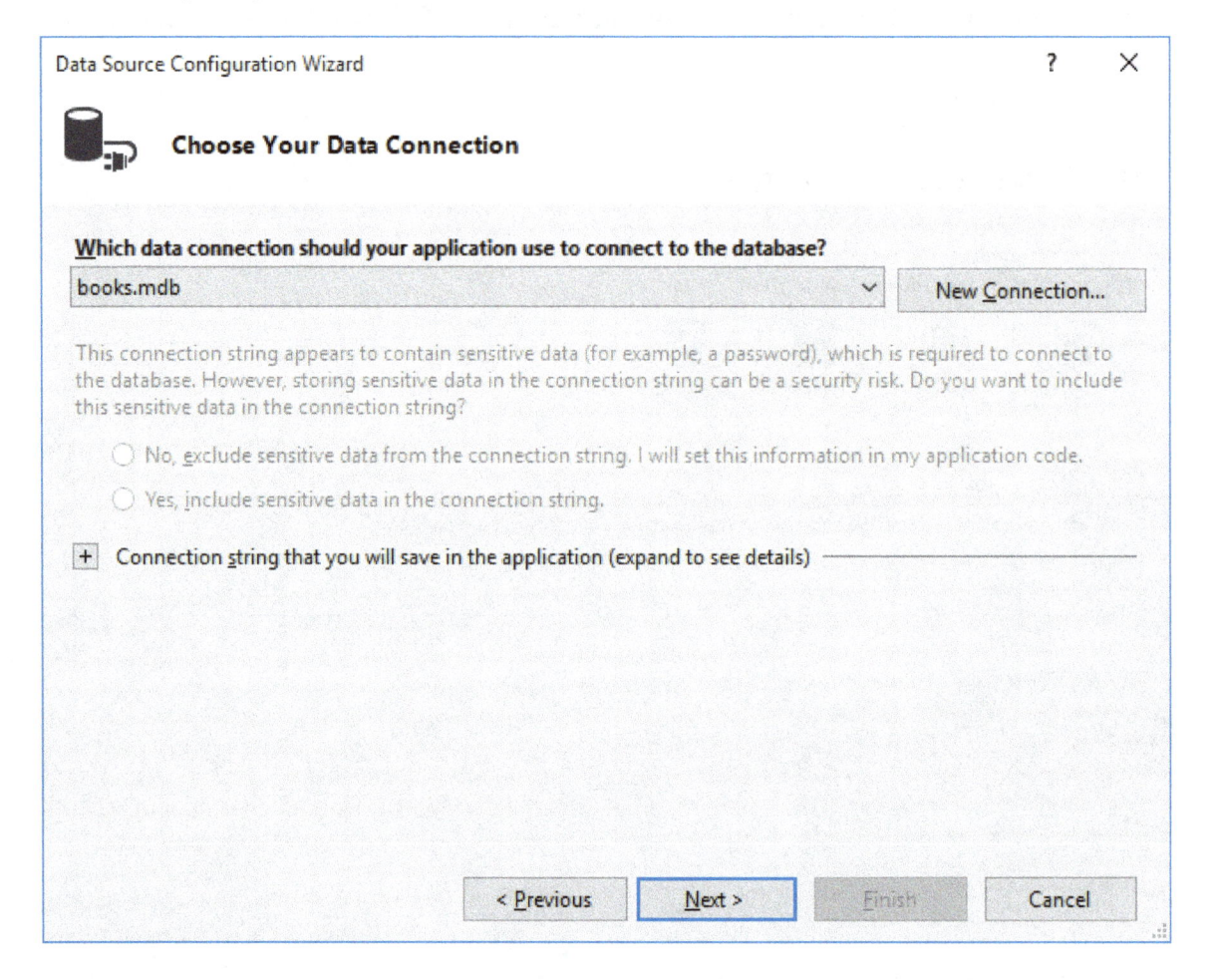

There may or may not be a connection listed in the drop down box. Here is where we will form a needed **Connection string** to connect to the database. Click **New Connection**.

Database Connection 3-61

In the next screen, you will see:

Add Connection

Enter information to connect to the selected data source or click "Change" to choose a different data source and/or provider.

Data source:

Microsoft Access Database File (OLE DB) [Change...]

Database file name:

[   ] [Browse...]

Log on to the database

User name: Admin

Password:

☐ Save my password

[Advanced...]

[Test Connection] [OK] [Cancel]

Make sure the **Data source** shows **Microsoft SQL Server**. If not, click **Change** to see:

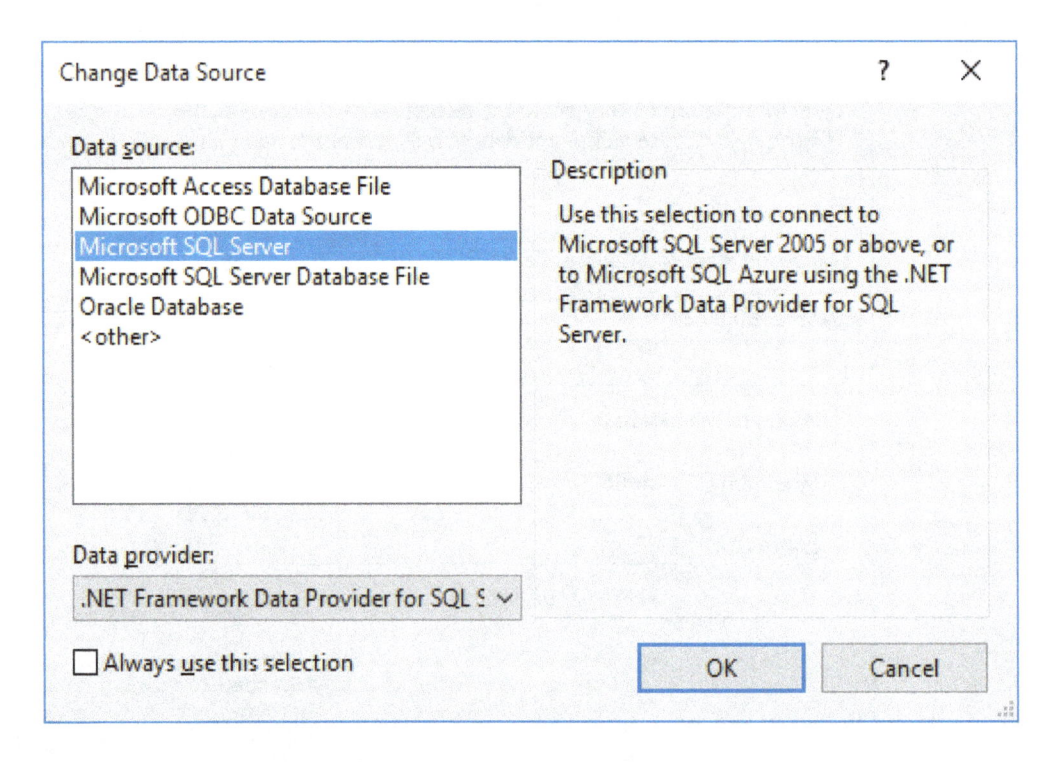

As shown, choose **Microsoft SQL Server**. Click **OK**.

You will return to the **Add Connection** window:

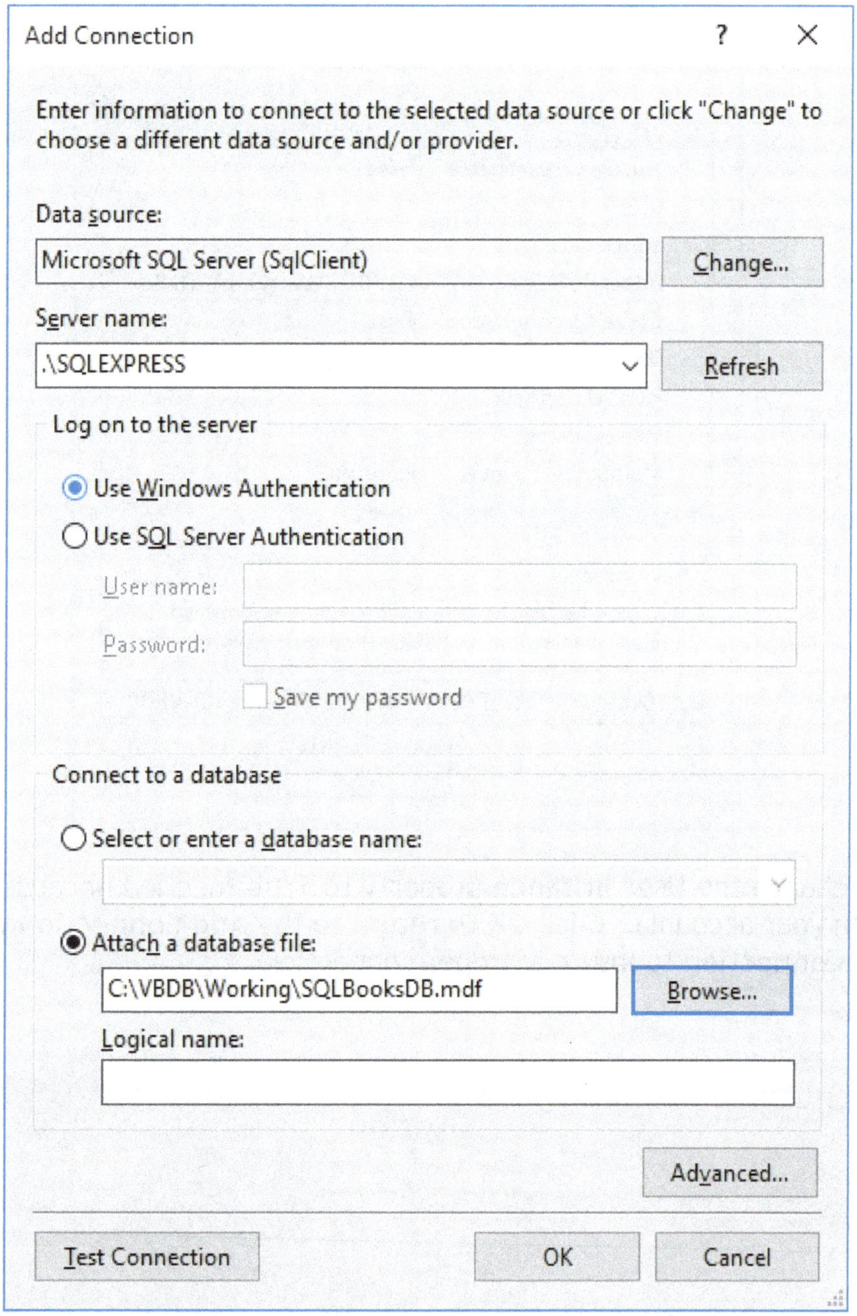

Type your SQL Server name in **Server Name** (default is **.\SQLEXPRESS**). Choose **Attach a database file** and click the **Browse** button and point to the **SQLBooksDB.mdf** database in your working folder - here it is **VBDB\Working**).

Click the **Advanced** button to see:

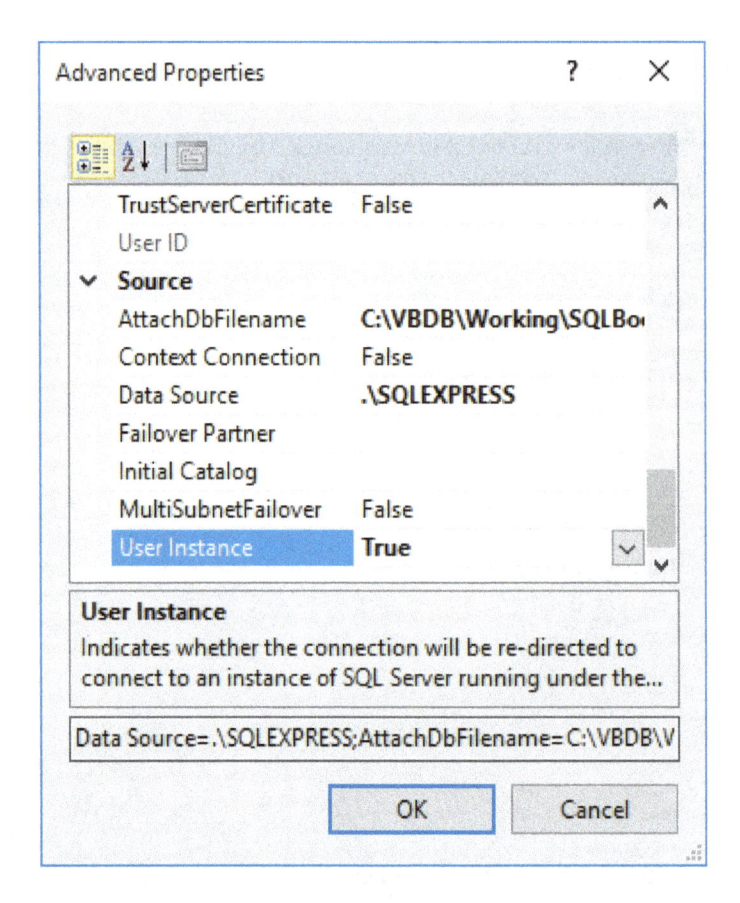

As shown, change the **User Instance** property to **True** (needed because SQL Server is on your account). Click **OK** to return to the **Add Connection** window. Click **Test Connection** to insure a proper connection.

Database Connection   3-65

Once the connection is verified, click **OK** and you will be returned to the **Data Source Configuration Wizard** main screen. Click **Next** and you may be asked if you want to copy the database to your project:

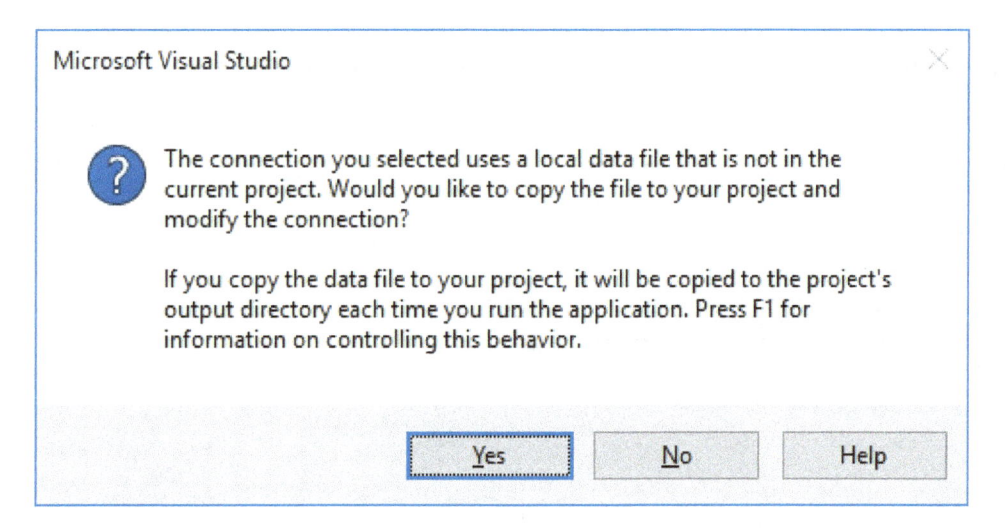

For our example, answer **No**.

3-66　　　　　　　　　Visual Basic and Databases

The next screen shows:

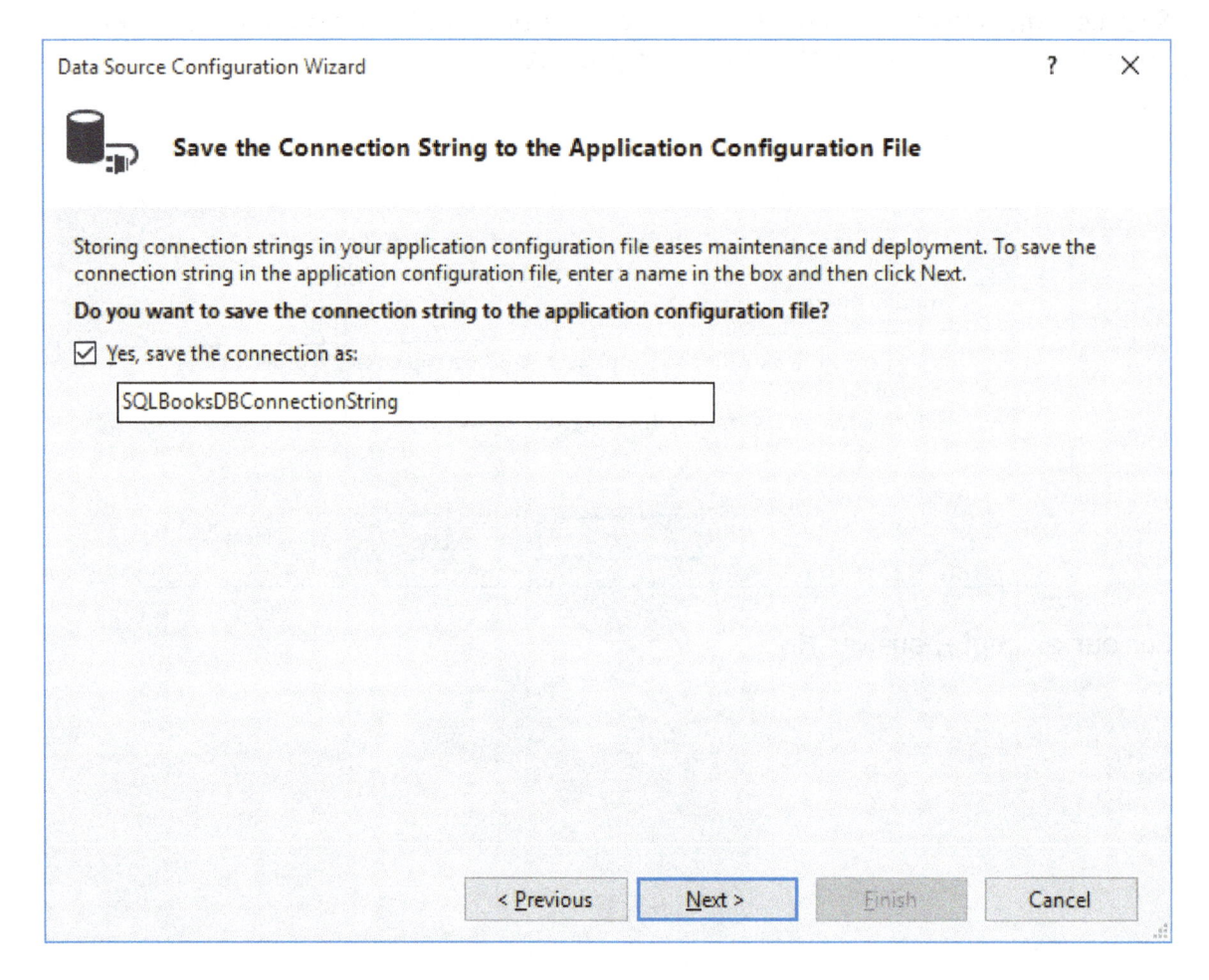

```
Data Source Configuration Wizard                                    ?   ×

   ▣   Save the Connection String to the Application Configuration File


   Storing connection strings in your application configuration file eases maintenance and deployment. To save the
   connection string in the application configuration file, enter a name in the box and then click Next.
   Do you want to save the connection string to the application configuration file?
   ☑ Yes, save the connection as:
     ┌─────────────────────────────────────┐
     │ SQLBooksDBConnectionString          │
     └─────────────────────────────────────┘




                                   < Previous    Next >    Finish     Cancel
```

The **connection string** specifies what database fields are used to form the dataset. Choose the default connection string and click **Next**. The database connection is finally complete.

Database Connection 3-67

3. We now need to specify the **DataSet** or table of data we want to generate. We want to choose the **Title, Year_Published, ISBN** and **PubID** fields in the **Titles** table. Expand the **Tables** object, then choose the **Titles** table and place checks next to the desired fields:

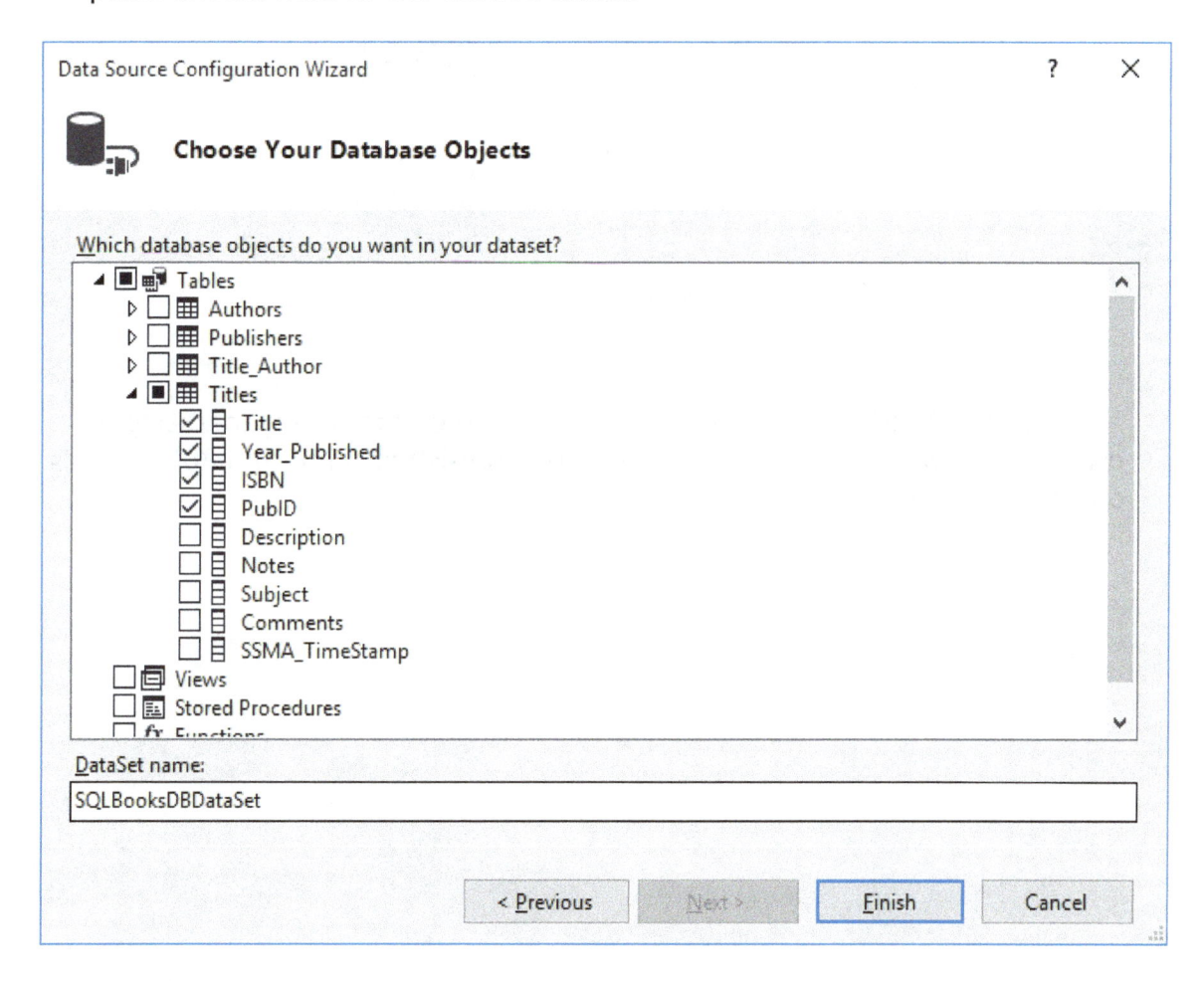

```
Data Source Configuration Wizard                                    ?   X

    Choose Your Database Objects

Which database objects do you want in your dataset?
  ▲ ■ Tables
     ▷ □ Authors
     ▷ □ Publishers
     ▷ □ Title_Author
     ▲ ■ Titles
           ☑ Title
           ☑ Year_Published
           ☑ ISBN
           ☑ PubID
           □ Description
           □ Notes
           □ Subject
           □ Comments
           □ SSMA_TimeStamp
     □ Views
     □ Stored Procedures
     □ fx Functions

DataSet name:
SQLBooksDBDataSet

                    < Previous    Next >    Finish    Cancel
```

Once these selections are done, click **Finish** to complete specification of the **DataSet**.

Visual Basic and Databases

4. Choose the **View** menu option, then **Other Windows** and click **Data Sources**. Pin this window to the IDE. Look in the **Data Sources** window in your project and you should see the newly created **DataSet** object (**SQLBooksDBDataSet**). The dataset contains one table (**Titles**):

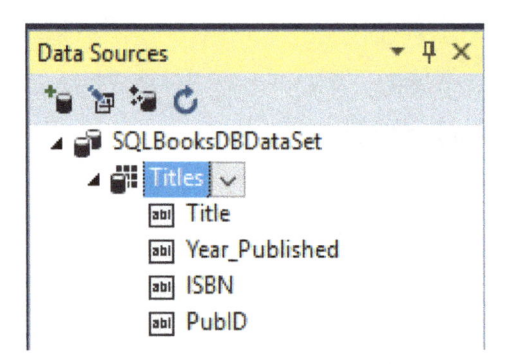

To form this **DataTable**, Visual Basic 'queried' the database (generating its own SQL statement) to pull the **Title, Year_Published, ISBN** and **PubID** fields out of the database.

Database Connection 3-69

5. Here's where the magic begins. Click the **Title** field in the **Data Sources** window, then drag and drop it onto the form. You will see:

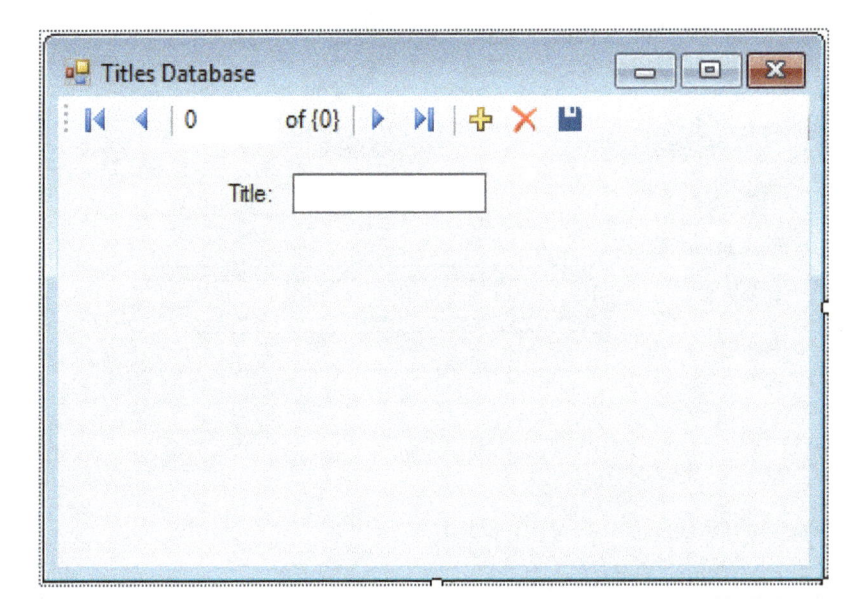

The wizard has created a label and a data bound text box for the **Title** field. It has also added a navigation tool at the top (you should recognize buttons to move to the first, previous, next and last records, respectively). Below the form are:

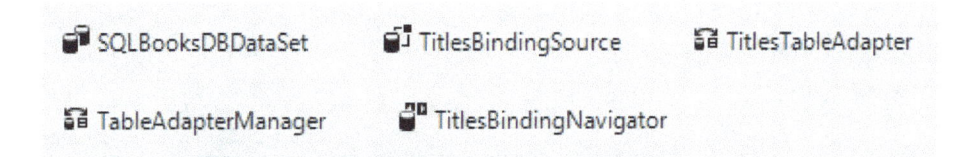

- SQLBooksDBDataSet
- TitlesBindingSource
- TitlesTableAdapter
- TableAdapterManager
- TitlesBindingNavigator

We recognize the **SQLBooksDBDataSet** object. The **TitlesTableAdapter** object is a **DataAdapter** that controls communication between the books database and the dataset. The **TitlesBindingSource** and **TitlesBindingNavigator** controls navigation through the dataset. The wizard has essentially done all the steps of doing a connection, establishing a command object, creating a data adapter, a data table and a navigation object. These are all steps we did with code in Example 3-1.

3-70   Visual Basic and Databases

6. Drag and drop the three other fields (**Year_Published**, **ISBN**, **PubID**) from the data source window onto the form. Resize things until it resembles this:

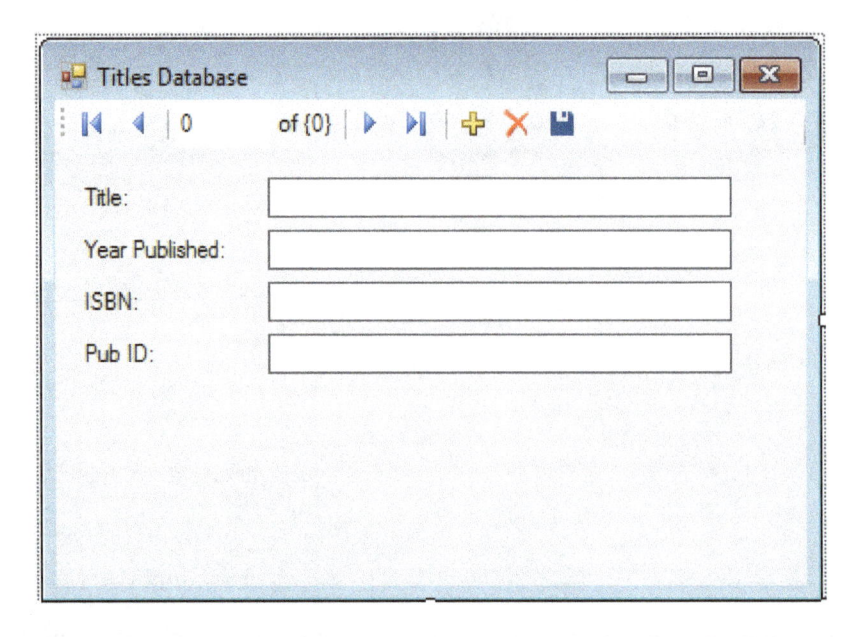

7. Save the application (saved in the **Example 3-2** folder in **VBDB\SQL Server\Class 3** folder). Run the application. Try out the navigation buttons. Notice how all the fields update with each click of a button. Here's the first record:

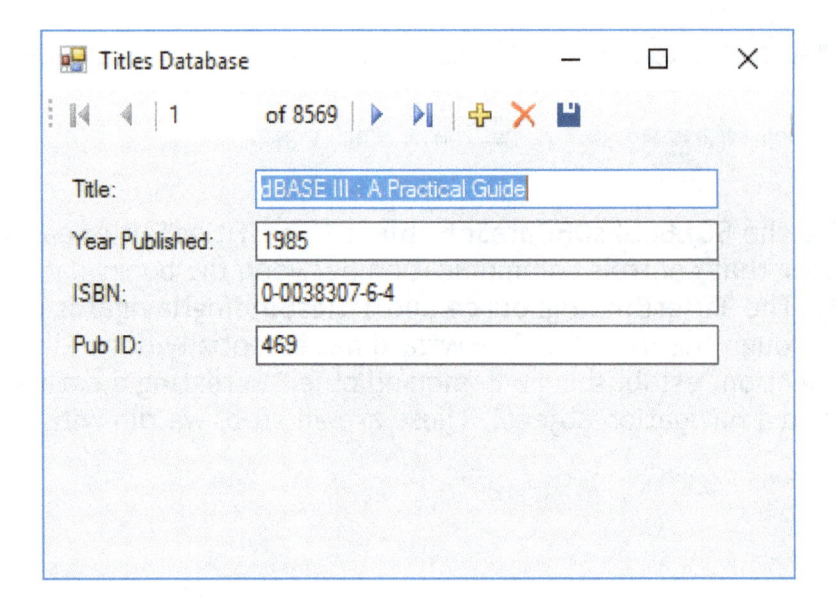

Here's the last record:

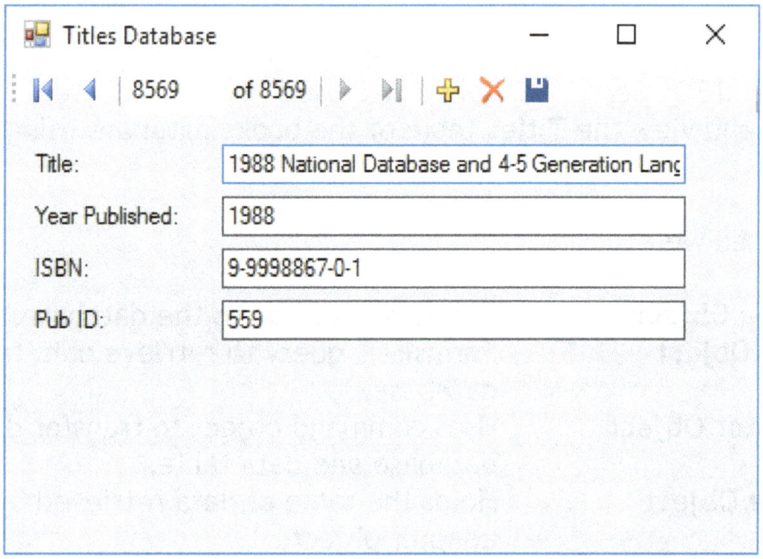
Titles Database
8569
of 8569
Title:
1988 National Database and 4-5 Generation Lang
Year Published:
1988
ISBN:
9-9998867-0-1
Pub ID:
559

There's lots of power with this data wizard. A tool to view the **Titles** table was built without writing a line of code. The power of the wizard is its downfall, however. If you don't like the appearance of the navigation tool, you can't use the wizard. All of the information used to build the database connection and other objects is hard-coded into the application. So, if the **SQLBooksDB.mdf** database is not in the specific folder designated when building the connection, the application will not work.

You decide where data wizards fit within your arsenal of database programming tools. I use them for quick personal applications and to test various database management tasks.

Summary

In this chapter, we finally used Visual Basic to connect to an actual database (both Access and SQL Server versions). We used several ADO .NET data objects to connect to and view the **Titles** table of the books database using data bound controls.

The objects used were:

Connection Object	Forms connection to the database.
Command Object	Forms SQL query to retrieve data table from database.
Data Adapter Object	Uses command object to transfer data between database and data table.
Data Table Object	Holds the table of data retrieved by the data adapter object.
Data Bound Controls	Controls 'bound' to fields of the data table object.
Currency Manager Object	Manages the controls bound to the data table. Provides both navigation and editing capabilities.

We looked at the Visual Basic data wizard. The wizard is good for quick prototyping of database applications, but its inflexibility for distribution purposes makes it unsuitable for our work here.

Even after all the work we've done, all we can do right now is view database tables, which in some applications is sufficient (think of your local library - they certainly don't want patrons changing information in their database). To build a complete database management system, we need to know SQL, the powerful language behind database queries. This is discussed in the next chapter.

If you're feeling overwhelmed by all the material presented thus far, don't worry - you'll see it many more times as you continue through this course and become a more proficient database programmer.

Example 3-3

Northwind Traders Database

A second sample database is included with these notes. The Access version is **NWindDB.accdb**, located in the **VBDB\Databases** folder. The SQL Server version (**SQLNWindDB.mdf**) can be downloaded from our web site, as explained in Chapter 2, or if you have a CD-ROM of these notes, it is also in the **VBDB\Databases** folder. This database is used by a fictional company (**Northwind Traders**) to handle its commerce. It has eight tables. In this exercise, we repeat the tasks of Example 3-1, using one table (**Customers**) in this database. The SQL statement (used in the command object) to do this is:

Select * from Customers

This example gives you further practice in using the ADO .NET data objects and data bound controls and allows you to study the structure of another database.

1. Copy **NWindDB.accdb** (or **SQLNWindDB.mdf**) to your working directory and start a new application. We'll develop a form where we can look through the **Customers** table in the Northwind Traders database. Place four label, four text boxes, and four buttons on the form.

2. Set the following properties for each control. For the data control and the four text boxes, make sure you set the properties in the order given.

Form1:
    Name   frmCustomers
    FormBorderStyle   FixedSingle
    StartPosition   CenterScreen
    Text   Customers Database

Label1:
    Text   Customer ID
Label2:
    Text   Company Name
Label3:
    Text   Contact Name
Label4:
    Text   Contact Title

TextBox1:
    Name   txtCustomerID
    BackColor   White
    ReadOnly   True
    MultiLine   True

TextBox2:
    Name   txtCompanyName
    BackColor   White
    ReadOnly   True
    MultiLine   True

TextBox3:
    Name   txtContactName
    BackColor   White
    ReadOnly   True
    MultiLine   True

TextBox4:
    Name   txtContactTitle
    BackColor   White
    ReadOnly   True
    MultiLine   True

Button1:
    Name   btnFirst
    Text   &First

Button2:
    Name   btnPrevious
    Text   &Previous

Button3:
    Name   btnNext
    Text   &Next

Button4:
    Name   btnLast
    Text   &Last

Database Connection

When done, the form will look something like this:

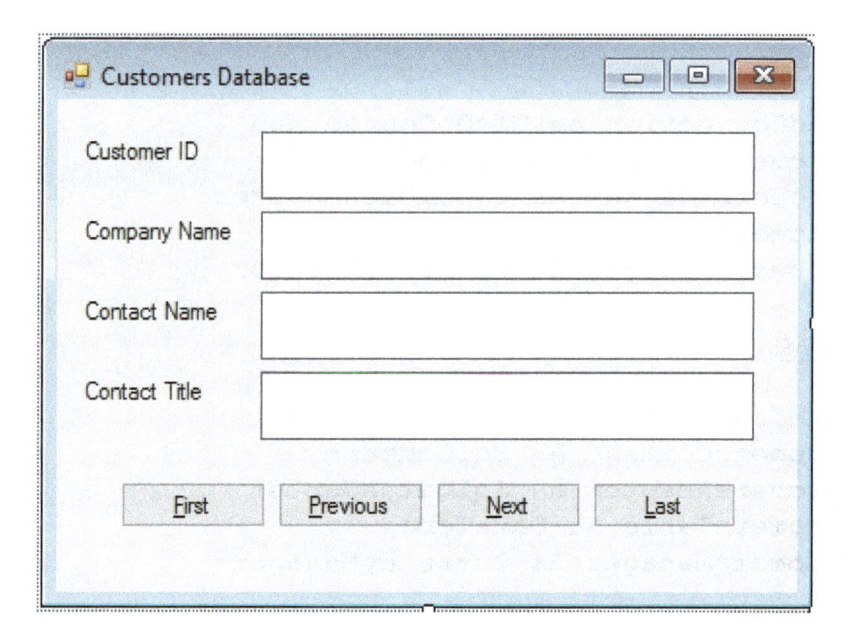

3. Add these lines at the top of the code window:

Access Database:

```
Imports System.Data
Imports System.Data.OleDb
```

SQL Server Database:

```
Imports System.Data
Imports System.Data.SqlClient
```

Visual Basic and Databases

4. Form level declarations to create data objects:

Access Database:

```
Dim NWindConnection As OleDbConnection
Dim CustomersCommand As OleDbCommand
Dim CustomersAdapter As OleDbDataAdapter
Dim CustomersTable As DataTable
Dim CustomersManager As CurrencyManager
```

~~Access~~ SQL SERVER Database:

```
Dim NWindConnection As SqlConnection
Dim CustomersCommand As SqlCommand
Dim CustomersAdapter As SqlDataAdapter
Dim CustomersTable As DataTable
Dim CustomersManager As CurrencyManager
```

Database Connection 3-77

5. Add this code the **frmCustomers Load** procedure:

Access Database:

```vb
Private Sub FrmCustomers_Load(ByVal sender As System.Object, ByVal e As System.EventArgs) Handles MyBase.Load
    'connect to NWind database
    NWindConnection = New OleDbConnection("Provider=Microsoft.ACE.OLEDB.12.0; Data Source = c:\VBDB\Working\NWindDB.accdb")
    NWindConnection.Open()
    'establish command object
    CustomersCommand = New OleDbCommand("Select * from Customers", NWindConnection)
    'establish data adapter/data table
    CustomersAdapter = New OleDbDataAdapter()
    CustomersAdapter.SelectCommand = CustomersCommand
    CustomersTable = New DataTable()
    CustomersAdapter.Fill(CustomersTable)
    'bind controls to data table
    txtCustomerID.DataBindings.Add("Text", CustomersTable, "CustomerID")
    txtCompanyName.DataBindings.Add("Text", CustomersTable, "CompanyName")
    txtContactName.DataBindings.Add("Text", CustomersTable, "ContactName")
    txtContactTitle.DataBindings.Add("Text", CustomersTable, "ContactTitle")
    'establish currency manager
    CustomersManager = DirectCast(Me.BindingContext(CustomersTable), CurrencyManager)
    'close the connection
    NWindConnection.Close()
    'dispose of the objects
    NWindConnection.Dispose()
    CustomersCommand.Dispose()
    CustomersAdapter.Dispose()
    CustomersTable.Dispose()
End Sub
```

SQL Server Database:

```vb
Private Sub FrmCustomers_Load(ByVal sender As System.Object, ByVal e As System.EventArgs) Handles MyBase.Load
    'connect to NWind database
    NWindConnection = New SqlConnection("Data Source=.\SQLEXPRESS;AttachDbFilename=C:\VBDB\Working\SQLNWindDB.mdf; Integrated Security=True; Connect Timeout=30; User Instance=True")
    NWindConnection.Open()
    'establish command object
    CustomersCommand = New SqlCommand("Select * from Customers", NWindConnection)
    'establish data adapter/data table
    CustomersAdapter = New SqlDataAdapter()
    CustomersAdapter.SelectCommand = CustomersCommand
    CustomersTable = New DataTable()
    CustomersAdapter.Fill(CustomersTable)
    'bind controls to data table
    txtCustomerID.DataBindings.Add("Text", CustomersTable, "CustomerID")
    txtCompanyName.DataBindings.Add("Text", CustomersTable, "CompanyName")
    txtContactName.DataBindings.Add("Text", CustomersTable, "ContactName")
    txtContactTitle.DataBindings.Add("Text", CustomersTable, "ContactTitle")
    'establish currency manager
    CustomersManager = DirectCast(Me.BindingContext(CustomersTable), CurrencyManager)
    'close the connection
    NWindConnection.Close()
    'dispose of the objects
    NWindConnection.Dispose()
    CustomersCommand.Dispose()
    CustomersAdapter.Dispose()
    CustomersTable.Dispose()
End Sub
```

Database Connection 3-79

6. Code for the four button **Click** events to allow navigation:

   ```
   Private Sub BtnFirst_Click(ByVal sender As System.Object, ByVal e As System.EventArgs) Handles btnFirst.Click
       CustomersManager.Position = 0
   End Sub

   Private Sub BtnPrevious_Click(ByVal sender As System.Object, ByVal e As System.EventArgs) Handles btnPrevious.Click
       CustomersManager.Position -= 1
   End Sub

   Private Sub BtnNext_Click(ByVal sender As System.Object, ByVal e As System.EventArgs) Handles btnNext.Click
       CustomersManager.Position += 1
   End Sub

   Private Sub BtnLast_Click(ByVal sender As System.Object, ByVal e As System.EventArgs) Handles btnLast.Click
       CustomersManager.Position = CustomersManager.Count - 1
   End Sub
   ```

7. Save the application (Access version saved in the **Example 3-3** folder in **VBDB\Access\Class 3** folder; SQL Server version saved in the **Example 3-3** folder in **VBDB\SQL Server\Class 3** folder). Run the application. Cycle through the various customers using the navigation buttons. Here's the last record:

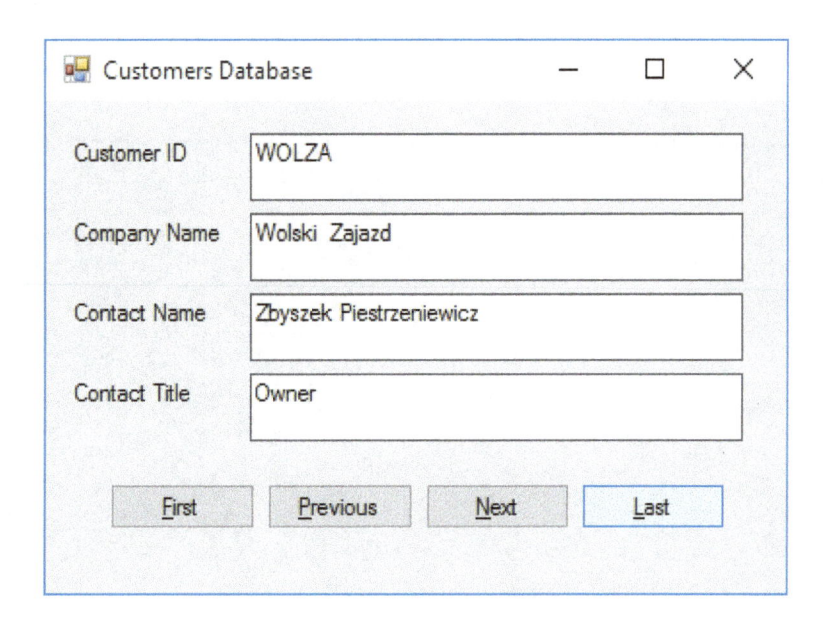

4

Database Queries with SQL

Review and Preview

At this point in our study, we can view any table that is part of a database (a **native table**). A powerful feature of any database management system is to have the ability to form any view of the data we desire. The formation of such **virtual tables** is discussed in this chapter.

Virtual data views are obtained by querying the database. The language used for such queries is the structured query language, or **SQL**. In this chapter, we will learn how to use SQL to extract desired information from a database. SQL is not just used with Visual Basic database applications. It is the standard language for database queries, hence all material learned here can be transferred to other database management systems.

SQL Background

SQL was developed at IBM in the early 1970's, coincident with relational database theory developed by E. F. Codd. SQL succeeded a previous database language called Sequel - hence, SQL is the "sequel to Sequel." Because of this, many programmers pronounce SQL as "sequel." The correct pronunciation is "ess-que-ell," that is, just say the letters.

SQL is a set of statements that tell a database engine (such as the ADO .NET engine with Visual Basic) what information the user wants displayed. The engine then processes that set of statements, as it sees fit, to provide the information. SQL statements fall into two categories: data manipulation language (**DML**) and data definition language (**DDL**). DDL statements can be used to define tables, indexes, and database relations. DML statements are used to select, sort, summarize, and make computations on data. We will discuss primarily DML statements.

SQL has been adopted as an **ANSI** (American National Standards Institute) standard. This means there is an established set of SQL statements that every database management system recognizes. Yet, even with this standard, each manufacturer has added its own 'dialect' to the standard. In these notes, we will use Microsoft SQL. When a statement or function does not agree with the ANSI standard, this will be pointed out to the reader.

Basics of SQL

SQL can be used with any database management system, not just Visual Basic. Hence, the syntax learned here will help any database programmer. SQL is a set of about 30 statements for database management tasks.

To query a database, we form a **SQL statement**. A statement is a string of SQL keywords and other information, such as database table and field names. This statement tells the database engine what information we want from the database. You do not have to tell the database engine how to get the information - it does all the hard work for you!

What can a SQL statement accomplish?

⇒ Sort records
⇒ Choose fields
⇒ Choose records
⇒ Cross reference tables
⇒ Perform calculations
⇒ Provide data for database reports
⇒ Modify data

Even though we don't even know what a SQL statement looks like yet, we need to set some rules on how to construct such statements. Then, we will look at how to use a SQL statement in a Visual Basic application.

All SQL **keywords** in a SQL statement will be typed in **upper case** letters. Even though SQL is 'case-insensitive,' this is good programming practice and allows us (and others) to differentiate between keywords and other information in a SQL statement.

SQL uses the term **row** to refer to a database **record** and the term **column** to refer to database **field**. This will not come into play in this class, but you should be aware of this difference if you read other books about SQL.

String information embedded within a SQL statement can be enclosed in double-quotes (") or single-quotes ('). With Visual Basic, you should only use single-quotes to enclose embedded strings. The reason for this is that the SQL statement is itself a string - so, in Visual Basic code, SQL statements must be enclosed in double-quotes. We enclose embedded strings with single-quotes to avoid confusion.

SQL supports the use of **wildcards** in forming data views. Here, we use the Microsoft SQL wildcard character, an asterisk (*). Use of wildcards will be illustrated in many examples. ANSI Standard SQL implementations use the percent sign (%) as a wildcard.

If a table or field name has an embedded space, that name must be enclosed in brackets ([]). For example, if the table name is **My Big Table**, in a SQL statement you would use:

[My Big Table]

This notation is not allowed in some SQL implementations. But in implementations that don't recognize brackets, embedded spaces in table and field names are not allowed, so it should never be a problem. A good rule of thumb is to avoid embedded spaces in table and field names if you can.

To refer to a particular field in a particular table in a SQL statement, use a dot notation:

TableName.FieldName

If either the table or field name has embedded spaces, it must be enclosed in brackets. Again, avoid embedded spaces if possible.

Now, we're ready to start forming SQL statements and using them with Visual Basic applications. One warning - SQL is a very powerful ally in obtaining and modifying data in a database. But, it can also be very destructive - a single SQL statement can wipe out an entire database! So, be careful and always provide safeguards against such potential destruction.

Where Does SQL Fit In Visual Basic?

In Chapter 3, we used a single SQL statement to look at some fields from the **Titles** table of the **BOOKS** database (**BooksDB.accdb** for Access, **SQLBooksDB.mdf** for SQL Server). The SQL statement was used to form a command object (based on a connection object), which in turn was used by a data adapter object to form a data table. The data table is then available for viewing using data bound controls.

The code involved in processing a SQL statement is (assumes all objects have been properly declared):

Access Database:

```
MyCommand = New OleDbCommand(MySQL, MyConnection)
MyAdapter.SelectCommand = MyCommand
MyAdapter.Fill(MyTable)
```

SQL Server Database:

```
MyCommand = New SqlCommand(MySQL, MyConnection)
MyAdapter.SelectCommand = MyCommand
MyAdapter.Fill(MyTable)
```

In this code, **MySQL** is the SQL statement applied against a connection object **MyConnection** (it is assumed that the connection object has been opened against a database). The resulting command object (**MyCommand**) is used by the data adapter (**MyAdapter**) to form the data table (**MyTable**). This table is then used for data binding.

A result of interest from a SQL query is the number of records returned (if any). The data table formed has that information in the following property:

```
MyTable.Rows.Count
```

Example 4-1

SQL Tester

Well, now we know some of the rules and syntax of SQL statements and how to use them with Visual Basic, but we still don't know what a SQL statement looks like (well, we saw a couple of examples in Chapter 3). We correct all that now and start learning more about SQL. To test SQL statements we form, we build this example which allows us to enter SQL statements and see the results of the formed database queries. The **BOOKS** database (Access - **BooksDB.accdb**, SQL Server – **SQLBooksDB.mdf**) is used in this example.

1. Start a new project. Add a text box control, two label controls, a button, and a data grid view control to the form. Wait, you say, what is a **DataGridView** control? The DataGridView control allows us to view and edit an entire database table by setting just one property (**DataSource**). Resize and position the controls so your form looks something like this:

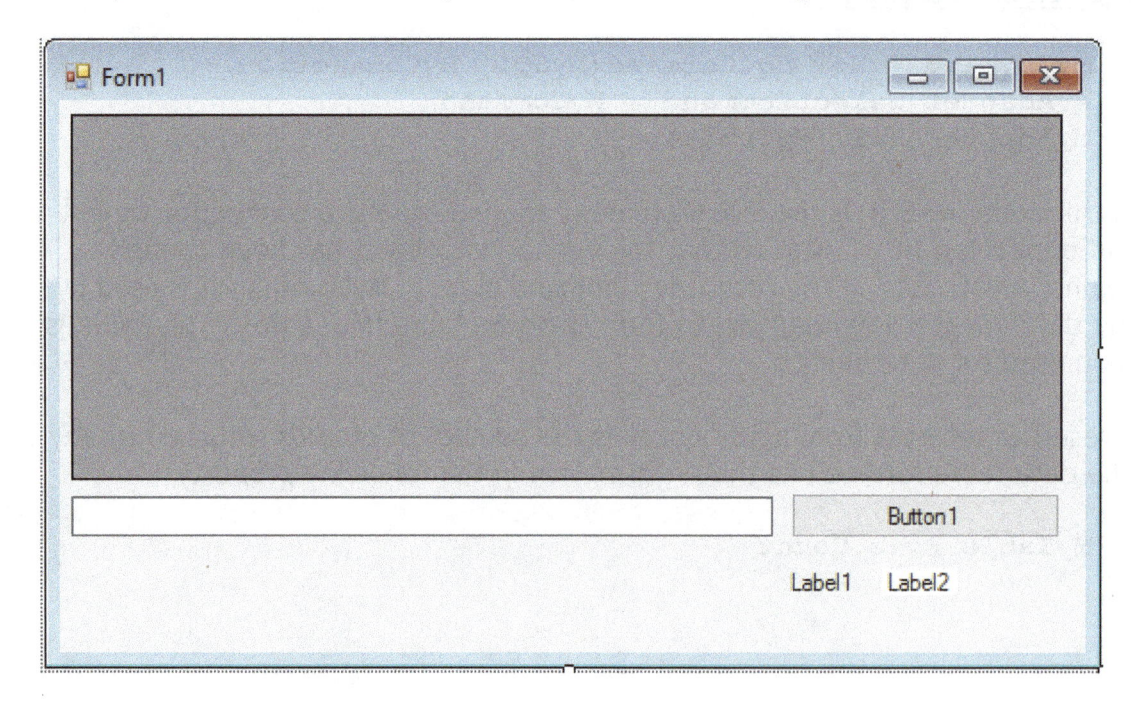

2. Set properties for the form and controls:

Form1:
    Name   frmSQLTester
    FormBorderStyle   FixedSingle
    StartPosition   CenterScreen
    Text   SQL Tester

Label1:
    AutoSize   False
    Text   Records Returned

Label2:
    Name   lblRecords
    AutoSize   False
    TextAlign   MiddleCenter
    BackColor   White
    BorderStyle   FixedSingle
    Text   0
    FontSize   12

Button1:
    Name   btnTest
    Text   Test SQL Statement
    TabStop   False

DataGridView1:
    Name   grdSQLTester
    TabStop   False

TextBox1:
    Name   txtSQLTester
    MultiLine   True
    ScrollBars   Vertical

When done, the form should look like this:

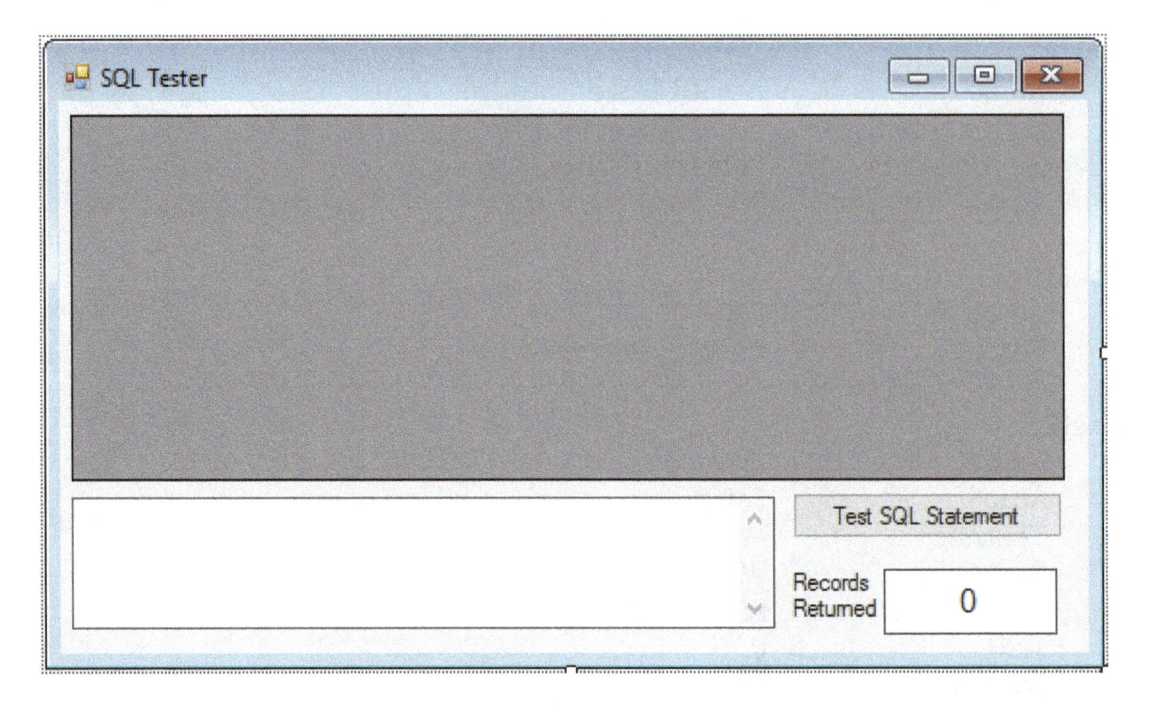

With this example, we will type SQL statements in the text box area, then click the **Test SQL Statement** button. The data grid will display the returned records, while the label control will display the number of records returned. We need some code to do all of this.

3. Add these two lines at the top of the code window to allow use of data objects:

<u>Access Database:</u>

```
Imports System.Data
Imports System.Data.OleDb
```

<u>SQL Server Database:</u>

```
Imports System.Data
Imports System.Data.SqlClient
```

Database Queries with SQL

4. Form level declaration for connection object:

Access Database:

```
Dim BooksConnection As OleDbConnection
```

SQL Server Database:

```
Dim BooksConnection As SqlConnection
```

5. Code for the **frmSQLTester Load** procedure that opens the database:

Access Database:

```
Private Sub FrmSQLTester_Load(ByVal sender As System.Object, ByVal e As System.EventArgs) Handles MyBase.Load
    'connect to books database
    BooksConnection = New OleDbConnection("Provider=Microsoft.ACE.OLEDB.12.0; Data Source = c:\VBDB\Working\BooksDB.accdb")
    BooksConnection.Open()
End Sub
```

SQL Server Database:

```
Private Sub FrmSQLTester_Load(ByVal sender As System.Object, ByVal e As System.EventArgs) Handles MyBase.Load
    'connect to books database
    BooksConnection = New SqlConnection("Data Source=.\SQLEXPRESS; AttachDbFilename=C:\VBDB\Working\SQLBooksDB.mdf; Integrated Security=True; Connect Timeout=30; User Instance=True")
    BooksConnection.Open()
End Sub
```

6. Code for the **frmSQLTester FormClosing** procedure:

```
  Private Sub FrmSQLTester_FormClosing(ByVal sender As
Object, ByVal e As
System.Windows.Forms.FormClosingEventArgs) Handles
Me.FormClosing
    BooksConnection.Close()
    BooksConnection.Dispose()
  End Sub
```

7. Code for the **btnTest Click** procedure:

Access Database:

```
  Private Sub BtnTest_Click(ByVal sender As System.Object,
ByVal e As System.EventArgs) Handles btnTest.Click
    Dim ResultsCommand As OleDbCommand = Nothing
    Dim ResultsAdapter As New OleDbDataAdapter
    Dim ResultsTable As New DataTable
    Try
      'establish command object and data adapter
      ResultsCommand = New OleDbCommand(txtSQLTester.Text,
BooksConnection)
      ResultsAdapter.SelectCommand = ResultsCommand
      ResultsAdapter.Fill(ResultsTable)
      'bind grid view to data table
      grdSQLTester.DataSource = ResultsTable
      lblRecords.Text = ResultsTable.Rows.Count.ToString
    Catch ex As Exception
      MessageBox.Show(ex.Message, "Error in Processing SQL",
MessageBoxButtons.OK, MessageBoxIcon.Error)
    End Try
    ResultsCommand.Dispose()
    ResultsAdapter.Dispose()
    ResultsTable.Dispose()
  End Sub
```

Database Queries with SQL

SQL Server Database:

```vb
  Private Sub BtnTest_Click(ByVal sender As System.Object, ByVal e As System.EventArgs) Handles btnTest.Click
    Dim ResultsCommand As SqlCommand = Nothing
    Dim ResultsAdapter As New SqlDataAdapter
    Dim ResultsTable As New DataTable
    Try
      'establish command object and data adapter
      ResultsCommand = New SqlCommand(txtSQLTester.Text, BooksConnection)
      ResultsAdapter.SelectCommand = ResultsCommand
      ResultsAdapter.Fill(ResultsTable)
      'bind grid view to data table
      grdSQLTester.DataSource = ResultsTable
      lblRecords.Text = ResultsTable.Rows.Count.ToString
    Catch ex As Exception
      MessageBox.Show(ex.Message, "Error in Processing SQL", MessageBoxButtons.OK, MessageBoxIcon.Error)
    End Try
    ResultsCommand.Dispose()
    ResultsAdapter.Dispose()
    ResultsTable.Dispose()
  End Sub
```

Let's spend some time seeing what's going on in this code. The first thing we do is use exception handling (the **Try/End Try** block). Without it, if we make a small error in a SQL statement, the program will stop. With it, we get a message indicating our mistake and are allowed to continue. Following error control, the SQL statement (from **txtSQLTester**) is processed by the data adapter (**ResultsAdapter**) and the data table (**ResultsTable**) established. The number of records is then displayed.

Be careful in typing SQL statements. Although we have exception handling in SQL Tester, if you make a mistake, the returned error messages are (many times) not of much help. If you get an error, the best thing to do is retype the SQL command, paying attention to spacing, spelling, and proper punctuation.

4-12   Visual Basic and Databases

8. Save the application (Access version saved in the **Example 4-1** folder in **VBDB\Access\Class 4** folder; SQL Server version saved in the **Example 4-1** folder in **VBDB\SQL Server\Class 4** folder) and run it. Type the only SQL statement you know at this time in the text box (**SELECT * FROM Titles**). Click **Test SQL Statement** and you should see (it may take several seconds for the records to appear):

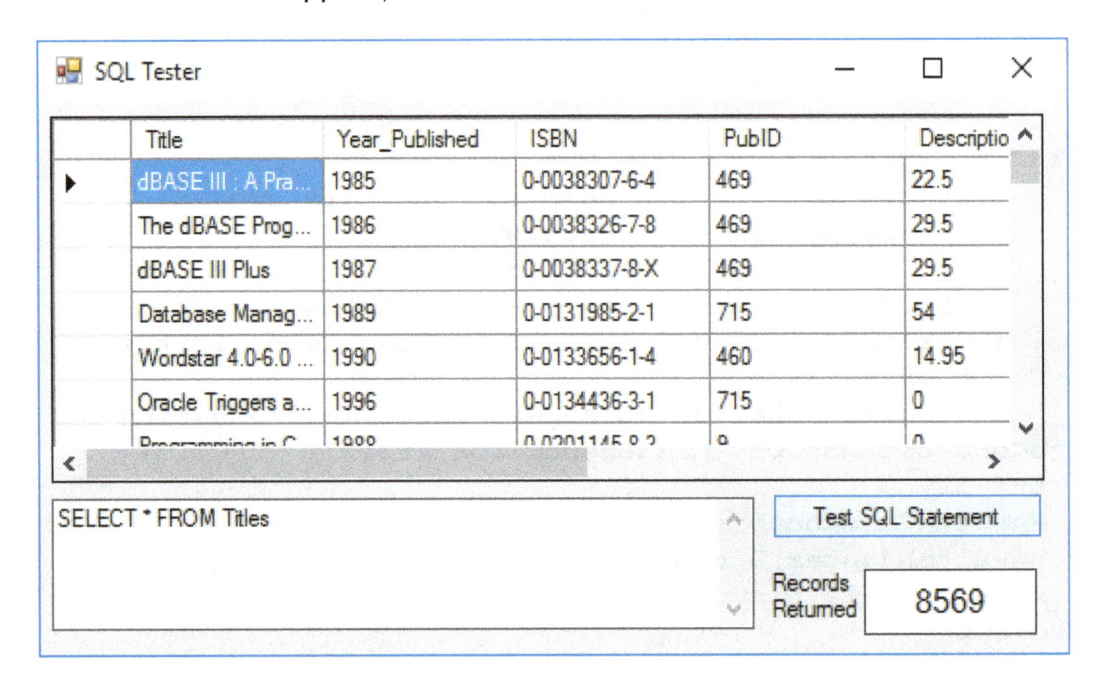

Title	Year_Published	ISBN	PubID	Descriptio
dBASE III : A Pra...	1985	0-0038307-6-4	469	22.5
The dBASE Prog...	1986	0-0038326-7-8	469	29.5
dBASE III Plus	1987	0-0038337-8-X	469	29.5
Database Manag...	1989	0-0131985-2-1	715	54
Wordstar 4.0-6.0 ...	1990	0-0133656-1-4	460	14.95
Oracle Triggers a...	1996	0-0134436-3-1	715	0

SELECT * FROM Titles

Records Returned: 8569

Note the data grid view control displays the entire table. You can scroll through the table or edit any values you choose. Any changes are automatically reflected in the underlying database. Column widths can be changed at run-time. Multiple row and column selections are possible. It's a very powerful tool. Please note **Records Returned** values for your results may be different, depending on the current data in the database.

Database Queries with SQL 4-13

Change the word **SELECT** to **SLECT** to make sure the error trapping works. You should see:

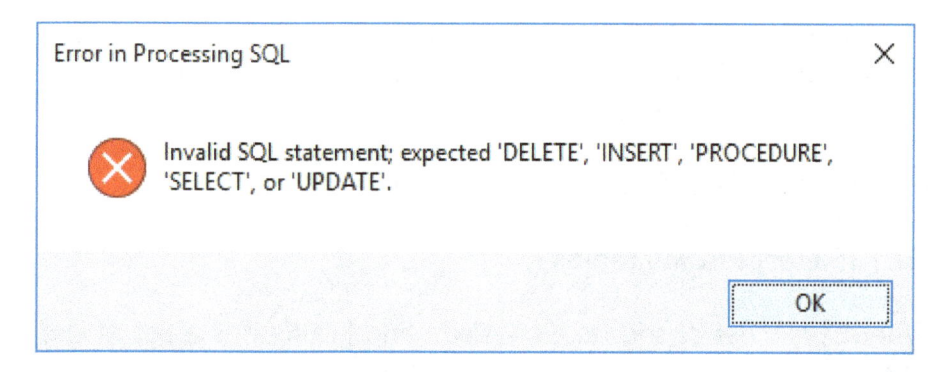

> **Error in Processing SQL**
>
> ❌ Invalid SQL statement; expected 'DELETE', 'INSERT', 'PROCEDURE', 'SELECT', or 'UPDATE'.
>
> [OK]

If using SQL Server, you may see:

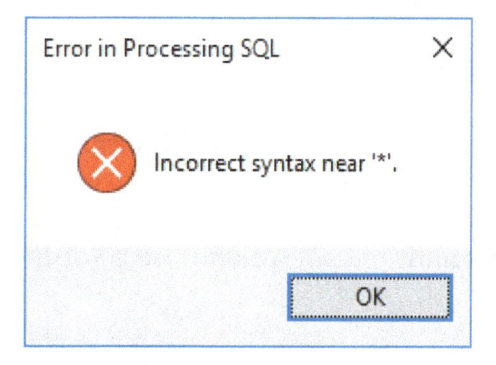

> **Error in Processing SQL**
>
> ❌ Incorrect syntax near '*'.
>
> [OK]

Now, let's use this SQL Tester to examine many kinds of SQL statements. When typing the statements, use upper case letters for the SQL keywords. Statements do not necessarily have to be on a single line - multiple line SQL statements are fine and usually make them easier to read and understand.

SELECT/FROM SQL Statement

The most commonly used SQL statement is the one we've been using as an example: the **SELECT/FROM** statement. This statement allows you to pick fields from one or more tables.

The syntax for a SELECT/FROM SQL statement is:

SELECT [Fields] **FROM** [Tables]

where [Fields] is a list of the fields desired and [Tables] is a list of the tables where the fields are to be found. The wildcard character (*) can be used for the fields list to select all fields from the listed table(s). For example, the statement we have been using:

SELECT * FROM Titles

selects and returns all fields from the **BOOKS** database **Titles** table. Look at all fields in the other tables (Authors, Publishers, Title_Author) using similar statements. Looking at each table will reacquaint you with the structure of the **BOOKS** database tables and fields. We will use a lot in the rest of this chapter.

Database Queries with SQL 4-15

If we only want selected fields from a table, we use a **field list**, which is a comma-delimited list of the fields desired, or:

SELECT Field1, Field2, Field3 **FROM** Table

will return three named fields from Table. Make sure you do not put a comma after the last field name. To obtain just the Title and Year_Published fields from the **BOOKS** database **Titles** table, use:

SELECT Title,Year_Published FROM Titles

Note the field names are not written using the prescribed dot notation of **Table.Field**. The table name omission is acceptable here because there is no confusion as to where the fields are coming from. When using multiple tables, we must use the dot notation.

Try this with the SQL tester and you will see just two fields are returned.

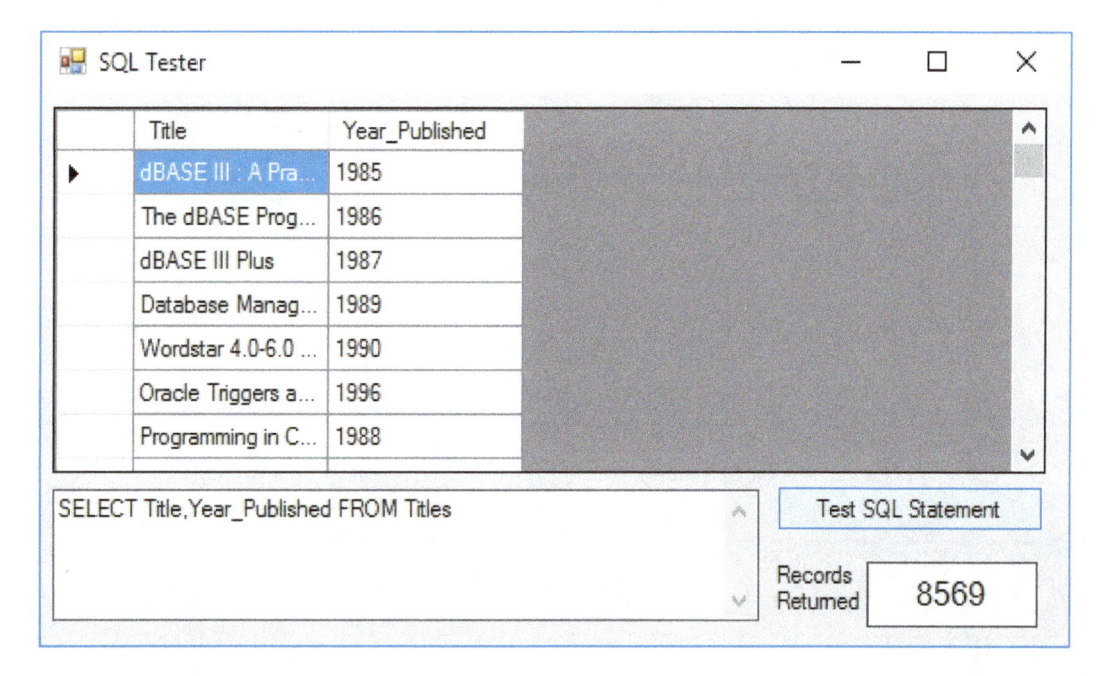

Title	Year_Published
dBASE III : A Pra...	1985
The dBASE Prog...	1986
dBASE III Plus	1987
Database Manag...	1989
Wordstar 4.0-6.0 ...	1990
Oracle Triggers a...	1996
Programming in C...	1988

SELECT Title,Year_Published FROM Titles

Records Returned: 8569

4-16 Visual Basic and Databases

The **DISTINCT** keyword can be used with SELECT to restrict the returned records to one per unique entry for the field. That is, there are no duplicate entries. As an example, first try this with the SQL tester:

SELECT PubID FROM Titles

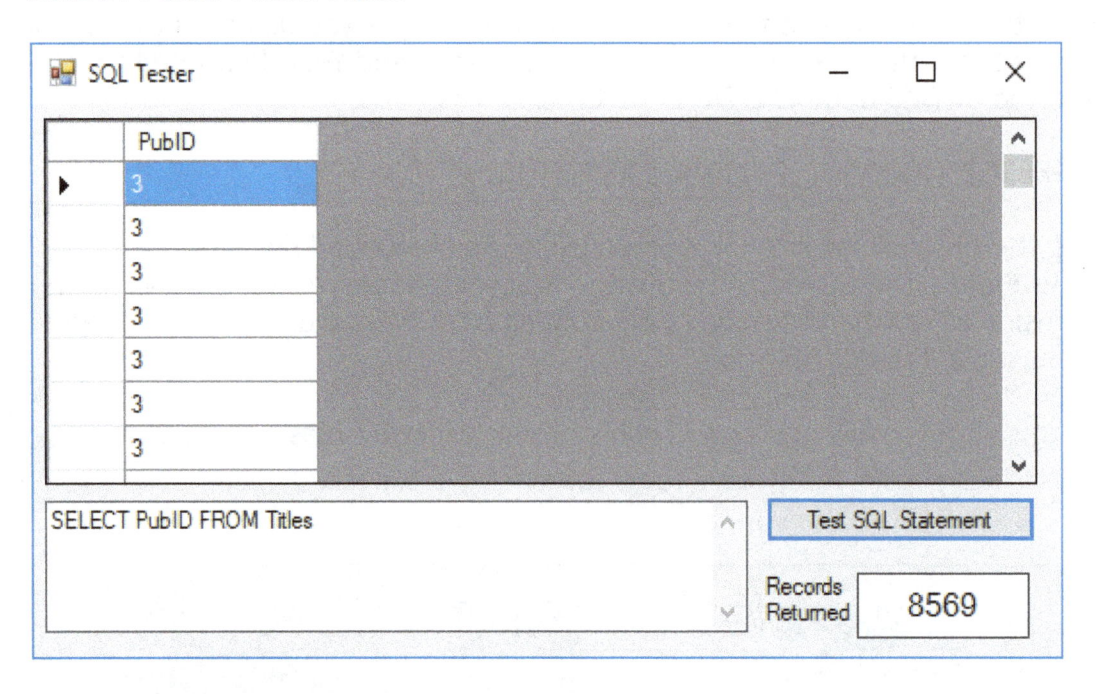

Database Queries with SQL 4-17

Now, try:

SELECT DISTINCT PubID FROM Titles

```
SQL Tester
PubID
▶  3
   4
   5
   6
   7
   8
   9

SELECT DISTINCT PubID FROM Titles        Test SQL Statement

                                          Records Returned  708
```

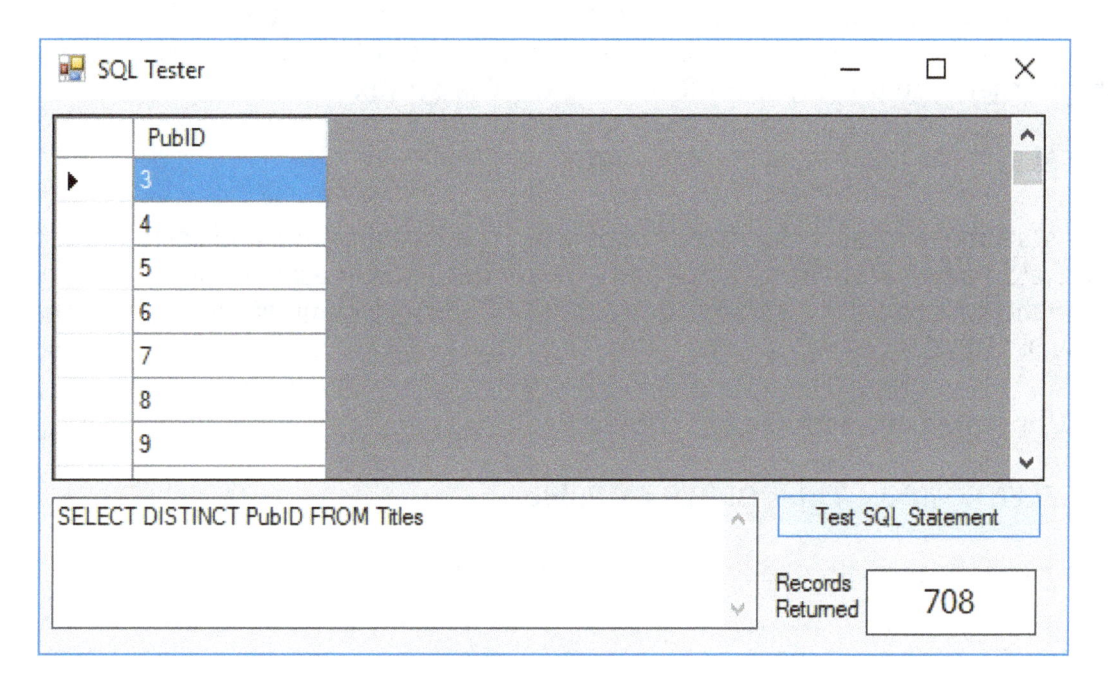

You should see far fewer records are returned - only distinct publishers are returned.

ORDER BY Clause

When you use a SELECT/FROM statement, the records are returned in the order they are found in the selected table(s). To sort the returned records in some other order, you use the **ORDER BY** clause. The syntax is:

SELECT [Fields] **FROM** [Tables] **ORDER BY** FieldSort

This statement selects the listed fields from the listed tables and sorts them by the field named FieldSort. By default, the ordering is in ascending order. If you want the sort to be in descending order, the FieldSort name is followed by the keyword **DESC**.

Try this statement with the SQL Tester:

SELECT * FROM Titles ORDER BY PubID

All records in the Titles table will be returned in order of Publisher ID.

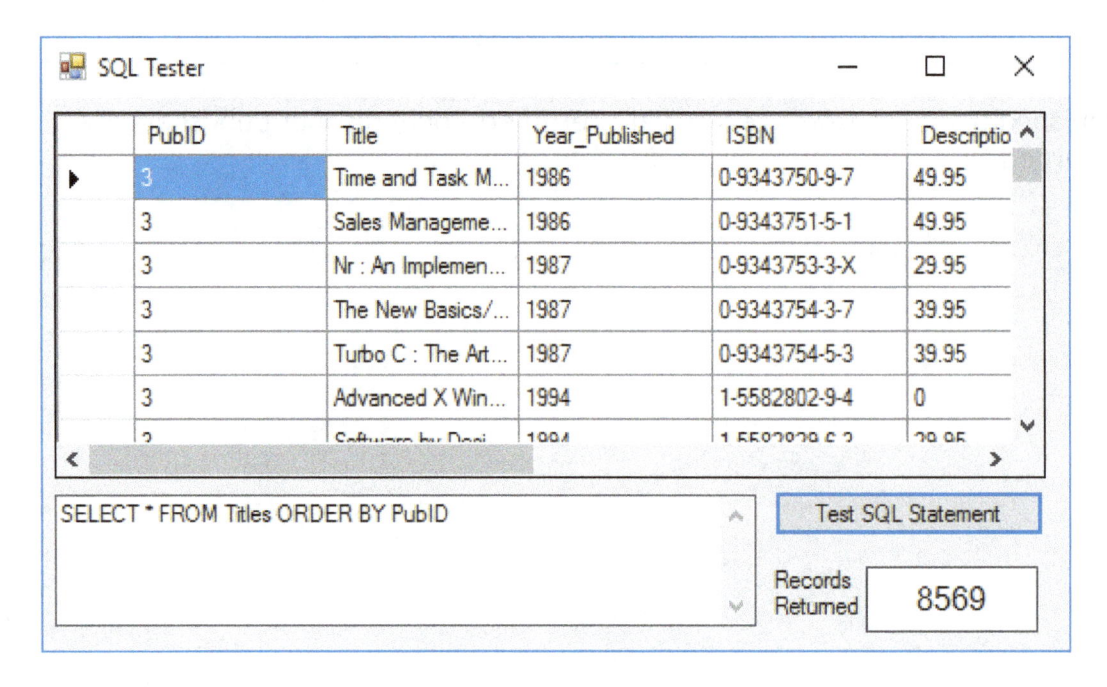

Try this and the order should be reversed:

SELECT * FROM Titles ORDER BY PubID DESC

Database Queries with SQL 4-19

You can use more than one field in the ORDER BY clause. SQL will create a data table based on all requested orderings. Try this with SQL tester:

SELECT * FROM Titles ORDER BY PubID,Title

The returned records will be in order of the publishers, with each publisher's titles in alphabetic order.

If you want to restrict the number of records returned by a SQL statement that orders the returned records, you can use the **TOP** keyword with SELECT. **TOP n** returns the first n records. **TOP n PERCENT** returns the first n percent of the returned records. If two or more records have the same order value, they are all returned. Use the SQL Tester and try:

SELECT TOP 20 * FROM Titles ORDER BY PubID,Title

Twenty books should be returned. Now, try:

SELECT TOP 20 PERCENT * FROM Titles ORDER BY PubID,Title

Far more books will be returned.

WHERE Clause

One of the most useful aspects of the SELECT/FROM SQL statement is its ability to limit the returned data table via the **WHERE** clause. This clause specifies some criteria that must be met in forming the data table. The syntax is:

SELECT [Fields] **FROM** [Tables] **WHERE** Criteria

The WHERE clause limits the number of returned records by allowing you to do logical checks on the value of any field(s). **Operators** used to perform these checks include:

<	Less than	<=	Less than or equal to
>	Greater than	>=	Greater than or equal to
=	Equal	<>	Not equal

Other operators are:

Between   Within a specified range
In   Specify a list of values
Like   Wild card matching

The WHERE clause can limit information displayed from one table or combine information from one or more tables. First, let's do some single table examples using SQL Tester.

Database Queries with SQL 4-21

Single Table WHERE Clause

Say we want to see all fields in the **BOOKS** database **Titles** table for books published after 1995. And, we want the returned records ordered by **Title**. The SQL statement to do this is (we'll type each clause on a separate line to clearly indicate what is going on - multiple line SQL statements are acceptable and, many times, desirable):

SELECT *
FROM Titles
WHERE Year_Published > 1995
ORDER BY Title

This is where the real power of SQL comes in. With this simple statement, the database engine quickly finds the desired records and sorts them - all without any coding on our part!

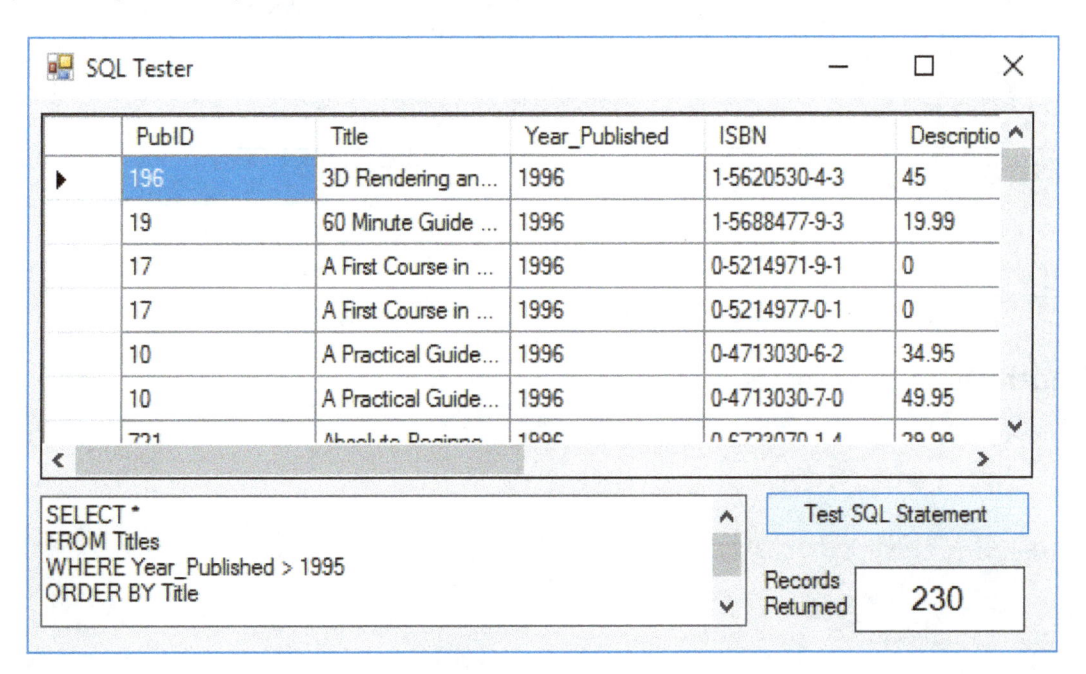

What if we want to know information about all the book publishers in the state of Washington. Try this SQL statement with the **BOOKS** Publishers table:

SELECT * FROM Publishers WHERE State = 'WA'

Note we enclosed the state name abbreviation (a string) in single quotes, as discussed earlier in this chapter. Try this SQL statement with the SQL tester and you should find one lonely publisher (BetaV) in the state of Washington!:

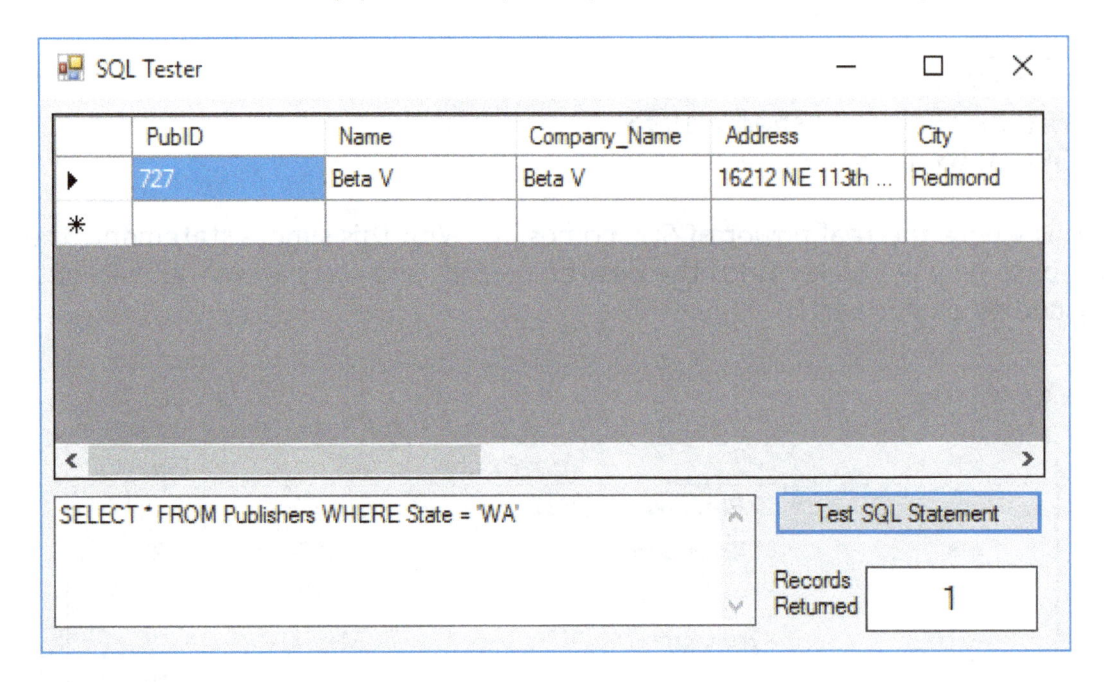

PubID	Name	Company_Name	Address	City
727	Beta V	Beta V	16212 NE 113th ...	Redmond

SELECT * FROM Publishers WHERE State = 'WA'

Records Returned: 1

Wonder where Microsoft is?

Database Queries with SQL 4-23

The **BETWEEN** keyword allows us to search for a range of values. Want all books published between 1995 and 1998? Use this SQL statement:

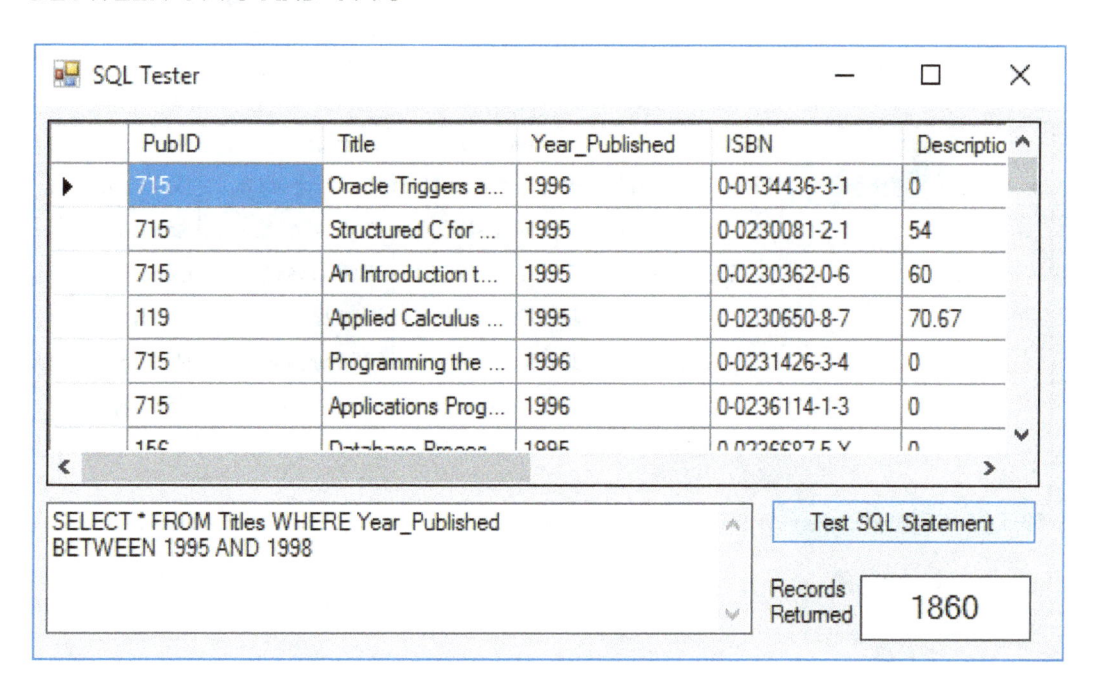

**SELECT * FROM Titles WHERE Year_Published
BETWEEN 1995 AND 1998**

PubID	Title	Year_Published	ISBN	Descriptio
715	Oracle Triggers a...	1996	0-0134436-3-1	0
715	Structured C for ...	1995	0-0230081-2-1	54
715	An Introduction t...	1995	0-0230362-0-6	60
119	Applied Calculus ...	1995	0-0230650-8-7	70.67
715	Programming the ...	1996	0-0231426-3-4	0
715	Applications Prog...	1996	0-0236114-1-3	0

SELECT * FROM Titles WHERE Year_Published BETWEEN 1995 AND 1998

Records Returned: 1860

The **IN** keyword lets us specify a comma-delimited list of desired values in the returned data table. Say, we want to know the publishers in New York, Massachusetts, and California. This SQL statement will do the trick:

SELECT * FROM Publishers WHERE State IN ('NY', 'MA', 'CA')

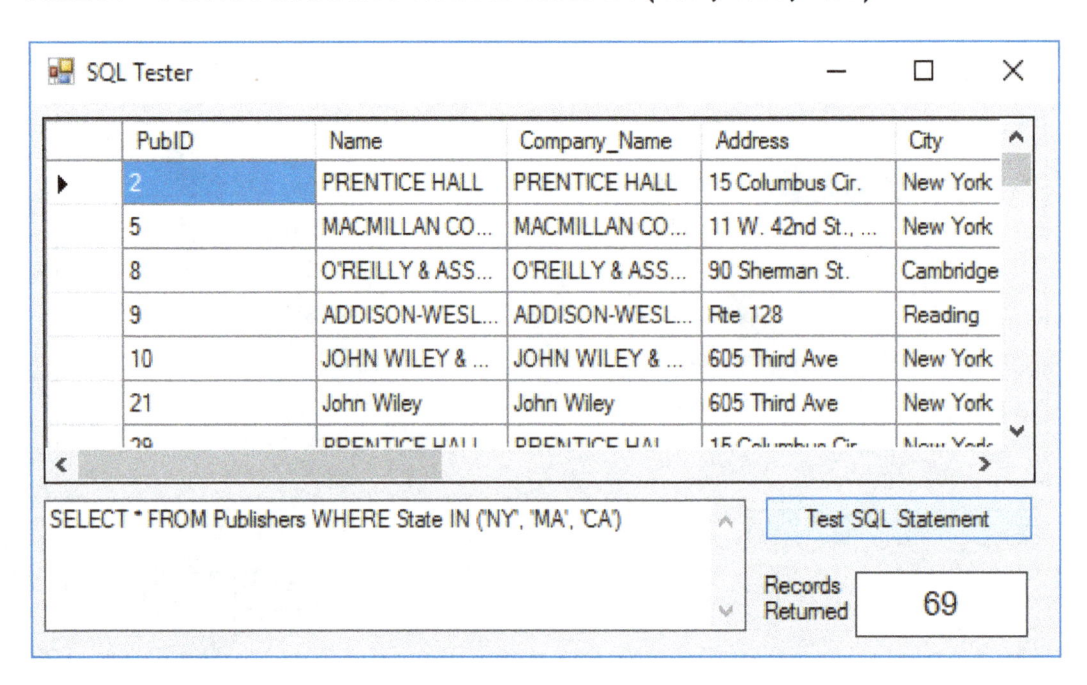

Database Queries with SQL 4-25

The **LIKE** keyword allows us to use wildcards in the WHERE clause. This lets us find similar fields. Recall, the Microsoft SQL wildcard character is the asterisk (*). For this example to work, you need to use % as a wildcard in the LIKE clause. The % is a SQL standard for wildcards. To find all authors with a 'g' anywhere in the their name, try:

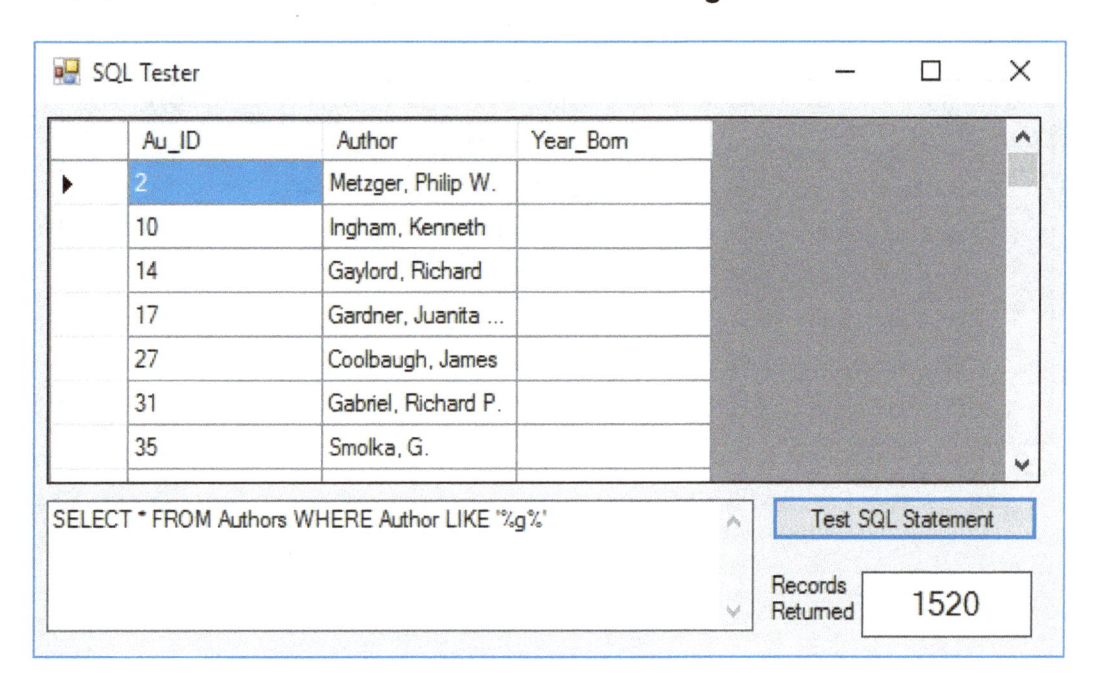

SELECT * FROM Authors WHERE Author LIKE '%g%'

Au_ID	Author	Year_Born
2	Metzger, Philip W.	
10	Ingham, Kenneth	
14	Gaylord, Richard	
17	Gardner, Juanita ...	
27	Coolbaugh, James	
31	Gabriel, Richard P.	
35	Smolka, G.	

SELECT * FROM Authors WHERE Author LIKE '%g%'

Records Returned: 1520

Multiple criteria are possible by using the logical operators **AND** and **OR**. For example, to find all books in the **Titles** table published after 1993 with a title that starts with the letters **Data**, we would use the SQL statement:

SELECT * FROM Titles
WHERE Year_Published > 1993 AND Title LIKE 'Data%'

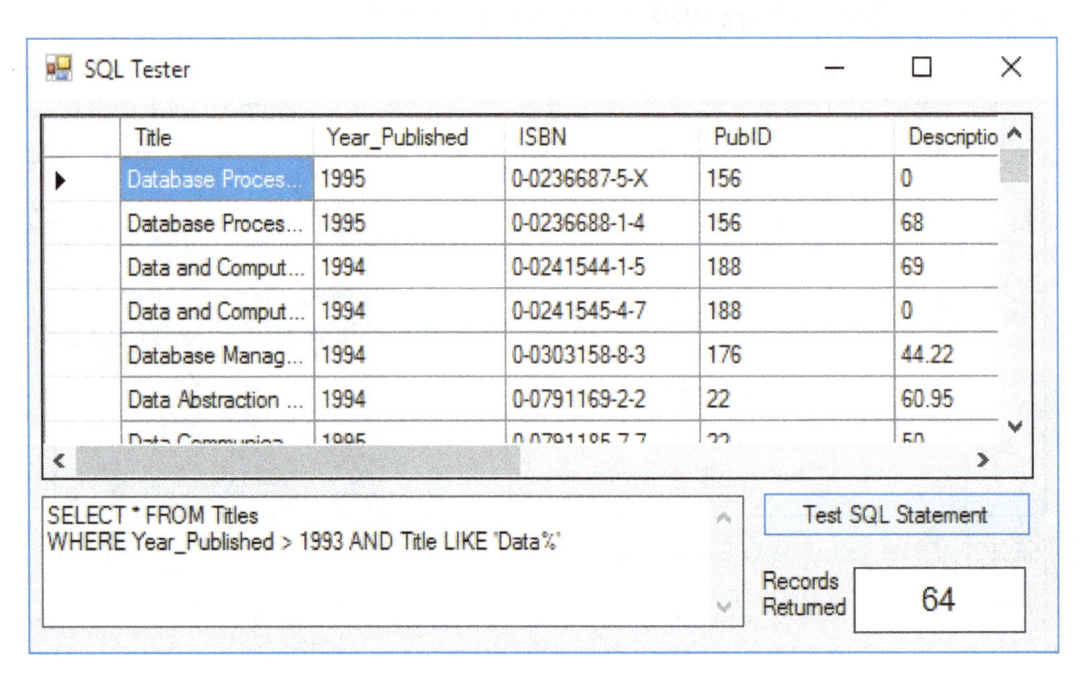

Multiple Table WHERE Clause

So far, almost everything we've done in this course has involved looking at a single native (built-in) table in a database. This has been valuable experience in helping us understand database design, learning how to use the Visual Basic database tools, and learning some simple SQL statements. Now, we begin looking at one of the biggest uses of database management systems - combining information from multiple tables within a database. SQL makes such combinations a simple task.

We still use the same SELECT/FROM syntax, along with the WHERE and ORDER BY clauses to form our new virtual tables:

SELECT [Fields]
FROM [Tables]
WHERE Criteria
ORDER BY [Fields]

The only difference here is there's more information in each SQL statement, resulting is some very long statements. The [Fields] list will have many fields, the [Tables] list will have multiple tables, and the Criteria will have several parts. The basic idea is to have the SQL statement specify what fields you want displayed (**SELECT**), what tables those fields are found in (**FROM**), how you want the tables to be combined (**WHERE**), and how you want them sorted (**ORDER BY**). Let's try an example.

Notice the Titles table does not list a book's publisher, but just publisher identification (PubID). What if we want to display a book's title (**Title** field in **Titles** table) and publisher (**Company_Name** in **Publishers** table) in the same data table? Let's build the SQL statement. First, the SELECT clause specifies the fields we want in our 'virtual' table:

    SELECT Titles.Title,Publishers.Company_Name

Note the use of dot notation to specify the desired fields. With multiple tables, this avoids any problems with naming ambiguities.

The FROM clause names the tables holding these fields:

    FROM Titles,Publishers

The WHERE clause declares what criteria must be met in combining the two tables. The usual selection is to match a **primary key** in one table with the corresponding **foreign key** in another table. Here, we want the publisher identification numbers from each table to match:

WHERE Titles.PubID = Publishers.PubID

Any records from the tables that do not match the WHERE criteria are not included in the returned data table.

Lastly, we declare how we want the resulting data table to be sorted:

ORDER BY Titles.Title

The complete SQL statement is thus:

SELECT Titles.Title,Publishers.Company_Name
FROM Titles,Publishers
WHERE Titles.PubID = Publishers.PubID
ORDER BY Titles.Title

Try this with the SQL tester.

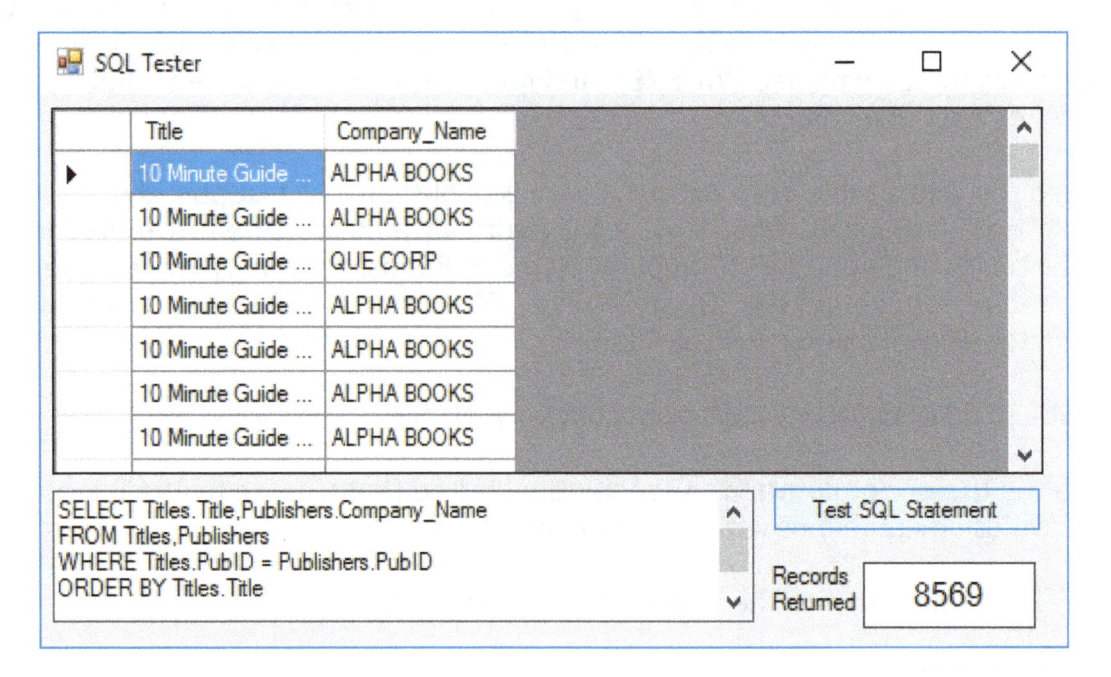

Database Queries with SQL 4-29

Are you amazed? You have just seen one of the real powers of using SQL with the ADO .NET database engine (or any database system, for that matter). We simply told the engine what we wanted (via the SQL statement) and it did all of the work for us - no coding needed! Let's do some more examples.

In the previous example, say you just want books published by Que Corporation. Modify the SQL statement to read (we added an AND clause):

SELECT Titles.Title,Publishers.Company_Name
FROM Titles,Publishers
WHERE Titles.PubID = Publishers.PubID
AND Publishers.Company_Name = 'QUE CORP'
ORDER BY Titles.Title

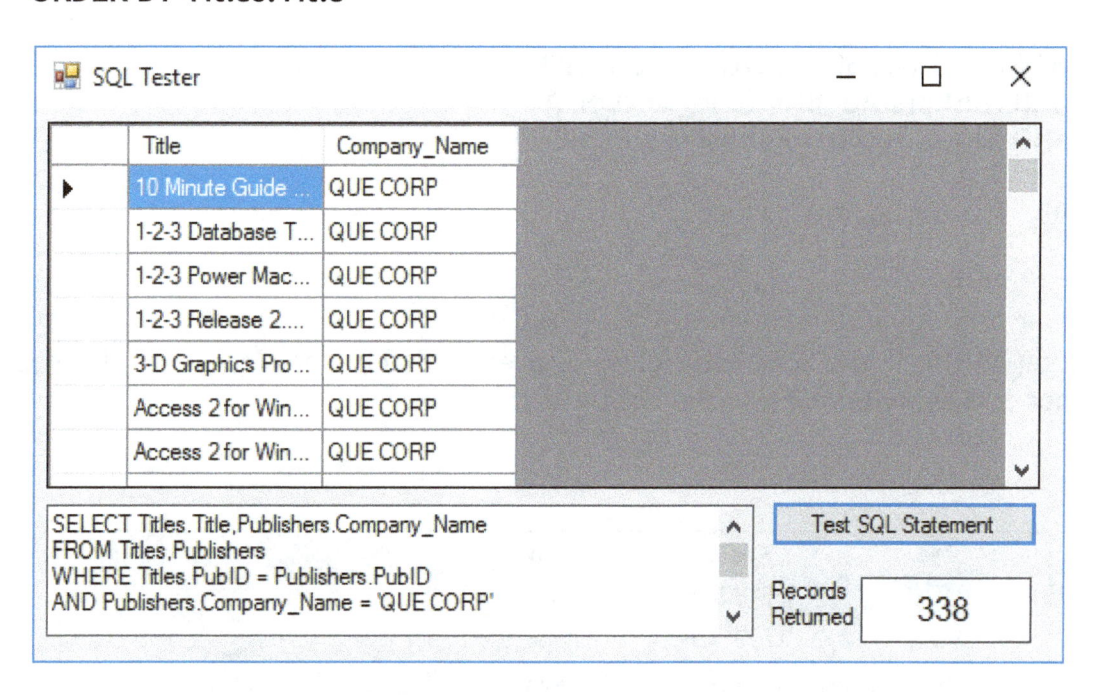

Title	Company_Name
10 Minute Guide ...	QUE CORP
1-2-3 Database T...	QUE CORP
1-2-3 Power Mac...	QUE CORP
1-2-3 Release 2....	QUE CORP
3-D Graphics Pro...	QUE CORP
Access 2 for Win...	QUE CORP
Access 2 for Win...	QUE CORP

Records Returned: 338

What if we want to list a book's title, publisher, <u>and</u> author, ordered by the author names? This requires using all four tables in the **BOOKS** database. Let's build the SQL statement. We want three fields:

SELECT Authors.Author,Titles.Title,Publishers.Company_Name

As mentioned, to retrieve this information requires all four tables:

FROM Authors,Titles,Publishers,Title_Author

We still need the publisher identification numbers to match, but now also need to make sure book titles (via the ISBN field) and author identification numbers match. The corresponding WHERE clause is:

WHERE Titles.ISBN = Title_Author.ISBN
AND Authors.Au_ID = Title_Author.Au_ID
AND Titles.PubID = Publishers.PubID

Finally, the results are sorted:

ORDER BY Authors.Author

Putting all this in the SQL tester gives us over 16,000 listings (one entry for every author and every book he or she wrote or co-wrote):

Database Queries with SQL   4-31

Such power! Can you imagine trying to write BASIC code to perform this record retrieval task?

If the displayed field name does not clearly describe the displayed information, you can **alias** the name, or change it to something more meaningful using the **AS** clause. As a simple example, try this:

SELECT Au_ID AS This_Author FROM Authors

Notice the displayed column is now **This_Author**.

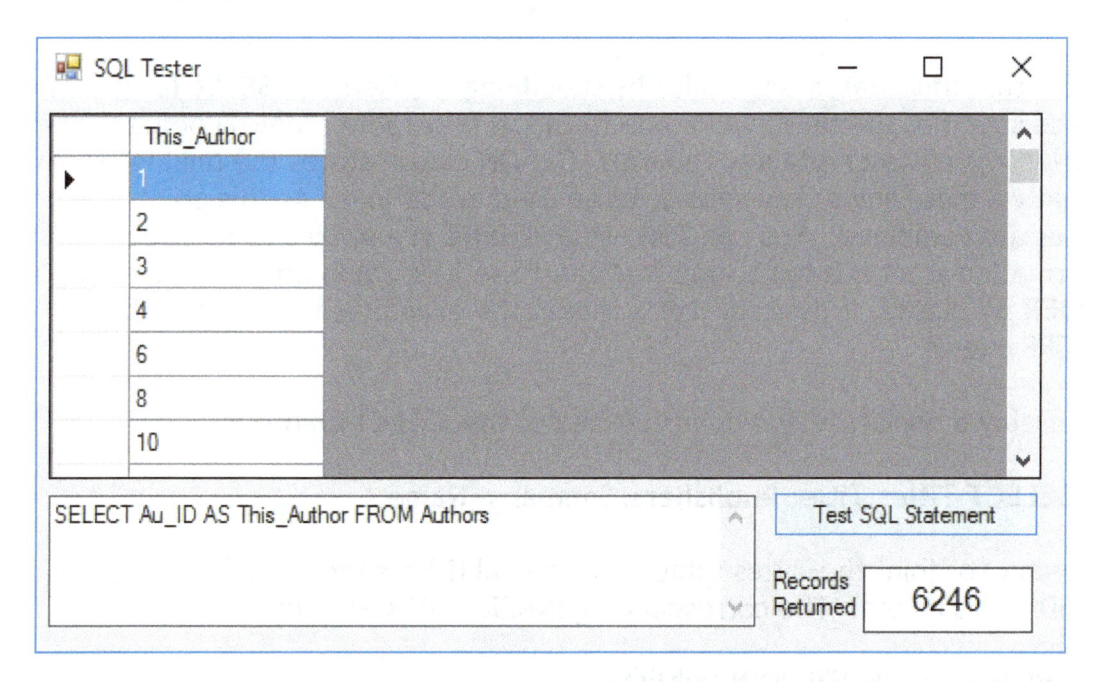

[SQL Tester window showing This_Author column with values 1, 2, 3, 4, 6, 8, 10; SQL statement "SELECT Au_ID AS This_Author FROM Authors"; Records Returned: 6246]

The field name is unaffected by aliasing - only the displayed name changes.

INNER JOIN Clause

When combining tables, the SQL **INNER JOIN** clause does the same work as the WHERE clause. The syntax for an INNER JOIN is a little different than that of the WHERE clause.

>   **SELECT** [Fields]
>   **FROM** Table1 **INNER JOIN** Table2 **ON** Linking Criteria
>   **WHERE** Criteria
>   **ORDER BY** [Fields]

This rather long statement begins by specifying the fields to **SELECT**. The **FROM** clause specifies the fields will come from the first table (Table1) being **INNER JOIN**ed with a second table (Table2). The **ON** clause states the linking criteria (usually a matching of key values) to be used in the join. At this point, the tables are combined. You can still use a **WHERE** clause to extract specific information from this table (you just can't use it to combine tables) and an **ORDER BY** clause, if desired. Let's repeat the examples just done with the WHERE clause.

To display a book title and publisher name, the SELECT clause is:

>   **SELECT Titles.Title, Publishers.Company_Name**

We want to 'join' the Titles table with the Publishers table, making sure the PubID fields match. The corresponding INNER JOIN statement is:

>   **FROM Titles INNER JOIN Publishers**
>   **ON Titles.PubID = Publishers.PubID**

Lastly, we order by the Title:

>   **ORDER BY Titles.Title**

Database Queries with SQL 4-33

Try this SQL statement in the SQL tester and you should obtain the same results seen earlier with the WHERE clause:

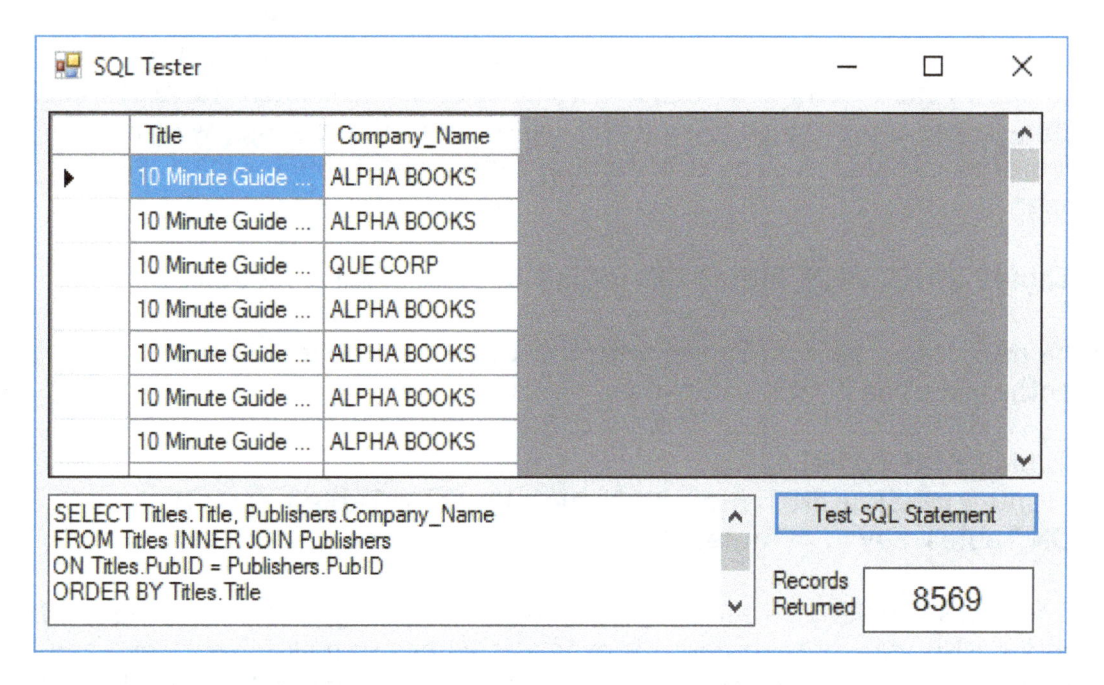

To illustrate use of the WHERE clause (to limit displayed records) in conjunction with the JOIN clause, try this modified SQL statement with SQL Tester:

    SELECT Titles.Title, Publishers.Company_Name
    FROM Titles INNER JOIN Publishers
    ON Titles.PubID = Publishers.PubID
    WHERE Publishers.Company_Name = 'QUE CORP'
    ORDER BY Titles.Title

Only QUE CORP publishers will be listed.

Use of the INNER JOIN clause to combine information from more than two tables is a little more complicated. The tables need be joined in stages, nesting the INNER JOIN clauses using parentheses for grouping. Assume we have three tables (**Table1**, **Table2**, **Table3**) we want to combine. Table1 and Table3 have a common key field for linking (**Key13**), as do Table2 and Table3 (**Key23**). Let's combine these three tables using INNER JOIN. In the first stage, we form a temporary table that is a result of joining Table2 and Table3 using Key23 for linking:

    Table2 INNER JOIN Table3 ON Table2.Key23 = Table3.Key23

In the next stage, we join Table1 with this temporary table (enclose it in parentheses) using Key13 for linking:

    Table1 INNER JOIN
    (Table2 INNER JOIN Table3 ON Table2.Key23 = Table3.Key23)
    ON Table1.Key13 = Table3.Key13

This nested statement is used in the SQL statement to specify the tables for field selection. Notice we've spread this over a few lines to make it clearer - any SQL processor can handle multiple line statements. The multiple table INNER JOIN can be generalized to more tables - just pay attention to what tables link with each other. Always make sure the tables you are joining, whether a temporary joined table or a database table, have a common key.

Remember the example we did earlier where we listed Author, Title, and Publisher in the **BOOKS** database? Let's build that SQL statement. First, SELECT the fields:

    SELECT Authors.Author,Titles.Title,Publishers.Company_Name

This is the same SELECT we used previously. Now, we need to form the FROM clause by combining four tables in three stages (one for each common key linking). In the first stage, combine the Publishers and Titles tables (PubID is common key):

    FROM Publishers INNER JOIN Titles
    ON Publishers.PubID=Titles.PubID

Database Queries with SQL 4-35

Now, join this temporary table (put its statement in parentheses) with the Title_Author table (ISBN is common key):

**FROM (Publishers INNER JOIN Titles
ON Publishers.PubID=Titles.PubID)
INNER JOIN Title_Author
ON Titles.ISBN=Title_Author.ISBN**

In the final stage, join the Authors table with this temporary table (enclose its statement in parentheses) using Au_ID as the key:

**FROM Authors INNER JOIN
((Publishers INNER JOIN Titles
ON Publishers.PubID=Titles.PubID)
INNER JOIN Title_Author
ON Titles.ISBN=Title_Author.ISBN)
ON Authors.Au_ID=Title_Author.Au_ID**

The **FROM** clause needed for the combined data view is now complete. The final line in the SQL statement orders the data:

ORDER BY Authors.Author

Whew! Try this full statement with the SQL tester and you should get the same results seen earlier using the WHERE clause.

OUTER JOIN Clause

The INNER JOIN only retrieves records that have a match on both sides of the JOIN. For example, with the **BOOKS** database, look at this INNER JOIN statement:

Publishers INNER JOIN Titles ON Publishers.PubID = Titles.PubID

In this statement, if there is a PubID in the Publishers table without a corresponding PubID in the Titles table, that value will not be in the returned data table. If you want all records returned, whether there is a match or not, you need to use what is called an **OUTER JOIN**. There are two forms for the OUTER JOIN.

A **RIGHT OUTER JOIN** includes all records from the second-named table (the right-most table), even if there are no matching values for records in the first-named (left-most table). Try this with SQL Tester:

**SELECT Titles.Title, Publishers.Company_Name
FROM Titles
RIGHT OUTER JOIN Publishers
ON Titles.PubID = Publishers.PubID
ORDER BY Titles.Title**

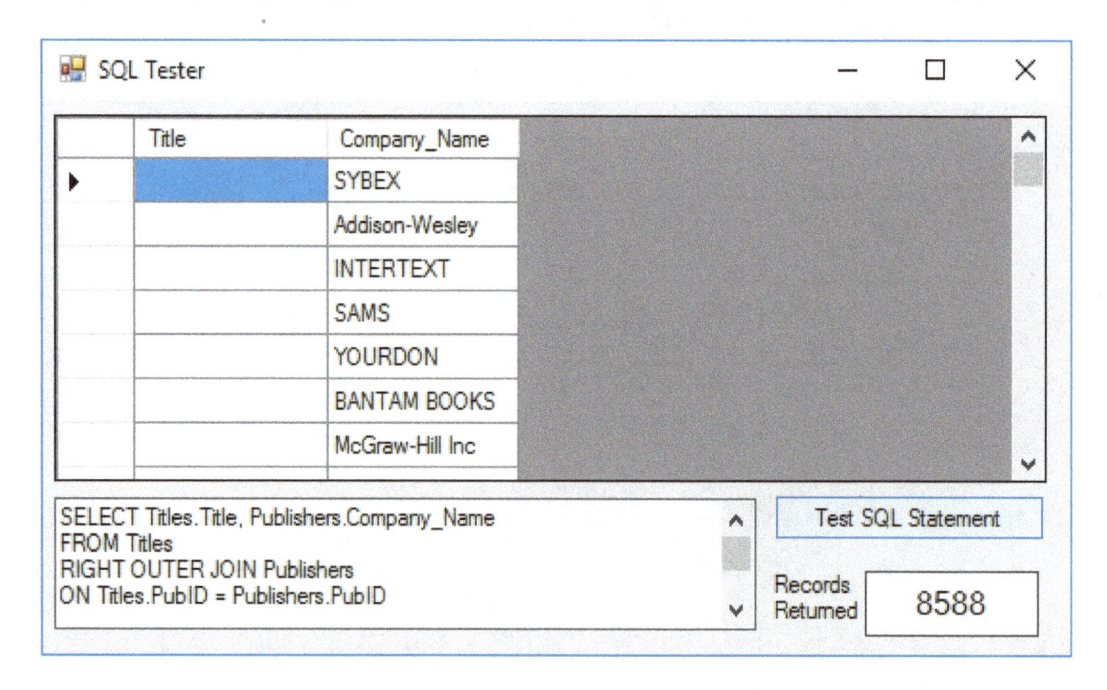

There are several publishers (about 19 or so) without corresponding titles in the database.

A **LEFT OUTER JOIN** includes all records from the first-named table (the left-most table), even if there are not matching values for records in the second-named (right-most table). Try this with SQL Tester:

SELECT Titles.Title, Publishers.Company_Name
FROM Titles
LEFT OUTER JOIN Publishers
ON Titles.PubID = Publishers.PubID
ORDER BY Titles.Title

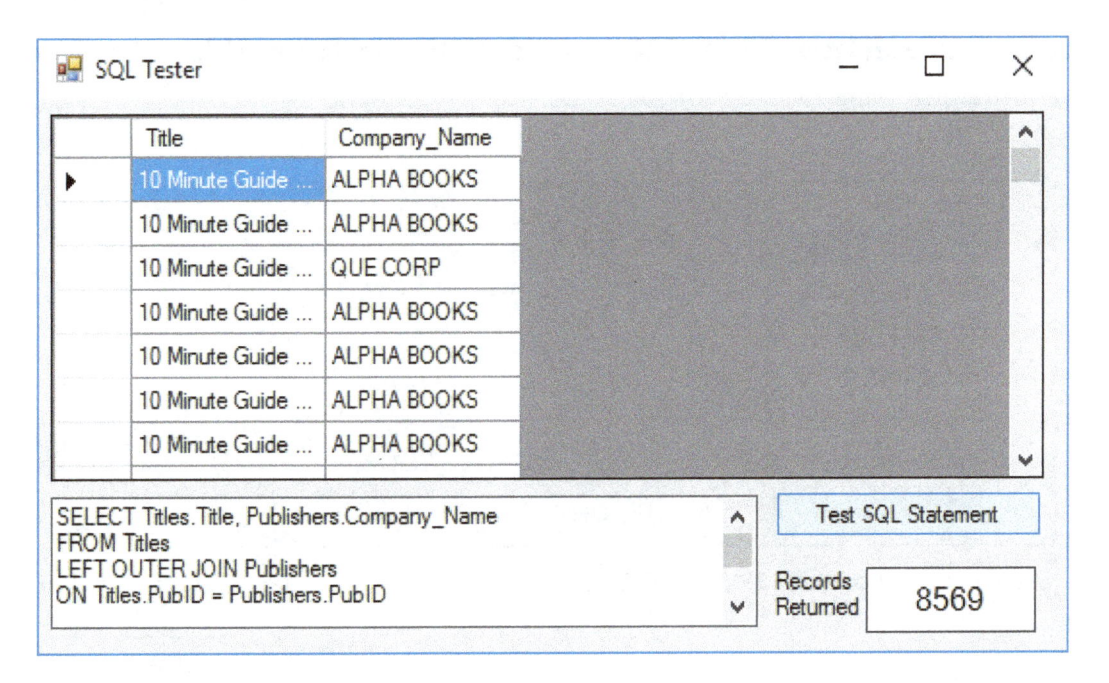

The returned data table is identical to that obtained with the INNER JOIN. Obviously, all books in the database have a corresponding publisher - that's actually a good thing.

Functions with SQL (Access Database)

The ADO .NET database engine allows you to use any valid BASIC function as part of a SQL statement with Access databases (see Access documentation for full list of such functions). This lets you modify the displayed information. It does not affect the underlying information in the database. As an example, say you want all book titles in the **BooksDB.accdb** database **Titles** table to be listed in upper case letters. Try this SQL statement with SQL Tester:

SELECT UCase(Titles.Title) FROM Titles ORDER BY Titles.Title

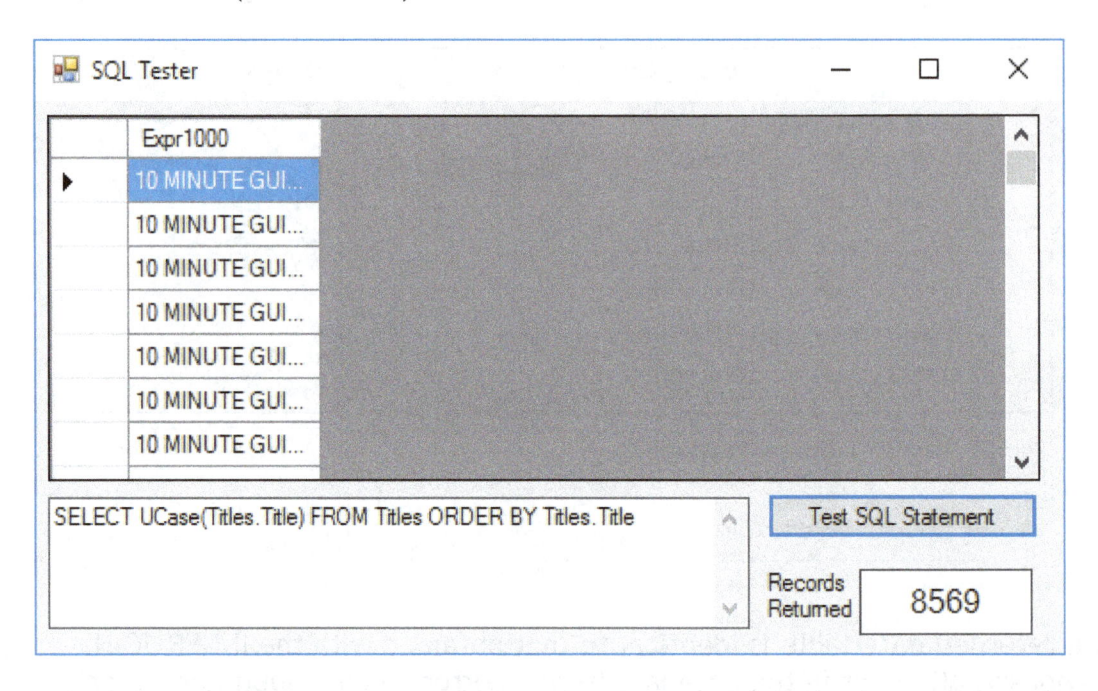

Notice SQL assigns a heading of **Expr1000** to this 'derived' field. We can use the alias feature of SQL change this heading to anything we want (except the name of an existing field). Try this:

SELECT UCase(Titles.Title) AS Title FROM Titles

Or, what if we had some process that could only use the 10 left-most characters of the book title. This SQL statement will do the trick:

SELECT Left(UCase(Titles.Title), 10) AS Title FROM Titles

You can also do BASIC math in a SQL statement. The **BOOKS** database **Authors** table has **Year_Born** as a field. This SQL statement will display each author and their age in 2006 (when this is being written):

SELECT Authors.Author,(2006-Authors.Year_Born) AS Age
FROM Authors

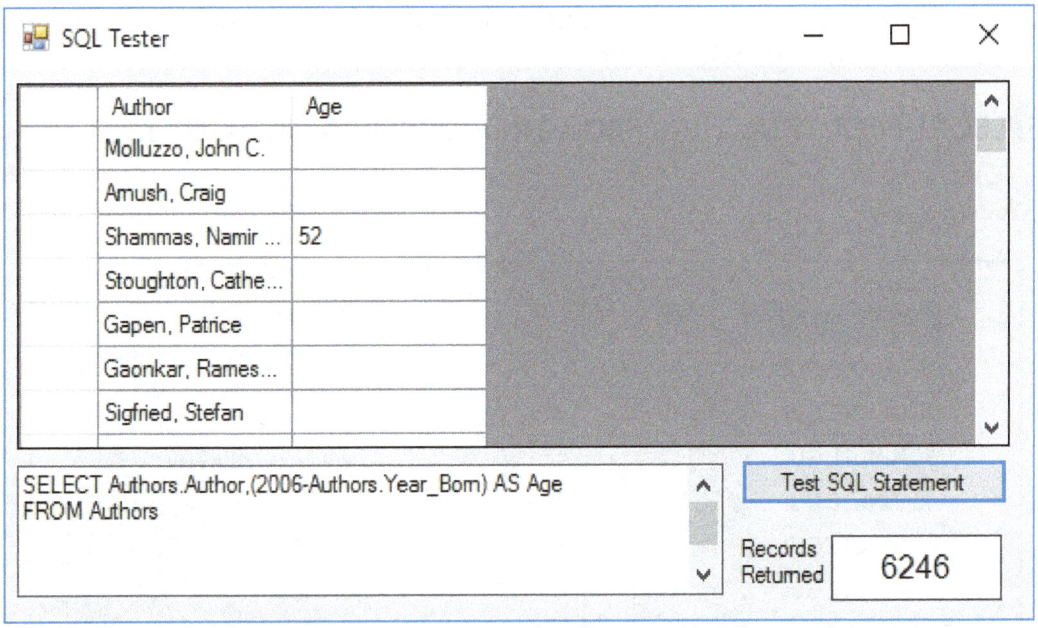
SQL Tester
Author
Age
Molluzzo, John C.
Amush, Craig
Shammas, Namir ...
52
Stoughton, Cathe...
Gapen, Patrice
Gaonkar, Rames...
Sigfried, Stefan
SELECT Authors.Author,(2006-Authors.Year_Born) AS Age
FROM Authors
Test SQL Statement
Records Returned
6246

Note that most of the listings do not have an Age value – I had to scroll down a bit to find one. The reason for this is because only a few of the author records have birth year entries - the entries are **NULL** (containing no information).

NULL is a special value meaning there is nothing there - this is not the same as an empty string or blank space. In our work, we will try to avoid placing NULLs in a database, but sometimes this is not possible or they may exist in other databases. You need to decide how to handle NULLs in your design. We will see examples where they cause problems. A NULL field can be tested using the SQL functions **IS NULL** and **IS NOT NULL**. We can add this to the SQL statement above to find just the Authors records with a birth year:

SELECT Authors.Author,(2006-Authors.Year_Born) AS Age
FROM Authors
WHERE Authors.Year_Born IS NOT NULL

You should now find 20 authors with ages listed.

Functions with SQL (SQL Server Database)

There are functions available for use as part of a SQL statement with SQL Server databases (consult SQL Server references for a full list of such functions). This lets you modify the displayed information. It does not affect the underlying information in the database. As an example, say you want all book titles in the **SQLBooksDB.mdf** database **Titles** table to be listed in upper case letters. Try this SQL statement with SQL Tester:

SELECT UPPER(Titles.Title) FROM Titles ORDER BY Titles.Title

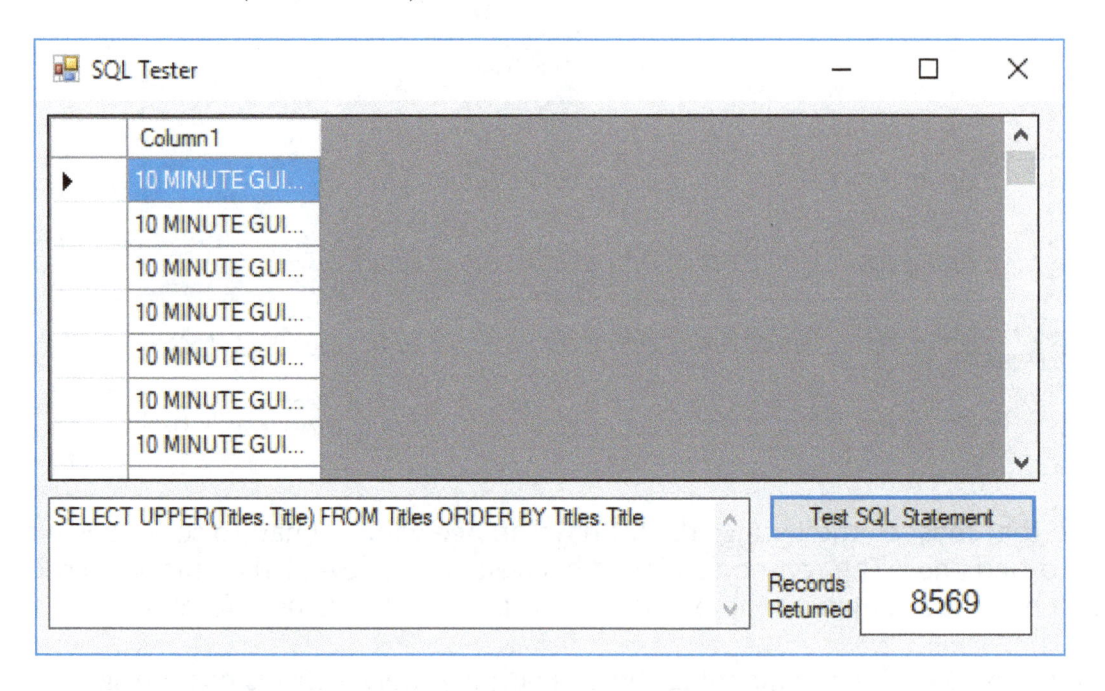

Notice SQL assigns a heading of **Column1** to this 'derived' field. We can use the alias feature of SQL change this heading to anything we want (except the name of an existing field). Try this:

SELECT UPPER(Titles.Title) AS Title FROM Titles

Or, what if we had some process that could only use the 10 left-most characters of the book title. This SQL statement will do the trick:

SELECT LEFT(UPPER(Titles.Title), 10) AS Title FROM Titles

Database Queries with SQL 4-41

You can also do BASIC math in a SQL statement. The **BOOKS** database **Authors** table has **Year_Born** as a field. This SQL statement will display each author and their age in 2006 (when this is being written):

SELECT Authors.Author,(2006-Authors.Year_Born) AS Age
FROM Authors

Author	Age
Laurel, Chris	
Fraize, Scott	
Trujillo, Stan	
Stevens, Al	66
Bulback, Fred	
Schildt, Herbert	
Smith, Tim	

SELECT Authors.Author,(2006-Authors.Year_Born) AS Age
FROM Authors

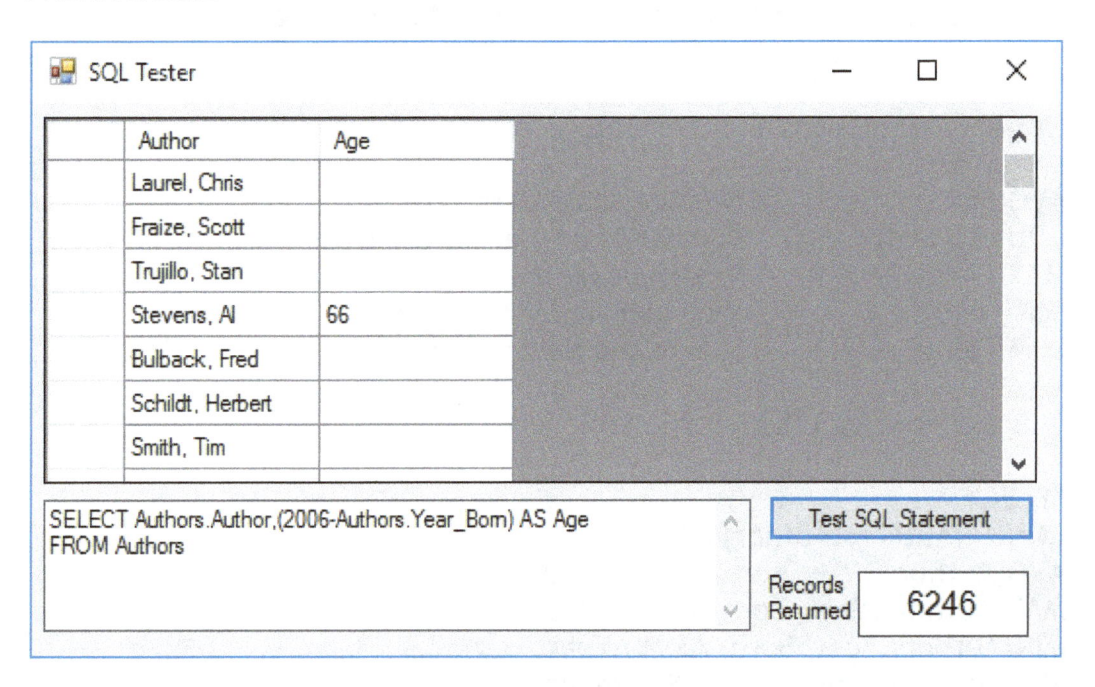

Records Returned: 6246

Note that most of the listings do not have an Age value – I had to scroll down a bit to find one. The reason for this is because only a few of the author records have birth year entries - the entries are **NULL** (containing no information).

NULL is a special value meaning there is nothing there - this is not the same as an empty string or blank space. In our work, we will try to avoid placing NULLs in a database, but sometimes this is not possible or they may exist in other databases. You need to decide how to handle NULLs in your design. We will see examples where they cause problems. A NULL field can be tested using the SQL functions **IS NULL** and **IS NOT NULL**. We can add this to the SQL statement above to find just the Authors records with a birth year:

SELECT Authors.Author,(2006-Authors.Year_Born) AS Age
FROM Authors
WHERE Authors.Year_Born IS NOT NULL

You should now find 20 authors with ages listed.

SQL Aggregate Functions

In addition to general functions, the ADO .NET database engine supports the standard **SQL aggregate functions** for Access databases. These are functions that let you compute summary statistics for fields in your database, alias the results, and display them in a data table. NULL fields are ignored by the aggregate functions.

The aggregate functions and their results are:

AVG(Field)	Average value of the field
COUNT(Field)	Number of entries for the field
MAX(Field)	Maximum value of the field
MIN(Field)	Minimum value of the field
SUM(Field)	Sum of the field values

Try this example with the Authors table:

SELECT
COUNT(Authors.Author) AS HowMany,
AVG(Authors.Year_Born) AS AveYear,
MAX(Authors.Year_Born) AS MaxYear,
MIN(Authors.Year_Born) AS MinYear,
SUM(Authors.Year_Born) AS SumYear
FROM Authors

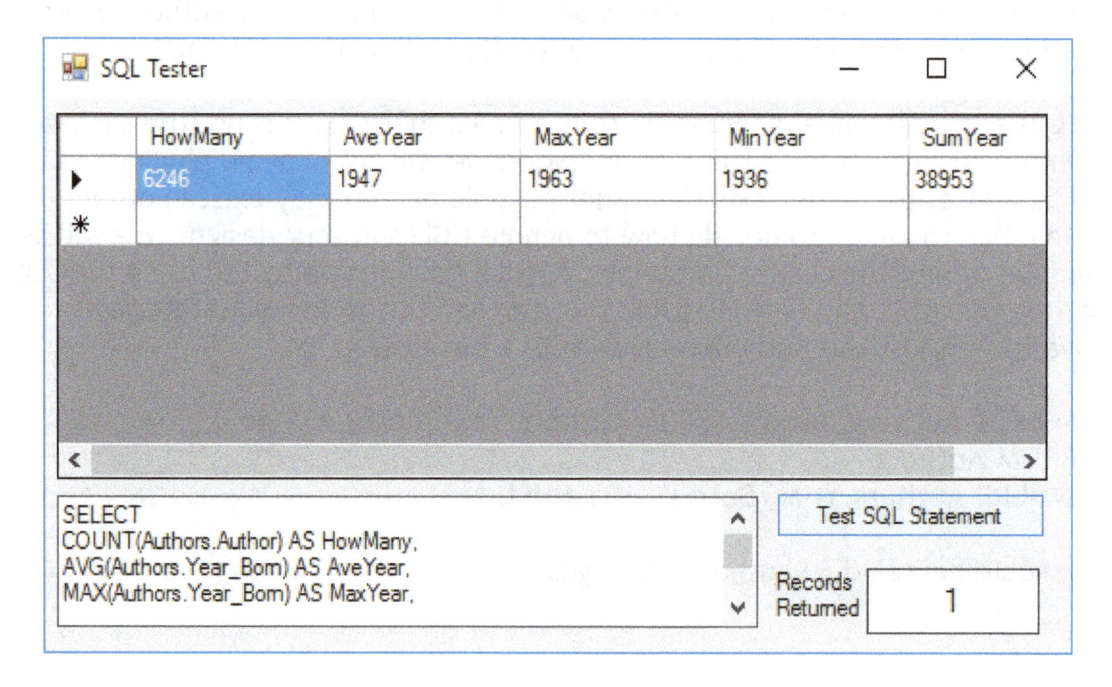

HowMany	AveYear	MaxYear	MinYear	SumYear
6246	1947	1963	1936	38953

Records Returned: 1

Database Queries with SQL 4-43

Aggregate functions can be used to group results. The **GROUP BY** clause lets you determine records with duplicate field values. Want to know how many publishers in your database are in each state? Try this SQL statement:

SELECT Publishers.State, Count(Publishers.State) as HowMany
FROM Publishers
GROUP BY Publishers.State

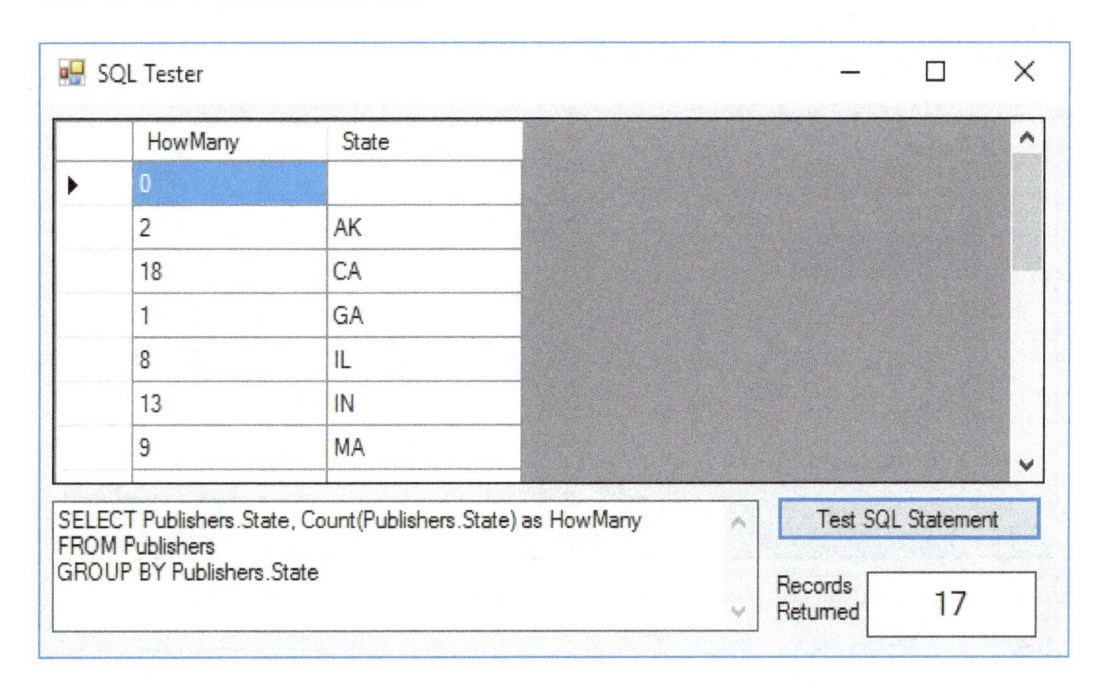

HowMany	State
0	
2	AK
18	CA
1	GA
8	IL
13	IN
9	MA

SELECT Publishers.State, Count(Publishers.State) as HowMany
FROM Publishers
GROUP BY Publishers.State

Records Returned: 17

You can use the HAVING qualifier to further reduce the grouping obtained with a GROUP BY clause. Say in the above example, you only want to display states starting with the letter M (a strange request, we know). This SQL statement will do the trick:

SELECT Publishers.State, Count(Publishers.State) as HowMany
FROM Publishers
GROUP BY Publishers.State
HAVING Publishers.State LIKE 'M%'

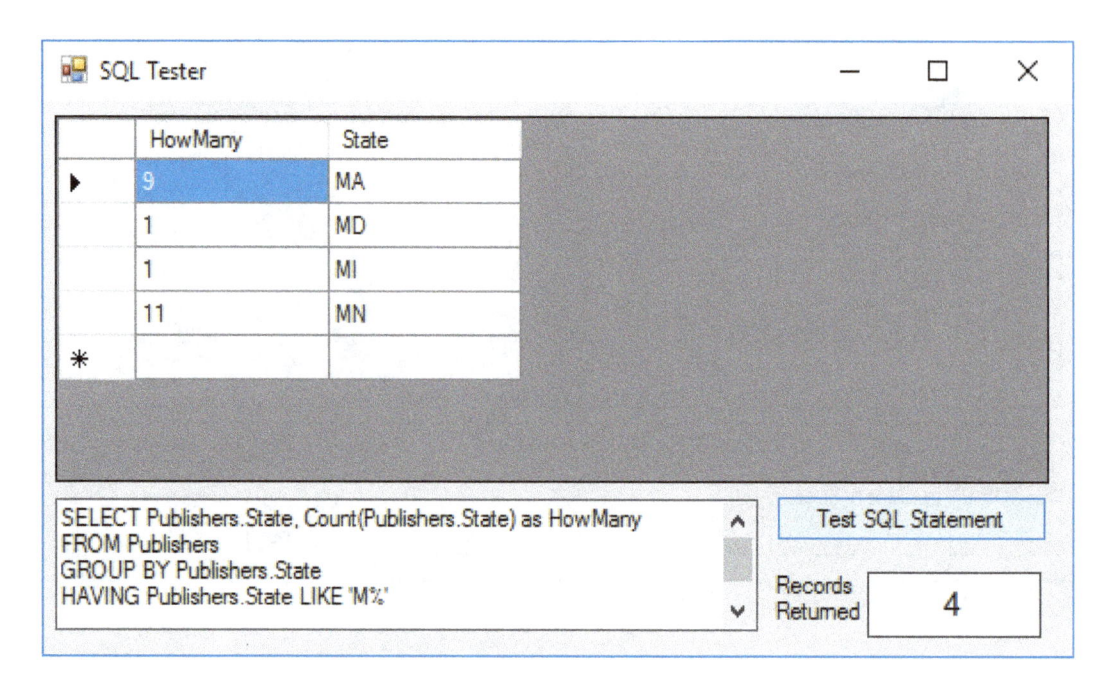

HowMany	State
9	MA
1	MD
1	MI
11	MN

Records Returned: 4

SQL Construction Tools

We've completed our review of the SQL language. There are other commands we haven't looked at. If you would like to know more, there are numerous references available for both ANSI standard SQL and the Microsoft version. You now know how to construct SQL statements to extract desired information from a multi-table database and you know how to read other's SQL statements.

You have seen that constructing SQL statements is, at times, a tedious process. To aid in the construction of such statements, there are several tools available for our use. We'll discuss two: one in **Microsoft Access** and one available with the **data wizard** (discussed in Chapter 3).

SQL Statements with Access

To build a SQL query using Microsoft Access, you obviously must have Access installed on your computer. As an example, we will build the SQL query that displays Author, Title, and Publisher for each book in the **BOOKS** database:

⇒ Start **Access** and open your copy of the **BooksDB.accdb**. Click the **Create** tab and select **Query Design** in the **Other** group, click **Open**.

⇒ In the **Show Table** form, add all four tables. When done, click **Close**. A split window appears with the four linked tables at the top (showing the relationships between primary and foreign keys) and a table in the lower portion.

⇒ In the lower portion of the window, click the first **Field** column, click the drop-down arrow and select **Authors.Author**. Under **Sort**, choose **Ascending** (sorting by Author). In the second column, click the drop-down arrow and select **Titles.Title**. In the third column, click the drop-down arrow and select **Publishers.Company_Name**. When done, you should see (I moved the tables around a bit):

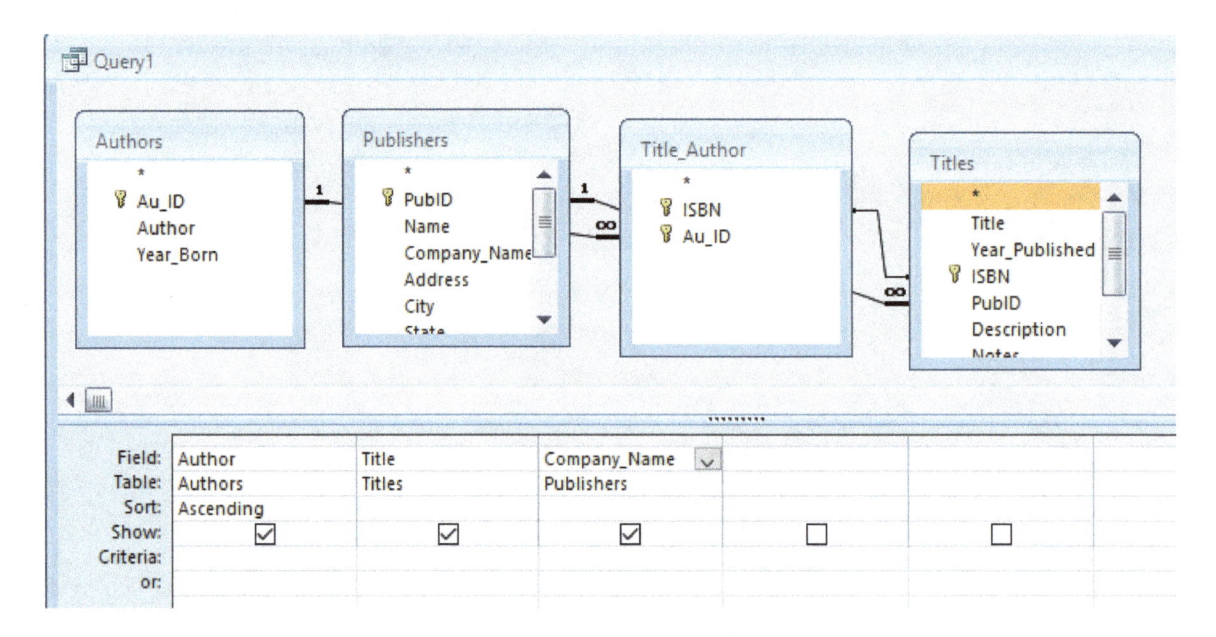

⇒ Click the exclamation point (!) with the **Run** caption on the Access toolbar to build the data table. Now, click **View** on the toolbar and select **SQL View**.

⇒ Like magic, the SQL statement that was used to develop the data table is displayed:

SELECT Authors.Author, Titles.Title, Publishers.Company_Name
FROM (Publishers INNER JOIN Titles ON Publishers.PubID = Titles.PubID) INNER JOIN (Authors INNER JOIN Title_Author ON Authors.Au_ID = Title_Author.Au_ID) ON Titles.ISBN = Title_Author.ISBN
ORDER BY Authors.Author;

Notice a couple of things about this query. First, it uses the **INNER JOIN** clause to combine tables. Second, notice the semicolon (;) at the end of the query. This is not needed and will be ignored by the ADO .NET database engine. You could now cut and paste the above query wherever you need it in your Visual Basic application. You may need to make some adjustments to the query to make sure it does not result in any syntax errors at run-time. Notice this generated query is very much like that developed earlier in these notes. It's similar because the author used Access to generate that query - you, too, should use the Access query building capabilities whenever you can. You are assured of a correct SQL statement, helping to minimize your programming headaches.

SQL Statements with the Data Wizard

In Chapter 3, we looked at the Visual Basic data wizard as a tool for building applications. Even though we won't be using the wizard to build applications (primarily to simplify distribution of our applications), it can be used to generate any SQL statements we might need.

The steps here are similar to those just used with Access (not unexpected since they probably use the same underlying code). And, even though this example uses **BooksDB.accdb**, it can also be done with the SQL Server version (**SQLBooksDB.mdf**). Start a new project in Visual Basic.

⇒ Choose the **Project** menu item, then **Add New Data Source**. Click **Next** on the screens until you see (we assume the connection still 'points' to the books database; if not, do the steps necessary):

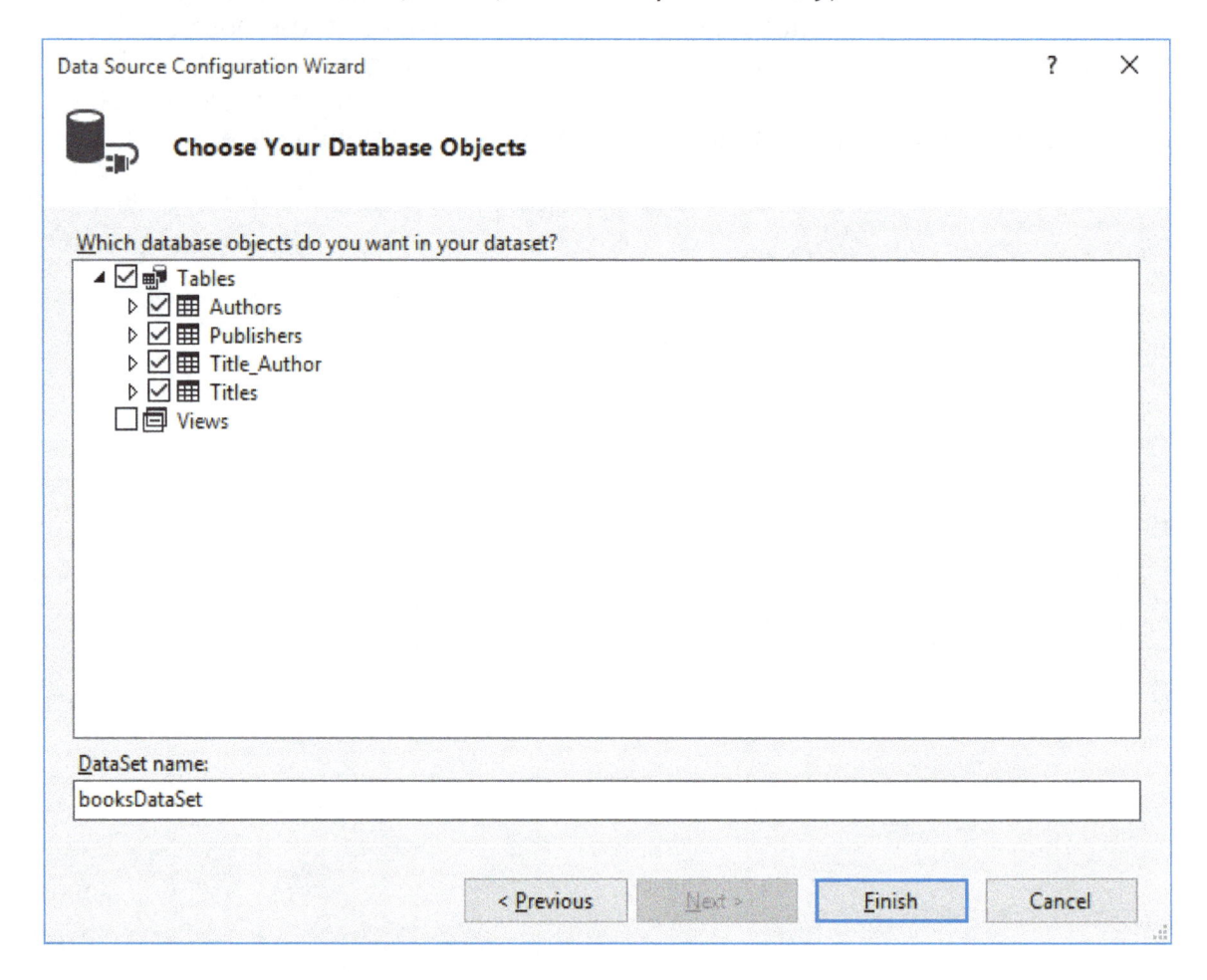

We need all tables in our dataset. Check **Authors**, **Publishers**, **Title_Author** and **Titles**. Then, click **Finish**.

Database Queries with SQL 4-49

A new dataset (**BooksDBDataSet**) will appear in the Data Sources window:

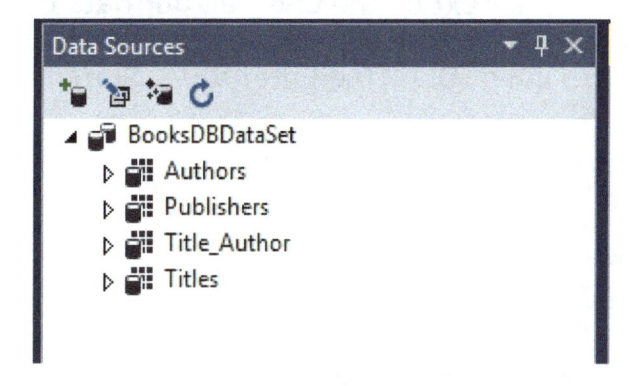

⇒ We now need to add a table adapter to generate the needed fields from the tables to form another table. Highlight the **BooksDBDataSet** in the **Data Sources** window and click the **Edit DataSet with Designer** button in the toolbar in that window. This window, displaying the four individual tables, will appear:

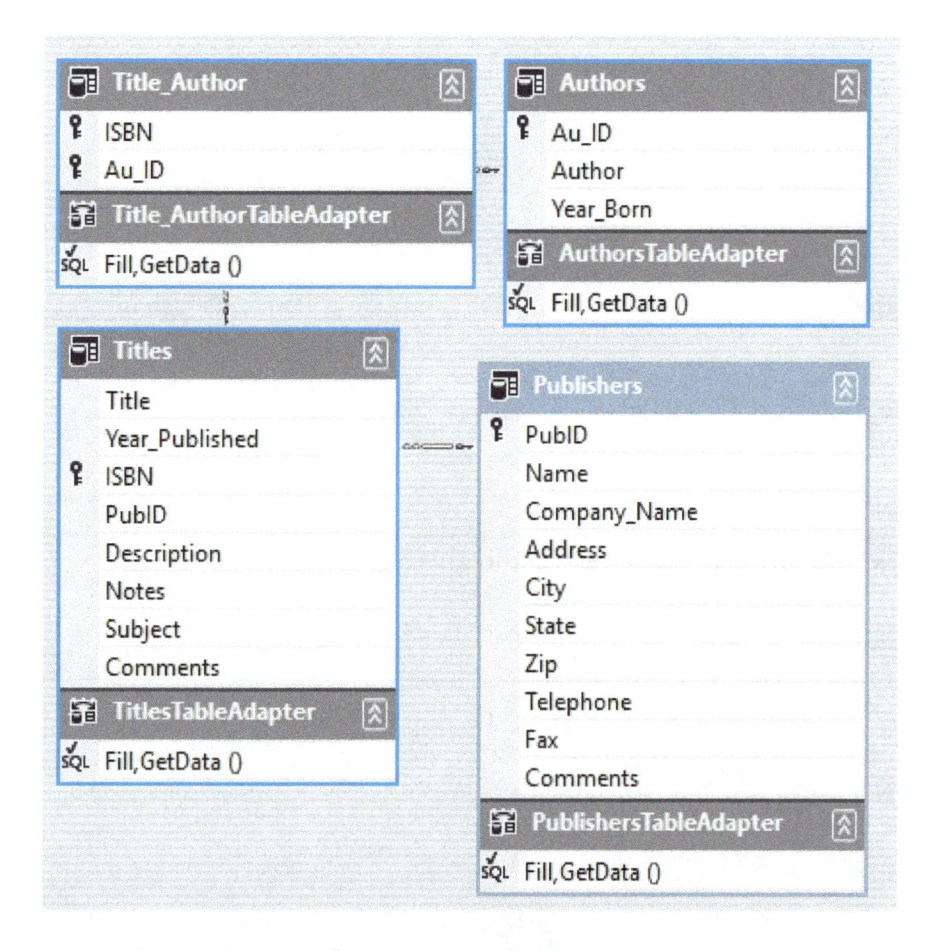

Our virtual table will include the **Author**, **Title**, and **Company_Name** fields. To build this table, we need a new **TableAdapter**. Right-click the display window, and choose **Add**, then **TableAdapter**.

4-50 Visual Basic and Databases

⇒ A new adapter will be added and the **TableAdapter Configuration Wizard** will start up. Click **Next** on the **Choose Your Data Connection** window and the subsequent **Choose a Command Type Window** (where we tell the adapter we are using SQL). The **Enter a SQL Statement** window will appear:

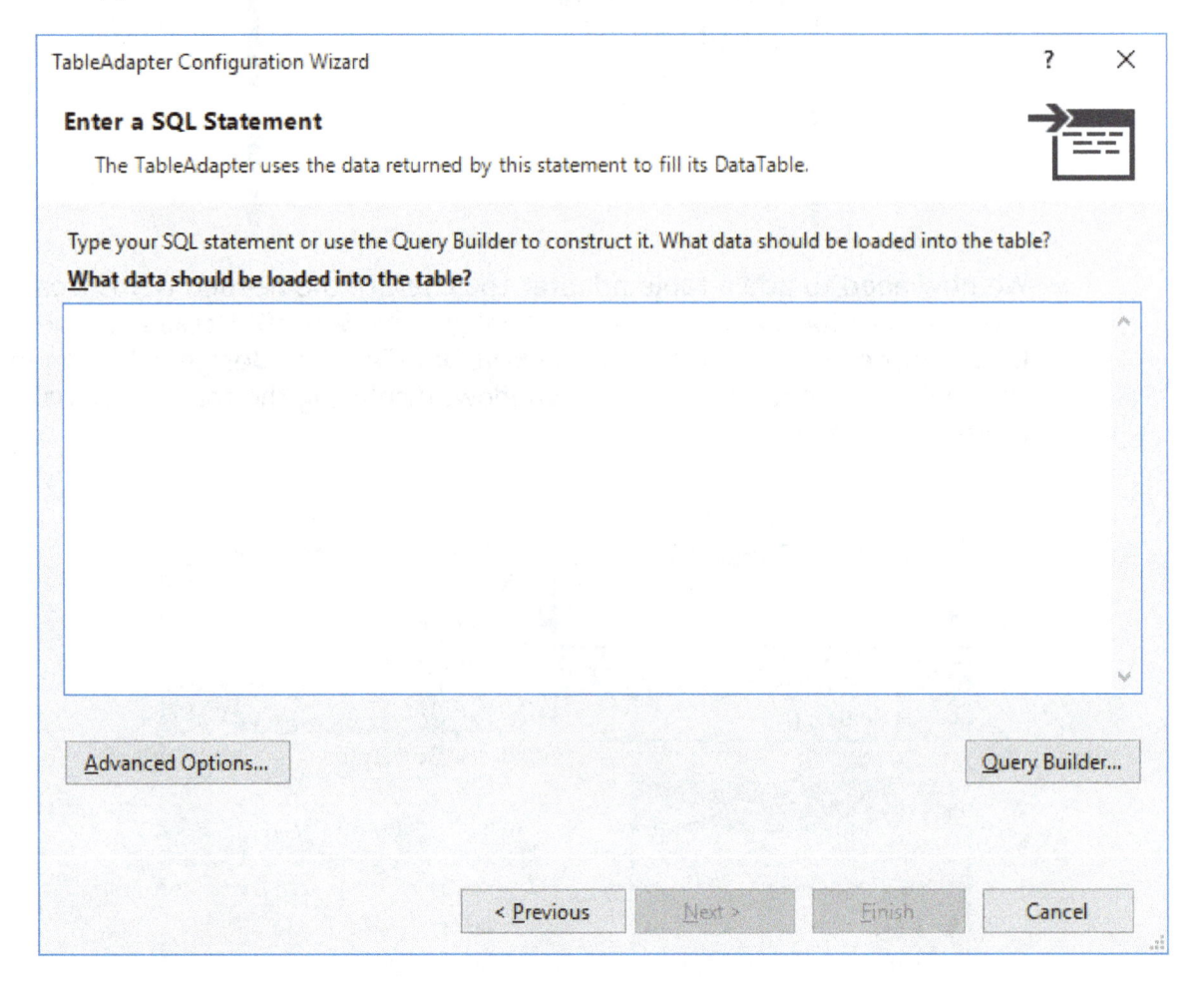

![TableAdapter Configuration Wizard - Enter a SQL Statement dialog box. The TableAdapter uses the data returned by this statement to fill its DataTable. Text reads: "Type your SQL statement or use the Query Builder to construct it. What data should be loaded into the table?" with a large empty text area below. Buttons at bottom: Advanced Options..., Query Builder..., < Previous, Next >, Finish, Cancel.]

Here's where we let the wizard build the SQL statement.

⇒ Click **Query Builder** to see:

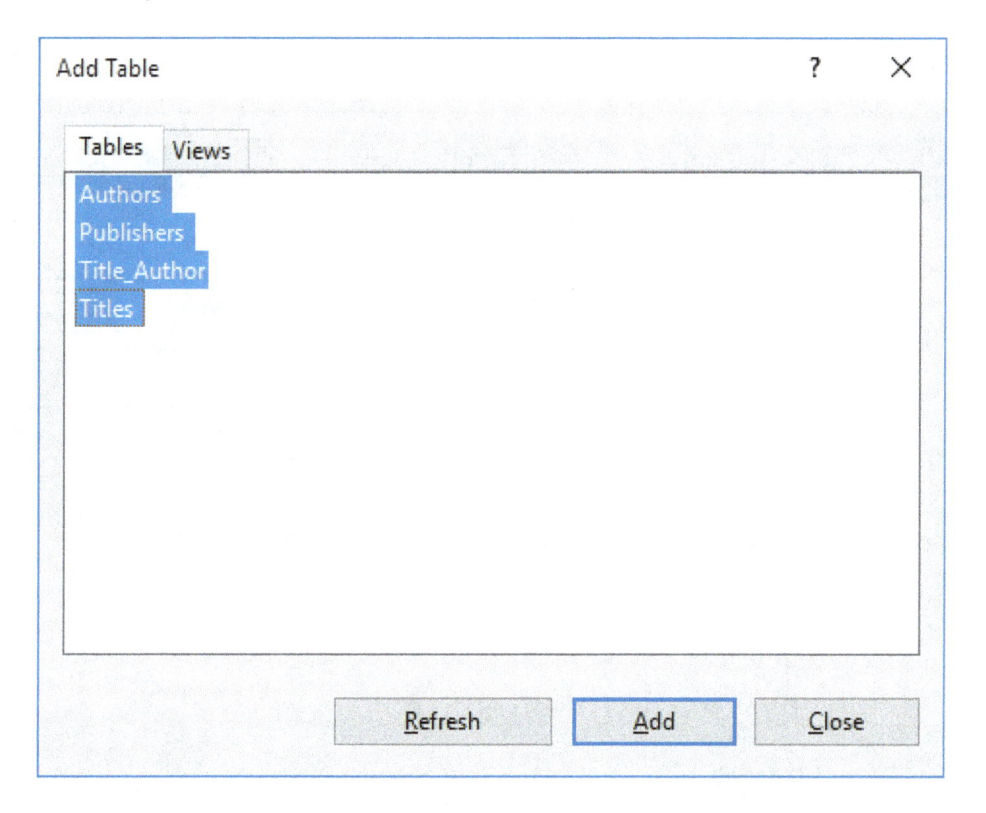

Select the **Authors**, **Publishers**, **Title_Author** and **Titles** tables and click **Add**.

⇒ Click **Close.** You will see:

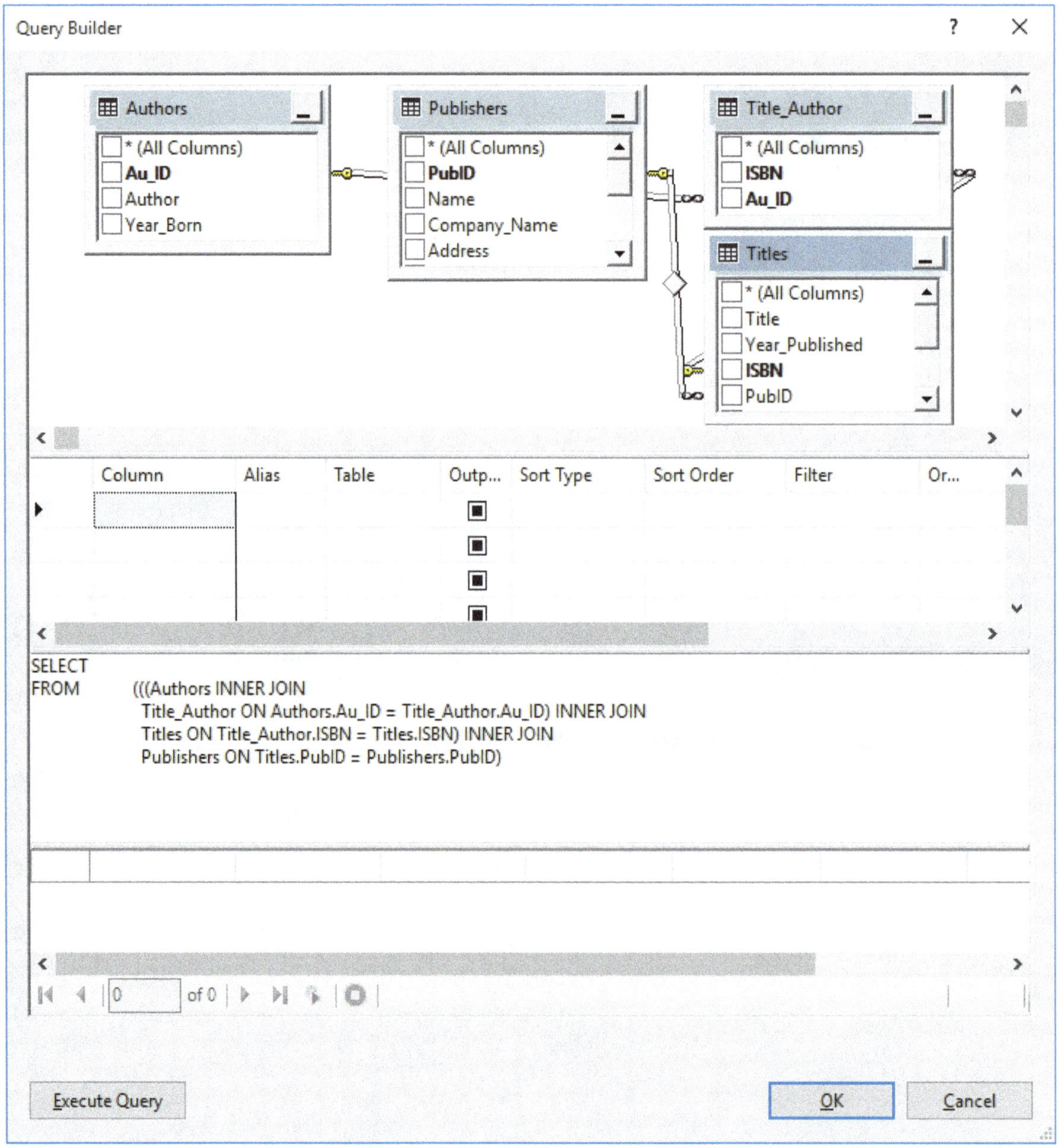
Query Builder
Authors
* (All Columns)
Au_ID
Author
Year_Born
Publishers
* (All Columns)
PubID
Name
Company_Name
Address
Title_Author
* (All Columns)
ISBN
Au_ID
Titles
* (All Columns)
Title
Year_Published
ISBN
PubID
Column
Alias
Table
Outp...
Sort Type
Sort Order
Filter
Or...
SELECT
FROM (((Authors INNER JOIN
Title_Author ON Authors.Au_ID = Title_Author.Au_ID) INNER JOIN
Titles ON Title_Author.ISBN = Titles.ISBN) INNER JOIN
Publishers ON Titles.PubID = Publishers.PubID)
0
of 0
Execute Query
OK
Cancel

The Query Builder is showing the relationships among the tables (i.e. how the **ISBN** value connects **Titles** with **Title_Author** and how **Au_ID** connects **Title_Author** with **Authors**, how **PubID** connects **Titles** with **Publishers**). Select **Title** in the **Titles** table. Select **Company_Name** in the **Publishers** table. Then, select **Author** in the **Authors** table. Once added, select a sort type of **Ascending** in the table below. This will sort the table according to Author name.

Database Queries with SQL 4-53

⇒ Once your selections are complete the window will appear as:

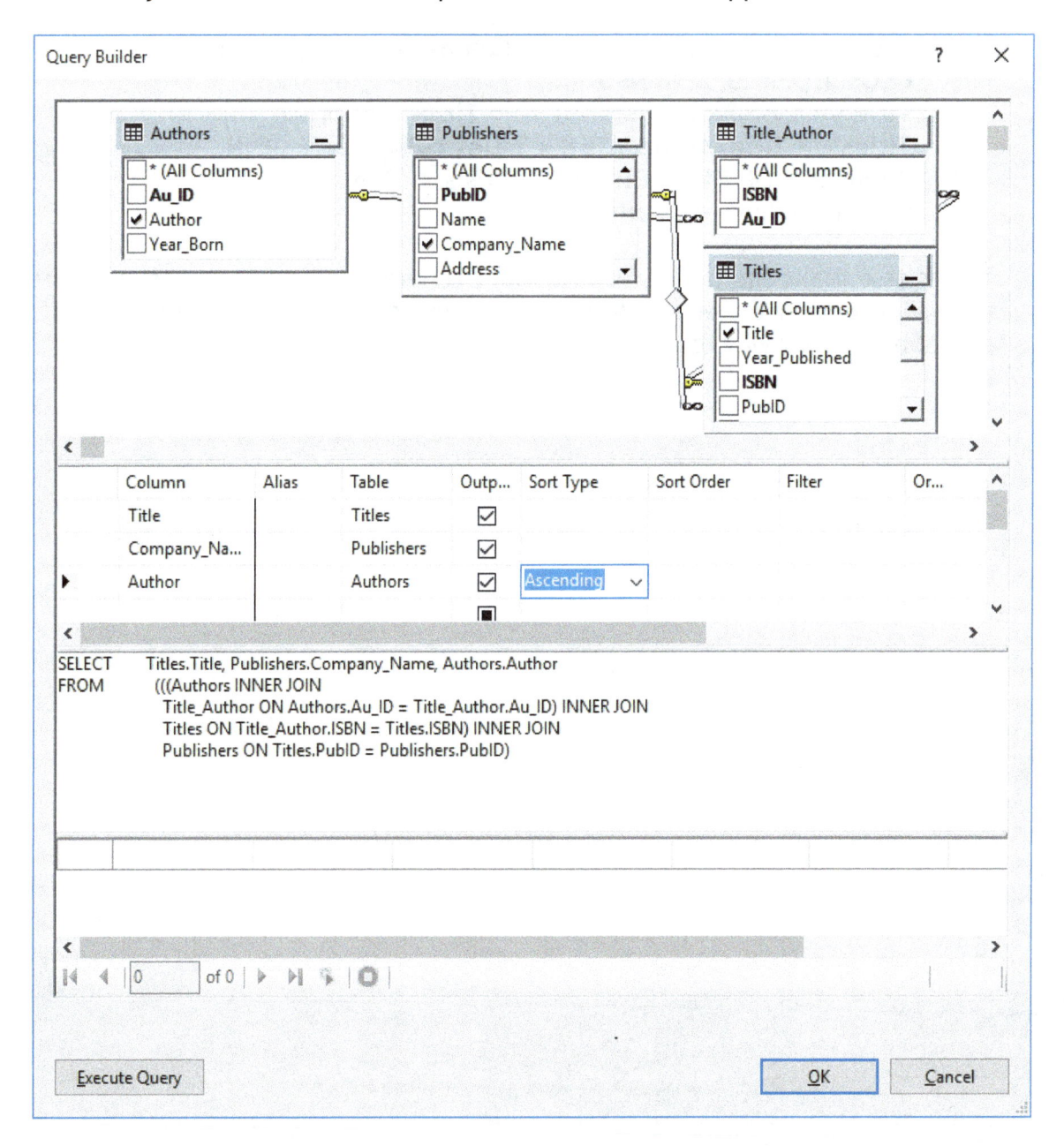

```
SELECT   Titles.Title, Publishers.Company_Name, Authors.Author
FROM     (((Authors INNER JOIN
         Title_Author ON Authors.Au_ID = Title_Author.Au_ID) INNER JOIN
         Titles ON Title_Author.ISBN = Titles.ISBN) INNER JOIN
         Publishers ON Titles.PubID = Publishers.PubID)
```

Click **OK** to see the following SQL statement is generated:

```
SELECT Titles.Title, Publishers.Company_Name, Authors.Author
FROM (((Authors INNER JOIN
Title_Author ON Authors.Au_ID = Title_Author.Au_ID) INNER JOIN
Titles ON Title_Author.ISBN = Titles.ISBN) INNER JOIN
Publishers ON Titles.PubID = Publishers.PubID)
ORDER BY Authors.Author
```

This is essentially the same SQL statement generated using Access (except there is no semicolon at the end). More steps were required. If you use Access, it's probably the best way to generate SQL statements.

Building SQL Commands in Code

In each example in this chapter, we formed a SQL command and processed it to obtain a returned data table (our virtual data view). What do you do if you don't know the SQL command prior to implementing it as a Visual Basic property? For example, the user of the books database may want to know all the publishers in Chicago. Or, the user may want to search the database for all authors whose name starts with a G.

In both of the above examples, we have no idea what the user will select. We need to provide the user a method to make a selection then, once the selection is made, build the SQL statement in Visual Basic. Fortunately, the BASIC language (used in all procedures) is rich with string handling functions and building such statements in code is a relatively straightforward process.

To build a SQL command in code, form all the known clauses as string variables. Once the user makes the selections forming the unknown information, using string concatenation operators (& or +) to place these selections in their proper position in the complete SQL statement. That statement can then be processed at run-time, using one of the methods discussed earlier in this chapter. The next example demonstrates this technique.

Example 4-2

Searching the Books Database

We build an application using the **BooksDB.accdb** (Access) or **SQLBooksDB.mdf** (SQL Server) books database that displays a book's author, title, and publisher. The user may display all books in the database or, alternately, search the database for books by particular authors (searching by the first letter of the last name, using buttons for selection). There is a lot to learn in this example. You'll see how to form a SQL command in code, how to get that statement into code, how to set up convenient search mechanisms, and how to build a nice interface, all topics covered in detail in Chapter 5.

1. Start a new project. Add a data view grid control and one button. Position and resize the controls until the form looks something like this:

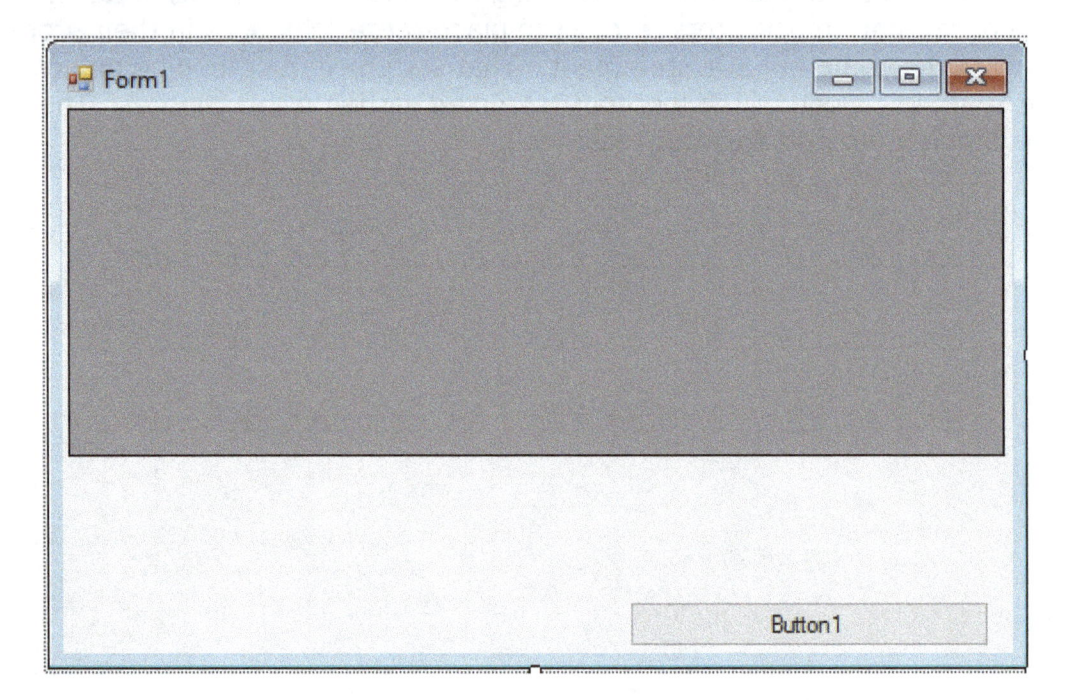

Make sure to leave space between the data grid and the button. We will use this space for two rows of button controls needed to search the database table.

2. Set properties for the form and controls:

Form1:
    Name   frmBooks
    FormBorderStyle   FixedSingle
    StartPosition   CenterScreen
    Text   Books Database

Button1:
    Name   btnAll
    Text   Show All Records

DataViewGrid1:
    Name   grdBooks
    AutoSizeColumnsMode Fill

At this point, the form should appear similar to this:

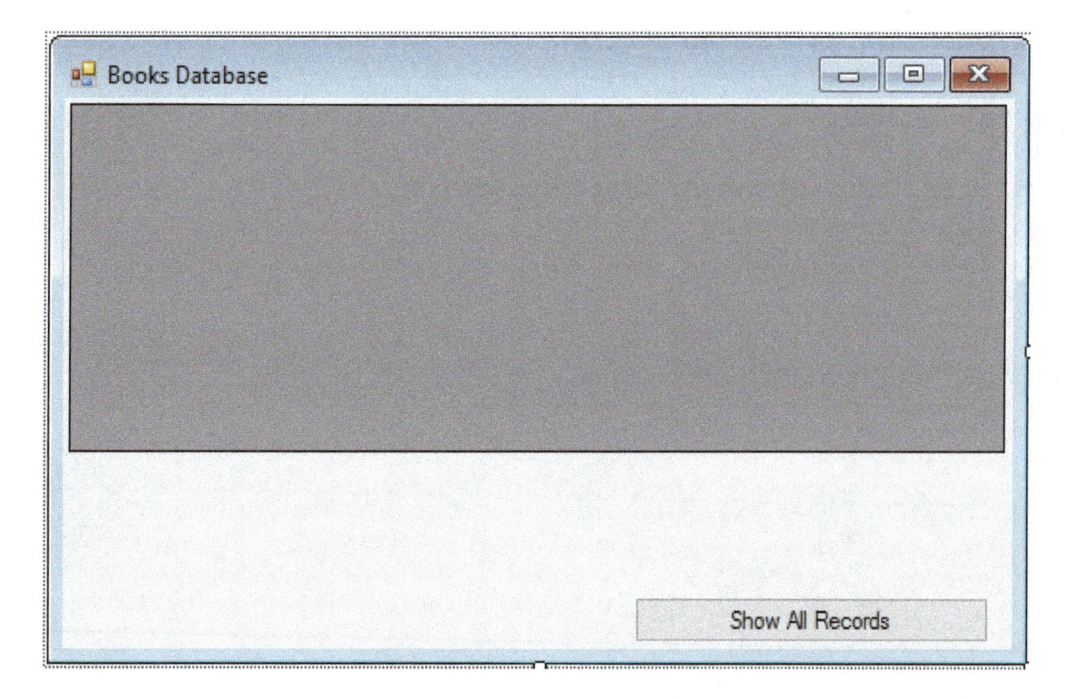

3. Add these two lines at the top of the code window to allow use of data objects:

Access Database:

```
Imports System.Data
Imports System.Data.OleDb
```

SQL Server Database:

```
Imports System.Data
Imports System.Data.SqlClient
```

4. Form level declarations:

Access Database:

```
Dim BooksConnection As OleDbConnection
Dim SQLAll As String
Dim btnRolodex(26) As Button
```

SQL Server Database:

```
Dim BooksConnection As SqlConnection
Dim SQLAll As String
Dim btnRolodex(26) As Button
```

SQLAll will be the variable that holds the default SQL statement. **btnRolodex** is an array of buttons used for searching.

Database Queries with SQL 4-59

5. Code for the **frmBooks Load** procedure:

Access Database:

```
  Private Sub FrmBooks_Load(ByVal sender As Object, ByVal e As System.EventArgs) Handles Me.Load
    'connect to books database
    BooksConnection = New OleDbConnection("Provider=Microsoft.ACE.OLEDB.12.0; Data Source = c:\VBDB\Working\BooksDB.accdb")
    BooksConnection.Open()
    'create Rolodex buttons for searching
    Dim W As Integer, LStart As Integer, L As Integer, T As Integer
    Dim ButtonHeight As Integer = 30 'found by trial and error
    Dim I As Integer
    'search buttons
    'determine button width (don't round up) - 13 on a row
    W = CInt(Me.ClientSize.Width / 14 - 0.5)
    'center buttons on form
    LStart = CInt(0.5 * (Me.ClientSize.Width - 13 * W))
    L = LStart
    T = grdBooks.Top + grdBooks.Height + 2
    'create and position 26 buttons
    For I = 1 To 26
      'create new pushbutton
      btnRolodex(I) = New Button()
      btnRolodex(I).TabStop = False
      'set text property
      btnRolodex(I).Text = Chr(64 + I)
      'position
      btnRolodex(I).Width = W
      btnRolodex(I).Height = ButtonHeight
      btnRolodex(I).Left = L
      btnRolodex(I).Top = T
      'give cool colors
      btnRolodex(I).BackColor = Color.Blue
      btnRolodex(I).ForeColor = Color.White
      'add button to form
      Me.Controls.Add(btnRolodex(I))
      'add event handler
      AddHandler btnRolodex(I).Click, AddressOf Me.btnSQL_Click
      'next left
      L += W
      If I = 13 Then
        'move to next row
```

```vb
        L = LStart
        T = T + ButtonHeight
      End If
    Next I
    'Build basic SQL statement
    SQLAll = "SELECT Authors.Author,Titles.Title,Publishers.Company_Name "
    SQLAll += "FROM Authors, Titles, Publishers, Title_Author "
    SQLAll += "WHERE Titles.ISBN = Title_Author.ISBN "
    SQLAll += "AND Authors.Au_ID = Title_Author.Au_ID "
    SQLAll += "AND Titles.PubID = Publishers.PubID "
    'show form and click on all records initially
    Me.Show()
    btnAll.PerformClick()
  End Sub
```

SQL Server Database:

```vb
  Private Sub FrmBooks_Load(ByVal sender As Object, ByVal e As System.EventArgs) Handles Me.Load
    'connect to books database
    BooksConnection = New SqlConnection("Data Source=.\SQLEXPRESS;AttachDbFilename=C:\VBDB\Working\SQLBooksDB.mdf; Integrated Security=True; Connect Timeout=30; User Instance=True")
    BooksConnection.Open()
    'create Rolodex buttons for searching
    Dim W As Integer, LStart As Integer, L As Integer, T As Integer
    Dim ButtonHeight As Integer = 30 'found by trial and error
    Dim I As Integer
    'search buttons
    'determine button width (don't round up) - 13 on a row
    W = CInt(Me.ClientSize.Width / 14 - 0.5)
    'center buttons on form
    LStart = CInt(0.5 * (Me.ClientSize.Width - 13 * W))
    L = LStart
    T = grdBooks.Top + grdBooks.Height + 2
    'create and position 26 buttons
    For I = 1 To 26
      'create new pushbutton
      btnRolodex(I) = New Button()
      btnRolodex(I).TabStop = False
      'set text property
      btnRolodex(I).Text = Chr(64 + I)
      'position
```

Database Queries with SQL

```
            btnRolodex(I).Width = W
            btnRolodex(I).Height = ButtonHeight
            btnRolodex(I).Left = L
            btnRolodex(I).Top = T
            'give cool colors
            btnRolodex(I).BackColor = Color.Blue
            btnRolodex(I).ForeColor = Color.White
            'add button to form
            Me.Controls.Add(btnRolodex(I))
            'add event handler
            AddHandler btnRolodex(I).Click, AddressOf
Me.btnSQL_Click
            'next left
            L += W
            If I = 13 Then
                'move to next row
                L = LStart
                T = T + ButtonHeight
            End If
        Next I
        'Build basic SQL statement
        SQLAll = "SELECT
Authors.Author,Titles.Title,Publishers.Company_Name "
        SQLAll += "FROM Authors, Titles, Publishers,
Title_Author "
        SQLAll += "WHERE Titles.ISBN = Title_Author.ISBN "
        SQLAll += "AND Authors.Au_ID = Title_Author.Au_ID "
        SQLAll += "AND Titles.PubID = Publishers.PubID "
        'show form and click on all records initially
        Me.Show()
        btnAll.PerformClick()
    End Sub
```

This routine creates the connection object and establishes the search buttons A through Z using the **btnRolodex** array. It determines button width and places them accordingly. Study the code that does this - it's very useful. This routine also builds the default SQL statement that gets the Author, Title, and Publisher from the database. Note the statement is built in several stages, each stage appending another clause to the statement. Note, particularly, each subsequent clause has a space at the end to make sure there are no 'run-ons' of keywords. Lastly, all records are displayed by 'clicking' on the **btnAll** control.

6. Code for the **frmBooks FormClosing** procedure:

```
  Private Sub FrmBooks_FormClosing(ByVal sender As Object,
ByVal e As System.Windows.Forms.FormClosingEventArgs)
Handles Me.FormClosing
     BooksConnection.Close()
     BooksConnection.Dispose()
  End Sub
```

7. Code for the **btnSQL Click** procedure (handles the **Click** event for all control buttons):

Access Database:

```
  Private Sub BtnSQL_Click(ByVal sender As System.Object,
ByVal e As System.EventArgs) Handles btnAll.Click
     Dim ResultsCommand As OleDbCommand = Nothing
     Dim ResultsAdapter As New OleDbDataAdapter
     Dim ResultsTable As New DataTable
     Dim SQLStatement As String
     'determine which button was clicked and form SQL
statement
     Dim ButtonClicked As Button
     ButtonClicked = CType(sender, Button)
     Select Case ButtonClicked.Text
       Case "Show All Records"
         SQLStatement = SQLAll
       Case "A" To "Y"
         'Letter key other than Z clicked
         'Append to SQLAll to limit records to letter clicked
         Dim Index As Integer = Asc(ButtonClicked.Text) - 64
         SQLStatement = SQLAll + "AND Authors.Author > '" +
btnrolodex(Index).Text + " ' "
         SQLStatement += "AND Authors.Author < '" +
btnRolodex(Index + 1).Text + " ' "
       Case Else
         'Z Clicked
         'Append to SQLAll to limit records to Z Authors
         SQLStatement = SQLAll + "AND Authors.Author > 'Z' "
     End Select
     SQLStatement += "ORDER BY Authors.Author"
     'apply SQL statement
     Try
        'establish command object and data adapter
        ResultsCommand = New OleDbCommand(SQLStatement,
BooksConnection)
        ResultsAdapter.SelectCommand = ResultsCommand
```

Database Queries with SQL

```vb
      ResultsAdapter.Fill(ResultsTable)
      'bind grid view to data table
      grdBooks.DataSource = ResultsTable
    Catch ex As Exception
      MessageBox.Show(ex.Message, "Error in Processing SQL",
MessageBoxButtons.OK, MessageBoxIcon.Error)
    End Try
    ResultsCommand.Dispose()
    ResultsAdapter.Dispose()
    ResultsTable.Dispose()
  End Sub
```

SQL Server Database:

```vb
  Private Sub BtnSQL_Click(ByVal sender As System.Object,
ByVal e As System.EventArgs) Handles btnAll.Click
    Dim ResultsCommand As SqlCommand = Nothing
    Dim ResultsAdapter As New SqlDataAdapter
    Dim ResultsTable As New DataTable
    Dim SQLStatement As String
    'determine which button was clicked and form SQL
statement
    Dim ButtonClicked As Button
    ButtonClicked = CType(sender, Button)
    Select Case ButtonClicked.Text
      Case "Show All Records"
        SQLStatement = SQLAll
      Case "A" To "Y"
        'Letter key other than Z clicked
        'Append to SQLAll to limit records to letter clicked
        Dim Index As Integer = Asc(ButtonClicked.Text) - 64
        SQLStatement = SQLAll + "AND Authors.Author > '" +
btnRolodex(Index).Text + " ' "
        SQLStatement += "AND Authors.Author < '" +
btnRolodex(Index + 1).Text + " ' "
      Case Else
        'Z Clicked
        'Append to SQLAll to limit records to Z Authors
        SQLStatement = SQLAll + "AND Authors.Author > 'Z' "
    End Select
    SQLStatement += "ORDER BY Authors.Author"
    'apply SQL statement
    Try
      'establish command object and data adapter
      ResultsCommand = New SqlCommand(SQLStatement,
BooksConnection)
      ResultsAdapter.SelectCommand = ResultsCommand
      ResultsAdapter.Fill(ResultsTable)
```

```
            'bind grid view to data table
            grdBooks.DataSource = ResultsTable
        Catch ex As Exception
            MessageBox.Show(ex.Message, "Error in Processing SQL", _
MessageBoxButtons.OK, MessageBoxIcon.Error)
        End Try
        ResultsCommand.Dispose()
        ResultsAdapter.Dispose()
        ResultsTable.Dispose()
    End Sub
```

This routine determines which button was clicked and forms the SQL statement. If the **'Show All Records'** button is clicked, all records are displayed. If a letter button is clicked, it determines which letter was clicked by the user and appends an additional test (using **AND**) to the WHERE clause in the default SQL statement. This test limits the returned records to author's names between the clicked letter and the next letter in the alphabet. Note that clicking Z is a special case. Once the SQL statement is formed, it is processed by the data adapter to form the data table.

Database Queries with SQL 4-65

8. Save the application (Access version saved in the **Example 4-2** folder in **VBDB\Access\Class 4** folder; SQL Server version saved in the **Example 4-2** folder in **VBDB\SQL Server\Class 4** folder). Run it. You should see:

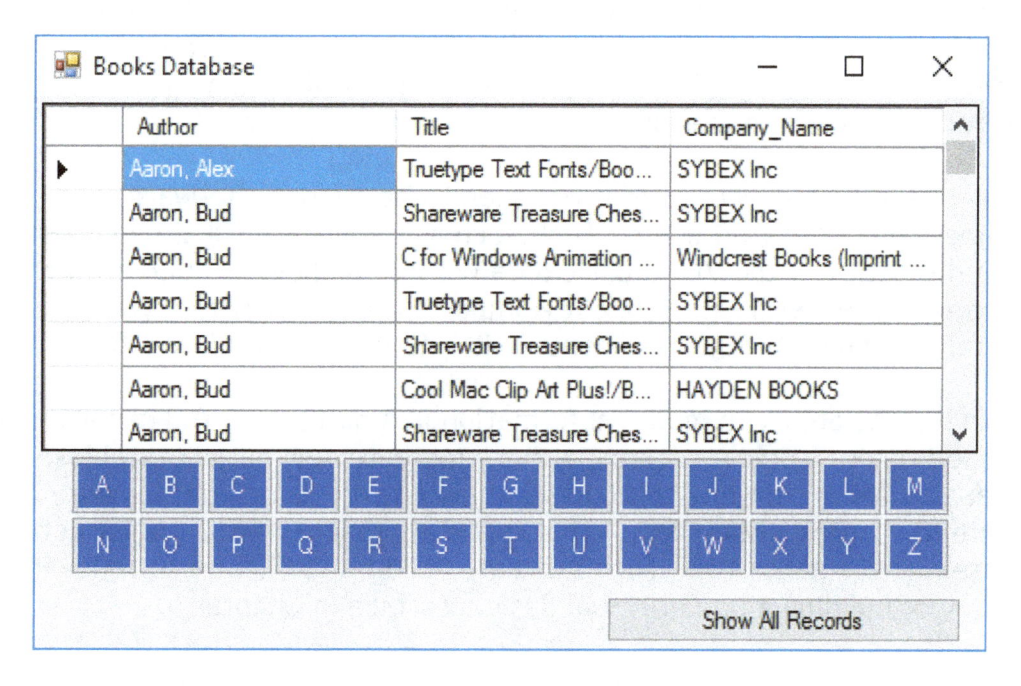

Notice how the search buttons are built and nicely displayed. Notice, too, that all records are displayed. Click one of the search buttons. Only records with author names matching the clicked letter will be displayed. Here's what I see when I click the 'G' button:

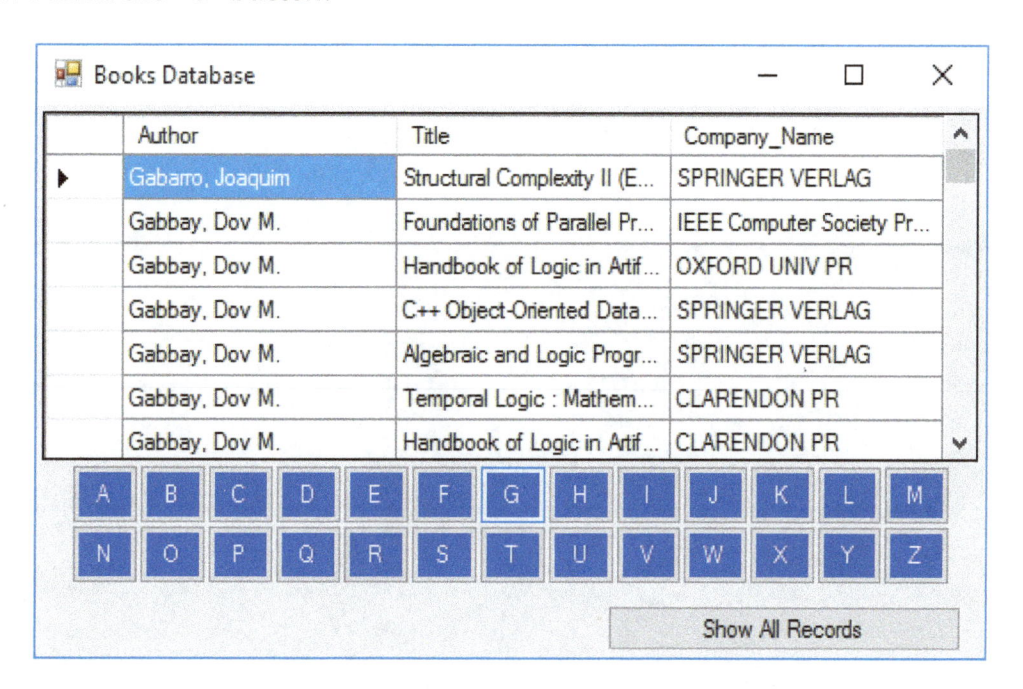

Summary

We're now done with our long journey into the world of SQL. This has been a relatively complete overview and you will learn more as you become a more proficient database programmer. SQL is at the heart of obtaining a virtual view of desired database information.

Forming this virtual view using SQL was seen to be a straightforward, and sometimes complicated, process. Tools such as the Access SQL Builder and the SQL Build function of the Visual Basic data wizard can help us build error free SQL queries. Even with such tools, it is important to know SQL so you can understand and modify SQL statements built and implemented by others.

SQL also has the ability to modify information in a database. You can also use SQL to add records, delete records, and even create new database tables. But, such capabilities are beyond this course. Besides, the same abilities are available to us using Visual Basic. That is the approach we will use for actual database management tasks. Such tasks are covered in Chapter 6, following a discussion of building a proper Visual Basic interface in Chapter 5.

Example 4-3

Northwind Traders Database

This example gives you more practice with SQL by looking at another database - the Northwind Traders database (Access - **NWindDB.accdb**; SQL Server – **SQLNWindDB.mdf**) studied in other chapters. This is an "open" exercise where you can do what you want until you feel you are more proficient in understanding SQL.

1. First, modify the SQL Tester in Example 4-1 so it uses the Northwind Traders Database (simply change the **ConnectionObject**):

Access Database:

```
NWindConnection = New
OleDbConnection("Provider=Microsoft.ACE.OLEDB.12.0; Data
Source = c:\VBDB\Working\NWindDB.accdb")
```

SQL Server Database:

```
NWindConnection = New SqlConnection("Data
Source=.\SQLEXPRESS;
AttachDbFilename=C:\VBDB\Working\SQLNWindDB.mdf; Integrated
Security=True; Connect Timeout=30; User Instance=True")
```

The connection object has been renamed for this example.

2. Save (Access version saved in the **Example 4-3** folder in **VBDB\Access\Class 4** folder; SQL Server version saved in the **Example 4-3** folder in **VBDB\SQL Server\Class 4** folder) and run your application. Now, try things. Use SQL to examine each of the eight tables (Categories, Customers, Employees, Order Details, Orders, Products, Shippers, Suppliers). Examine each field. Try selecting specific fields from tables. Try ordering the results. Try combining tables to show various information. Try the SQL aggregate functions to do some math. Use Access's or the data wizard's ability to generate SQL statements. Cut and paste those statements into SQL Tester to try them.

Here's the result from finding all fields in the **Customers** table:

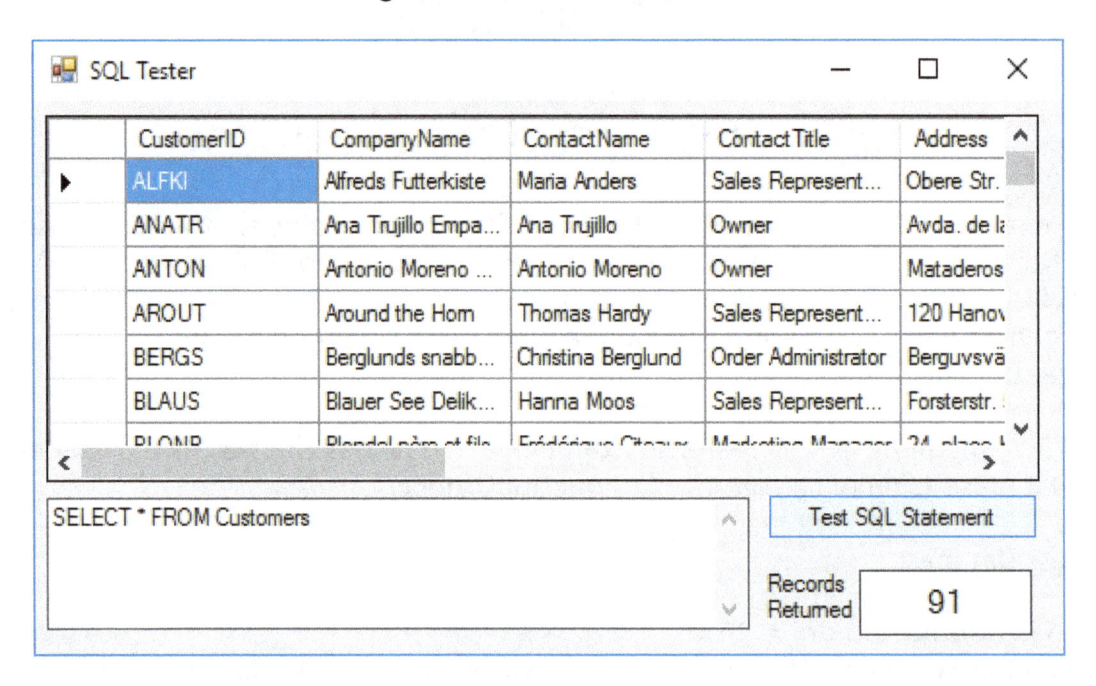

and here's the same from the **Products** table:

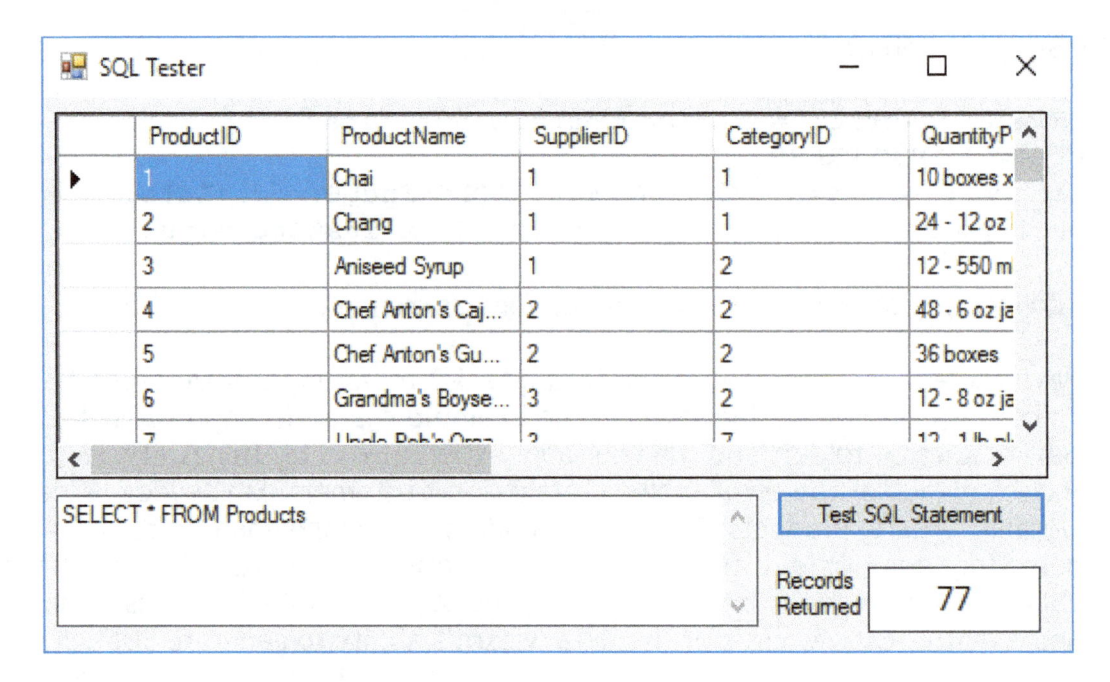

5

Visual Basic Interface Design

Review and Preview

At this point in the course, we can use Visual Basic to connect to a database and SQL statements allow us to obtain any view of the database information we desire. But, that's all we can do - view the data.

We now want to know how to allow a user to interact with the data - obtain alternate views, modify it, add to it, delete it. To do this, we need a well-designed user interface.

In this chapter, we look at some design considerations for the Visual Basic front-end. We examine the toolbox controls and Visual Basic coding techniques needed to build a useful interface and application. Several examples illustrate use of the tools and techniques.

Interface Design Philosophy

The design philosophy for a proper application interface is very basic - keep it as **simple** as possible and as **intuitive** as possible. By doing this, you will save yourself (the programmer) and your users a lot of problems. This may be an obvious statement, but you would be surprised at how many programmers do not follow it.

A first consideration should be to determine what **processes** and **functions** you want your application to perform. What are the **inputs** and **outputs**? Develop a framework or flow chart of all your application's processes. Possible functions of a database interface include: data entry, searching, deleting information, adding information, editing information, sorting data, and printing capabilities.

Decide if multiple **forms** are required. Decide what **controls** from the Visual Basic toolbox you need. Do the built-in Visual Basic tools and functions meet your needs? Do you need to develop some tools or functions of your own? Do you need to acquire some third-party controls?

Minimize the possibility of user errors. This is a very important step. The fewer errors your user can make, the less error checking you have to do. If a particular input calls for numeric data, make sure your user can't type in his name. Choose 'point and click' type tools whenever they can be used to replace tools requiring the user to type in something. For example, let the user point at a month of the year, rather than have the user type in the month. If you can avoid letting your user type anything, do it! Every "typed input" requires some kind of validation that means extra work on your part.

At all steps in the application, make it **intuitive** to the user what he or she is to do. Don't make or let the user guess. You, as the programmer, control the flow of information from the user to the program and vice versa. Maintain that control at all times. Try to anticipate all possible ways a user can mess up in using your application. It's fairly easy to write an application that works properly when the user does everything correctly. It's difficult to write an application that can handle all the possible wrong things a user can do and still not bomb out. And, although it is difficult, it is straightforward and just a matter of following your common sense.

Visual Basic Interface Design 5-3

Make your interface appealing to the user. Use tolerable colors and don't get carried away with too many font types. Make sure there are no misspellings (a personal pet peeve). Make the interface consistent with other Windows applications. Familiarity is good in program design. It is quite proper to 'borrow' ideas from other applications.

Although not part of the interface the user sees, you should make your code readable and traceable - future code modifiers will thank you. Choose meaningful variable and control names. Use comments to explain what you are doing. Consider developing reusable code - modules with utility outside your current development. This will save you time in future developments.

Debug your application completely before distributing it. There's nothing worse than having a user call you to point out flaws in your application. A good way to find all the bugs is to let several people try the code - a mini beta-testing program. Let's illustrate some of these philosophies with an example.

Example 5-1

Mailing List Revisited

Open and run the mailing list example built in Chapter 1 (**Example 1-1**, also saved in the **Example 5-1** folder in the **VBDB\General\Class 5** folder). It illustrates many of the interface design philosophies just discussed. Notice the program flow - how it directs the user about what to do and minimizes the possibility of errors. In particular, note:

⇒ You cannot type **Address Information** unless the timer has started (controlled via the **Enabled** property of **grpMail**).
⇒ When the Address Information frame is active, the cursor appears in the first text box, so the user starts typing the Name field first (controlled with the **txtName** text box **Focus** method).
⇒ After the user types information in each text box, hitting <Enter> or <Tab> automatically moves them to the next text box (controlled with the **Focus** method).
⇒ After the user types in the last text box (**Zip**), the focus moves to the **Accept** button, so a simple <Enter> accepts the mailing label (using **Focus** on the **btnAccept** button).

Notice how the program flow leads the user through the input process. Regarding the timer portion of the application, notice the **Pause** button is faded (**Enabled** is **False**) initially and is only active (**Enabled** is **True**) when the timer is running. The other timer control buttons toggle accordingly.

There is some validation of inputs in this application also. If there are not five values input, a message box appears informing the user of his error. And, only numbers can be typed when **txtZip** is active (done in the **KeyPress** event). This is the box for the **Zip** that can only be a number. It would probably be more proper to also make sure the entered zip matches either the five or nine digit zip code format. Another validation possible would be to provide a list box control with the 50 states (apologies to our foreign readers for using a provincial example) to choose from instead of asking the user to type in a state name.

Visual Basic Interface Design 5-5

Regarding the code in the example, notice the use of comments to explain what is happening in each procedure. This helps others read and understand your code. It also helps you know what you were doing when you look back on the code a year later. Also notice that selection of proper variable and control names aids in understanding what is going on in the code portion of the application. Now, let's look at interface design in more detail.

Visual Basic Standard Controls

The first step in building a Visual Basic interface is to 'draw' the application on a form. We place the required controls on the form, set properties, and write BASIC code for the needed event and general procedures. As the interface designer, you need to decide which controls best meet your needs regarding efficiency, applicability, and minimization of error possibilities.

In this section, we briefly look at the standard Visual Basic controls. We examine how they might be used in a database 'front-end' and present some of the important properties, events, and methods associated with these controls. This information is provided as a quick review of what is available in the Visual Basic toolbox - a "one-stop" reference to standard controls and how they are used with databases. A later look at more advanced controls will complete the reference.

Form Control

The **Form** is where the user interface is drawn. It is central to the development of Visual Basic applications, whether for databases or other uses.

Form **Properties:**

Name	Gets or sets the name of the form (three letter prefix for form name is **frm**).
AcceptButton	Gets or sets the button on the form that is clicked when the user presses the <Enter> key.
BackColor	Get or sets the form background color.
CancelButton	Gets or sets the button control that is clicked when the user presses the <Esc> key.
ControlBox	Gets or sets a value indicating whether a control box is displayed in the caption bar of the form.
Enabled	If False, all controls on form are disabled.
Font	Gets or sets font name, style, size.
ForeColor	Gets or sets color of text or graphics.
FormBorderStyle	Sets the form border to be fixed or sizeable.
Height	Height of form in pixels.
Help	Gets or sets a value indicating whether a Help button should be displayed in the caption box of the form.
Icon	Gets or sets the icon for the form.
Left	Distance from left of screen to left edge of form, in pixels.
MaximizeButton	Gets or sets a value indicating whether the maximize button is displayed in the caption bar of the form.
MinimizeButton	Gets or sets a value indicating whether the minimize button is displayed in the caption bar of the form.
StartPosition	Gets or sets the starting position of the form when the application is running.
Text	Gets or sets the form window title.
Top	Distance from top of screen to top edge of form, in pixels.
Width	Width of form in pixels.

Form **Methods**:

Close	Closes the form.
Focus	Sets focus to the form.
Hide	Hides the form.
Refresh	Forces the form to immediately repaint itself.
Show	Makes the form display by setting the Visible property to True.

The normal syntax for invoking a method is to type the control name, a dot, then the method name. For form methods, the name to use is **Me**. This is a Visual Basic keyword used to refer to a form. Hence, to close a form, use:

```
Me.Close()
```

Form **Events**:

Activated	Occurs when the form is activated in code or by the user.
Click	Occurs when the form is clicked by the user.
FormClosing	Occurs when the form is closing.
DoubleClick	Occurs when the form is double clicked.
Load	Occurs before a form is displayed for the first time.
Paint	Occurs when the form is redrawn.

To access a form event in the Code window, select **(FormName Events)**.

Typical use of **Form** object (for each control in this, and following chapters, we will provide information for how that control is typically used):

- Set the **Name** and **Text** properties
- Set the **StartPosition** property (in this course, this property will almost always be set to **CenterScreen**)
- Set the **FormBorderStyle** to some value. In this course, we will mostly use **FixedSingle** forms. You can have resizable forms in Visual Basic (and there are useful properties that help with this task), but we will not use resizable forms in this course.
- Write any needed initialization code in the form's **Load** event. To access this event in the Code window, double-click the form or select the **(FormName Events)** object, then the **Load** event.

Button Control

[ab] Button

The **button** is probably the most widely used control. It is used to begin, interrupt, or end a particular process. With **databases**, it is used to **navigate** among records, **add** records, and **delete** records.

Button **Properties**:

Name	Gets or sets the name of the button (three letter prefix for button name is **btn**).
BackColor	Get or sets the button background color.
Enabled	If False, button is visible, but cannot accept clicks.
Font	Gets or sets font name, style, size.
ForeColor	Gets or sets color of text or graphics.
Image	Gets or sets the image that is displayed on a button control.
Text	Gets or sets string displayed on button.
TextAlign	Gets or sets the alignment of the text on the button control.

Button **Methods**:

Focus	Sets focus to the button.
PerformClick	Generates a Click event for a button.

Button **Events**:

Click	Event triggered when button is selected either by clicking on it or by pressing the access key.

Typical use of **Button** control:

➢ Set the **Name** and **Text** property.
➢ Write code in the button's **Click** event.
➢ You may also want to change the **Font**, **Backcolor** and **Forecolor** properties.

Label Control

A Label

A **label** is a control you use to display text. The text in a label can be changed at run-time in response to events. It is widely used in **database** applications for **information display**.

Label **Properties:**

Name	Gets or sets the name of the label (three letter prefix for label name is **lbl**).
AutoSize	Gets or sets a value indicating whether the label is automatically resized to display its entire contents.
BackColor	Get or sets the label background color.
BorderStyle	Gets or sets the border style for the label.
Font	Gets or sets font name, style, size.
ForeColor	Gets or sets color of text or graphics.
Text	Gets or sets string displayed on label.
TextAlign	Gets or sets the alignment of text in the label.

Note, by default, the label control has no resizing handles. To resize the label, set AutoSize to False.

Label **Methods:**

Refresh	Forces an update of the label control contents.

Label **Events:**

Click	Event triggered when user clicks on a label.
DblClick	Event triggered when user double-clicks on a label.

Visual Basic Interface Design

Typical use of **Label** control for static, unchanging display:

- Set the **Name** (though not really necessary for static display) and **Text** property.
- You may also want to change the **Font**, **Backcolor** and **Forecolor** properties.

Typical use of **Label** control for changing display:

- Set the **Name** property. Initialize **Text** to desired string.
- Set **AutoSize** to **False**, resize control and select desired value for **TextAlign**.
- Assign **Text** property (String type) in code where needed.
- You may also want to change the **Font**, **Backcolor** and **Forecolor** properties.

TextBox Control

A **text box** is used to display information entered at design time, by a user at run-time, or assigned within code. The displayed text may be edited. This is the tool used in **database** applications for **editing** fields.

TextBox **Properties**:

Name	Gets or sets the name of the text box (three letter prefix for text box name is **txt**).
BackColor	Get or sets the text box background color.
BorderStyle	Gets or sets the border style for the text box.
Font	Gets or sets font name, style, size.
ForeColor	Gets or sets color of text or graphics.
HideSelection	Gets or sets a value indicating whether the selected text in the text box control remains highlighted when the control loses focus.
Lines	Gets or sets the lines of text in a text box control.
MaxLength	Gets or sets the maximum number of characters the user can type into the text box control.
MultiLine	Gets or sets a value indicating whether this is a multiline text box control.
PasswordChar	Gets or sets the character used to mask characters of a password in a single-line TextBox control.
ReadOnly	Gets or sets a value indicating whether text in the text box is read-only.
ScrollBars	Gets or sets which scroll bars should appear in a multiline TextBox control.
SelectedText	Gets or sets a value indicating the currently selected text in the control.
SelectionLength	Gets or sets the number of characters selected in the text box.
SelectionStart	Gets or sets the starting point of text selected in the text box.
Text	Gets or sets the current text in the text box.
TextAlign	Gets or sets the alignment of text in the text box.
TextLength	Gets length of text in text box.

Visual Basic Interface Design 5-13

TextBox **Methods**:

AppendText	Appends text to the current text of text box.
Clear	Clears all text in text box.
Focus	Places the cursor in a specified text box.
SelectAll	Selects all text in text box.
Undo	Undoes the last edit operation in the text box.

TextBox **Events**:

KeyDown	Occurs when a key is pressed down while the control has focus.
KeyPress	Occurs when a key is pressed while the control has focus – used for key trapping.
Leave	Triggered when the user leaves the text box. This is a good place to examine the contents of a text box after editing.
TextChanged	Occurs when the Text property value has changed.

Typical use of **TextBox** control as display control:

- Set the **Name** property. Initialize **Text** property to desired string.
- Set **ReadOnly** property to **True**.
- If displaying more than one line, set **MultiLine** property to **True**.
- Assign **Text** property in code where needed.
- You may also want to change the **Font**, **Backcolor** and **Forecolor** properties.

Typical use of **TextBox** control as input device:

- Set the **Name** property. Initialize **Text** property to desired string.
- If it is possible to input multiple lines, set **MultiLine** property to **True**.
- In code, give **Focus** to control when needed. Provide key trapping code in **KeyPress** event. Read **Text** property when **Leave** event occurs.
- You may also want to change the **Font**, **Backcolor** and **Forecolor** properties.

CheckBox Control

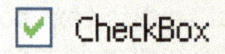

Check boxes provide a way to make choices from a list of potential candidates. Some, all, or none of the choices in a group may be selected. With **databases**, check boxes are used for many kinds of **choices**.

CheckBox **Properties:**

Name	Gets or sets the name of the check box (three letter prefix for check box name is **chk**).
AutoSize	Gets or sets a value indicating whether the check box is automatically resized to display its entire contents.
BackColor	Get or sets the check box background color.
Checked	Gets or sets a value indicating whether the check box is in the checked state.
Font	Gets or sets font name, style, size.
ForeColor	Gets or sets color of text or graphics.
Text	Gets or sets string displayed next to check box.
TextAlign	Gets or sets the alignment of text of the check box.

CheckBox **Methods:**

Focus	Moves focus to this check box.

CheckBox **Events:**

CheckedChanged	Occurs when the value of the Checked property changes, whether in code or when a check box is clicked.
Click	Triggered when a check box is clicked. **Checked** property is automatically changed by Visual Basic.

Typical use of **CheckBox** control:

- Set the **Name** and **Text** property. Initialize the **Checked** property.
- Monitor **Click** or **CheckChanged** event to determine when button is clicked. At any time, read **Checked** property to determine check box state.
- You may also want to change the **Font**, **Backcolor** and **Forecolor** properties.

RadioButton Control

Radio buttons provide the capability to make a mutually exclusive choice among a group of potential candidate choices. Hence, radio buttons work as a group, only one of which can have a True (or selected) value. Radio buttons on a form work as an independent group as do groups of options buttons within panels and group boxes. Radio buttons are not data bound controls, yet they can still be used for a variety of **options** in database interfaces.

RadioButton **Properties**:

Name	Gets or sets the name of the radio button (three letter prefix for radio button name is **rdo**).
AutoSize	Gets or sets a value indicating whether the radio button is automatically resized to display its entire contents.
BackColor	Get or sets the radio button background color.
Checked	Gets or sets a value indicating whether the radio button is checked.
Font	Gets or sets font name, style, size.
ForeColor	Gets or sets color of text or graphics.
TextAlign	Gets or sets the alignment of text of the radio button.

RadioButton **Methods**:

Focus	Moves focus to this radio button.
PerformClick	Generates a Click event for the button, simulating a click by a user.

RadioButton **Events**:

CheckedChanged	Occurs when the value of the Checked property changes, whether in code or when a radio button is clicked.
Click	Triggered when a button is clicked. **Checked** property is automatically changed by Visual Basic.

Typical use of **RadioButton** control:

- Establish a group of radio buttons.
- For each button in the group, set the **Name** (give each button a similar name to identify them with the group) and **Text** property. You might also change the **Font**, **BackColor** and **Forecolor** properties.
- Initialize the **Checked** property of one button to **True.**
- Monitor the **Click** or **CheckChanged** event of each radio button in the group to determine when a button is clicked. The 'last clicked' button in the group will always have a **Checked** property of **True.**

GroupBox Control

Group boxes provide a way of grouping related controls on a form. Radio buttons within a group box act independently of other radio buttons in an application.

GroupBox **Properties:**

Name	Gets or sets the name of the group box (three letter prefix for group box name is **grp**).
BackColor	Get or sets the group box background color.
Enabled	Gets or sets a value indicating whether the group box is enabled. If False, all controls in the group box are disabled.
Font	Gets or sets font name, style, size.
ForeColor	Gets or sets color of text.
Text	Gets or sets string displayed in title region of group box.
Visible	If False, hides the group box (and all its controls).

The GroupBox control has some methods and events, but these are rarely used. We are more concerned with the methods and events associated with the controls in the group box.

Typical use of **GroupBox** control:

- Set **Name** and **Text** property (perhaps changing **Font**, **BackColor** and **ForeColor** properties).
- Place desired controls in group box. Monitor events of controls in group box using usual techniques.

Panel Control

☐ Panel

The **Panel** control is another Visual Basic grouping control. It is nearly identical to the **GroupBox** control in behavior. The Panel control lacks a Text property (titling information), but has optional scrolling capabilities. Radio buttons in the Panel control act as an independent group. Panel controls can also be used to display graphics (lines, curves, shapes, animations).

Panel **Properties**:

Name	Gets or sets the name of the panel (three letter prefix for panel name is **pnl**).
AutoScroll	Gets or sets a value indicating whether the panel will allow the user to scroll to any controls placed outside of its visible boundaries.
BackColor	Get or sets the panel background color.
BorderStyle	Get or set the panel border style.
Enabled	Gets or sets a value indicating whether the panel is enabled. If False, all controls in the panel are disabled.
Visible	If False, hides the panel (and all its controls).

Like the GroupBox control, the Panel control has some methods and events, but these are rarely used (we will see a few Panel events in later graphics chapters). We usually only are concerned with the methods and events associated with the controls in the panel.

Typical use of **Panel** control:

> Set **Name** property.
> Place desired controls in panel control.
> Monitor events of controls in panel using usual techniques.

PictureBox Control

The **picture box** allows you to place graphics information on a form. In a **database**, picture boxes are used to store **graphic** data.

PictureBox **Properties**:

Name	Gets or sets the name of the picture box (three letter prefix for picture box name is **pic**).
BackColor	Get or sets the picture box background color.
BorderStyle	Indicates the border style for the picture box.
Height	Height of picture box in pixels.
Image	Establishes the graphics file to display in the picture box (jpeg, gif, bmp files).
Left	Distance from left edge of form to left edge of picture box, in pixels.
SizeMode	Indicates how the image is displayed.
Top	Distance bottom of form title bar area to top edge of picture box, in pixels.
Width	Width of picture box in pixels.

PictureBox **Events**:

Click	Triggered when a picture box is clicked.

Typical use of **PictureBox** control for displaying images:

- Set the **Name** and **SizeMode** property (most often, **StretchImage**).
- Set **Image** property, either in design mode or at run-time, remembering icon files are not automatically displayed.

Example 5-2

Authors Table Input Form

In Chapter 6, we will build a complete database management system for the books database. Each table in the database will require some kind of input form. In this chapter, we build such a form for the **Authors** table. Even though it is a very simple table (only three fields: **Au_ID**, **Author**, **Year_Born**), it provides an excellent basis to illustrate many of the steps of proper interface design. The SQL statement needed by the command object to retrieve the fields (sorted by **Author**) is:

SELECT * FROM Authors ORDER BY Author

We need an input form that allows a user to edit an existing record, delete an existing record or add a new record. The form should also allow navigation from one record to another. The steps to follow:

1. Start a new application. We need three label controls and three text boxes to display the fields. We need two buttons to move from one record to the next. We need five buttons to control editing features and one button to allow us to stop editing. Place these controls on a form. The layout should resemble:

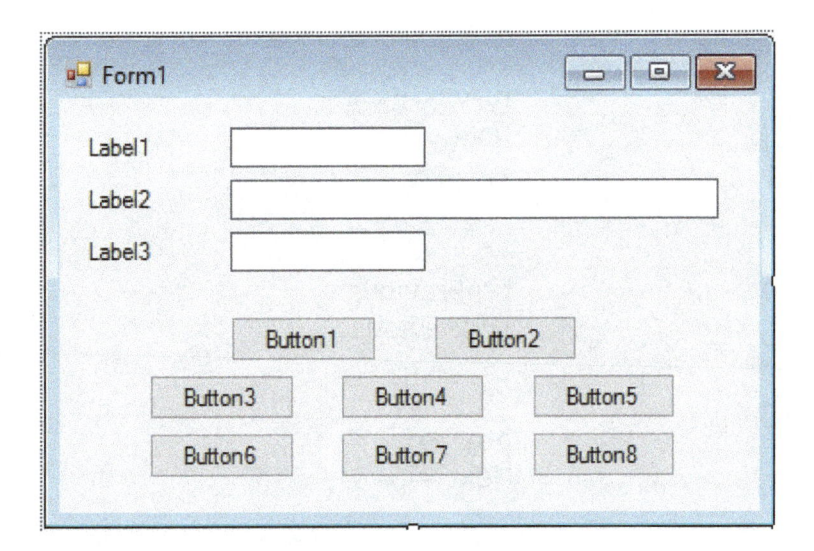

2. Set these properties for the form and controls:

Form1:
- Name   frmAuthors
- FormBorderStyle   FixedSingle
- StartPosition   CenterScreen
- Text   Authors

Label1:
- Text   Author ID

TextBox1:
- Name   txtAuthorID
- BackColor   White
- ReadOnly   True

Label2:
- Text   Author Name

TextBox2:
- Name   txtAuthorName
- BackColor   White
- ReadOnly   True

Label3:
- Text   Year Born

TextBox3:
- Name   txtYearBorn
- BackColor   White
- ReadOnly   True

Button1:
- Name   btnPrevious
- Text   <= Previous

Button2:
- Name   btnNext
- Text   Next =>

Button3:
    Name   btnEdit
    Text   &Edit

Button4:
    Name   btnSave
    Text   &Save

Button5:
    Name   btnCancel
    Text   &Cancel

Button6:
    Name   btnAddNew
    Text   &Add New

Button7:
    Name   btnDelete
    Text   &Delete

Button8:
    Name   btnDone
    Text   Do&ne

Note, we 'lock' (**ReadOnly** = **True**) all the text boxes. We will unlock them when we (as the programmer) decide the user can change a value (remember, we are in control). At this point, the form should appear as:

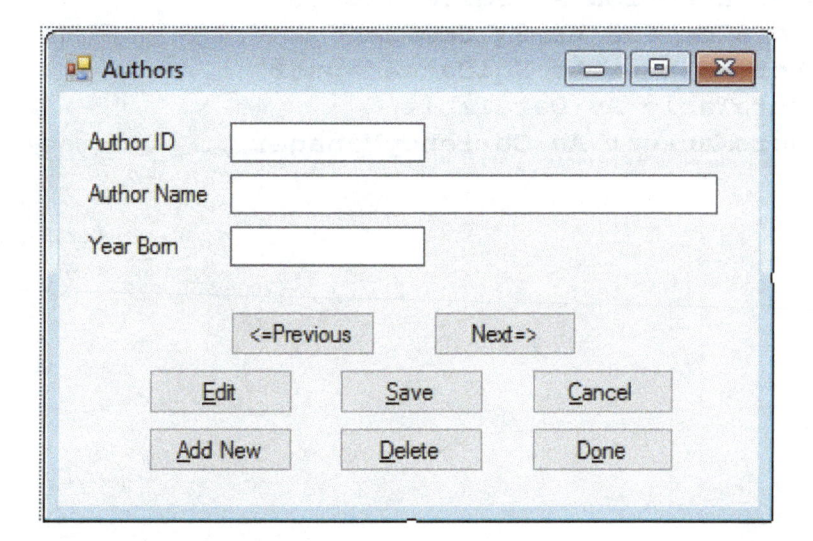

3. We will add features to this input application as we progress through the chapter. At this point, we add code to form the data table and allow us to navigate through the **Authors** table records. Add these two lines at the top of the code window:

Access Database:

```
Imports System.Data
Imports System.Data.OleDb
```

SQL Server Database:

```
Imports System.Data
Imports System.Data.SqlClient
```

4. Form level declarations to create data objects:

Access Database:

```
Dim BooksConnection As OleDbConnection
Dim AuthorsCommand As OleDbCommand
Dim AuthorsAdapter As OleDbDataAdapter
Dim AuthorsTable As DataTable
Dim AuthorsManager As CurrencyManager
```

SQL Server Database:

```
Dim BooksConnection As SqlConnection
Dim AuthorsCommand As SqlCommand
Dim AuthorsAdapter As SqlDataAdapter
Dim AuthorsTable As DataTable
Dim AuthorsManager As CurrencyManager
```

Visual Basic Interface Design 5-25

5. Add this code the **frmAuthors Load** procedure:

Access Database:

```
  Private Sub FrmAuthors_Load(ByVal sender As System.Object, ByVal e As System.EventArgs) Handles MyBase.Load
      'connect to books database
      BooksConnection = New OleDbConnection("Provider=Microsoft.ACE.OLEDB.12.0; Data Source = c:\VBDB\Working\BooksDB.accdb")
      BooksConnection.Open()
      'establish command object
      AuthorsCommand = New OleDbCommand("Select * from Authors ORDER BY Author", BooksConnection)
      'establish data adapter/data table
      AuthorsAdapter = New OleDbDataAdapter()
      AuthorsAdapter.SelectCommand = AuthorsCommand
      AuthorsTable = New DataTable()
      AuthorsAdapter.Fill(AuthorsTable)
      'bind controls to data table
      txtAuthorID.DataBindings.Add("Text", AuthorsTable, "Au_ID")
      txtAuthorName.DataBindings.Add("Text", AuthorsTable, "Author")
      txtYearBorn.DataBindings.Add("Text", AuthorsTable, "Year_Born")
      'establish currency manager
      AuthorsManager = DirectCast(Me.BindingContext(AuthorsTable), CurrencyManager)
    End Sub
```

SQL Server Database:

```
   Private Sub FrmAuthors_Load(ByVal sender As System.Object, ByVal e As System.EventArgs) Handles MyBase.Load
     'connect to books database
     BooksConnection = New SqlConnection("Data Source=.\SQLEXPRESS; AttachDbFilename=C:\VBDB\Working\SQLBooksDB.mdf; Integrated Security=True; Connect Timeout=30; User Instance=True")
     BooksConnection.Open()
     'establish command object
     AuthorsCommand = New SqlCommand("Select * from Authors ORDER BY Author", BooksConnection)
     'establish data adapter/data table
     AuthorsAdapter = New SqlDataAdapter()
     AuthorsAdapter.SelectCommand = AuthorsCommand
     AuthorsTable = New DataTable()
     AuthorsAdapter.Fill(AuthorsTable)
     'bind controls to data table
     txtAuthorID.DataBindings.Add("Text", AuthorsTable, "Au_ID")
     txtAuthorName.DataBindings.Add("Text", AuthorsTable, "Author")
     txtYearBorn.DataBindings.Add("Text", AuthorsTable, "Year_Born")
     'establish currency manager
     AuthorsManager = DirectCast(Me.BindingContext(AuthorsTable), CurrencyManager)
   End Sub
```

This code creates the needed data objects to open the database and form the **Authors** table (includes all fields ordered by Author). It then binds the controls to the currency manager object. This code is identical to code seen in the previous two chapters.

Visual Basic Interface Design 5-27

6. Add this code to the **frmAuthors Closing** event procedure to close the database connection:

```
Private Sub FrmAuthors_FormClosing(ByVal sender As Object,
ByVal e As System.Windows.Forms.FormClosingEventArgs)
Handles Me.FormClosing
    'close the connection
    BooksConnection.Close()
    'dispose of the objects
    BooksConnection.Dispose()
    AuthorsCommand.Dispose()
    AuthorsAdapter.Dispose()
    AuthorsTable.Dispose()
End Sub
```

7. Code for the two button **Click** events to allow navigation:

```
Private Sub BtnPrevious_Click(ByVal sender As
System.Object, ByVal e As System.EventArgs) Handles
btnPrevious.Click
    AuthorsManager.Position -= 1
End Sub

Private Sub BtnNext_Click(ByVal sender As System.Object,
ByVal e As System.EventArgs) Handles btnNext.Click
    AuthorsManager.Position += 1
End Sub
```

8. Save the application (Access version saved in the **Example 5-2** folder in **VBDB\Access\Class 5** folder; SQL Server version saved in the **Example 5-2** folder in **VBDB\SQL Server\Class 5** folder). Run it. Here is the first record:

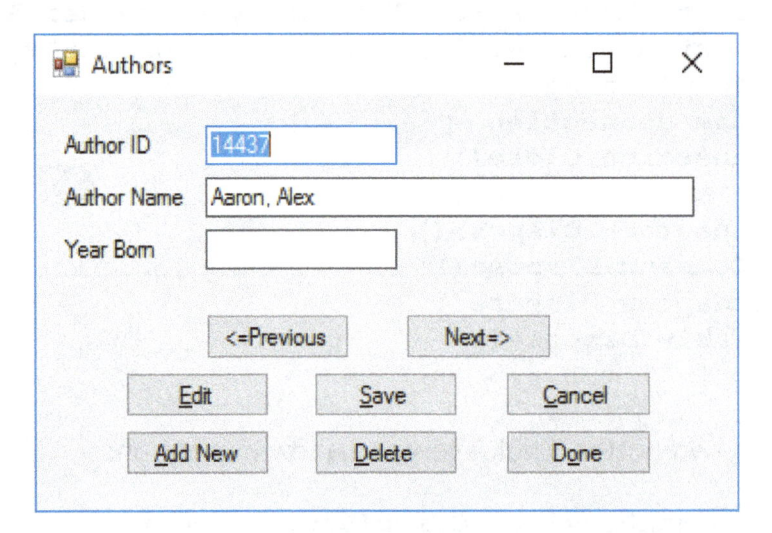

Navigate among the records. Note you cannot edit anything. The text boxes are read-only. As we progress through this chapter (and the next), we will continue to add features to this example until it is complete.

MessageBox Object

Many times, in a database application, you will want to impart some information to your user. That information may be a courtesy message ("New record written") or a question requiring feedback ("Do you really want to delete this record?"). Visual Basic (and Windows) provides an excellent medium for providing such information – the **MessageBox** object.

You've seen message boxes if you've ever used a Windows application. Think of all the examples you've seen. For example, message boxes are used to ask you if you wish to save a file before exiting and to warn you if a disk drive is not ready. For example, if while writing these notes in Microsoft Word, I attempt to exit, I see this message box:

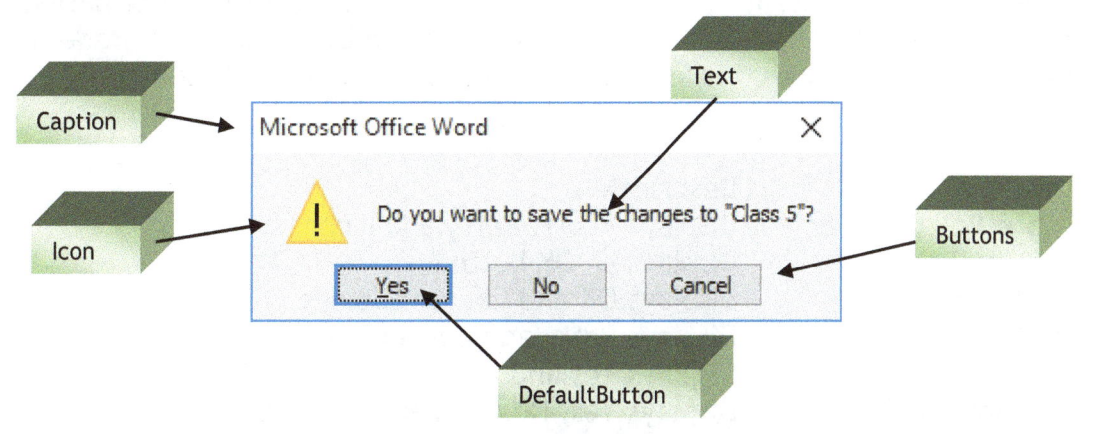

In this message box, the different parts that you control have been labeled. You will see how you can format a message box any way you desire.

To use the **MessageBox** object, you decide what the **Text** of the message should be, what **Caption** you desire, what **Icon** and **Buttons** are appropriate, and which **DefaultButton** you want. To display the message box in code, you use the MessageBox **Show** method.

The MessageBox is **overloaded** with several ways to implement the **Show** method. Some of the more common ways are:

```
MessageBox.Show(Text)
MessageBox.Show(Text, Caption)
MessageBox.Show(Text, Caption, Buttons)
MessageBox.Show(Text, Caption, Buttons, Icon)
MessageBox.Show(Text, Caption, Buttons, Icon,
DefaultButton)
```

In these implementations, if **DefaultButton** is omitted, the first button is default. If **Icon** is omitted, no icon is displayed. If **Buttons** is omitted, an 'OK' button is displayed. And, if **Caption** is omitted, no caption is displayed.

You decide what you want for the message box **Text** and **Caption** information (string data types). The other arguments are defined by Visual Basic predefined constants. The **Buttons** constants are defined by the **MessageBoxButtons** constants:

Member	Description
AbortRetryIgnore	Displays Abort, Retry and Ignore buttons
OK	Displays an OK button
OKCancel	Displays OK and Cancel buttons
RetryCancel	Displays Retry and Cancel buttons
YesNo	Displays Yes and No buttons
YesNoCancel	Displays Yes, No and Cancel buttons

The syntax for specifying a choice of buttons is the usual dot-notation:

MessageBoxButtons.Member

So, to display an OK and Cancel button, the constant is:

```
MessageBoxButtons.OKCancel
```

You don't have to remember this, however. When typing the code, the Intellisense feature will provide a drop-down list of button choices when you reach that argument! This will happen for all the arguments in the MessageBox object.

Visual Basic Interface Design 5-31

The displayed Icon is established by the **MessageBoxIcon** constants:

Member	Description
IconAsterisk	Displays an information icon
IconInformation	Displays an information icon
IconError	Displays an error icon (white X in red circle)
IconHand	Displays an error icon
IconNone	Display no icon
IconStop	Displays an error icon
IconExclamation	Displays an exclamation point icon
IconWarning	Displays an exclamation point icon
IconQuestion	Displays a question mark icon

To specify an icon, the syntax is:

MessageBoxIcon.Member

Note there are eight different members of the **MessageBoxIcon** constants, but only four icons (information, error, exclamation, question) available. This is because the current Windows operating system only offers four icons. Future implementations may offer more.

When a message box is displayed, one of the displayed buttons will have focus or be the default button. If the user presses <Enter>, this button is selected. You specify which button is default using the **MessageBoxDefaultButton** constants:

Member	Description
Button1	First button in message box is default
Button2	Second button in message box is default
Button3	Third button in message box is default

To specify a default button, the syntax is:

MessageBoxDefaultButton.Member

The specified default button is relative to the displayed buttons, left to right. So, if you have Yes, No and Cancel buttons displayed and the second button is selected as default, the No button will have focus (be default). Always try to make the default response the "least damaging," if the user just blindly accepts it.

When you invoke the **Show** method of the MessageBox object, the method returns a value from the **DialogResult** constants. The available members are:

Member	Description
Abort	The Abort button was selected
Cancel	The Cancel button was selected
Ignore	The Ignore button was selected
No	The No button was selected
OK	The OK button was selected
Retry	The Retry button was selected
Yes	The Yes button was selected

MessageBox **Example**:

This little code snippet (the first line is very long):

```
If MessageBox.Show("This is an example of a message box",
"Message Box Example", MessageBoxButtons.OKCancel,
MessageBoxIcon.Information,
MessageBoxDefaultButton.Button1) =
Windows.Forms.DialogResult.OK Then
   'everything is OK
Else
   'cancel was pressed
End If
```

displays this message box:

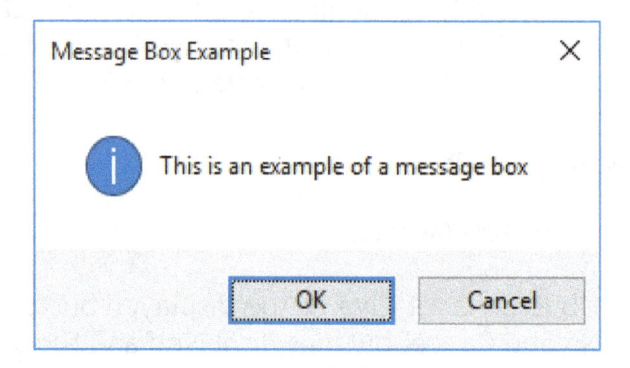

Of course, you would need to add code for the different tasks depending on whether **OK** or **Cancel** is clicked by the user.

Visual Basic Interface Design 5-33

Another MessageBox **Example**:

Many times, you just want to display a quick message to the user with no need for feedback (just an OK button). This code does the job:

```
MessageBox.Show("Quick message for you.", "Hey You!")
```

The resulting message box:

Notice there is no icon and the OK button (default if no button specified) is shown. Also, notice in the code, there is no need to read the returned value - we know what it is! You will find a lot of uses for this simple form of the message box (with perhaps some kind of icon) as you progress in this course.

Message boxes should be used whenever your application needs to inform the user of action or requires user feedback to continue. It is probably better to have too many message boxes, than too few. You always want to make sure your application is performing as it should and the more information you have, the better.

Example 5-3

Authors Table Input Form (Message Box)

There are two places where we could use message boxes in the Authors Table example. A simple box after saving an update to let the user know the save occurred and one related to deleting records.

1. Load Example 5-2 completed earlier. We will modify this example to include message boxes.

2. Use this code in the **btnSave Click** event:

```
Private Sub BtnSave_Click(ByVal sender As System.Object, ByVal e As System.EventArgs) Handles btnSave.Click
    MessageBox.Show("Record saved.", "Save", MessageBoxButtons.OK, MessageBoxIcon.Information)
End Sub
```

Obviously, there will be more code in this event as we continue with this example. This code just implements the message box.

3. Use this code in the **btnDelete Click** event:

```
Private Sub BtnDelete_Click(ByVal sender As System.Object, ByVal e As System.EventArgs) Handles btnDelete.Click
    Dim Response As Windows.Forms.DialogResult
    Response = MessageBox.Show("Are you sure you want to delete this record?", "Delete", MessageBoxButtons.YesNo, MessageBoxIcon.Question, MessageBoxDefaultButton.Button2)
    If Response = Windows.Forms.DialogResult.No Then
        Exit Sub
    End If
End Sub
```

Note we exit the procedure if the user selects **No**. And, notice the **No** button is default – this makes the user think a bit before hitting **Enter**. Like above, there will be more code in this procedure as we proceed.

Visual Basic Interface Design   5-35

4. Save the application (Access version saved in the **Example 5-3** folder in **VBDB\Access\Class 5** folder; SQL Server version saved in the **Example 5-3** folder in **VBDB\SQL Server\Class 5** folder) and run it. Click the **Save** button and you will see:

> Save
>
> ⓘ Record saved.
>
> [OK]

Click **OK**, then try clicking the **Delete** button to see:

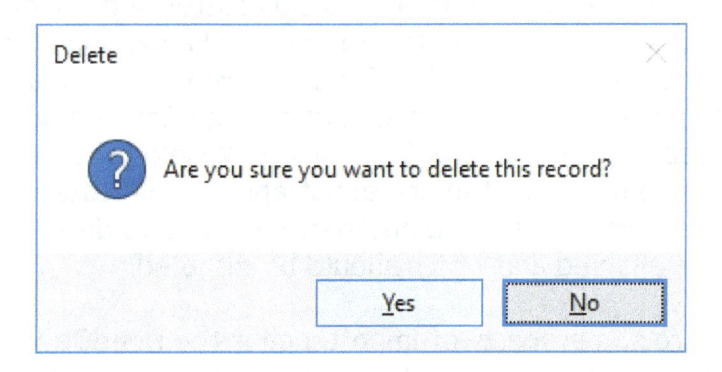

> Delete
>
> ❓ Are you sure you want to delete this record?
>
> [Yes] [No]

Application State

When presenting a Visual Basic database interface to a user, it should be obvious, to the user, what needs to be done. Options should be intuitive and the possibility of mistakes minimized, if not completely eliminated. To maintain this obvious quality, you should always be aware of what **state** your application is in.

Application state implies knowing just what is currently being done within the interface. Are you adding a record, editing a record, deleting a record, or perhaps leaving the application? Once you know the state the application is in, you adjust the interface so that options needed for that particular state are available to the user. You also need to know when and how to transition from one state to another.

What options are adjusted to reflect application state? A primary option is a control's **Enabled** property. By setting **Enabled** to **False**, you disable a control, making it unavailable to the user. So, if the user is not able to save a current record, the button that does the save should have an Enabled property of False. A more drastic disabling of a control is setting its Visible property to False. In this case, there is no misunderstanding about application state. As the application moves from one state to another, you need to determine which controls should be enabled and which should be disabled.

For **text box** controls, a property of importance is the **ReadOnly** property. If a value in a text box is not to be edited, set ReadOnly to True. When editing is allowed (the state changes), toggle the ReadOnly property to False. For text boxes that are always read-only (used for display, not editing purposes), use color (red is good) to indicate they are not accessible. When editing in a text box, use the **Focus** method to place the cursor in the box, making it the active control (giving it focus) and saving the user a mouse click. The **Focus** method can also be used to programmatically move the user from one text box to the next in a desired order.

Another mechanism for moving from one control to another in a prescribed order is the **TabIndex** property, in conjunction with **TabStop**. If **TabStop** is **True**, TabIndex defines the order controls become active (only one control can be active at a time) as the <**Tab**> key is pressed (the order is reversed when <**Shift**>-<**Tab**> is pressed). When controls are placed on a form at design time, they are assigned a TabIndex value with TabStop = True. If you don't want a control to be made active with <Tab>, you need to reset its TabStop property to False. If the assigned order is not acceptable, reset the TabIndex properties for the desired controls, starting with a low number and increasing that value with each control added to the <Tab> sequence. A primary application for <Tab> sequencing is moving from one text box to the next in a detailed input form.

If the concepts of control focus and tab movements are new or unfamiliar, try this. Start a new application in Visual Basic. Add three buttons (**Button1**, **Button2, Button3**), then three text boxes (**Text1**, **Text2, Text3**). Run the application. The first button (Button1) should have focus (a little outline box is around the Text). If you press <Enter> at this point, this button is 'clicked.' Press the <Tab> key and the focus moves to the second button. Press <Tab> twice. The focus should now be in the first text box (the cursor is in the box). Keep pressing <Tab> and watch the focus move from one control to the other, always in the same order. Pressing <Shift>-<Tab> reverses the order. Now, for each button, set the **TabStop** property to **False** (removing them from the tab sequence). Re-run the application and you should note the focus only shifts among the text boxes. Try resetting the **TabIndex** properties of the text boxes to change the shift direction. Always use the idea of focus in your applications to indicate to the user what control is active.

All of this application state talk may sound complicated, but it really isn't. Again, it's all just a matter of common sense. After you design your interface, sit back and step through your application in the Visual Basic environment, exercising every option available. With each option, ask yourself what the user needs to see. Implement the necessary logic to make sure this is all the user sees. Make sure moves from one state to another are apparent and correct. Try lots of things until you are comfortable with the finished product. The Visual Basic environment makes performing such tasks quite easy.

Example 5-4

Authors Table Input Form (Application State)

The Authors Table Input Form can operate in one of three states: **View** state, **Add** state or **Edit** state. In **View** state, the user can navigate from record to record, switch to Edit state, add and/or delete records, or exit the application. In **View** state, data cannot be changed. In both **Add** and **Edit** states, no navigation should be possible, data can be changed, and the user should have access to the **Save** and **Cancel** functions. Each of these states can be implemented using button **Enabled** properties and text box **ReadOnly** properties. We use **TabIndex** (and **TabOrder**) to control shift of focus in the text box controls. We will use a general procedure to allow switching from one state to another.

1. Open Example 5-3 in the Visual Basic environment. We will modify this example to include state considerations.

2. Remove the buttons from tab sequencing by setting all (eight buttons) of their **TabStop** properties to **False**. Also set **TabStop** to **False** for the **txtAuthorID** text box (we will not edit this value - we'll explain why later). Set **TabIndex** for **txtAuthorName** to **1** and **TabIndex** for **txtYearBorn** to **2**.

Visual Basic Interface Design 5-39

3. Add a general Sub procedure named **SetState** with string argument **AppState**. Add this code to the **SetState** procedure:

```
Private Sub SetState(ByVal AppState As String)
  Select Case AppState
    Case "View"
      txtAuthorID.BackColor = Color.White
      txtAuthorID.ForeColor = Color.Black
      txtAuthorName.ReadOnly = True
      txtYearBorn.ReadOnly = True
      btnPrevious.Enabled = True
      btnNext.Enabled = True
      btnAddNew.Enabled = True
      btnSave.Enabled = False
      btnCancel.Enabled = False
      btnEdit.Enabled = True
      btnDelete.Enabled = True
      btnDone.Enabled = True
      txtAuthorName.Focus()
    Case "Add", "Edit"
      txtAuthorID.BackColor = Color.Red
      txtAuthorID.ForeColor = Color.White
      txtAuthorName.ReadOnly = False
      txtYearBorn.ReadOnly = False
      btnPrevious.Enabled = False
      btnNext.Enabled = False
      btnAddNew.Enabled = False
      btnSave.Enabled = True
      btnCancel.Enabled = True
      btnEdit.Enabled = False
      btnDelete.Enabled = False
      btnDone.Enabled = False
      txtAuthorName.Focus()
  End Select
End Sub
```

This code sets the application in View, Add or Edit state. Note which buttons are available and which are not. Notice the **Author ID** box is red in Add and Edit state to indicate it cannot be changed. Notice that the Add and Edit states are the same (for now) and are just a 'toggling' of the View state – this will occur quite often – a great place for 'cut and paste' coding. We now need to modify the application code to use this procedure to move from state to state.

4. We want to be in the **View** state when the application is initialized. Add these two lines at the bottom of the **frmAuthors Load** event:

```
Me.Show()
Call SetState("View")
```

5. When the **Add New** button is clicked, we want to switch to **Add** state. Add this line of code at the top of the **btnAddNew Click** event procedure:

```
Call SetState("Add")
```

6. When the **Edit** button is clicked, we switch to **Edit** state. Add this line of code at the top of the **btnEdit Click** event procedure:

```
Call SetState("Edit")
```

7. Following a **Cancel** or **Save** operation (in **Add** or **Edit** state), we want to return to **View** state. Place this line at the end of the **btnCancel Click** and **btnSave Click** event procedures:

```
Call SetState("View")
```

The **Delete** button does not need any change of state code - it only works in **View** state and stays in that state following a delete.

Visual Basic Interface Design 5-41

8. We're almost done. This is a small change, but an important one that gives your application a professional touch. Notice that if you click the **Previous** button and the pointer is at the first record, nothing changes. Similarly, at the end of the data table, if you click **Next**, nothing happens. This lack of change might confuse the user. To give the user some feedback that they've reached a limit, I like to provide some audible feedback. Make the shaded changes to the **btnPrevious** and **btnNext Click** event procedures to play a beep when the user bumps into a limit:

```
Private Sub BtnPrevious_Click(ByVal sender As System.Object, ByVal e As System.EventArgs) Handles btnPrevious.Click
    If AuthorsManager.Position = 0 Then Console.Beep()
    AuthorsManager.Position -= 1
End Sub

Private Sub BtnNext_Click(ByVal sender As System.Object, ByVal e As System.EventArgs) Handles btnNext.Click
    If AuthorsManager.Position = AuthorsManager.Count - 1 Then Console.Beep()
    AuthorsManager.Position += 1
End Sub
```

9. Save and run the application (Access version saved in the **Example 5-4** folder in **VBDB\Access\Class 5** folder; SQL Server version saved in the **Example 5-4** folder in **VBDB\SQL Server\Class 5** folder). The initial (**View**) state is:

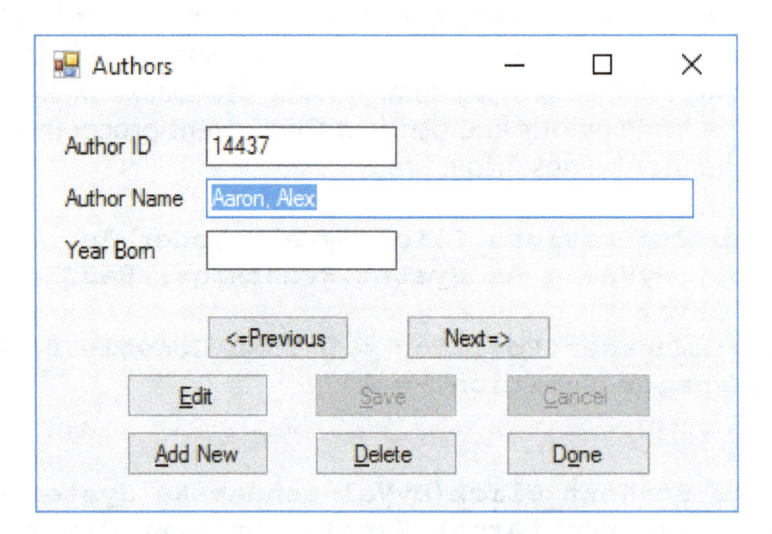

Notice how the various buttons change state as different functions are accessed on the interface form. In **Add** and **Edit** state (the ID box is red), check the tab order of the two text boxes (a very short tab order!):

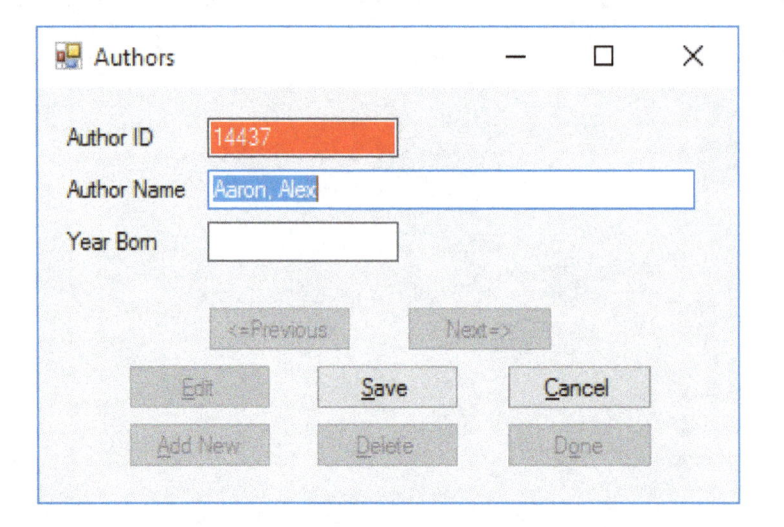

In each state, it is obvious to the user what functions are available and when they are available. Do you hear the beep when you try to move past a limit at the end or beginning of the data table?

Entry Validation

Throughout your work with databases, you will find that viewing database information is an easy task with Visual Basic. Things quickly become difficult, though, when you want to modify information in a database. And, things become very difficult when you allow your user to type information. That's why, if at all possible, don't allow your user to type things. Use point and click type controls whenever possible.

Checking input information from a user requires programming on your part. You must ensure information being put in a database is correct. There are two steps to checking information from a user: **entry** validation and **input** validation. Entry validation is associated with text box controls and checks for proper keystrokes. Input validation is associated with several control types and checks to make sure entries and choices meet certain requirements. In this section, we address entry validation. Input validation is addressed in the next section of this chapter.

As mentioned, entry validation checks for proper keystrokes. For example, if a numerical entry is needed, only allow the pressing of number keys. If spaces are not allowed, don't allow them. If an input must be in upper case letters, don't allow lower case letters to be typed. Restricting keystrokes is referred to as **key trapping**.

Key Trapping

Key trapping is done in the **KeyPress** event procedure of a text box control. Such a procedure has the form (for a text box named **txtExample**):

```
Private Sub TxtExample_KeyPress(ByVal sender As Object,
ByVal e As System.Windows.Forms.KeyPressEventArgs) Handles
txtExample.KeyPress
    .
    .
    .
End Sub
```

What happens in this procedure is that every time a key is pressed in the corresponding text box, the **KeyPressEventArgs** class passes the key that has been pressed into the procedure via the **Char** type **e.KeyChar** property. Recall the **Char** type is used to represent a single character. We can thus examine this key. If it is an acceptable key, we set the **e.Handled** property to **False**. This tells Visual Basic that this procedure has not been handled and the KeyPress should be allowed. If an unacceptable key is detected, we set **e.Handled** to **True**. This 'tricks' Visual Basic into thinking the KeyPress event has already been handled and the pressed key is ignored.

We need some way of distinguishing what keys are pressed. The usual alphabetic, numeric and character keys are fairly simple to detect. To help detect other keys, known as control keys, Visual Basic has predefined values in the **ControlChars** module. Some values for these keys we will use:

Value	Definition
ControlChars.Back	Backspace
ControlChars.Cr	Carriage return (<Enter> key)
ControlChars.NullChar	Null character
ControlChars.Quote	Double quote
ControlChars.Tab	Tab

As an example, let's say we have text box (**txtExample**) and we only want to enter numbers or a decimal point. There are several ways to build a key trapping routine. I suggest a Select Case structure that, based on different values of **e.KeyChar**, takes different steps. If e.KeyChar represents a number, a decimal point or a backspace key (always include backspace or the user won't be able to edit the text box properly), we will allow the keypress (e.Handled = False). Otherwise, we will set e.Handled = True to ignore the keypress (we also add a beep). The code to do this is:

```
Private Sub TxtExample_KeyPress(ByVal sender As Object, ByVal e As System.Windows.Forms.KeyPressEventArgs) Handles txtExample.KeyPress
  Select Case e.KeyChar
    Case CChar("0") To CChar("9"), CChar("."), ControlChars.Back
      'Acceptable keystrokes
      e.Handled = False
    Case Else
      e.Handled = True
      Console.Beep()
  End Select
End Sub
```

Note the use of the **CChar** function to convert single characters to Char type variables, the same type as e.KeyChar. And, note ControlChars.Back is not on a separate line in the code window, it is just displayed that way here due to page margins.

Example 5-5

Authors Table Input Form (Entry Validation)

In the Authors Table Input Form, the **Year Born** field can only be numeric data.

1. Load Example 5-4 completed earlier. We will modify this example to include entry validation.

2. Use this code to the **txtYearBorn KeyPress** event (make sure you select the proper event in the code window – don't use the Change event!):

```
Private Sub TxtYearBorn_KeyPress(ByVal sender As System.Object, ByVal e As System.Windows.Forms.KeyPressEventArgs) Handles txtYearBorn.KeyPress
    Select Case e.KeyChar
      Case CChar("0") To CChar("9"), ControlChars.Back
        'Acceptable keystrokes
        e.Handled = False
      Case Else
        e.Handled = True
        Console.Beep()
    End Select
End Sub
```

3. Save and run the application (Access version saved in the **Example 5-5** folder in **VBDB\Access\Class 5** folder; SQL Server version saved in the **Example 5-5** folder in **VBDB\SQL Server\Class 5** folder). Click **Edit** to switch to Edit state. Click the **Year Born** text box. Try some typing. You should only be able to type numbers (or use the backspace key) in the Year Born entry box. You should hear a beep sound when you type an incorrect key.

Input Validation

In the example just studied, although the user can only input numeric data for the Year Born field, there is no guarantee the final input would be acceptable. What if the input year is past the current year? What if the year is 1492? A second step in validation is to check values in context. Do the input values make sense? Do the values meet established rules? This step is **input validation**.

Some common validation rules are:

⇒ Is this field required? If a field is required and no input is provided, this could cause problems.
⇒ Is the input within an established range? For example, if entering a day number for the month of April, is the value between 1 and 30?
⇒ Is the input the proper length? Social security numbers (including hyphens) require 11 characters. If 11 characters are not detected, the input is not a valid social security number. The BASIC **Len** function can be used here, as can a text box **MaxLength** property (to limit the length).
⇒ Is the input conditional? Some fields only need to be filled in if other fields are filled in. For example, if a user clicks to ship to another address, you need to make sure that address exists.
⇒ Is the input a primary key? If so, and the user has the capability of entering a value, we must insure it is a unique value. Each primary key value in a table must be different.

The amount of input validation required is dependent on the particular field. Many times, there is none needed. You, as the programmer, need to examine each input field and answer the questions posed above: is the field required, must it be within a range, is it length restricted, is it conditional? Any Yes answers require BASIC code to do the validation. You will probably find additional questions as you develop your database skills.

Where does the validation code go? It really depends on how you implement database editing. We will discuss this topic in detail in Chapter 6. For our example we have been creating, we will write a general procedure named **ValidateData** that is called in the **Click** event of the **Save** button. The user clicks this button when done editing, making it a great place to check validity. If any validation rules are violated, we don't allow the requested change(s).

We see entry and input validation require a bit of programming on our part. But, it is worth it. Field validation insures the integrity of the information we are putting in a database. We always need to maintain that integrity. And, one last time for emphasis (are you getting the idea this is important) – if you can eliminate user typing – do it!

Visual Basic Interface Design

5-49

Example 5-6

Authors Table Input Form (Input Validation)

As mentioned, the **Year Born** must be validated. We will make sure that, if an input is attempted (we won't require a year be input), the year has no more than four characters, is not greater than the current year and is greater than 150 years prior to the current year (by not hard coding a minimum year, the code automatically upgrades itself). We will also make sure the user enters an Author Name.

1. Load Example 5-5 completed earlier. We will modify this example to include input validation.

2. Set **MaxLength** property for **txtYearBorn** text box to **4**.

3. Add a function named **ValidateData** that returns a Boolean argument (if True, all validation rules were met). Add this code:

```
Private Function ValidateData() As Boolean
   Dim Message As String = ""
   Dim InputYear As Integer, CurrentYear As Integer
   Dim AllOK As Boolean = True
   'Check for name
   If txtAuthorName.Text.Trim = "" Then
     Message = "You must enter an Author Name." + ControlChars.CrLf
     txtAuthorName.Focus()
     AllOK = False
   End If
   'Check length and range on Year Born
   If txtYearBorn.Text.Trim <> "" Then
     InputYear = CInt(Val(txtYearBorn.Text))
     CurrentYear = CInt(Val(Format(Now, "yyyy")))
     If InputYear > CurrentYear Or InputYear < CurrentYear - 150 Then
       Message += "Year born must be between" + Str(CurrentYear - 150) + " and" + Str(CurrentYear)
       txtYearBorn.Focus()
       AllOK = False
     End If
   End If
   If Not (AllOK) Then
     MessageBox.Show(Message, "Validation Error", MessageBoxButtons.OK, MessageBoxIcon.Information)
   End If
   Return (AllOK)
End Function
```

In this code, we first check to see if an **Author Name** is entered and then validate the **Year Born** field. If either validation rule is violated, the variable **AllOK** is set to **False** and a message box displayed. If any of this code is unfamiliar, try Visual Basic on-line help for assistance.

Visual Basic Interface Design 5-51

4. Modify the **btnSave_Click** event to read (new line is shaded):

```
Private Sub BtnSave_Click(ByVal sender As System.Object, ByVal e As System.EventArgs) Handles btnSave.Click
    If Not (ValidateData()) Then Exit Sub
    MessageBox.Show("Record saved.", "Save", MessageBoxButtons.OK, MessageBoxIcon.Information)
    Call SetState("View")
```

In the new line of code, if the **ValidateData** function returns a **False**, the data is not valid and we exit the procedure.

4. Save and run the application. Click **Edit** and blank out the **Author Name**. Click **Save**. A message box should appear:

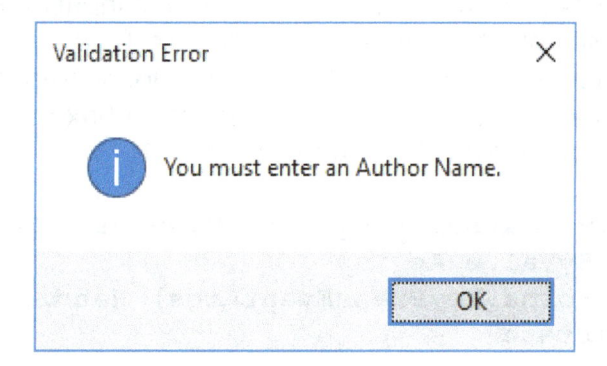

> Validation Error
>
> You must enter an Author Name.
>
> OK

Click **OK** and the focus is reset on the **Author Name** text box, helping the user. Type an invalid numeric value in the **Year Born** box. Click **Save**. A new message should be displayed:

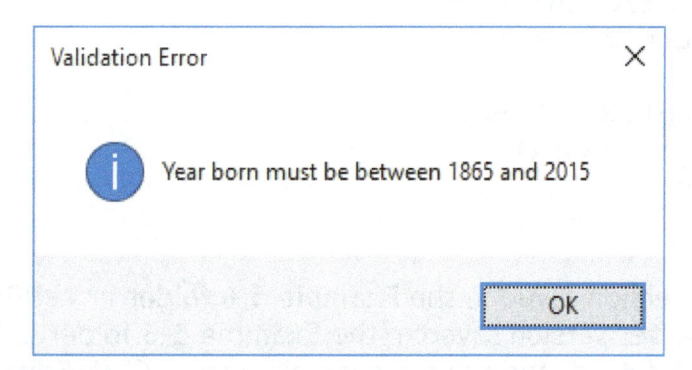

> Validation Error
>
> Year born must be between 1865 and 2015
>
> OK

If you attempt a year, you must either enter a valid value or click **Cancel**. Try a valid year and valid name – make sure they are accepted.

5. After typing a new Author name, to type a Year Born, you need to click in that text box. This clicking (especially when working with lots of text boxes) is cumbersome. A preferred method would be a programmatic shift of focus. Add this code at the top of the **txtAuthorName KeyPress** event:

```
Private Sub TxtAuthorName_KeyPress(ByVal sender As Object, ByVal e As System.Windows.Forms.KeyPressEventArgs) Handles txtAuthorName.KeyPress
    If e.KeyChar = ControlChars.Cr Then
      txtYearBorn.Focus()
    End If
End Sub
```

In this code, if the <Enter> key is pressed, the focus is shifted from the Author text box to the Year Born text box (if a valid name is input). This programmatic change of focus is used all the time in database interfaces. Users like to see the focus move when they press <Enter>. It is an additional step in maintaining proper application state. To shift from the Year Born box to the Author box, add the shaded code to the **txtYearBorn KeyPress** event:

```
Private Sub TxtYearBorn_KeyPress(ByVal sender As System.Object, ByVal e As System.Windows.Forms.KeyPressEventArgs) Handles txtYearBorn.KeyPress
    Select Case e.KeyChar
      Case CChar("0") To CChar("9"), ControlChars.Back
        'Acceptable keystrokes
        e.Handled = False
      Case ControlChars.Cr
        txtAuthorName.Focus()
      Case Else
        e.Handled = True
        Console.Beep()
    End Select
End Sub
```

6. Save (Access version saved in the **Example 5-6** folder in **VBDB\Access\Class 5** folder; SQL Server version saved in the **Example 5-6** folder in **VBDB\SQL Server\Class 5** folder) and run the example again. Click **Edit**. Notice how the focus shifts between the two text boxes as you change the values and press <Enter>. Pressing <Tab> should also change the focus appropriately.

Error Trapping and Handling

Even with a well-designed, 'user-proof' interface, errors can still occur. This is especially true when working with databases. Occasionally, data cannot be written to, or deleted from, the database or invalid fields are encountered. Without any action on our part, these **run-time errors** might bring our application to an unceremonious end. If, however, we recognize an error has occurred and inform the user of the problem, we might be able to recover.

Error trapping and handling must be implemented in <u>every</u> procedure in your application where you think it might be needed. Visual Basic does not allow global error trapping. At a minimum, you should implement error trapping and handling in every procedure that writes to or reads from the database.

Visual Basic uses a structured approach to trapping and handling errors. The structure is referred to as a **Try/Catch/Finally** block. And the annotated syntax for using this block is:

>**Try**
> 'here is code you try where some kind of error may occur
>**Catch** *Exception* **AS** *Type*
> 'if error described by *Exception* of *Type* occurs, process this code
>**Catch**
> 'if any other error occurs, process this code
>**Finally**
> 'Execute this code whether error occurred or not
> 'this block is optional
>**End Try**

The above code works from the top, down. It 'tries' the code between **Try** and the first **Catch** statement. If no error is encountered, any code in the **Finally** block will be executed and the program will continue after the **End Try** statement. If an error (exception) occurs, the program will look to find, if any, the first **Catch** statement (you can have multiple Catch statements) that matches the exception that occurred. If one is found, the code in that respective block is executed (code to help clear up the error - the error handling), then the code in the **Finally** block, then program execution continues after **End Try**. If an error occurs that doesn't match a particular exception, the code in the 'generic' **Catch** block is executed, followed by the code in the **Finally** block. And, program execution continues after the **End Try** statement.

This structure can be used to trap and handle any **Type** of exception defined in the Visual Basic **Exception** class. There are hundreds of possible exceptions related to data access, input and output functions, graphics functions, data types and numerical computations. Here is a list of example exception types (their names are descriptive of the corresponding error condition):

```
ArgumentException                 ArgumentNullException
ArgumentOutOfRangeException       ArithmeticException
ArrayTypeMismatchException        DivideByZeroException
DllNotFoundException              Exception
FormatException                   IndexOutOfRangeException
IO.DirectoryNotFoundException     IO.EndOfStreamException
IO.FileNotFoundException          IO.IOException
OutOfMemoryException              OverflowException
```

Let's take a closer look at the **Catch** block. When you define a Catch block, you specify a name for the exception and define the exception type you want to catch. For example, if want to catch a **DivideByZeroException**, we use:

```
Catch MyException As DivideByZeroException
    'Code to execute if divide by zero occurs
```

If in the **Try** block, a divide by zero occurs, the code following this **Catch** statement will be executed. You would probably put a message box here to tell the user what happened and provide him or her with options of how to fix the problem. To help with the messaging capability, the variable you define as the exception (**MyException**, in this case) has a **Message** property you can use.

A **Try/End Try** loop may be exited using the **Exit Try** statement. Be aware any code in the **Finally** block will still be executed even if an Exit Try is encountered. Once the Finally code is executed, program execution continues after the End Try statement.

Example of **Try/End Try** block to catch an end-of-file error:

```
Try
   'Code to open file
Catch EOFError As IO.EndOfStreamException
   MessageBox.Show(EOFError.Message)
Finally
   'Code to close file (even if error occurred)
End Try
```

Example of a **generic** error trapping routine:

```
Try
   'Code to try
Catch MyException As Exception
   MessageBox.Show(MyException.Message)
Finally
   'Code to execute before leaving block
End Try
```

We've only taken a brief look at the structured run-time error handling capabilities of Visual Basic. It is difficult to be more specific without knowing just what an application's purpose is. You need to know what type of errors you are looking for and what corrective actions should be taken if these errors are encountered. As you build and run your own applications, you will encounter run-time errors. These errors may be due to errors in your code. If so, fix them. But, they may also be errors that arise due to some invalid inputs from your user, because a file does not meet certain specifications or because a disk drive is not ready. You need to use error handling to keep such errors from shutting down your application, leaving your user in a frustrated state.

Example 5-7

Authors Table Input Form (Error Trapping)

As mentioned, error trapping and handling should be included within every procedure where database information is read or written. It should also be included in procedures where database files are being opened or saved.

1. Load Example 5-6 completed earlier. We will modify this example to include error trapping handling

2. Modify the **frmAuthors Load** procedure to incorporate error handling. Changes are shaded:

Access Database:

```
Private Sub FrmAuthors_Load(ByVal sender As System.Object, ByVal e As System.EventArgs) Handles MyBase.Load
    Try
        'connect to books database
        BooksConnection = New OleDbConnection("Provider=Microsoft.ACE.OLEDB.12.0; Data Source = c:\VBDB\Working\BooksDB.accdb")
        BooksConnection.Open()
        'establish command object
        AuthorsCommand = New OleDbCommand("Select * from Authors ORDER BY Author", BooksConnection)
        'establish data adapter/data table
        AuthorsAdapter = New OleDbDataAdapter()
        AuthorsAdapter.SelectCommand = AuthorsCommand
        AuthorsTable = New DataTable()
        AuthorsAdapter.Fill(AuthorsTable)
        'bind controls to data table
        txtAuthorID.DataBindings.Add("Text", AuthorsTable, "Au_ID")
        txtAuthorName.DataBindings.Add("Text", AuthorsTable, "Author")
        txtYearBorn.DataBindings.Add("Text", AuthorsTable, "Year_Born")
        'establish currency manager
        AuthorsManager = DirectCast(Me.BindingContext(AuthorsTable), CurrencyManager)
    Catch ex As Exception
        MessageBox.Show(ex.Message, "Error establishing Authors table.", MessageBoxButtons.OK, MessageBoxIcon.Error)
```

```vb
      Exit Sub
    End Try
    Me.Show()
    Call SetState("View")
  End Sub
```

SQL Server Database:

```vb
  Private Sub FrmAuthors_Load(ByVal sender As System.Object, ByVal e As System.EventArgs) Handles MyBase.Load
    Try
      'connect to books database
      BooksConnection = New SqlConnection("Data Source=.\SQLEXPRESS; AttachDbFilename=C:\VBDB\Working\SQLBooksDB.mdf; Integrated Security=True; Connect Timeout=30; User Instance=True")
      BooksConnection.Open()
      'establish command object
      AuthorsCommand = New SqlCommand("Select * from Authors ORDER BY Author", BooksConnection)
      'establish data adapter/data table
      AuthorsAdapter = New SqlDataAdapter()
      AuthorsAdapter.SelectCommand = AuthorsCommand
      AuthorsTable = New DataTable()
      AuthorsAdapter.Fill(AuthorsTable)
      'bind controls to data table
      txtAuthorID.DataBindings.Add("Text", AuthorsTable, "Au_ID")
      txtAuthorName.DataBindings.Add("Text", AuthorsTable, "Author")
      txtYearBorn.DataBindings.Add("Text", AuthorsTable, "Year_Born")
      'establish currency manager
      AuthorsManager = DirectCast(Me.BindingContext(AuthorsTable), CurrencyManager)
    Catch ex As Exception
      MessageBox.Show(ex.Message, "Error establishing Authors table.", MessageBoxButtons.OK, MessageBoxIcon.Error)
      Exit Sub
    End Try
    Me.Show()
    Call SetState("View")
  End Sub
```

3. Modify the **btnAddNew Click**, **btnSave Click**, and **btnDelete Click** event procedures to allow error trapping and handling. Use the generic code developed in this section, taking advantage of 'cut and paste' editing. The changes are shaded:

```
Private Sub BtnAddNew_Click(ByVal sender As System.Object, ByVal e As System.EventArgs) Handles btnAddNew.Click
    Try
      Call SetState("Add")
    Catch ex As Exception
      MessageBox.Show("Error adding record.", "Error", MessageBoxButtons.OK, MessageBoxIcon.Error)
    End Try
  End Sub

    Private Sub BtnSave_Click(ByVal sender As System.Object, ByVal e As System.EventArgs) Handles btnSave.Click
    If Not (ValidateData()) Then Exit Sub
    Try
    MessageBox.Show("Record saved.", "Save", MessageBoxButtons.OK, MessageBoxIcon.Information)
      Call SetState("View")
    Catch ex As Exception
      MessageBox.Show("Error saving record.", "Error", MessageBoxButtons.OK, MessageBoxIcon.Error)
    End Try
  End Sub

    Private Sub BtnDelete_Click(ByVal sender As System.Object, ByVal e As System.EventArgs) Handles btnDelete.Click
    Dim Response As Windows.Forms.DialogResult
    Response = MessageBox.Show("Are you sure you want to delete this record?", "Delete", MessageBoxButtons.YesNo, MessageBoxIcon.Question, MessageBoxDefaultButton.Button2)
    If Response = Windows.Forms.DialogResult.No Then
      Exit Sub
    End If
    Try
    Catch ex As Exception
      MessageBox.Show("Error deleting record.", "Error", MessageBoxButtons.OK, MessageBoxIcon.Error)
    End Try
  End Sub
```

4. Save the application (Access version saved in the **Example 5-7** folder in **VBDB\Access\Class 5** folder; SQL Server version saved in the **Example 5-7** folder in **VBDB\SQL Server\Class 5** folder).

Access Database:

In the connection string, change the database name to **BooksDB1.accdb**. Run the application. The error trapping should display this message telling us it can't find the database:

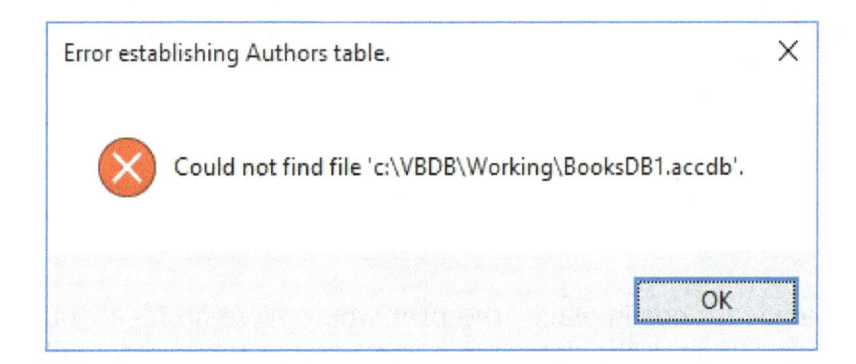

> Error establishing Authors table.
>
> Could not find file 'c:\VBDB\Working\BooksDB1.accdb'.
>
> OK

If error trapping were not in place, the user would have no idea what caused the program to stop. Change the database name back to the correct value (**BooksDB.accdb**).

SQL Server Database:

In the connection string, change the database name to **SQLBooksDB1.mdf**. Run the application. The error trapping should display this message telling us it can't find the database:

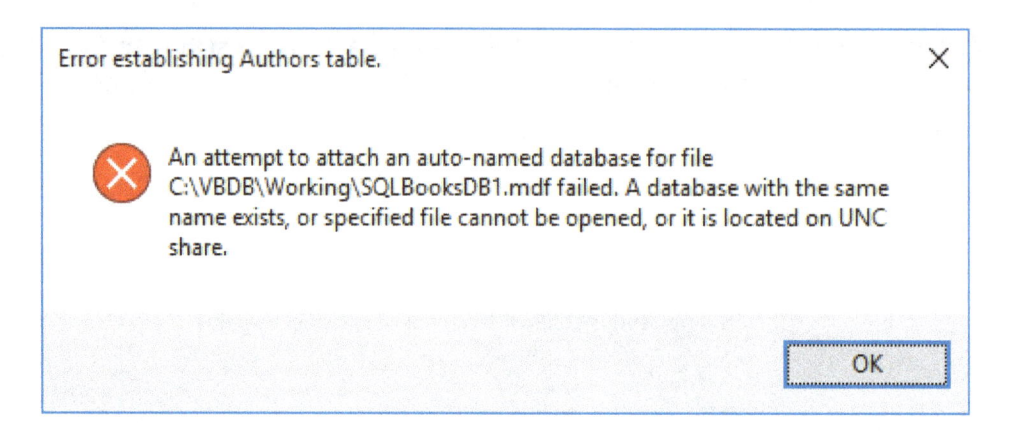

> **Error establishing Authors table.**
>
> An attempt to attach an auto-named database for file C:\VBDB\Working\SQLBooksDB1.mdf failed. A database with the same name exists, or specified file cannot be opened, or it is located on UNC share.
>
> OK

If error trapping were not in place, the user would have no idea what caused the program to stop. Change the database name back to the correct value (**SQLBooksDB.mdf**).

On-Line Help Systems

So, at this point, we know how to build a powerful, intuitive interface, insure valid inputs, and handle any run-time errors that might occur. Even with all this work, there still may be times when the user is stumped as to what to do next. Instinct tells the user to press the **<F1>** function key. Long ago, someone in the old DOS world decided this would be the magic "Help Me!" key. Users expect help when pressing <F1> (I'm sure you rely on it a lot when using Visual Basic). If nothing appears after pressing <F1>, user frustration sets in – not a good thing.

All applications written (other than those for your personal use) should include some form of an on-line help system. It doesn't have to be elegant, but it should be there. Adding a **help file** to your Visual Basic application will give it real polish, as well as making it easier to use. In this section, we will show you how to build a very basic on-line help system for your database applications. This system will simply have a list of help topics the user can choose from.

We create what is known as an **HTML help** system. HTML stands for **hypertext markup language** and is the 'programming' language of choice for generating web pages. This language will be used to generate and display the topics displayed in the help system. Fortunately, we won't need to learn much (if any) HTML. Building an HTML help system involves several files and several steps. In diagram form, we have:

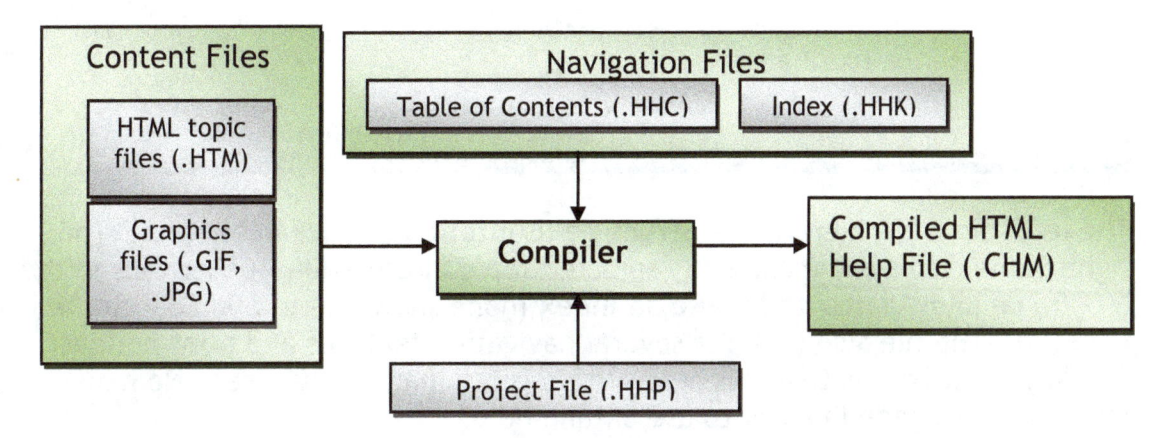

We need to create topic files (**.HTM** files) for each topic in our help system. (We could also add graphics.) These topics are organized by a Table of Contents file (**.HHC**) and Index file (**.HHK**). The Project File (**.HHP**) specifies the components of a help project. All of these files are 'compiled' to create the finished help file (**.CHM**). This file is the file that can be opened for viewing the finished help system.

The developed help system is similar to help systems used by all Windows applications. As an example, here is a help system (.CHM file) that explains how to add or remove programs from your computer:

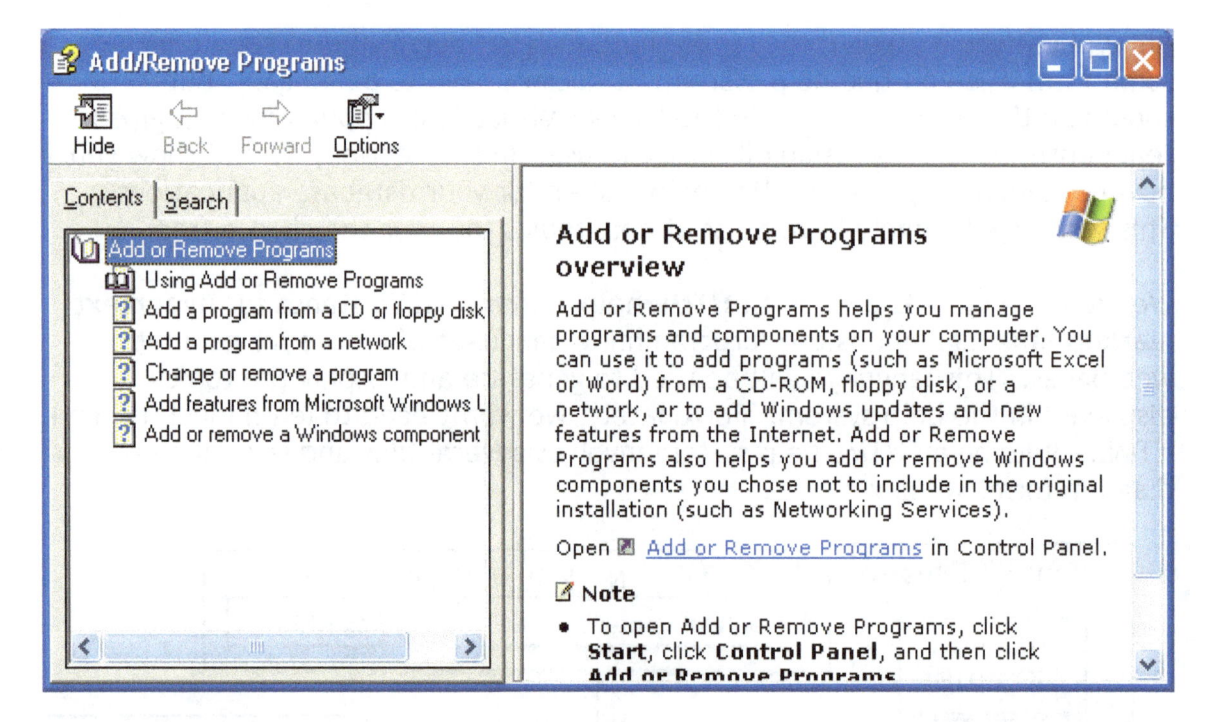

The left frame is a hierarchical structure (**Contents**) of clickable topics. The right frame displays the currently selected topic information. Other tabs in the left frame allow a user to browse an **Index** (none shown here) and **Search** the help file. The file also features several navigation features and print options. The key point here is that this help system is familiar to your user. No new instruction is needed in how to use on-line help.

We will build an HTML help system similar to the one displayed above, but with minimal features. Learning how to build a full-featured help system would be a course in itself. In this chapter, we will learn how to create text-only topics, add a contents file, create a project file and see how to compile the entire package into a useful (if simple) help system.

Creating a Help File

We could create a help system using only text editors if we knew the required structure for the various files. We won't take that approach. The on-line help system will be built using the **Microsoft HTML Help Workshop**. This is a free product from Microsoft that greatly simplifies the building of a help system. The workshop lets you build and organize all the files needed for building the help system. Once built, simple clicks allow compiling and viewing of the help system.

So, obviously, you need to have the workshop installed on your computer. The **HTML Help Workshop** can be downloaded from various Microsoft web sites. To find a download link, go to Microsoft's web site (http://www.microsoft.com). Search on **"HTML Help"** – the search results should display a topic **HTML Downloads**. Select that link and you will be led to a place where you can do the download. Once downloaded, install the workshop as directed.

Creating a complete help file is a major task and sometimes takes as much time as creating the application itself! Because of this, we will only skim over the steps involved, generate a simple example, and provide guidance for further reference. There are five major steps involved in building your own help file:

1. Create your application and develop a hierarchical list of help system topics. This list would consist of headings and topics under specific headings.
2. Create the **topic files** (**HTM** extensions). Please make sure you spell and grammar check your topic files. If there are mistakes in your help system, your user base may not have much confidence in the care you showed in developing your application.
3. Create a **Table of Contents** (**HHC** extension).
4. Create the **Help Project File** (**HHP** extension).
5. Compile the help file to create your finished help system (**CHM** extension).

Step 1 is application-dependent. Here, we'll look at how to use the HTML Help Workshop to complete the last four steps.

Starting the HTML Help Workshop

We will demonstrate the use of the **HTML Help Workshop** to build a very basic help system. The help file will have two headings. Each heading will have three sub-topics:

Heading 1
Topic 1
Topic 2
Topic 3
Heading 2
Topic 1
Topic 2
Topic 3

Though simple, the steps followed here can be used to build an adequate help system. All of the files created while building this help system can be found in the **VBDB\General\Class 5\Sample Help** folder.

If properly installed, there will be an entry for the help workshop on your computer's **Programs** menu. Click **Start**, then **Programs**. Select **HTML Help Workshop**, then **HTML Help Workshop** again. This dialog box should appear:

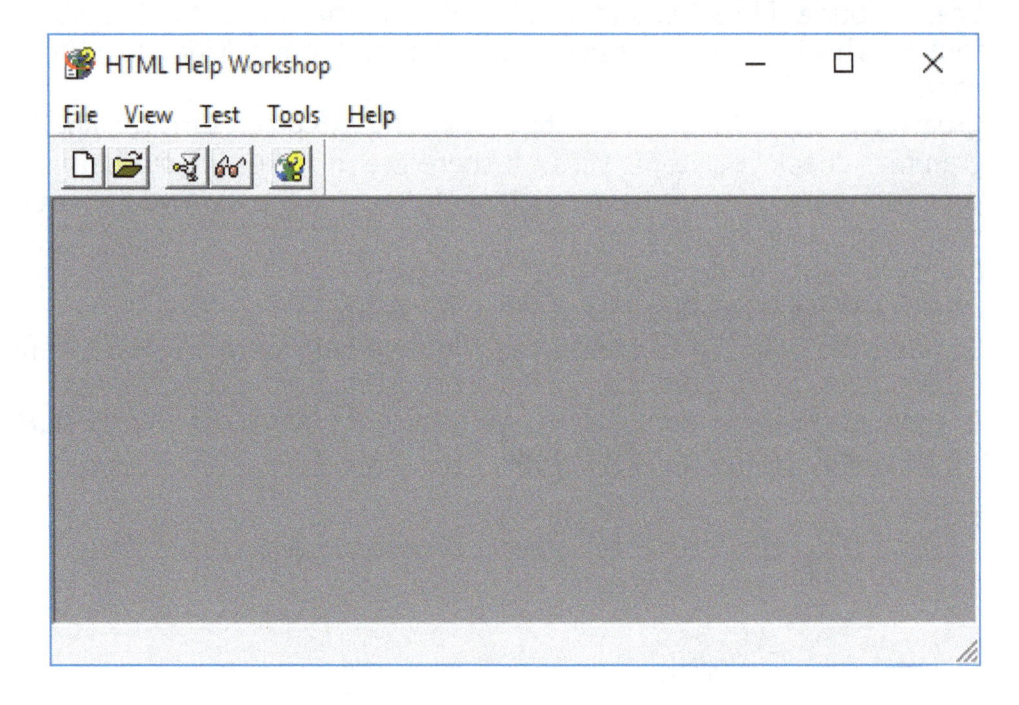

Visual Basic Interface Design 5-65

We want to start a new project. Select **New** under the **File** menu. In the selection box that appears, choose **Project** and click **OK**. A cute little **New Project Wizard** appears:

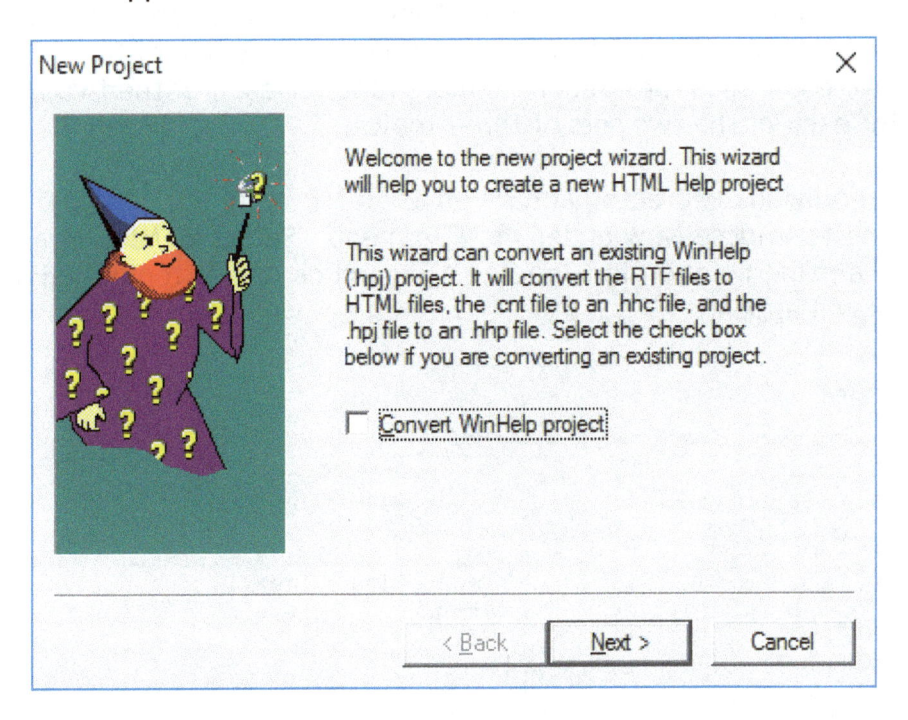

All we need to tell the wizard at this point is the name of our project file. Click **Next**. On the next screen, find (or create) the folder to hold your files (again, I used **VBDB\General\Class 5\Sample Help**) and use the project name **Sample**. Click **Next** two times (make no further selections), then **Finish**. The file **Sample.hhp** is created and you will see:

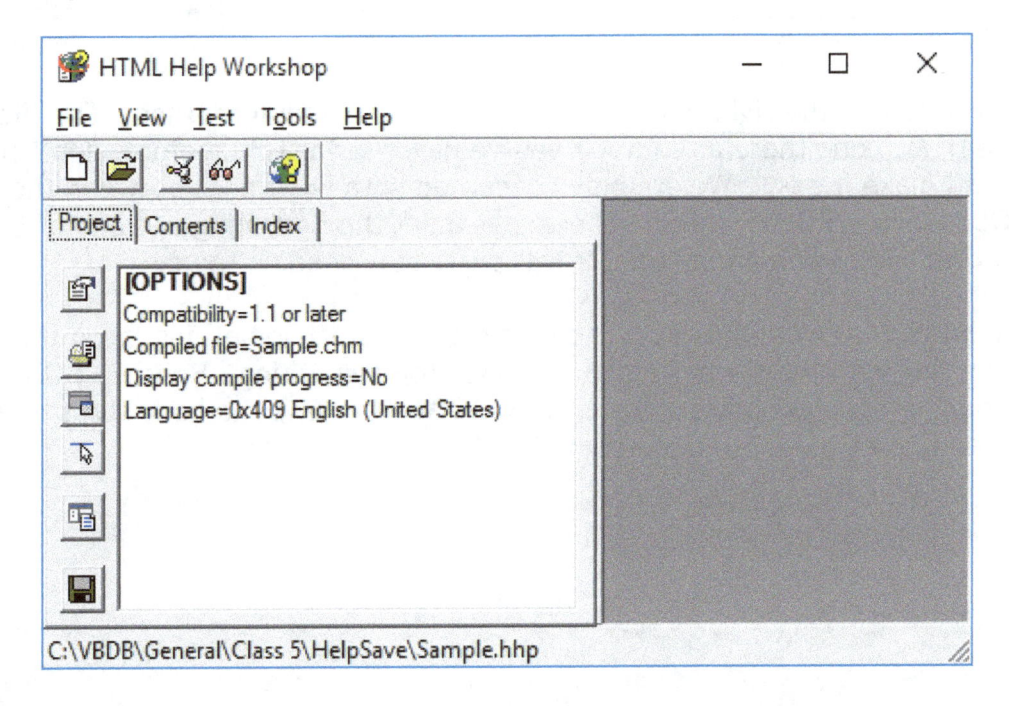

Creating Topic Files

At this point, we are ready to create our topic files. These are the files your user can view for help on topics listed in the contents region of the help system. We will have eight such files in our example (one for each of the two headings and one for each of the two sets of three topics).

Each file is individually created and saved as an HTM file. To create the first file (for Heading 1), choose **New** under the **File** menu. Select **HTML File** and click **OK**. Enter a name for the file (**Heading 1**) and click **OK**. A topic file HTML framework will appear:

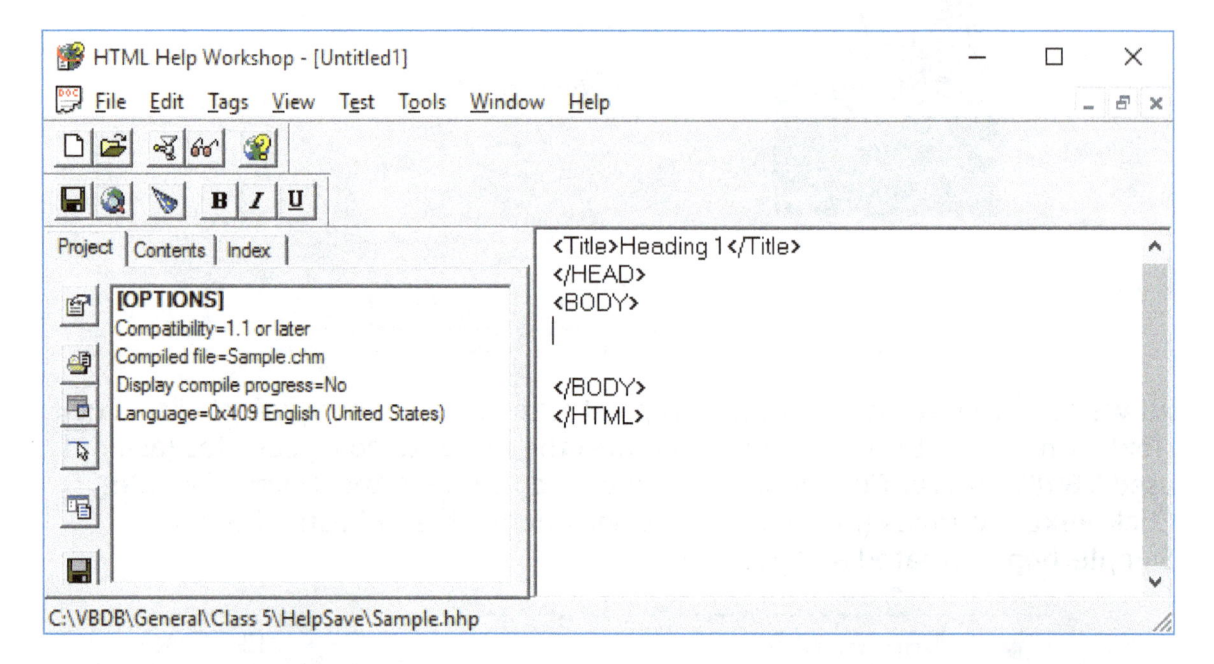

The window on the right is where you type your topic information. The file has some HTML code there already. If you've never seen HTML before, don't panic. We will make it easy. We are only concerned with what goes between the **<BODY>** and **</BODY>** 'tags'. These tags mark the beginning and end of the text displayed when a user selects this particular heading topic.

Most HTML tags work in pairs. The first tag says start something, then the second tag with the slash preface **</>** says stop something. Hence, **<BODY>** says the body of the text starts here. The **</BODY>** tag says the body stops here. It's really pretty easy to understand HTML.

Visual Basic Interface Design   5-67

It would help to know just a little more HTML to make your text have a nice appearance. To change the font, use the **FONT** tag:

    <FONT FACE="FontName" SIZE="FontSize">

where **FontName** is the name of the desired font and **FontSize** the desired size. Notice this is very similar to the **Font** constructor in Visual Basic. When you are done with one font and want to specify a new one, you must use a **</FONT>** tag before specifying the new font. To bold text, use the **<STRONG>** and **</STRONG>** tags. To delineate a paragraph in HTML, use the **<P>** and **</P>** tags. To cause a line break, use **
**. There is no corresponding </BR> tag.

So, using our minimal HTML knowledge (if you know more, use it), we can create our first topic file. The HTML I used to create the first topic (**Heading1**) is:

```
<BODY>
<STRONG>
This is Heading 1
</STRONG>
<P>
This is where I explain what the subtopics available under this heading are.
</P>
</BODY>
```

This HTML will create this finished topic:

This is Heading 1

This is where I explain what the subtopics available under this heading are.

When done typing this first topic, choose **Close File** under the **File** menu. Select a file name (I used **Heading1.HTM**) to use and save the topic file. Of course, at any time, you can reopen, modify and resave any topic file.

You repeat the above process for every topic in your help system. That is, create a new file, type your topic and save it. You will have an HTM file for every topic in your help system. For our example, create seven more HTM files using whatever text and formatting you desire. The files I created are saved as: **Heading1.HTM, Topic11.HTM, Topic12.HTM, Topic13.HTM, Heading2.HTM, Topic21.HTM, Topic22.HTM, Topic23.HTM.**

Creating HTML topic files using the Help Workshop is a bit tedious. You need to use HTML tags and don't really know what your topic file will look like until you've completed the help system. Using a **WYSIWYG** (what you see is what you get) editor is a better choice. Such editors allow you to create HTML files without knowing any HTML. You just type the file in a normal word processing-type environment, then save it in HTML format. There are several WYSIWYG HTML editors available. Check Internet download sites for options. Also, most word processors offer an option to save a document as an HTML file. I always use a WYSIWYG editor for topic files. I simply save each topic file in the same folder as my help system files, just as if I was using the built-in editor.

Next, we create a **Table of Contents** file. But, before leaving your topic files, make sure they are as complete and accurate as possible. And, again, please check for misspellings - nothing scares a user more than a poorly prepared help file. They quickly draw the conclusion that if the help system is not built with care, the application must also be sloppily built.

Creating Table of Contents File

The **Table of Contents** file specifies the hierarchy of topics to display when the help system's **Contents** tab is selected. In the **HTML Help Workshop**, choose the **New** option under the **File** menu. Choose **Table of Contents**, then click **OK**. The following window appears:

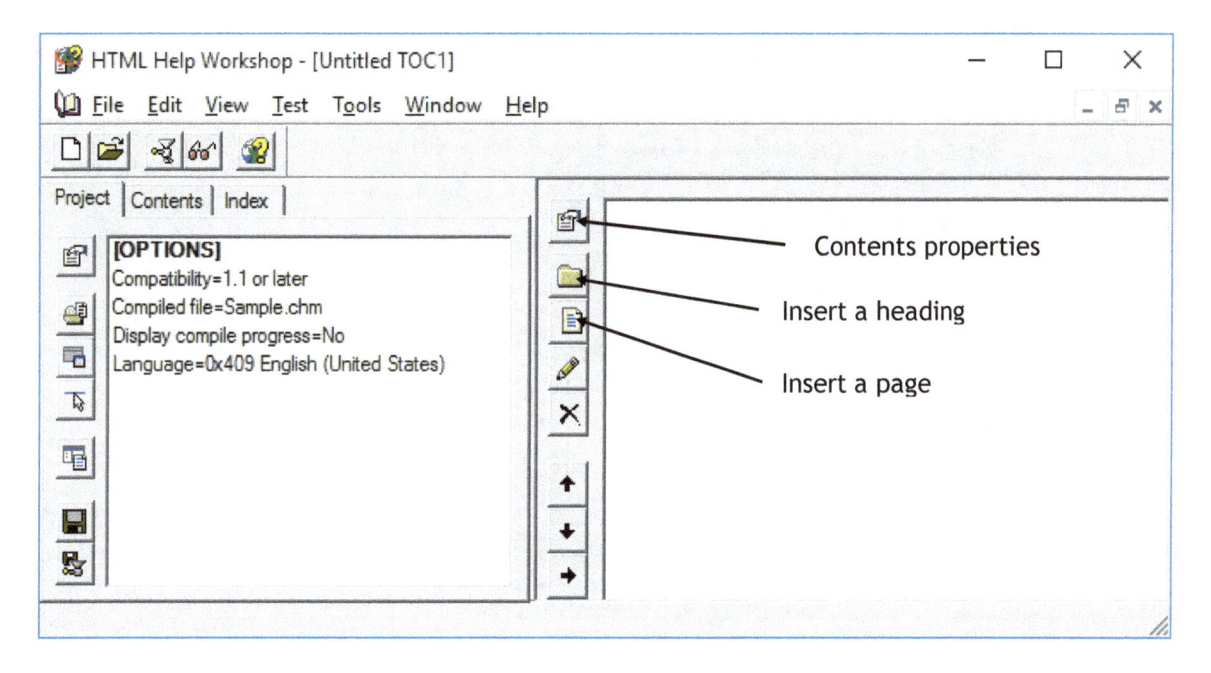

- Contents properties
- Insert a heading
- Insert a page

5-70   Visual Basic and Databases

We want to add two headings with three topics under each. To insert a heading, in the right frame, click the toolbar button with a folder (**Insert a heading**). This window appears:

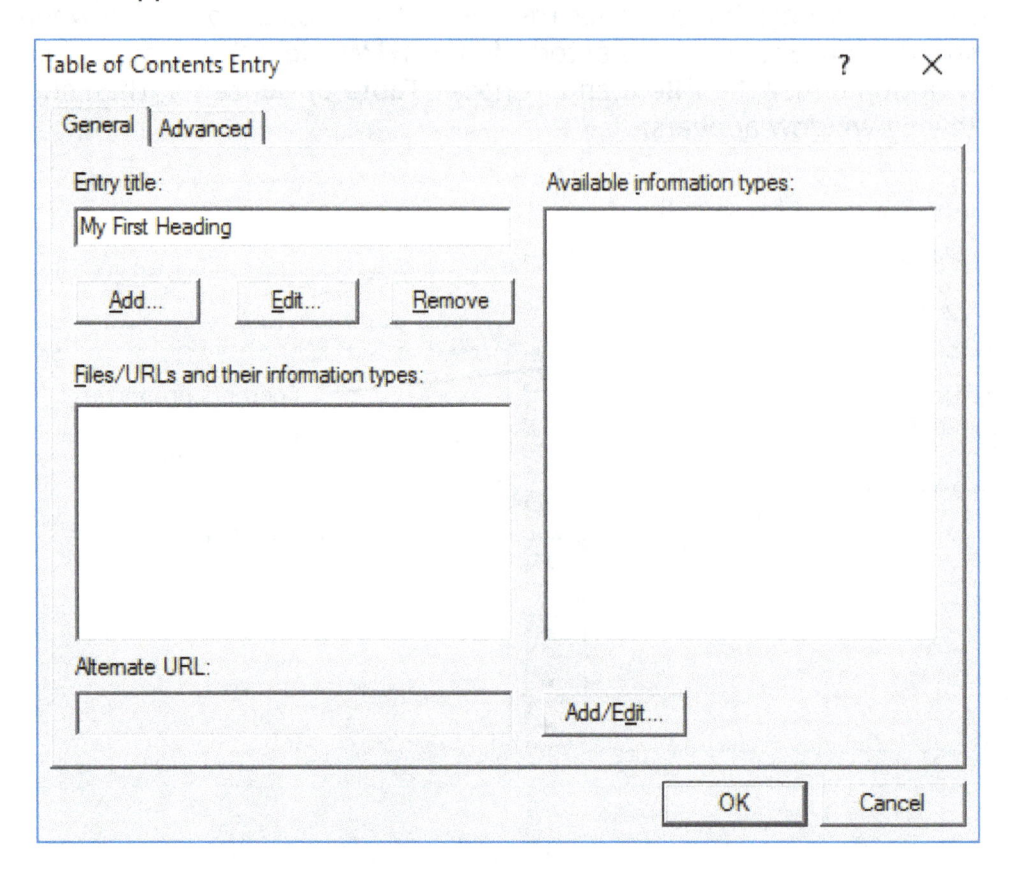

Type a title for the entry in **Entry title** (this is what will appear in the **Contents** – I used **My First Heading**).

You also need to link this topic to its topic file (HTM file). To do this, click **Add** and this appears:

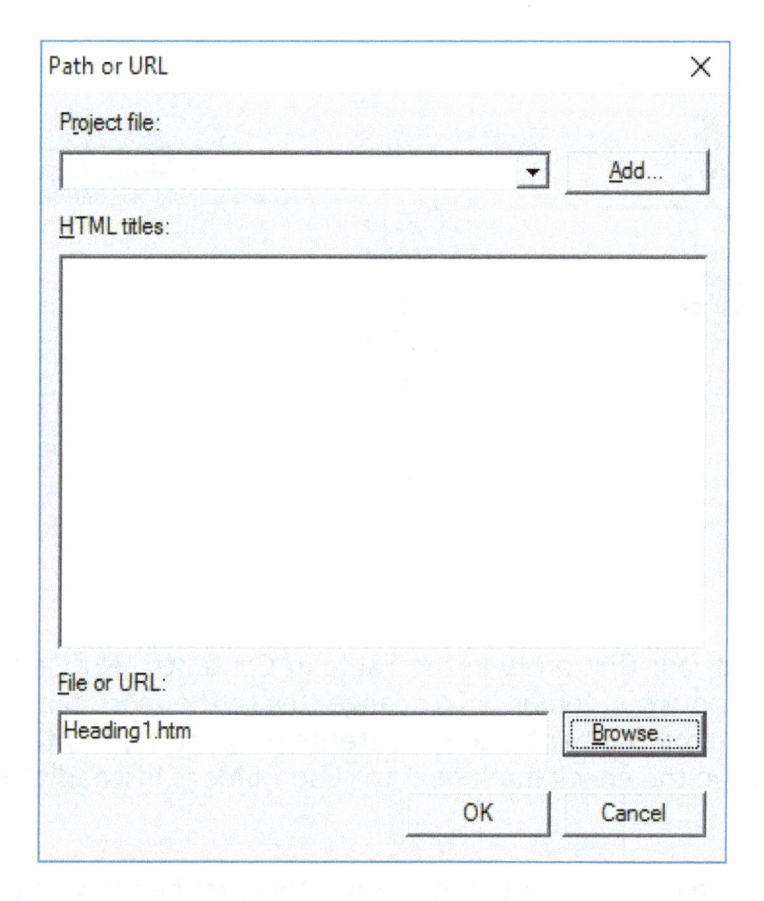

Click the Browse button and 'point' to the corresponding topic file (**Heading1.HTM** in this case). Click **OK** to close this window.

Click **OK** to close the Table of Contents entry window and you'll now see:

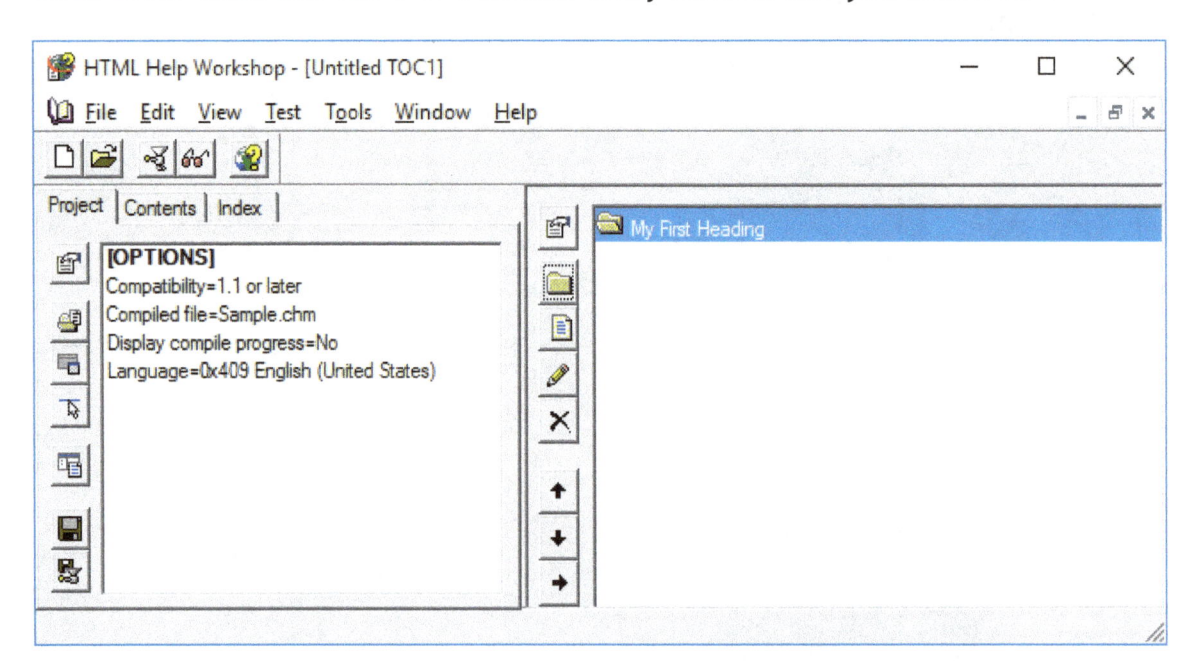

You've created your first entry in the Table of Contents. Notice the icon next to the heading is an 'open folder.' To change this to the more familiar 'open book,' click the top toolbar button (**Contents properties**). In the window that appears, remove the check mark next to '**Use Folders Instead of Books**,' and click **OK**.

Now, we need to enter our first topic under this first heading. Click the toolbar button (**Insert a page**) under the heading button. This dialog will appear:

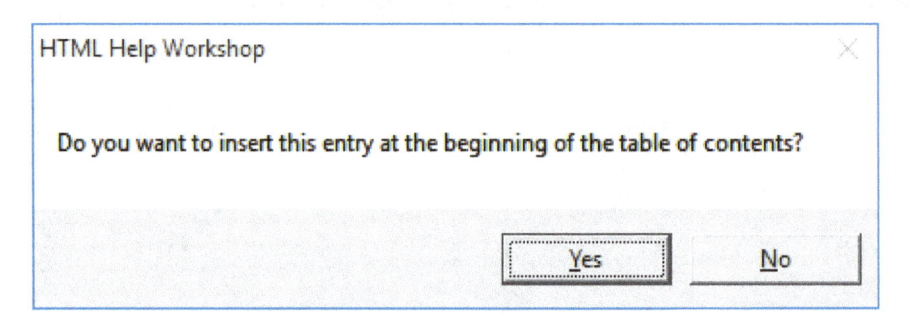

Answer **No** – we want the entry after the heading topic. At this point, you follow the same steps followed for the heading: enter a title and add a link to the topic file.

Visual Basic Interface Design 5-73

Add Table of Contents entries for all topic files in our little example. Use whatever titling information you choose. When you enter the second heading, it will be listed under the third topic in the first heading. To move it to the left (making it a major heading), right-click the heading and choose **Move Left**, the left arrow button on the toolbar). When done, I have this:

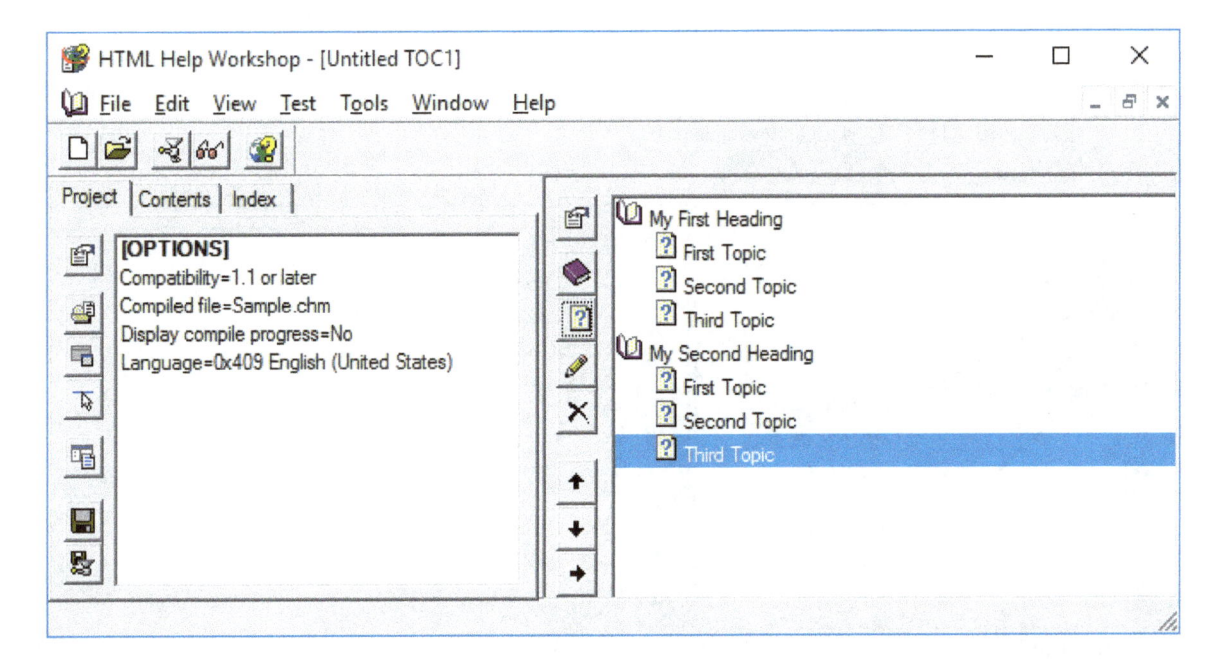

Save the contents file. Choose **Close File** under the **File** menu and assign a name of **Sample.HHC** to this contents file.

Compiling the Help File

We're almost ready to compile and create our help system. Before doing this, we need to add entries to the **Project** file. The project file at this point appears as:

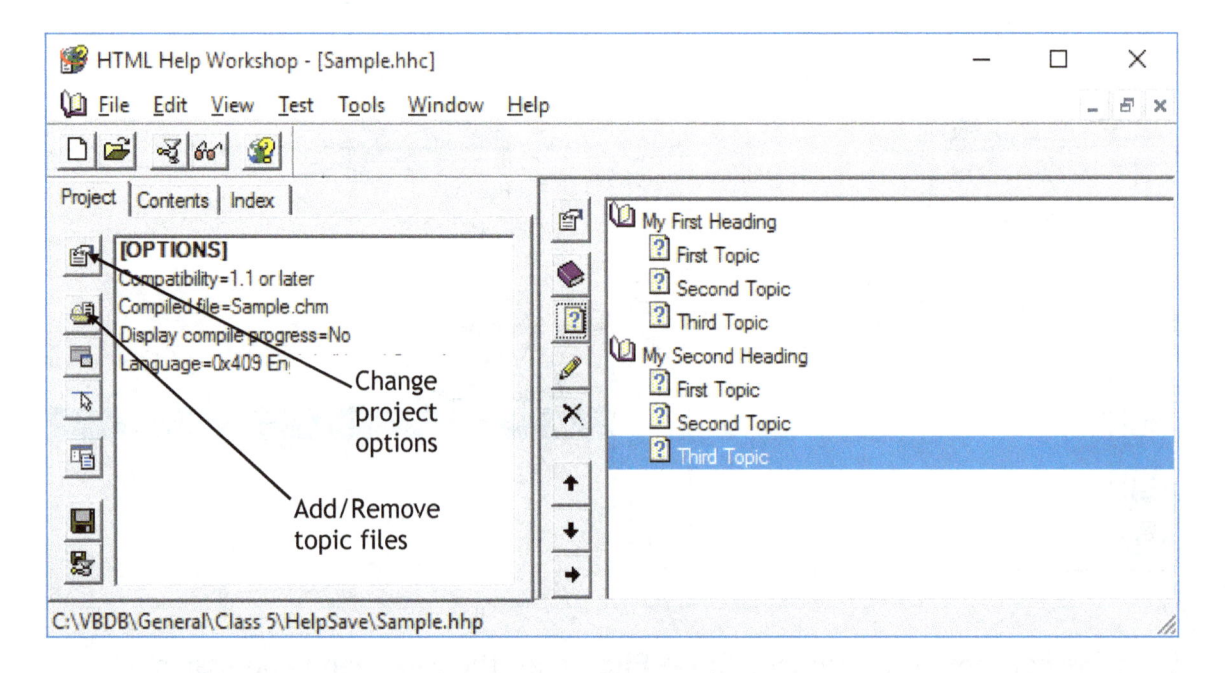

We first need to add our topic files. To do this, choose the **Add/remove topic files** toolbar button. In the window that appears, click **Add**, then select all topics files. You should see:

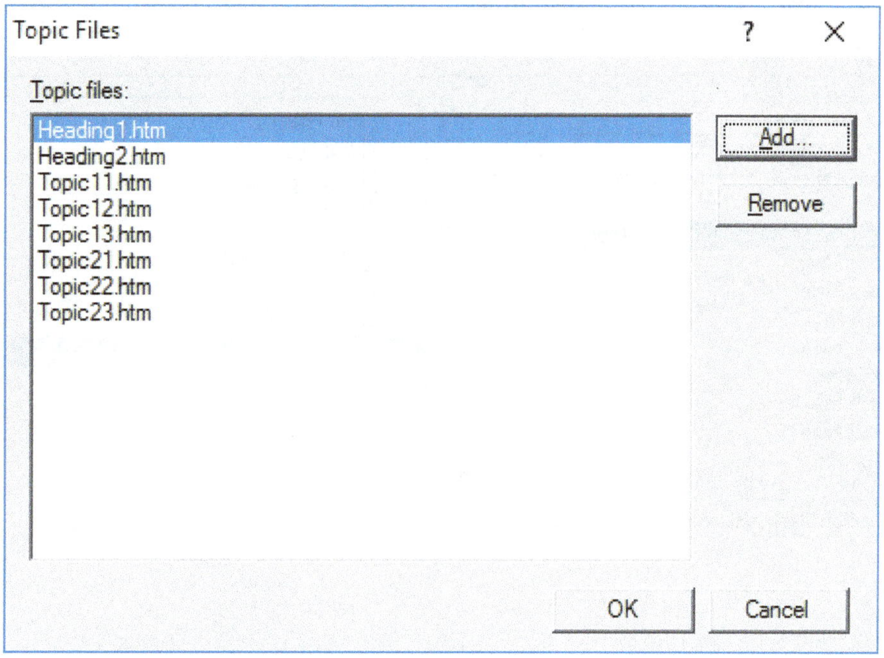
Topic Files
Topic files:
Heading1.htm
Heading2.htm
Topic11.htm
Topic12.htm
Topic13.htm
Topic21.htm
Topic22.htm
Topic23.htm
Add...
Remove
OK
Cancel

Click **OK.**

Now, the project file has the topic files added:

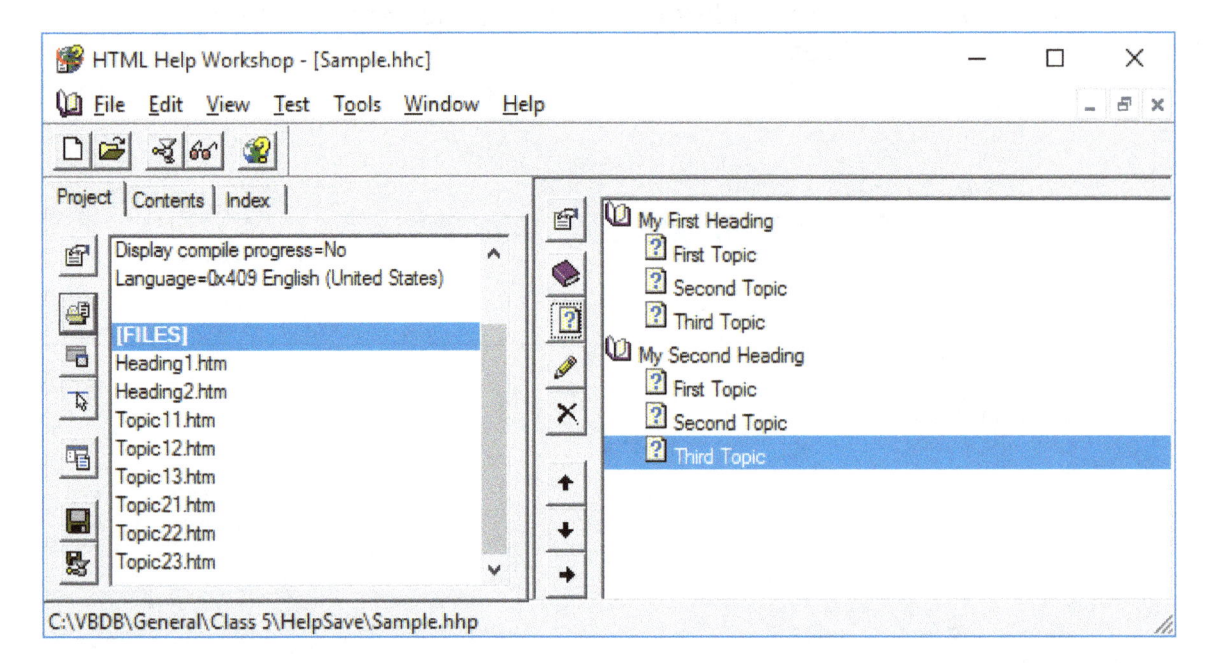

Now, we specify the **Table of Contents** file and set a few other properties. Click the **Change project options** toolbar button. Click the **General** tab and type a title for your help system (I used **My Sample Help File**) and specify the default file (**Heading1.htm**):

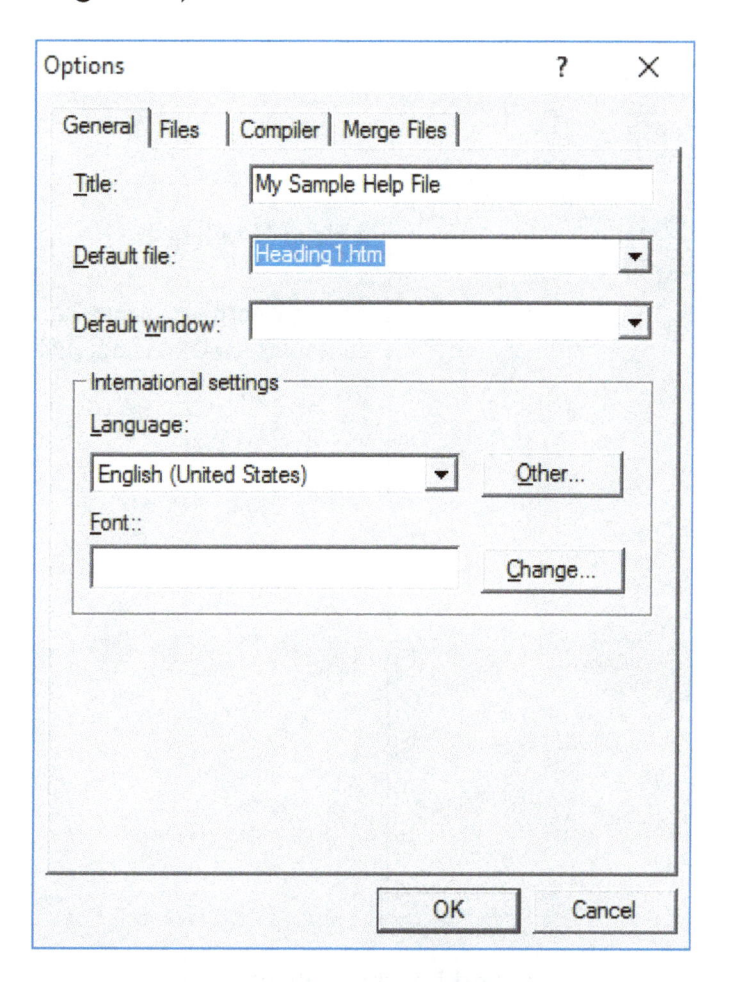

Click on the **Files** tab and select **Sample.hhc** as your contents file. Click **OK** to complete specification of your project file. At this point, save all files by choosing **Save Project** under the **File** menu.

We can now compile our project into the finished product – a complete HTML help system. To do this, click the **Compile HTML file** button (resembles a meat grinder) on the workshop toolbar. **Browse** so your project file (**Sample.hhp**) is selected. Choose **Compile** in the resulting window and things start 'grinding.' If no errors are reported, you should now have a **CHM** file in your directory. If errors did occur, you need to fix any reported problems.

At long last, we can view our finished product. Click on the **View compiled file** button (a pair of sunglasses) on the workshop toolbar. **Browse** so your help file (**Sample.chm**) is selected. Choose **View**, and this will appear (I've expanded the headings to show the topics):

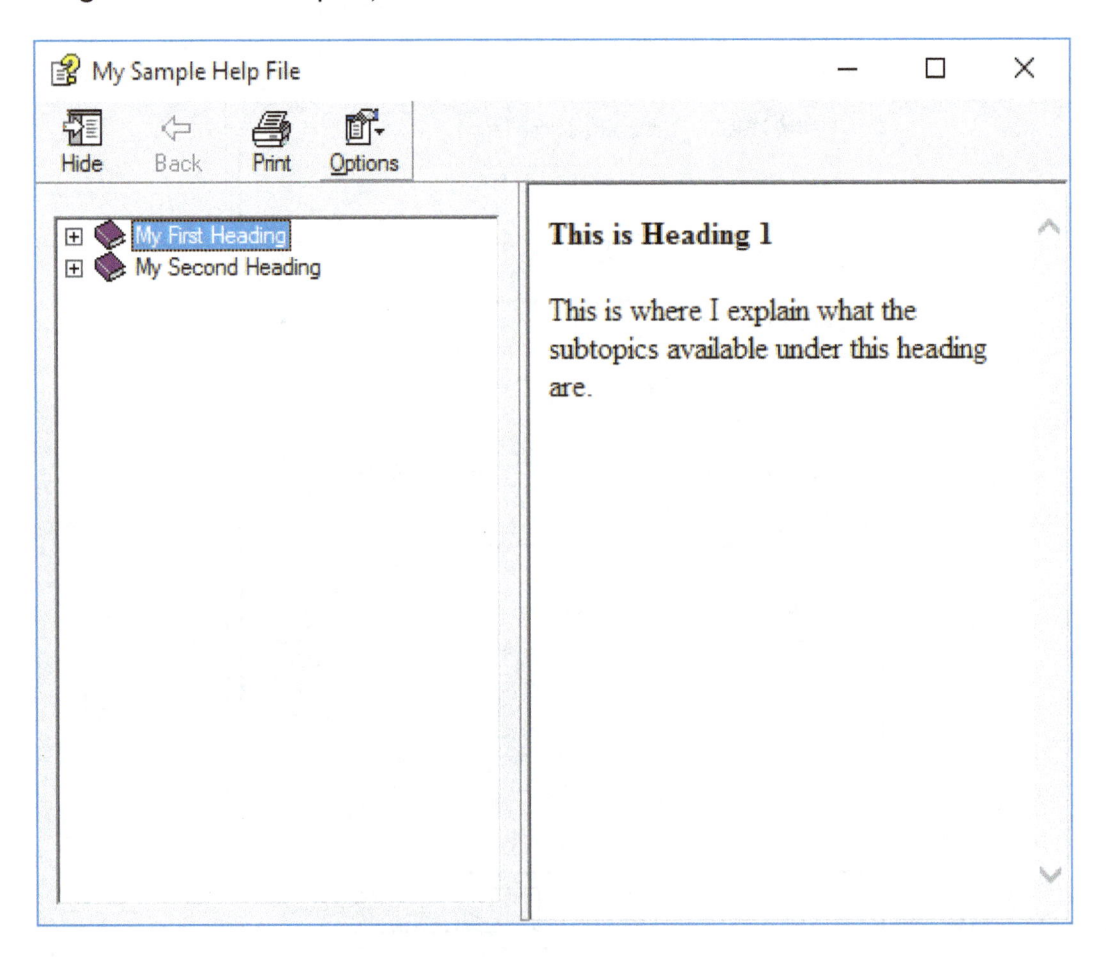

Click to see the various topics and headings displayed.

After all this work, you still only have a simple help file, nothing that rivals those seen in most applications. But, it is a very adequate help system. To improve your help system, you need to add more features. Investigate the HTML Help Workshop for information on tasks such as adding an index file, using context-sensitive help, adding search capabilities and adding graphics to the help system.

HelpProvider Control

[F1] HelpProvider

Once we have a completed HTML help system, we need to connect our Visual Basic application to the help file. You need to decide how you want your application to interact with the help system. We will demonstrate a simple approach. We will have the help system appear when the user presses <F1> or clicks some control related to obtaining help (menu item, button control). The Visual Basic **HelpProvider** control provides this connection.

HelpProvider **Properties**:

Name	Gets or sets the name of the help provider control (three letter prefix for label name is **hlp**).
HelpNamespace	Complete path to compiled help file (**CHM** file)

The **HelpNamespace** property is usually established at run-time. The help file is often installed in the application directory (**Bin\Debug** folder). If this is the case, we can use the **Application.StartupPath** parameter to establish **HelpNamespace**. You also must include the help file in any deployment package you build for your application.

To have the help file appear when a user presses <**F1**>, we set the **HelpNavigator** property of the application form to **TableofContents**. With this setting, the help file will appear displaying the **Table of Contents**, set to the default form.

To have the help file appear in a **Click** event, we use the **ShowHelp** method of the **Help** object. The Visual Basic **Help** object allows us to display HTML help files. To replicate the **<F1>** functionality above, we use the syntax:

```
Help.ShowHelp(Me, HelpProvider.HelpNamespace)
```

This line of code will display the specified help file.

Typical use of **HelpProvider** control:

> ➤ Set the **Name** property.
> ➤ Set **HelpNameSpace** property in code (file is usually in **Bin** folder of application).
> ➤ Set **HelpNavigator** property for form to **TableofContents**.
> ➤ Write code for events meant to display the help file (use **Help.ShowHelp**).

The steps above provide minimal, but sufficient, access to an HTML help system. If you need more functionality (context-sensitive help, help on individual controls, pop-up help, adding help to dialog boxes), consult the Visual Basic documentation on the **Help Provider** control.

Visual Basic Interface Design   5-81

Example 5-8

Authors Table Input Form (On-Line Help)

We will build a simple help system for our Authors Table Input Form and attach it to our application. Refer back to the notes to complete each step listed here.

1. Using an editor, prepare a single topic file (saved as **authors.htm** in the **VBDB\General\Class 5\Example 5-8\HelpFile** folder):

Authors Input Form

Available options for managing Authors database table:

Add New Record

Click the **Add New** button to add a record to the Authors database. Type in the Author Name (required), then Year Born (optional). Click **Save** to save the new record; click **Cancel** to ignore the new record.

Edit Record

Click the **Edit** button to edit the displayed record. Make any needed changes. The Author Name is required and the Year Born is optional. Click **Save** to save the changes; click **Cancel** to ignore the changes.

Delete Record

Click the **Delete** button to delete the displayed record.

Exit Program

Click the **Done** button to quit the application.

---

2. Using HTML Help Workshop, build a help project file, adding the topic file (no contents file) (**authors.hhp** in the **VBDB\General\Class 5\Example 5-8\HelpFile** folder).

3. Using HTML Help Workshop, compile and build the project file (**authors.chm** in the **VBDB\General\Class 5\Example 5-8\HelpFile** folder).

5-82   Visual Basic and Databases

4. Load Example 5-7 completed earlier. We will modify this example to include our help system. Copy **authors.chm** to the application's **Bin\Debug** folder (**Bin\x86\Debug** for **Access** version - you may have to create the folder first). Add a help provider control to the project – name it **hlpAuthors**. Set the **HelpNavigator** property of **frmAuthors** to **TableofContents**.

5. Add the shaded code near the top of the **frmAuthors Load** procedure. This code points to the help file in the project's application folder:

Access Database:

```
    Private Sub FrmAuthors_Load(ByVal sender As System.Object, ByVal e As System.EventArgs) Handles MyBase.Load
        Try
            'point to help file
            hlpAuthors.HelpNamespace = Application.StartupPath + "\authors.chm"
            'connect to books database
            BooksConnection = New OleDbConnection("Provider=Microsoft.ACE.OLEDB.12.0; Data Source = c:\VBDB\Working\BooksDB.accdb")
            BooksConnection.Open()
            'establish command object
              .
              .
              .
    End Sub
```

Visual Basic Interface Design   5-83

SQL Server Database:

```
  Private Sub FrmAuthors_Load(ByVal sender As System.Object,
ByVal e As System.EventArgs) Handles MyBase.Load
    Try
      'point to help file
      hlpAuthors.HelpNamespace = Application.StartupPath +
"\authors.chm"
      'connect to books database
      BooksConnection = New SqlConnection("Data
Source=.\SQLEXPRESS;
AttachDbFilename=C:\VBDB\Working\SQLBooksDB.mdf; Integrated
Security=True; Connect Timeout=30; User Instance=True")
      BooksConnection.Open()
       .
       .
       .
  End Sub
```

6. Add a button to the form. Assign a **Text** of **&Help** and a **Name** of **btnHelp**. The form now looks like this:

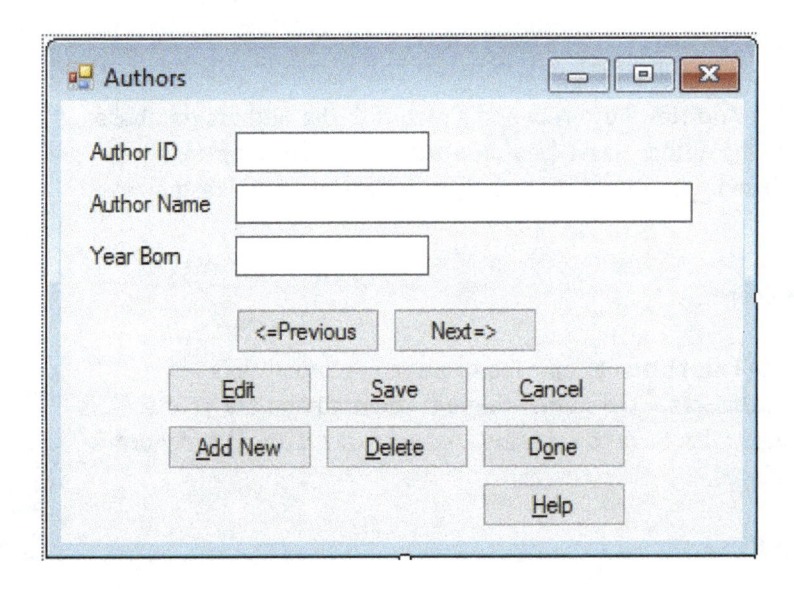

7. Use this code in the **btnHelp_Click** event to display the help file:

   ```
   Private Sub BtnHelp_Click(ByVal sender As System.Object, ByVal e As System.EventArgs) Handles btnHelp.Click
       Help.ShowHelp(Me, hlpAuthors.HelpNamespace)
   End Sub
   ```

8. Save (Access version saved in the **Example 5-8** folder in **VBDB\Access\Class 5** folder; SQL Server version saved in the **Example 5-8** folder in **VBDB\SQL Server\Class 5** folder) and run the application. Press <**F1**> or click **Help**. With either, you should see the help file:

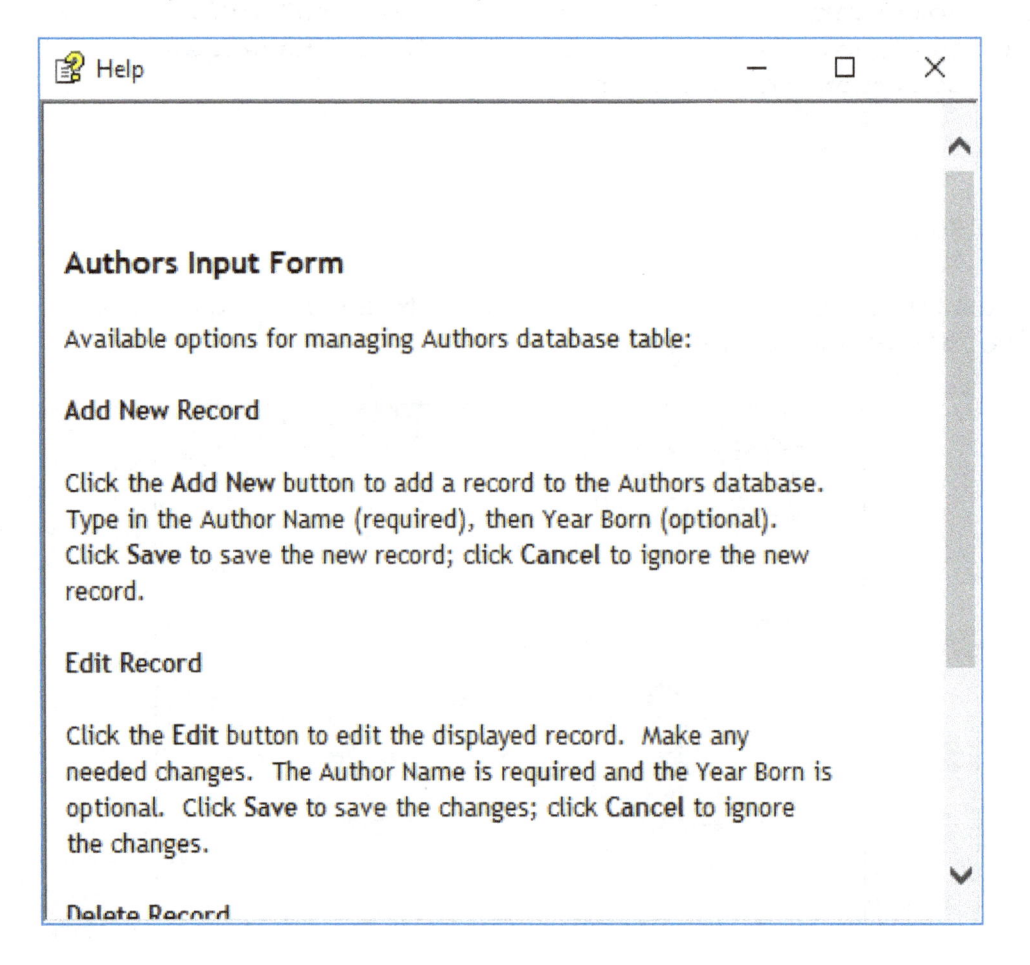

Application Testing

Our discussion of Visual Basic interface design has, for now, come to an end. And, we have a fairly complete interface for the books database Authors table. We, obviously, still need the remainder of the code that goes behind the buttons. We'll do that in the next chapter.

Once you have completed an application, you need to test it to make sure it performs as expected. If you are careful in building your application, no big surprises should appear in this final testing. In fact, the Visual Basic environment helps achieve this goal. The event-driven nature of Visual Basic makes it easy to build an application in stages, testing and debugging each stage as it is built. In other words, you don't have to have a complete application before testing can begin. We have done this with the Authors table example.

The event-driven nature of Visual Basic also makes it easy to modify an application. We will see in Chapter 6, as we modify the books database example, that we have made some omissions and errors in our design. But these omissions and errors will be easily corrected using the Visual Basic environment. These corrections will give you additional insight into application building and testing process.

Let others (particularly potential users) try your application and see if its use is as obvious as you planned it to be. Are the inputs and outputs of the project appropriate? Is application state clear? Implement and retest any necessary changes, based on user feedback. And, keep track of all feedback after you 'release' your application. This information can be used in future updates of your product.

Before leaving this chapter, let's look at some other Visual Basic controls that you might like to use in your database interface arsenal.

Other Controls

In addition to the standard Visual Basic controls discussed earlier in this chapter, there are many **other controls** that can be used to build a database interface. If not in the toolbox, these controls will have to be added to the Visual Basic toolbox before they can be used.

To load a control, make sure the toolbox is visible in the development environment. Choose **Choose Toolbox Items** from the Visual Basic **Tools** menu. Select **.NET Framework Components** in the resulting dialog:

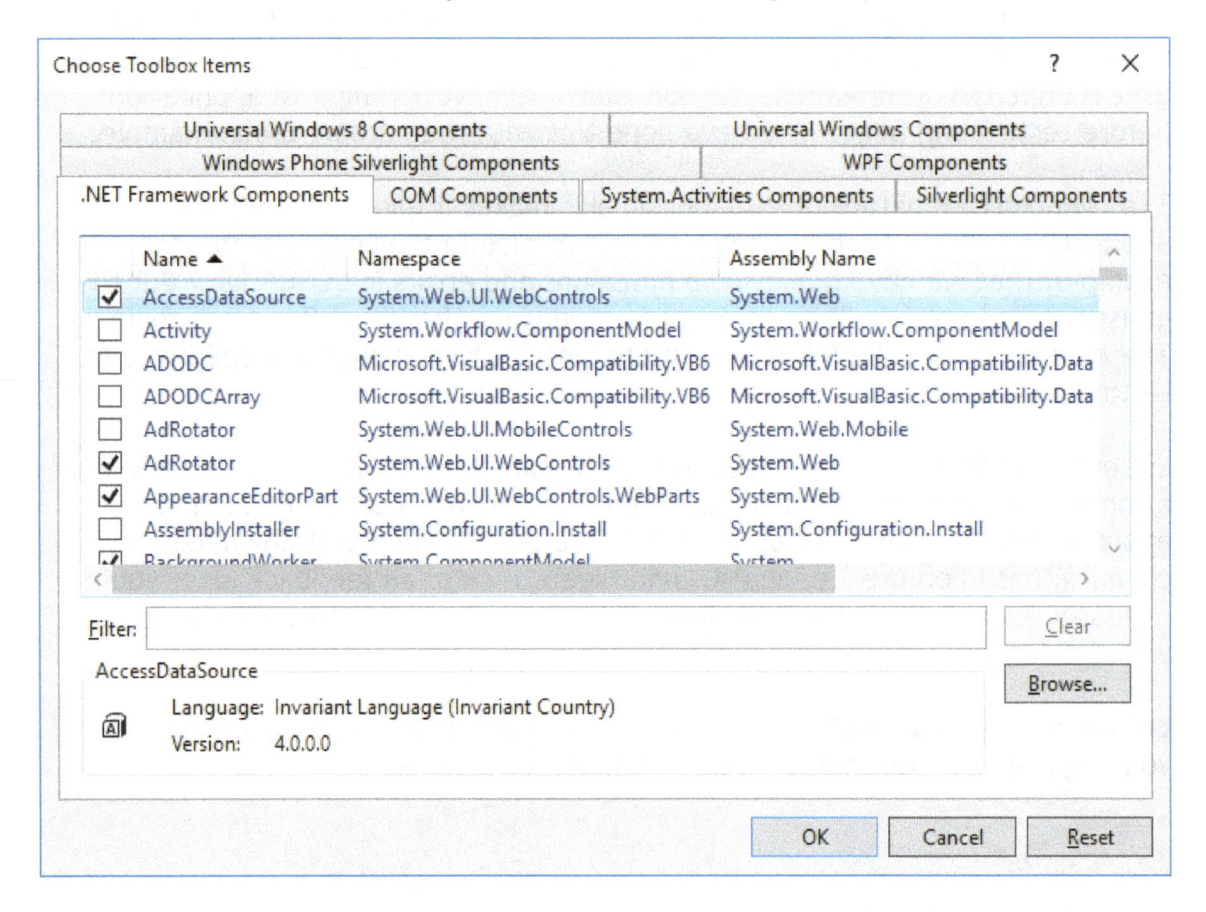

To add a control or controls, select the check box next to the desired selection(s). When done, choose **OK** and the selected control(s) will now appear in the toolbox. The Visual Basic on-line help system can provide details for usage.

Here, we look at several other controls (some data bound, some not) and how they can be used with a Visual Basic interface.

MaskedTextBox Control

#_ MaskedTextBox

The **masked text box control** is a data bound control used to prompt users for data input using a mask pattern. It works like a text box, but the mask allows you to specify exactly the desired input format. In a **database**, this control could be used to prompt for a date, a time, number, or currency value. Or it could be used to prompt for something that follows a pattern, like a phone number or social security number. Use of this control can eliminate many of the entry validation problems mentioned earlier in the chapter. If needed, to load this control into the toolbox, select **MaskedTextBox** from the **.NET Framework Components** dialog box.

Masked Text Box **Properties**:

Mask	Determines the type of information that is input into the control. It uses characters to define the type of input. Check on-line help for mask formatting.
PromptChar	Character used for missing information.
Text	Contains data entered into the control (including all prompt characters of the input mask). This is the property bound to the database.
TextMaskFormat	Used to indicate if the **Text** property includes literal and prompts used.

Masked Text Box **Events**:

Leave	Event called when the user leaves the control.
LostFocus	Event called when control loses focus.
MaskInputRejected	Event called when the data being entered by the user does not match the input mask.

Typical use of **MaskedTextBox** control:

> - Set the **Name** property. Initialize **Text** property to desired string. Set **Mask** property.
> - In code, give **Focus** to control when needed. Read **Text** property when **Leave** event occurs.
> - You may also want to change the **Font**, **Backcolor** and **Forecolor** properties.

This control features built-in input validation to lessen your tasks as a programmer. We will use the masked edit control in some of our example applications in later chapters.

NumericUpDown Control

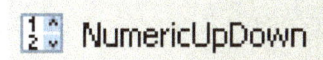

[1̃2̃] NumericUpDown

The **NumericUpDown** control is used to obtain a numeric input. It looks like a text box control with two small arrows. Clicking the arrows changes the displayed value, which ranges from a specified minimum to a specified maximum. The user can even type in a value, if desired. Such controls are useful for supplying a date in a month or are used as volume controls in some Windows multimedia applications.

NumericUpDown **Properties**:

Name	Gets or sets the name of the numeric updown (three letter prefix for numeric updown name is **nud**).
BackColor	Get or sets the numeric updown background color.
BorderStyle	Gets or sets the border style for the updown control.
Font	Gets or sets font name, style, size.
ForeColor	Gets or sets color of text or graphics.
Increment	Gets or sets the value to increment or decrement the updown control when the up or down buttons are clicked.
Maximum	Gets or sets the maximum value for the updown control.
Minimum	Gets or sets the minimum value for the updown control.
ReadOnly	Gets or sets a value indicating whether the text may be changed by the use of the up or down buttons only.
TextAlign	Gets or sets the alignment of text in the numeric updown.
Value	Gets or sets the value assigned to the updown control.

NumericUpDown **Methods**:

DownButton   Decrements the value of the updown control.
UpButton   Increments the value of the updown control.

NumericUpDown **Events**:

Leave   Occurs when the updown control loses focus.
ValueChanged   Occurs when the Value property has been changed in some way.

The **Value** property can be changed by clicking either of the arrows or, optionally by typing a value. If using the arrows, the value will always lie between **Minimum** and **Maximum**. If the user can type in a value, you have no control over what value is typed. However, once the control loses focus, the typed value will be compared to Minimum and Maximum and any adjustments made. Hence, if you allow typed values, only check the Value property in the Leave event.

Typical use of **NumericUpDown** control:

> Set the **Name, Minimum** and **Maximum** properties. Initialize **Value** property. Decide on value for **ReadOnly**.
> Monitor **ValueChanged** (or **Leave**) event for changes in Value.
> You may also want to change the **Font, Backcolor** and **Forecolor** properties.

The NumericUpDown control is a 'point-and-click' type control that can be used in place of a user's typed input. We will use the NumericUpDown control in some of our example applications in later chapters.

TabControl Control

📁 TabControl

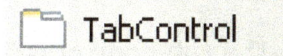

The **TabControl** control provides an easy way to present several dialogs or screens of information on a single form. This is the same interface seen in many commercial Windows applications. The tab control provides a group of tabs, each of which acts as a container (works just like a group box or panel) for other controls. In particular, groups of radio buttons within a tab 'page' operate as an independent group. Only one tab can be active at a time. Using this control is easy. Just build each tab container as a separate group: add controls, set properties, and write code like you do for any application. Navigation from one tab to the next is simple: just click on the corresponding tab.

TabControl **Properties:**

Name	Gets or sets the name of the tab control (three letter prefix for control name is **tab**).
BackColor	Get or sets the tab control background color.
BorderStyle	Gets or sets the border style for the tab control.
Font	Gets or sets font name, style, size.
ForeColor	Gets or sets color of text or graphics.
ItemSize	Size structure determining tab size.
SelectedIndex	Gets or sets the currently displayed tab index.
SizeMode	Determines how tabs are sized.
TabPages	Collection describing each tab page.

TabControl **Events**:

    SelectedIndexChanged   Occurs when the **SelectedIndex** property changes.

The most important property for the tab control is **TabPages**. It is used to design each tab (known as a **TabPage**). Choosing the **TabPages** property in the Properties window and clicking the ellipsis that appears will display the **TabPage Collection Editor**. With this editor, you can add, delete, insert and move tab pages. To add a tab page, click the **Add** button. A name and index will be assigned to a tab. There are two tabs added initially so the editor appears like this:

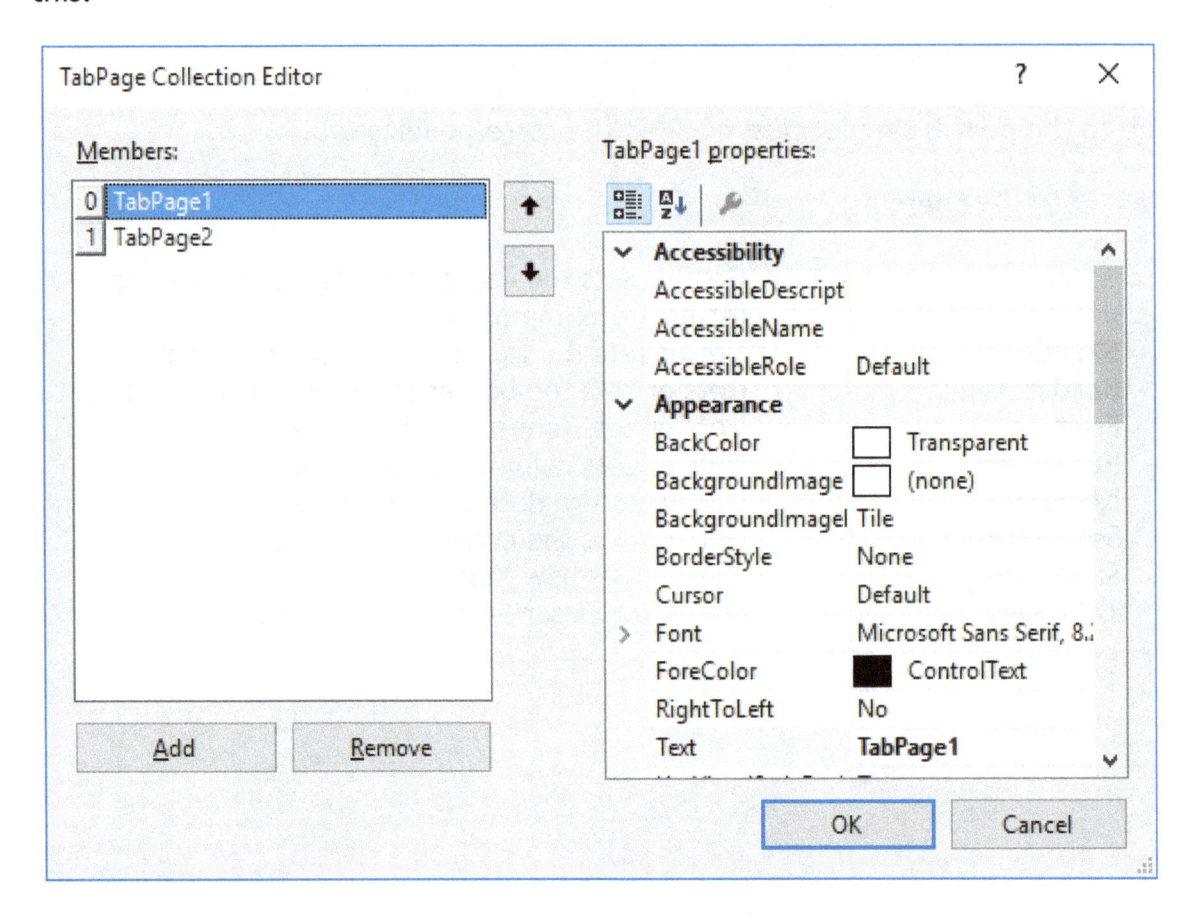

Add as many tab pages as you like. The tab page 'array' is zero-based; hence, if you have N tabs, the first is index 0, the last index N – 1. You can change any property you desire in the **Properties** area.

Visual Basic Interface Design 5-93

TabPage **Properties**:

Name	Gets or sets the name of the tab page (three letter prefix for control name is **tab**).
BackColor	Get or sets the tab page background color.
BorderStyle	Gets or sets the border style for the tab page.
Font	Gets or sets font name, style, size.
ForeColor	Gets or sets color of text or graphics.
Text	Titling information appearing on tab.

When done, click **OK** to leave the TabPage Collection Editor.

The next step is to add controls to each 'page' of the tab control. This is straightforward. Simply display the desired tab page by clicking on the tab. Then place controls on the tab page, treating the page like a group box or panel control. Make sure your controls become 'attached' to the tab page. You can still place controls on the form that are not associated with any tab. As the programmer, you need to know which tab is active (**SelectedIndex** property). And, you need to keep track of which controls are available with each tab page.

Typical use of **TabControl** control:

- Set the **Name** property and size appropriately.
- Establish each tab page using the **TabPage Collection Editor**.
- Add controls to tabs and form.
- Write code for the various events associated with controls on the tab control and form.

The tab control is becoming a very popular control in Windows applications. It allows you to put a lot of 'input power' into a single form - minimizing the need for multi-form applications. We will use the tab control in a Weather Monitor example in Chapter 10.

ToolStrip (Toolbar) Control

ToolStrip

Almost all Windows applications these days use toolbars. A toolbar provides quick access to the most frequently used menu commands in an application. In a database application, it could be used to add, delete, or edit records. It could be used to access database reports or obtain different database views. The **ToolStrip** control (also referred to as the **Toolbar** control) is a mini-application in itself. It provides everything you need to design and implement a toolbar into your application. Possible uses for this control include: provide a consistent interface between applications with matching toolbars, place commonly used functions in an easily-accessed space and provide an intuitive, graphical interface for your application.

ToolStrip **Properties**:

Name	Gets or sets the name of the toolstrip (toolbar) control (three letter prefix for label name is **tlb**).
BackColor	Background color of toolstrip.
Items	Gets the collection of controls assigned to the toolstrip control.
LayoutStyle	Establishes whether toolbar is vertical or horizontal.
Dock	Establishes location of toolbar on form.

Visual Basic Interface Design 5-95

The primary property of concern is the **Items** collection. This establishes each item in the toolbar. Choosing the **Items** property in the Properties window and clicking the ellipsis that appears will display the **Items Collection Editor**. With this editor, you can add, delete, insert and move items. We will look at adding just two types of items: **ToolStripButton** and **ToolStripSeparator** (used to separate tool bar buttons). To add a button, make sure **ToolStripButton** appears in the drop-down box and click the **Add** button. A name will be assigned to a button. After adding one button, the editor will look like this:

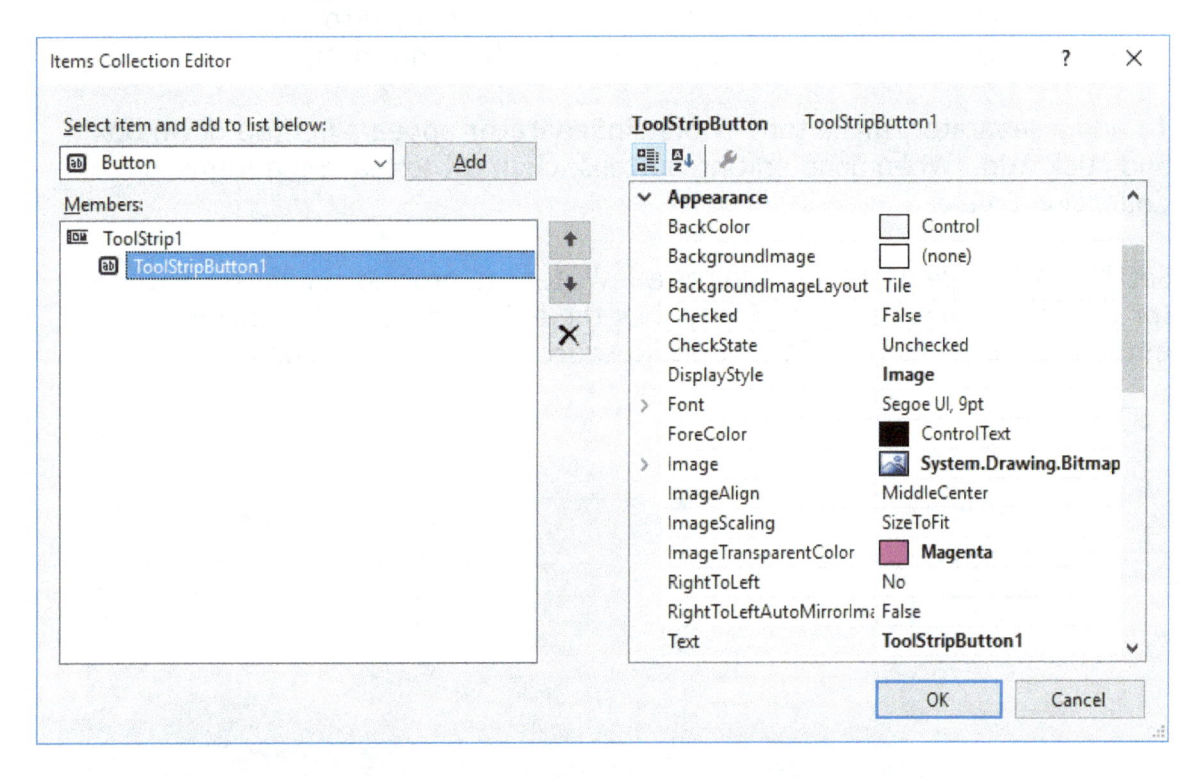

Add as many buttons as you like. You can change any property you desire in the **Properties** area.

ToolStripButton Properties:

Name	Gets or sets the name of the button (three letter prefix for control name is **tlb**).
DisplayStyle	Sets whether image, text or both are displayed on button.
Image	Image to display on button.
Text	Caption information on the button, often blank.
TextImageRelation	Where text appears relative to image.
ToolTipText	Text to display in button tool tip.

To add a separator, make sure **ToolStripSeparator** appears in drop-down box and click **Add**. When done editing buttons, click **OK** to leave the Items Collection Editor.

Setting the **Image** property requires a few steps (a process similar to that used for the picture box control). First, click the ellipsis next to the **Image** property in the property window. This **Select Resource** window will appear:

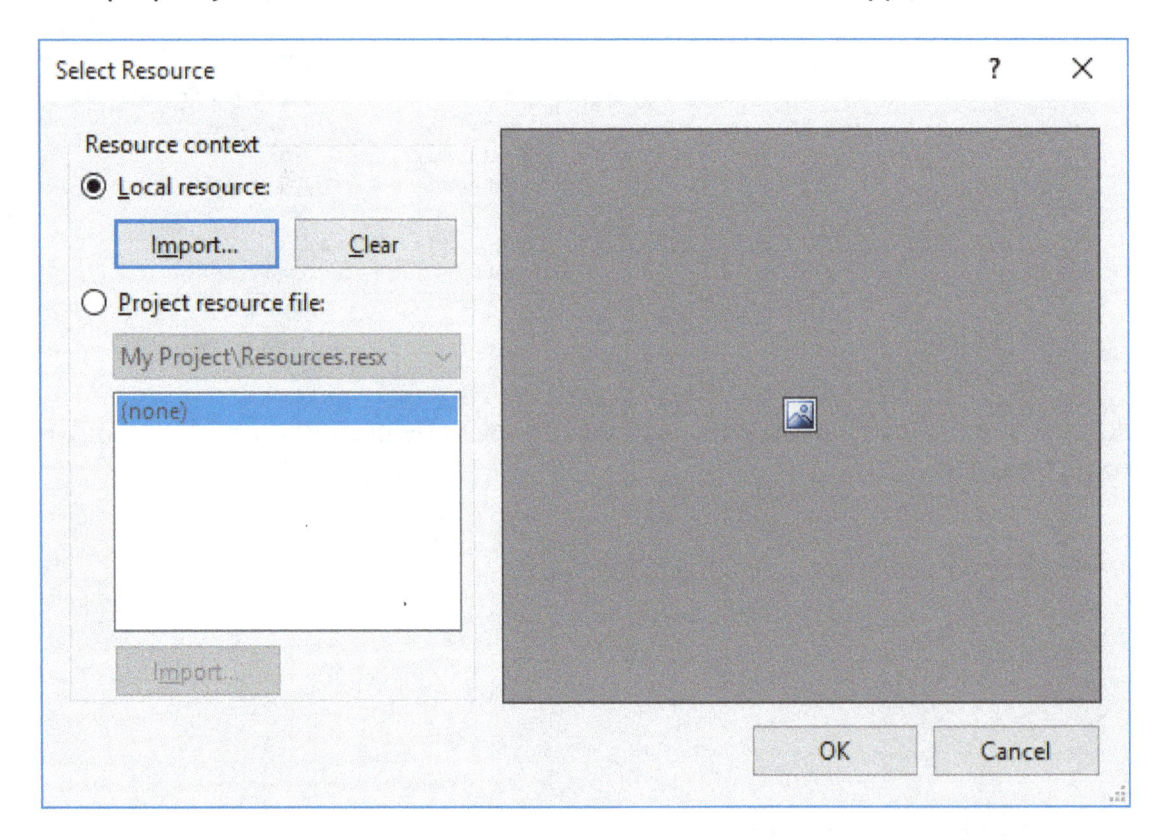

The images will be a local resource, so select the **Local resource** radio button and click the **Import** button.

Visual Basic Interface Design   5-97

An **Open** window will display graphics files (if you want to see an **ico** file, you must change **Files of type** to **All Files**). In the **VBDB\General\Class 5** folder is a folder named **Toolbar Graphics**. In this folder, there are many bitmap files for toolbar use:

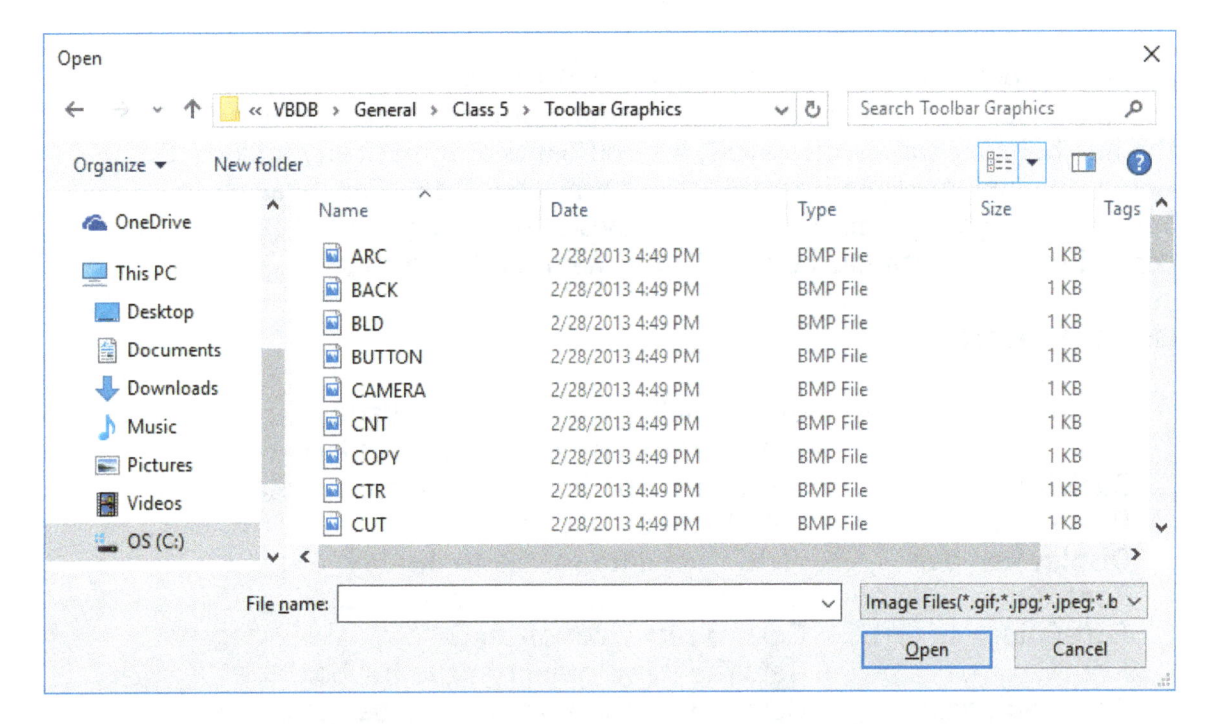

Select the desired file and click **Open**. Once an image is selected, click **OK** in the **Select Resource** window. It will be assigned to the **Image** property

After setting up the toolbar, you need to write code for the **Click** event for each toolbar button. This event is the same **Click** event we encounter for button controls.

Typical use of **ToolStrip** control:

> ➤ Set the **Name** property and desired location.
> ➤ Decide on image, text, and tooltip text for each button.
> ➤ Establish each button/separator using the **Items Collection Editor**.
> ➤ Write code for the each toolbar button's **Click** event.

The toolbar is a very powerful and professional tool. And, it's easy to implement and use. Try to use it whenever it fits the design of your interface.

ListBox Control

A **ListBox** control displays a list of items (with as many items as you like) from which the user can select one or more items. If the number of items exceeds the number that can be displayed, a scroll bar is automatically added. Both single item and multiple item selections are supported. For database applications, you can display multiple rows of data (a given field) in the same control (see the **DataSource** and **DisplayMember** properties).

ListBox **Properties**:

Name	Gets or sets the name of the list box (three letter prefix for list box name is **lst**).
BackColor	Get or sets the list box background color.
DataSource	Data table to bind control to.
DisplayMember	Field from data source to display.
Font	Gets or sets font name, style, size.
ForeColor	Gets or sets color of text.
Items	Gets the Items object of the list box.
SelectedIndex	Gets or sets the zero-based index of the currently selected item in a list box.
SelectedIndices	Zero-based array of indices of all currently selected items in the list box.
SelectedItem	Gets or sets the currently selected item in the list box.
SelectedItems	SelectedItems object of the list box.
SelectedValue	The value provided by/to the ValueMember for data binding.
SelectionMode	Gets or sets the method in which items are selected in list box (allows single or multiple selections).
Sorted	Gets or sets a value indicating whether the items in list box are sorted alphabetically.
Text	Text of currently selected item in list box.
TopIndex	Gets or sets the index of the first visible item in list box.
ValueMember	The data source field corresponding to same record shown by DisplayMember.

ListBox **Methods**:

ClearSelected	Unselects all items in the list box.
FindString	Finds the first item in the list box that starts with the specified string.
GetSelected	Returns a value indicating whether the specified item is selected.
SetSelected	Selects or clears the selection for the specified item in a list box.

ListBox **Events**:

SelectedIndexChanged	Occurs when the SelectedIndex property has changed.

One use for the data bound list control is to fill the list (**DisplayMember**) from a database table (**DataSource**), then allow selections. This allows us to list all values of a particular field in a database table. The selections can be used by any control on a form, whether it is data bound or not. For the **BooksDB.accdb** database **Authors** table we've been using, if we display the **Author** field, a list box will show:

```
Aaron, Alex
Aaron, Bud
Aarts, Jan
Abas, S.J.
Abbey, Michael
Abdelguerfi, Mahdi
Abel, David
Abel, Peter
Abelson, Amanda
Abelson, Harold
Abernethy, Kenneth
Abernety, Ken
Abiteboul, S.
Abiteboul, Serge
Abnous, Raxmik
Abnous, Razmik
```

More complex data binding (using the **SelectedValue** and **ValueMember** properties) is possible. We will look at this complex binding as we develop a management system for the books database in later chapters (see Example 6-9).

Some further discussion is need to use the list box **Items** object, **SelectedItems** object and **SelectionMode** property. The Items object has its own properties to specify the items in the list box. It also has its own methods for adding and deleting items in the list box. Two properties of use: **Item** is a zero-based array of the items in the list and **Count** is the number of items in the list. Hence, the first item in a list box named **lstExample** is:

    lstExample.Items.Item(0)

The last item in the list is:

    lstExample.Items.Item(lstExample.Items.Count - 1)

The minus one is needed because of the zero-based array.

To add an item to a list box, use the **Add** method, to delete an item, use the **Remove** or **RemoveAt** method and to clear a list box use the **Clear** method. For our example list box, the respective commands are:

Add Item:	`lstExample.Items.Add(ItemToAdd)`
Delete Item:	`lstExample.Items.Remove(ItemToRemove)`
	`lstExample.Items.RemoveAt(IndexofItemToRemove)`
Clear list box:	`lstExample.Items.Clear`

List boxes normally list string data types, though other types are possible. Note, when removing items, that indices for subsequent items in the list change following a removal.

In a similar fashion, the **SelectedItems** object has its own properties to specify the currently selected items in the list box Of particular use is **Count** which tells you how many items are selected. This value, in conjunction with the SelectedIndices array, identifies the set of selected items.

The **SelectionMode** property specifies whether you want single item selection or multiple selections. When the property is **SelectionMode.One**, you can select only one item (works like a group of radio buttons). When the SelectionMode property is set to **SelectionMode.MultiExtended**, pressing <Shift> and clicking the mouse or pressing <Shift> and one of the arrow keys extends the selection from the previously selected item to the current item. Pressing <Ctrl> and clicking the mouse selects or deselects an item in the list. When the property is set to **SelectionMode.MultiSimple**, a mouse click or pressing the spacebar selects or deselects an item in the list.

Typical use of **ListBox** control:

- Set **Name** property, **SelectionMode** property and populate **Items** object (usually in **Form_Load** procedure).
- If using with database, set **DataSource** property to desired data table and **DisplayMember** property to corresponding data table field.
- Monitor **SelectedIndexChanged** event for individual selections.
- Use **SelectedIndex** and **SelectIndices** properties to determine selected items.

ComboBox Control

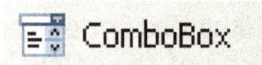

		ComboBox

The **combo box control** is nearly identical to the list box, hence we won't look at a separate set of properties or another example. A primary difference between the two controls is the way data is displayed - the combo control has a list box portion and a text box portion that displays the selected item. And, with the combo control, the user is (optionally) given the opportunity to type in a choice not in the list box.

As mentioned, data display is different with the combo control. Display is established by the **DropDownStyle** property:

Style	Description
DropDown	Drop-down list box, user can change selection
Simple	Displayed list box, user can change selection
DropDownList	Drop-down list box, user cannot change selection

When using the **Simple** style, make sure you sufficiently size the control (so the list box portion appears) when it is placed on the form.

Typical use of **ComboBox** control:

> - Set **Name** property, **DropDownStyle** property and populate **Items** object (usually in **Form_Load** procedure).
> - If using with database, set **DataSource** property to desired data table and **DisplayMember** property to corresponding data table field.
> - Monitor **SelectedIndexChanged** event for individual selections.
> - Use **SelectedIndex** or **Text** properties to determine selected item.

When should you use the combo control instead of the list box control? The combo control is an excellent data entry control. Its advantage over the list box is that it provides experienced users the ability to type in values they know are correct, speeding up the data entry process. The list box control does not allow any typing. It is also a good control when you are short on form space. Using the **DropDownList** style replicates the functionality of the list box control without needing space for the list box.

DataGridView Control

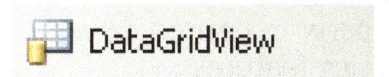

The **data grid view control** tool is one of the most useful data bound controls. It can display an entire database table. The table can then be edited as desired. Recall we used this control in our SQL Tester program in Chapter 4.

The data bound grid control is in a class by itself, when considering its capabilities. It is essentially a separate, highly functional program. It has one primary property:

DataSource   Name of the data table to display.

The data grid view control is a collection of **DataColumn** objects, corresponding to fields in the table, and **DataRow** objects, corresponding to records. Cells can be accessed and edited via mouse operations or programmatically.

For the **BooksDB.accdb** database, if we display the **Authors** table (**DataSource** property) we've been using in a data grid view, we will see:

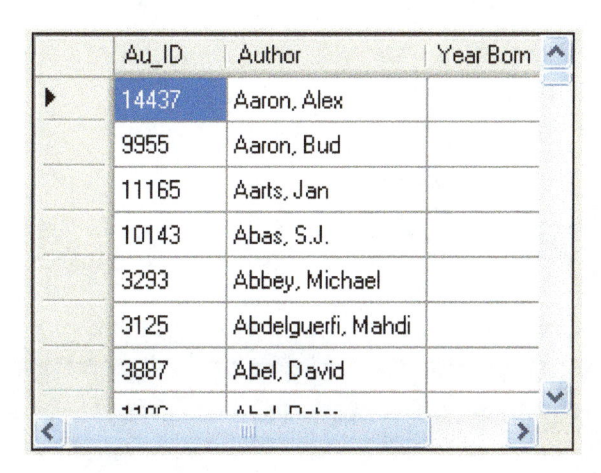

Au_ID	Author	Year Born
14437	Aaron, Alex	
9955	Aaron, Bud	
11165	Aarts, Jan	
10143	Abas, S.J.	
3293	Abbey, Michael	
3125	Abdelguerfi, Mahdi	
3887	Abel, David	

Typical use of **DataGridView** control:

> ➢ Set **Name** property.
> ➢ Set **DataSource** property to desired data table.
> ➢ Add any desired editing features.

You are encouraged to further study the data grid view control (properties, events, methods) as you progress in your database studies. We will use it in applications studied in later chapters.

MonthCalendar Control

MonthCalendar

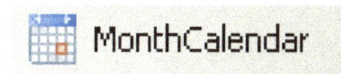

The **MonthCalendar** control allows a user to select a date. It is a very easy to use interface – just point and click. This control is useful for ordering information, making reservations or choosing the current date. It can be used to select a single date or a range of dates.

MonthCalendar **Properties:**

Name	Gets or sets the name of the month calendar (three letter prefix for label name is **cal**).
BackColor	Get or sets the month calendar background color.
CalendarDimensions	Gets or sets the number of columns and rows of months displayed.
FirstDayOfWeek	Gets or sets the first day of the week as displayed in the month calendar.
Font	Gets or sets font name, style, size.
ForeColor	Gets or sets color of text or graphics.
MaxDate	Gets or sets the maximum allowable date.
MaxSelectionCount	The maximum number of days that can be selected in a month calendar control.
MinDate	Gets or sets the minimum allowable date.
SelectionEnd	Gets or sets the end date of the selected range of dates.
SelectionRange	Retrieves the selected range of dates for a month calendar control.
SelectionStart	Gets or sets the start date of the selected range of dates.
ShowToday	Gets or sets a value indicating whether the date represent by the TodayDate property is shown at the bottom of the control.
ShowTodayCircle	Gets or sets a value indicating whether today's date is circled.
TodayDate	Gets or sets the value that is used by MonthCalendar as today's date.

MonthCalendar **Methods:**

> **SetDate**   Sets date as the current selected date.

MonthCalendar **Events:**

> **DateChanged**   Occurs when the date in the MonthCalendar changes.
> **DateSelected**   Occurs when a date is selected.

Typical use of **MonthCalendar** control:

- ➢ Set the **Name** property. Set **MaxSelectionCount** (set to 1 if just picking a single date).
- ➢ Monitor **DateChanged** and/or **DateSelected** events to determine date value(s). Values are between **SelectionStart** and **SelectionEnd** properties.

DateTimePicker Control

DateTimePicker

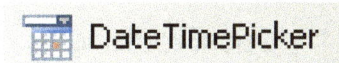

The **DateTimePicker** control works like the MonthCalendar control with a different interface and formatting options. It allows the user to select a single date. The selected date appears in a combo box. The calendar portion is available as a 'drop down.' This control can also be used to select a time; we won't look at that option.

DateTimePicker **Properties:**

Name	Gets or sets the name of the date/time picker control (three letter prefix for label name is **dtp**).
BackColor	Get or sets the control background color.
Font	Gets or sets font name, style, size.
ForeColor	Gets or sets color of text or graphics.
Format	Gets or sets the format of the date displayed in the control.
MaxDate	Gets or sets the maximum allowable date.
MinDate	Gets or sets the minimum allowable date.
Value	Gets or sets the date value assigned to the control.

DateTimePicker **Events:**

ValueChanged   Occurs when the **Value** property changes.

Typical use of **DateTimePicker** control:

- Set the **Name** and Format properties.
- When needed, read **Value** property for selected date.

OpenFileDialog Control

OpenFileDialog

In all examples studied in this course, the database name has been assumed to be known at design time (before running the application). There will be times when this is not true. For example, say a schoolteacher uses a database application to keep track of grades. There will database files for each class. When the teacher starts the application, he or she needs to specify which particular database file is being accessed and that file needs to be opened at run-time. Not only do we need the capability to open a user specified file, but we also need to be able to save database files with user specified names.

What we need from the user, whether opening or saving files is a complete path to the filename of interest. We could provide a text box and ask the user to type the path, but that's only asking for trouble. We would have to validate existence of drives, directories, and files! Fortunately, we can use the Windows standard interface for working with files. Visual Basic provides this interface through the **common dialog controls**. These controls display the same interface you see when opening or saving a file in any Windows application. Such an interface is familiar to any Windows user and gives your application a professional look. And, some context-sensitive help is available while the interface is displayed. Let's look first at the **open file dialog control**.

OpenFileDialog **Properties**:

Name	Gets or sets the name of the open file dialog (I usually name this control **dlgOpen**).
AddExtension	Gets or sets a value indicating whether the dialog box automatically adds an extension to a file name if the user omits the extension.
CheckFileExists	Gets or sets a value indicating whether the dialog box displays a warning if the user specifies a file name that does not exist.
CheckPathExists	Gets or sets a value indicating whether the dialog box displays a warning if the user specifies a path that does not exist.
DefaultExt	Gets or sets the default file extension.
FileName	Gets or sets a string containing the file name selected in the file dialog box.
Filter	Gets or sets the current file name filter string, which determines the choices that appear in "Files of type" box.
FilterIndex	Gets or sets the index of the filter currently selected in the file dialog box.
InitialDirectory	Gets or sets the initial directory displayed by the file dialog box.
Title	Gets or sets the file dialog box title.

OpenFileDialog **Methods**:

ShowDialog	Displays the dialog box. Returned value indicates which button was clicked by user (**OK** or **Cancel**).

To use the **OpenFileDialog** control, we add it to our application the same as any control. Since the OpenFileDialog control has no immediate user interface (you control when it appears), the control does not appear on the form at design time. Such Visual Basic appear in a 'tray' below the form in the IDE Design window. Once added, we set a few properties. Then, we write code to make the dialog box appear when desired. The user then makes selections and closes the dialog box. At this point, we use the provided information for our tasks.

The **ShowDialog** method is used to display the **OpenFileDialog** control. For a control named **dlgOpen**, the appropriate code is:

```
dlgOpen.ShowDialog()
```

And the displayed dialog box is similar to this:

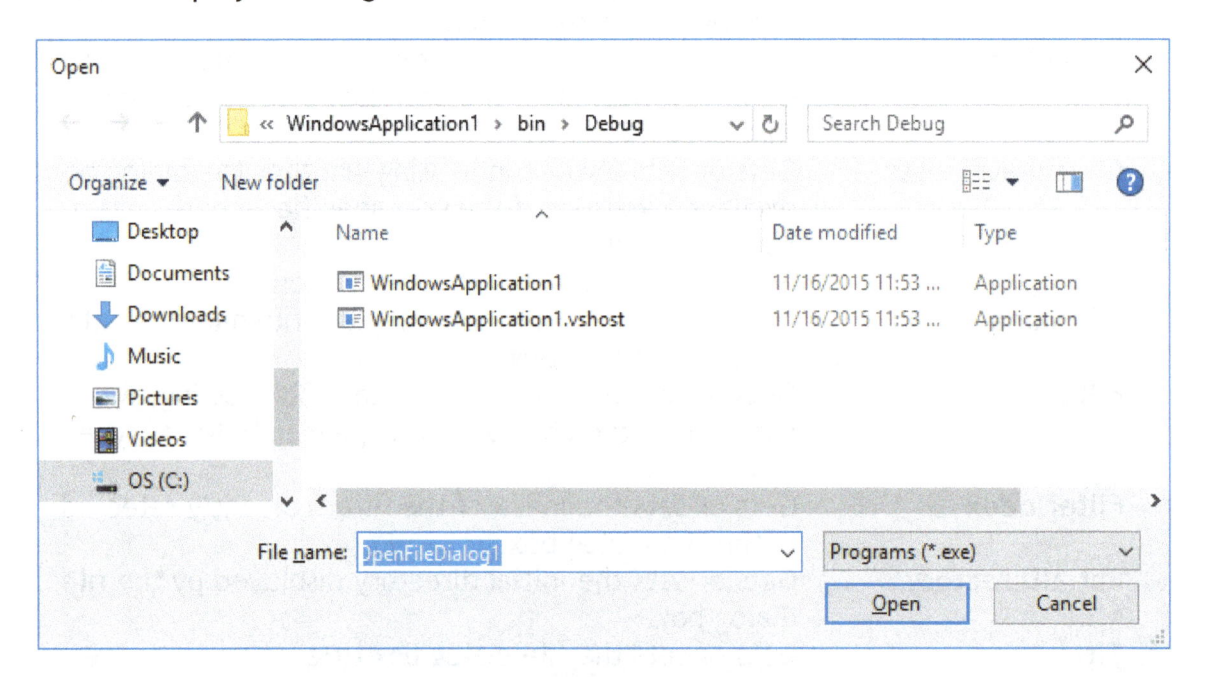

The user selects a file using the dialog control (or types a name in the **File name** box). The file type is selected form the **Files of type** box next to the **File name** box (values here set with the **Filter** property). Once selected, the **Open** button is clicked. **Cancel** can be clicked to cancel the open operation. The ShowDialog method returns the clicked button. It returns **DialogResult.OK** if Open is clicked and returns **DialogResult.Cancel** if Cancel is clicked. The nice thing about this control is that it can validate the file name before it is returned to the application. The **FileName** property contains the complete path to the selected file.

Typical use of **OpenFileDialog** control:

> ➢ Set the **Name, Filter**, and **Title** properties.
> ➢ Use **ShowDialog** method to display dialog box.
> ➢ Read **FileName** property to determine selected file

SaveFileDialog Control

SaveFileDialog

To obtain a file name for saving we use the **SaveFileDialog** control. This control insures that any path selected for saving a file exists and that if an existing file is selected, the user has agreed to overwriting that file.

SaveFileDialog **Properties:**

Name	Gets or sets the name of the save file dialog (I usually name this control **dlgSave**).
AddExtension	Indicates whether the dialog box automatically adds an extension to a file name if the user omits the extension.
CheckFileExists	Indicates whether the whether the dialog box displays a warning if the user specifies a file name that does not exist. Useful if you want the user to save to an existing file.
CheckPathExists	Indicates whether the dialog box displays a warning if the user specifies a path that does not exist.
CreatePrompt	Indicates whether the dialog box prompts the user for permission to create a file if the user specifies a file that does not exist.
DefaultExt	Gets or sets the default file extension.
FileName	Gets or sets a string containing the file name selected in the file dialog box.
Filter	Gets or sets the current file name filter string, which determines the choices that appear in "Files of type" box.
FilterIndex	Gets or sets the index of the filter currently selected in the file dialog box.
InitialDirectory	Gets or sets the initial directory displayed by the file dialog box.
OverwritePrompt	Indicates whether the dialog box displays a warning if the user specifies a file name that already exists. Default value is True.
Title	Gets or sets the file dialog box title.

SaveFileDialog **Methods**:

    ShowDialog   Displays the dialog box. Returned value indicates which button was clicked by user (**OK** or **Cancel**).

The **SaveFileDialog** control will appear in the tray area of the design window. The **ShowDialog** method is used to display the **SaveFileDialog** control. For a control named **dlgSave**, the appropriate code is:

```
dlgSave.ShowDialog()
```

And the displayed dialog box is similar to this:

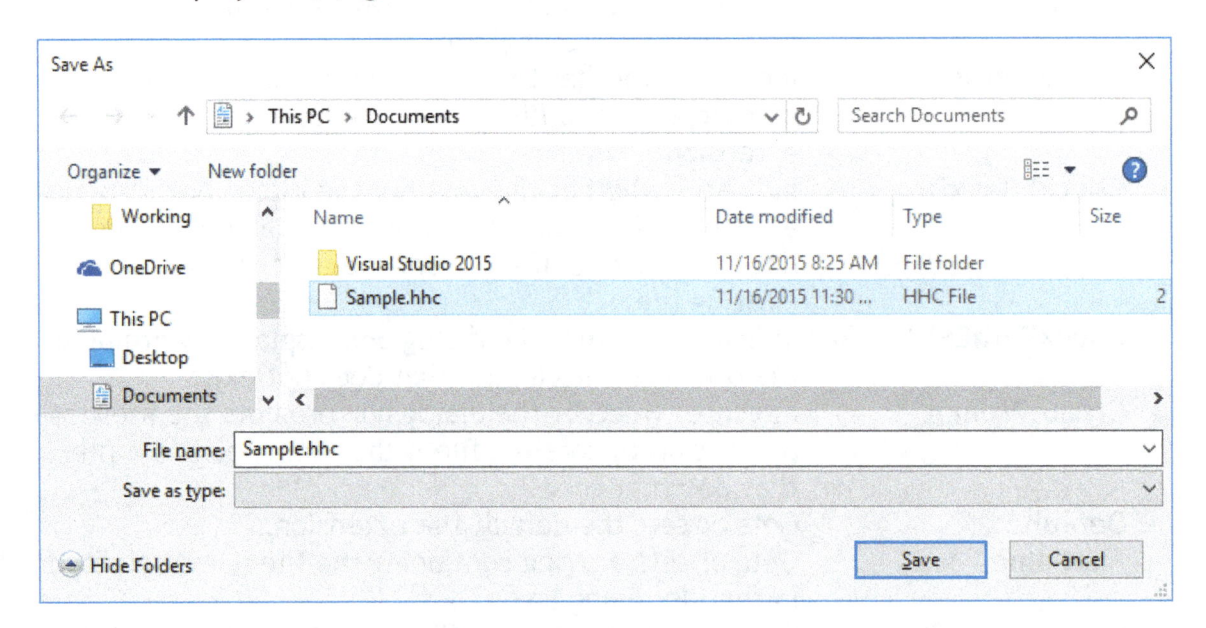

Visual Basic Interface Design 5-113

The user types a name in the File name box (or selects a file using the dialog control). The file type is selected form the **Files of type** box (values here set with the **Filter** property). Once selected, the **Save** button is clicked. **Cancel** can be clicked to cancel the save operation. If the user selects an existing file and clicks **Save**, the following dialog will appear:

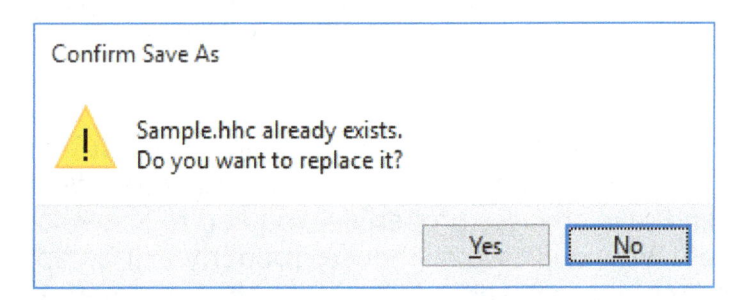

> Confirm Save As
>
> ⚠ Sample.hhc already exists.
> Do you want to replace it?
>
> [Yes] [No]

This is the aforementioned protection against inadvertently overwriting an existing file.

The ShowDialog method returns the clicked button. It returns **DialogResult.OK** if Save is clicked and returns **DialogResult.Cancel** if Cancel is clicked. The **FileName** property contains the complete path to the selected file.

Typical use of **SaveFileDialog** control:

- Set the **Name, DefaultExt, Filter**, and **Title** properties.
- Use **ShowDialog** method to display dialog box.
- Read **FileName** property to determine selected file

Summary

There is wealth of material covered here. You now have a complete reference to the Visual Basic toolbox and how those tools can be used for proper interface design. The Visual Basic interface is very important and we wanted to make sure you have many tools at your disposal. This will make your (and your user's) task much easier.

Even with all this work, our interface is not complete. We still need code that allows us to edit, add, and delete records from a database. We need to know how to validate and save changes properly. We need to know how to 'undo' unwanted changes. We need to know how to properly exit an application. These topics, and more, are covered in the next chapter where we learn to design the total database management system.

Example 5-9

Publishers Table Input Form

In this chapter, we built the framework for an interface that allows us to maintain the **Authors** table in the books database (Access- **BooksDB.accdb**, SQL Server – **SQLBooksDB.mdf**). This framework will be modified in the next chapter and implemented as part of a complete database management system. This database management system will also need interfaces to maintain the **Publishers** and **Titles** tables. The Titles table interface is a little tricky, in that it uses foreign keys to reference information in other tables. We will develop this interface in the next chapter. As an exercise here, we will begin the interface to maintain the **Publishers** table.

We will follow the same steps used in this chapter to build the Authors table input form:

- Build interface
- Add message box(es)
- Code application state
- Perform entry validation
- Perform input validation
- Add error trapping and handling
- Add on-line help system
- Application testing

Rather than starting from scratch, however, we will follow a 'tried and true' programming method – adapting an existing application to a new use. The Publishers table interface will essentially be the same as the Authors table interface. It will just have more (and different) input fields. Adapting an existing application saves us programmers a lot of time. You do have to make sure the modification implements the needs of the new application while at the same time eliminates vestiges of the old application. This exercise illustrates the modification steps followed and crosschecks required. An important step: **Save** your work often. You want to make sure your changes are always there.

Build Interface

1. Make a copy of the **Example 5-8** project folder (the last version of the **Authors** table input form). Rename the newly copied folder to something else (I used **Example 5-9**). We now have a copy of the **Authors** table input form project to modify to a **Publishers** table input form. Open the copied project in Visual Basic. The Publishers table has ten (10) fields that must be input:

   PubID
   Name
   Company_Name
   Address
   City
   State
   Zip
   Telephone
   Fax
   Comments

   The SQL statement needed by the command object to retrieve these fields (sorted by the **Name** field) is:

   SELECT * FROM Publishers ORDER BY Name

   We need a label and text box for each field. Resize the form so it is much taller (tall enough to hold ten labels and text boxes). Move the buttons to the bottom of the resized form. Don't worry where things are right now – they can always be resized and/or moved later.

Visual Basic Interface Design 5-117

2. Change these properties on the existing form, labels and text box controls as:

frmAuthors (current name):
    Name   frmPublishers
    Text   Publishers

Label1 (current name):
    Text   Publisher ID

txtAuthorID (current name):
    Name   txtPubID

Label2 (current name):
    Text   Name

txtAuthorName (current name):
    Name   txtPubName

Label3 (current name):
    Text   Company Name

txtYearBorn (current name):
    Name   txtCompanyName
    MaxLength   32767

3. Add seven additional label and text box controls. Set these properties:

Label4:
    Text   Address

TextBox1:
    Name   txtPubAddress
    BackColor   White
    ReadOnly   True
    TabIndex   3

Label5:
    Text   City

TextBox2:
    Name   txtPubCity
    BackColor   White
    ReadOnly   True
    TabIndex   4

Label6:
    Text   State

TextBox3:
    Name   txtPubState
    BackColor   White
    ReadOnly   True
    TabIndex   5

Label7:
    Text   Zip

TextBox4:
    Name   txtPubZip
    BackColor   White
    ReadOnly   True
    TabIndex   6

Label8:
    Text   Telephone

TextBox5:
    Name   txtPubTelephone
    BackColor   White
    ReadOnly   True
    TabIndex   7

Visual Basic Interface Design 5-119

Label9:
    Text   FAX

TextBox6:
    Name   txtPubFAX
    BackColor   White
    ReadOnly   True
    TabIndex   8

Label10:
    Text   Comments

TextBox7:
    Name   txtPubComments
    BackColor   White
    ReadOnly   True
    TabIndex   9

At this point, my modified form looks like this:

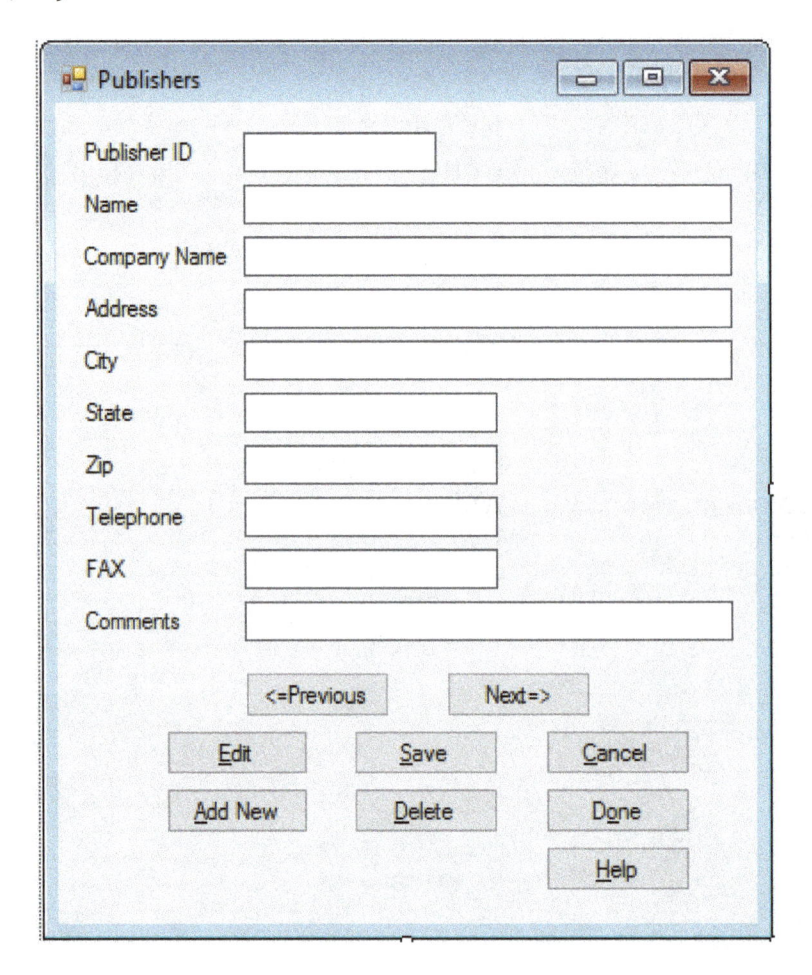

The interface looks good. Let's eliminate the vestiges (old code) from the application and add any needed new code.

Visual Basic Interface Design 5-121

4. We rename the data objects to reflect the **Publishers** table. Make the shaded changes to the Form level declarations:

Access Database:

```
Dim BooksConnection As OleDbConnection
Dim PublishersCommand As OleDbCommand
Dim PublishersAdapter As OleDbDataAdapter
Dim PublishersTable As DataTable
Dim PublishersManager As CurrencyManager
```

SQL Server Database:

```
Dim BooksConnection As SqlConnection
Dim PublishersCommand As SqlCommand
Dim PublishersAdapter As SqlDataAdapter
Dim PublishersTable As DataTable
Dim PublishersManager As CurrencyManager
```

5. Make the shaded changes to the Form **Load** event procedure:

Access Database:

```
Private Sub FrmPublishers_Load(ByVal sender As System.Object, ByVal e As System.EventArgs) Handles MyBase.Load
    Try
        'point to help file
        hlpAuthors.HelpNamespace = Application.StartupPath + "\authors.chm"
        'connect to books database
        BooksConnection = New OleDbConnection("Provider=Microsoft.ACE.OLEDB.12.0; Data Source = c:\VBDB\Working\BooksDB.accdb")
        BooksConnection.Open()
        'establish command object
        PublishersCommand = New OleDbCommand("Select * from Publishers ORDER BY Name", BooksConnection)
        'establish data adapter/data table
        PublishersAdapter = New OleDbDataAdapter()
        PublishersAdapter.SelectCommand = PublishersCommand
        PublishersTable = New DataTable()
        PublishersAdapter.Fill(PublishersTable)
        'bind controls to data table
        txtPubID.DataBindings.Add("Text", PublishersTable, "PubID")
```

```vb
      txtPubName.DataBindings.Add("Text", PublishersTable, "Name")
      txtCompanyName.DataBindings.Add("Text", PublishersTable, "Company_Name")
      txtPubAddress.DataBindings.Add("Text", PublishersTable, "Address")
      txtPubCity.DataBindings.Add("Text", PublishersTable, "City")
      txtPubState.DataBindings.Add("Text", PublishersTable, "State")
      txtPubZip.DataBindings.Add("Text", PublishersTable, "Zip")
      txtPubTelephone.DataBindings.Add("Text", PublishersTable, "Telephone")
      txtPubFAX.DataBindings.Add("Text", PublishersTable, "FAX")
      txtPubComments.DataBindings.Add("Text", PublishersTable, "Comments")
      'establish currency manager
      PublishersManager = DirectCast(Me.BindingContext(PublishersTable), CurrencyManager)
    Catch ex As Exception
      MessageBox.Show(ex.Message, "Error establishing Publishers table.", MessageBoxButtons.OK, MessageBoxIcon.Error)
      Exit Sub
    End Try
    Me.Show()
    Call SetState("View")
  End Sub
```

SQL Server Database:

```vb
  Private Sub FrmPublishers_Load(ByVal sender As System.Object, ByVal e As System.EventArgs) Handles MyBase.Load
    Try
      'point to help file
      hlpPublishers.HelpNamespace = Application.StartupPath + "\publishers.chm"
      'connect to books database
      BooksConnection = New SqlConnection("Data Source=.\SQLEXPRESS; AttachDbFilename=C:\VBDB\Working\SQLBooksDB.mdf; Integrated Security=True; Connect Timeout=30; User Instance=True")
      BooksConnection.Open()
      'establish command object
```

```vb
            PublishersCommand = New SqlCommand("Select * from
Publishers ORDER BY Name", BooksConnection)
            'establish data adapter/data table
            PublishersAdapter = New SqlDataAdapter()
            PublishersAdapter.SelectCommand = PublishersCommand
            PublishersTable = New DataTable()
            PublishersAdapter.Fill(PublishersTable)
            'bind controls to data table
            txtPubID.DataBindings.Add("Text", PublishersTable,
"PubID")
            txtPubName.DataBindings.Add("Text", PublishersTable,
"Name")
            txtCompanyName.DataBindings.Add("Text",
PublishersTable, "Company_Name")
            txtPubAddress.DataBindings.Add("Text",
PublishersTable, "Address")
            txtPubCity.DataBindings.Add("Text", PublishersTable,
"City")
            txtPubState.DataBindings.Add("Text", PublishersTable,
"State")
            txtPubZip.DataBindings.Add("Text", PublishersTable,
"Zip")
            txtPubTelephone.DataBindings.Add("Text",
PublishersTable, "Telephone")
            txtPubFAX.DataBindings.Add("Text", PublishersTable,
"FAX")
            txtPubComments.DataBindings.Add("Text",
PublishersTable, "Comments")
            'establish currency manager
            PublishersManager =
DirectCast(Me.BindingContext(PublishersTable),
CurrencyManager)
        Catch ex As Exception
            MessageBox.Show(ex.Message, "Error establishing
Publishers table.", MessageBoxButtons.OK,
MessageBoxIcon.Error)
            Exit Sub
        End Try
        Me.Show()
        Call SetState("View")
    End Sub
```

These changes reflect the new data object naming, the new SQL string and the proper data binding for the text box controls.

Visual Basic and Databases

6. Make the shaded name change in the **FormClosing** procedure:

```
Private Sub FrmPublishers_FormClosing(ByVal sender As
Object, ByVal e As
System.Windows.Forms.FormClosingEventArgs) Handles
Me.FormClosing
    'close the connection
    BooksConnection.Close()
    'dispose of the objects
    BooksConnection.Dispose()
    PublishersCommand.Dispose()
    PublishersAdapter.Dispose()
    PublishersTable.Dispose()
End Sub
```

7. Make the shaded changes to the **btnPrevious** and **btnNext Click** event procedures to reflect new name for currency manager:

```
Private Sub BtnPrevious_Click(ByVal sender As
System.Object, ByVal e As System.EventArgs) Handles
btnPrevious.Click
    If PublishersManager.Position = 0 Then Console.Beep()
    PublishersManager.Position -= 1
End Sub

Private Sub BtnNext_Click(ByVal sender As System.Object,
ByVal e As System.EventArgs) Handles btnNext.Click
    If PublishersManager.Position = PublishersManager.Count
- 1 Then Console.Beep()
    PublishersManager.Position += 1
End Sub
```

Visual Basic Interface Design 5-125

Add Message Box(es)

In its current state, all the message boxes within our code, except one, are generic in nature. These generic message boxes can be left as is. The one exception is the message box we added to inform the user if they typed an invalid date for the old **Year Born** field. This message box will be deleted in the next step.

Code Application State

1. In this step, we modify the code to reflect proper application state. We will eliminate all old code, so when we are done the application will run without errors. The biggest changes are in the **SetState** procedure. The modification locks and unlocks the text boxes (using the ReadOnly property), depending on state. The procedure is (new code is shaded):

```
Private Sub SetState(ByVal AppState As String)
  Select Case AppState
    Case "View"
        txtPubID.BackColor = Color.White
        txtPubID.ForeColor = Color.Black
        txtPubName.ReadOnly = True
        txtCompanyName.ReadOnly = True
        txtPubAddress.ReadOnly = True
        txtPubCity.ReadOnly = True
        txtPubState.ReadOnly = True
        txtPubZip.ReadOnly = True
        txtPubTelephone.ReadOnly = True
        txtPubFAX.ReadOnly = True
        txtPubComments.ReadOnly = True
        btnPrevious.Enabled = True
        btnNext.Enabled = True
        btnAddNew.Enabled = True
        btnSave.Enabled = False
        btnCancel.Enabled = False
        btnEdit.Enabled = True
        btnDelete.Enabled = True
        btnDone.Enabled = True
        txtPubName.Focus()
    Case "Add", "Edit"
        txtPubID.BackColor = Color.Red
        txtPubID.ForeColor = Color.White
        txtPubName.ReadOnly = False
        txtCompanyName.ReadOnly = False
        txtPubAddress.ReadOnly = False
        txtPubCity.ReadOnly = False
        txtPubState.ReadOnly = False
        txtPubZip.ReadOnly = False
        txtPubTelephone.ReadOnly = False
        txtPubFAX.ReadOnly = False
        txtPubComments.ReadOnly = False
        btnPrevious.Enabled = False
        btnNext.Enabled = False
        btnAddNew.Enabled = False
        btnSave.Enabled = True
```

Visual Basic Interface Design 5-127

```
                btnCancel.Enabled = True
                btnEdit.Enabled = False
                btnDelete.Enabled = False
                btnDone.Enabled = False
                txtPubName.Focus()
        End Select
    End Sub
```

2. Eliminate the **txtAuthorName KeyPress** and **txtYearBorn KeyPress** event procedures since these controls no longer exist. Add this **txtInput KeyPress** event procedure (called by all nine editable controls). This implements the code to programmatically move from text box to text box using the <Enter> key (as an alternate to using <Tab>):

```
Private Sub TxtInput_KeyPress(ByVal sender As
System.Object, ByVal e As
System.Windows.Forms.KeyPressEventArgs) Handles
txtPubName.KeyPress, txtPubZip.KeyPress,
txtPubTelephone.KeyPress, txtPubState.KeyPress,
txtPubFAX.KeyPress, txtPubComments.KeyPress,
txtPubCity.KeyPress, txtPubAddress.KeyPress,
txtCompanyName.KeyPress
    Dim WhichBox As TextBox = CType(sender, TextBox)
    If e.KeyChar = ControlChars.Cr Then
      Select Case WhichBox.Name
        Case "txtPubName"
           txtCompanyName.Focus()
        Case "txtCompanyName"
           txtPubAddress.Focus()
        Case "txtPubAddress"
           txtPubCity.Focus()
        Case "txtPubCity"
           txtPubState.Focus()
        Case "txtPubState"
           txtPubZip.Focus()
        Case "txtPubZip"
           txtPubTelephone.Focus()
        Case "txtPubTelephone"
           txtPubFAX.Focus()
        Case "txtPubFAX"
           txtPubComments.Focus()
        Case "txtPubComments"
           txtPubName.Focus()
      End Select
    End If
End Sub
```

5-128　Visual Basic and Databases

3. Save and run the application. You should now be able to move from record to record and use the other buttons to switch from state to state (don't click **Save** or **Help** yet). Here's what I see for the first record (not all fields will have values):

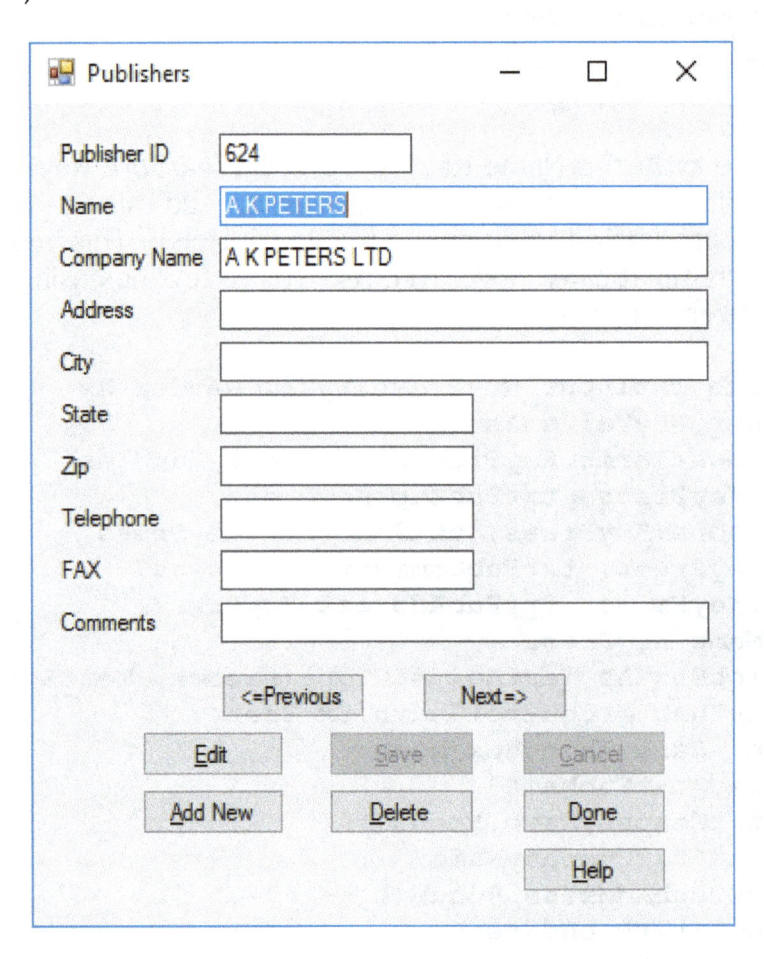

Perform Entry Validation

We need to eliminate any old entry validations done and add required new ones. The only field that appears to need entry validation is **Zip** (it only uses numbers and hyphens, for 9 digit zips). We won't add any validation, though. Why? Perhaps, in the future, the post office will develop a zip code with letters. We want to be ready for this possibility. And, other countries have a wide variety of zip formats. Since we are doing nothing but displaying this value, validation is not that important. If we were doing math with a value or using it in some other function, validation would take on greater importance.

The old validation we need to eliminate is in the **KeyPress** event procedure for the **txtYearBorn** control. That procedure has already been eliminated.

Perform Input Validation

Again, we need to eliminate any old input validations done and add required new ones. All of the inputs here are generic in nature and don't need much validation. We will just insure a publisher **Name** field is entered.

1. Modify the **ValidateData** procedure to read (just eliminate the **Year Born** validation and modify the old **Author Name** validation a bit):

```
Private Function ValidateData() As Boolean
   Dim Message As String = ""
   Dim AllOK As Boolean = True
   'Check for name
   If txtPubName.Text.Trim = "" Then
     Message = "You must enter an Publisher Name." + ControlChars.CrLf
     txtPubName.Focus()
     AllOK = False
   End If
   If Not (AllOK) Then
     MessageBox.Show(Message, "Validation Error", MessageBoxButtons.OK, MessageBoxIcon.Information)
   End If
   Return (AllOK)
End Function
```

You may be asking – isn't the **PubID** field important enough to be validated? Well, yes, but being a primary key, it is treated differently. We will see how to handle this in Chapter 6.

2. Save the application and run it. Click **Edit**. Blank out the **Publisher Name** field and click **Save**. This message box should appear:

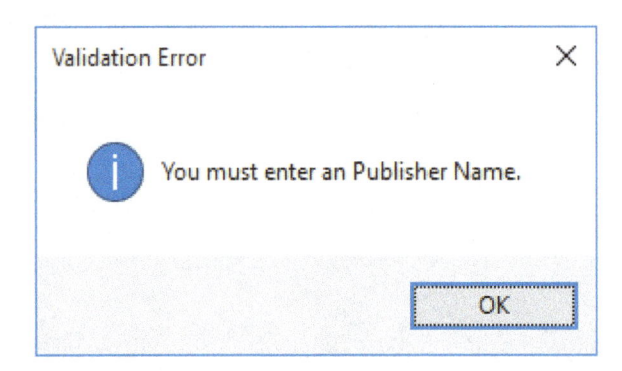

Stop the application.

Add Error Trapping and Handling

The error trapping and handling code in the old application still applies to the new application, hence no change is needed here. This is often the case in modifying existing applications. For other applications, you may need to modify existing error trapping schemes or add new ones.

Add On-Line Help System

Use the HTML Help Workshop to develop a help system named **Publishers.chm**.

1. In an editor program, prepare a single HTML topic file (**Publishers.htm**). The topic I used is:

Publishers Input Form

Available options for managing Publishers database table:

Add New Record

Click the **Add New** button to add a record to the Publishers database. Type in the requested fields. The Publisher Name is a required field. Click **Save** to save the new record; click **Cancel** to ignore the new record.

Edit Record

Click the **Edit** button to edit the displayed record. Make any needed changes. The Publisher Name is a required field. Click **Save** to save the changes; click **Cancel** to ignore the changes.

Delete Record

Click the **Delete** button to delete the displayed record.

Exit Program

Click the **Done** button to quit the application.

---

2. In the HTML Help Workshop, prepare a project file (**Publishers.hhp**). Compile the help file (**Publishers.chm**). All the help files are saved in the **VBDB\General\Class 5\Example 5-9\HelpFile** folder. Copy **Publishers.chm** to your application's **Bin\Debug** folder (**Bin\x86\Debug** for **Access** version).

Visual Basic Interface Design 5-133

3. Go back to your application in Visual Basic. Change the **Name** of the help provider control to **hlpPublishers**. Make the shaded change near the top of the **frmPublishers Load** procedure:

```
Private Sub FrmPublishers_Load(ByVal sender As
System.Object, ByVal e As System.EventArgs) Handles
MyBase.Load
    Try
        'point to help file
        hlpPublishers.HelpNamespace = Application.StartupPath
+ "\publishers.chm"
        'connect to books database
        .
        .
        .
    End Sub
```

And make the shaded change to the **btnHelp Click** procedure:

```
Private Sub BtnHelp_Click(ByVal sender As System.Object,
ByVal e As System.EventArgs) Handles btnHelp.Click
    Help.ShowHelp(Me, hlpPublishers.HelpNamespace)
End Sub
```

5-134　　　Visual Basic and Databases

4. Save the application. Run it. Make sure both the **<F1>** key and **Help** button bring up the help system properly:

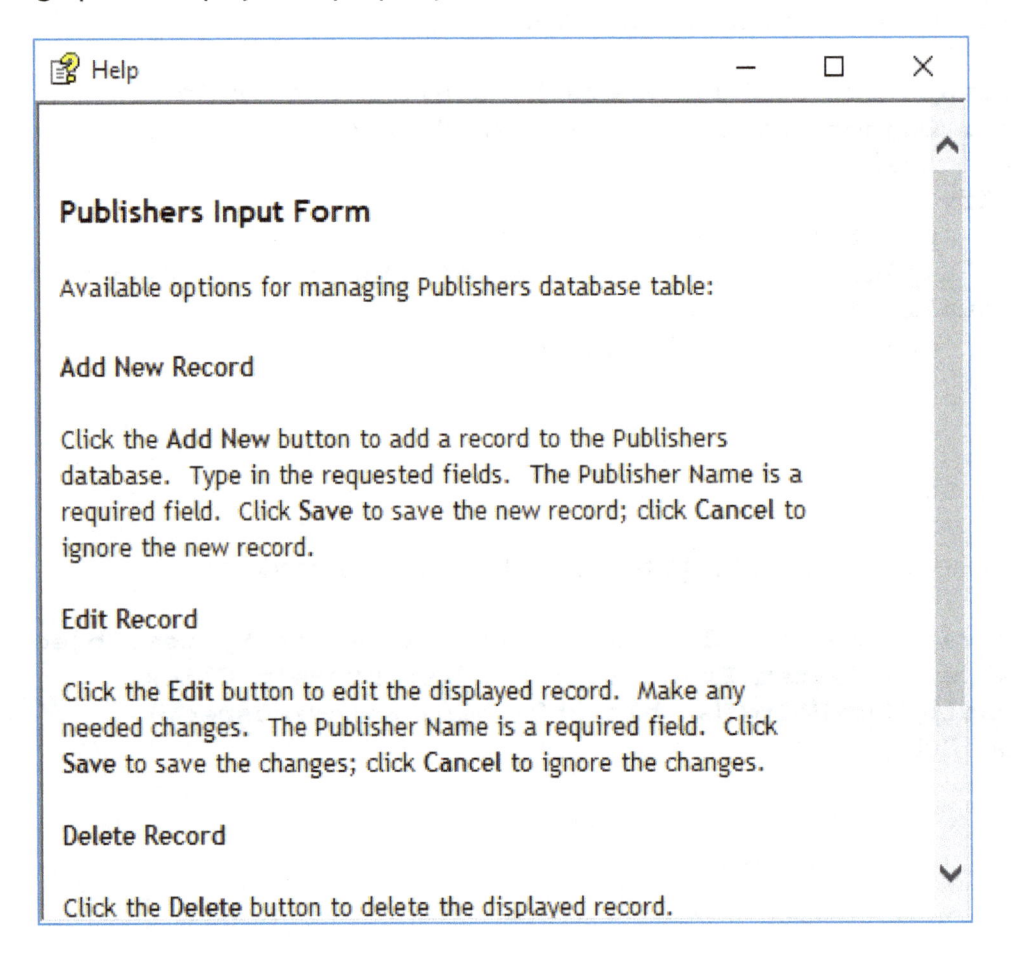

> **Help**
>
> **Publishers Input Form**
>
> Available options for managing Publishers database table:
>
> **Add New Record**
>
> Click the **Add New** button to add a record to the Publishers database. Type in the requested fields. The Publisher Name is a required field. Click **Save** to save the new record; click **Cancel** to ignore the new record.
>
> **Edit Record**
>
> Click the **Edit** button to edit the displayed record. Make any needed changes. The Publisher Name is a required field. Click **Save** to save the changes; click **Cancel** to ignore the changes.
>
> **Delete Record**
>
> Click the **Delete** button to delete the displayed record.

Application Testing

If you did all the above steps carefully, the application should be running properly. If not, make the changes required to get it running. Here's one of the first records I found with most of the fields:

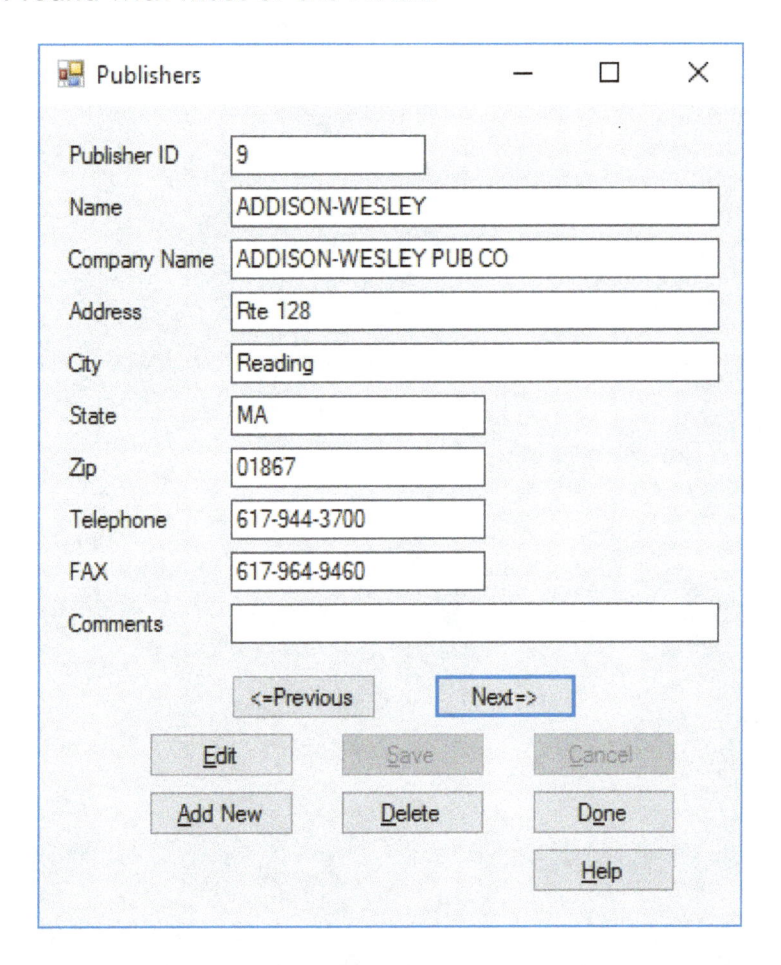

```
Publishers                                    —   □   ×

Publisher ID    [9          ]
Name            [ADDISON-WESLEY              ]
Company Name    [ADDISON-WESLEY PUB CO       ]
Address         [Rte 128                     ]
City            [Reading                     ]
State           [MA                          ]
Zip             [01867                       ]
Telephone       [617-944-3700                ]
FAX             [617-964-9460                ]
Comments        [                            ]

              [ <=Previous ]  [ Next=> ]
              [   Edit    ]  [  Save  ]  [ Cancel ]
              [  Add New  ]  [ Delete ]  [  Done  ]
                                         [  Help  ]
```

As with the Authors form, we still need code to add the database management functions. This is addressed in the next chapter. The final Access version of this example is saved in the **Example 5-9** folder in **VBDB\Access\Class 5** folder. The final SQL Server version of this example is saved in the **Example 5-9** folder in **VBDB\SQL Server\Class 5** folder.

6

Database Management

Review and Preview

After the first five chapters, we have the ability to open databases and obtain any virtual view (using SQL) of the data desired. We have an abundance of tools at our disposal to help in these views. We also have the ability to build a useful, intuitive Visual Basic interface. But, we still can't modify the data in the database.

In this chapter, we learn the steps involved in database management. We learn how to edit data, add data, delete data, and search a database. Using this knowledge, we build a complete database management system for the books database.

Database Management Tasks

As mentioned way back in Chapter 1, the tasks of a **database management** system (**DBMS**) are really quite simple. In concept, there are only a few things you can do with a database:

1. **View** the data
2. Modify (**edit**) the data
3. **Add** some data
4. **Delete** some data
5. **Find** some data of interest

At this point in our study, we've covered topic 1 (viewing data) in some detail. In this section, we tackle the next three topics. The final topic (finding data) is covered later in the chapter.

The ADO .NET engine that is part of the Visual Basic environment simplifies database management techniques significantly. We only need to know a few object methods. Using ADO .NET and the currency manager object, we look at how to edit, add, or delete data. As we implement these database management techniques, we still consider proper interface design methods and intuitive program flow.

Editing Database Records

Database **editing** entails the modification of one or more fields in one or more records within a data table. This data table is formed as a result of the ADO .NET data connection object processing some SQL statement. Editing data is a simple task in Visual Basic - there are three steps:

1. Display the record and associated fields to edit.
2. Make desired changes.
3. Save the changes.

Once Steps 1 and 2 are complete, Step 3 is automatic (if you allow it). After editing, when you move to another record, using programmatic navigation or through some other action, ADO .NET (via the currency manager and data adapter) saves the changes. This automatic saving of changes is great for basic applications, but it makes editing a little too simple. We will be more systematic in editing records. This will save us many headaches. The steps we will follow to edit a record are:

1. Display the record and associated fields to edit.
2. Make desired changes.
3. Validate changes.
4. Save the changes (or, optionally, cancel the edit operation).

To display the record, we use programmatic navigation or some search technique. Once the proper record is displayed, it is automatically in edit mode. Once in edit mode, the user can change any and all displayed fields, using whatever Visual Basic data bound control is used to represent the field.

After an edit, we need to perform proper input and entry validation to insure all validation rules are met. ADO .NET does not provide any specific event procedures for validation. You, the programmer, need to provide all validation code and decide where to place this code. Just make sure validations are done before any new information is written to the database.

In most cases, you will want to give the user the option of **saving** changes and/or **canceling** any edits. To **save** edits, use the currency manager's **EndCurrentEdit** method. Assume a currency manager named **MyManager**, the syntax to save the current record is:

```
MyManager.EndCurrentEdit()
```

This will save the values in the data bound controls tied to the currency manager. This does not save the new values in the database (it only saves the local data table copy).

To save changes in the database, we use the data adapter's **Update** method. If the data adapter **MyAdapter** is connected to a data table named **MyTable**, the syntax to save changes is:

```
MyAdapter.Update(MyTable)
```

For this line of code to operate properly, it needs an 'update command' that is formed using:

Access Database:

```
Dim MyAdapterUpdate As New OleDbCommandBuilder(MyAdapter)
```

SQL Server Database:

```
Dim MyAdapterUpdate As New SqlCommandBuilder(MyAdapter)
```

This declaration is made before using the **Update** method (it also forms proper delete and insert commands needed by the adapter). This save procedure is usually done when an application is closed.

To **cancel** any changes made while editing, you use the currency manager's **CancelCurrentEdit** method. The syntax is:

```
MyManager.CancelCurrentEdit()
```

After this, the data bound controls are reset to their 'pre-edit' values.

Phone Contact Database

For many examples in this chapter, we will use a practice database named **PhoneDB.accdb,** included with the sample code (in the **VBDB\Databases** folder). The SQL Server version (**SQLPhoneDB.mdf**) is also in the **VBDB\Databases** folder. This is a simple database of contacts, containing names and phone numbers with three fields (**ContactID, ContactName,** and **ContactNumber**) in a single table named **PhoneTable**. Using this sample lets us edit, add, and delete records without worrying about destroying something important, like the books database.

The phone database **PhoneTable** table has 26 records:

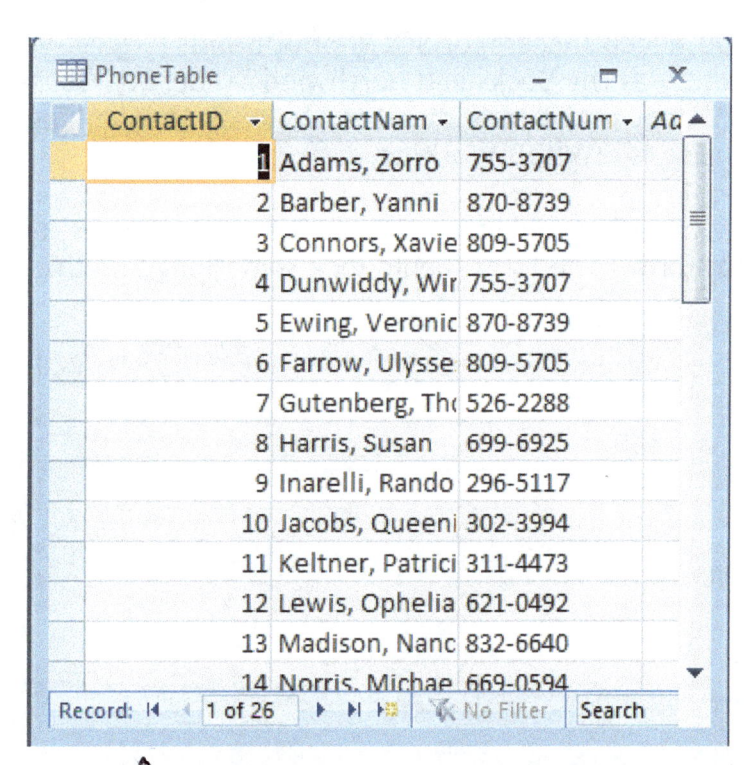

ContactID	ContactName	ContactNumber
1	Adams, Zorro	755-3707
2	Barber, Yanni	870-8739
3	Connors, Xavie	809-5705
4	Dunwiddy, Wir	755-3707
5	Ewing, Veronic	870-8739
6	Farrow, Ulysse	809-5705
7	Gutenberg, Th(	526-2288
8	Harris, Susan	699-6925
9	Inarelli, Rando	296-5117
10	Jacobs, Queeni	302-3994
11	Keltner, Patrici	311-4473
12	Lewis, Ophelia	621-0492
13	Madison, Nanc	832-6640
14	Norris, Michae	669-0594

ContactName and **ContactName** [NUMBER] are simple string fields. **ContactID** is a **primary key** and is **auto-numbering,** insuring a unique value for each record. The ADO .NET database engine assigns the value and we will not let the user change it.

Example 6-1

Editing Database Records

Let's look at some of the coding and considerations used in editing database records. We will use the phone datatabase with its single table **PhoneTable**. To retrieve the fields from this table (ordered by **ContactName**), we use this SQL statement:

Select * from PhoneTable ORDER BY ContactName

1. Copy **PhoneDB.accdb** (Access) or **SQLPhoneDB.mdf** (SQL Server) to the same working directory as the Books and Northwind Traders databases (this lets us keep a 'clean' copy in the code directory). Recall the working directory we've been using is **c:\VBDB\Working**.

2. Start a new application. Add three labels, three text boxes, and four buttons to the project form. The form should look something like this:

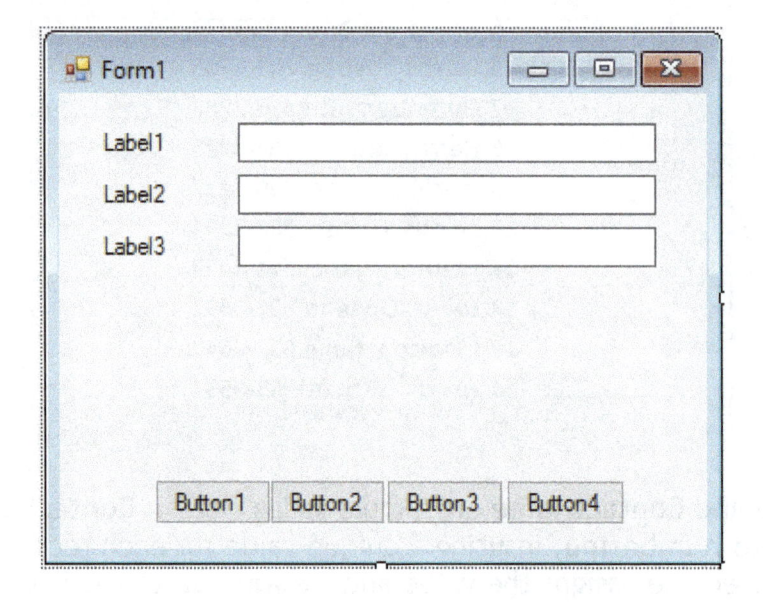

Database Management

Set the following properties for each control:

Form1:
Name	frmPhoneDB
FormBorderStyle	FixedSingle
StartPosition	CenterScreen
Text	Phone DBMS

Label1:
Text	ID

TextBox1:
Name	txtID
BackColor	White

Label2:
Text	Name

TextBox2:
Name	txtName
BackColor	White

Label3:
Text	Number

TextBox3:
Name	txtNumber
BackColor	White

Button1:
Name	btnFirst
Text	|<
FontStyle	Bold

Button2:
Name	btnPrevious
Text	<
FontStyle	Bold

Button3:
Name	btnNext
Text	>
FontStyle	Bold

Button4:
Name	btnLast
Text	>|
FontStyle	Bold

When done, my form looks like this:

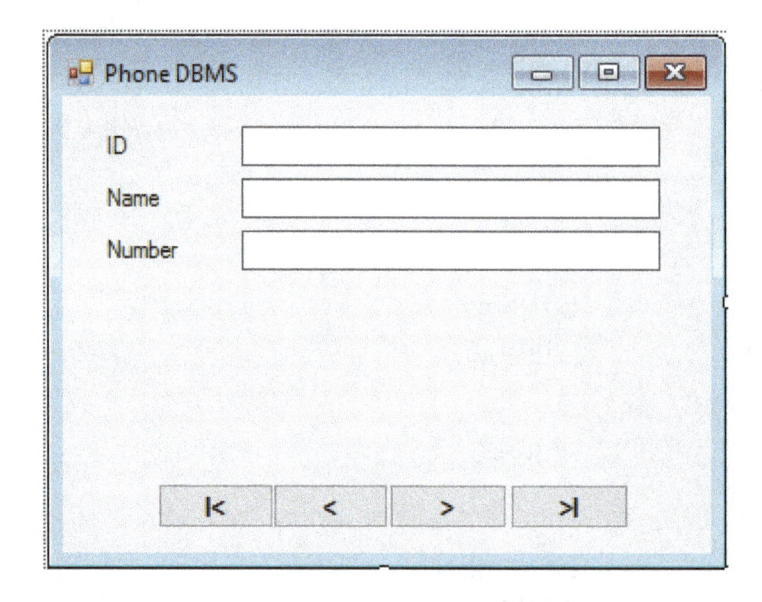

3. Add these lines at the top of the code window:

<u>Access Database:</u>

```
Imports System.Data
Imports System.Data.OleDb
```

<u>SQL Server Database:</u>

```
Imports System.Data
Imports System.Data.SqlClient
```

Database Management 6-9

4. Form level declarations to create data object:

Access Database:

```
Dim PhoneConnection As OleDbConnection
Dim PhoneCommand As OleDbCommand
Dim PhoneAdapter As OleDbDataAdapter
Dim PhoneTable As DataTable
Dim PhoneManager As CurrencyManager
```

SQL Server Database:

```
Dim PhoneConnection As SqlConnection
Dim PhoneCommand As SqlCommand
Dim PhoneAdapter As SqlDataAdapter
Dim PhoneTable As DataTable
Dim PhoneManager As CurrencyManager
```

6-10 Visual Basic and Databases

5. Add this code to the **frmPhoneDB Load** event procedure (creates data objects and binds controls):

Access Database:

```
  Private Sub FrmPhoneDB_Load(ByVal sender As System.Object, ByVal e As System.EventArgs) Handles MyBase.Load
    'connect to Phone database
    PhoneConnection = New OleDbConnection("Provider=Microsoft.ACE.OLEDB.12.0; Data Source = c:\VBDB\Working\PhoneDB.accdb")
    PhoneConnection.Open()
    'establish command object
    PhoneCommand = New OleDbCommand("Select * from PhoneTable ORDER BY ContactName", PhoneConnection)
    'establish data adapter/data table
    PhoneAdapter = New OleDbDataAdapter()
    PhoneAdapter.SelectCommand = PhoneCommand
    PhoneTable = New DataTable()
    PhoneAdapter.Fill(PhoneTable)
    'bind controls to data table
    txtID.DataBindings.Add("Text", PhoneTable, "ContactID")
    txtName.DataBindings.Add("Text", PhoneTable, "ContactName")
    txtNumber.DataBindings.Add("Text", PhoneTable, "ContactNumber")
    'establish currency manager
    PhoneManager = DirectCast(Me.BindingContext(PhoneTable), CurrencyManager)
  End Sub
```

SQL Server Database:

```
   Private Sub FrmPhoneDB_Load(ByVal sender As System.Object, ByVal e As System.EventArgs) Handles MyBase.Load
      'connect to Phone database
      PhoneConnection = New SqlConnection("Data Source=.\SQLEXPRESS; AttachDbFilename=C:\VBDB\Working\SQLPhoneDB.mdf; Integrated Security=True; Connect Timeout=30; User Instance=True")
      PhoneConnection.Open()
      'establish command object
      PhoneCommand = New SqlCommand("Select * from PhoneTable ORDER BY ContactName", PhoneConnection)
      'establish data adapter/data table
      PhoneAdapter = New SqlDataAdapter()
      PhoneAdapter.SelectCommand = PhoneCommand
      PhoneTable = New DataTable()
      PhoneAdapter.Fill(PhoneTable)
      'bind controls to data table
      txtID.DataBindings.Add("Text", PhoneTable, "ContactID")
      txtName.DataBindings.Add("Text", PhoneTable, "ContactName")
      txtNumber.DataBindings.Add("Text", PhoneTable, "ContactNumber")
      'establish currency manager
      PhoneManager = DirectCast(Me.BindingContext(PhoneTable), CurrencyManager)
   End Sub
```

6-12   Visual Basic and Databases

6. Add this code to the **frmPhoneDB FormClosing** event procedure to save any changes to the database and close the connection:

Access Database:

```
Private Sub FrmPhoneDB_FormClosing(ByVal sender As Object, ByVal e As System.Windows.Forms.FormClosingEventArgs) Handles Me.FormClosing
    Try
      'save the updated phone table
      Dim PhoneAdapterCommands As New OleDbCommandBuilder(PhoneAdapter)
      PhoneAdapter.Update(PhoneTable)
    Catch ex As Exception
      MessageBox.Show("Error saving database to file:" + ControlChars.CrLf + ex.Message, "Save Error", MessageBoxButtons.OK, MessageBoxIcon.Error)
    End Try
    'close the connection
    PhoneConnection.Close()
    'dispose of the objects
    PhoneConnection.Dispose()
    PhoneCommand.Dispose()
    PhoneAdapter.Dispose()
    PhoneTable.Dispose()
  End Sub
```

Database Management

SQL Server Database:

```
Private Sub FrmPhoneDB_FormClosing(ByVal sender As Object, ByVal e As System.Windows.Forms.FormClosingEventArgs) Handles Me.FormClosing
    Try
        'save the updated phone table
        Dim PhoneAdapterCommands As New SqlCommandBuilder(PhoneAdapter)
        PhoneAdapter.Update(PhoneTable)
    Catch ex As Exception
        MessageBox.Show("Error saving database to file:" + ControlChars.CrLf + ex.Message, "Save Error", MessageBoxButtons.OK, MessageBoxIcon.Error)
    End Try
    'close the connection
    PhoneConnection.Close()
    'dispose of the objects
    PhoneConnection.Dispose()
    PhoneCommand.Dispose()
    PhoneAdapter.Dispose()
    PhoneTable.Dispose()
End Sub
```

This code uses command objects (**PhoneAdapterCommands**) and the data adapter **Update** method to save any changes to the database.

7. Lastly, add code for the four navigation buttons **Click** events:

```
Private Sub BtnPrevious_Click(ByVal sender As System.Object, ByVal e As System.EventArgs) Handles btnPrevious.Click
    PhoneManager.Position -= 1
End Sub

Private Sub BtnNext_Click(ByVal sender As System.Object, ByVal e As System.EventArgs) Handles btnNext.Click
    PhoneManager.Position += 1
End Sub

Private Sub BtnFirst_Click(ByVal sender As System.Object, ByVal e As System.EventArgs) Handles btnFirst.Click
    PhoneManager.Position = 0
End Sub

Private Sub BtnLast_Click(ByVal sender As System.Object, ByVal e As System.EventArgs) Handles btnLast.Click
    PhoneManager.Position = PhoneManager.Count - 1
End Sub
```

Database Management 6-15

8. Save the application (Access version saved in the **Example 6-1** folder in **VBDB\Access\Class 6** folder; SQL Server version saved in the **Example 6-1** folder in **VBDB\SQL Server\Class 6** folder) and run it. Here's the first record:

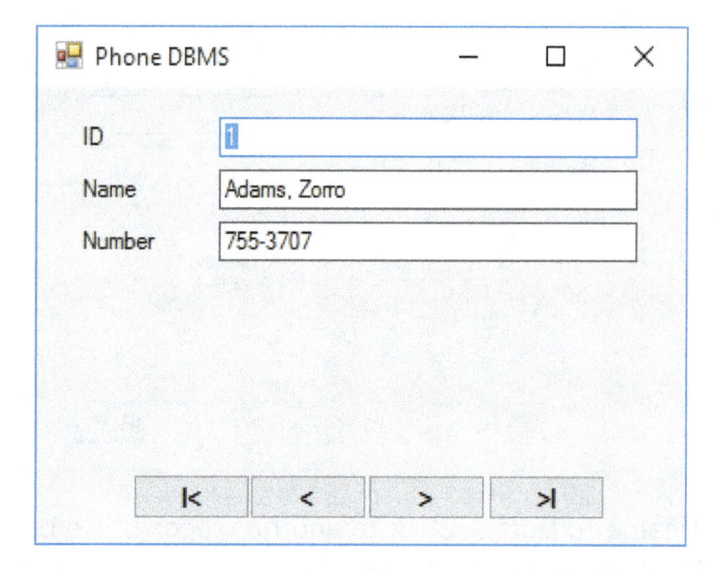

Scroll through the records (using the navigation buttons) to become familiar with the listings. Notice the records are sorted by name.

Go to the last record (click the >| arrow). The **Name** should be **Zuffi, Adam**:

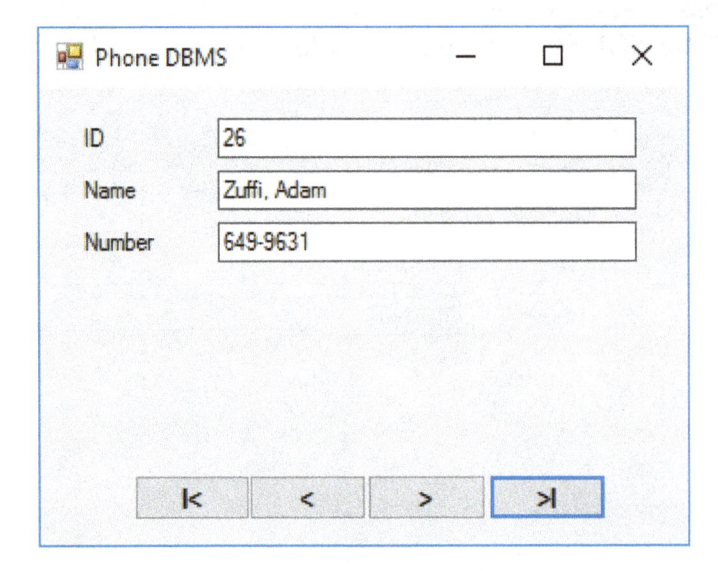

Change the last name to **Duffi**. Click to another record. Go back to the last record and you will see the name change is reflected in the displayed record:

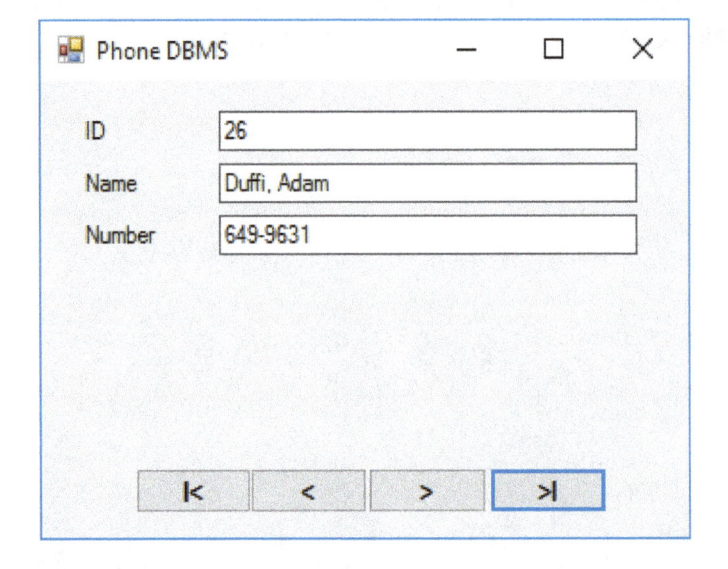

If you were to stop the application at this point, the change would be saved to the database. Change the last name back to **Zuffi**, and then stop the application (click the **X** in the upper corner of the form).

Database Management 6-17

Do you see how easy it is to edit and save a record? As we mentioned, it's too easy. The user may not be aware any changes are being saved. Recall, when we discussed proper interface design, we decided that all user tasks should be obvious and we should lead the user through these tasks. In this example, the user should tell us when they want to **edit** a record and when they want to **save** it. It should not be possible to change a record until the user decides to change it. Let's put in these modifications.

1. First, set the **ReadOnly** property for all text boxes to **True** (we will decide when to change this to False, to allow editing). Now, add three buttons, with these properties:

Button1:
    Name   btnEdit
    Text   Edit

Button2:
    Name   btnSave
    Text   Save
    Enabled   False

Button3:
    Name   btnCancel
    Text   Cancel
    Enabled   False

Now, the form looks like this:

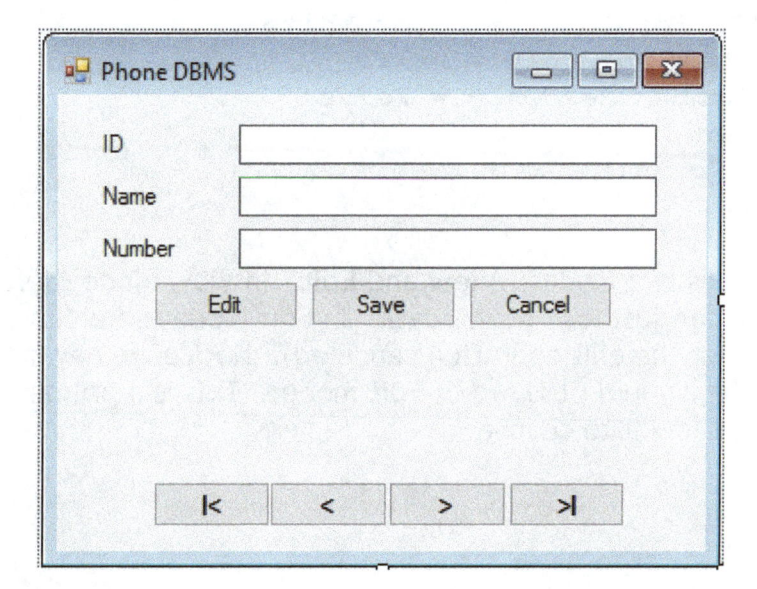

2. We'll use the concept of **application state** (we often use the term **mode** as a synonym for **state**) introduced in Chapter 5. Insert a procedure named **SetState** with a string argument **AppState**. Place this code in that procedure:

```
Private Sub SetState(ByVal AppState As String)
  Select Case AppState
    Case "View"
      btnFirst.Enabled = True
      btnPrevious.Enabled = True
      btnNext.Enabled = True
      btnLast.Enabled = True
      btnEdit.Enabled = True
      btnSave.Enabled = False
      btnCancel.Enabled = False
      txtID.BackColor = Color.White
      txtID.ForeColor = Color.Black
      txtName.ReadOnly = True
      txtNumber.ReadOnly = True
    Case "Edit"
      btnFirst.Enabled = False
      btnPrevious.Enabled = False
      btnNext.Enabled = False
      btnLast.Enabled = False
      btnEdit.Enabled = False
      btnSave.Enabled = True
      btnCancel.Enabled = True
      txtID.BackColor = Color.Red
      txtID.ForeColor = Color.White
      txtName.ReadOnly = False
      txtNumber.ReadOnly = False
  End Select
  txtName.Focus()
End Sub
```

This procedure has two modes: **View** and **Edit**. In View mode (default when the form loads), we can just look at the data. In Edit mode, data can be changed, and then saved (or the edit operation canceled). Notice we never 'unlock' the text box with the ID field (it is red in **Edit** mode). This is a primary database key and we will not allow it to change.

Database Management 6-19

3. Add this line at the end of the **frmPhoneDB Load** procedure to put the form in **View** mode initially:

    ```
    Call SetState("View")
    ```

This puts the form in **View** mode initially.

4. Place this code in the **btnEdit Click** event procedure:

    ```
    Private Sub BtnEdit_Click(ByVal sender As System.Object, ByVal e As System.EventArgs) Handles btnEdit.Click
       Call SetState("Edit")
    End Sub
    ```

This code places the form in **Edit** mode and allows the data table to be edited.

5. Place this code in the **btnSave Click** event procedure:

    ```
    Private Sub BtnSave_Click(ByVal sender As System.Object, ByVal e As System.EventArgs) Handles btnSave.Click
       PhoneManager.EndCurrentEdit()
       Call SetState("View")
    End Sub
    ```

This code saves changes in the bound controls by invoking the currency manager **EndCurrentEdit** method. It resets the application state to **View** mode.

6. Place this code in the **btnCancel Click** event procedure:

    ```
    Private Sub BtnCancel_Click(ByVal sender As System.Object, ByVal e As System.EventArgs) Handles btnCancel.Click
       PhoneManager.CancelCurrentEdit()
       Call SetState("View")
    End Sub
    ```

This code cancels the edit operation and resets the application state to **View** mode.

7. Resave the modified application. Run it. Go to the last record (remember **Zuffi, Adam**?). Try to change the name – you shouldn't be able to since the text box is locked. Click **Edit**. The form is in **Edit** mode:

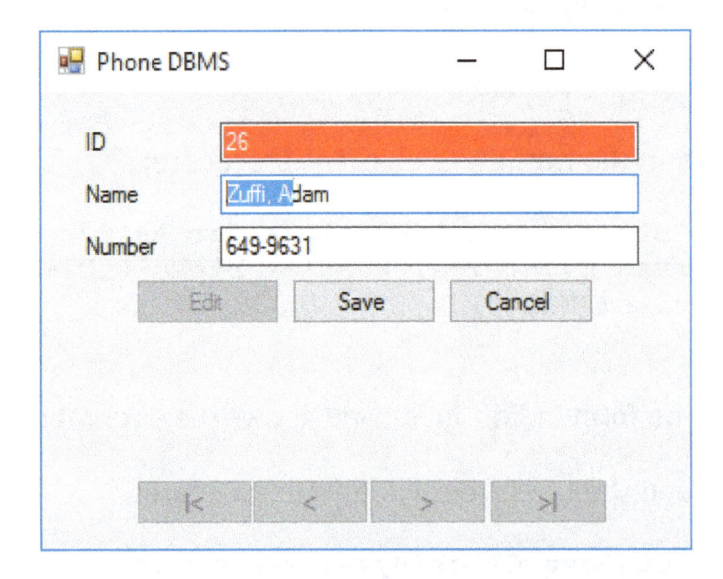

Change the last name to **Duffi**. Click **Cancel**. Notice the Name field is set back to **Zuffi** and the form is restored to viewing mode. Nothing has changed. Click **Edit** again. Change the last name to **Duffi**. Click **Save**. The form returns to viewing mode and the name change is reflected in the displayed record. Do you see how use of this interface is clear? Notice, though, that the records have not been re-sorted. That is, the 'Duffi' entry is still the last record. Stop the application.

Database Management 6-21

8. Re-start the application. Go to the last record. Where's Adam 'Duffi'? Scroll through the records to the 'D' listings – he should be there. When we re-opened the database with the original SQL command (**SELECT * FROM PhoneTable ORDER BY ContactName**), the new name was properly sorted with the other records. Change **Duffi** back to **Zuffi** (use **Edit**, then **Save**) and stop the application. To properly sort edits at the time they are made, we use the data table **Sort** method. Stop the application and add this line of code after the **'EndCurrentEdit'** line in the **btnSave_Click** event procedure:

   ```
   PhoneTable.DefaultView.Sort = "ContactName"
   ```

Run the application. Go to the last record (**Zuffi**). Change **Zuffi** to **Duffi** and click **Save**. The form will show the record preceding the one we changed (**Yarrow, Betty**):

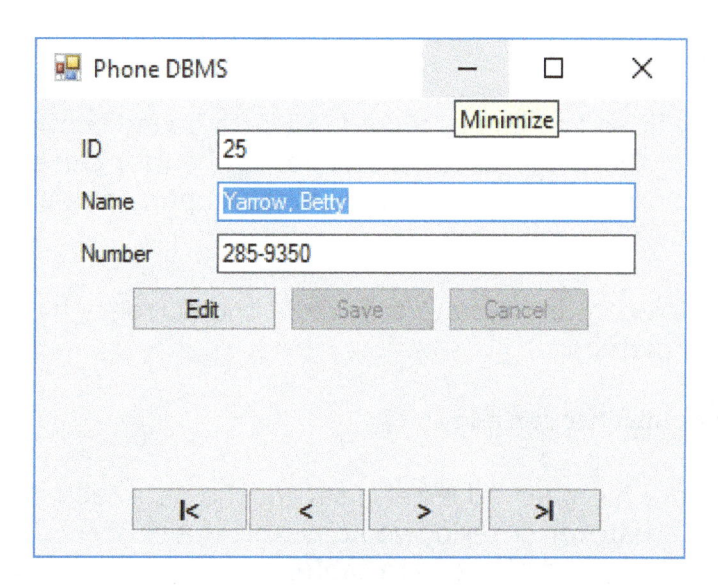

Move to the 'D' entries and you'll see **Duffi** is now in the proper location without having to stop the application). Why was the Yarrow entry shown instead of the Duffi record? After the re-sort, the pointer is left at the end (where it was prior to the edit). If we want to display the Duffi record after the sort, we need to search the sorted records to see where it was placed. We explain how to do this later in the chapter. Stop and save the application (Access version saved in **Example 6-1** folder of **VBDB\Access\Class 6** folder; SQL Server version saved in **Example 6-1** folder of **VBDB\SQL Server\Class 6** folder). Before you leave this example, run it once more and changing Mr. Zuffi's name back.

Adding Database Records

Adding a record to a database data table is closely related to the editing process just discussed. The only difference is we are editing a new empty record. The steps we will follow to add a new record are:

1. Add and display an empty record and associated fields.
2. Place field data in displayed controls.
3. Validate data.
4. Save the data (or, optionally, cancel the add operation).

To add a record to the data table, use the currency manager object's **AddNew** method. For a currency manager named **MyManager**, the code is:

```
MyManager.AddNew()
```

This statement will add an empty record (all data bound controls are blanked out) at the end of the data table. At this point, the user can enter new values. Once new values are entered, the same validation procedures discussed for editing records must be followed.

To **save** the new record in the data table, use the currency manager object's **EndCurrentEdit** method:

```
MyManager.EndCurrentEdit()
```

After a new record has been added and saved, the data table should be re-sorted based on whatever criterion you choose. If a re-sort is not done, the new record remains at the end of the data table.

Database Management 6-23

If the user decides to **cancel** the addition of a new record, use the currency manager **CancelCurrentEdit** method. For our example currency manager, the code to do this is:

```
MyManager.CancelCurrentEdit()
```

This removes the new record from the 'editing buffer.' We still need to do a little extra work. Why? Prior to adding a record, the user was viewing a particular record. We would like that same record to be displayed after the add operation is canceled. We can do this by storing a record's **bookmark** prior to the adding a record. A bookmark is a placeholder in database management tasks. Then, if the 'add operation' is canceled, we restore the bookmark. The code to store the bookmark (the **Position** property of the currency manager) is:

```
MyBookmark = MyManager.Position
```

Note this requires a variable **MyBookmark** (of type **Integer**) to save the bookmark. To restore the bookmark, reverse the sides of the relation:

```
MyManager.Position = MyBookmark
```

Example 6-2

Adding Database Records

Let's modify the previous example (Example 6-1) to include the ability to add records to the phone number list.

1. Add a button. Set **Name** to **btnAdd** and **Text** to **Add New**. The form should look like this (I've resized the form a bit):

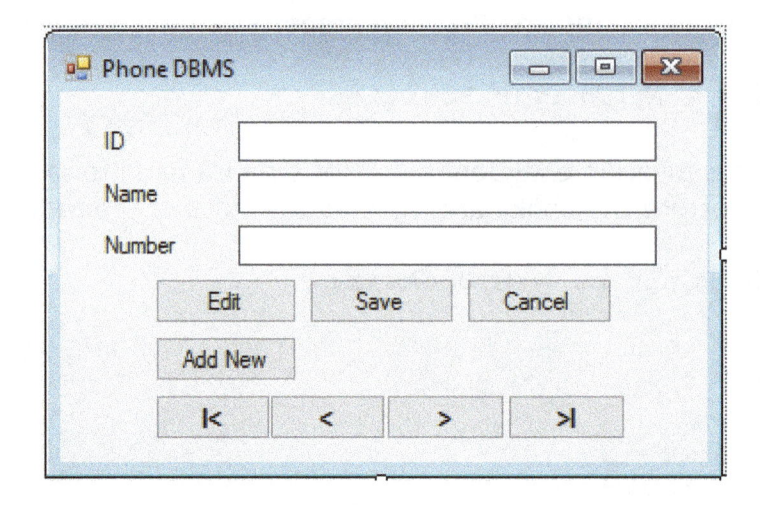

2. Place this line with the form level declarations. These variables will store the application state and any bookmark we use.

   ```
   Dim MyState As String, MyBookmark As Integer
   ```

3. Place this code in the **btnAdd Click** event procedure:

   ```
   Private Sub BtnAdd_Click(ByVal sender As System.Object, ByVal e As System.EventArgs) Handles btnAdd.Click
       MyBookmark = PhoneManager.Position
       Call SetState("Add")
       PhoneManager.AddNew()
   End Sub
   ```

This code first sets the bookmark in case the operation is later canceled. It then places the application in **AddNew** mode and adds a blank record.

Database Management 6-25

4. Modify the **btnCancel Click** code to differentiate between canceling during **Edit** mode and **Add** mode (new code is shaded):

```
Private Sub BtnCancel_Click(ByVal sender As System.Object, ByVal e As System.EventArgs) Handles btnCancel.Click
    PhoneManager.CancelCurrentEdit()
    If MyState = "Add" Then
      PhoneManager.Position = MyBookmark
    End If
    Call SetState("View")
End Sub
```

In this code, if in **Edit** mode, nothing has changed. If in **Add** mode, the record addition is canceled and the saved bookmark is restored. In either case, the user is returned to the **View** state. **MyState** is a variable defined in the next routine.

5. Modify the **SetState** procedure so the state is saved in **MyState**, the new **Add** state is recognized, and the enabled property of the **Add New** button is properly toggled (new code is shaded):

```
Private Sub SetState(ByVal AppState As String)
    MyState = AppState
    Select Case AppState
      Case "View"
        btnFirst.Enabled = True
        btnPrevious.Enabled = True
        btnNext.Enabled = True
        btnLast.Enabled = True
        btnEdit.Enabled = True
        btnSave.Enabled = False
        btnCancel.Enabled = False
        btnAdd.Enabled = True
        txtID.BackColor = Color.White
        txtID.ForeColor = Color.Black
        txtName.ReadOnly = True
        txtNumber.ReadOnly = True
      Case "Add", "Edit"
        btnFirst.Enabled = False
        btnPrevious.Enabled = False
        btnNext.Enabled = False
        btnLast.Enabled = False
        btnEdit.Enabled = False
        btnSave.Enabled = True
        btnCancel.Enabled = True
        btnAdd.Enabled = False
        txtID.BackColor = Color.Red
        txtID.ForeColor = Color.White
        txtName.ReadOnly = False
        txtNumber.ReadOnly = False
    End Select
    txtName.Focus()
End Sub
```

Database Management 6-27

6. Save the application (Access version saved in the **Example 6-2** folder in **VBDB\Access\Class 6** folder; SQL Server version saved in the **Example 6-2** folder in **VBDB\SQL Server\Class 6** folder). Run it. Click **Add New**. Note that all three textboxes (**ID**, **Name** and **Number**) are blank:

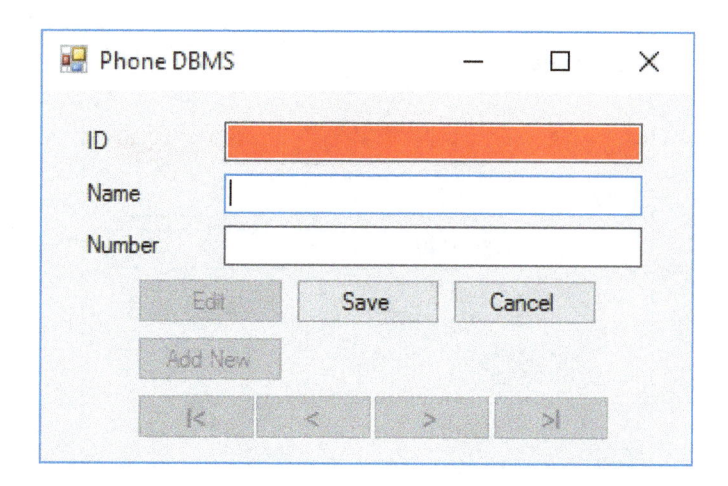

Recall the **ContactID** field is a primary key and is autonumbering. Why, then, isn't an ID value generated and displayed? A 'feature' of ADO .NET is that it does not generate such a value until the modified row is written back to the database (the data adapter is updated). In this example, we don't save the database until we end the application, so these values will not be seen until the database is reopened.

7. Type in a name (Last Name, First Name) and a phone number. (I'm sure that you have realized we should have some input and entry validation for the phone number field, but we're ignoring it for this simple example.) Here's my new record:

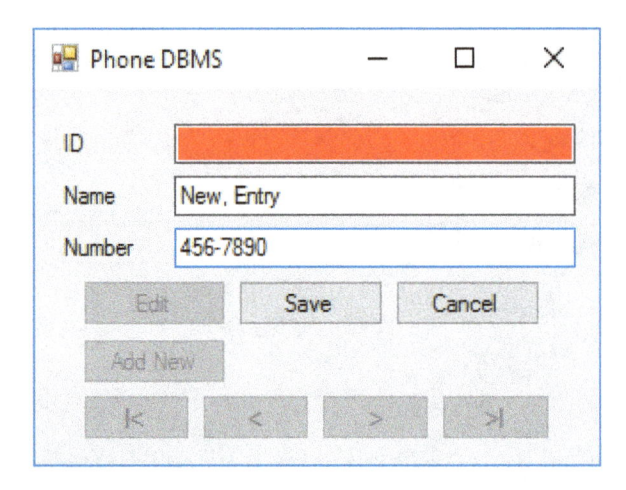

Notice there is no **ID**. Click **Save**. The application returns to **View** state, displaying some other record. As mentioned earlier, we will learn how to display the newly added record later in the chapter. Click **Add New** again. Type in a new record, but this time click **Cancel**. The displayed record should be the same one seen prior to clicking **Add New**. Users like to see such results. Scroll through the records – the canceled record should be nowhere to be found. The added record should still be there. Stop the application.

Database Management 6-29

8. Run the application again and find the newly added entry. The **ID** (132 in my example) should be there:

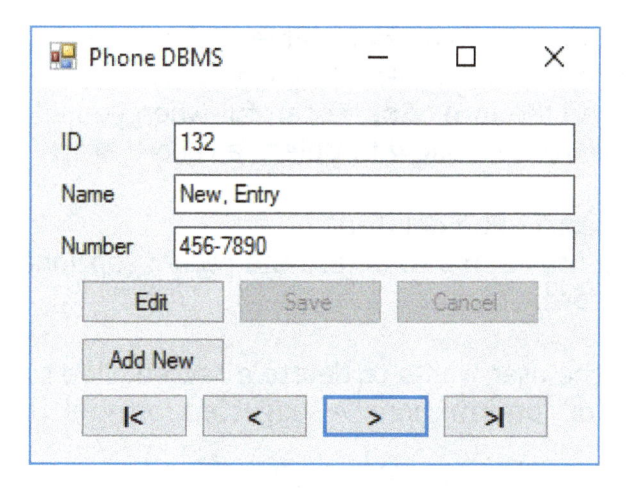

Stop and save the application. This lack of ID display when adding a record is not a big problem, just an inconvenience. A user cannot edit or modify this value in any way (it is used by the database for searching), so there is really no reason to display it.

Deleting Database Records

Deleting a record from a database data table is simple and potentially dangerous. Once a record is deleted, it cannot be recovered (unless you write Visual Basic code to do the job). So, be careful when you allow record deletions. The steps we will follow to delete a record are:

1. Display the record to be deleted.
2. Make sure the user wants to delete the record (optional, but crucial).
3. Delete the record.

We want to be sure the user wants to delete a record. We suggest the use of a message box to ask for confirmation. A suggested form for the message box is:

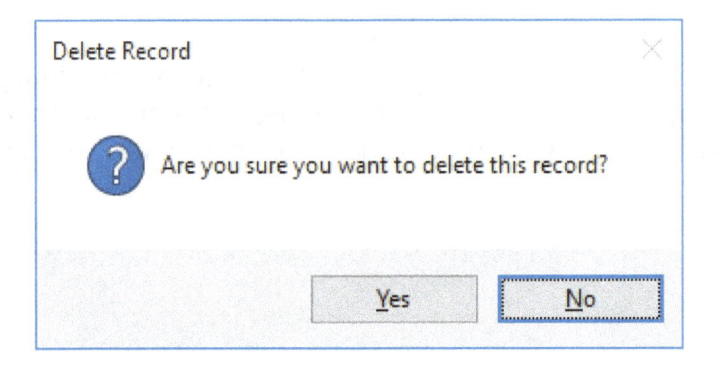

The code snippet to generate this message box is:

```
MessageBox.Show("Are you sure you want to delete this
record?", "Delete Record", MessageBoxButtons.YesNo,
MessageBoxIcon.Question, MessageBoxDefaultButton.Button2)
```

Note we make the **No** button default. We want the user to have to click **Yes** to delete a record. If the user responds **No** to this box, we simply exit the procedure the delete operation is in. If the response is **Yes**, we continue with the deletion.

To delete a record from a data table, use the currency manager object's **RemoveAt** method. For a currency manager named **MyManager**, the code is:

```
MyManager.RemoveAt(MyManager.Position)
```

This code irrevocably deletes the displayed record (the record at **MyManager.Position**).

Example 6-3

Deleting Database Records

1. Let's modify the previous example (Example 6-2) to include the ability to delete records from the phone number list.

2. Add a button. Set **Name** to **btnDelete** and **Text** to **Delete**. The form should look like this:

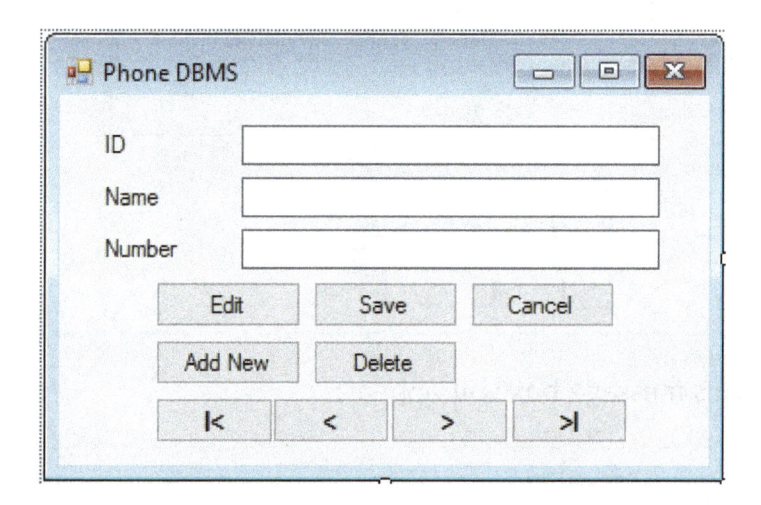

3. Place this code in the **btnDelete Click** event procedure:

```
Private Sub BtnDelete_Click(ByVal sender As System.Object, ByVal e As System.EventArgs) Handles btnDelete.Click
    If MessageBox.Show("Are you sure you want to delete this record?", "Delete Record", MessageBoxButtons.YesNo, MessageBoxIcon.Question, MessageBoxDefaultButton.Button2) = Windows.Forms.DialogResult.Yes Then
        PhoneManager.RemoveAt(PhoneManager.Position)
    End If
    Call SetState("View")
End Sub
```

This code confirms the deletion using a message box. If user responds with **Yes**, the deletion is done. If **No**, nothing happens. The application is always returned to **View** mode.

4. Modify the **SetState** procedure to set the **btnDelete** button **Enabled** property to **True** in **View** mode, **False** in **Add/Edit** mode.

5. Save the application (Access version saved in the **Example 6-3** folder in **VBDB\Access\Class 6** folder; SQL Server version saved in the **Example 6-3** folder in **VBDB\SQL Server\Class 6** folder). Run it. Click **Add New** and add your name and phone number. Click **Save**. Now scroll through the records until your name is displayed. My screen shows:

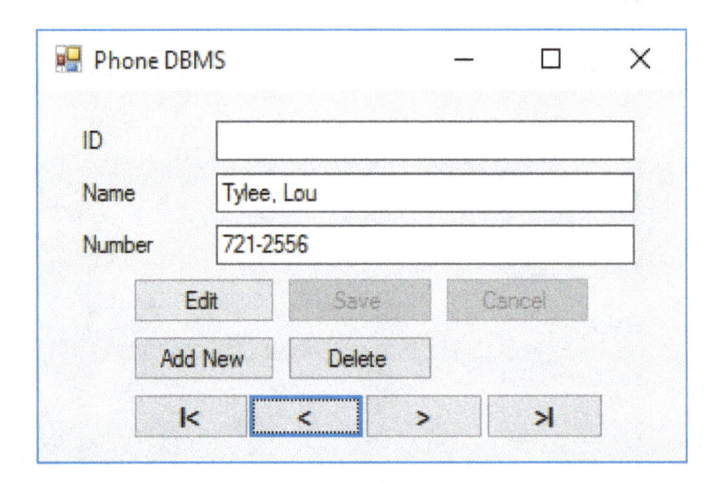

Click **Delete**. This message box will appear:

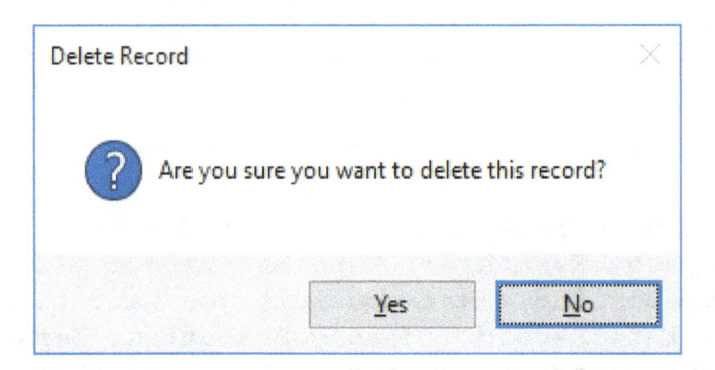

Respond **No** to the message box. Your entry is still displayed. Click **Delete** again, but this time respond **Yes** to the message box. You are deleted from the database! Note another record is now displayed. Stop the application.

Finding Records in a Database

There are many times in database management tasks you might like to locate certain records in a database. As an example, in the little phone database we've been using a user may want to find a particular person to call. Or, in the books database, a user may need to find all books published by a particular author. Or, after adding a record to and resorting a data table, you would like to find that record and display it.

One way to **find records** in a database is via a SQL query. A SQL query returns all records that match particular criteria and needs a requerying of the database (making it slow for large databases). Such searches were discussed in Chapter 5. In this section, we are concerned with finding a single record in an established data table. There are two ways to accomplish such a task. First, we will use the data table **Find** method.

The data table **Find** method will only perform searches on the column by which the data is sorted. This is exactly what we need for the phone database, since we sort by names and are searching by names. More complex searches require more complex techniques (discussed next).

If we have a data table (**MyTable**) sorted on the field **MySortField** and are searching for **MyValue**, the syntax for the **Find** method is:

```
Dim MyRow As Integer
MyTable.DefaultView.Sort = MySortField
MyRow = MyTable.DefaultView.Find(MyValue)
```

This method returns the first row (**MyRow**) in the data table containing the desired field value. If no such row is found, a negative one (-1) is returned. Setting the currency manager **Position** property to **MyRow** will properly rebind controls.

The **Find** method is easy to use, but limited. If we want to find a row based on more complex criteria or based on a column other than the one the data is sorted on, we use the data table's **Select** method. The syntax is:

```
Dim MyRows() As DataRow
MyRows = MyTable.Select(Criteria)
```

where **Criteria** is a Boolean expression of the search criteria. The method returns an array of rows (**MyRows**) containing each row in the data table that matches the criteria.

The search **Criteria** is a string expression like the **WHERE** clause in SQL. It specifies requirements for the search. The usual form is to compare one or more fields to a desired value. As an example, using the phone database, if we want to find a person named **Smith** (**ContactName** field), we would use:

Criteria = "ContactName = 'Smith'"

Note the use of single quotes around the embedded string. If you are unsure of the complete field name, you can use the **LIKE** keyword with the wildcard character (*). Say, in the above example, you are unsure if the name you are looking for is Smith or Smyth. A search criteria to find either is:

Criteria = "ContactName LIKE 'Sm*'"

How do you know if a search is successful? You check the length of the returned row array. If, after a **Select** method, that length is greater than 0, the search was successful. One problem with the **Select** method is that is doesn't provide corresponding row numbers within the data table (like the **Find** method did). It only tells us what the rows are that match the search criteria. To find corresponding row numbers (to allow positioning of a currency manager), we need to do a little work. The code is not difficult, just a bit awkward.

Database Management

Assuming the returned rows array (**MyRows**) is of non-zero length and the default view of the data table is sorted by **MySortField**, the corresponding row number for the first row in the array is:

```
Dim FirstRow As Integer
FirstRow =
MyTable.DefaultView.Find(MyRows(0).Item(MySortField))
```

This code uses the **Find** method to locate the first row (**FirstRow**) that contains the **MySortField** value found in **MyRows(0)**. As we said, it's awkward, but it works. After finding **FirstRow**, you set the currency manager's **Position** property to that value to properly rebind all controls.

Example 6-4

Finding Database Records

In the phone database we have been using, we noted one drawback when editing and adding records to the data table. After saving changes, the currency manager does not necessarily point to the record we just edited or added. We can now correct that drawback using the data table **Find** method.

1. Open Example 6-3 (the phone database example we've been building).

2. Modify the **btnSave Click** event procedure to implement a search, following resorting of the saved data table (new code is shaded):

```
Private Sub BtnSave_Click(ByVal sender As System.Object, ByVal e As System.EventArgs) Handles btnSave.Click
    Dim SavedName As String = txtName.Text
    Dim SavedRow As Integer
    PhoneManager.EndCurrentEdit()
    PhoneTable.DefaultView.Sort = "ContactName"
    SavedRow = PhoneTable.DefaultView.Find(SavedName)
    PhoneManager.Position = SavedRow
    Call SetState("View")
End Sub
```

When we enter this procedure, we have decided to save the displayed information. Before ending the edit, we save the **ContactName** field (contained in the **txtName** text box) in the variable **SavedName**. After ending the edit (saving the data table), we search for that saved name using the **Find** method. The returned row (**SavedRow**) is used to reposition the currency manager. Notice we didn't check to see if **SavedRow** is valid, since we are guaranteed a successful search. In other searches, you would want to make sure **SavedRow** is not -1 before continuing.

3. Save the application (Access version saved in the **Example 6-4** folder in **VBDB\Access\Class 6** folder; SQL Server version saved in the **Example 6-4** folder in **VBDB\SQL Server\Class 6** folder) and run it. **Edit** a record. Click **Save**. Note the displayed record is now the newly edited record. Try the same thing with **Add New**.

Modifying Records in Code

There are times you might like to change information in database records using BASIC code. As an example, say you want to transfer information from a data file to your database (we do that in the last chapter). Or, perhaps you want to transfer information from one database into another. Or, maybe you need to update some fields in your database. And, in an extreme case, you might want to delete all the records in your database. All of these tasks can be performed with BASIC code.

To modify a database using code, you simply determine what tasks need to be accomplished and what code you need to accomplish those tasks. What code do you have at your disposal? The same code you have been using for database management tasks:

- ⇒ The currency manager **Position** property can be used to navigate among the database records.
- ⇒ **AddNew** can be used to add a record.
- ⇒ **RemoveAt** can be used to delete a record.
- ⇒ **EndCurrentEdit** can be used to update a data table.
- ⇒ **Find** can be used to locate records.
- ⇒ The data adapter **Update** method can be used to save changes in the database.

Write the code in the same manner you would have a user perform the tasks. And take advantage of any code you might already have in your application. For example, if you add a record in code and want to save it, simply call your **Save** event (if it exists). As you progress in database programming, you will find many places you want to automate database management procedures. This is exactly what modifying data in code does for you.

There are many properties and methods that allow us to view, edit and modify a data table without using a currency manager. One very useful property is the data table's **Rows** collection. This collection contains all rows in the data table. The **DataRow** object allows us to examine (or establish) fields in each row of the data table. To see all values of a field (**MyField**) in a table (**MyTable**), you could use this code snippet:

```
Dim MyRow As DataRow
    .
    .
For Each MyRow In MyTable.Rows
    .
    'Field is available in variable MyRow.Item(MyField)
    .
Next
```

In this snippet, **MyField** is a string data type. The code uses a special form of the **For/Next** loop that goes through all elements of the **Rows** collection. Such code could be used to make bulk changes to a database. For example, you could use it to add area codes to all your phone numbers or change the case of particular fields. We do that in the next example.

In addition to direct editing of data rows, you can use the data row object to add a row to a data table. To add a row to **MyTable**, use this code:

```
Dim NewRow As DataRow
NewRow = MyTable.NewRow()

'Add fields using
NewRow.Item(MyField) = FieldValue

'After adding all fields add row
MyTable.Rows.Add(NewRow)
```

To delete row **N** from a data table (**MyTable**), simply use:

```
MyTable.Rows(N).Delete()
```

Example 6-5

Modifying Records in Code

Notice the phone numbers in the phone database we have been using do not have area codes listed. It is for local calls. If we want to expand our database to allow calls outside our area code, we need to add area codes to all the existing numbers. We could run the application and edit all records, one at a time, adding an area code, or we could do it in code. Let's try it.

1. Re-open Example 6-4. Add this code at the bottom of the **frmPhoneDB Load** procedure:

```
Dim PhoneRow As DataRow
For Each PhoneRow In PhoneTable.Rows
   PhoneRow.Item("ContactNumber") = "(206) " +
PhoneRow.Item("ContactNumber").ToString
Next
```

In this code, we go through each row in the data table (**PhoneTable**) and change the **ContactNumber** field, adding a (206) area code

2. Save (Access version saved in the **Example 6-5** folder in **VBDB\Access\Class 6** folder; SQL Server version saved in the **Example 6-5** folder in **VBDB\SQL Server\Class 6** folder) and run the application. Notice all the phone numbers now have area codes. Here's our old friend Adam Zuffi:

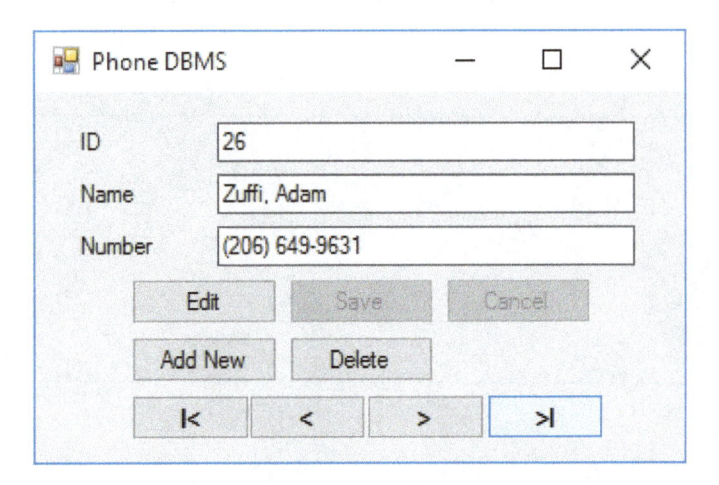

3. If desired, replace the line of code adding area codes with this one:

   ```
   PhoneRow.Item("ContactNumber") =
   Mid(PhoneRow.Item("ContactNumber").ToString, 7)
   ```

   Run the application again. This line strips off the area codes to restore the database to its original state. Once you are done making all the modifications, remove the code that changes the **ContactNumber**. If you don't, you will get changes each time you run the program. In the saved version of this project, all lines changing phone numbers are commented out.

Stopping a Database Application

In all applications we have built in this class, execution can be stopped in one of four ways:

1. Using the Visual Basic toolbar **End** button.
2. Clicking the **control box** in the upper left hand corner of the form and choosing **Close**.
3. Pressing **Alt-<F4>**.
4. Clicking the **X** in the upper right corner of the application form.

When others use our applications, the Visual Basic **End** button will not be available, the control box may or may not be visible, and all users may not know they can use **Alt-<F4>** or the X button to stop. We need a way to clearly indicate to a user how to stop an application.

The most straightforward way to stop an application is to provide a button to click. You choose the caption. Some captions that are used in Windows applications are **Exit**, **Stop**, **Close**, and **Done**. We will use a **Text** property of **Done**. We will **Name** our button **btnDone**. So, all we need is code to put in the **btnDone Click** event procedure. The code is very simple:

```
Private Sub BtnDone_Click(ByVal sender As System.Object,
ByVal e As System.EventArgs) Handles btnDone.Click
  Me.Close()
End Sub
```

How's that for simple? One line of code stops the application. This line tells the form to close itself (**Me**).

With regard to application state, the **Done** button should be disabled during any editing. We want to make sure our users have saved any changes made to the database before stopping the application. This is easily controlled using the button's **Enabled** property. But there's a problem. We can keep the user from clicking **Done** at an inappropriate time, but we can't stop the user from using one of the three other ways to stop the application (control box, **Alt-<F4>**, x). And, we can't prevent the user from completely shutting down the Windows operating system! Fortunately, Visual Basic provides a procedure that allows us to intercept any attempt to close a form and decide if that attempt is appropriate. The procedure is form's **FormClosing** event.

The **FormClosing** procedure is invoked prior to closing the form. We have been using this procedure to save changes to the database and close connections. Now, we'll add capability to insure the user can close the form. The **FormClosing** procedure has the form:

```
Private Sub My_FormClosing(ByVal sender As Object, ByVal e
As System.Windows.Forms.FormClosingEventArgs) Handles
Me.FormClosing
    .
    .
    .
End Sub
```

The **e** argument (of type **FormClosingEventArgs**) has two properties: **e.Cancel** and **e.CloseReason**. If **e.Cancel** is **False**, when the procedure is exited, the closing continues. If **e.Cancel** is **True**, the closing process is canceled.

e.CloseReason tells us what invoked the closing event:

ApplicationExitCall	The Exit method of the Application class was invoked.
FormOwnerClosing	The owner form is closing.
None	The cause of the closure was not defined or could not be determined.
TaskManagerClosing	The Microsoft Windows Task Manager is closing the application.
UserClosing	The user is closing the form through the user interface (UI), for example by clicking the Close button on the form window, selecting Close from the window's control menu, or pressing ALT+F4.
WindowsShutDown	The operating system is closing all applications before shutting down.

So, how do we use this event procedure? With regard to database management, we simply check to see if any editing functions are in progress. If so, we inform the user with a message box and cancel the closing process (set **e.Cancel** to **True**). If no editing is being done, we allow the closing to continue. That is, we do nothing. The next example illustrates its use.

Example 6-6

Stopping a Database Application

We add stopping ability to the phone database example we have been using.

1. Re-open Example 6-4 (the project version that doesn't modify the phone numbers). Add a button with a **Name** of **btnDone** and **Text** of **Done**. The form will look like this:

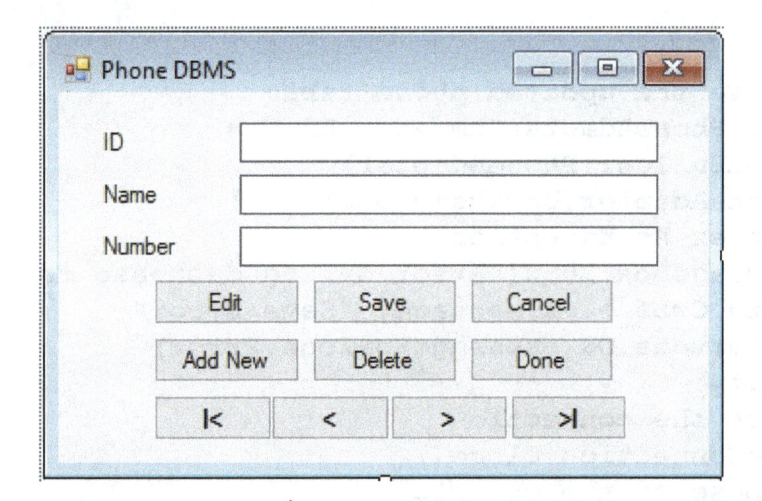

2. Place this code in the **btnDone Click** procedure:

   ```
   Private Sub BtnDone_Click(ByVal sender As System.Object,
   ByVal e As System.EventArgs) Handles btnDone.Click
      Me.Close()
   End Sub
   ```

3. Modify the **SetState** procedure to set the **btnDone** button **Enabled** property to **True** in **View** mode, **False** in **Add/Edit** mode.

6-44 Visual Basic and Databases

4. Add the shaded code to the **frmPhoneDB Closing** procedure:

Access Database:

```
  Private Sub FrmPhoneDB_FormClosing(ByVal sender As Object,
ByVal e As System.Windows.Forms.FormClosingEventArgs)
Handles Me.FormClosing
    If MyState = "Edit" Or MyState = "Add" Then
      MessageBox.Show("You must finish the current edit
before stopping the application.", "", MessageBoxButtons.OK,
MessageBoxIcon.Information)
      e.Cancel = True
    Else
      Try
        'save the updated phone table
        Dim PhoneAdapterCommands As New
OleDbCommandBuilder(PhoneAdapter)
        PhoneAdapter.Update(PhoneTable)
      Catch ex As Exception
        MessageBox.Show("Error saving database to file:" +
ControlChars.CrLf + ex.Message, "Save Error",
MessageBoxButtons.OK, MessageBoxIcon.Error)
      End Try
      'close the connection
      PhoneConnection.Close()
      'dispose of the objects
      PhoneConnection.Dispose()
      PhoneCommand.Dispose()
      PhoneAdapter.Dispose()
      PhoneTable.Dispose()
    End If
  End Sub
```

Database Management 6-45

SQL Server Database:

```
Private Sub FrmPhoneDB_FormClosing(ByVal sender As Object, ByVal e As System.Windows.Forms.FormClosingEventArgs) Handles Me.FormClosing
    If MyState = "Edit" Or MyState = "Add" Then
        MessageBox.Show("You must finish the current edit before stopping the application.", "", MessageBoxButtons.OK, MessageBoxIcon.Information)
        e.Cancel = True
    Else
        Try
            'save the updated phone table
            Dim PhoneAdapterCommands As New SqlCommandBuilder(PhoneAdapter)
            PhoneAdapter.Update(PhoneTable)
        Catch ex As Exception
            MessageBox.Show("Error saving database to file:" + ControlChars.CrLf + ex.Message, "Save Error", MessageBoxButtons.OK, MessageBoxIcon.Error)
        End Try
        'close the connection
        PhoneConnection.Close()
        'dispose of the objects
        PhoneConnection.Dispose()
        PhoneCommand.Dispose()
        PhoneAdapter.Dispose()
        PhoneTable.Dispose()
    End If
End Sub
```

If the application is in **Edit** or **Add** mode, the user is editing a record and we don't want the application to stop. We inform the user of the problem and cancel the closing process.

6-46   **Visual Basic and Databases**

5. Save (Access version saved in the **Example 6-6** folder in **VBDB\Access\Class 6** folder; SQL Server version version saved in the **Example 6-6** folder in **VBDB\SQL Server\Class 6** folder) the application and run it. Click **Edit**. Notice the **Done** button is disabled:

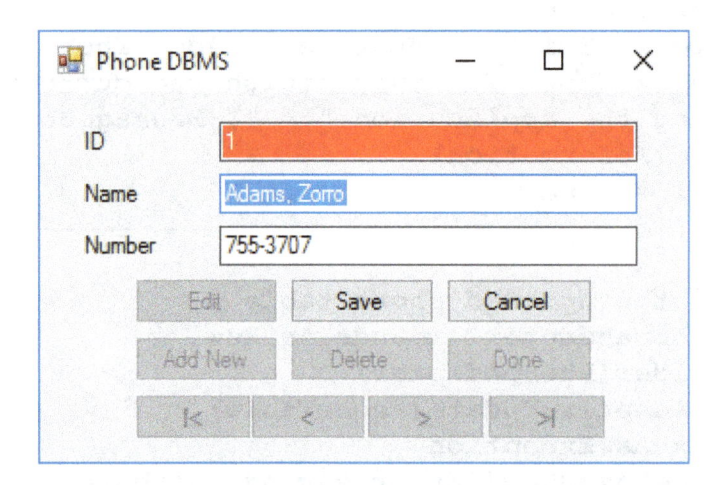

Click the **X** in the upper right corner of the form. This should not stop the application. This message box will appear:

Click **OK** to return to the database screen. Click **Cancel**. Now, try **X** again. The application should stop. Try the other ways (including the **Done** button) to stop the application, both in **View** mode and **Edit** mode. Make sure everything works properly.

Example 6-7

Authors Table Input Form

At long last, we can use our new database management knowledge to complete the input forms begun in Chapter 6 for the books database (Access - **BooksDB.accdb**, SQL Server - **SQLBooksDB.mdf**). In this example, we tackle the **Authors** Table. In the next example, we'll complete the **Publishers** Table. We will do the modifications in stages, testing each stage as we proceed.

Additional Navigation Capabilities

Recall, in Chapter 6, we stated that part of proper interface design was recognizing you might have omitted needed features. And, the Visual Basic environment makes correcting these omissions a simple task. The Authors table input form only has two navigation buttons – one to move to the **Previous** record and one to move to the **Next** record. This may limit us. We will add the ability to move to the beginning and end of the data table. Adding these additional navigation capabilities is a good example of correcting an omission.

1. Load Example 5-8 (the last version of the **Authors** table input form). Add two buttons. Set these properties:

Button1:
    Name   btnFirst
    Text |< First

Button2:
    Name   btnLast
    Text   Last >|

Change the **btnPrevious** button's **Text** to **< Previous** and **btnNext** button's **Text** to **Next >** (remove the = signs). The form looks like this:

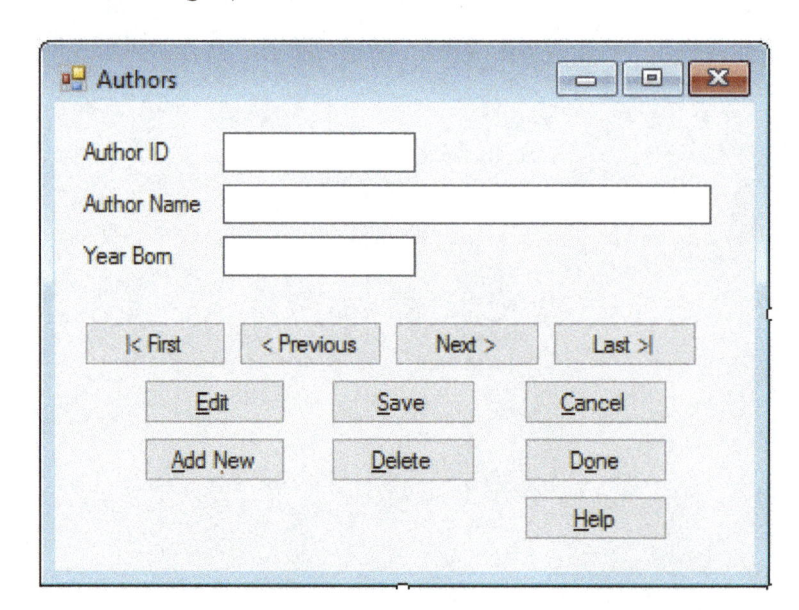

Database Management   6-49

2. Add this code to the **btnFirst Click** procedure:

```
Private Sub BtnFirst_Click(ByVal sender As System.Object, ByVal e As System.EventArgs) Handles btnFirst.Click
    AuthorsManager.Position = 0
End Sub
```

Add this code to the **btnLast Click** procedure:

```
Private Sub BtnLast_Click(ByVal sender As System.Object, ByVal e As System.EventArgs) Handles btnLast.Click
    AuthorsManager.Position = AuthorsManager.Count - 1
End Sub
```

3. Go to the **SetState** procedure. Make sure the **First** and **Last** buttons are enabled in **View** mode and disabled in **Add** and **Edit** mode (the same as the **Previous** and **Next** buttons).

4. Save the application (Access version saved in the **Example 6-7** folder in **VBDB\Access\Class 6** folder; SQL Server version saved in the **Example 6-7** folder in **VBDB\SQL Server\Class 6** folder). Run it. Your should see:

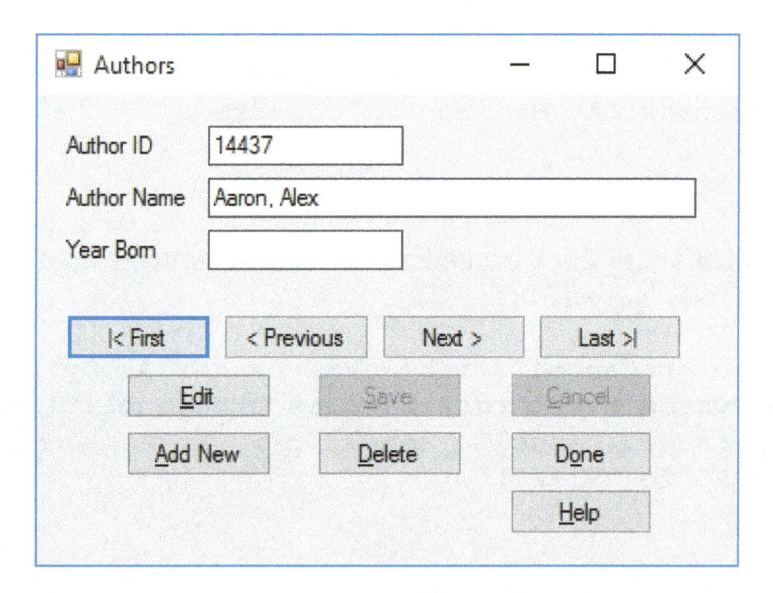

Make sure the new navigation buttons work correctly (both moving through the records and enabling/disabling as states change).

Editing Records

We now add editing capability and the corresponding abilities to save and/or cancel an edit.

1. Modify the **btnSave Click** procedure to save edits and reposition the pointer to the edited record (new lines of code are shaded):

```
Private Sub BtnSave_Click(ByVal sender As System.Object, ByVal e As System.EventArgs) Handles btnSave.Click
    If Not (ValidateData()) Then Exit Sub
    Dim SavedName As String = txtAuthorName.Text
    Dim SavedRow As Integer
    Try
      AuthorsManager.EndCurrentEdit()
      AuthorsTable.DefaultView.Sort = "Author"
      SavedRow = AuthorsTable.DefaultView.Find(SavedName)
      AuthorsManager.Position = SavedRow
      MessageBox.Show("Record saved.", "Save", MessageBoxButtons.OK, MessageBoxIcon.Information)
      Call SetState("View")
    Catch ex As Exception
      MessageBox.Show("Error saving record.", "Error", MessageBoxButtons.OK, MessageBoxIcon.Error)
    End Try
End Sub
```

2. Modify the **btnCancel Click** procedure to restore controls if edit is canceled (new line of code is shaded):

```
Private Sub BtnCancel_Click(ByVal sender As System.Object, ByVal e As System.EventArgs) Handles btnCancel.Click
    AuthorsManager.CancelCurrentEdit()
    Call SetState("View")
End Sub
```

Database Management 6-51

3. Add the shaded code to **frmAuthors FormClosing** procedure to save any changes to the database file:

Access Database:

```
Private Sub FrmAuthors_FormClosing(ByVal sender As Object, ByVal e As System.Windows.Forms.FormClosingEventArgs) Handles Me.FormClosing
    Try
        'save changes to database
        Dim AuthorsAdapterCommands As New OleDbCommandBuilder(AuthorsAdapter)
        AuthorsAdapter.Update(AuthorsTable)
    Catch ex As Exception
        MessageBox.Show("Error saving database to file:" + ControlChars.CrLf + ex.Message, "Save Error", MessageBoxButtons.OK, MessageBoxIcon.Error)
    End Try
    'close the connection
    BooksConnection.Close()
    'dispose of the objects
    BooksConnection.Dispose()
    AuthorsCommand.Dispose()
    AuthorsAdapter.Dispose()
    AuthorsTable.Dispose()
End Sub
```

SQL Server Database:

```
  Private Sub FrmAuthors_FormClosing(ByVal sender As Object,
ByVal e As System.Windows.Forms.FormClosingEventArgs)
Handles Me.FormClosing
    Try
      'save changes to database
      Dim AuthorsAdapterCommands As New
SqlCommandBuilder(AuthorsAdapter)
      AuthorsAdapter.Update(AuthorsTable)
    Catch ex As Exception
      MessageBox.Show("Error saving database to file:" +
ControlChars.CrLf + ex.Message, "Save Error",
MessageBoxButtons.OK, MessageBoxIcon.Error)
    End Try
    'close the connection
    BooksConnection.Close()
    'dispose of the objects
    BooksConnection.Dispose()
    AuthorsCommand.Dispose()
    AuthorsAdapter.Dispose()
    AuthorsTable.Dispose()
End Sub
```

4. Save the application. Run it. Make sure the **Edit** feature works – try changing an author's name. Make sure **Cancel** works properly.

Adding Records

We now implement the ability to add records to the database.

1. Add this line in the form level declarations:

   ```
   Dim MyState As String, MyBookmark As Integer
   ```

2. Add this line of code at the top of the **SetState** procedure:

   ```
   MyState = AppState
   ```

3. Modify the **btnAddNew Click** procedure to add records (new code is shaded):

   ```
   Private Sub BtnAddNew_Click(ByVal sender As System.Object, ByVal e As System.EventArgs) Handles btnAddNew.Click
       Try
           MyBookmark = AuthorsManager.Position
           AuthorsManager.AddNew()
           Call SetState("Add")
       Catch ex As Exception
           MessageBox.Show("Error adding record.", "Error", MessageBoxButtons.OK, MessageBoxIcon.Error)
       End Try
   End Sub
   ```

4. Modify the **btnCancel Click** code to differentiate between canceling during **Edit** mode and **Add** mode (new code is shaded):

   ```
   Private Sub BtnCancel_Click(ByVal sender As System.Object, ByVal e As System.EventArgs) Handles btnCancel.Click
       AuthorsManager.CancelCurrentEdit()
       If MyState = "Add" Then
           AuthorsManager.Position = MyBookmark
       End If
       Call SetState("View")
   End Sub
   ```

5. Save the application and run it. Click **Add New**. Notice all text boxes are blank (including the **Author ID** box; recall this primary key value will be assigned by ADO .NET when the database is resaved). Type in a name and year (if desired). Click **Save**. You should see:

Click **OK** and the new record should be displayed. I added myself:

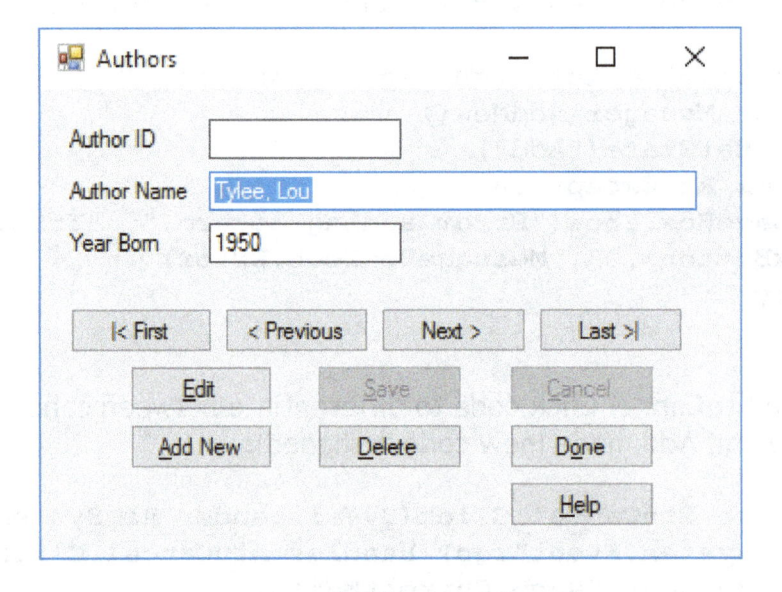

Deleting Records

We now add the ability to delete records from the **Authors** table.

1. Modify the **btnDelete Click** procedure to delete the record if the user responds **Yes** to the message box (new code is shaded):

```
Private Sub BtnDelete_Click(ByVal sender As System.Object, ByVal e As System.EventArgs) Handles btnDelete.Click
    Dim Response As Windows.Forms.DialogResult
    Response = MessageBox.Show("Are you sure you want to delete this record?", "Delete", MessageBoxButtons.YesNo, MessageBoxIcon.Question, MessageBoxDefaultButton.Button2)
    If Response = Windows.Forms.DialogResult.No Then
       Exit Sub
    End If
    Try
       AuthorsManager.RemoveAt(AuthorsManager.Position)
    Catch ex As Exception
       MessageBox.Show("Error deleting record.", "Error", MessageBoxButtons.OK, MessageBoxIcon.Error)
    End Try
End Sub
```

2. Save the application and run it. Make sure both the **Yes** and **No** responses to the message box give the proper results. Only delete records you added in testing the **Add New** function. If you try to delete an original author in the table, you will see this message box when you stop the application (from the **FormClosing** event):

Access Database:

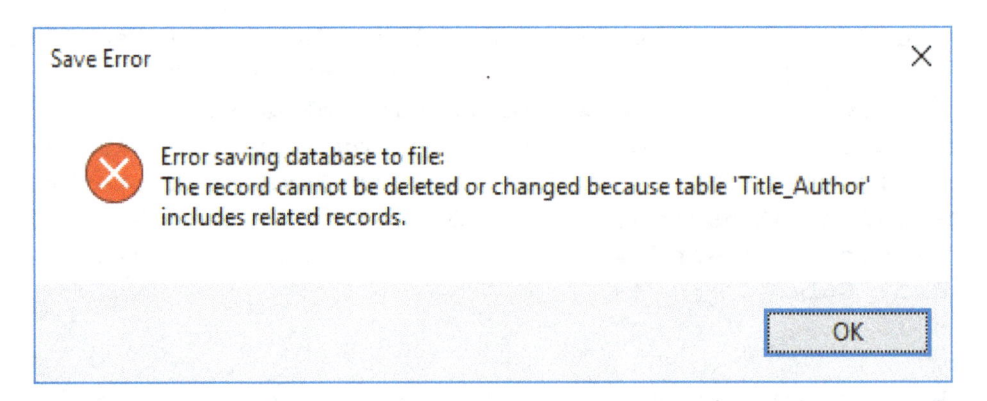

> Save Error
>
> ❌ Error saving database to file:
> The record cannot be deleted or changed because table 'Title_Author' includes related records.
>
> OK

SQL Server Database:

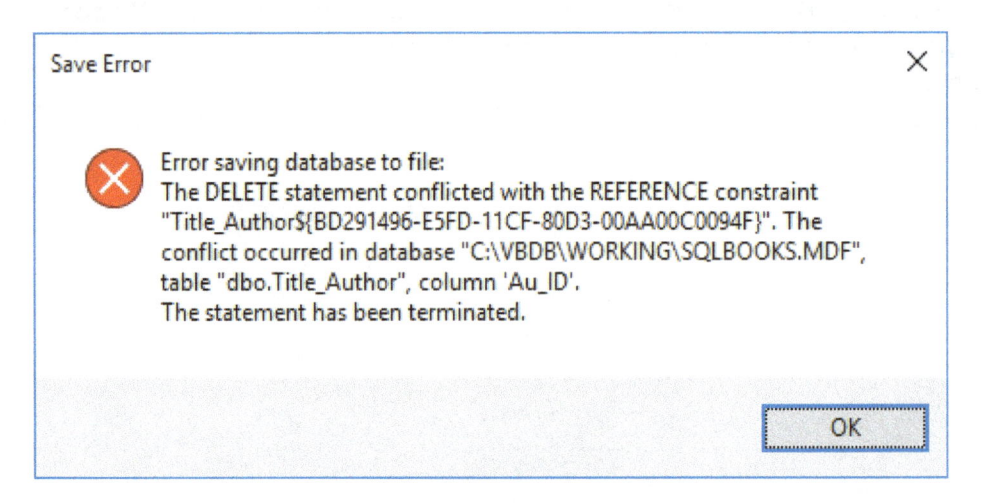

> Save Error
>
> ❌ Error saving database to file:
> The DELETE statement conflicted with the REFERENCE constraint "Title_Author${BD291496-E5FD-11CF-80D3-00AA00C0094F}". The conflict occurred in database "C:\VBDB\WORKING\SQLBOOKS.MDF", table "dbo.Title_Author", column 'Au_ID'.
> The statement has been terminated.
>
> OK

This is preventing you from deleting an author that is used by other tables. An author record can only be deleted if no other table uses it. This preserves your database's integrity.

Stopping the Application

The final modification step is to implement the correct stopping code.

1. Place this code in the **btnDone Click** procedure:

```
Private Sub BtnDone_Click(ByVal sender As System.Object, ByVal e As System.EventArgs) Handles btnDone.Click
   Me.Close()
End Sub
```

2. Add the shaded code to the **frmAuthors FormClosing** procedure to insure we don't close in the middle of an edit:

Access Database:

```
Private Sub FrmAuthors_FormClosing(ByVal sender As Object, ByVal e As System.Windows.Forms.FormClosingEventArgs) Handles Me.FormClosing
    If MyState = "Edit" Or MyState = "Add" Then
      MessageBox.Show("You must finish the current edit before stopping the application.", "", MessageBoxButtons.OK, MessageBoxIcon.Information)
      e.Cancel = True
    Else
      Try
        'save changes to database
        Dim AuthorsAdapterCommands As New OleDbCommandBuilder(AuthorsAdapter)
        AuthorsAdapter.Update(AuthorsTable)
      Catch ex As Exception
        MessageBox.Show("Error saving database to file:" + ControlChars.CrLf + ex.Message, "Save Error", MessageBoxButtons.OK, MessageBoxIcon.Error)
      End Try
      'close the connection
      BooksConnection.Close()
      'dispose of the objects
      BooksConnection.Dispose()
      AuthorsCommand.Dispose()
      AuthorsAdapter.Dispose()
      AuthorsTable.Dispose()
    End If
End Sub
```

SQL Server Database:

```
  Private Sub FrmAuthors_FormClosing(ByVal sender As Object,
ByVal e As System.Windows.Forms.FormClosingEventArgs)
Handles Me.FormClosing
    If MyState = "Edit" Or MyState = "Add" Then
      MessageBox.Show("You must finish the current edit
before stopping the application.", "", MessageBoxButtons.OK,
MessageBoxIcon.Information)
      e.Cancel = True
    Else
      Try
        'save changes to database
        Dim AuthorsAdapterCommands As New
SqlCommandBuilder(AuthorsAdapter)
        AuthorsAdapter.Update(AuthorsTable)
      Catch ex As Exception
        MessageBox.Show("Error saving database to file:" +
ControlChars.CrLf + ex.Message, "Save Error",
MessageBoxButtons.OK, MessageBoxIcon.Error)
      End Try
      'close the connection
      BooksConnection.Close()
      'dispose of the objects
      BooksConnection.Dispose()
      AuthorsCommand.Dispose()
      AuthorsAdapter.Dispose()
      AuthorsTable.Dispose()
    End If
  End Sub
```

3. Save the application and run it. Make sure the **Done** button works properly. Make sure you can't exit the application while in **Edit** or **Add** mode. Make sure all functions work properly.

The **Authors** Table Input Form application is now complete (final Access version is saved in the **Example 6-7** folder in **VBDB\Access\Class 6** folder; SQL Server version is saved in the **Example 6-7** folder in **VBDB\SQL Server\Class 6** folder). Hopefully, you see the great advantage in using the Visual Basic interface to build and test an application. The event-driven nature allows building of the interface in stages. This greatly simplifies testing and debugging of the application. We will use this form as part of a complete books database management system in the final example of this chapter.

Example 6-8

Publishers Table Input Form

We now add database management capabilities to the **Publishers** Table Input Form developed in Example 5-9 in Chapter 5. This table, in conjunction with the **Authors** Table Input Form just completed, will be part of a complete books database management system. You will notice the steps are essentially identical to those followed for the Authors table.

Additional Navigation Capabilities

We add the ability to move to the beginning and end of the data table.

1. Open Example 5-9 (the Publishers table input form). Add two buttons. Set these properties:

Button1:
    Name   btnFirst
    Text |< First

Button2:
    Name   btnLast
    Text   Last >|

Change the **btnPrevious** button's **Text** to **< Previous** and **btnNext** button's **Text** to **Next >** (we just eliminated the = signs). The form looks like this:

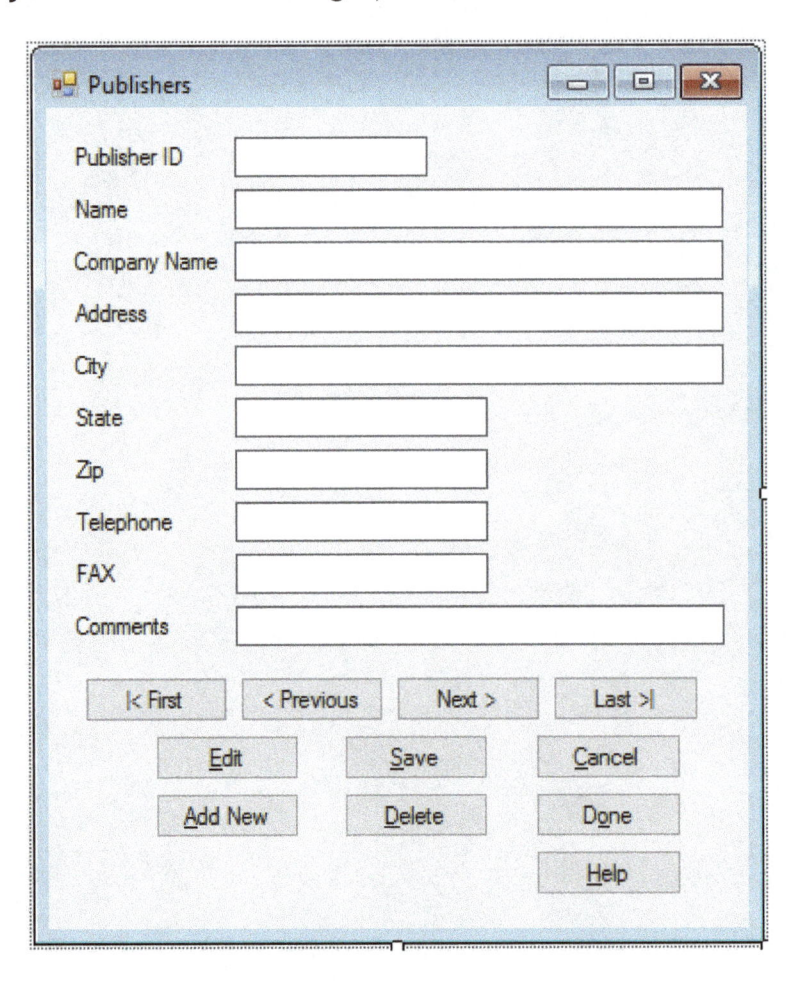

Database Management

2. Add this code to the **btnFirst Click** procedure:

```
Private Sub BtnFirst_Click(ByVal sender As System.Object, ByVal e As System.EventArgs) Handles btnFirst.Click
    PublishersManager.Position = 0
End Sub
```

Add this code to the **btnLast Click** procedure:

```
Private Sub BtnLast_Click(ByVal sender As System.Object, ByVal e As System.EventArgs) Handles btnLast.Click
    PublishersManager.Position = PublishersManager.Count - 1
End Sub
```

3. Go to the **SetState** procedure. Make sure the **First** and **Last** buttons are enabled in **View** mode and disabled in **Add** and **Edit** mode (the same as the **Previous** and **Next** buttons).

Visual Basic and Databases

4. Save the application (Access version saved in the **Example 6-8** folder in the **VBDB\Access\Class 6** folder; SQL Server version saved in the **Example 6-8** folder in the **VBDB\ SQL Server\Class 6** folder). Run it. You should see:

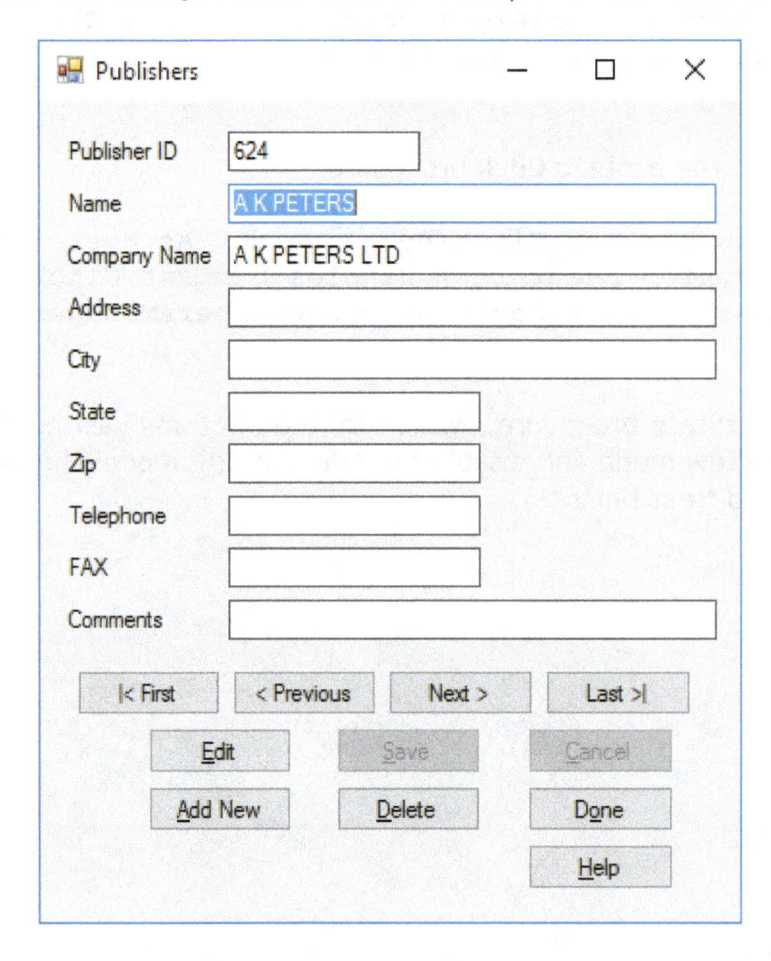

Make sure the new navigation buttons work correctly (both moving through the records and enabling/disabling as states change).

Database Management

6-63

Editing Records

We now add editing capability and the corresponding abilities to save and/or cancel an edit.

1. Modify the **btnSave Click** procedure to save edit and reposition pointer to the edited record (new lines of code are shaded):

```
Private Sub BtnSave_Click(ByVal sender As System.Object,
ByVal e As System.EventArgs) Handles btnSave.Click
    If Not (ValidateData()) Then Exit Sub
    Dim SavedName As String = txtPubName.Text
    Dim SavedRow As Integer
    Try
      PublishersManager.EndCurrentEdit()
      PublishersTable.DefaultView.Sort = "Name"
      SavedRow = PublishersTable.DefaultView.Find(SavedName)
      PublishersManager.Position = SavedRow
      MessageBox.Show("Record saved.", "Save",
MessageBoxButtons.OK, MessageBoxIcon.Information)
      Call SetState("View")
    Catch ex As Exception
      MessageBox.Show("Error saving record.", "Error",
MessageBoxButtons.OK, MessageBoxIcon.Error)
    End Try
  End Sub
```

2. Modify the **btnCancel Click** procedure to restore controls if edit is canceled (new line of code is italicized):

```
Private Sub BtnCancel_Click(ByVal sender As System.Object,
ByVal e As System.EventArgs) Handles btnCancel.Click
    PublishersManager.CancelCurrentEdit()
    Call SetState("View")
  End Sub
```

3. Add the shaded code to the **frmPublishers FormClosing** procedure to save any changes to the database file:

Access Database:

```
   Private Sub FrmPublishers_FormClosing(ByVal sender As
Object, ByVal e As
System.Windows.Forms.FormClosingEventArgs) Handles
Me.FormClosing
      Try
         'save changes to database
         Dim PublishersAdapterCommands As New
OleDbCommandBuilder(PublishersAdapter)
         PublishersAdapter.Update(PublishersTable)
      Catch ex As Exception
         MessageBox.Show("Error saving database to file:" +
ControlChars.CrLf + ex.Message, "Save Error",
MessageBoxButtons.OK, MessageBoxIcon.Error)
      End Try
'close the connection
      BooksConnection.Close()
      'dispose of the objects
      BooksConnection.Dispose()
      PublishersCommand.Dispose()
      PublishersAdapter.Dispose()
      PublishersTable.Dispose()
   End Sub
```

Database Management 6-65

SQL Server Database:

```vb
   Private Sub FrmPublishers_FormClosing(ByVal sender As
Object, ByVal e As
System.Windows.Forms.FormClosingEventArgs) Handles
Me.FormClosing
      Try
        'save changes to database
        Dim PublishersAdapterCommands As New
SqlCommandBuilder(PublishersAdapter)
        PublishersAdapter.Update(PublishersTable)
      Catch ex As Exception
        MessageBox.Show("Error saving database to file:" +
ControlChars.CrLf + ex.Message, "Save Error",
MessageBoxButtons.OK, MessageBoxIcon.Error)
      End Try
      'close the connection
      BooksConnection.Close()
      'dispose of the objects
      BooksConnection.Dispose()
      PublishersCommand.Dispose()
      PublishersAdapter.Dispose()
      PublishersTable.Dispose()
End Sub
```

4. Save the application. Run it. Make sure the **Edit** feature works – try changing a publisher's name. Make sure **Cancel** works properly.

Adding Records

We now implement the ability to add records to the database.

1. Add this line in the form level declarations:

   ```
   Dim MyState As String, MyBookmark As Integer
   ```

2. Add this line of code at the top of the **SetState** procedure:

   ```
   MyState = AppState
   ```

3. Modify the **btnAddNew Click** procedure to add records (new code is shaded):

   ```
   Private Sub BtnAddNew_Click(ByVal sender As System.Object, ByVal e As System.EventArgs) Handles btnAddNew.Click
       Try
           MyBookmark = PublishersManager.Position
           PublishersManager.AddNew()
           Call SetState("Add")
       Catch ex As Exception
           MessageBox.Show("Error adding record.", "Error", MessageBoxButtons.OK, MessageBoxIcon.Error)
       End Try
   End Sub
   ```

4. Modify the **btnCancel Click** code to differentiate between canceling during **Edit** mode and **Add** mode (new code is shaded):

   ```
   Private Sub BtnCancel_Click(ByVal sender As System.Object, ByVal e As System.EventArgs) Handles btnCancel.Click
       PublishersManager.CancelCurrentEdit()
       If MyState = "Add" Then
           PublishersManager.Position = MyBookmark
       End If
       Call SetState("View")
   End Sub
   ```

Database Management 6-67

5. Save the application and run it. Click **Add New**. Again, all the text boxes are blank. The **Publisher ID** (a non-editable primary key) will be assigned once the database file is saved. Type in some information (add at least a **Name** value). Click **Save** and you will see:

[Save dialog: "Record saved." with OK button]

Click **OK** and the new record will be displayed. I added my company (KIDware):

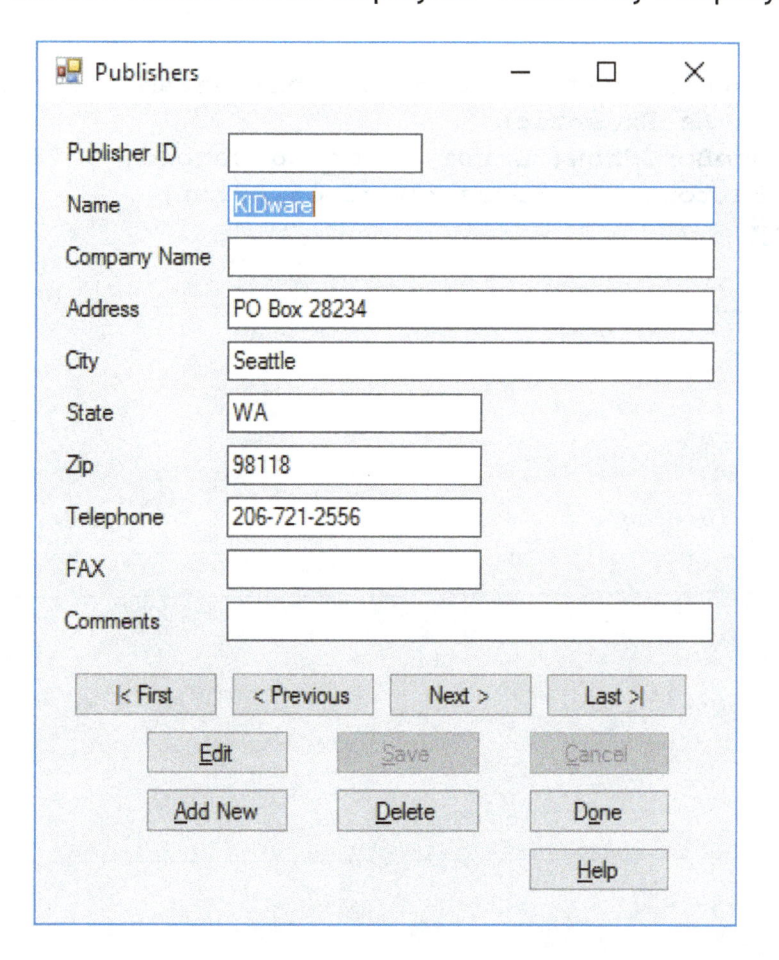

[Publishers form showing:
- Publisher ID: (blank)
- Name: KIDware
- Company Name: (blank)
- Address: PO Box 28234
- City: Seattle
- State: WA
- Zip: 98118
- Telephone: 206-721-2556
- FAX: (blank)
- Comments: (blank)
Buttons: |< First, < Previous, Next >, Last >|, Edit, Save, Cancel, Add New, Delete, Done, Help]

Deleting Records

We now add the ability to delete records from the Publishers table.

1. Modify the **btnDelete Click** procedure to delete the record if the user responds **Yes** to the message box (new code is shaded):

```
Private Sub BtnDelete_Click(ByVal sender As System.Object, ByVal e As System.EventArgs) Handles btnDelete.Click
    Dim Response As Windows.Forms.DialogResult
    Response = MessageBox.Show("Are you sure you want to delete this record?", "Delete", MessageBoxButtons.YesNo, MessageBoxIcon.Question, MessageBoxDefaultButton.Button2)
    If Response = Windows.Forms.DialogResult.No Then
      Exit Sub
    End If
    Try
      PublishersManager.RemoveAt(PublishersManager.Position)
    Catch ex As Exception
      MessageBox.Show("Error deleting record.", "Error", MessageBoxButtons.OK, MessageBoxIcon.Error)
    End Try
  End Sub
```

Database Management 6-69

2. Save the application and run it. Make sure both the **Yes** and **No** responses to the message box give the proper results. Delete a record. Only delete records you added in testing the **Add New** function. If you delete an original publisher in the table, you will see this message box when you stop the application (from the **FormClosing** event):

Access Database:

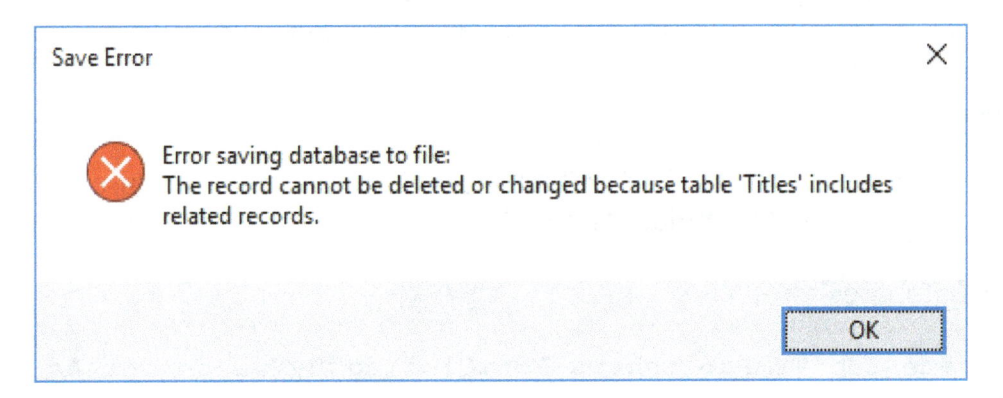

> **Save Error** ✕
>
> ❌ Error saving database to file:
> The record cannot be deleted or changed because table 'Titles' includes related records.
>
> [OK]

SQL Server Database:

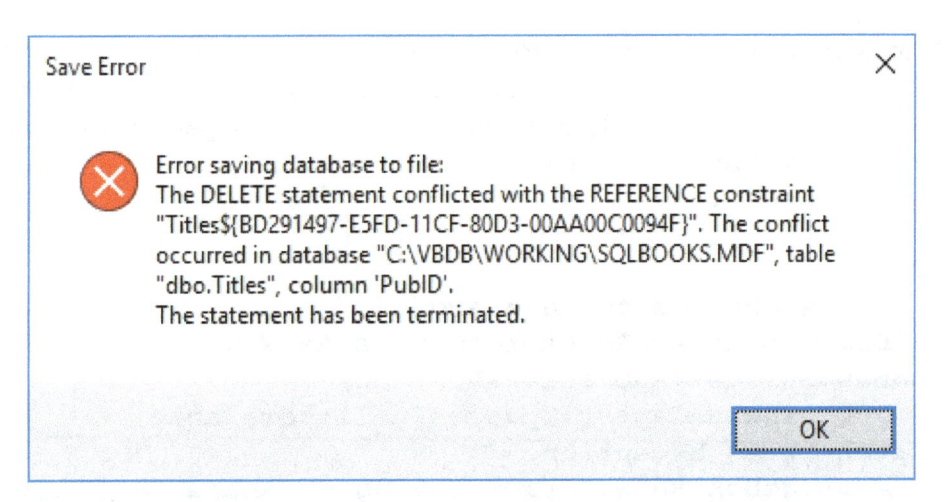

> **Save Error** ✕
>
> ❌ Error saving database to file:
> The DELETE statement conflicted with the REFERENCE constraint "Titles${BD291497-E5FD-11CF-80D3-00AA00C0094F}". The conflict occurred in database "C:\VBDB\WORKING\SQLBOOKS.MDF", table "dbo.Titles", column 'PubID'.
> The statement has been terminated.
>
> [OK]

You cannot delete publishers that are used by other tables. This would destroy the integrity of your database.

Stopping the Application

The final modification step is to implement the correct stopping code.

1. Place this code in the **btnDone Click** procedure:

```
Private Sub BtnDone_Click(ByVal sender As System.Object, ByVal e As System.EventArgs) Handles btnDone.Click
    Me.Close()
End Sub
```

2. Add the shaded code to the **frmPublishers FormClosing** procedure to insure we don't close in the middle of an edit:

Access Database:

```
Private Sub FrmPublishers_FormClosing(ByVal sender As Object, ByVal e As System.Windows.Forms.FormClosingEventArgs) Handles Me.FormClosing
    If MyState = "Edit" Or MyState = "Add" Then
        MessageBox.Show("You must finish the current edit before stopping the application.", "", MessageBoxButtons.OK, MessageBoxIcon.Information)
        e.Cancel = True
    Else
        Try
            'save changes to database
            Dim PublishersAdapterCommands As New OleDbCommandBuilder(PublishersAdapter)
            PublishersAdapter.Update(PublishersTable)
        Catch ex As Exception
            MessageBox.Show("Error saving database to file:" + ControlChars.CrLf + ex.Message, "Save Error", MessageBoxButtons.OK, MessageBoxIcon.Error)
        End Try
        'close the connection
        BooksConnection.Close()
        'dispose of the connection object
        BooksConnection.Dispose()
    End If
End Sub
```

Database Management

SQL Server Database:

```vb
  Private Sub FrmPublishers_FormClosing(ByVal sender As
Object, ByVal e As
System.Windows.Forms.FormClosingEventArgs) Handles
Me.FormClosing
    If MyState = "Edit" Or MyState = "Add" Then
      MessageBox.Show("You must finish the current edit
before stopping the application.", "", MessageBoxButtons.OK,
MessageBoxIcon.Information)
      e.Cancel = True
    Else
      Try
        'save changes to database
        Dim PublishersAdapterCommands As New
SqlCommandBuilder(PublishersAdapter)
        PublishersAdapter.Update(PublishersTable)
      Catch ex As Exception
        MessageBox.Show("Error saving database to file:" +
ControlChars.CrLf + ex.Message, "Save Error",
MessageBoxButtons.OK, MessageBoxIcon.Error)
      End Try
      'close the connection
      BooksConnection.Close()
      'dispose of the objects
      BooksConnection.Dispose()
      PublishersCommand.Dispose()
      PublishersAdapter.Dispose()
      PublishersTable.Dispose()
    End If
  End Sub
```

3. Save the application and run it. Make sure the **Done** button works properly. Make sure you can't exit the application while in **Edit** or **Add** mode. Make sure all functions work properly.

The **Publishers** Table Input Form application is now complete (final Access version is saved in the **Example 6-8** folder in **VBDB\Access\Class 6** folder; SQL Server version is saved in the **Example 6-8** folder in **VBDB\SQL Server\Class 6** folder). We will use this form as part of a complete books database management system in the final example of this chapter.

Multiple Table Database Management

We have seen that adding database management capabilities to a single data table form is a straightforward process. There are certain procedures for editing, adding, and deleting records. And, the ADO .NET database engine makes implementing these procedures a simple task. Most databases, however, contain multiple tables within a single file. New complications arise when adding database management capabilities to these **relational databases**. Some things you need to do are:

- Display information from multiple tables on a single form
- Use a selected record to change information in another table or form
- Coordinate saving updates to many tables
- Handle more than one data adapter
- Provide access to other editing forms

In this section, we provide some general rules for attacking **multiple table database** management. The most important rule to follow in multiple table database management is the same rule followed with single tables. Understand your database application and what you are trying to do. Plan ahead. Be systematic in your application development. Understand how changes in one table may affect other tables. Use the Visual Basic environment to your advantage. Do your development in stages and test each stage as your proceed. Try your ideas until things work like you want them to. You'll do lots of iterating on ideas you may have. Make sure the use of your application is obvious and intuitive to the user. As we said, these are the same rules followed with single tables. There are just more things to consider with multiple tables.

Database Keys

Recall **keys** connect tables in a relational database. **Primary** keys are unique one-to-one identifiers. **Foreign** keys are many-to-one identifiers used in various tables to point back to database information. You need to know which fields in your database are keys and whether they are primary or foreign. In our single table examples (the Authors table and Publishers table for **BOOKS** database), we did not let the user modify the primary key (**Au_ID** and **PubID**) fields. These are numbers automatically assigned by the ADO .NET engine (auto-incrementing) to insure unique values. We continue that restriction here – the user will not be allowed to edit primary keys. In multiple table databases, the user will have the option to change foreign keys. This is acceptable.

Extra care concerning **keys** must be taken when deleting records in a multiple table situation. If you delete a record (with a primary key) that foreign key entries in other records need, those 'foreign' records would lose the information provided by the deleted record. These are called **orphan** records – they are incomplete. This compromises the **integrity** of your database – not a good thing. For example, in the books database, if you delete a **Publisher** entry, all books in the **Titles** table using that publisher will no longer have access to the publisher's information. Before you delete a record with a primary key, make sure no other records rely on the information needed by the 'about to be deleted' record. Fortunately, the ADO .NET engine helps you avoid orphans by not allowing data adapter updates (saving back to the original database) if needed primary key entries are deleted. We saw this with error message received in the Authors and Publishers table examples.

You may occasionally have 'primary records' not referred to by any 'foreign record'. That's acceptable; there is no loss of integrity in this case. The database just has an extra entry that may be used at some time.

Database Modifications

Since we are working with many database tables (and, hence, many data tables) at a time, we must always be aware of how changes in one particular data table may affect other data tables. This is where the power of the ADO .NET database engine can help or may come back to haunt you. As an example using the books database (and we'll see this in the next example), say you form a data table (using SQL) displaying book titles and publisher names (connecting two tables using **PubID**). If you change a publisher's name in that data table, the ADO .NET database engine will write that change in the Publishers table for every entry with the same **PubID**. Every book in the database with that particular publisher will be connected with the new publisher name. You may change thousands of records with one little entry! This is good if you really want to change the publisher name, but dangerous if it was an inadvertent change. So, as we said, be careful and systematic in building your interface with multiple tables.

There are also cases where you may have to coordinate changes among various database tables using BASIC code. This arises if you use controls that are not data bound or if you can't form a complete updateable data table using SQL. An example with the books database (Example 6-9) is related to the fact that there may be multiple authors for a particular book. We would like to display, edit, and update all authors in our data table. This cannot be done solely with SQL; we must also use code. There are no general rules for coordinating table modifications - every case is different. Just decide what you need to do and try to do it. If it works, great! If not, try again, using the Visual Basic environment as your virtual test bench.

Final Application

The final application in this chapter will illustrate many of the operations just outlined for multiple table database management. This final application completes our books database application by incorporating the **Titles** and **Title_Author** table to tie everything together. It will make use of the **Authors** and **Publishers** forms built in earlier examples. Pay close attention to the steps followed to attack the application. You will encounter similar problems and operations in database applications you build in the future.

Be aware this is not the only possible way to incorporate the books database tables into a management system. We have our ways of doing things and you will develop your own ways. All programmers have their styles. Feel free to modify this example to fit your style.

Example 6-9

Books Database Management System

In previous examples in this chapter, we have developed Visual Basic forms (interfaces) that allow management of the **Authors** and **Publishers** tables in the books database (Access - **BooksDB.accdb**, SQL Server - **SQLBooksDB.mdf**). To complete this database management system, we need a form (it will rely on the Authors and Publishers forms) to allow a user to edit, add, and delete information about individual book titles. This involves using multiple tables (not only the **Authors** and **Publishers** tables, but also the **Titles** and **Title_Author** tables). We develop that final form in this example.

This is not a simple project. As such, we will proceed in stages checking our work as we go. This is very typical of the process followed in building complicated Visual Basic projects. As we proceed, we will try to explain not only what we are doing, but also why we are doing it. We believe you will find this pedagogical approach is of benefit to you, the student trying to learn database management techniques.

As an aid in developing this database management system, we repeat a diagram first viewed in Chapter 2 that illustrates the four tables of the **BOOKS** database:

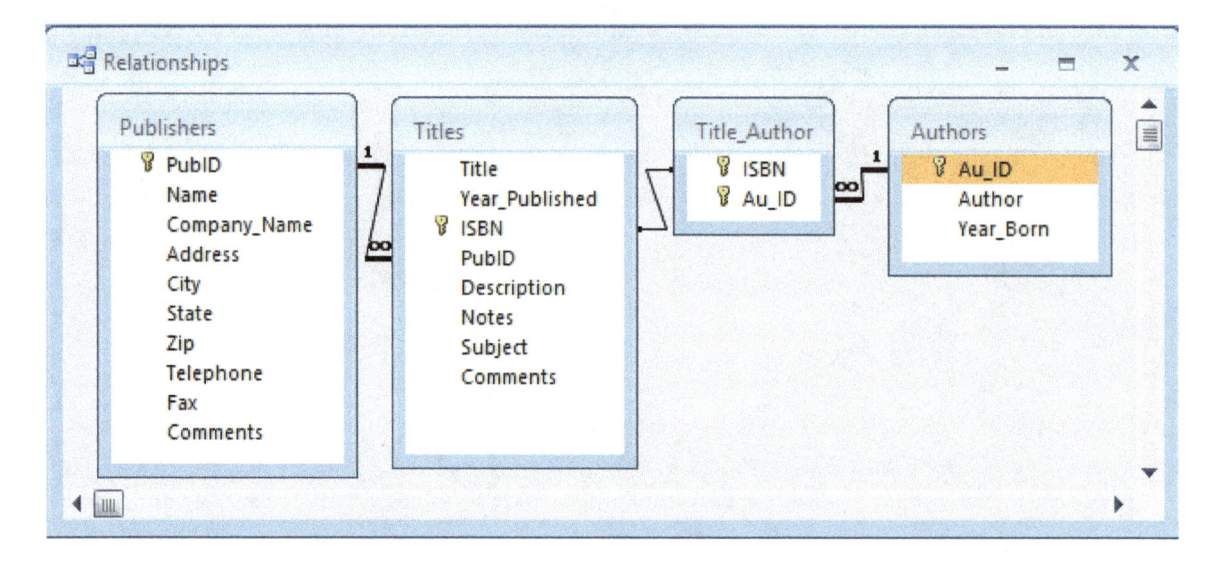

This table shows the fields for each table and how the database keys connect the tables. Referring to this table throughout this example will help you understand the steps we take.

Basic Book Titles Input Form

We begin by constructing and testing a basic input form for book titles. What information would we want to input about a book? Such basic information as title, date of publication, author, and publisher would be a start. Much of this information can be gleaned from the books database **Titles** table. Recall this is a table we haven't dealt with yet in building our application. This table has eight fields:

> **Title**
> **Year_Published**
> **ISBN**
> **PubID**
> **Description**
> **Notes**
> **Subject**
> **Comments**

The SQL statement needed by the command object to retrieve the fields (sorted by the **Title** field) is:

SELECT * FROM Titles ORDER BY Title

If this field's list had the author's name(s) and publisher name, it would be a complete list for an input form. But, it doesn't.

How do we get the author and publisher? We could use SQL to form a virtual view of the data using all of the tables in the books database. The **PubID** field, in conjunction with the **Publishers** table, will give us the Publisher's name. The **ISBN** field, in conjunction with the **Title_Author** table (another one we haven't used yet) and the **Authors** table, can provide author information. We will ignore these omissions for now and just build a basic input form for the information in the Titles table. This will be a good first step.

Recall how (in Example 5-9) we built the **Publishers** input form by modifying the **Authors** input form, rather than starting from scratch. We'll follow that same approach here. We'll take a copy of the **Publishers** input form application and modify it to become the new **Titles** input form. You'll see how quick and easy such a modification is.

6-78　　　　　　　　　　Visual Basic and Databases

The steps are:

1. Make a copy of the Example 6-8 project folder (our final version of the **Publishers** input form). Rename the copied folder something else (I used **Example 6-9**). Open this resaved project. Rename the single form in the project **TitleForm.vb**. We now have a renamed copy of the **Publishers** input form to modify. Our first iteration on the **Titles** form will allow the input of seven fields:

   Title, Year_Published, ISBN, Description, Notes, Subject, Comments

   We have purposely not included **PubID** in this list. We will add it when we discuss obtaining a Publisher name in the next section of this example.

2. Open the form. Delete the label and text box controls for **Telephone**, **FAX**, and **Comments**. Change these properties on the existing form labels and text box controls:

frmPublishers (current name):
    Name   frmTitles
    Text   Titles

Label1 (current name):
    Text   Title

txtPubID (current name):
    Name   txtTitle
    TabIndex   0
    TabStop   True

Label2 (current name):
    Text   Year Published

txtPubName (current name):
    Name   txtYear
    TabIndex   1
    TabStop   True

Database Management 6-79

Label3 (current name):
    Text   ISBN

txtCompanyName (current name):
    Name   txtISBN
    TabIndex   2
    TabStop   True

Label4 (current name):
    Text   Description

txtPubAddress (current name):
    Name   txt Description
    TabIndex   3
    TabStop   True

Label5 (current name):
    Text   Notes

txtPubCity (current name):
    Name   txtNotes
    TabIndex   4
    TabStop   True

Label6 (current name):
    Text   Subject

txtPubState (current name):
    Name   txtSubject
    TabIndex   5
    TabStop   True

Label7 (current name):
    Text   Comments

txtPubZip (current name):
    Name   txtComments
    TabIndex   6
    TabStop   True

3. Move the controls around and resize the form until it looks something like this:

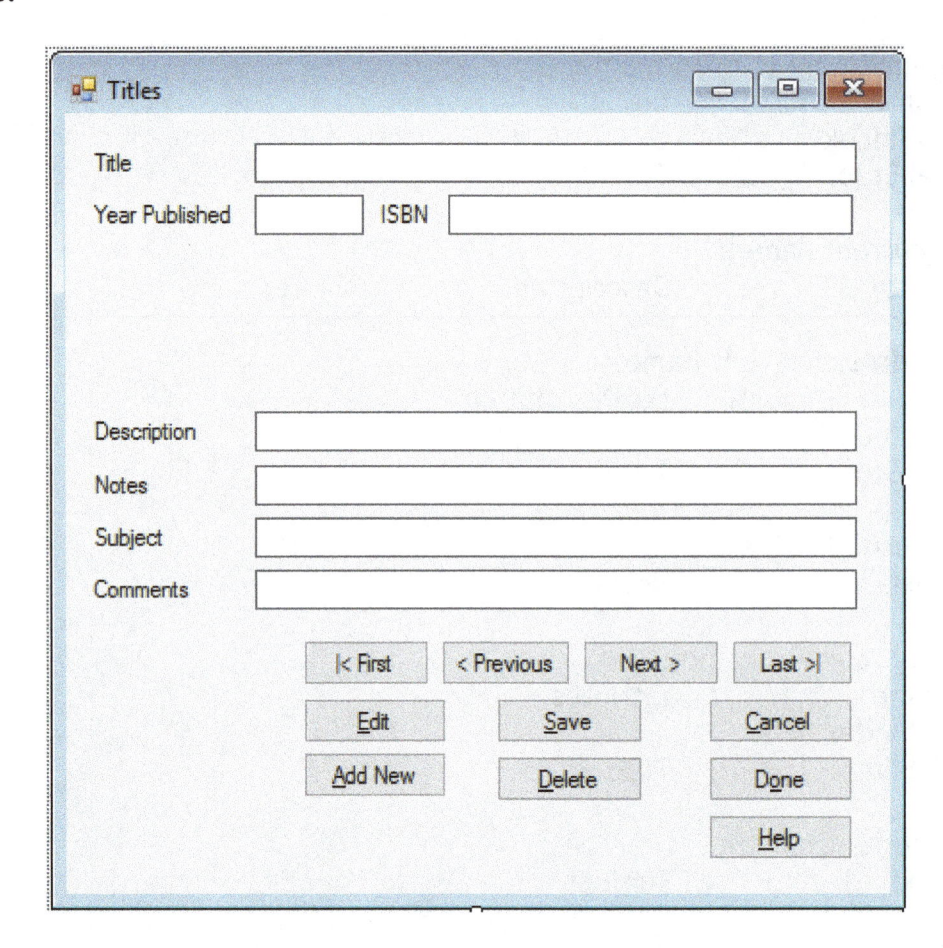

I've resized and relocated the buttons at the bottom of the form too. We're saving space to add author and publisher information and a search capability at a later time.

Database Management 6-81

4. We rename the data objects to reflect the **Titles** table. Make the shaded changes to the form level declarations:

Access Database:

```
Dim BooksConnection As OleDbConnection
Dim TitlesCommand As OleDbCommand
Dim TitlesAdapter As OleDbDataAdapter
Dim TitlesTable As DataTable
Dim TitlesManager As CurrencyManager
Dim MyState As String, MyBookmark As Integer
```

SQL Server Database:

```
Dim BooksConnection As SqlConnection
Dim TitlesCommand As SqlCommand
Dim TitlesAdapter As SqlDataAdapter
Dim TitlesTable As DataTable
Dim TitlesManager As CurrencyManager
Dim MyState As String, MyBookmark As Integer
```

6-82   **Visual Basic and Databases**

5. Make the shaded changes to the form **Load** event procedure:

Access Database:

```
Private Sub FrmTitles_Load(ByVal sender As System.Object, ByVal e As System.EventArgs) Handles MyBase.Load
    Try
        'point to help file
        hlpPublishers.HelpNamespace = Application.StartupPath + "\publishers.chm"
        'connect to books database
        BooksConnection = New OleDbConnection("Provider=Microsoft.ACE.OLEDB.12.0; Data Source = c:\VBDB\Working\BooksDB.accdb")
        BooksConnection.Open()
        'establish command object
        TitlesCommand = New OleDbCommand("Select * from Titles ORDER BY Title", BooksConnection)
        'establish data adapter/data table
        TitlesAdapter = New OleDbDataAdapter()
        TitlesAdapter.SelectCommand = TitlesCommand
        TitlesTable = New DataTable()
        TitlesAdapter.Fill(TitlesTable)
        'bind controls to data table
        txtTitle.DataBindings.Add("Text", TitlesTable, "Title")
        txtYear.DataBindings.Add("Text", TitlesTable, "Year_Published")
        txtISBN.DataBindings.Add("Text", TitlesTable, "ISBN")
        txtDescription.DataBindings.Add("Text", TitlesTable, "Description")
        txtNotes.DataBindings.Add("Text", TitlesTable, "Notes")
        txtSubject.DataBindings.Add("Text", TitlesTable, "Subject")
        txtComments.DataBindings.Add("Text", TitlesTable, "Comments")
        'establish currency manager
        TitlesManager = DirectCast(Me.BindingContext(TitlesTable), CurrencyManager)
    Catch ex As Exception
        MessageBox.Show(ex.Message, "Error establishing Titles table.", MessageBoxButtons.OK, MessageBoxIcon.Error)
        Exit Sub
    End Try
    Me.Show()
    Call SetState("View")
End Sub
```

SQL Server Database:

```vb
  Private Sub FrmTitles_Load(ByVal sender As System.Object, ByVal e As System.EventArgs) Handles MyBase.Load
    Try
      'point to help file
      hlpPublishers.HelpNamespace = Application.StartupPath + "\publishers.chm"
      'connect to books database
      BooksConnection = New SqlConnection("Data Source=.\SQLEXPRESS; AttachDbFilename=C:\VBDB\Working\SQLBooksDB.mdf; Integrated Security=True; Connect Timeout=30; User Instance=True")
      BooksConnection.Open()
      'establish command object
      TitlesCommand = New SqlCommand("Select * from Titles ORDER BY Title", BooksConnection)
      'establish data adapter/data table
      TitlesAdapter = New SqlDataAdapter()
      TitlesAdapter.SelectCommand = TitlesCommand
      TitlesTable = New DataTable()
      TitlesAdapter.Fill(TitlesTable)
      'bind controls to data table
      txtTitle.DataBindings.Add("Text", TitlesTable, "Title")
      txtYear.DataBindings.Add("Text", TitlesTable, "Year_Published")
      txtISBN.DataBindings.Add("Text", TitlesTable, "ISBN")
      txtDescription.DataBindings.Add("Text", TitlesTable, "Description")
      txtNotes.DataBindings.Add("Text", TitlesTable, "Notes")
      txtSubject.DataBindings.Add("Text", TitlesTable, "Subject")
      txtComments.DataBindings.Add("Text", TitlesTable, "Comments")
      'establish currency manager
      TitlesManager = DirectCast(Me.BindingContext(TitlesTable), CurrencyManager)
    Catch ex As Exception
      MessageBox.Show(ex.Message, "Error establishing Titles table.", MessageBoxButtons.OK, MessageBoxIcon.Error)
      Exit Sub
    End Try
    Me.Show()
    Call SetState("View")
  End Sub
```

These changes reflect the new data object naming, the new SQL command string and the proper data binding for the text box controls. Yes, we know we're still pointing to the Publishers help system – we'll fix this later.

6. Make similar changes to the form **FormClosing** procedure:

Access Database:

```
  Private Sub FrmTitles_FormClosing(ByVal sender As Object, ByVal e As System.Windows.Forms.FormClosingEventArgs) Handles Me.FormClosing
    If MyState = "Edit" Or MyState = "Add" Then
      MessageBox.Show("You must finish the current edit before stopping the application.", "", MessageBoxButtons.OK, MessageBoxIcon.Information)
      e.Cancel = True
    Else
      Try
        'save changes to database
        Dim TitlesAdapterCommands As New OleDbCommandBuilder(TitlesAdapter)
        TitlesAdapter.Update(TitlesTable)
      Catch ex As Exception
        MessageBox.Show("Error saving database to file:" + ControlChars.CrLf + ex.Message, "Save Error", MessageBoxButtons.OK, MessageBoxIcon.Error)
      End Try
      'close the connection
      BooksConnection.Close()
      'dispose of objects
      BooksConnection.Dispose()
      TitlesCommand.Dispose()
      TitlesAdapter.Dispose()
      TitlesTable.Dispose()
    End If
  End Sub
```

Database Management 6-85

SQL Server Database:

```vb
    Private Sub FrmTitles_FormClosing(ByVal sender As Object, ByVal e As System.Windows.Forms.FormClosingEventArgs) Handles Me.FormClosing
        If MyState = "Edit" Or MyState = "Add" Then
            MessageBox.Show("You must finish the current edit before stopping the application.", "", MessageBoxButtons.OK, MessageBoxIcon.Information)
            e.Cancel = True
        Else
            Try
                'save changes to database
                Dim TitlesAdapterCommands As New SqlCommandBuilder(TitlesAdapter)
                TitlesAdapter.Update(TitlesTable)
            Catch ex As Exception
                MessageBox.Show("Error saving database to file:" + ControlChars.CrLf + ex.Message, "Save Error", MessageBoxButtons.OK, MessageBoxIcon.Error)
            End Try
            'close the connection
            BooksConnection.Close()
            'dispose of objects
            BooksConnection.Dispose()
            TitlesCommand.Dispose()
            TitlesAdapter.Dispose()
            TitlesTable.Dispose()
        End If
    End Sub
```

7. Make the shaded changes to the four procedures for navigation:

```
Private Sub BtnFirst_Click(ByVal sender As System.Object, ByVal e As System.EventArgs) Handles btnFirst.Click
    TitlesManager.Position = 0
End Sub

Private Sub BtnPrevious_Click(ByVal sender As System.Object, ByVal e As System.EventArgs) Handles btnPrevious.Click
    If TitlesManager.Position = 0 Then Console.Beep()
    TitlesManager.Position -= 1
End Sub

Private Sub BtnNext_Click(ByVal sender As System.Object, ByVal e As System.EventArgs) Handles btnNext.Click
    If TitlesManager.Position = TitlesManager.Count - 1 Then Console.Beep()
    TitlesManager.Position += 1
End Sub

Private Sub BtnLast_Click(ByVal sender As System.Object, ByVal e As System.EventArgs) Handles btnLast.Click
    TitlesManager.Position = TitlesManager.Count - 1
End Sub
```

8. Eliminate code in the **txtInput KeyPress** event (for now). We'll add code here when we're further along in the application development.

9. Change the **ValidateData** function to just three lines of code (for now):

```
Private Function ValidateData() As Boolean
    Dim Message As String = ""
    Dim AllOK As Boolean = True
    Return (AllOK)
End Function
```

Database Management 6-87

10. Modify the **SetState** procedure (new code is shaded):

```
Private Sub SetState(ByVal AppState As String)
   MyState = AppState
   Select Case AppState
      Case "View"
         txtTitle.ReadOnly = True
         txtYear.ReadOnly = True
         txtISBN.ReadOnly = True
         txtISBN.TabStop = True
         txtISBN.BackColor = Color.White
         txtISBN.ForeColor = Color.Black
         txtDescription.ReadOnly = True
         txtNotes.ReadOnly = True
         txtSubject.ReadOnly = True
         txtComments.ReadOnly = True
         btnFirst.Enabled = True
         btnPrevious.Enabled = True
         btnNext.Enabled = True
         btnLast.Enabled = True
         btnAddNew.Enabled = True
         btnSave.Enabled = False
         btnCancel.Enabled = False
         btnEdit.Enabled = True
         btnDelete.Enabled = True
         btnDone.Enabled = True
         txtTitle.Focus()
      Case "Add", "Edit"
         txtTitle.ReadOnly = False
         txtYear.ReadOnly = False
         txtISBN.ReadOnly = False
         If MyState = "Edit" Then
            txtISBN.BackColor = Color.Red
            txtISBN.ForeColor = Color.White
            txtISBN.ReadOnly = True
            txtISBN.TabStop = False
         Else
            txtISBN.TabStop = True
         End If
         txtDescription.ReadOnly = False
         txtNotes.ReadOnly = False
         txtSubject.ReadOnly = False
         txtComments.ReadOnly = False
         btnFirst.Enabled = False
         btnPrevious.Enabled = False
         btnNext.Enabled = False
         btnLast.Enabled = False
         btnAddNew.Enabled = False
```

```
          btnSave.Enabled = True
          btnCancel.Enabled = True
          btnEdit.Enabled = False
          btnDelete.Enabled = False
          btnDone.Enabled = False
          txtTitle.Focus()
    End Select
End Sub
```

This code reflects the new names on the text boxes. Also, we set **ReadOnly** to **True** for the **txtISBN** control **Edit** mode (and change it to red). This is the box where ISBN (a primary key identifying a book) is entered. Recall we will not allow editing of primary keys. We only want to enter a value here in **Add** mode.

11. Make the shaded changes to the **btnAddNew Click**, **btnDelete Click** and **btnCancel Click** procedures to reflect data object names:

```
Private Sub BtnAddNew_Click(ByVal sender As System.Object, ByVal e As System.EventArgs) Handles btnAddNew.Click
    Try
        MyBookmark = TitlesManager.Position
        TitlesManager.AddNew()
        Call SetState("Add")
    Catch ex As Exception
        MessageBox.Show("Error adding record.", "Error", MessageBoxButtons.OK, MessageBoxIcon.Error)
    End Try
End Sub
```

Database Management 6-89

```vb
Private Sub BtnDelete_Click(ByVal sender As System.Object, ByVal e As System.EventArgs) Handles btnDelete.Click
    Dim Response As Windows.Forms.DialogResult
    Response = MessageBox.Show("Are you sure you want to delete this record?", "Delete", MessageBoxButtons.YesNo, MessageBoxIcon.Question, MessageBoxDefaultButton.Button2)
    If Response = Windows.Forms.DialogResult.No Then
      Exit Sub
    End If
    Try
      TitlesManager.RemoveAt(TitlesManager.Position)
    Catch ex As Exception
      MessageBox.Show("Error deleting record.", "Error", MessageBoxButtons.OK, MessageBoxIcon.Error)
    End Try
  End Sub

  Private Sub BtnCancel_Click(ByVal sender As System.Object, ByVal e As System.EventArgs) Handles btnCancel.Click
    TitlesManager.CancelCurrentEdit()
    If MyState = "Add" Then
      TitlesManager.Position = MyBookmark
    End If
    Call SetState("View")
  End Sub
```

12. Modify the **btnSave Click** event procedure to reflect the new data objects and search the **Titles** table for the new record (we search on the first field, **Title**) following a save (new code is shaded):

```
Private Sub BtnSave_Click(ByVal sender As System.Object, ByVal e As System.EventArgs) Handles btnSave.Click
    If Not (ValidateData()) Then Exit Sub
    Dim SavedName As String = txtTitle.Text
    Dim SavedRow As Integer
    Try
        TitlesManager.EndCurrentEdit()
        TitlesTable.DefaultView.Sort = "Title"
        SavedRow = TitlesTable.DefaultView.Find(SavedName)
        TitlesManager.Position = SavedRow
        MessageBox.Show("Record saved.", "Save", MessageBoxButtons.OK, MessageBoxIcon.Information)
        Call SetState("View")
    Catch ex As Exception
        MessageBox.Show("Error saving record.", "Error", MessageBoxButtons.OK, MessageBoxIcon.Error)
    End Try
End Sub
```

Database Management 6-91

13. Save the application (Access version saved in the **Example 6-9** folder in the **VBDB\Access\Class 6** folder; SQL Server version saved in the **Example 6-9** folder in the **VBDB\SQL Server\Class 6** folder). Run it. You should see this form:

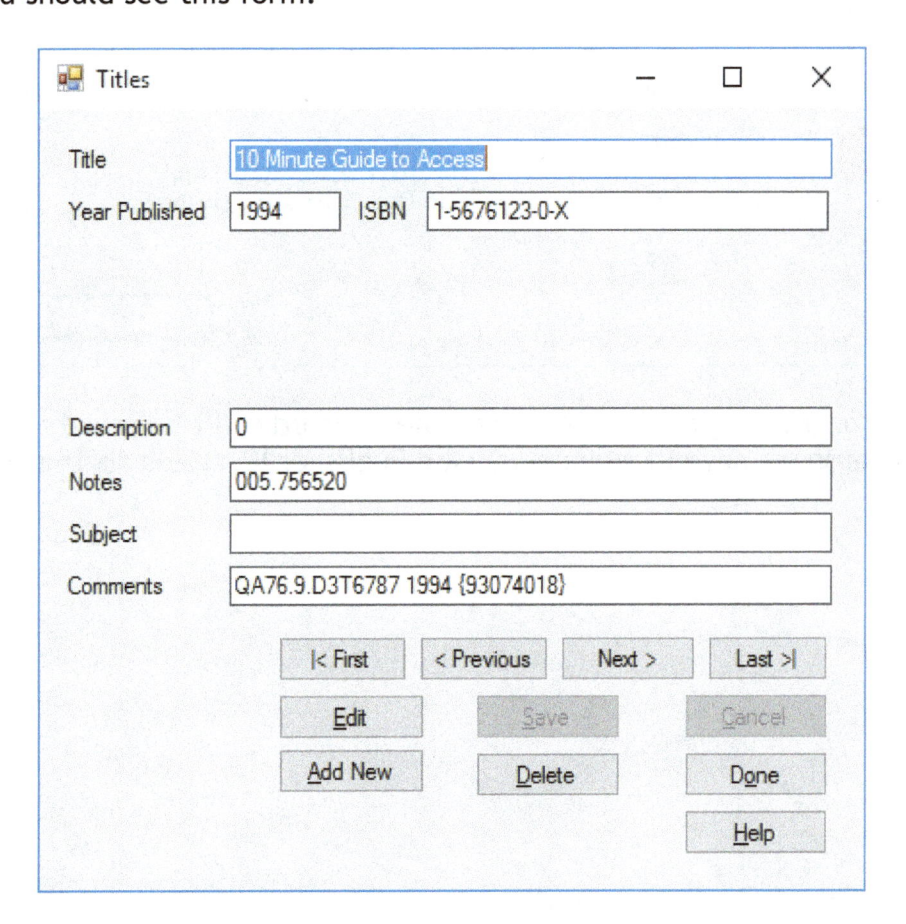

Scroll through the records using the navigation buttons. Try **editing** a record (make sure both the **Save** and **Cancel** functions work).

Try **adding** a record. Type a title and click **Save**. Then exit the application. You should see this error message (will be different if using SQL Server):

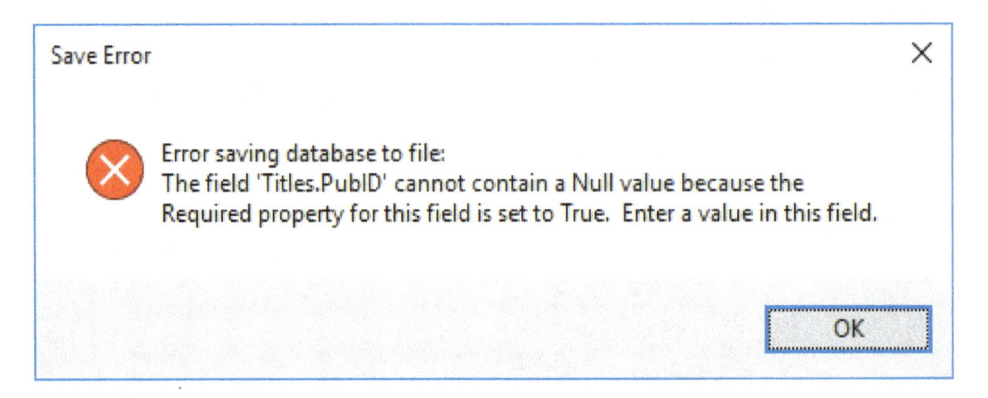

> **Save Error** ✕
>
> ❌ Error saving database to file:
> The field 'Titles.PubID' cannot contain a Null value because the
> Required property for this field is set to True. Enter a value in this field.
>
> [OK]

This is our error trapping code telling us the new record can't be saved to the database because we haven't supplied a valid Publisher ID. We'll fix this soon.

Finding Records

The **Titles** table has over 8,500 entries. If we wanted to edit an entry that began with the letter 'N', we would need to use the **Next** arrow about 4,000 times before we found the desired record! This is not acceptable. We need a faster way to locate records. We will add the ability to search for book titles that begin with certain letters. This will let a user get close to a title they might be looking for. And, while we are at it, we will add the ability to display the number of records in our data table. Users like to know how many records they are working with.

1. Add a group box at the lower left corner of the **Titles** input form. Place a label, a text box and button in the group box. Set these properties:

GroupBox1:
    Name   grpFindTitle
    Text   Find Title

Label1:
    AutoSize   False
    Text   Type first few letters of Title

TextBox1:
    Name   txtFind
    TabStop   False

Button1:
    Name   btnFind
    Text   Find
    TabStop   False

When done, the modified form should look like this:

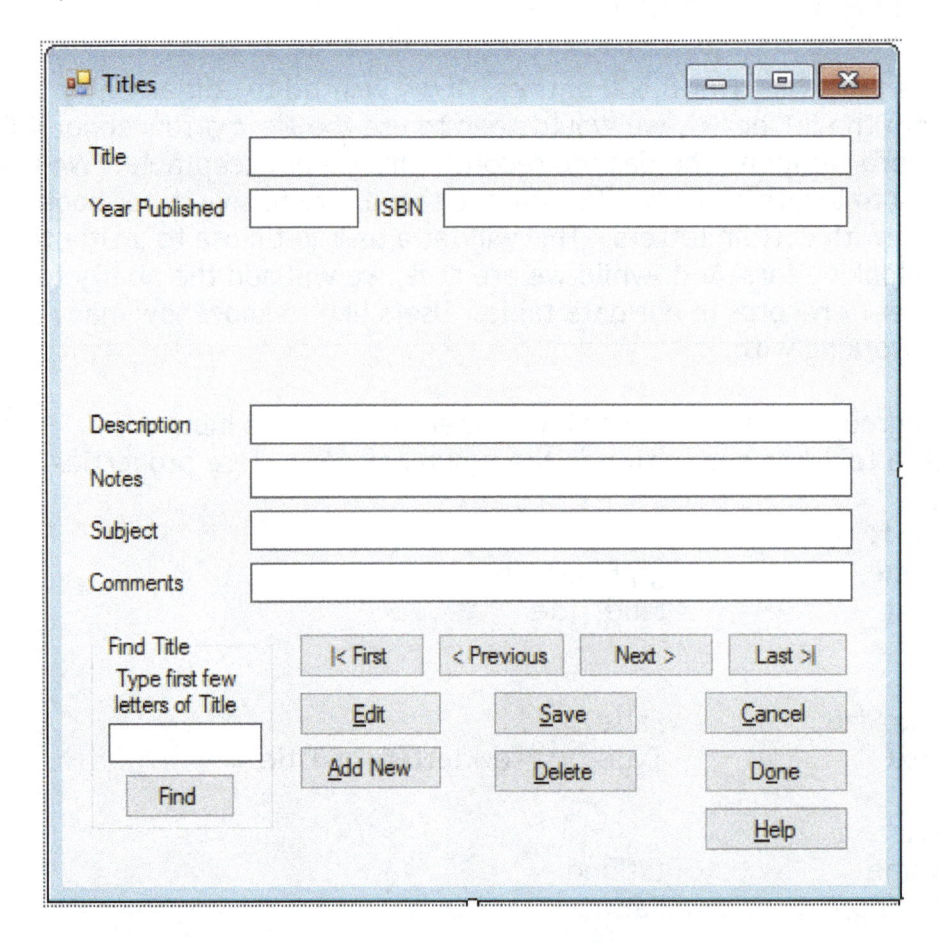

2. In the **SetState** procedure, enable the **Find Title** group box in **View** mode, disable it in **Add** and **Edit** mode. Use the **grpFindTitle Enabled** property.

Database Management 6-95

3. Add this code to the **btnFind Click** event procedure:

```
Private Sub BtnFind_Click(ByVal sender As System.Object, ByVal e As System.EventArgs) Handles btnFind.Click
    If txtFind.Text = "" Then Exit Sub
    Dim SavedRow As Integer = TitlesManager.Position
    Dim FoundRows() As DataRow
    TitlesTable.DefaultView.Sort = "Title"
    FoundRows = TitlesTable.Select("Title LIKE '" + txtFind.Text + "*'")
    If FoundRows.Length = 0 Then
       TitlesManager.Position = SavedRow
    Else
       TitlesManager.Position = TitlesTable.DefaultView.Find(FoundRows(0).Item("Title"))
    End If
End Sub
```

This routine first saves the position of the currency manager. It then uses the **Select** method of the data table to find all rows with a **Title** field **LIKE** the input letter(s) (we append the wild card character, *). If the search is not successful, the saved position is restored.

6-96　　　　　　　　　　Visual Basic and Databases

4. Save the application and run it. Type **N** in text box of the **Find Title** group box. Click **Find**. You should see the first N title:

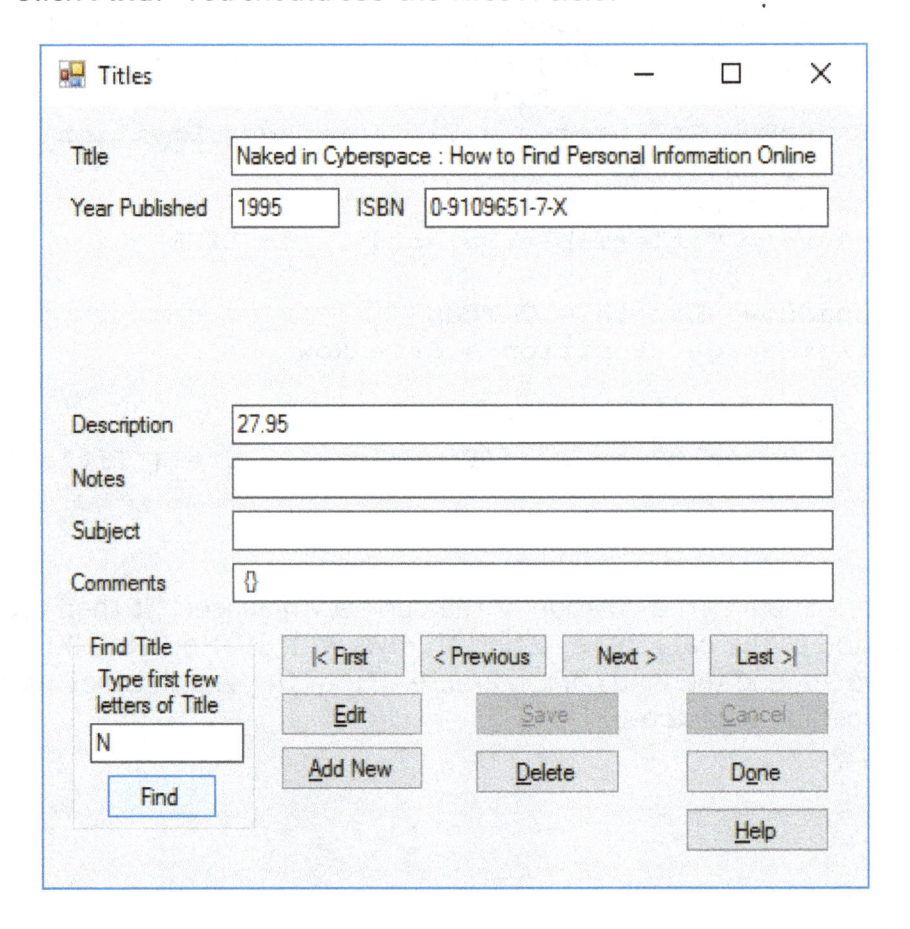

Try other searches. Notice what happens when a search is not successful. Stop the application.

Navigation Information

We'll now add code to keep track of and display which record you are viewing and the total number of records in the **Titles** data table.

1. Add a general procedure named **SetText** to your application. Use this code:

   ```
   Private Sub SetText()
     Me.Text = "Titles - Record" + Str(TitlesManager.Position + 1) + " of" + Str(TitlesManager.Count) + " Records"
   End Sub
   ```

   This sets the form **Text** property to reflect the current record (**Position**) and the total number of records (**Count**).

2. Add this single line of code at the bottom of the **frmTitles Load** to initialize the display of the number of records:

   ```
   Call SetText()
   ```

3. When we move to a new record, the currency manager position changes so we need to update the title bar information. Add this line of code at the end of the **btnFind Click, btnFirst Click, btnPrevious Click, btnNext Click** and **btnLast Click** event procedures:

   ```
   Call SetText()
   ```

4. When we add, save or delete a record, the number of records and current position may change. Also, if we cancel adding a record, there will be changes. Add this line of code at the end of the **btnAddNew Click, btnSave Click, btnCancel Click** and **btnDelete Click** event procedures to reflect this change:

   ```
   Call SetText()
   ```

5. Save the application. Run it. Note navigation information is now displayed in the form's title bar area:

   Titles - Record 1 of 8569 Records

Later, when we add publisher and author information, we can see how adding records and deleting records changes the number of records.

Adding Publisher Name

Earlier, when we tried to add and save a record to the **Titles** table, we received an error message stating no **PubID** field was supplied. We will correct that problem now. As indicated, each title in the books database requires a **PubID** (or Publisher identification) number. This is a foreign key related to the primary key in the **Publishers** table. This key tells us who the publisher of the book is.

For existing records, the PubID value is known and can be changed, since it is a foreign key. For added records, the user must supply a value. But, how does a user know the PubID value for a book's publisher? He or she probably doesn't. But, the user should know the name of the publisher. Rather than ask the user to supply a PubID, it would be preferable to have the user supply the name of the publisher and let the database engine supply the corresponding PubID. Similarly, when a user navigates to an existing record, we would prefer to see the publisher name rather than the corresponding PubID value.

Can we do this? Of course. Recall this is just what the **combo box**, studied in Chapter 5, can do for us. Go back and review that material. The basic idea is that we use the **Name** field of the **Publishers** table to fill the list portion of the combo box. When the user picks a name, we want the combo box to pass the corresponding **PubID** to the **Titles** table. Then, when a user navigates to a record, we want the corresponding **PubID** sent to the combo box to display the corresponding publisher name. Let's try it.

1. Add another label control and a combo box to the **Titles** input form. The form should look like this:

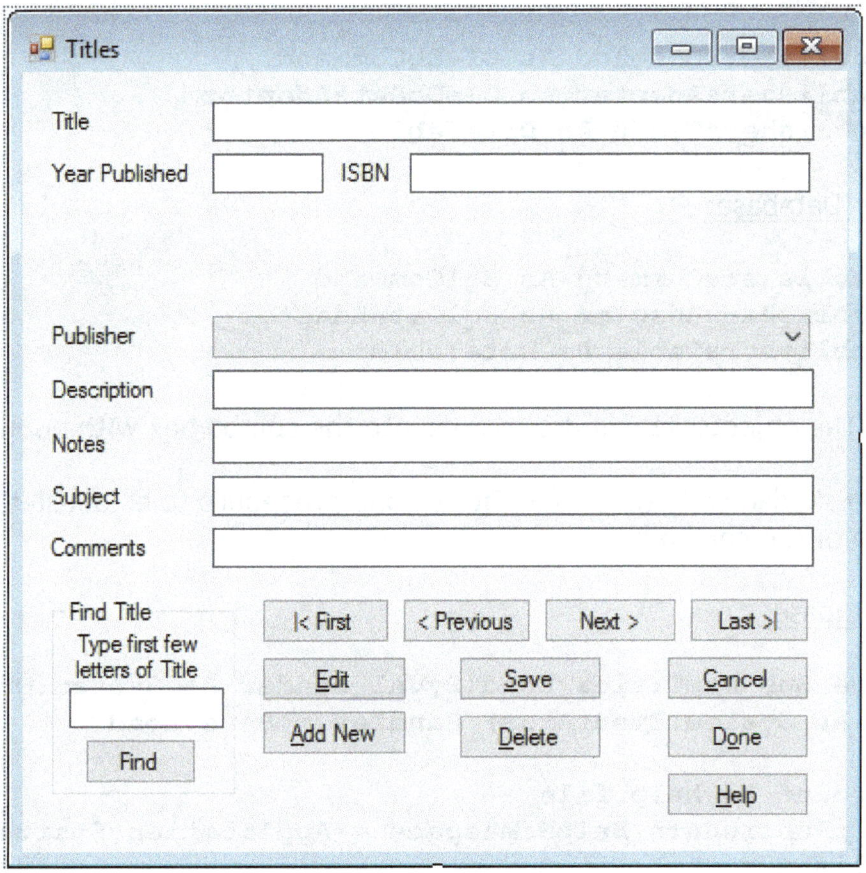
Titles
Title
Year Published
ISBN
Publisher
Description
Notes
Subject
Comments
Find Title
Type first few letters of Title
Find
|< First
< Previous
Next >
Last >|
Edit
Save
Cancel
Add New
Delete
Done
Help

2. The new control's have these properties:

Label1:

Text	Publisher

ComboBox1:

Name	cboPublisher
BackColor	White (changed so we can see values when **Enabled** is **False**)
DropDownStyle	DropdownList

3. Add these lines in the form level declarations:

Access Database:

```
Dim PublishersCommand As OleDbCommand
Dim PublishersAdapter As OleDbDataAdapter
Dim PublishersTable As DataTable
```

SQL Server Database:

```
Dim PublishersCommand As SqlCommand
Dim PublishersAdapter As SqlDataAdapter
Dim PublishersTable As DataTable
```

These are the objects we will use to populate the combo box with publishers.

4. Add the shaded code to the **frmTitles Load** procedure to establish the proper binding of the combo box:

Access Database:

```
Private Sub FrmTitles_Load(ByVal sender As System.Object, ByVal e As System.EventArgs) Handles MyBase.Load
    Try
        'point to help file
        hlpPublishers.HelpNamespace = Application.StartupPath + "\publishers.chm"
        'connect to books database
        BooksConnection = New OleDbConnection("Provider=Microsoft.ACE.OLEDB.12.0; Data Source = c:\VBDB\Working\BooksDB.accdb")
        BooksConnection.Open()
        'establish command object
        TitlesCommand = New OleDbCommand("Select * from Titles ORDER BY Title", BooksConnection)
        'establish data adapter/data table
        TitlesAdapter = New OleDbDataAdapter()
        TitlesAdapter.SelectCommand = TitlesCommand
        TitlesTable = New DataTable()
        TitlesAdapter.Fill(TitlesTable)
        'bind controls to data table
        txtTitle.DataBindings.Add("Text", TitlesTable, "Title")
        txtYear.DataBindings.Add("Text", TitlesTable, "Year_Published")
        txtISBN.DataBindings.Add("Text", TitlesTable, "ISBN")
```

```vbnet
        txtDescription.DataBindings.Add("Text", TitlesTable, "Description")
        txtNotes.DataBindings.Add("Text", TitlesTable, "Notes")
        txtSubject.DataBindings.Add("Text", TitlesTable, "Subject")
        txtComments.DataBindings.Add("Text", TitlesTable, "Comments")
        'establish currency manager
        TitlesManager = DirectCast(Me.BindingContext(TitlesTable), CurrencyManager)
        'establish publisher table/combo box to pick publisher
        PublishersCommand = New OleDbCommand("Select * from Publishers ORDER BY Name", BooksConnection)
        PublishersAdapter = New OleDbDataAdapter()
        PublishersAdapter.SelectCommand = PublishersCommand
        PublishersTable = New DataTable()
        PublishersAdapter.Fill(PublishersTable)
        cboPublisher.DataSource = PublishersTable
        cboPublisher.DisplayMember = "Name"
        cboPublisher.ValueMember = "PubID"
        cboPublisher.DataBindings.Add("SelectedValue", TitlesTable, "PubID")
    Catch ex As Exception
        MessageBox.Show(ex.Message, "Error establishing Titles table.", MessageBoxButtons.OK, MessageBoxIcon.Error)
        Exit Sub
    End Try
    Me.Show()
    Call SetState("View")
    Call SetText()
End Sub
```

SQL Server Database:

```vbnet
Private Sub FrmTitles_Load(ByVal sender As System.Object, ByVal e As System.EventArgs) Handles MyBase.Load
    Try
        'point to help file
        hlpPublishers.HelpNamespace = Application.StartupPath + "\publishers.chm"
        'connect to books database
        BooksConnection = New SqlConnection("Data Source=.\SQLEXPRESS;AttachDbFilename=C:\VBDB\Working\SQLBooksDB.mdf;Integrated Security=True;Connect Timeout=30;User Instance=True")
        BooksConnection.Open()
        'establish command object
```

```vb
        TitlesCommand = New SqlCommand("Select * from Titles
ORDER BY Title", BooksConnection)
        'establish data adapter/data table
        TitlesAdapter = New SqlDataAdapter()
        TitlesAdapter.SelectCommand = TitlesCommand
        TitlesTable = New DataTable()
        TitlesAdapter.Fill(TitlesTable)
        'bind controls to data table
        txtTitle.DataBindings.Add("Text", TitlesTable,
"Title")
        txtYear.DataBindings.Add("Text", TitlesTable,
"Year_Published")
        txtISBN.DataBindings.Add("Text", TitlesTable, "ISBN")
        txtDescription.DataBindings.Add("Text", TitlesTable,
"Description")
        txtNotes.DataBindings.Add("Text", TitlesTable,
"Notes")
        txtSubject.DataBindings.Add("Text", TitlesTable,
"Subject")
        txtComments.DataBindings.Add("Text", TitlesTable,
"Comments")
        'establish currency manager
        TitlesManager =
DirectCast(Me.BindingContext(TitlesTable), CurrencyManager)
        'establish publisher table/combo box to pick publisher
        PublishersCommand = New SqlCommand("Select * from
Publishers ORDER BY Name", BooksConnection)
        PublishersAdapter = New SqlDataAdapter()
        PublishersAdapter.SelectCommand = PublishersCommand
        PublishersTable = New DataTable()
        PublishersAdapter.Fill(PublishersTable)
        cboPublisher.DataSource = PublishersTable
        cboPublisher.DisplayMember = "Name"
        cboPublisher.ValueMember = "PubID"
        cboPublisher.DataBindings.Add("SelectedValue",
TitlesTable, "PubID")
      Catch ex As Exception
        MessageBox.Show(ex.Message, "Error establishing Titles
table.", MessageBoxButtons.OK, MessageBoxIcon.Error)
        Exit Sub
      End Try
      Me.Show()
      Call SetState("View")
      Call SetText()
    End Sub
```

Let's review what we did here in the added code. The first few lines are used to get a **PublishersTable** object (the **Publishers** table in the books database) to bind the combo box to (**DataSource** property). These should be familiar steps by now. The drop-down list portion of the combo box will display the **Name** field (**DisplayMember** property) from the **Publisher** table. The displayed names in the combo box correspond to the **PubID** field (**ValueMember** property). The last line in the added code is the key to everything:

```
cboPublisher.DataBindings.Add("SelectedValue",
TitlesTable, "PubID")
```

This statement binds the **SelectedValue** property of the combo box (which holds the value of the **PubID**) to the **PubID** field in the **TitlesTable** object. This insures that when a title is displayed, the proper publisher is displayed and when the user picks a publisher name, the **Titles** table will get the proper **PubID** value.

5. Add the shaded lines to the **frmTitles Closing** event procedure to dispose of the newly added objects:

Access Database:

```
  Private Sub FrmTitles_FormClosing(ByVal sender As Object, ByVal e As System.Windows.Forms.FormClosingEventArgs) Handles Me.FormClosing
    If MyState = "Edit" Or MyState = "Add" Then
      MessageBox.Show("You must finish the current edit before stopping the application.", "", MessageBoxButtons.OK, MessageBoxIcon.Information)
      e.Cancel = True
    Else
      Try
        'save changes to database
        Dim TitlesAdapterCommands As New OleDbCommandBuilder(TitlesAdapter)
        TitlesAdapter.Update(TitlesTable)
      Catch ex As Exception
        MessageBox.Show("Error saving database to file:" + ControlChars.CrLf + ex.Message, "Save Error", MessageBoxButtons.OK, MessageBoxIcon.Error)
      End Try
      'close the connection
      BooksConnection.Close()
      'dispose of objects
      BooksConnection.Dispose()
      TitlesCommand.Dispose()
      TitlesAdapter.Dispose()
      TitlesTable.Dispose()
      PublishersCommand.Dispose()
      PublishersAdapter.Dispose()
      PublishersTable.Dispose()
    End If
  End Sub
```

Database Management 6-105

SQL Server Database:

```
   Private Sub FrmTitles_FormClosing(ByVal sender As Object,
ByVal e As System.Windows.Forms.FormClosingEventArgs)
Handles Me.FormClosing
     If MyState = "Edit" Or MyState = "Add" Then
        MessageBox.Show("You must finish the current edit
before stopping the application.", "", MessageBoxButtons.OK,
MessageBoxIcon.Information)
        e.Cancel = True
     Else
       Try
         'save changes to database
         Dim TitlesAdapterCommands As New
SqlCommandBuilder(TitlesAdapter)
         TitlesAdapter.Update(TitlesTable)
       Catch ex As Exception
         MessageBox.Show("Error saving database to file:" +
ControlChars.CrLf + ex.Message, "Save Error",
MessageBoxButtons.OK, MessageBoxIcon.Error)
       End Try
       'close the connection
       BooksConnection.Close()
       'dispose of objects
       BooksConnection.Dispose()
       TitlesCommand.Dispose()
       TitlesAdapter.Dispose()
       TitlesTable.Dispose()
       PublishersCommand.Dispose()
       PublishersAdapter.Dispose()
       PublishersTable.Dispose()
     End If
   End Sub
```

6. Modify the **SetState** procedure so the combo box is disabled in **View** mode and enabled in **Add** and **Edit** modes.

7. Save the application and run it. You should now see a **Publisher** listed (it is 'grayed out' since it can't be edited in **View** mode):

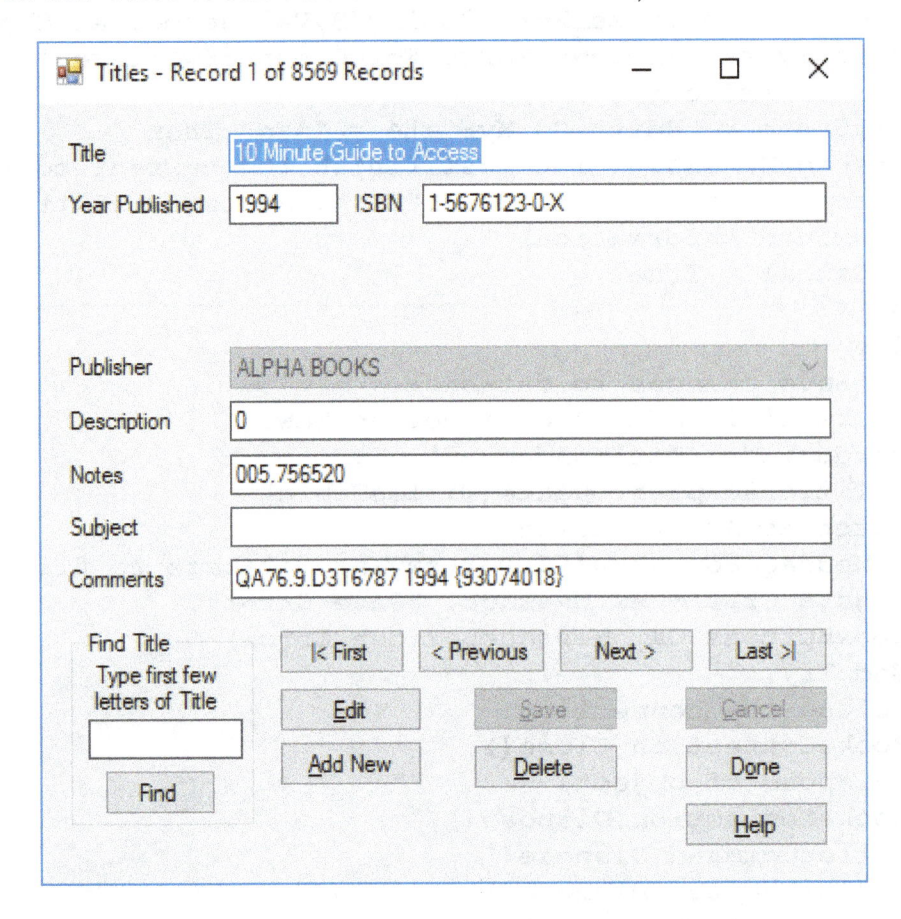

You can scroll through the records and notice how the combo box properly displays the publisher name.

8. Let's try changing a publisher. Write down the name of the publisher for the displayed record. Click **Edit**. Click the drop-down arrow for the combo box. (When the drop-down box is displayed, you can press the first letter of the name, if you know it, for faster navigation among the names. This only works in **Edit** mode, the list is disabled in **View** mode.) Click on a new publisher. Click **Save**. Your book now has a new publisher – it's that easy. Change the name back to the correct one. You should make sure the **Cancel** option operates correctly too.

Database Management 6-107

9. Let's try adding a title (including publisher) to the database. Click **Add New**. Type in a **Title** and select a **Publisher**. Click **Save**. Close the application, trying to write the changes back to the database. Did this show up (or something similar for SQL Server)?

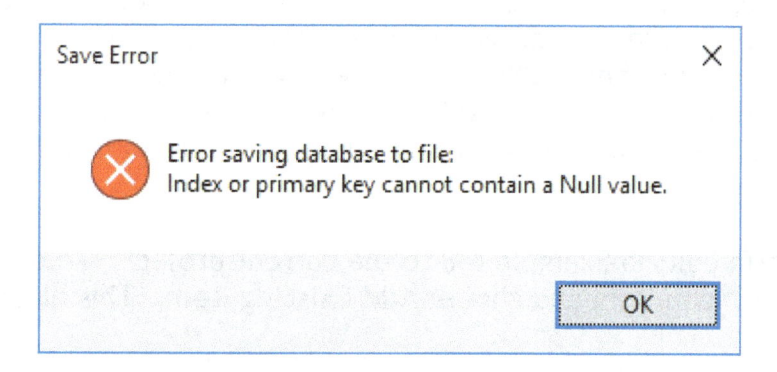

> **Save Error** ×
>
> ❌ Error saving database to file:
> Index or primary key cannot contain a Null value.
>
> [OK]

The primary key it is referring to is the **ISBN** field. This is the primary key identifying every title in the **Titles** table. We must supply a value. Start the application again. Click **Add New**. Type in some value for **ISBN** (don't worry what it is). Click **Save**. Your new book has been added to the database. Notice, too, that the number of records (in the title bar) has increased by one. Delete the book you just added. Use the **Find Title** feature, if needed. Stop the application

Adding Publisher Editing

What if the user can't find the publisher they want in the drop-down list? This could often happen when adding new titles to the database. If the desired publisher name is not in the list, we need to either edit a current entry or add a new entry to the **Publishers** table. Once the new publisher name is in the Publishers table, it will be available for use in the **Titles** input form. And, guess what? We've already built the form that lets us edit the **Publishers** table in Example 6-8.

1. Add the form built in Example 6-8 to the current project. To do this, click the **Project** menu item and choose **Add Existing Item**. This dialog should appear:

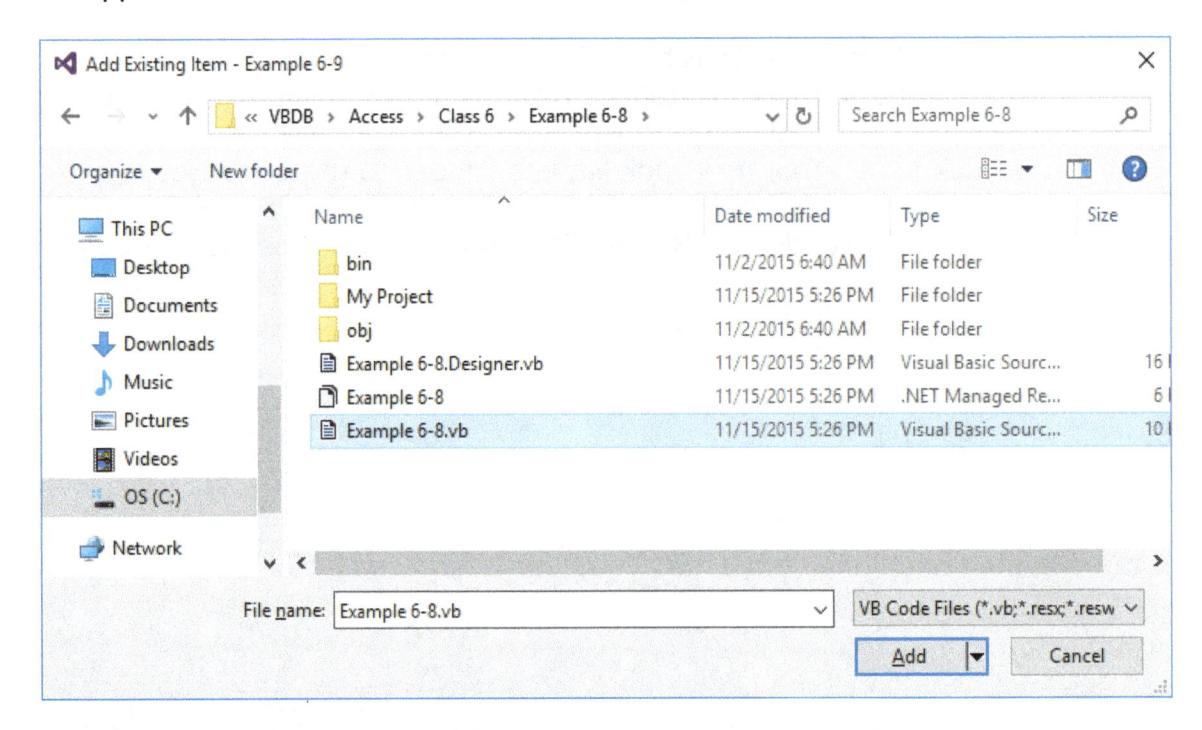

As shown, navigate to the **Example 6-8** project folder (you may have named it something else) and select the **vb** file (not the **Designer.vb** file) in that folder. Click **Add**.

The file will appear in the **Solution Explorer** window as part of the project:

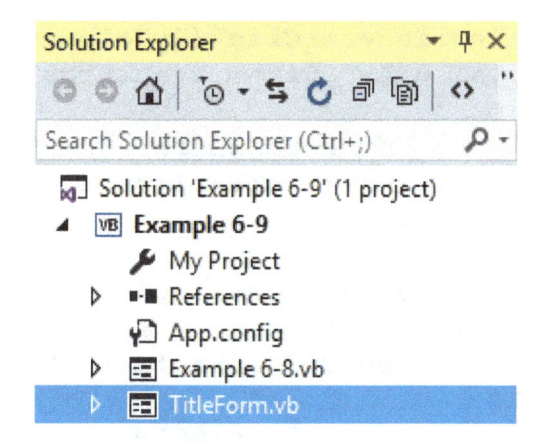

Rename this form **PublisherForm.vb**.

2. On the **Titles** input form, add a button to the left of the **Help** button. Give it a **Name** property of **btnPublishers** and a **Text** property of **&Publishers**. Add this code to the **btnPublishers Click** event:

Access Database:

```
  Private Sub BtnPublishers_Click(ByVal sender As
System.Object, ByVal e As System.EventArgs) Handles
btnPublishers.Click
    Dim PubForm As New frmPublishers
    Dim PubSave As String = cboPublisher.Text
    PubForm.ShowDialog()
    PubForm.Dispose()
    'need to regenerate publishers data
    BooksConnection.Close()
    BooksConnection = New
OleDbConnection("Provider=Microsoft.ACE.OLEDB.12.0; Data
Source = c:\VBDB\Working\BooksDB.accdb")
    BooksConnection.Open()
    PublishersAdapter.SelectCommand = PublishersCommand
    PublishersTable = New DataTable()
    PublishersAdapter.Fill(PublishersTable)
    cboPublisher.DataSource = PublishersTable
    cboPublisher.Text = PubSave
  End Sub
```

SQL Server Database:

```
  Private Sub BtnPublishers_Click(ByVal sender As System.Object, ByVal e As System.EventArgs) Handles btnPublishers.Click
    Dim PubForm As New frmPublishers
    Dim PubSave As String = cboPublisher.Text
    PubForm.ShowDialog()
    PubForm.Dispose()
    'need to regenerate publishers data
    BooksConnection.Close()
    BooksConnection = New SqlConnection("Data Source=.\SQLEXPRESS; AttachDbFilename=C:\VBDB\Working\SQLBooksDB.mdf; Integrated Security=True; Connect Timeout=30; User Instance=True")
    BooksConnection.Open()
    PublishersAdapter.SelectCommand = PublishersCommand
    PublishersTable = New DataTable()
    PublishersAdapter.Fill(PublishersTable)
    cboPublisher.DataSource = PublishersTable
    cboPublisher.Text = PubSave
  End Sub
```

This code displays the **Publishers** input form to allow any editing necessary. Before displaying the form, the current publisher choice is saved (**PubSave**). When the **Titles** form becomes active again, there may be new values in the database (from editing the **Publishers** table). To see these changes, we close our connection to the database, then reopen it, recreating the **PublishersTable** object bound to the publisher combo box. We then reset the combo box to the saved value.

3. Save the application and run it. Click **Add New**. A blank record appears. Type a book **Title** and an **ISBN**. Assume the publisher name you want is not in the drop-down list. Click the **Publishers** button. The Publishers input form appears. Click **Add New**. Add a publisher using this input form. Click **Save**. Click **Done**. The **Titles** form reappears. You should still be in **Add** mode with your new title displayed. Click the drop-down button and pick your new publisher. Click **Save**. Your new book title is saved and your newly added publisher will be available for all future users. The database engine does all the saving work. Here's my form after adding a new book with a new publisher:

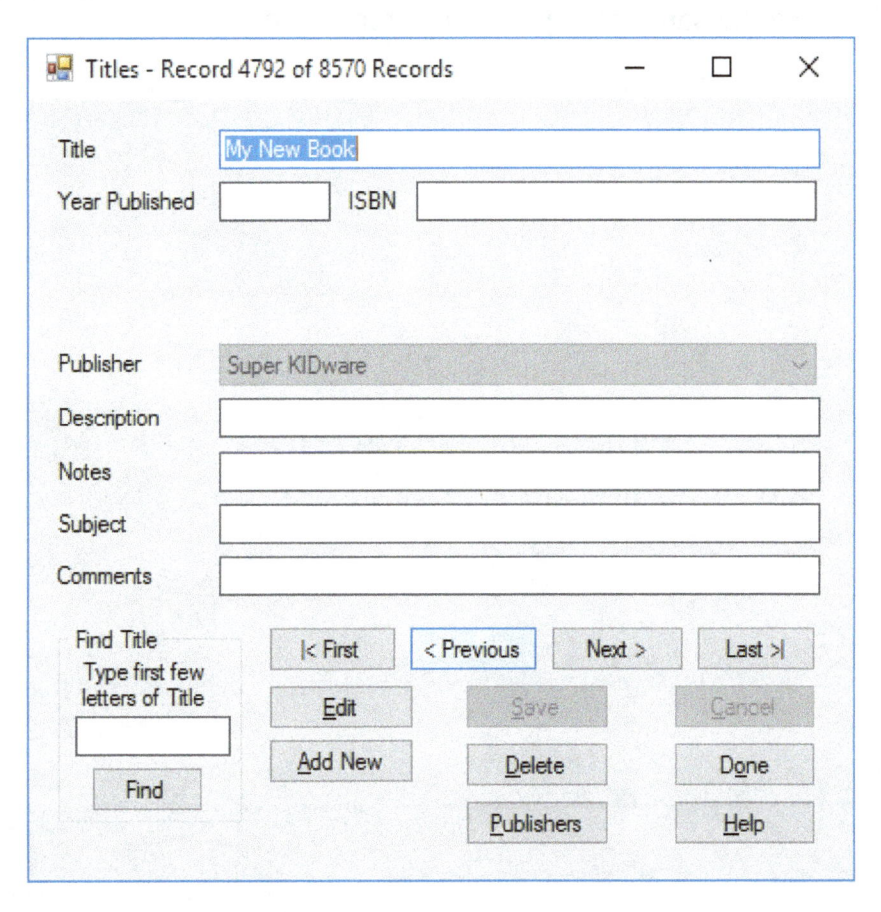

Don't try using the Publisher Input Form **Help** button yet. It may not work, but we'll fix that at the end of this chapter. And, there is one other problem with the **Publishers** input form you may or may not have noticed. We earlier noted the same problem with the Titles form. The Publishers form has many entries. If you want to find a particular one, the only tools at your disposal are the four navigation buttons. Let's add a find capability identical to that used in the Titles table. That is, if the user types the first few letters of a Publishers name, the program will find the record. And, while we're at it, let's also add the ability to display the navigational information (current record and number of records). And, since we'll need the same capabilities for the Authors input form, we'll make the same changes on that form, too

Modify Publishers Input Form

1. Make sure the **Publishers** (saved as **frmPublisher.vb**) input form is in the Visual Basic design window. Add a group box to the lower left corner of the form. Place a label, a text box and button in the group box. Set these properties:

GroupBox1:
    Name   grpFindPublisher
    Text   Find Publisher

Label1:
    AutoSize   False
    Text   Type first few letters of Publisher Name

TextBox1:
    Name   txtFind
    TabStop   False

Button1:
    Name   btnFind
    Text   Find
    TabStop   False

When done, the modified form should look like this (I had to make my form a little longer):

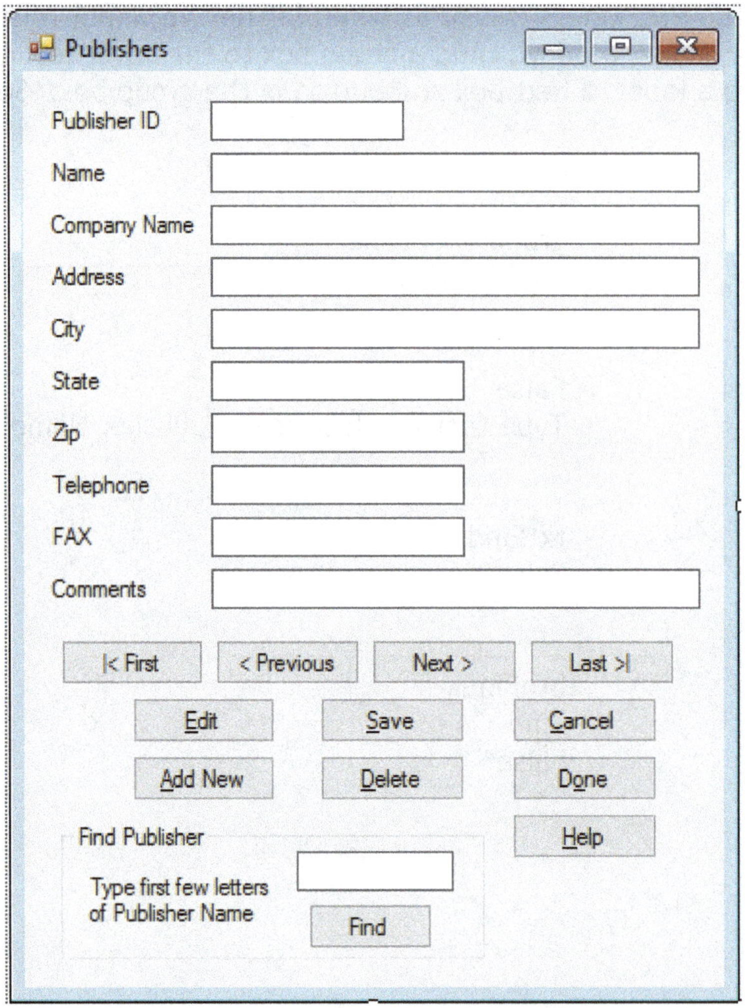
Publishers
Publisher ID
Name
Company Name
Address
City
State
Zip
Telephone
FAX
Comments
|< First
< Previous
Next >
Last >|
Edit
Save
Cancel
Add New
Delete
Done
Find Publisher
Type first few letters of Publisher Name
Find
Help

2. In the **SetState** procedure, enable the **Find Publisher** group box in **View** mode, disable it in **Add** and **Edit** mode. Use the **grpFindPublisher Enabled** property.

3. Add this code to the **btnFind Click** event procedure:

```
Private Sub BtnFind_Click(ByVal sender As System.Object, ByVal e As System.EventArgs) Handles btnFind.Click
    If txtFind.Text = "" Then Exit Sub
    Dim SavedRow As Integer = PublishersManager.Position
    Dim FoundRows() As DataRow
    PublishersTable.DefaultView.Sort = "Name"
    FoundRows = PublishersTable.Select("Name LIKE '" + txtFind.Text + "*'")
    If FoundRows.Length = 0 Then
       PublishersManager.Position = SavedRow
    Else
       PublishersManager.Position = PublishersTable.DefaultView.Find(FoundRows(0).Item("Name"))
    End If
End Sub
```

This code is identical to that used in the **Titles** table. It first saves the position of the currency manager. It then uses the **Select** method of the data table to find all rows with a **Name** field **LIKE** the input letter(s) (we append the wild card character, *). If the search is not successful, the saved position is restored.

6-116　　　　　　　　　Visual Basic and Databases

4. Save the form. Rerun the **Titles** table application. Click **Publishers**. Try out the **Find** function. Make sure it works properly. Here, I found Super KIDware:

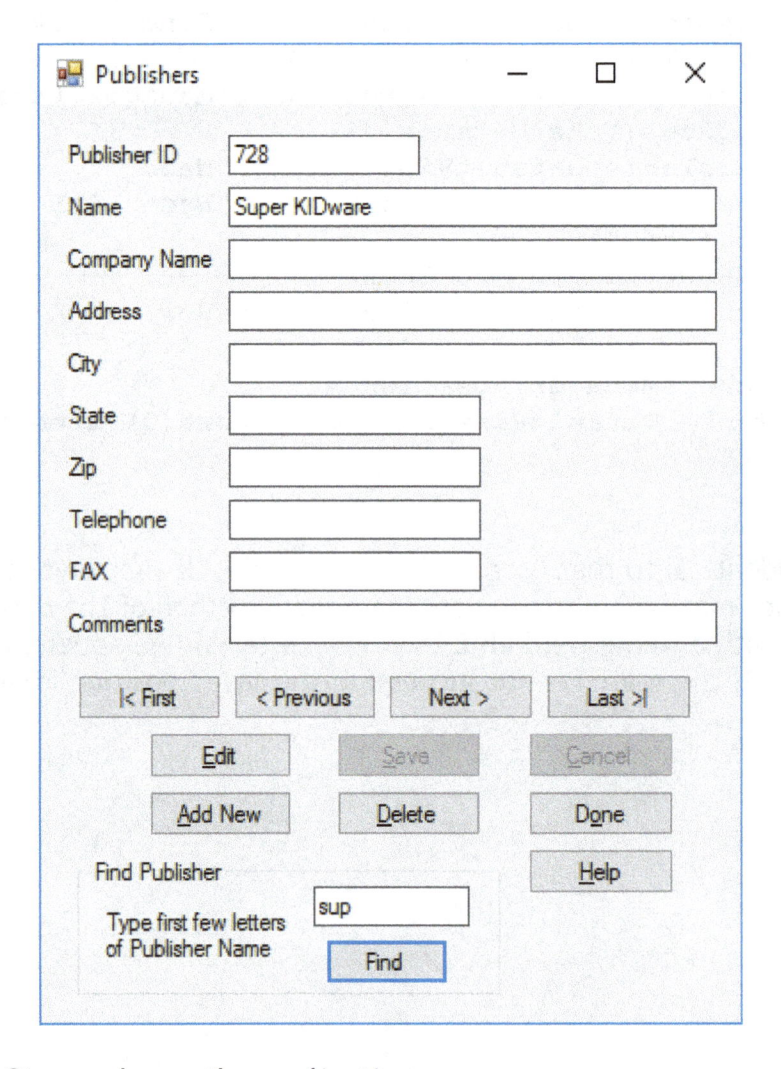

Click **Done**. Stop and save the application.

We'll now add code to keep track of and display the number of records in the **Publishers** data table.

1. Add a general procedure named **SetText** to your application. Use this code:

```
Private Sub SetText()
   Me.Text = "Publishers - Record" +
Str(PublishersManager.Position + 1) + " of" +
Str(PublishersManager.Count) + " Records"
End Sub
```

This sets the form **Text** property to reflect the current record (**Position**) and the total number of records (**Count**).

2. Add this single line of code at the bottom of the **frmPublishers Load** to initialize the display of the number of records:

```
Call SetText()
```

3. When we move to a new record, the currency manager position changes so we need to update the title bar information. Add this line of code at the end of the **btnFind Click**, **btnFirst Click**, **btnPrevious Click**, **btnNext Click** and **btnLast Click** event procedures:

```
Call SetText()
```

4. When we add, save or delete a record, the number of records and current position may change. Also, if we cancel adding a record, there will be changes. Add this line of code at the end of the **btnAddNew Click, btnSave Click, btnCancel Click** and **btnDelete Click** event procedures to reflect this change:

```
Call SetText()
```

5. Save the form and run the application. Click **Publishers**. Note navigation information is now displayed in the form's title bar area:

   Publishers - Record 1 of 728 Records

As you add or delete publishers, this number will change. Add a phony publisher, then delete it to make sure this feature works. When done, stop and save the application.

Modify Authors Input Form

We will soon need the ability to edit, add, and delete authors in the books database **Authors** table. We will want the ability to search using the Authors input form and know how many records there are. So, we'll now modify the Authors input form in the same manner we just modified the Publishers input form. Then, the modified form will be available for author editing.

1. Add the form from Example 6-7 to your project (the last incarnation of the Authors input form; you may have saved it in a different location) to the current project. Save this form as **AuthorForm.vb**.

2. Add a group box to the lower left corner of the form. Place a label, a text box and button in the group box. Set these properties:

GroupBox1:
    Name   grpFindAuthor
    Text   Find Author

Label1:
    AutoSize   False
    Text   Type first few letters of Author Name

TextBox1:
    Name   txtFind
    TabStop   False

Button1:
    Name   btnFind
    Text   Find
    TabStop   False

Database Management 6-119

When done, the modified form should look like this (I had to make my form a little longer):

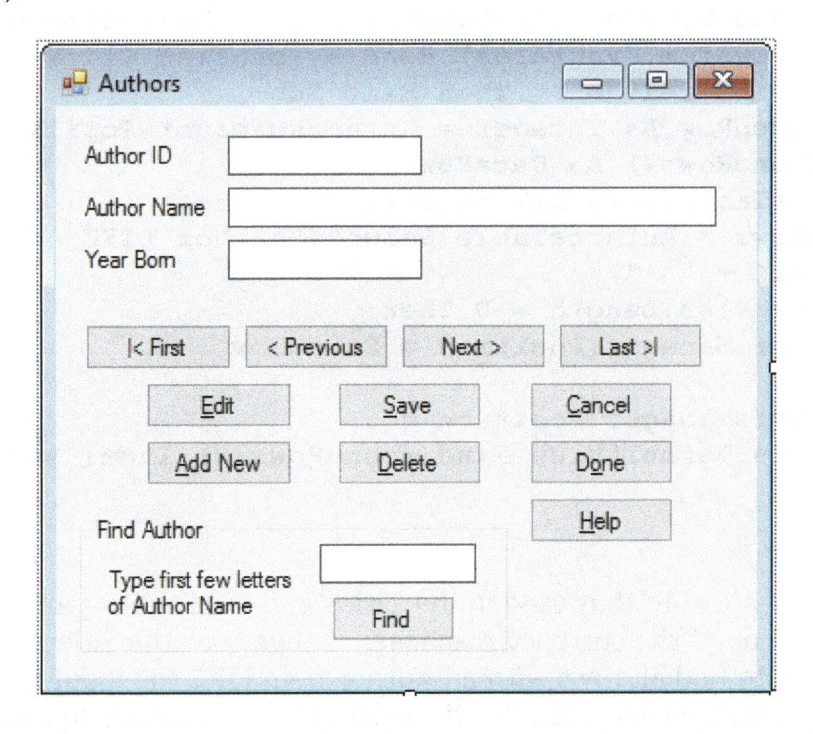

3. In the **SetState** procedure, enable the **Find Author** group box in **View** mode, disable it in **Add** and **Edit** mode. Use the **grpFindAuthor Enabled** property.

4. Add this code to the **btnFind Click** event procedure:

```
Private Sub BtnFind_Click(ByVal sender As System.Object, ByVal e As System.EventArgs) Handles btnFind.Click
    If txtFind.Text = "" Then Exit Sub
    Dim SavedRow As Integer = AuthorsManager.Position
    Dim FoundRows() As DataRow
    AuthorsTable.DefaultView.Sort = "Author"
    FoundRows = AuthorsTable.Select("Author LIKE '" + txtFind.Text + "*'")
    If FoundRows.Length = 0 Then
       AuthorsManager.Position = SavedRow
    Else
       AuthorsManager.Position = AuthorsTable.DefaultView.Find(FoundRows(0).Item("Author"))
    End If
  End Sub
```

This code is identical to that used in the **Titles** and **Publishers** table. It first saves the position of the currency manager. It then uses the **Select** method of the data table to find all rows with an **Author** field **LIKE** the input letter(s) (we append the wild card character, *). If the search is not successful, the saved position is restored.

Database Management 6-121

5. Save the form. Click the **Project** menu, then **Project Properties**. Change **Startup Object** to **frmAuthors**:

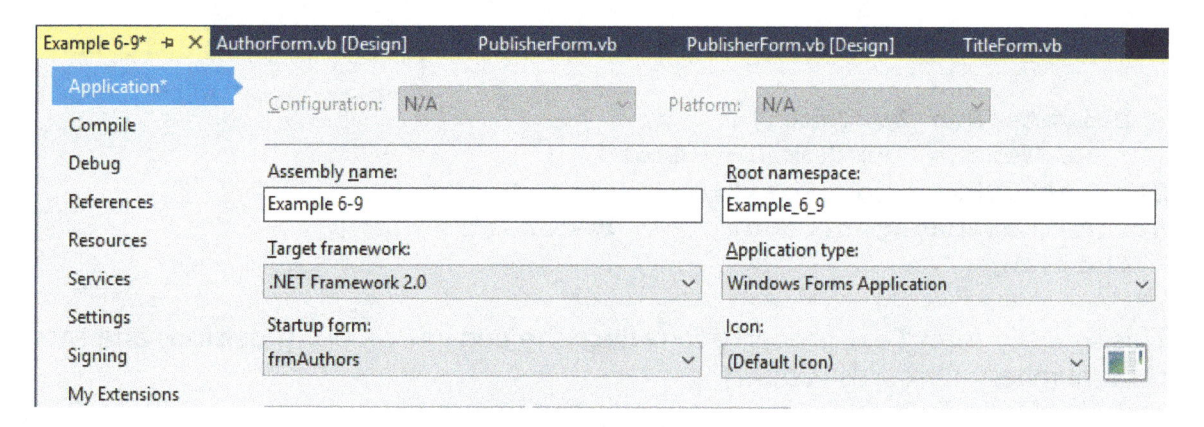

We are temporarily changing the startup form to test our changes to the **Authors** input form. Run the application. The Authors form should appear. Try out the **Find** function. Make sure it works properly. Here, I found myself (added a while back):

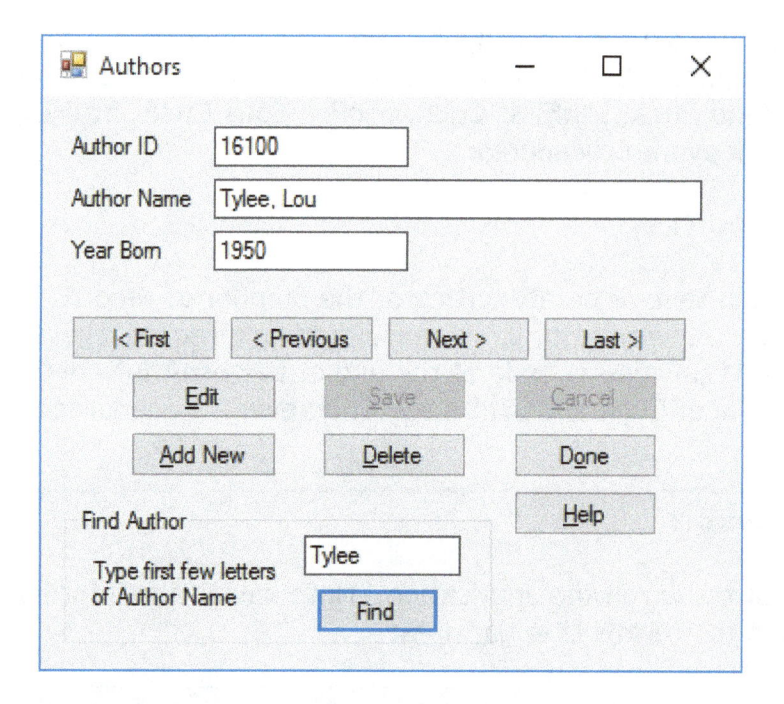

Click **Done**. Stop and save the application. Like the Publisher form, the Author form's **Help** button may not work yet, but it will before we finish the application.

We'll now add code to keep track of and display the number of records in the **Authors** table.

1. Add a general procedure named **SetText** to your application. Use this code:

   ```
   Private Sub SetText()
      Me.Text = "Authors - Record" + Str(AuthorsManager.Position + 1) + " of" + Str(AuthorsManager.Count) + " Records"
   End Sub
   ```

   This sets the form **Text** property to reflect the current record (**Position**) and the total number of records (**Count**).

2. Add this single line of code at the bottom of the **frmAuthors Load** to initialize the display of the number of records:

   ```
   Call SetText()
   ```

3. When we move to a new record, the currency manager position changes so we need to update the title bar information. Add this line of code at the end of the **btnFind Click**, **btnFirst Click**, **btnPrevious Click**, **btnNext Click** and **btnLast Click** event procedures:

   ```
   Call SetText()
   ```

4. When we add, save or delete a record, the number of records and current position may change. Also, if we cancel adding a record, there will be changes. Add this line of code at the end of the **btnAddNew Click, btnSave Click, btnCancel Click** and **btnDelete Click** event procedures to reflect this change:

   ```
   Call SetText()
   ```

5. Save the form and run the application. Note navigation information is now displayed in the form's title bar area:

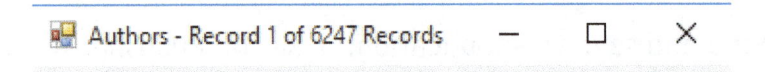

   Authors - Record 1 of 6247 Records   — ☐ ✕

As you add or delete Authors, this number will change. Add a phony Author, then delete it to make sure this feature works. When done, stop the application. Reset the **Startup Object** to **frmTitles**. Make sure it is saved. We leave this example for a bit, while we build a little 'helper' project.

Adding Author Names

This marathon example continues. We're ready to add **author names** to the **Titles** input form. Notice we say author <u>names</u>, not <u>name</u>. That is, books may have more than one author. This fact makes managing author names a difficult task. Difficult, but not impossible. Let's begin to tackle the problem.

First, you might be asking how do we know there may be more than one author listed for a particular book title? If you go way back to Chapter 2, where we took our first look at the books database, note there were **8,569** titles in the **Titles** table, meaning there are 8,569 unique **ISBN** values (the primary key). Yet, in the **Title_Author** table, matching **ISBN** values with author identification numbers (**Au_ID**), there are **16,056** entries! This means there is not a unique Au_ID value for each ISBN value. This database obviously allows multiple Au_ID values for each ISBN value.

The next question is: how many authors could be listed for each title? We need to know this to build our input form. Unfortunately, the answer to this question is not obvious, unless the person who built the database is around to ask. But, using our Visual Basic database programming skills, we can play detective and find out the answer. We build a little project that opens the books database and goes through the **Title_Author** table counting how many authors are listed for each title (**ISBN** value). You might think this is a daunting task, but Visual Basic makes it simple.

Example 6-10

Database Detective - Author Search

1. Again, make sure the Books DBMS Project (**Example 6-9**) is saved. Start a new project. Add a list box control (**ListBox1**). We won't worry about setting proper properties. My form looks like this:

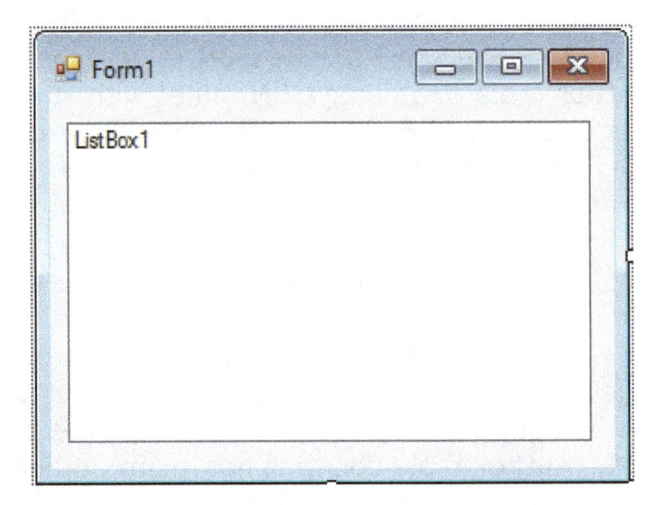

2. Add these lines at the top of the code window:

Access Database:

```
Imports System.Data
Imports System.Data.OleDb
```

SQL Server Database:

```
Imports System.Data
Imports System.Data.SqlClient
```

Database Management 6-125

3. Put this code in the **Form1 Load** event procedure:

Access Database:

```vb
Private Sub Form1_Load(ByVal sender As System.Object, ByVal e As System.EventArgs) Handles MyBase.Load
    Dim BooksConnection As OleDbConnection
    Dim ISBNCommand As OleDbCommand
    Dim ISBNAdapter As OleDbDataAdapter
    Dim ISBNTable As DataTable
    'connect to books database
    BooksConnection = New OleDbConnection("Provider=Microsoft.ACE.OLEDB.12.0; Data Source = c:\VBDB\Working\BooksDB.accdb")
    BooksConnection.Open()
    'establish command object
    ISBNCommand = New OleDbCommand("Select * from Title_Author ORDER BY ISBN", BooksConnection)
    'establish data adapter/data table
    ISBNAdapter = New OleDbDataAdapter()
    ISBNAdapter.SelectCommand = ISBNCommand
    ISBNTable = New DataTable()
    ISBNAdapter.Fill(ISBNTable)
    'Count authors
    Dim Author As Integer
    Dim AuthorCount(10) As Integer
    Dim LastISBN As String
    LastISBN = ""
    'Allow for up to 10 authors per title
    For Author = 1 To 10
      AuthorCount(Author) = 0
    Next Author
    Author = 1
    Dim MyRow As DataRow
    'Check each listing for repeated ISBN
    For Each MyRow In ISBNTable.Rows
      If MyRow.Item("ISBN").Equals(LastISBN) Then
        'If ISBN repeated, additional author
        Author += 1
      Else
        'No more authors for this ISBN
        AuthorCount(Author) += 1
        Author = 1
        LastISBN = MyRow.Item("ISBN").ToString
      End If
    Next
    'display results
    For Author = 1 To 10
```

```vb
            ListBox1.Items.Add(Str(AuthorCount(Author)) + " Books
 with" + Str(Author) + " Authors")
      Next Author
      'dispose
      BooksConnection.Close()
      BooksConnection.Dispose()
      ISBNCommand.Dispose()
      ISBNAdapter.Dispose()
      ISBNTable.Dispose()
   End Sub
```

SQL Server Database:

```vb
   Private Sub Form1_Load(ByVal sender As System.Object,
 ByVal e As System.EventArgs) Handles MyBase.Load
      Dim BooksConnection As SqlConnection
      Dim ISBNCommand As SqlCommand
      Dim ISBNAdapter As SqlDataAdapter
      Dim ISBNTable As DataTable
      'connect to books database
      BooksConnection = New SqlConnection("Data
 Source=.\SQLEXPRESS;
 AttachDbFilename=C:\VBDB\Working\SQLBooksDB.mdf; Integrated
 Security=True; Connect Timeout=30; User Instance=True")
      BooksConnection.Open()
      'establish command object
      ISBNCommand = New SqlCommand("Select * from Title_Author
 ORDER BY ISBN", BooksConnection)
      'establish data adapter/data table
      ISBNAdapter = New SqlDataAdapter()
      ISBNAdapter.SelectCommand = ISBNCommand
      ISBNTable = New DataTable()
      ISBNAdapter.Fill(ISBNTable)
      'Count authors
      Dim Author As Integer
      Dim AuthorCount(10) As Integer
      Dim LastISBN As String
      LastISBN = ""
      'Allow for up to 10 authors per title
      For Author = 1 To 10
         AuthorCount(Author) = 0
      Next Author
      Author = 1
      Dim MyRow As DataRow
      'Check each listing for repeated ISBN
      For Each MyRow In ISBNTable.Rows
         If MyRow.Item("ISBN").Equals(LastISBN) Then
            'If ISBN repeated, additional author
```

```
            Author += 1
        Else
            'No more authors for this ISBN
            AuthorCount(Author) += 1
            Author = 1
            LastISBN = MyRow.Item("ISBN").ToString
        End If
    Next
    'display results
    For Author = 1 To 10
        ListBox1.Items.Add(Str(AuthorCount(Author)) + " Books with" + Str(Author) + " Authors")
    Next Author
    'dispose
    BooksConnection.Close()
    BooksConnection.Dispose()
    ISBNCommand.Dispose()
    ISBNAdapter.Dispose()
    ISBNTable.Dispose()
End Sub
```

The idea behind this code is simple. Using familiar code, we load the **Title_Author** table into a data table object (**ISBNTable**) ordered by **ISBN**. The SQL statement that does this is:

SELECT * FROM Title_Author ORDER BY ISBN

We then go through the data table, one record at a time. If the current ISBN value is the same as the one before (**LastISBN**), we have an additional author. If not, we are looking at a new book. The index of the array **AuthorCount()** keeps track of how many books have that number of authors. We allow for up to 10 authors per book. We initially set all array elements to zero. Once, we check all the records, we present the summary in the list box.

4. Save and run the example. You should see (after a bit of disk whirring):

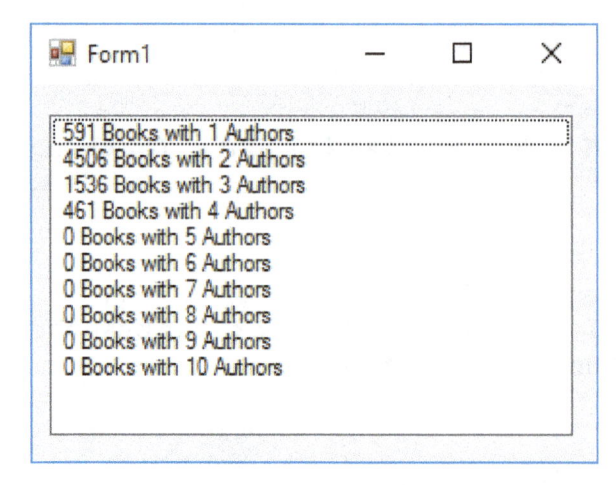

```
591 Books with 1 Authors
4506 Books with 2 Authors
1536 Books with 3 Authors
461 Books with 4 Authors
0 Books with 5 Authors
0 Books with 6 Authors
0 Books with 7 Authors
0 Books with 8 Authors
0 Books with 9 Authors
0 Books with 10 Authors
```

This table shows that, at most, there are four authors for a book. We will allow for that. It's a good check in examples like this to make sure the reported math is correct.

Can you see that this table covers all 16,056 entries in the **Title_Author** table? (Hint: multiply the number of authors by the number of books and add.) Note this code cannot show us how many books have zero authors, since such a book would not have a listing in the **Title_Author** table. To find this information, note there are 7,094 books (591 + 4506 + 1536 + 461) with 1 to 4 authors. Recall the **Titles** table has 8569 listings, hence 1,475 books (8,569 - 7,094) have zero authors. All of these numbers assume you have not modified any entries in the original **Titles** or **Title_Author** tables in the books database file.

The Access version of this example is saved in the **Example 6-10** folder in the **VBDB\Access\Class 6** folder. The SQL Server version is saved in the **Example 6-10** folder in the **VBDB\SQL Server\Class 6** folder.

Viewing Author Selections

Our quick example shows that we need to be able to handle up to **four authors** on the **Titles** input form. But, notice the books database **Titles** table has no author information. So, if we input authors on the Titles input form, what do we do with the information? We need to somehow connect the **Titles** table (via the **ISBN** field) to the **Title_Author** table (which matches **ISBN** to **Au_ID**) to the **Authors** table (which has author information, particularly the **Author**). Perhaps, a true SQL expert could construct a query where the Titles input form displays all the book title information along with the corresponding author(s). Then, all database management tasks would be automated via the database engine. But, I, not being a SQL expert, don't know how to do that. If you do, give it a try. Here, we will use a more ad hoc approach using our Visual Basic programming skills to develop a solution. We'll go slow, taking it in small steps.

The basic requirement from the user is up to four author identification numbers (**Au_ID** fields) for each title in the **Titles** table. These values will be matched with the corresponding title **ISBN** field in the **Title_Author** table. Like the Publisher information we added earlier in this example, we would not expect a user to know a particular author's identification number, but we would expect him or her to know the author's name. Hence, it looks like data bound combo boxes (listing author names to choose from) would be a good place to start.

1. Re-open the BOOKS DBMS application we have been working on (Example 6-9). Open the **Titles** form. Add four label controls and four combo boxes to the form. Set these properties:

   Label1:
       Text   Author 1

   Label2:
       Text   Author 2

   Label3:
       Text   Author 3

   Label4:
       Text   Author 4

ComboBox1:
- Name — cboAuthor1
- BackColor — White (changed so we can see values when **Enabled** is **False**)
- DropDownStyle — DropdownList

ComboBox2:
- Name — cboAuthor2
- BackColor — White (changed so we can see values when **Enabled** is **False**)
- DropDownStyle — DropdownList

ComboBox3:
- Name — cboAuthor3
- BackColor — White (changed so we can see values when **Enabled** is **False**)
- DropDownStyle — DropdownList

ComboBox4:
- Name — cboAuthor4
- BackColor — White (changed so we can see values when **Enabled** is **False**)
- DropDownStyle — DropdownList

Database Management

My completed form looks like this:

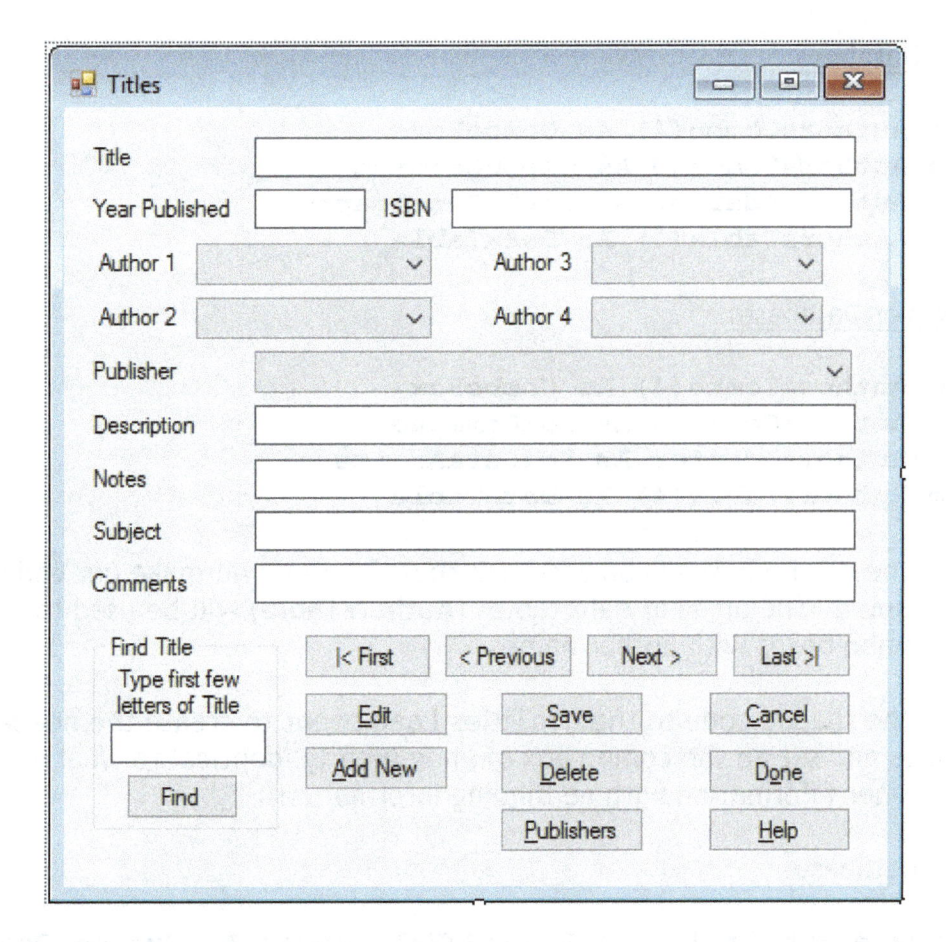

We will add four data table objects to provide a list of author names for the user to choose from in each of the four combo boxes.

6-132　　Visual Basic and Databases

2. Add these declarations at the form level:

Access Database:

```
Dim AuthorsCombo(4) As ComboBox
Dim AuthorsCommand As OleDbCommand
Dim AuthorsAdapter As OleDbDataAdapter
Dim AuthorsTable(4) As DataTable
```

SQL Server Database:

```
Dim AuthorsCombo(4) As ComboBox
Dim AuthorsCommand As SqlCommand
Dim AuthorsAdapter As SqlDataAdapter
Dim AuthorsTable(4) As DataTable
```

Putting the combo boxes in an array (**AuthorsCombo**) will make our coding a little simpler. The array of data tables (**AuthorsTable**) will be used to populate these combo boxes with author names.

3. Add the shaded code to the **frmTitles Load** event to create the needed data tables and set up the combo box binding (nearly identical to what we did for publisher information with no binding information):

Access Database:

```
  Private Sub FrmTitles_Load(ByVal sender As System.Object, ByVal e As System.EventArgs) Handles MyBase.Load
    Try
      'point to help file
      hlpPublishers.HelpNamespace = Application.StartupPath + "\publishers.chm"
      'connect to books database
      BooksConnection = New OleDbConnection("Provider=Microsoft.ACE.OLEDB.12.0; Data Source = c:\VBDB\Working\BooksDB.accdb")
      BooksConnection.Open()
      'establish command object
      TitlesCommand = New OleDbCommand("Select * from Titles ORDER BY Title", BooksConnection)
      'establish data adapter/data table
      TitlesAdapter = New OleDbDataAdapter()
      TitlesAdapter.SelectCommand = TitlesCommand
      TitlesTable = New DataTable()
      TitlesAdapter.Fill(TitlesTable)
      'bind controls to data table
```

Database Management

```vb
        txtTitle.DataBindings.Add("Text", TitlesTable, "Title")
        txtYear.DataBindings.Add("Text", TitlesTable, "Year_Published")
        txtISBN.DataBindings.Add("Text", TitlesTable, "ISBN")
        txtDescription.DataBindings.Add("Text", TitlesTable, "Description")
        txtNotes.DataBindings.Add("Text", TitlesTable, "Notes")
        txtSubject.DataBindings.Add("Text", TitlesTable, "Subject")
        txtComments.DataBindings.Add("Text", TitlesTable, "Comments")
        'establish currency manager
        TitlesManager = DirectCast(Me.BindingContext(TitlesTable), CurrencyManager)
        'establish publisher table/combo box to pick publisher
        PublishersCommand = New OleDbCommand("Select * from Publishers ORDER BY Name", BooksConnection)
        PublishersAdapter = New OleDbDataAdapter()
        PublishersAdapter.SelectCommand = PublishersCommand
        PublishersTable = New DataTable()
        PublishersAdapter.Fill(PublishersTable)
        cboPublisher.DataSource = PublishersTable
        cboPublisher.DisplayMember = "Name"
        cboPublisher.ValueMember = "PubID"
        cboPublisher.DataBindings.Add("SelectedValue", TitlesTable, "PubID")
        'set up combo box array
        AuthorsCombo(1) = cboAuthor1
        AuthorsCombo(2) = cboAuthor2
        AuthorsCombo(3) = cboAuthor3
        AuthorsCombo(4) = cboAuthor4
        AuthorsCommand = New OleDbCommand("Select * from Authors ORDER BY Author", BooksConnection)
        AuthorsAdapter = New OleDbDataAdapter()
        AuthorsAdapter.SelectCommand = AuthorsCommand
        Dim I As Integer
        For I = 1 To 4
          'establish author table/combo boxes to pick author
          AuthorsTable(I) = New DataTable()
          AuthorsAdapter.Fill(AuthorsTable(I))
          AuthorsCombo(I).DataSource = AuthorsTable(I)
          AuthorsCombo(I).DisplayMember = "Author"
          AuthorsCombo(I).ValueMember = "Au_ID"
          'set all to no selection
          AuthorsCombo(I).SelectedIndex = -1
        Next I
```

```
      Catch ex As Exception
        MessageBox.Show(ex.Message, "Error establishing Titles
table.", MessageBoxButtons.OK, MessageBoxIcon.Error)
        Exit Sub
      End Try
      Me.Show()
      Call SetState("View")
      Call SetText()
   End Sub
```

SQL Server Database:

```
   Private Sub FrmTitles_Load(ByVal sender As System.Object,
ByVal e As System.EventArgs) Handles MyBase.Load
      Try
         'point to help file
         hlpPublishers.HelpNamespace = Application.StartupPath
+ "\publishers.chm"
         'connect to books database
         BooksConnection = New SqlConnection("Data
Source=.\SQLEXPRESS;
AttachDbFilename=C:\VBDB\Working\SQLBooksDB.mdf; Integrated
Security=True; Connect Timeout=30; User Instance=True")
         BooksConnection.Open()
         'establish command object
         TitlesCommand = New SqlCommand("Select * from Titles
ORDER BY Title", BooksConnection)
         'establish data adapter/data table
         TitlesAdapter = New SqlDataAdapter()
         TitlesAdapter.SelectCommand = TitlesCommand
         TitlesTable = New DataTable()
         TitlesAdapter.Fill(TitlesTable)
         'bind controls to data table
         txtTitle.DataBindings.Add("Text", TitlesTable,
"Title")
         txtYear.DataBindings.Add("Text", TitlesTable,
"Year_Published")
         txtISBN.DataBindings.Add("Text", TitlesTable, "ISBN")
         txtDescription.DataBindings.Add("Text", TitlesTable,
"Description")
         txtNotes.DataBindings.Add("Text", TitlesTable,
"Notes")
         txtSubject.DataBindings.Add("Text", TitlesTable,
"Subject")
         txtComments.DataBindings.Add("Text", TitlesTable,
"Comments")
         'establish currency manager
```

Database Management 6-135

```vb
        TitlesManager = _
DirectCast(Me.BindingContext(TitlesTable), CurrencyManager)
        'establish publisher table/combo box to pick publisher
        PublishersCommand = New SqlCommand("Select * from _
Publishers ORDER BY Name", BooksConnection)
        PublishersAdapter = New SqlDataAdapter()
        PublishersAdapter.SelectCommand = PublishersCommand
        PublishersTable = New DataTable()
        PublishersAdapter.Fill(PublishersTable)
        cboPublisher.DataSource = PublishersTable
        cboPublisher.DisplayMember = "Name"
        cboPublisher.ValueMember = "PubID"
        cboPublisher.DataBindings.Add("SelectedValue", _
TitlesTable, "PubID")
        'set up array
        AuthorsCombo(1) = cboAuthor1
        AuthorsCombo(2) = cboAuthor2
        AuthorsCombo(3) = cboAuthor3
        AuthorsCombo(4) = cboAuthor4
        Dim I As Integer
        AuthorsCommand = New SqlCommand("Select * from Authors _
ORDER BY Author", BooksConnection)
        AuthorsAdapter = New SqlDataAdapter()
        AuthorsAdapter.SelectCommand = AuthorsCommand
        For I = 1 To 4
          'establish author table/combo boxes to pick author
          AuthorsTable(I) = New DataTable()
          AuthorsAdapter.Fill(AuthorsTable(I))
          AuthorsCombo(I).DataSource = AuthorsTable(I)
          AuthorsCombo(I).DisplayMember = "Author"
          AuthorsCombo(I).ValueMember = "Au_ID"
          'set all to no selection
          AuthorsCombo(I).SelectedIndex = -1
        Next I
    Catch ex As Exception
      MessageBox.Show(ex.Message, "Error establishing Titles _
table.", MessageBoxButtons.OK, MessageBoxIcon.Error)
      Exit Sub
    End Try
    Me.Show()
    Call SetState("View")
    Call SetText()
  End Sub
```

4. Add these lines at the bottom of the **frmTitles Closing** procedure to dispose of our new objects:

   ```
   AuthorsCommand.Dispose()
   AuthorsAdapter.Dispose()
   AuthorsTable(1).Dispose()
   AuthorsTable(2).Dispose()
   AuthorsTable(3).Dispose()
   AuthorsTable(4).Dispose()
   ```

5. Modify the **SetState** procedure to disable the four combo boxes in **View** mode. Enable the combo boxes in **Add** and **Edit** mode.

Database Management 6-137

6. Save the application and run it. There's a chance the **Authors** form will appear instead of the **Titles** form. This will happen if you forgot to reset the startup form when testing the Authors form. To get the proper startup form, click the **Project** menu, then **Project Properties**. Change the **Startup Object** to **frmTitles**. Click **OK**. Once the proper form appears, no authors will be listed – we need some code to do that. Click **Edit**. Click a combo box to see the drop down author lists:

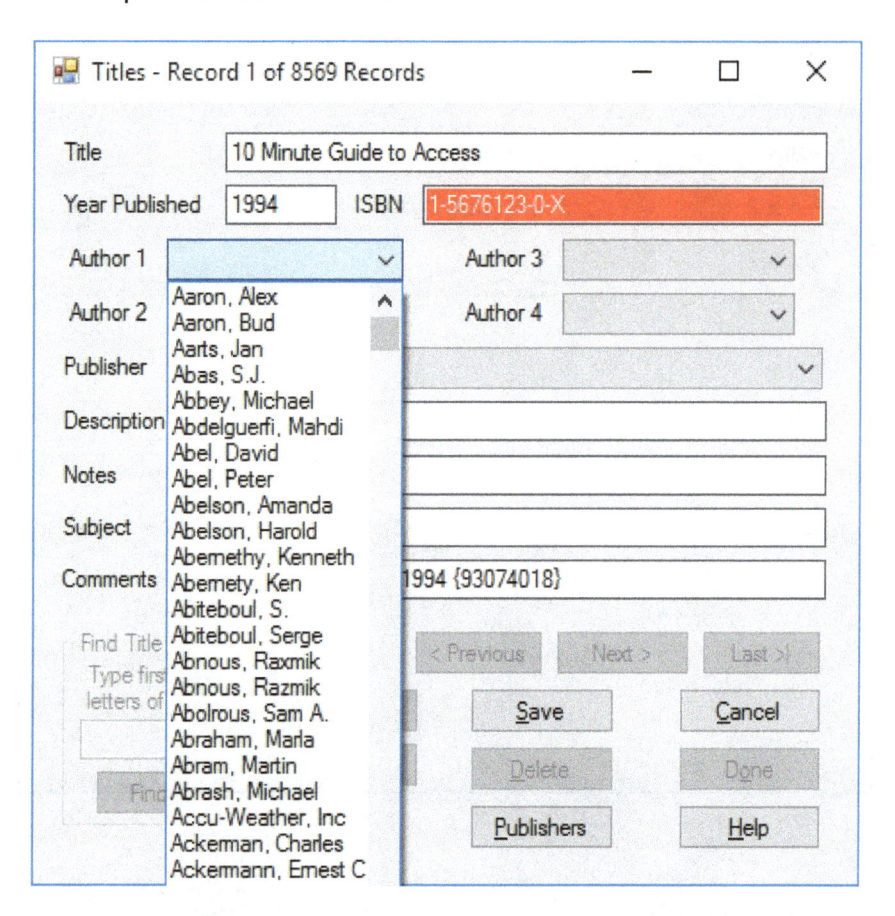

Change one of the authors (any changing won't be saved) just to see how the interface works. When the drop-down box is displayed, you can press the first letter of the last name, if you know it, for faster navigation among the names. This only works in **Edit** mode, the list is disabled in **View** mode. Notice you can't delete a selected author. We'll correct that now. Stop the application.

6-138   Visual Basic and Databases

7. Next to each combo box, place a small button control. **Name** the buttons **btnXAuthor1, btnXAuthor2, btnXAuthor3, btnXAuthor4** and give each button a **Text** of **X** (use a bold font). Set each button's **TabStop** to **False**. The form looks like this now:

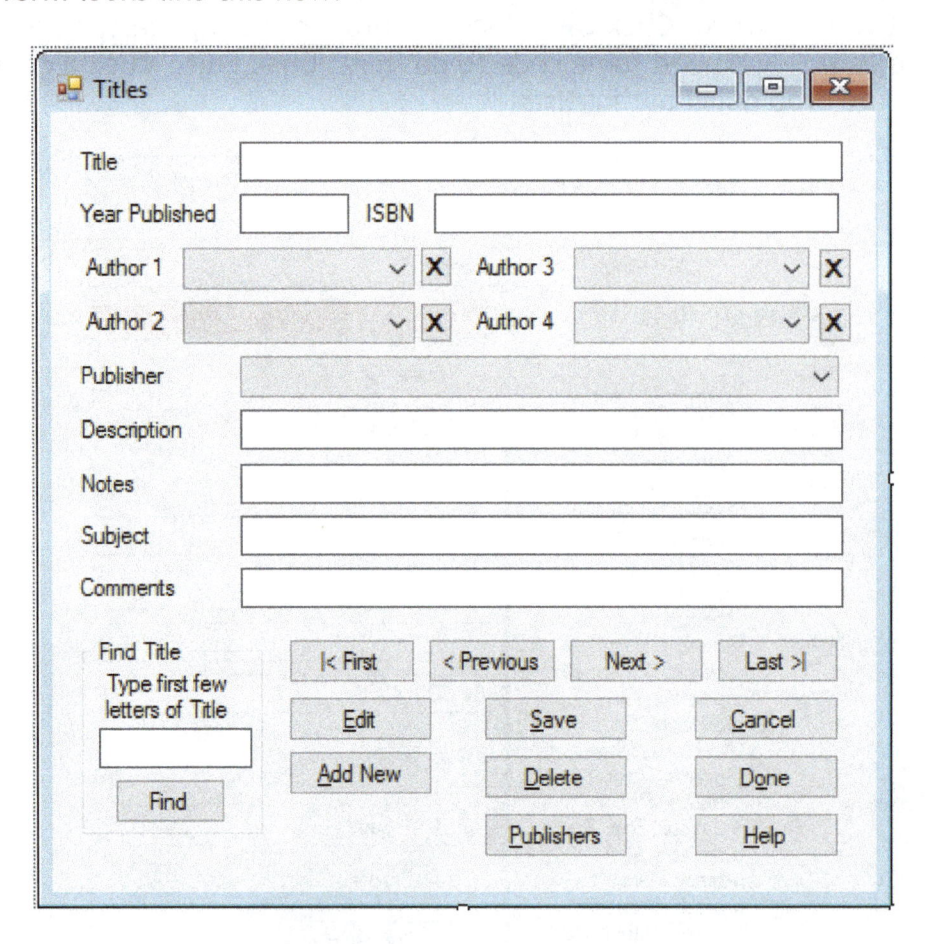

Database Management

8. In the **SetState** procedure, **Enable** these buttons in **Add** and **Edit** mode, disable them in **View** mode. Add this code to the **btnXAuthor Click** procedure (handles the click on any of the four buttons):

```
Private Sub BtnXAuthor_Click(ByVal sender As
System.Object, ByVal e As System.EventArgs) Handles
btnXAuthor1.Click, btnXAuthor4.Click, btnXAuthor3.Click,
btnXAuthor2.Click
    Dim WhichButton As Button = CType(sender, Button)
    Select Case WhichButton.Name
      Case "btnXAuthor1"
        cboAuthor1.SelectedIndex = -1
      Case "btnXAuthor2"
        cboAuthor2.SelectedIndex = -1
      Case "btnXAuthor3"
        cboAuthor3.SelectedIndex = -1
      Case "btnXAuthor4"
        cboAuthor4.SelectedIndex = -1
    End Select
End Sub
```

When a button is clicked, the corresponding combo box selection is cleared.

9. Save the application and run it. Click **Edit**. Choose an author. Then, click the **X** button to delete it. The deletion won't be saved. We need some code to do that.

Viewing Author Names

As a next step, we want the proper author(s) to appear as each title is listed on the **Titles** form. This is where some tricky coding and paying attention to details comes into play. For a particular title, we would like to form a small version of the **Title_Author** table (using another data adapter) like this that shows the author identifications for the title (referenced by its ISBN value):

ISBN	Au_ID

The **ISBN** value will be the same for each row with up to four **Au_ID** values. To form the table, we use our old friend SQL. For our example, assume the displayed record has an ISBN value of **SearchString**. The SQL statement to form the above table is:

SELECT Title_Author.* FROM Title_Author
WHERE Title_Author.ISBN = 'SearchString'

After processing this SQL statement, we determine how many records (if any) are in the resulting data table. For each record, we set the **ValueSelected** property of the corresponding combo box control to **Au_ID**. By doing this, the author name will magically appear! Let's write this code.

1. Return to the BOOKS DBMS application. Add this code in the form level declarations to create the objects we need:

Access Database:

```
Dim ISBNAuthorsCommand As OleDbCommand
Dim ISBNAuthorsAdapter As OleDbDataAdapter
Dim ISBNAuthorsTable As DataTable
```

SQL Server Database:

```
Dim ISBNAuthorsCommand As SqlCommand
Dim ISBNAuthorsAdapter As SqlDataAdapter
Dim ISBNAuthorsTable As DataTable
```

2. Add the general procedure **GetAuthors** to retrieve the authors for the current record:

Access Database:

```
Private Sub GetAuthors()
  Dim I As Integer
  Dim SQLStatement As String = "SELECT Title_Author.* FROM Title_Author WHERE Title_Author.ISBN = '" + txtISBN.Text + "'"
  For I = 1 To 4
    AuthorsCombo(I).SelectedIndex = -1
  Next
  'establish author table/combo boxes to pick author
  ISBNAuthorsCommand = New OleDbCommand(SQLStatement, BooksConnection)
  ISBNAuthorsAdapter = New OleDbDataAdapter()
  ISBNAuthorsAdapter.SelectCommand = ISBNAuthorsCommand
  ISBNAuthorsTable = New DataTable()
  ISBNAuthorsAdapter.Fill(ISBNAuthorsTable)
  If ISBNAuthorsTable.Rows.Count = 0 Then
    Exit Sub
  End If
  For I = 1 To ISBNAuthorsTable.Rows.Count
    AuthorsCombo(I).SelectedValue = ISBNAuthorsTable.Rows(I - 1).Item("Au_ID").ToString
  Next I
End Sub
```

SQL Server Database:

```
  Private Sub GetAuthors()
    Dim I As Integer
    Dim SQLStatement As String = "SELECT Title_Author.* FROM Title_Author WHERE Title_Author.ISBN = '" + txtISBN.Text + "'"
    For I = 1 To 4
      AuthorsCombo(I).SelectedIndex = -1
    Next
    'establish author table/combo boxes to pick author
    ISBNAuthorsCommand = New SqlCommand(SQLStatement, BooksConnection)
    ISBNAuthorsAdapter = New SqlDataAdapter()
    ISBNAuthorsAdapter.SelectCommand = ISBNAuthorsCommand
    ISBNAuthorsTable = New DataTable()
    ISBNAuthorsAdapter.Fill(ISBNAuthorsTable)
    If ISBNAuthorsTable.Rows.Count = 0 Then
      Exit Sub
    End If
    For I = 1 To ISBNAuthorsTable.Rows.Count
      AuthorsCombo(I).SelectedValue = ISBNAuthorsTable.Rows(I - 1).Item("Au_ID").ToString
    Next I
  End Sub
```

In this code, we form the SQL statement for the given ISBN value, blank out the combo boxes and form the data table. For each author, we set the combo box **SelectedValue** property to the **Au_ID** value.

Database Management 6-143

3. Add these lines to the bottom of the **frmTitles Closing** event procedure to dispose of our new objects when done:

   ```
   ISBNAuthorsCommand.Dispose()
   ISBNAuthorsAdapter.Dispose()
   ISBNAuthorsTable.Dispose()
   ```

4. Add this single line of code at the bottom of the **frmTitles Load** to initialize the author display:

   ```
   Call GetAuthors()
   ```

5. When we move to a new record, the currency manager position changes so we need to update the authors. Add this line of code at the end of the **btnFind Click, btnFirst Click, btnPrevious Click, btnNext Click** and **btnLast Click** event procedures:

   ```
   Call GetAuthors()
   ```

6. When we delete a record, the displayed information changes. Add this line of code at the end of the **btnDelete Click** event procedure to reflect this change:

   ```
   Call GetAuthors()
   ```

7. When we cancel an edit, the author combo boxes need to be returned to their 'unedited values.' Add this line of code at the end of the **btnCancel Click** event procedure:

   ```
   Call GetAuthors()
   ```

8. When adding a new title to the database (clicking **Add New**), we need to blank out the author combo boxes. Add this code at the top of the **btnAddNew Click** procedure:

   ```
   cboAuthor1.SelectedIndex = -1
   cboAuthor2.SelectedIndex = -1
   cboAuthor3.SelectedIndex = -1
   cboAuthor4.SelectedIndex = -1
   ```

9. Save the application and run it. Scroll through the records. Notice for each title, the author(s) can be seen. Here's a record we looked at way back in Chapter 2 (when we looked at relational databases):

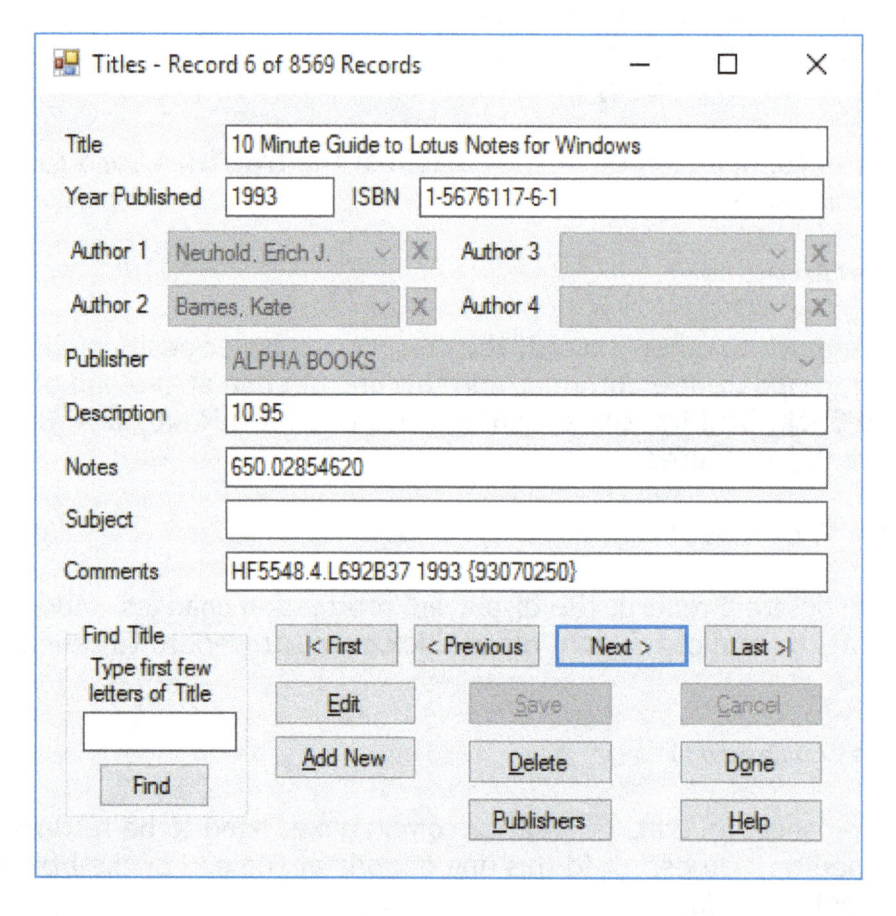

The author names appear shaded because they cannot be edited in **View** mode. It may take a while to display each record, depending on the speed of processing the SQL statement. Click one of the author drop-down boxes. Notice the listed author is selected.

Saving Author Names

We can now list and modify any author(s) associated with a particular book, but we don't have the capability to save any modifications. How do we know if the user has changed any book authors, requiring a **Save**? We don't, but we could write code to determine if any author names have been changed, added or deleted. We'll take a simpler approach. When a **Save** is invoked, we create a new author data table populated with the displayed author names (actually the **Au_ID** values and corresponding **ISBN** values needed by the **Title_Author** table). The ADO .NET engine will then incorporate these changes into the database. This is another good example of using Visual Basic to automate database management tasks.

1. Return to the DBMS project. Add the shaded code to the **btnSave Click** event procedure:

Access Database:

```
  Private Sub BtnSave_Click(ByVal sender As System.Object,
ByVal e As System.EventArgs) Handles btnSave.Click
    If Not (ValidateData()) Then Exit Sub
    Dim SavedName As String = txtTitle.Text
    Dim SavedRow As Integer
    Try
      TitlesManager.EndCurrentEdit()
      Dim I As Integer
      Dim ISBNCommandUpdate As New
OleDbCommandBuilder(ISBNAuthorsAdapter)
      'delete all rows of data table then repopulate
      If ISBNAuthorsTable.Rows.Count <> 0 Then
        For I = 0 To ISBNAuthorsTable.Rows.Count - 1
          ISBNAuthorsTable.Rows(I).Delete()
        Next
        ISBNAuthorsAdapter.Update(ISBNAuthorsTable)
      End If
      For I = 1 To 4
        If AuthorsCombo(I).SelectedIndex <> -1 Then
          ISBNAuthorsTable.Rows.Add()
          ISBNAuthorsTable.Rows(ISBNAuthorsTable.Rows.Count
- 1).Item("ISBN") = txtISBN.Text
          ISBNAuthorsTable.Rows(ISBNAuthorsTable.Rows.Count
- 1).Item("Au_ID") = AuthorsCombo(I).SelectedValue
        End If
      Next
      ISBNAuthorsAdapter.Update(ISBNAuthorsTable)
      TitlesTable.DefaultView.Sort = "Title"
```

```
      SavedRow = TitlesTable.DefaultView.Find(SavedName)
      TitlesManager.Position = SavedRow
      MessageBox.Show("Record saved.", "Save",
MessageBoxButtons.OK, MessageBoxIcon.Information)
      Call SetState("View")
    Catch ex As Exception
      MessageBox.Show("Error saving record.", "Error",
MessageBoxButtons.OK, MessageBoxIcon.Error)
      MessageBox.Show(ex.Message)
    End Try
    Call SetText()
  End Sub
```

SQL Server Database:

```
  Private Sub BtnSave_Click(ByVal sender As System.Object,
ByVal e As System.EventArgs) Handles btnSave.Click
    If Not (ValidateData()) Then Exit Sub
    Dim SavedName As String = txtTitle.Text
    Dim SavedRow As Integer
    Try
      TitlesManager.EndCurrentEdit()
      Dim I As Integer
      Dim ISBNCommandUpdate As New
SqlCommandBuilder(ISBNAuthorsAdapter)
      'delete all rows of data table then repopulate
      If ISBNAuthorsTable.Rows.Count <> 0 Then
        For I = 0 To ISBNAuthorsTable.Rows.Count - 1
          ISBNAuthorsTable.Rows(I).Delete()
        Next
        ISBNAuthorsAdapter.Update(ISBNAuthorsTable)
      End If
      For I = 1 To 4
        If AuthorsCombo(I).SelectedIndex <> -1 Then
          ISBNAuthorsTable.Rows.Add()
          ISBNAuthorsTable.Rows(ISBNAuthorsTable.Rows.Count
- 1).Item("ISBN") = txtISBN.Text
          ISBNAuthorsTable.Rows(ISBNAuthorsTable.Rows.Count
- 1).Item("Au_ID") = AuthorsCombo(I).SelectedValue
        End If
      Next
      ISBNAuthorsAdapter.Update(ISBNAuthorsTable)
      TitlesTable.DefaultView.Sort = "Title"
      SavedRow = TitlesTable.DefaultView.Find(SavedName)
      TitlesManager.Position = SavedRow
      MessageBox.Show("Record saved.", "Save",
MessageBoxButtons.OK, MessageBoxIcon.Information)
      Call SetState("View")
```

```
    Catch ex As Exception
        MessageBox.Show("Error saving record.", "Error",
MessageBoxButtons.OK, MessageBoxIcon.Error)
        MessageBox.Show(ex.Message)
    End Try
    Call SetText()
End Sub
```

The new code first deletes all records. It then looks at all four combo boxes for author names. If a combo box holds a name, a record is added to the data table and proper field values (**ISBN**, **Au_ID**) established. The data adapter holding the data table is then updated to save the changes to the database.

2. Save the project. Run it. Try all functions. Add a title, fill in the fields and save it. Here's a listing for this book (**Visual Basic and Databases**):

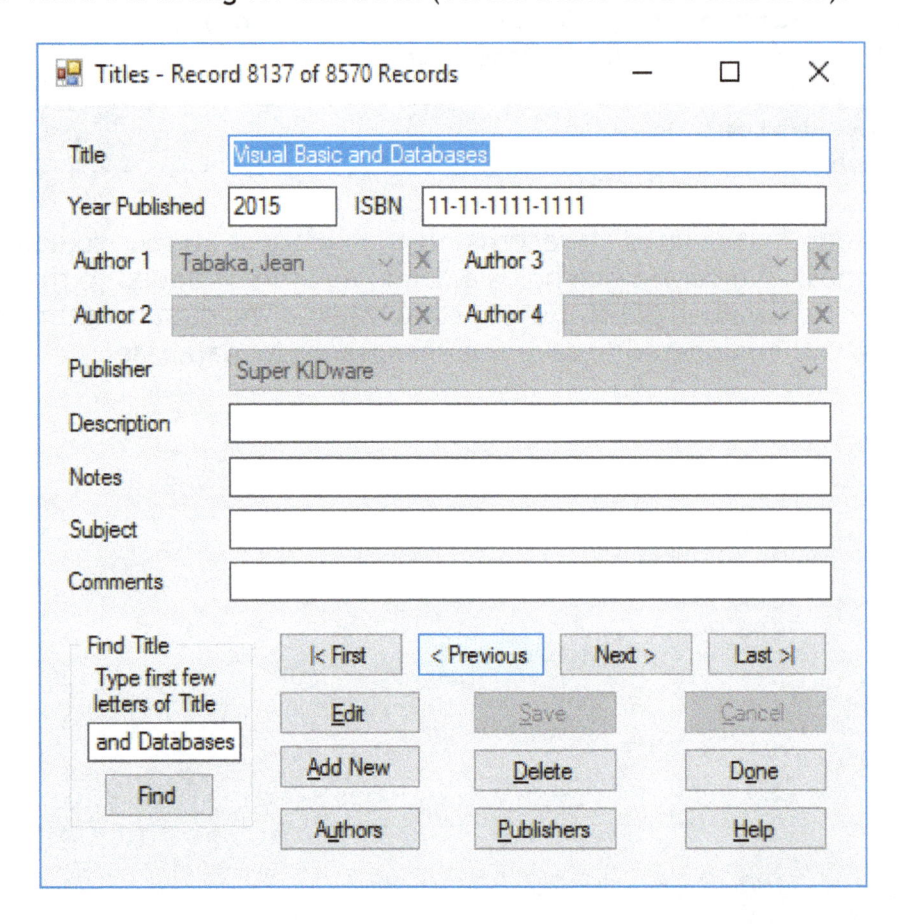

[Screenshot: Titles - Record 8137 of 8570 Records. Title: Visual Basic and Databases. Year Published: 2015. ISBN: 11-11-1111-1111. Author 1: Tabaka, Jean. Publisher: Super KIDware. Find Title - Type first few letters of Title: "and Databases". Buttons: First, Previous, Next, Last, Edit, Save, Cancel, Add New, Delete, Done, Authors, Publishers, Help.]

I made up an author since I'm not listed – we'll fix that next. Return to that record to see how the author(s) were saved. Make sure the **Cancel** function works with both **Add** and **Edit** modes.

Adding Author Editing

We readdress a problem encountered earlier with the **Publisher** entry. What if the user can't find the author they want in the drop-down list? This could often happen when adding new titles to the database. If the desired author name is not in the list, we need to either edit a current entry or add a new entry to the **Authors** table. Once the new author name is in the Authors table, it will be available for use in the **Titles** input form. Editing is done using the **Authors** input form modified and saved earlier as **AuthorForm.vb**.

1. Make sure **TitleForm.vb** is in the Visual Basic form window. On the Titles input form, add a button to the left of the **Publishers** button. Give it a **Name** property of **btnAuthors** and a **Text** property of A&uthors.

Add this code to the **btnAuthors Click** event:

Access Database:

```
  Private Sub BtnAuthors_Click(ByVal sender As
System.Object, ByVal e As System.EventArgs) Handles
btnAuthors.Click
    Dim AuthorsForm As New frmAuthors
    Dim AuthorsSave(4) As String
    AuthorsSave(1) = AuthorsCombo(1).Text
    AuthorsSave(2) = AuthorsCombo(2).Text
    AuthorsSave(3) = AuthorsCombo(3).Text
    AuthorsSave(4) = AuthorsCombo(4).Text
    Dim I As Integer
    AuthorsForm.ShowDialog()
    AuthorsForm.Dispose()
    'need to regenerate authors data
    BooksConnection.Close()
    BooksConnection = New
OleDbConnection("Provider=Microsoft.ACE.OLEDB.12.0; Data
Source = c:\VBDB\Working\BooksDB.accdb")
    BooksConnection.Open()
    AuthorsAdapter.SelectCommand = AuthorsCommand
    For I = 1 To 4
      AuthorsTable(I) = New DataTable()
      AuthorsAdapter.Fill(AuthorsTable(I))
      AuthorsCombo(I).DataSource = AuthorsTable(I)
      If AuthorsSave(I) <> "" Then
        AuthorsCombo(I).Text = AuthorsSave(I)
      Else
        AuthorsCombo(I).SelectedIndex = -1
      End If
    Next
  End Sub
```

SQL Server Database:

```
   Private Sub BtnAuthors_Click(ByVal sender As
System.Object, ByVal e As System.EventArgs) Handles
btnAuthors.Click
     Dim AuthorsForm As New frmAuthors
     Dim AuthorsSave(4) As String
     AuthorsSave(1) = AuthorsCombo(1).Text
     AuthorsSave(2) = AuthorsCombo(2).Text
     AuthorsSave(3) = AuthorsCombo(3).Text
     AuthorsSave(4) = AuthorsCombo(4).Text
     Dim I As Integer
     AuthorsForm.ShowDialog()
     AuthorsForm.Dispose()
     'need to regenerate authors data
     BooksConnection.Close()
     BooksConnection = New SqlConnection("Data
Source=.\SQLEXPRESS;
AttachDbFilename=C:\VBDB\Working\SQLBooksDB.mdf; Integrated
Security=True; Connect Timeout=30; User Instance=True")
     BooksConnection.Open()
     AuthorsAdapter.SelectCommand = AuthorsCommand
     For I = 1 To 4
       AuthorsTable(I) = New DataTable()
       AuthorsAdapter.Fill(AuthorsTable(I))
       AuthorsCombo(I).DataSource = AuthorsTable(I)
       If AuthorsSave(I) <> "" Then
         AuthorsCombo(I).Text = AuthorsSave(I)
       Else
         AuthorsCombo(I).SelectedIndex = -1
       End If
     Next
   End Sub
```

This code displays the **Authors** input form to allow any editing necessary. Before displaying the form, the current author choices are saved (**AuthorsSave** array). When the **Titles** form becomes active again, there may be new values in the database (from editing the **Authors** table). To see these changes, we close our connection to the database, then reopen it, recreating the **AuthorsTable()** objects bound to the author combo boxes. The saved values are then used to reestablish author choices.

2. Save the application and run it. Click **Add New**. A blank record appears. Type a book **Title**, an **ISBN**, and select a **Publisher**. Assume the author name you want is not in the drop-down list. Click the **Authors** button. The Authors input form appears. Click **Add New**. Add an author using this input form. Click **Save**. Click **Done**. The **Titles** form reappears (it may take a while to rebuild). You should still be in **Add** mode with your new title displayed. Click the drop-down button and pick your new author. Click **Save**. Your new book title is saved and your newly added author will be available for all future users. The database engine does all the saving work. Here's my form after editing the listing built for this book (**Visual Basic and Databases**) after adding me to the **Authors** table:

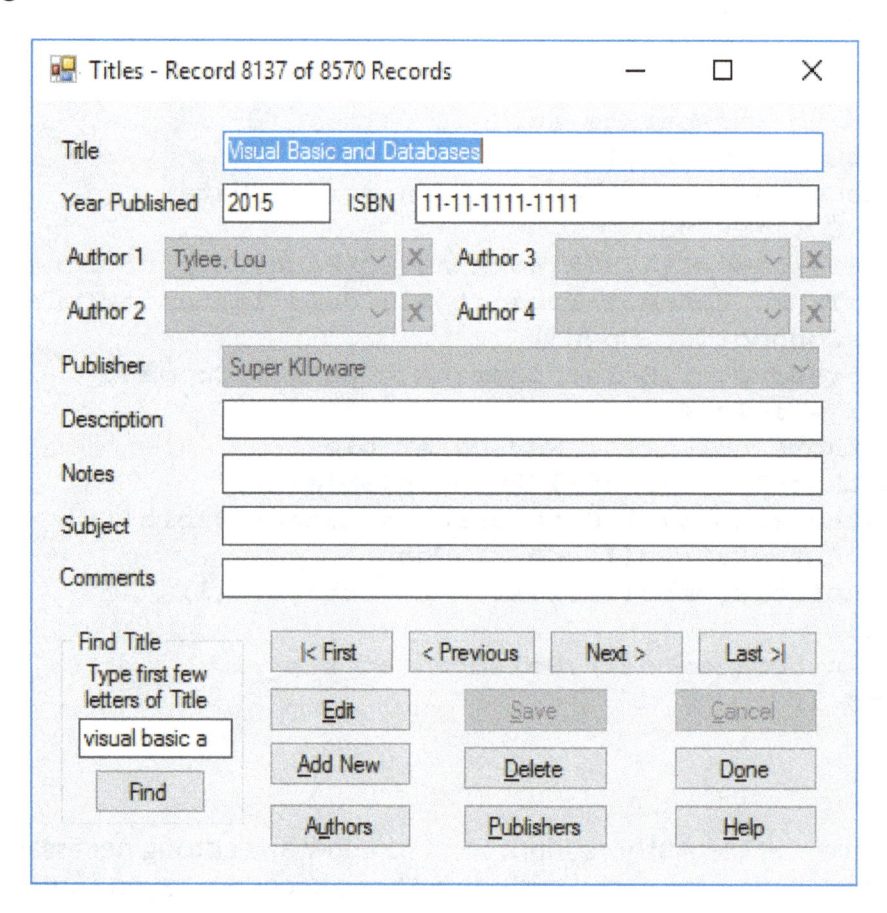

Input Control Navigation

As the user enters data on the **Titles** form, there should be logical movement from one control to the next. This is easily accomplished using the control **TabIndex** property and a little code in **KeyPress** events.

1. Return to the DBMS application. Establish the following **TabIndex** values for each control used for input (this will set a logical progression from one control to the next):

Control Name	TabIndex
txtTitle	0
txtYear	1
txtISBN	2
cboAuthor1	3
cboAuthor2	4
cboAuthor3	5
cboAuthor4	6
cboPublisher	7
txtDescription	8
txtNotes	9
txtSubject	10
txtComments	11

2. Save the application and run it. Tab through the controls and notice the sequencing in **View**, **Edit** and **Add** modes.

3. Add this code to the **cboPublisher KeyPress** event procedure:

```
Private Sub CboPublisher_KeyPress(ByVal sender As
System.Object, ByVal e As
System.Windows.Forms.KeyPressEventArgs) Handles
cboPublisher.KeyPress
   If e.KeyChar = ControlChars.Cr Then
      txtDescription.Focus()
   End If
End Sub
```

Add this code to the **cboAuthor KeyPress** event procedure (invoked by all four author combo boxes):

```
Private Sub CboAuthor_KeyPress(ByVal sender As Object, ByVal e As System.Windows.Forms.KeyPressEventArgs) Handles cboAuthor1.KeyPress, cboAuthor4.KeyPress, cboAuthor3.KeyPress, cboAuthor2.KeyPress
    Dim WhichComboBox As ComboBox = CType(sender, ComboBox)
    Select Case WhichComboBox.Name
      Case "cboAuthor1"
        cboAuthor2.Focus()
      Case "cboAuthor2"
        cboAuthor3.Focus()
      Case "cboAuthor3"
        cboAuthor4.Focus()
      Case "cboAuthor4"
        cboPublisher.Focus()
    End Select
End Sub
```

Add this code to the **txtInput KeyPress** event procedure (invoked by all text box inputs):

```
  Private Sub TxtInput_KeyPress(ByVal sender As
System.Object, ByVal e As
System.Windows.Forms.KeyPressEventArgs) Handles
txtTitle.KeyPress, txtYear.KeyPress, txtSubject.KeyPress,
txtNotes.KeyPress, txtISBN.KeyPress,
txtDescription.KeyPress, txtComments.KeyPress
    Dim WhichTextBox As TextBox = CType(sender, TextBox)
    If e.KeyChar = ControlChars.Cr Then
      Select Case WhichTextBox.Name
        Case "txtTitle"
          txtYear.Focus()
        Case "txtYear"
          If MyState = "Add" Then
            txtISBN.Focus()
          Else
            cboAuthor1.Focus()
          End If
        Case "txtISBN"
          cboAuthor1.Focus()
        Case "txtDescription"
          txtNotes.Focus()
        Case "txtNotes"
          txtSubject.Focus()
        Case "txtSubject"
          txtComments.Focus()
        Case "txtComments"
          txtTitle.Focus()
      End Select
    End If
End Sub
```

All of the above code detects if **<Enter>** is clicked and moves the focus accordingly. This adds another way to move from control to control. Note ISBN (**txtISBN**) can only be accessed in **Add** mode.

4. Save the application and run it. Note how pressing **<Enter>** moves you from control to control in a logical order.

Entry and Input Validation

In earlier work, we implemented entry and input validation for the **Authors** and **Authors** input forms. We now need similar validation for the **Titles** input form. The validation rules we will apply are:

- A **Title** must be entered.
- If a **Year Published** is entered, it must be valid.
- An **ISBN** value must be entered and have a specified format.
- A **Publisher** must be entered.

We will develop a procedure that checks these validation rules. The procedure will be called prior to saving a record. We first validate the **Title** field.

1. Return to the BOOKS DBMS application. Make sure you are working with the **Titles** table. Modify the **ValidateData** procedure to check for existence of a **Title** (**txtTitle**; new code is shaded):

```
Private Function ValidateData() As Boolean
    Dim Message As String = ""
    Dim AllOK As Boolean = True
    If txtTitle.Text = "" Then
      Message = "You must input a Title." + ControlChars.CrLf
      txtTitle.Focus()
      AllOK = False
    End If
    If Not (AllOK) Then
      MessageBox.Show(Message, "Validation Error", MessageBoxButtons.OK, MessageBoxIcon.Information)
    End If
    Return (AllOK)
End Function
```

Recall this function is invoked prior to saving a record permanently. If a **False** is returned, the data is not valid.

Database Management 6-157

2. Save the application. Run it. Click **Add New**, then **Save**. Make sure the message box appears:

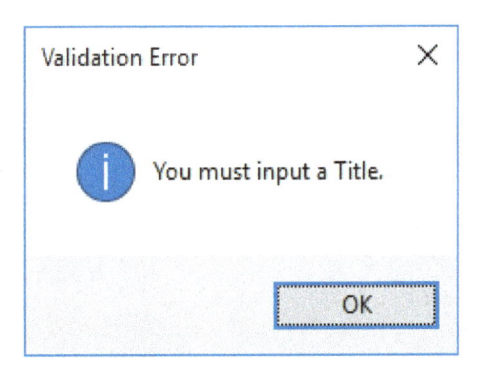

Click **OK**. Click **Cancel**. Click **Add New** and type in a **Title**. Click **Save**. You may get a message concerning the lack of a **PubID** field. This is coming from our error-trapping routine. We will fix the problem soon. Stop the application.

We'll now validate the **Year Published** field (**txtYear**).

1. Set the **MaxLength** property for **txtYear** to **4**. Add this code to the end of the **txtInput KeyPress** event to insure only numbers are typed in this box.

```
If WhichTextBox.Name = "txtYear" Then
   If (e.KeyChar >= CChar("0") And e.KeyChar <= CChar("9")) Or e.KeyChar = ControlChars.Back Then
      e.Handled = False
   Else
      Console.Beep()
      e.Handled = True
   End If
End If
```

6-158　　Visual Basic and Databases

2. Modify the code added earlier in the **ValidateData** procedure to check for a valid date value (most borrowed from the **Authors** form code). Changes are shaded:

```
Private Function ValidateData() As Boolean
   Dim Message As String = ""
   Dim AllOK As Boolean = True
   If txtTitle.Text = "" Then
      Message = "You must input a Title." + ControlChars.CrLf
      txtTitle.Focus()
      AllOK = False
   End If
   Dim InputYear As Integer, CurrentYear As Integer
   'Check length and range on Year Published
   If txtYear.Text.Trim <> "" Then
      InputYear = CInt(Val(txtYear.Text))
      CurrentYear = CInt(Val(Format(Now, "yyyy")))
      If InputYear > CurrentYear Or InputYear < CurrentYear - 150 Then
         Message += "Year published must be between" + Str(CurrentYear - 150) + " and" + Str(CurrentYear)
         txtYear.Focus()
         AllOK = False
      End If
   End If
   If Not (AllOK) Then
      MessageBox.Show(Message, "Validation Error", MessageBoxButtons.OK, MessageBoxIcon.Information)
   End If
   Return (AllOK)
End Function
```

3. Save the application and run it. Click **Add New**. Type in a Title. Type in valid years and invalid years. Click **Save**. Make sure the **Year Published** validation works correctly. You may still get the missing PubID error. Stop the application.

Next, we validate the **ISBN** field (**txtISBN**). This value is fixed length, with a specific format. The ISBN is always a 13-character string with hyphens at positions 2, 10, and 12. The other positions are assumed to have either numbers or upper case letters. Those who know more about ISBN values may want to implement different rules about what characters can be used in different positions. Remember the masked text box control described back in Chapter 5? This is an excellent place to use such a control. We need to replace the existing text box, but the work is worth it. This happens all the time in building applications. At some point, you may discover one control does a better job than the one you have been using and you need to do a replacement.

1. Return to the project. Delete the **txtISBN** textbox control. Add a masked text box control to the form and resize it to fit the position held by the previous control. Set these properties:

Name	txtISBN
Mask	>A-AAAAAAA-A-A (allows numbers and upper case letters)
TabIndex	2

By giving the control the same name, we can use the existing code.

2. Add this **txtISBN KeyPress** event procedure:

```
Private Sub TxtISBN_KeyPress(ByVal sender As
System.Object, ByVal e As
System.Windows.Forms.KeyPressEventArgs) Handles
txtISBN.KeyPress
    If e.KeyChar = ControlChars.Cr Then
      cboAuthor1.Focus()
    End If
End Sub
```

We can't use the existing **txtInput KeyPress** procedure since it only works with text box controls, not masked text box controls.

The form with the new control will look like this (note the mask):

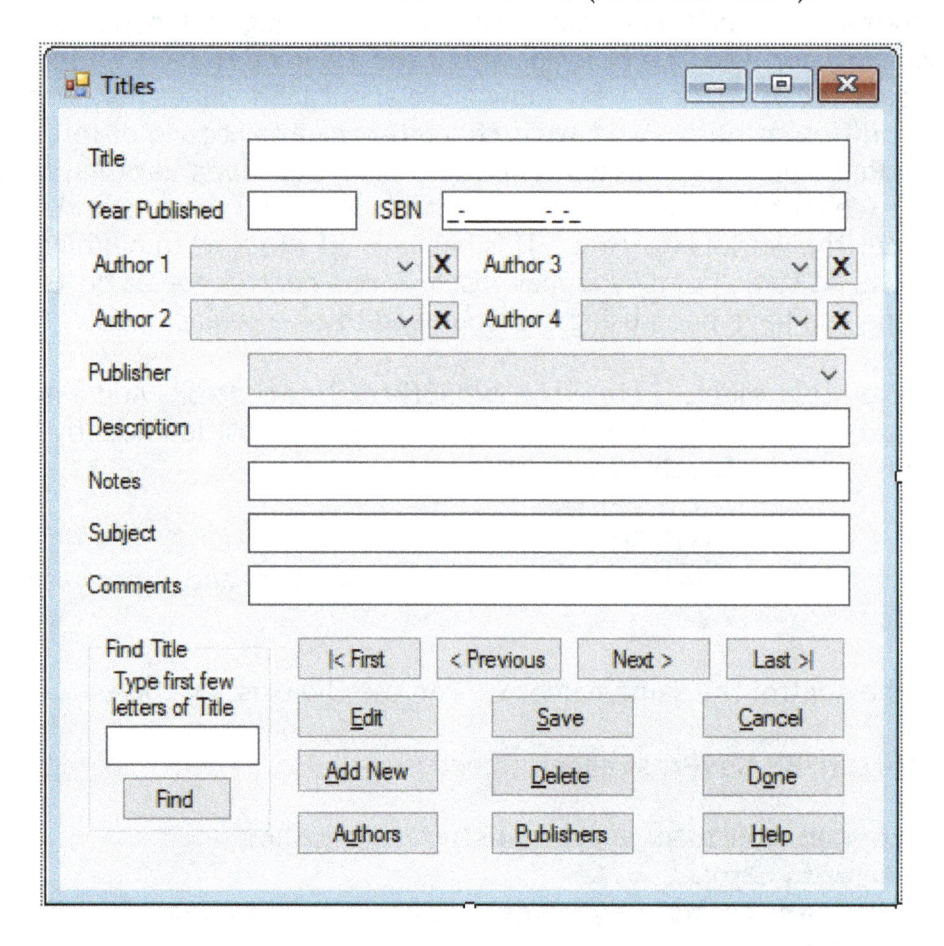

3. Save the application and run it. Make sure the navigation among the controls works under all application states (**View, Edit, Add**). Click **Add New**. Type in a **Title** and **Year Published**. Tab to the **ISBN** field. Type in a value. Notice how the masked control makes entry simple. Here's a value I entered for the book I've been editing:

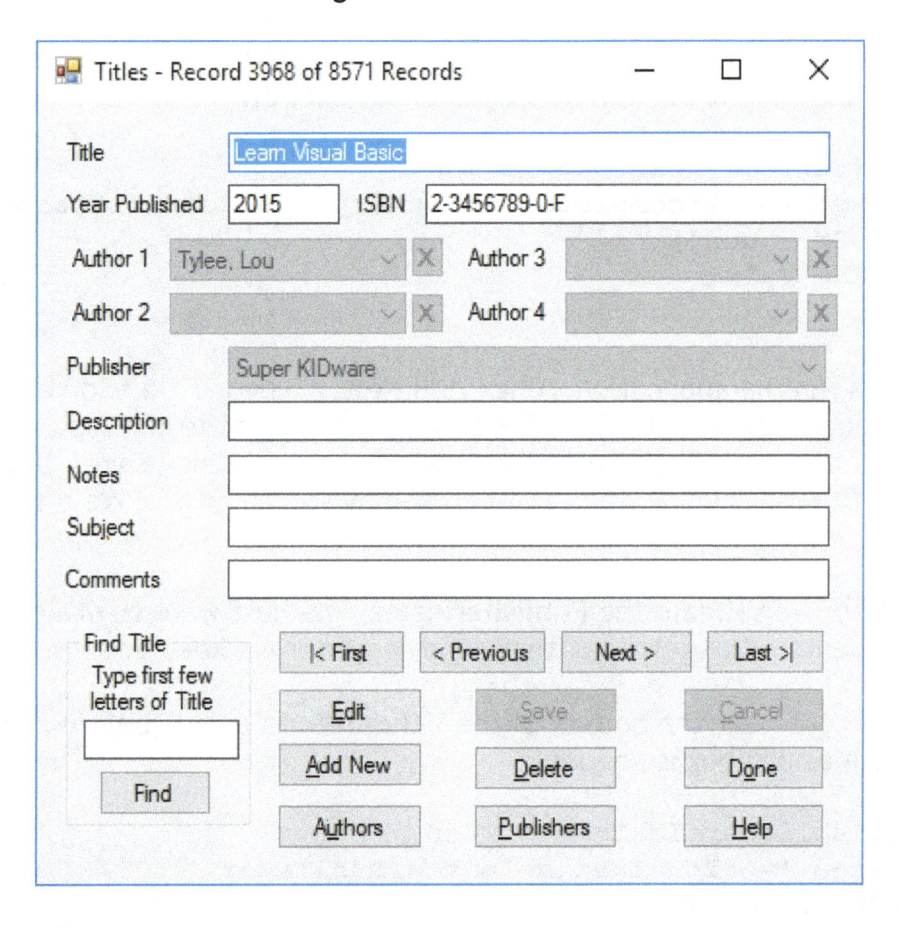

Stop the application.

How do we validate the value in the masked edit control? The control insures valid characters are typed and that they are positioned correctly. The only validation we need to do is check that all characters are filled in. To do this, we check the length of the **Text** property. If the length of the Text property is 13 characters (includes the three hyphens), it is assumed to be valid.

1. Add this validation code near the bottom of the **ValidateData** procedure (before checking to see if a message box is needed):

   ```
   If Len(txtISBN.Text) <> 13 Then
     Message += "Incomplete ISBN entry." + ControlChars.CrLf
     txtISBN.Focus()
     AllOK = False
   End If
   ```

2. Save and run the application. Click **Add New**. Type a Title and Year Published value. Try out the **ISBN** masked text box control. Type an incomplete entry. Click **Save**. Complete the entry. Click **Save**. Did it work properly? Yeah, I know, the **PubID** error may still show up. We'll fix that now.

As a last step, we validate the **Publisher** name. We just want to make sure a publisher is entered to get rid of that annoying error we keep getting.

1. Add this code near the bottom of the **ValidateData** event (before checking to see if a message box is needed):

   ```
   If cboPublisher.Text = "" Then
     Message += "You must select a Publisher."
     cboPublisher.Focus
     AllOK = False
   End If
   ```

2. Save and run the application. You should now test all four of the validation rules. When satisfied they are working properly, we'll do one more thing to wrap up this mammoth example.

Titles Form On-Line Help

Recall that the **Help** buttons on the **Authors** input form and the **Publishers** input form may not work. And, the **Help** button on the main **Titles** input form definitely won't work because we haven't developed an on-line help system for that form yet. Let's solve all these problems now and finish the **Books Database Management System**.

Every Visual Basic application can have just one help file. We need to combine the Authors and Publishers help files with one developed here for the Titles table. This complete file, properly divided into topics, will form the books database help system. Refer back to the Chapter 5 notes to complete each step listed here.

1. Using FrontPage or a similar product, write a topic file for the Titles form (saved as **titles.htm** in the **VBDB\General\Class 6\Example 6-9\HelpFile** folder). The topics and text I used are:

> **Titles Input Form**
>
> Available options for managing Titles database table:
>
> **Edit Record**
>
> Click the **Edit** button to edit the displayed record. Make any needed changes. The Title, ISBN and Publisher fields are required, all others are optional. Click **Save** to save the changes; click **Cancel** to ignore the changes.
>
> **Add New Record**
>
> Click the **Add New** button to add a record to the Titles database. Type in a Title (required), Year Published, ISBN (required), Description, Notes, Subject, and Comments. Use the drop-down boxes to select up to four authors. Use the drop-down box to also select a Publisher (required). Click **Save** to save the new record; click **Cancel** to ignore the new record.
>
> **Delete Record**
>
> Click the **Delete** button to delete the displayed record.
>
> **Find**
>
> Type a few starting letters in the text box and click **Find** to help locate a particular title.
>
> **Authors**
>
> Click the **Authors** button to display the Authors input form if you need to change, add, or delete entries in the Authors database table.
> **Publishers**

> Click the **Publishers** button to display the Publishers input form if you need to change, add, or delete entries in the Publishers database table.
>
> **Exit Program**
>
> Click the **Done** button to quit the application.

2. Copy the **authors.htm** (Example 6-7) and **publishers.htm** (Example 6-8) topic files into the same folder as **titles.htm**.

3. Using the HTML Help Workshop, create a project file for this example. Name it **books.hhp**.

4. Using the HTML Help Workshop, create a contents file for this example. Name it **books.hhc**. Have one topic for each of the three input forms.

5. Using the HTML Help Workshop, save and compile your help file (named **books.chm** in the the **VBDB\General\Class 6\Example 6-9\HelpFile** folder). Copy this file to the Books DBMS project **Bin\Debug** folder (**Bin\x86\Debug** for **Access** version).

Database Management   6-165

6. Load the books database application (**Example 6-9**). Display the **Titles** form. Rename the help provider control **hlpBooks**. Make the shaded change near the top of the **frmTitles Load** procedure:

```
Private Sub FrmTitles_Load(ByVal sender As System.Object,
ByVal e As System.EventArgs) Handles MyBase.Load
    Try
        'point to help file
        hlpBooks.HelpNamespace = Application.StartupPath +
"\books.chm"
        'connect to books database
        .
        .
End Sub
```

And make the shaded change to the **btnHelp Click** procedure:

```
Private Sub BtnHelp_Click(ByVal sender As System.Object,
ByVal e As System.EventArgs) Handles btnHelp.Click
    Help.ShowHelp(Me, hlpBooks.HelpNamespace)
End Sub
```

7. Display the **Authors** form. We need to point it to the new help file. Make the shaded change near the top of the **frmAuthors Load** procedure:

```
Private Sub FrmAuthors_Load(ByVal sender As System.Object,
ByVal e As System.EventArgs) Handles MyBase.Load
    Try
        'point to help file
        hlpAuthors.HelpNamespace = Application.StartupPath +
"\books.chm"
        'connect to books database
        .
        .
End Sub
```

8. Display the **Publishers** form. We also need to point it to the new help file. Make the shaded change near the top of the **frmPublishers Load** procedure:

```
  Private Sub FrmPublishers_Load(ByVal sender As
System.Object, ByVal e As System.EventArgs) Handles
MyBase.Load
    Try
      'point to help file
      hlpPublishers.HelpNamespace = Application.StartupPath
+ "\books.chm"
      'connect to books database
      .
      .
    End Sub
```

9. Save and run the application (final Access version saved in **VBDB\Access\Class 6\Example 6-9** folder; SQL Server version saved in **VBDB\SQL Server\Class 6\Example 6-9** folder). Click **Help**. You should see:

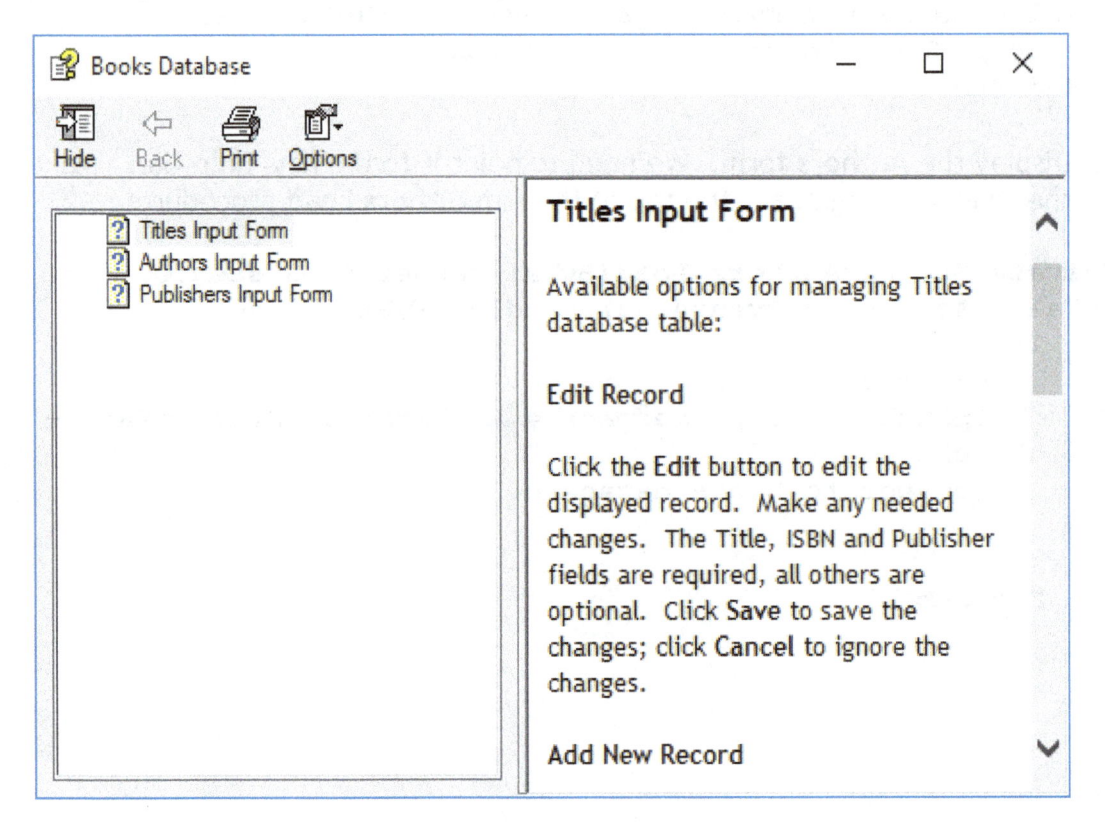

Make sure help works with the **Authors** and **Publishers** forms. And, guess what the Books Database Management System is complete!

Summary

In this chapter, you built a very large application. You learned how to edit, add, and delete records in both single table and multiple table databases. You learned how to find records of interest. The books database management system you built would rival a mid-size commercial application, regarding its capabilities. Congratulations if you worked through this detailed example.

In this chapter, you learned that, though building a database management system is a long and detailed process, it is relatively straightforward. There is a set procedure to follow in implementing any database management task. The Visual Basic environment, with its event-driven nature, allows us to build an application in stages. This ability lets us build part of the application, test it, and proceed. There is no need to build an entire application before it can be tested.

Still remaining in our database studies are the topics of database reports, distributing applications, and database design. And, later on in the course, we'll build three complete database projects.

7

Database Reports

Review and Preview

We have seen that using the ADO .NET data objects, in conjunction with Visual Basic, allows us to build a solid, well-functioning database management system. We are able to edit, add, delete, and/or find records within any database.

Once you have gone to all the trouble of managing a database, it is nice to have the ability to obtain printed or displayed information from your data. The vehicle for obtaining such information is known as a **database report**. In this chapter, we look at how to use Visual Basic code to obtain database reports.

PrintDocument Object

Users expect to have the ability to obtain printed copies of information contained within a database. This information is in the form of **database reports**. Generating reports is a straightforward task. You just need to determine what information you want in the report and how you want it to be presented. We look at using the Visual Basic **PrintDocument** object for database reports.

The Visual Basic **PrintDocument** object provides a virtual space where you can place information to be printed. This information is placed in the space using Visual Basic properties and methods. You just write code to put information where you want it. The PrintDocument object does not take advantage of any data bound controls or database access techniques. You need to do that in code. The PrintDocument object is good for quick data report generation and allows lots of flexibility in what can be displayed. It also allows you to take advantage of several print-related common dialog controls. And, you don't have to learn anything new. Using it only requires your Visual Basic knowledge.

The **PrintDocument** object (in the **Drawing.Printing** namespace) controls the printing process and has four important properties:

Property	Description
DefaultPageSettings	Indicates default page settings for the document.
DocumentName	Indicates the name displayed while the document is printing.
PrintController	Indicates the print controller that guides the printing process.
PrinterSettings	Indicates the printer that prints the document.

The steps to print a document (which may include text and graphics) using the **PrintDocument** object are:

- Declare a **PrintDocument** object
- Create a **PrintDocument** object
- Set any properties desired.
- Print the document using the **Print** method of the **PrintDocument** object.

The first three steps are straightforward. To declare and create a **PrintDocument** object named **MyDocument**, use:

```
Dim MyDocument As Drawing.Printing.PrintDocument
  .
  .
MyDocument = New Drawing.Printing.PrintDocument()
```

Any properties needed usually come from print dialog boxes we'll examine in a bit.

The last step poses the question: how does the **PrintDocument** object print with the **Print** method? Printing is done in a general Visual Basic procedure associated with the **PrintDocument.PrintPage** event. This is a procedure you must create and write. The procedure tells the **PrintDocument** object what goes on each page of your document. Once the procedure is written, you need to add the event handler in code so the **PrintDocument** object knows where to go when it's ready to print a page. It may sound confusing now, but once you've done a little printing, it's very straightforward.

The general Visual Basic procedure for printing your pages (**MyPrintPage** in this case) must be of the form:

```
Private Sub MyPrintPage(ByVal sender As Object, ByVal e As
Drawing.Printing.PrintPageEventArgs)
  .
  .
End Sub
```

In this procedure, you 'construct' each page that the **PrintDocument** object is to print. And, you'll see the code in this procedure is familiar.

In the **MyPrintPage** procedure, the argument **e** (of type **Drawing.Printing.PrintPageEventArgs**) has many properties with information about the printing process. The most important property is the **graphics object**:

```
e.Graphics
```

PrintDocument provides us with a graphics object to 'draw' each page we want to print. We can draw lines, rectangles, images and even text! We'll look at how to do this in detail next. But, first, let's review how to establish and use the **PrintDocument** object.

Here is an annotated code segment that establishes a **PrintDocument** object (**MyDocument**) and connects it to a procedure named **MyPrintPage** that provides the pages to print via the graphics object:

```
'Declare the document
Dim MyDocument As Drawing.Printing.PrintDocument
    .
    .
    .
'Create the document and name it
MyDocument = New Drawing.Printing.PrintDocument()
MyDocument.DocumentName = "My Document"
    .
    .
    .
'You could set other properties here
    .
    .
    .
'Add code handler
AddHandler MyDocument.PrintPage, AddressOf Me.MyPrintPage
'Print document
MyDocument.Print()
'Dispose of document when done printing
MyDocument.Dispose()
```

This code assumes the procedure **MyPrintPage** is available. Let's see how to build such a procedure.

Printing Document Pages

The **PrintDocument** object provides (in its **PrintPage** event) a graphics object (**e.Graphics**) for 'drawing' our pages. And, that's just what we do using graphics methods. For each page in our printed document, we draw the desired text information (**DrawString** method), any lines (**DrawLine** method), rectangles (**DrawRectangle** method) or images (**DrawImage** method).

Once a page is completely drawn to the graphics object, we 'tell' the **PrintDocument** object to print it. We repeat this process for each page we want to print. This does require a little bit of work on your part. You must know how many pages your document has and what goes on each page. I usually define a page number variable to help keep track of the current page being drawn.

Once a page is complete, there are two possibilities: there are more pages to print or there are no more pages to print. The **e.HasMorePages** property (Boolean) is used to specify which possibility exists. If a page is complete and there are still more pages to print, use:

```
e.HasMorePages = True
```

In this case, the **PrintDocument** object will return to the **PrintPages** event for the next page. If the page is complete and printing is complete (no more pages), use:

```
e.HasMorePages = False
```

This tells the **PrintDocument** object its job is done. At this point, you should dispose of the **PrintDocument** object.

Let's look at the graphics object for a single page. The boundaries of the printed page are defined by the **e.MarginBounds** properties (these are established by the **PrinterSettings** property):

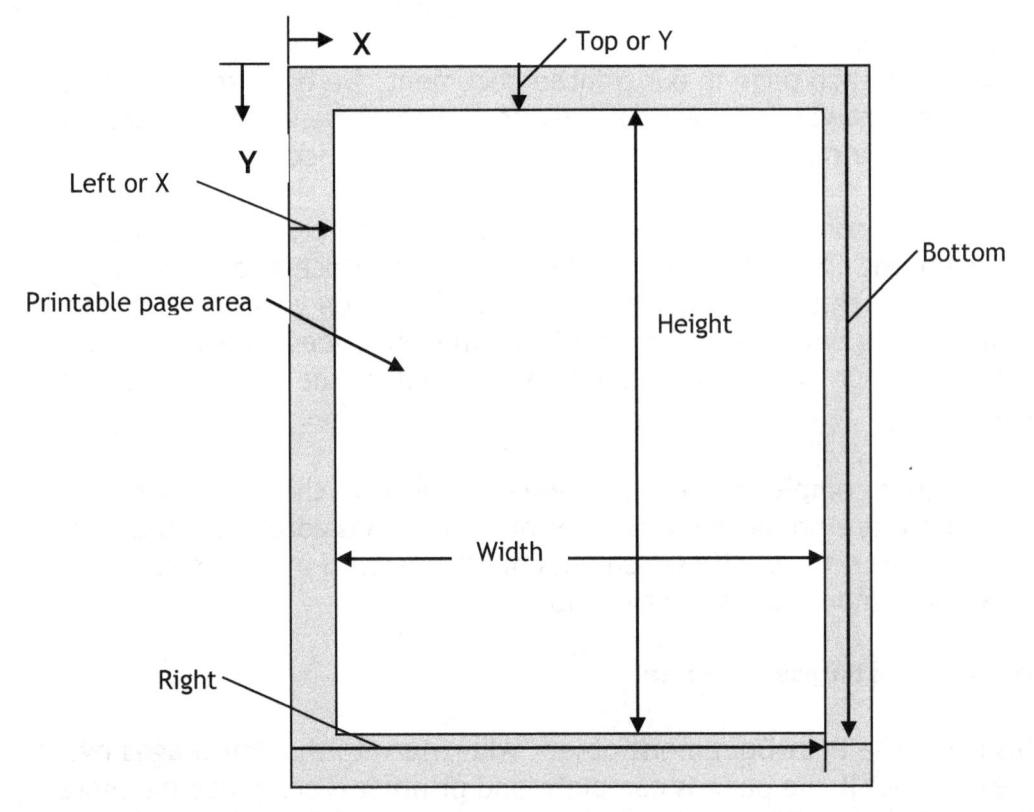

This becomes our palette for positioning items on a page. All properties are in 1/100th of an inch. Horizontal position is governed by **X** (increases from 0 to the right) and vertical position is governed by **Y** (increases from 0 to the bottom).

The process for each page is to decide "what goes where" and then position the desired information using the appropriate graphics method. There are many Visual Basic graphics methods. Here, we limit the discussion to printing text, lines, rectangles and images. Before discussing the graphics methods, we need to provide information on two useful objects: **Pen** and **Brush**.

Pen Object

Some of the printing graphics methods require a **Pen** object. This virtual pen is just like the pen you use to write and draw. You can choose color and width of the pen. You can use pens built into Visual Basic or create your own pen.

In many cases, the pen objects built into Visual Basic are sufficient. The **Pens** class will draw a line **1** pixel wide in a color you choose. If the selected color is **ColorName**, the syntax to refer to such a pen is:

```
Drawing.Pens.ColorName
```

To create your own **Pen** object (in **Drawing** namespace), you first declare the pen using:

```
Dim MyPen As Drawing.Pen
```

The pen is then created using the **Pen** constructor:

```
MyPen = New Drawing.Pen(Color, Width)
```

where **Color** is the color your new pen will draw in and **Width** is the integer width of the line (in pixels) drawn. This pen will draw a solid line. The **Color** argument can be one of the built-in colors or one generated with the **FromArgb** function.

Once created, you can change the color and width at any time using the **Color** and **Width** properties of the pen object. The syntax is:

```
MyPen.Color = NewColor
MyPen.Width = NewWidth
```

Here, **NewColor** is a newly specified color and **NewWidth** is a new integer pen width.

When done drawing with a pen object, it should be disposed using the **Dispose** method:

```
MyPen.Dispose()
```

Brush Object

Filling of regions and printing text in Visual Basic is done with a **Brush** object. Like the Pen object, a brush is just like a brush you use to paint - just pick a color. You can use brushes built into Visual Basic or create your own brush.

In most cases, the brush objects built into Visual Basic are sufficient. The **Brushes** class provides brush objects that paint using one of the 141 built-in colors. The syntax to refer to such a brush is:

```
Drawing.Brushes.ColorName
```

To create your own **Brush** object (from the **Drawing** namespace), you first declare the brush using:

```
Dim MyBrush As Drawing.Brush
```

The solid color brush is then created using the **SolidBrush** constructor:

```
MyBrush = New Drawing.SolidBrush(Color)
```

where **Color** is the color your new brush will paint with. This color argument can be one of the built-in colors or one generated with the **FromArgb** function.

Once created, you can change the color of a brush any time using the **Color** property of the brush object. The syntax is:

```
MyBrush.Color = NewColor
```

where **NewColor** is a newly specified color.

When done painting with a brush object, it should be disposed using the **Dispose** method:

```
MyBrush.Dispose()
```

Graphics Methods

To place text on the graphics object (**e.Graphics**), use the **DrawString** method. To place the string **MyString** at position (**X, Y**), using the font object **MyFont** and brush object **MyBrush**, the syntax is:

```
e.Graphics.DrawString(MyString, MyFont, MyBrush, X, Y)
```

With this statement, you can place any text, anywhere you like, with any font, any color and any brush style. You just need to make the desired specifications. Each line of text on a printed page will require a **DrawString** statement.

There are two methods for determining the size of strings. This is helpful for both vertical and horizontal placement of text on a page. To determine the height (in pixels) of a particular font, use:

```
MyFont.GetHeight(e.Graphics)
```

If you need width and height of a string use:

```
e.Graphics.MeasureString(MyString, MyFont)
```

This method returns a **SizeF** structure with two properties: **Width** and **Height** (both in hundredths of an inch). These two properties are useful for justifying (left, right, center, vertical) text strings.

Many times, you use lines in a document to delineate various sections. To draw a line on the graphics object, use the **DrawLine** method:

```
e.Graphics.DrawLine(MyPen, x1, y1, x2, y2)
```

This statement will draw a line from (**x1, y1**) to (**x2, y2**) using the pen object **MyPen**.

To draw a rectangle (used with tables or graphics regions), use the **DrawRectangle** method:

```
e.Graphics.DrawRectangle(MyPen, x1, y1, x2, y2)
```

This statement will draw a rectangle with upper left corner at (**x1, y1**) and lower right corner at (**x2, y2**) using the pen object **MyPen**.

The **DrawImage** method is used to position an image (**MyImage**) object on a page. The syntax is:

```
e.Graphics.DrawImage(MyImage, X, Y, Width, Height)
```

The upper left corner of **MyImage** will be at (**X, Y**) with the specified **Width** and **Height**. Any image will be scaled to fit the specified region.

If **DrawImage** is to be used to print the contents of a panel control hosting a graphics object (we'll do this in Chapter 10), you must insure the graphics are persistent. We review those steps. For a panel named **pnlExample**, establish the **BackgroundImage** as an empty bitmap:

```
pnlExample.BackgroundImage = New
Drawing.Bitmap(pnlExample.ClientSize.Width,
pnlExample.ClientSize.Height,
Drawing.Imaging.PixelFormat.Format24bppRgb)
```

Then, establish the drawing object **MyObject** using:

```
MyObject =
Drawing.Graphics.FromImage(pnlExample.BackgroundImage)
```

Now, any graphics methods applied to this object will be persistent. To maintain this persistence, after each drawing operation to this object, use:

```
MyObject.Refresh()
```

The image in this object can then be printed with the **DrawImage** method:

```
e.Graphics.DrawImage(pnlExample.BackgroundImage, X, Y,
Width, Height)
```

The upper left corner of the image will be at (**X, Y**) with the specified **Width** and **Height**. The image will be scaled to fit the specified region.

The use of each graphics method (and the **Pen** and **Brush** objects) will be illustrated in this chapter's examples. The best way to learn how to print in Visual Basic is to do lots of it. You'll develop your own approaches and techniques as you gain familiarity. You might want to see how some of the other graphics methods (**DrawEllipse**, **DrawLines**, **DrawCurves**) might work with printing. Or, look at different brush and pen objects.

Many print jobs just involve the user clicking a button marked **'Print'** and the results appear on printed page with no further interaction. If more interaction is desired, there are three dialog controls that help specify desired printing job properties: **PageSetupDialog**, **PrintDialog**, and **PrintPreviewDialog**. Using these controls adds more code to your application. You must take any user inputs and implement these values in your program. We'll show what each control can do and let you decide if you want to use them in your work. The **PrintPreviewDialog** control is especially cool!!

PageSetupDialog Control

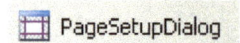

The **PageSetupDialog** control allows the user to set various parameters regarding a printing task. This is the same dialog box that appears in most Windows applications. Users can set border and margin adjustments, headers and footers, and portrait vs. landscape orientation.

PageSetupDialog **Properties**:

Name	Gets or sets the name of the page setup dialog (I usually name this control **dlgSetup**).
AllowMargins	Gets or sets a value indicating whether the margins section of the dialog box is enabled.
AllowOrientation	Gets or sets a value indicating whether the orientation section of the dialog box (landscape vs. portrait) is enabled.
AllowPaper	Gets or sets a value indicating whether the paper section of the dialog box (paper size and paper source) is enabled.
AllowPrinter	Gets or sets a value indicating whether the Printer button is enabled.
Document	Gets or sets a value indicating the PrintDocument to get page settings from.
MinMargins	Gets or sets a value indicating the minimum margins the user is allowed to select, in hundredths of an inch.
PageSettings	Gets or sets a value indicating the page settings to modify.
PrinterSettings	Gets or sets the printer settings the dialog box is to modify when the user clicks the Printer button

FontDialog **Methods**:

ShowDialog	Displays the dialog box. Returned value indicates which button was clicked by user (**OK** or **Cancel**).

Database Reports 7-13

To use the **PageSetupDialog** control, we add it to our application the same as any control. It will appear in the tray below the form. Once added, we set a few properties. Then, we write code to make the dialog box appear when desired. The user then makes selections and closes the dialog box. At this point, we use the provided information for our tasks.

The **ShowDialog** method is used to display the **PageSetupDialog** control. For a control named **dlgSetup**, the appropriate code is:

```
dlgSetup.ShowDialog()
```

And the displayed dialog box is:

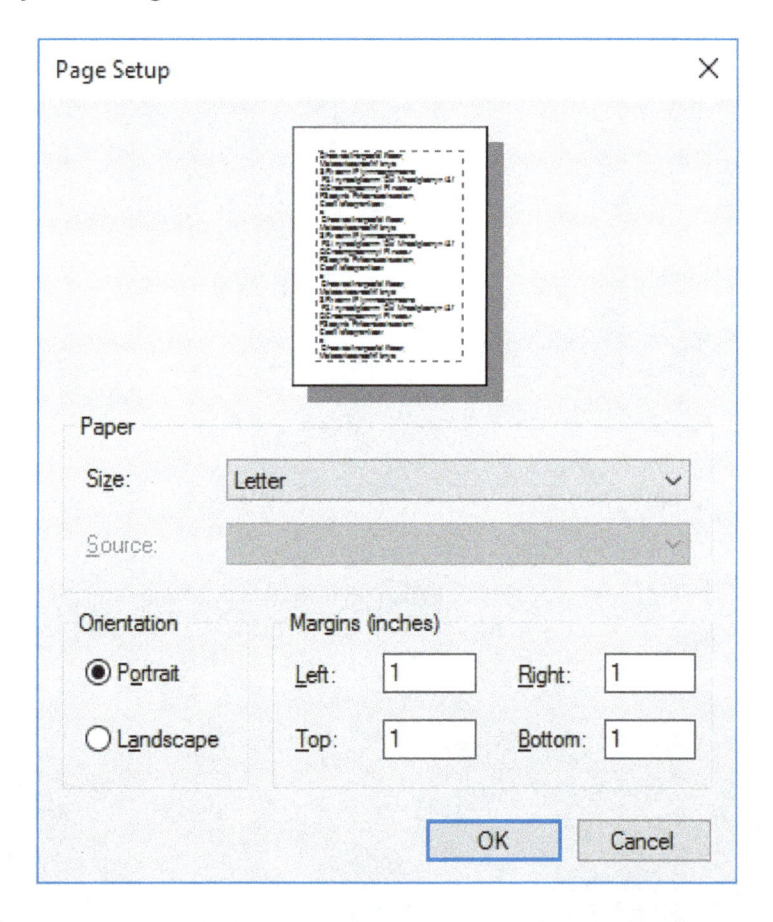

The user makes any desired choices. Once complete, the **OK** button is clicked. At this point, various properties are available for use (namely **PageSettings** and **PrinterSettings**). **Cancel** can be clicked to cancel the changes. The ShowDialog method returns the clicked button. It returns **DialogResult.OK** if OK is clicked and returns **DialogResult.Cancel** if Cancel is clicked.

Typical use of **PageSetupDialog** control:

- Set the **Name** property. Decide what options should be available.
- Use **ShowDialog** method to display dialog box, prior to printing.
- Use **PageSettings** and **PrinterSetting** properties to change printed output.

PrintDialog Control

The **PrintDialog** control allows the user to select which printer to use, choose page orientation, printed page range and number of copies. This is the same dialog box that appears in many Windows applications.

PrintDialog **Properties**:

Name	Gets or sets the name of the print dialog (I usually name this control **dlgPrint**).
AllowPrintToFile	Gets or sets a value indicating whether the Print to file check box is enabled.
AllowSelection	Gets or sets a value indicating whether the From... To... Page option button is enabled.
AllowSomePages	Gets or sets a value indicating whether the Pages option button is enabled.
Document	Gets or sets a value indicating the PrintDocument used to obtain PrinterSettings.
PrinterSettings	Gets or sets the PrinterSettings the dialog box is to modify.
PrintToFile	Gets or sets a value indicating whether the Print to file check box is checked

PrintDialog **Methods**:

ShowDialog	Displays the dialog box. Returned value indicates which button was clicked by user (**OK** or **Cancel**).

To use the **PrintDialog** control, we add it to our application the same as any control. It will appear in the tray below the form. Once added, we set a few properties. Then, we write code to make the dialog box appear when desired. The user then makes selections and closes the dialog box. At this point, we use the provided information for our tasks.

The **ShowDialog** method is used to display the **PrintDialog** control. For a control named **dlgPrint**, the appropriate code is:

```
dlgPrint.ShowDialog()
```

And the displayed dialog box is:

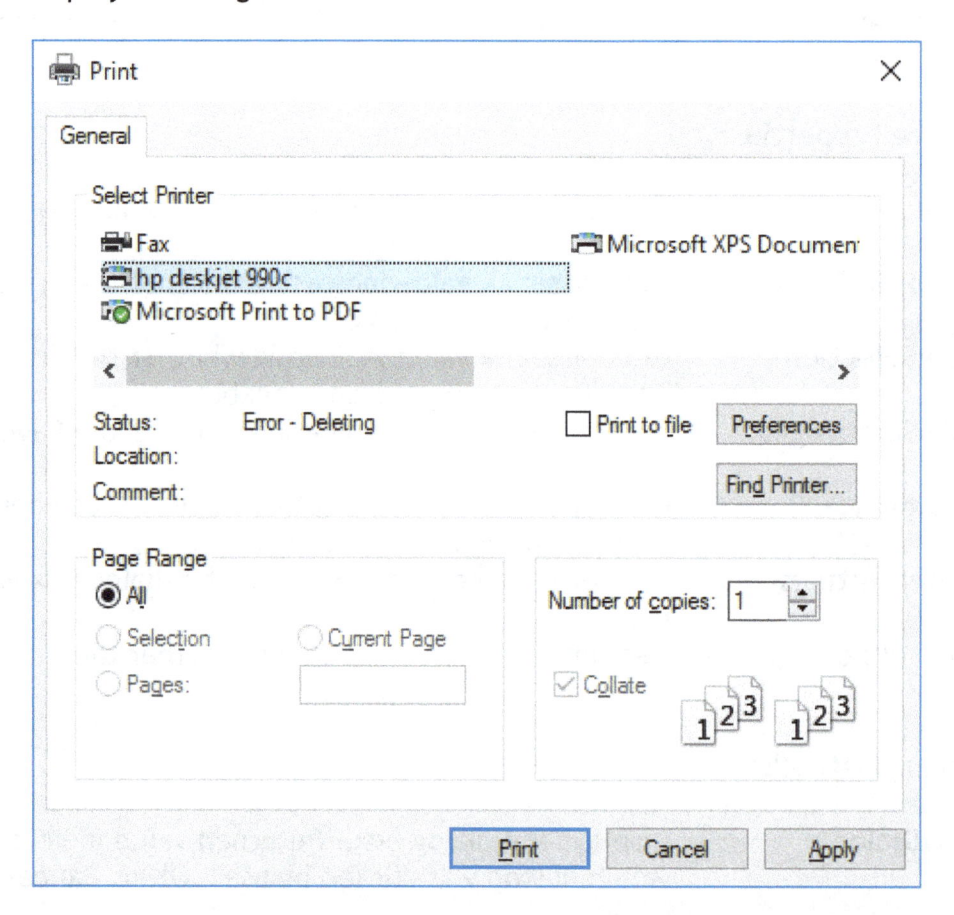

The user makes any desired choices. Once complete, the **OK** button is clicked. At this point, various properties are available for use (namely **PrinterSettings**). **Cancel** can be clicked to cancel the changes. The ShowDialog method returns the clicked button. It returns **DialogResult.OK** if OK is clicked and returns **DialogResult.Cancel** if Cancel is clicked.

Typical use of **PrintDialog** control:

> ➢ Set the **Name** property. Decide what options should be available.
> ➢ Use **ShowDialog** method to display dialog box, prior to printing with the PrintDocument object.
> ➢ Use **PrinterSettings** properties to change printed output.

PrintPreviewDialog Control

PrintPreviewDialog

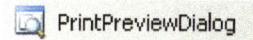

The **PrintPreviewDialog** control is a great addition to Visual Basic. It lets the user see printed output in preview mode. They can view all pages, format page views and zoom in on or out of any. The previewed document can also be printed from this control. This is also a useful "temporary" control for a programmer to use while developing printing routines. By viewing printed pages in a preview mode, rather than on a printed page, many trees are saved as you fine tune your printing code.

PrintPreviewDialog **Properties**:

Name	Gets or sets the name of the print preview dialog (I usually name this control **dlgPreview**)
AcceptButton	Gets or sets the button on the form that is clicked when the user presses the <Enter> key.
Document	Gets or sets the document to preview.
Text	Gets or sets the text associated with this control.

PrintPreviewDialog **Methods**:

ShowDialog	Displays the dialog box. Returned value indicates which button was clicked by user (**OK** or **Cancel**).

To use the **PrintDialog** control, we add it to our application the same as any control. It will appear in the tray below the form. Once added, we set a few properties, primarily **Document**. Make sure the **PrintPage** event Is properly coded for the selected **Document**. Add code to make the dialog box appear when desired. The document pages will be generated and the user can see them in the preview window.

The **ShowDialog** method is used to display the **PrintPreviewDialog** control. For a control named **dlgPreview**, the appropriate code is:

```
dlgPreview.ShowDialog()
```

And the displayed dialog box (with no document) is:

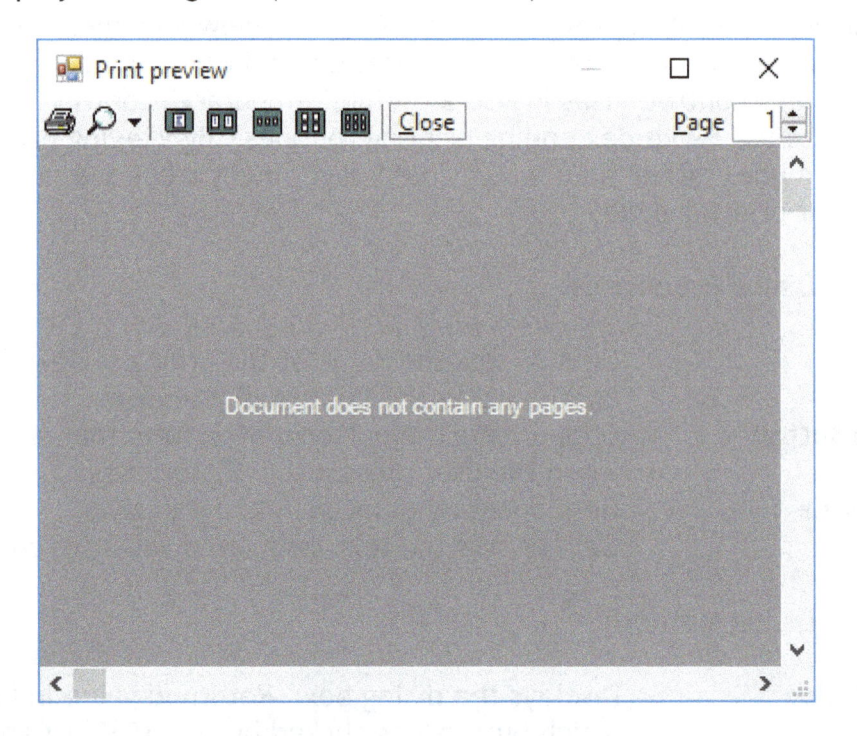

The user can use the various layout, zoom and print options in previewing the displayed document. When done, the user closes the dialog control.

Typical use of **PrintPreviewDialog** control:

> ➢ Set the **Name** property. Set the **Document** property.
> ➢ Use **ShowDialog** method to display dialog box and see the previewed document.

PrintDocument Object with Databases

You may be asking yourself, how does all this **PrintDocument** object information work with **database** management systems? It's really pretty simple. It's just a matter of following a few straightforward (though, many times, detailed) steps.

First, determine what information from the database you want in your database report. Do you want to print all fields and all records? If so, you need to develop code to cycle through the records of interest. Do you want just individual records? Determine, where in your Visual Basic application, this information is located. Usually, it's found in properties of the controls on your form(s).

Second, determine the layout for each page of your database report. My approach is to sketch it out on a piece of standard-sized graph paper. This is a good reference when writing the code – the next step.

Third, add control(s) and code to your Visual Basic application to access the database report printing routine. This is usually a button with a **Click** event containing the printing code.

Lastly, write the Visual Basic code that establishes each page of your database report. This code usually goes in its own procedure. Use positioning properties (the **e** argument in the **PrintPage** event procedure) to place all information in desired positions. A nice thing about the **PrintDocument** object is that there is no need to place information sequentially. That is, you don't have to start at the top and work your way down. You can place information anywhere on the page in any order. When the page is complete, it is sent to the printer using the **e.HasMorePages** property. You will find that you need to write lots of code, but it's very easy code to write. Let's look at each of these steps with an example.

The first example (Example 7-1) we build here is simple, printing a single page. When the user clicks a button to print, the report goes directly to their default printer. With large database reports, spanning many pages, this is not a good idea. The user should be given an interface that allows him or her to know how big a print job is ahead. Based on this information, the user should be able to decide whether to continue printing the entire report or select portions of the report. The **PrintPreviewDialog** control provides such utility. In Examples 7-2 and 7-3, we give an example using this control as a printing interface.

Example 7-1

Database Report

In this example, we use the books database management system built in Chapter 6. We will add the capability to print any book title's displayed record.

1. If you like, make a copy of the books database management system built in **Example 6-9** before starting this example. Open that project. Make sure the **Titles** form is active. Add a button and a picture box control. Set these properties:

Button1:
    Name   btnPrintRecord
    Text   Print &Record

PictureBox1:
    Name   picBooks
    Image   Books.wmf (in **VBDB\General\Class 7\Example 7-1** folder)
    SizeMode   StretchImage
    Visible   False

Visual Basic and Databases

The picture box will provide a graphic to print on the database report. My form looks like this:

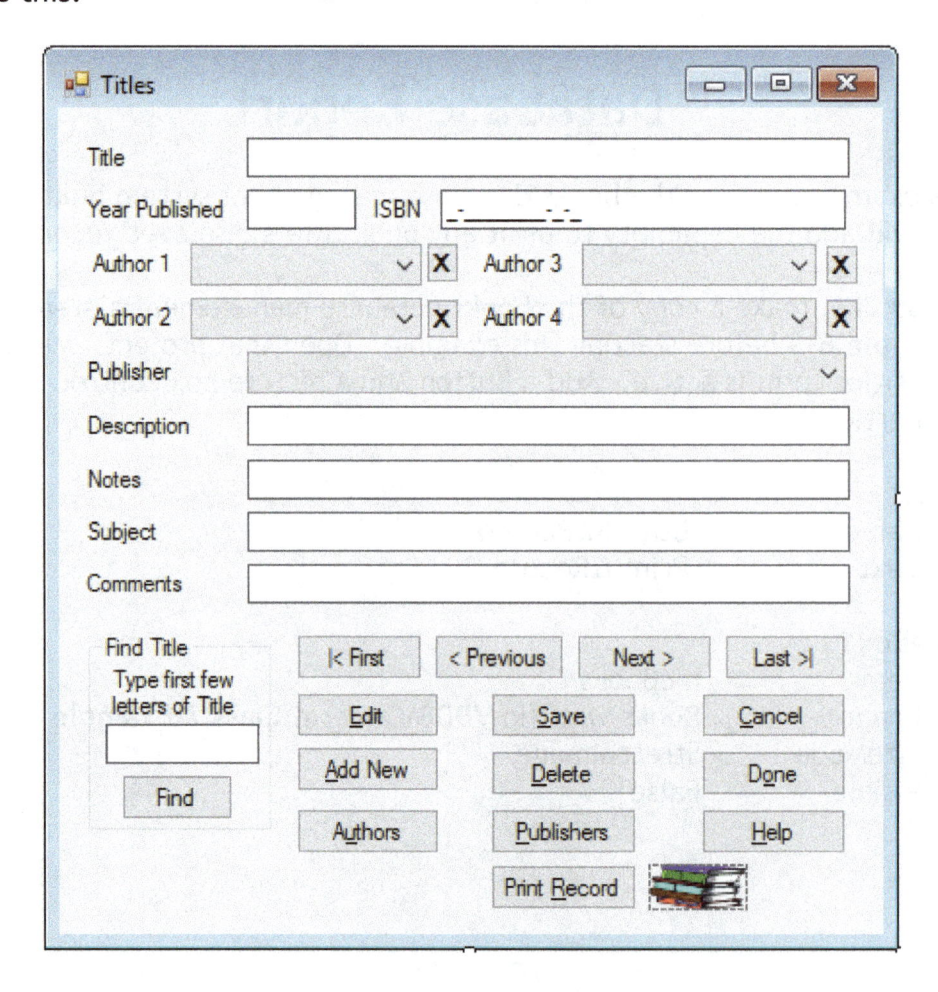

Database Reports

2. Put this code in the **btnPrintRecord Click** event:

```
Private Sub BtnPrintRecord_Click(ByVal sender As System.Object, ByVal e As System.EventArgs) Handles btnPrintRecord.Click
    'Declare the document
    Dim RecordDocument As Drawing.Printing.PrintDocument
    'Create the document and name it
    RecordDocument = New Drawing.Printing.PrintDocument()
    RecordDocument.DocumentName = "Titles Record"
    'Add code handler
    AddHandler RecordDocument.PrintPage, AddressOf Me.PrintRecordPage
    'Print document
    RecordDocument.Print()
    'Dispose of document when done printing
    RecordDocument.Dispose()
End Sub
```

This code sets up the **PrintDocument** object (**RecordDocument**) to print using the information in the **PrintRecordPage** procedure.

3. Add this code to the **PrintRecordPage** event procedure:

```
Private Sub PrintRecordPage(ByVal sender As Object, ByVal e As Drawing.Printing.PrintPageEventArgs)
    'print graphic and heading (1 inch in height)
    Dim MyPen As New Pen(Color.Black, 3)
    e.Graphics.DrawRectangle(MyPen, e.MarginBounds.Left, e.MarginBounds.Top, e.MarginBounds.Width, 100)
    e.Graphics.DrawImage(picBooks.Image, e.MarginBounds.Left + 10, e.MarginBounds.Top + 10, 80, 80)
    'print heading
    Dim S As String = "BOOKS DATABASE"
    Dim MyFont As Font = New Font("Arial", 24, FontStyle.Bold)
    Dim SSize As SizeF = e.Graphics.MeasureString(S, MyFont)
    e.Graphics.DrawString(S, MyFont, Brushes.Black, e.MarginBounds.Left + 100 + CInt(0.5 * (e.MarginBounds.Width - 100 - SSize.Width)), e.MarginBounds.Top + CInt(0.5 * (100 - SSize.Height)))
    MyFont = New Font("Arial", 12, FontStyle.Regular)
    Dim Y As Integer = 300
    Dim DY As Integer = CInt(e.Graphics.MeasureString("S", MyFont).Height)
    'print title
    e.Graphics.DrawString("Title: " + txtTitle.Text, MyFont, Brushes.Black, e.MarginBounds.Left, Y)
    'print authors
    Y += 2 * DY
    e.Graphics.DrawString("Author(s): ", MyFont, Brushes.Black, e.MarginBounds.Left, Y)
    Dim X As Integer = e.MarginBounds.Left + CInt(e.Graphics.MeasureString("Author(s): ", MyFont).Width)
    Dim I As Integer
    If ISBNAuthorsTable.Rows.Count <> 0 Then
      For I = 1 To ISBNAuthorsTable.Rows.Count
        e.Graphics.DrawString(AuthorsCombo(I).Text, MyFont, Brushes.Black, X, Y)
        Y += DY
      Next I
    Else
      e.Graphics.DrawString("None", MyFont, Brushes.Black, X, Y)
      Y += DY
    End If
    X = e.MarginBounds.Left
    Y += DY
    'Print other fields
```

```
        e.Graphics.DrawString("ISBN: " + txtISBN.Text, MyFont,
Brushes.Black, X, Y)
        Y += 2 * DY
        e.Graphics.DrawString("Year Published: " + txtYear.Text,
MyFont, Brushes.Black, X, Y)
        Y += 2 * DY
        e.Graphics.DrawString("Publisher: " + cboPublisher.Text,
MyFont, Brushes.Black, X, Y)
        Y += 2 * DY
        e.Graphics.DrawString("Description: " +
txtDescription.Text, MyFont, Brushes.Black, X, Y)
        Y += 2 * DY
        e.Graphics.DrawString("Notes: " + txtNotes.Text, MyFont,
Brushes.Black, X, Y)
        Y += 2 * DY
        e.Graphics.DrawString("Subject: " + txtSubject.Text,
MyFont, Brushes.Black, X, Y)
        Y += 2 * DY
        e.Graphics.DrawString("Comments: " + txtComments.Text,
MyFont, Brushes.Black, X, Y)
        e.HasMorePages = False
    End Sub
```

Yes, this is a lot of code, but you should see that it is very easy to follow what's going on. First a header is printed within a rectangle (the width of the page margins). The **DrawImage** method puts the graphic in the header. Every field is printed in sequence. We determine position and print the field. Note how **MeasureString** is used to position the heading and line up the author names. The numbers I used in the above code were determined by trial-and-error, something you do a lot with the **PrintDocument** object.

7-26　　　Visual Basic and Databases

4. Save (Access version saved in **Example 7-1** folder in **VBDB\Access\Class 7** folder; SQL Server version saved in **Example 7-1** folder in **VBDB\SQL Server\Class 7** folder) and run the application. Select a title using the navigation buttons. Here's one I picked:

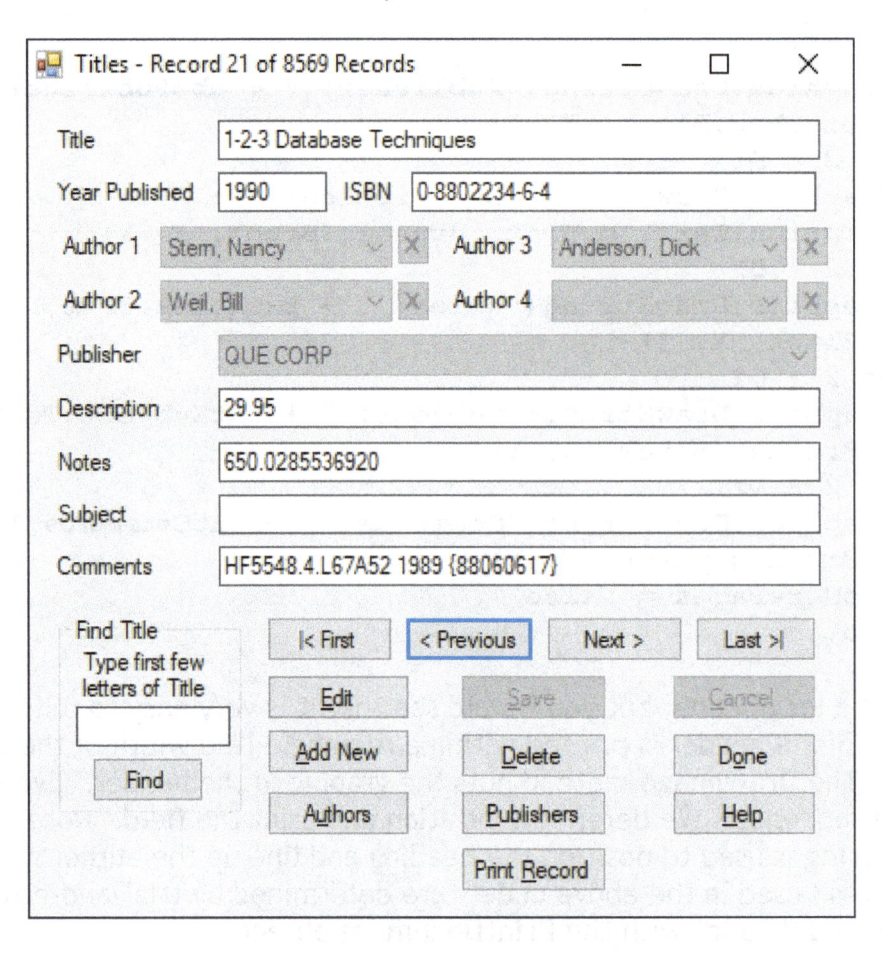

Database Reports 7-27

Click **Print Record**. Your printer should start making noise and a page will pop out. Here's what I got for the displayed record (I cropped out the white space):

BOOKS DATABASE

Title: 1-2-3 Database Techniques

Author(s): Stern, Nancy
Weil, Bill
Anderson, Dick

ISBN: 0-8802234-6-4

Year Published: 1990

Publisher: QUE CORP

Description: 29.95

Notes: 650.0285536920

Subject:

Comments: HF5548.4.L67A52 1989 {88060617}

As mentioned, you can add a **PrintPreviewDialog** control to this application to view the page before printing (we'll use one in the next example). That's how I got the above graphic. Try it if you are adventurous.

Example 7-2

Titles Listing

A single page document with one record is not that exciting. Let's add the capability of printing out every title in our database (including the first author). This will be a very large printout, so we'll use a **PrintPreviewDialog** control to allow the user to decide just what to print.

1. Return to Example 7-1. Display the **Titles** form. Add a button and a print preview dialog control to the project (the dialog control will be below the form). Set these properties:

Button1:
    Name   btnPrintTitles
    Text   Print &Titles

PrintPreviewDialog1:
    Name   dlgPreview

Database Reports 7-29

The form now looks like this:

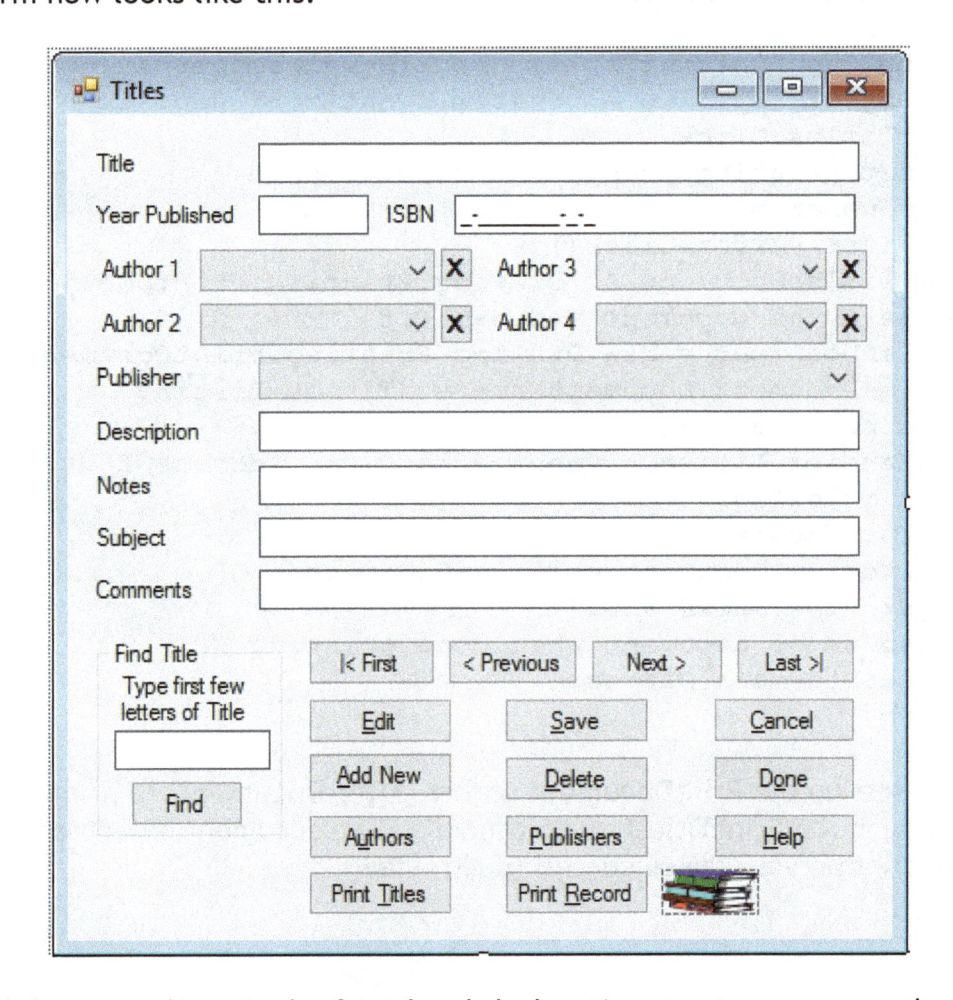

2. Add these two lines in the form level declarations to store page number information:

```
Dim PageNumber As Integer
Const TitlesPerPage As Integer = 45
```

7-30   Visual Basic and Databases

3. Put this code in the **btnPrintTitles Click** event:

```
Private Sub BtnPrintTitles_Click(ByVal sender As System.Object, ByVal e As System.EventArgs) Handles btnPrintTitles.Click
    'Start printing process at first record
    PageNumber = 1
    btnFirst.PerformClick()
    Dim TitlesDocument As Drawing.Printing.PrintDocument
    'Create the document and name it
    TitlesDocument = New Drawing.Printing.PrintDocument()
    TitlesDocument.DocumentName = "Titles Listing"
    'Add code handler
    AddHandler TitlesDocument.PrintPage, AddressOf Me.PrintTitlesPage
    'Print document
    dlgPreview.Document = TitlesDocument
    dlgPreview.ShowDialog()
    'Dispose of document when done printing
    TitlesDocument.Dispose()
End Sub
```

This code sets up the **PrintDocument** object (**TitlesDocument**) to print using the information in the **PrintTitlesPage** procedure. The document object is opened with the print preview dialog control (**dlgPreview**).

4. Add this code to the **PrintTitlesPage** event procedure:

```
Private Sub PrintTitlesPage(ByVal sender As Object, ByVal e As Drawing.Printing.PrintPageEventArgs)
    'here you decide what goes on each page and draw it there
    'print headings
    Dim MyFont As Drawing.Font = New Font("Courier New", 14, FontStyle.Bold)
    e.Graphics.DrawString("Titles - Page" + Str(PageNumber), MyFont, Brushes.Black, e.MarginBounds.Left, e.MarginBounds.Top)
    MyFont = New Font("Courier New", 12, FontStyle.Underline)
    Dim Y As Integer = CInt(e.MarginBounds.Top + 50)
    e.Graphics.DrawString("Title", MyFont, Brushes.Black, e.MarginBounds.Left, Y)
    e.Graphics.DrawString("Author", MyFont, Brushes.Black, e.MarginBounds.Left + CInt(0.6 * (e.MarginBounds.Width)), Y)
    Y += CInt(2 * MyFont.GetHeight)
    MyFont = New Font("Courier New", 12, FontStyle.Regular)
    Dim IEnd As Integer = TitlesPerPage * PageNumber
    If IEnd > TitlesTable.Rows.Count Then
      IEnd = TitlesTable.Rows.Count
      e.HasMorePages = False
    Else
      e.HasMorePages = True
    End If
    Dim I As Integer
    For I = 1 + TitlesPerPage * (PageNumber - 1) To IEnd
      'programmatically move through all the records
      e.Graphics.DrawString(Mid(txtTitle.Text, 1, 35), MyFont, Brushes.Black, e.MarginBounds.Left, Y)
      e.Graphics.DrawString(Mid(cboAuthor1.Text, 1, 20), MyFont, Brushes.Black, e.MarginBounds.Left + CInt(0.6 * (e.MarginBounds.Width)), Y)
      btnNext.PerformClick()
      Y += CInt(MyFont.GetHeight)
    Next I
    If e.HasMorePages Then
      PageNumber += 1
    Else
      PageNumber = 1
    End If
  End Sub
```

This code puts a header on each page. It programmatically moves through all the records (by simulated clicks on the **btnNext** button). As control moves through the records, the corresponding title and author values are printed (they are truncated using the **Mid** function so they fit on a line). When done, we need to reset **PageNumber** to 1 to allow for correct printing (if you really want to print out all these pages). If we didn't do this, only the last page would print.

5. Save (Access version saved in **Example 7-2** folder in **VBDB\Access\Class 7** folder; SQL Server version saved in **Example 7-2** folder in **VBDB\SQL Server\Class 7** folder) and run the application. Click **Print Titles** and sit back. You should see a status box indicating progress:

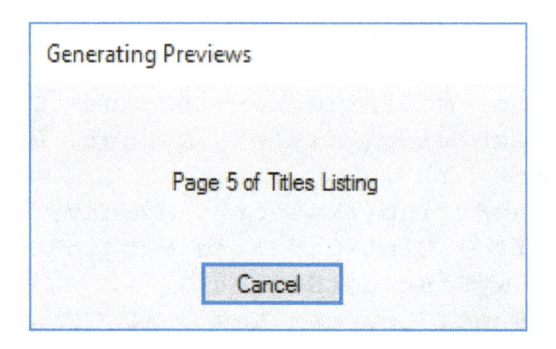

It would take a while to wait for all pages (nearly 200 of them!) to appear in the preview control. At some point, click **Cancel**.

The pages can be previewed in the displayed control. Here's the fifth page:

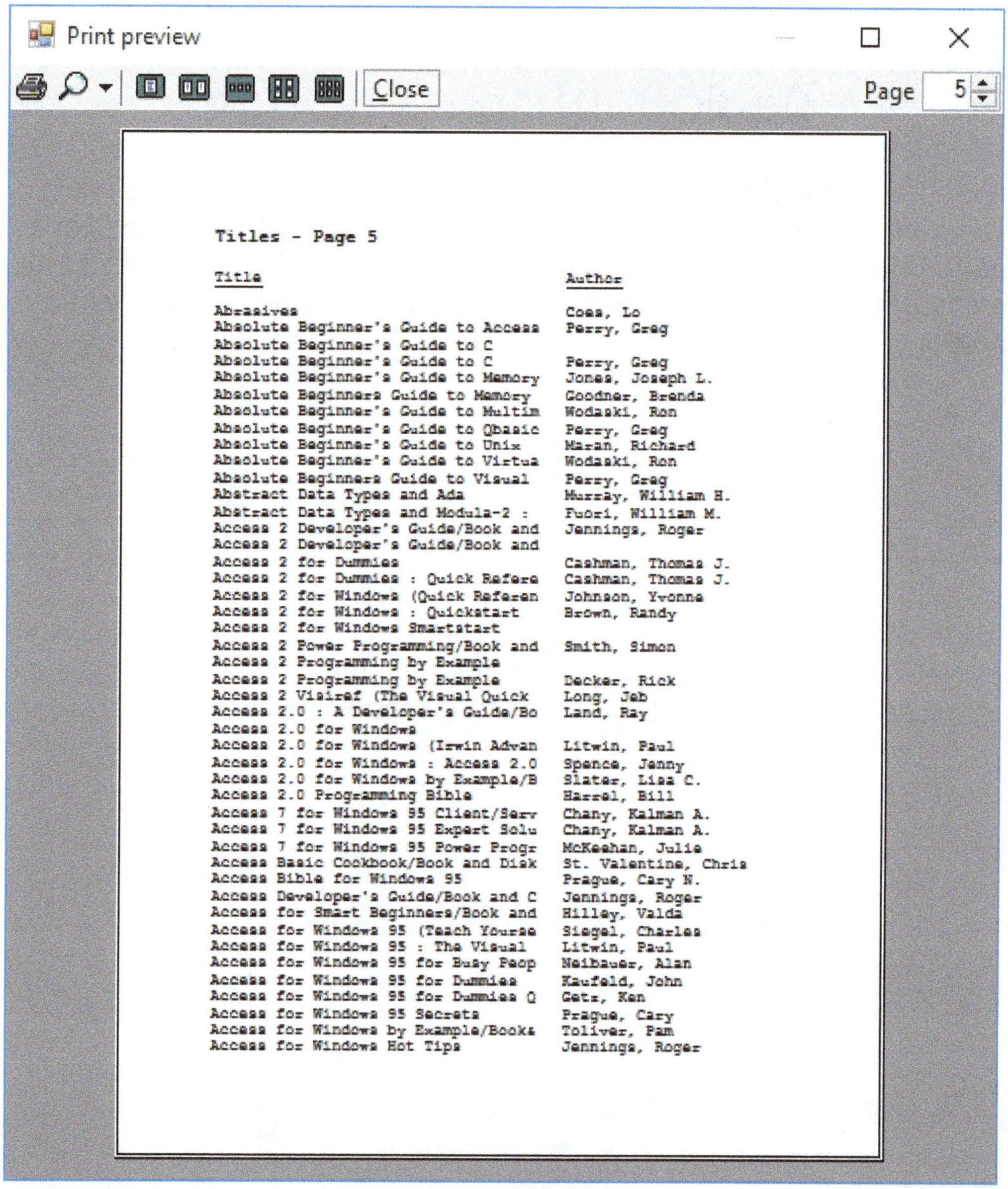
Print preview
Close
Page 5
Titles - Page 5
Title
Author
Abrasives Coes, Lo
Absolute Beginner's Guide to Access Perry, Greg
Absolute Beginner's Guide to C
Absolute Beginner's Guide to C Perry, Greg
Absolute Beginner's Guide to Memory Jones, Joseph L.
Absolute Beginners Guide to Memory Goodner, Brenda
Absolute Beginner's Guide to Multim Wodaski, Ron
Absolute Beginner's Guide to Qbasic Perry, Greg
Absolute Beginner's Guide to Unix Maran, Richard
Absolute Beginner's Guide to Virtua Wodaski, Ron
Absolute Beginners Guide to Visual Perry, Greg
Abstract Data Types and Ada Murray, William H.
Abstract Data Types and Modula-2 : Fuori, William M.
Access 2 Developer's Guide/Book and Jennings, Roger
Access 2 Developer's Guide/Book and
Access 2 for Dummies Cashman, Thomas J.
Access 2 for Dummies : Quick Refere Cashman, Thomas J.
Access 2 for Windows (Quick Referen Johnson, Yvonne
Access 2 for Windows : Quickstart Brown, Randy
Access 2 for Windows Smartstart
Access 2 Power Programming/Book and Smith, Simon
Access 2 Programming by Example
Access 2 Programming by Example Decker, Rick
Access 2 Visiref (The Visual Quick Long, Jeb
Access 2.0 : A Developer's Guide/Bo Land, Ray
Access 2.0 for Windows
Access 2.0 for Windows (Irwin Advan Litwin, Paul
Access 2.0 for Windows : Access 2.0 Spence, Jenny
Access 2.0 for Windows by Example/B Slater, Lisa C.
Access 2.0 Programming Bible Harrel, Bill
Access 7 for Windows 95 Client/Serv Chany, Kalman A.
Access 7 for Windows 95 Expert Solu Chany, Kalman A.
Access 7 for Windows 95 Power Progr McKeehan, Julie
Access Basic Cookbook/Book and Disk St. Valentine, Chris
Access Bible for Windows 95 Prague, Cary N.
Access Developer's Guide/Book and C Jennings, Roger
Access for Smart Beginners/Book and Hilley, Valda
Access for Windows 95 (Teach Yourse Siegel, Charles
Access for Windows 95 : The Visual Litwin, Paul
Access for Windows 95 for Busy Peop Neibauer, Alan
Access for Windows 95 for Dummies Kaufeld, John
Access for Windows 95 for Dummies Q Getz, Ken
Access for Windows 95 Secrets Prague, Cary
Access for Windows by Example/Books Toliver, Pam
Access for Windows Hot Tips Jennings, Roger

The **PrintDocument** object, with a need to programmatically move through all the records, slows us down. You could let the user somehow limit how many pages to print. We'll look at a way to do that in the final example.

Example 7-3

Book Publishers Listing

For more practice in developing database reports and designing Visual Basic interfaces, we build a database report for the **Publishers** table in the books database. This will be a multiple page report listing publisher name and mailing address information. The following fields will be in the report for each publisher:

Name
Address
City
State
Zip

Each page will have multiple publishers (seven to a page). Since this is a large table (over 700 records), the user will be able to limit the number of available printed records by specifying the first letter of the Publisher name.

Database Reports
7-35

User Interface

The interface we build for the book publishers listing will be simple, consisting of twenty-seven buttons (each representing a single letter of the alphabet). Wait, you say, there are only 26 letters in the alphabet! You're right. The 27th button will be used for publisher names beginning with non-alphabetic characters. When the user clicks a button, the application will display the publisher pages in a print preview control. Then, the user can choose to print any, or all, pages. The finished interface will be built in code. Let's do it.

1. Start a new Visual Basic application with just a form and a print preview dialog control. Set these properties:

Form1:
    Name   frmPubs
    BorderStyle   FixedSingle
    StartPosition   CenterScreen
    Text   Book Publishers Listing

PrintPreviewDialog1:
    Name   dlgPreview

Size the form so it looks similar to this:

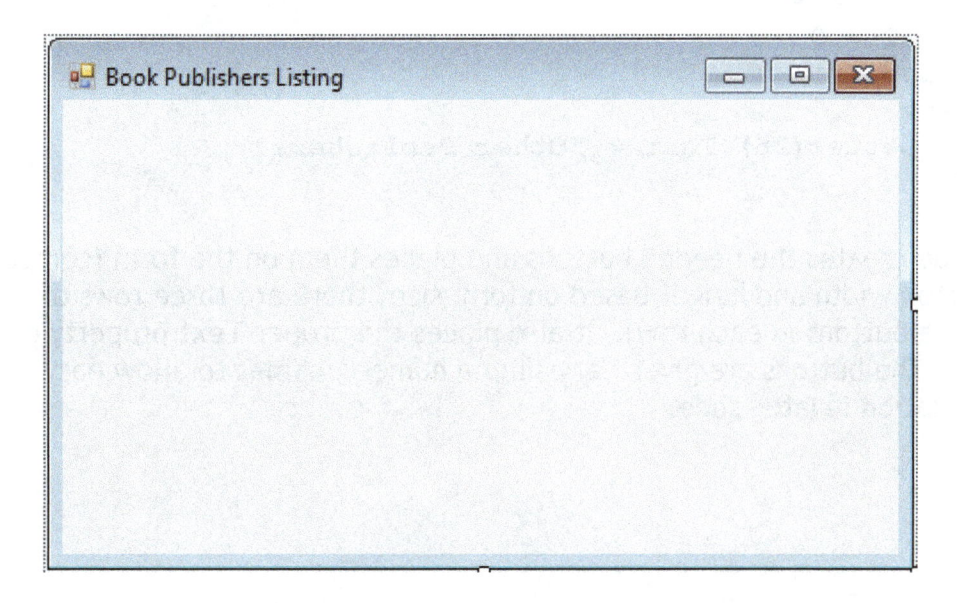

2. Use this code in the **frmPubs Load** procedure:

```
  Private Sub FrmPubs_Load(ByVal sender As System.Object, ByVal e As System.EventArgs) Handles MyBase.Load
    'Build interface
    Dim btnLetter(26) As Button
    Dim I As Integer
    Dim L As Integer = 0
    Dim W As Integer = CInt(Me.ClientRectangle.Width / 3 - 0.5)
    Dim T As Integer = 0
    Dim H As Integer = CInt(Me.ClientRectangle.Height / 9 - 0.5)
    For I = 0 To 26
      btnLetter(I) = New Button
      btnLetter(I).Name = I.ToString
      btnLetter(I).Left = L
      btnLetter(I).Width = W
      btnLetter(I).Top = T
      btnLetter(I).Height = H
      btnLetter(I).Text = Chr(I + 65) + " Publishers"
      Me.Controls.Add(btnLetter(I))
      T += H
      If I = 8 Or I = 17 Then
        L += W
        T = 0
      End If
    Next
    btnLetter(26).Text = "Other Publishers"
  End Sub
```

This code creates the needed buttons and places them on the form (computing the button width and height based on form size; there are three rows of buttons with nine buttons in each row). It also places the proper **Text** property on each button. The buttons are given very simple numeric names to allow easy identification in later code.

Database Reports 7-37

3. Save the application (Access version saved in **Example 7-3** folder in **VBDB\Access\Class 7** folder; SQL Server version saved in **Example 7-3** folder in **VBDB\SQL Server\Class 7** folder). Run it and you'll see the buttons appear as they should. My form at run-time looks like this:

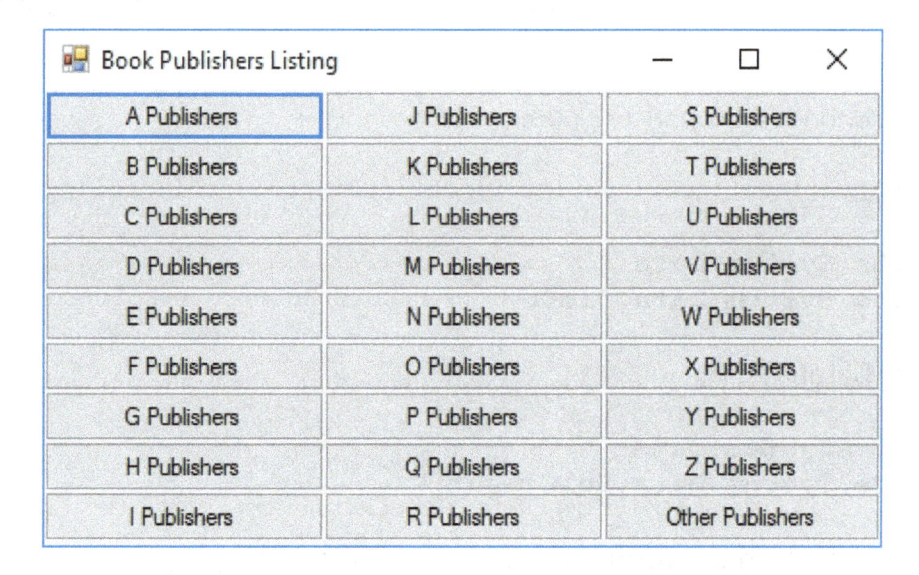

A Publishers	J Publishers	S Publishers
B Publishers	K Publishers	T Publishers
C Publishers	L Publishers	U Publishers
D Publishers	M Publishers	V Publishers
E Publishers	N Publishers	W Publishers
F Publishers	O Publishers	X Publishers
G Publishers	P Publishers	Y Publishers
H Publishers	Q Publishers	Z Publishers
I Publishers	R Publishers	Other Publishers

Book Publishers Listing

This completes the interface framework. Notice this is a cute little way to get a letter input from a user. You may find other applications where similar interfaces may be useful.

Database Connection and Printing

Now, we'll connect to the **Publishers** table in **BooksDB.accdb** (or **SQLBooksDB.mdf**) and use the **PrintDocument** object to print the **Publishers** database report.

1. Add these lines at top of the code window:

Access Database:

```
Imports System.Data
Imports System.Data.OleDb
```

SQL Server Database:

```
Imports System.Data
Imports System.Data.SqlClient
```

2. Add these lines in the form level declarations to declare the needed data objects and establish print parameters:

Access Database:

```
Dim BooksConnection As OleDbConnection
Dim PublishersCommand As OleDbCommand
Dim PublishersAdapter As OleDbDataAdapter
Dim PublishersTable As DataTable
Dim PageNumber As Integer
Const RecordsPerPage As Integer = 6
```

SQL Server Database:

```
Dim BooksConnection As SqlConnection
Dim PublishersCommand As SqlCommand
Dim PublishersAdapter As SqlDataAdapter
Dim PublishersTable As DataTable
Dim PageNumber As Integer
Const RecordsPerPage As Integer = 6
```

Database Reports 7-39

3. Add the shaded code to the **frmPubs Load** procedure to attach the buttons to a **Click** event procedure (**BtnLetter_Click**) and to open the books database:

<u>Access Database:</u>

```
Private Sub FrmPubs_Load(ByVal sender As System.Object, ByVal e As System.EventArgs) Handles MyBase.Load
    'Build interface
    Dim btnLetter(26) As Button
    Dim I As Integer
    Dim L As Integer = 0
    Dim W As Integer = CInt(Me.ClientRectangle.Width / 3 - 0.5)
    Dim T As Integer = 0
    Dim H As Integer = CInt(Me.ClientRectangle.Height / 9 - 0.5)
    For I = 0 To 26
      btnLetter(I) = New Button
      btnLetter(I).Name = I.ToString
      btnLetter(I).Left = L
      btnLetter(I).Width = W
      btnLetter(I).Top = T
      btnLetter(I).Height = H
      btnLetter(I).Text = Chr(I + 65) + " Publishers"
      Me.Controls.Add(btnLetter(I))
      AddHandler btnLetter(I).Click, AddressOf Me.BtnLetter_Click
      T += H
      If I = 8 Or I = 17 Then
        L += W
        T = 0
      End If
    Next
    btnLetter(26).Text = "Other Publishers"
    'connect to books database
    BooksConnection = New OleDbConnection("Provider=Microsoft.ACE.OLEDB.12.0; Data Source = c:\VBDB\Working\BooksDB.accdb")
    BooksConnection.Open()
  End Sub
```

SQL Server Database:

```
  Private Sub FrmPubs_Load(ByVal sender As System.Object, ByVal e As System.EventArgs) Handles MyBase.Load
    'Build interface
    Dim btnLetter(26) As Button
    Dim I As Integer
    Dim L As Integer = 0
    Dim W As Integer = CInt(Me.ClientRectangle.Width / 3 - 0.5)
    Dim T As Integer = 0
    Dim H As Integer = CInt(Me.ClientRectangle.Height / 9 - 0.5)
    For I = 0 To 26
      btnLetter(I) = New Button
      btnLetter(I).Name = I.ToString
      btnLetter(I).Left = L
      btnLetter(I).Width = W
      btnLetter(I).Top = T
      btnLetter(I).Height = H
      btnLetter(I).Text = Chr(I + 65) + " Publishers"
      Me.Controls.Add(btnLetter(I))
      AddHandler btnLetter(I).Click, AddressOf Me.btnLetter_Click
      T += H
      If I = 8 Or I = 17 Then
        L += W
        T = 0
      End If
    Next
    btnLetter(26).Text = "Other Publishers"
    'connect to books database
    BooksConnection = New SqlConnection("Data Source=.\SQLEXPRESS; AttachDbFilename=C:\VBDB\Working\SQLBooksDB.mdf; Integrated Security=True; Connect Timeout=30; User Instance=True")
    BooksConnection.Open()
  End Sub
```

4. Add this code to the **frmPubs FormClosing** event to dispose of the data objects:

```
Private Sub FrmPubs_FormClosing(ByVal sender As
System.Object, ByVal e As
System.Windows.Forms.FormClosingEventArgs) Handles
MyBase.FormClosing
    'dispose of objects
    BooksConnection.Close()
    BooksConnection.Dispose()
    PublishersCommand.Dispose()
    PublishersAdapter.Dispose()
    PublishersTable.Dispose()
End Sub
```

5. Add this code to the **BtnLetter_Click** event procedure (handles a click on any of the 27 buttons):

Access Database:

```
  Private Sub BtnLetter_Click(ByVal sender As System.Object, ByVal e As System.EventArgs)
    Dim WhichButton As Button = CType(sender, Button)
    'Retrieve records
    Dim Sql As String = "SELECT * FROM Publishers "
    Dim Index As Integer = CInt(WhichButton.Name)
    Select Case Index
      Case 0 To 24 ' A to Y
        Sql += "WHERE Name >= '" + Chr(Index + 65) + "' AND Name < '" + Chr(Index + 65 + 1) + "'"
      Case 25 'Z
        Sql += "WHERE Name >= 'Z'"
      Case 26 'Other
        Sql += "WHERE Name < 'A'"
    End Select
    Sql += " ORDER BY Name"
    PublishersCommand = New OleDbCommand(Sql, BooksConnection)
    'establish data adapter/data table
    PublishersAdapter = New OleDbDataAdapter()
    PublishersAdapter.SelectCommand = PublishersCommand
    PublishersTable = New DataTable()
    PublishersAdapter.Fill(PublishersTable)
    'set up printdocument
    Dim PublishersDocument As Drawing.Printing.PrintDocument
    'Create the document and name it
    PublishersDocument = New Drawing.Printing.PrintDocument()
    PublishersDocument.DocumentName = "Publishers Listing"
    'Add code handler
    AddHandler PublishersDocument.PrintPage, AddressOf Me.PrintPublishersPage
    'Print document
    PageNumber = 1
    dlgPreview.Document = PublishersDocument
    dlgPreview.ShowDialog()
    'Dispose of object when done printing
    PublishersDocument.Dispose()
  End Sub
```

Database Reports

SQL Server Database:

```vb
   Private Sub BtnLetter_Click(ByVal sender As System.Object, ByVal e As System.EventArgs)
      Dim WhichButton As Button = CType(sender, Button)
      'Retrieve records
      Dim Sql As String = "SELECT * FROM Publishers "
      Dim Index As Integer = CInt(WhichButton.Name)
      Select Case Index
        Case 0 To 24 ' A to Y
          Sql += "WHERE Name >= '" + Chr(Index + 65) + "' AND Name < '" + Chr(Index + 65 + 1) + "'"
        Case 25 'Z
          Sql += "WHERE Name >= 'Z'"
        Case 26 'Other
          Sql += "WHERE Name < 'A'"
      End Select
      Sql += " ORDER BY Name"
      PublishersCommand = New SqlCommand(Sql, BooksConnection)
      'establish data adapter/data table
      PublishersAdapter = New SqlDataAdapter()
      PublishersAdapter.SelectCommand = PublishersCommand
      PublishersTable = New DataTable()
      PublishersAdapter.Fill(PublishersTable)
      'set up printdocument
      Dim PublishersDocument As Drawing.Printing.PrintDocument
      'Create the document and name it
      PublishersDocument = New Drawing.Printing.PrintDocument()
      PublishersDocument.DocumentName = "Publishers Listing"
      'Add code handler
      AddHandler PublishersDocument.PrintPage, AddressOf Me.PrintPublishersPage
      'Print document
      PageNumber = 1
      dlgPreview.Document = PublishersDocument
      dlgPreview.ShowDialog()
      'Dispose of object when done printing
      PublishersDocument.Dispose()
   End Sub
```

7-44 Visual Basic and Databases

This code forms a SQL statement based on the button clicked. For example, if the user clicks '**M Publishers**', the SQL statement formed is:

```
SQL = "SELECT * FROM Publishers WHERE Name >= 'M' AND Name < 'N' ORDER BY Name"
```

The data table object (**PublishersTable**) containing the corresponding records is formed. This is the table that provides the printed results in **PublishersDocument**.

6. Add this code to the **PrintPublishersPage** general procedure.

```
Private Sub PrintPublishersPage(ByVal sender As Object, ByVal e As Drawing.Printing.PrintPageEventArgs)
    'print headings
    Dim MyFont As Drawing.Font = New Font("Arial", 18, FontStyle.Bold)
    Dim Y As Integer = CInt(e.MarginBounds.Top)
    e.Graphics.DrawString("Book Publishers Listing - " + Date.Now.ToString, MyFont, Brushes.Black, e.MarginBounds.Left, Y)
    Y += CInt(MyFont.GetHeight)
    e.Graphics.DrawString("Page" + Str(PageNumber), MyFont, Brushes.Black, e.MarginBounds.Left, Y)
    Y += CInt(MyFont.GetHeight) + 10
    e.Graphics.DrawLine(Pens.Black, e.MarginBounds.Left, Y, e.MarginBounds.Right, Y)
    Y += CInt(MyFont.GetHeight)
    MyFont = New Font("Courier New", 12, FontStyle.Regular)
    Dim IEnd As Integer = RecordsPerPage * PageNumber
    If IEnd > PublishersTable.Rows.Count Then
      IEnd = PublishersTable.Rows.Count
      e.HasMorePages = False
    Else
      e.HasMorePages = True
    End If
    Dim I As Integer
    For I = RecordsPerPage * (PageNumber - 1) To IEnd - 1
      'display current record
      e.Graphics.DrawString("Publisher: " + PublishersTable.Rows(I).Item("Name").ToString, MyFont, Brushes.Black, e.MarginBounds.Left, Y)
      Y += CInt(MyFont.GetHeight)
      e.Graphics.DrawString("Address:    " + PublishersTable.Rows(I).Item("Address").ToString, MyFont, Brushes.Black, e.MarginBounds.Left, Y)
      Y += CInt(MyFont.GetHeight)
```

Database Reports 7-45

```
      e.Graphics.DrawString("City:          " + _
PublishersTable.Rows(I).Item("City").ToString, MyFont, _
Brushes.Black, e.MarginBounds.Left, Y)
      Y += CInt(MyFont.GetHeight)
      e.Graphics.DrawString("State:         " + _
PublishersTable.Rows(I).Item("State").ToString, MyFont, _
Brushes.Black, e.MarginBounds.Left, Y)
      Y += CInt(MyFont.GetHeight)
      e.Graphics.DrawString("Zip:           " + _
PublishersTable.Rows(I).Item("Zip").ToString, MyFont, _
Brushes.Black, e.MarginBounds.Left, Y)
      Y += CInt(MyFont.GetHeight)
      Y += 2 * CInt(MyFont.GetHeight)
    Next I
    If e.HasMorePages Then
      PageNumber += 1
    Else
      PageNumber = 1
    End If
  End Sub
```

Here, we print some header information, then we cycle through the records, placing **RecordsPerPage** entries on each page. You should be able to identify what is going on in this code. Note, again, we reset the **PageNumber** to 1 once printing is complete. This allows for correct printing of the pages, if desired.

7. Save (Access version saved in **Example 7-3** folder in **VBDB\Access\Class 7** folder; SQL Server version saved in **Example 7-3** folder in **VBDB\SQL Server\Class 7** folder) and run the application. Click **M Publishers** – 11 pages should appear:

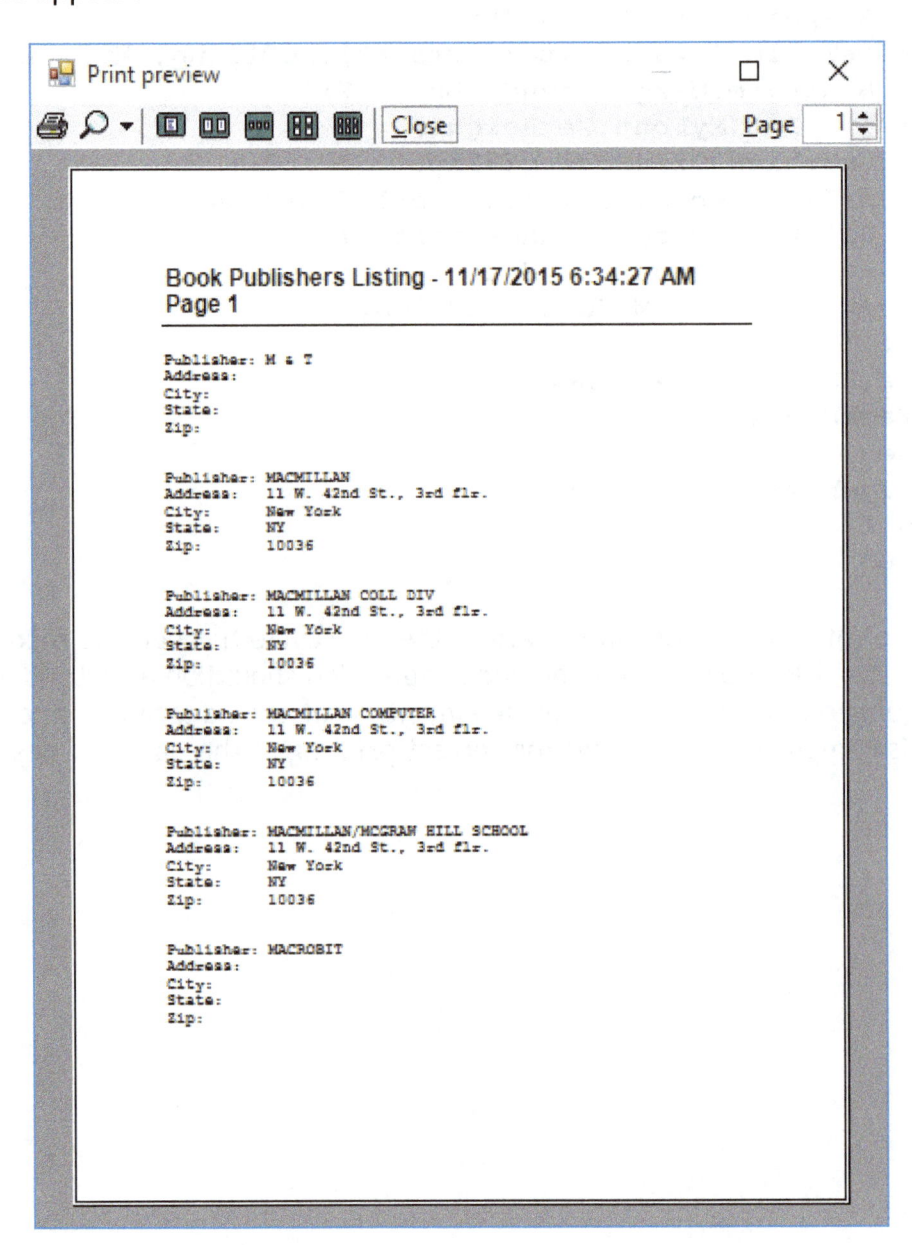

Try printing some records if you like.

Other Approaches to Database Reports

Though straightforward, using the **PrintDocument** object for developing database reports is tedious and the resulting print process is, at times, slow. There are other possibilities available for building reports you might want to consider.

Visual Basic has a built-in database reporting capability. The **ReportViewer** works with the data objects to build reports with a graphical interface. Its capabilities are excellent, with future upgrades and support guaranteed. It is available for download from Microsoft.

CrystalReportViewer is a third-party product that generates data reports using a structured system. CrystalReportViewer was included with past versions of Visual Basic, but is no longer available for Visual Studio. CrystalReportViewer provides extensive connections to database structure. The big disadvantage to CrystalReportViewer is its complexity. And, there's the question of support. If it is not included with future Visual Basic upgrades, you would need to purchase a copy to support your legacy code.

There are several reporting tools that also work with SQL Server databases. One possibility is the **Report Designer** included with the **SQL Server Business Intelligence Development Studio** (a free Microsoft download). Consult Microsoft's website for details.

The internet offers several tutorials for using **ReportViewer**, **Report Designer** for SQL Server and **CrystalReportViewer**. We suggest you look into these other tools if you are interested.

Summary

In this chapter, we have looked using the Visual Basic **PrintDocument** object for developing database reports.

Using the PrintDocument object is easy and doesn't require any knowledge beyond Visual Basic. But, lots of code is required and performance is slow for large databases, such as our books database.

We will see more examples of database reports in Chapter 10.

8

Distributing a Database Application

Review and Preview

At this point in the course, you have the skills to create a complete database management system, including printed reports. It's time to share your capabilities and products with others. The applications you have built have been executed within the Visual Basic environment.

In this chapter, you learn the steps of developing a stand-alone application that can be run on any Windows-based machine – even machines without Visual Basic.

Several topics are covered: accessing database files in code, adding an icon to an application, creating a stand-alone executable, and creating a distribution package (which can be distributed via CD-ROM or downloaded files).

Accessing Database Files in Code

When we develop a Visual Basic application, all files used (including project, form, code and database files) are saved in directories (folders) we specify in our computing environment. To distribute our applications, we need to make them independent of the directory structure used. A first step in achieving this independence is to delete any directory structure used within our code.

In these notes, we have placed database files in our working directory. And, we have 'hard-wired' that location in code when we develop the connection object. We can't expect a user to be so kind as to place their copy of the database in a directory with the same path name we use. We need some way to determine database location. And, once we know this location, we need to use that location to open the database in code. That is, we must delete the 'hard-wiring' we have been using.

We look at two ways of determining the location of a database file: (1) placing the database in the application directory and (2) allowing the user to specify the location using an open file dialog box. Once location is known, we look at how to open the database (and establish associated connection objects tables) in Visual Basic code.

Important: In each case, do not delete directory structure from your application until you are sure it works in your design environment. Then, make the changes provided in these notes to properly locate and open database files in code.

Database File in Application Path

The easiest way to solve the problem of finding a database file is to place it in the same path (directory) as the application itself. That directory is the **Bin\Debug** folder in a project (**Bin\x86\Debug** for 32 bit applications like the ones using **Access** databases), specified by **Application.StartupPath**. We have used this before to specify the location of help files needed by an application.

Access Database:

To create a connection object (**MyConnection**) connected to an Access database (**MyDataBase.accdb**) located in the application folder, we would use:

```
MyConnection = New
OleDbConnection("Provider=Microsoft.ACE.OLEDB.12.0; Data
Source = " + Application.StartupPath +
"\MyDataBase.accdb")
```

Everything else in the code remains the same. It's that easy. The additional slash (\) is needed because the **Application.StartupPath** property does not have a terminating slash. You do need to remember to copy your database to the proper folder.

SQL Server Database:

To create a connection object (**MyConnection**) connected to a SQL Server database (**MySQLDataBase.mdf**) located in the application folder, we would use:

```
MyConnection = New SqlConnection("Data Source=SQLInstance;
AttachDbFilename=" + Application.StartupPath +
"\MySQLDatabase.mdf; Integrated Security=True; Connect
Timeout=30; User Instance=True")
```

where **SQLInstance** is the name of your SQL Server instance (set when installed; if using default SQL Server Express settings, name is **.\SQLEXPRESS**). Everything else in the code remains the same. It's that easy. The additional slash (\) is needed because the **Application.StartupPath** property does not have a terminating slash. You do need to remember to copy your database to the proper folder.

Example 8-1

Opening Database Files in Application Directory

In this example, we will modify the Books Database Management System (including the **Titles**, **Authors**, and **Publishers** input forms) developed in Chapter 6 and modified in Chapter 7, to open the books database file from the application directory. These modifications will make our application independent of the directories we used to build the application. This is a needed step to make our application distributable

1. Open the latest version of the books database management system in **Example 7-2.** Place a working copy of books database (Access - **BooksDB.accdb**; SQL Server - **SQLBooksDB.mdf**) into the **Bin\Debug** folder for the application (**Bin\x86\Debug** for **Access**).

2. Make the **Titles** form active. In the **frmTitles Load** procedure, make the shaded modification:

Access Database:

```
   Private Sub FrmTitles_Load(ByVal sender As System.Object, ByVal e As System.EventArgs) Handles MyBase.Load
      Try
         'point to help file
         hlpBooks.HelpNamespace = Application.StartupPath + "\books.chm"
         'connect to books database
         BooksConnection = New OleDbConnection("Provider=Microsoft.ACE.OLEDB.12.0; Data Source = " + Application.StartupPath + "\BooksDB.accdb")
         BooksConnection.Open()
            .
            .
   End Sub
```

Distributing a Database Application 8-5

SQL Server Database:

```vb
Private Sub FrmTitles_Load(ByVal sender As System.Object, ByVal e As System.EventArgs) Handles MyBase.Load
    Try
        'point to help file
        hlpBooks.HelpNamespace = Application.StartupPath + "\books.chm"
        'connect to books database
        BooksConnection = New SqlConnection("Data Source=.\SQLEXPRESS; AttachDbFilename=" + Application.StartupPath + "\SQLBooksDB.mdf; Integrated Security=True; Connect Timeout=30; User Instance=True")
        BooksConnection.Open()
        .
        .
End Sub
```

This removes the directory dependency from the code.

3. Make similar changes in the **btnAuthors Click** and **btnPublishers Click** event procedures:

<u>Access Database:</u>

```
  Private Sub BtnAuthors_Click(ByVal sender As System.Object, ByVal e As System.EventArgs) Handles btnAuthors.Click
    .
    .
    'need to regenerate authors data
    BooksConnection.Close()
    BooksConnection = New OleDbConnection("Provider=Microsoft.ACE.OLEDB.12.0; Data Source = " + Application.StartupPath + "\BooksDB.accdb")
    BooksConnection.Open()
    .
    .
  End Sub

  Private Sub BtnPublishers_Click(ByVal sender As System.Object, ByVal e As System.EventArgs) Handles btnPublishers.Click
    .
    .
    'need to regenerate publishers data
    BooksConnection.Close()
    BooksConnection = New OleDbConnection("Provider=Microsoft.ACE.OLEDB.12.0; Data Source = " + Application.StartupPath + "\BooksDB.accdb")
    BooksConnection.Open()
    .
    .
  End Sub
```

Distributing a Database Application 8-7

SQL Server Database:

```vb
Private Sub BtnAuthors_Click(ByVal sender As
System.Object, ByVal e As System.EventArgs) Handles
btnAuthors.Click
    .
    .
    'need to regenerate authors data
    BooksConnection.Close()
    BooksConnection = New SqlConnection("Data
Source=.\SQLEXPRESS; AttachDbFilename=" +
Application.StartupPath + "\SQLBooksDB.mdf; Integrated
Security=True; Connect Timeout=30; User Instance=True")
    BooksConnection.Open()
    .
    .
End Sub

Private Sub BtnPublishers_Click(ByVal sender As
System.Object, ByVal e As System.EventArgs) Handles
btnPublishers.Click
    .
    .
    'need to regenerate publishers data
    BooksConnection.Close()
    BooksConnection = New SqlConnection("Data
Source=.\SQLEXPRESS; AttachDbFilename=" +
Application.StartupPath + "\SQLBooksDB.mdf; Integrated
Security=True; Connect Timeout=30; User Instance=True")
    BooksConnection.Open()
    .
    .
End Sub
```

8-8   Visual Basic and Databases

4. Now, make the **Publishers** form active. In the **frmPublishers Load** procedure, make the same shaded modification:

Access Database:

```
  Private Sub FrmPublishers_Load(ByVal sender As
System.Object, ByVal e As System.EventArgs) Handles
MyBase.Load
    Try
      'point to help file
      hlpPublishers.HelpNamespace = Application.StartupPath
+ "\books.chm"
      'connect to books database
      BooksConnection = New
OleDbConnection("Provider=Microsoft.ACE.OLEDB.12.0; Data
Source = " + Application.StartupPath + "\BooksDB.accdb")
      BooksConnection.Open()
      .
      .
  End Sub
```

SQL Server Database:

```
  Private Sub FrmPublishers_Load(ByVal sender As
System.Object, ByVal e As System.EventArgs) Handles
MyBase.Load
    Try
      'point to help file
      hlpPublishers.HelpNamespace = Application.StartupPath
+ "\books.chm"
      'connect to books database
      BooksConnection = New SqlConnection("Data
Source=.\SQLEXPRESS; AttachDbFilename=" +
Application.StartupPath + "\SQLBooksDB.mdf; Integrated
Security=True; Connect Timeout=30; User Instance=True")
      BooksConnection.Open()
      .
      .
  End Sub
```

5. Save application (Access version saved in the **Example 8-1** folder in **VBDB\Access\Class 8** folder; SQL Server version saved in the **Example 8-1** folder in **VBDB\SQL Server\Class 8** folder) and run the application. When the **Titles** form appears, click the **Publishers** button and make sure the database file opens properly. Stop the application.

Distributing a Database Application 8-9

6. Finally, make the **Authors** form active. In the **frmAuthors Load** procedure, make the same shaded modification:

Access Database:

```
  Private Sub FrmAuthors_Load(ByVal sender As System.Object, ByVal e As System.EventArgs) Handles MyBase.Load
    Try
      'point to help file
      hlpAuthors.HelpNamespace = Application.StartupPath + "\books.chm"
      'connect to books database
      BooksConnection = New OleDbConnection("Provider=Microsoft.ACE.OLEDB.12.0; Data Source = " + Application.StartupPath + "\BooksDB.accdb")
      BooksConnection.Open()
      .
      .
  End Sub
```

SQL Server Database:

```
  Private Sub FrmAuthors_Load(ByVal sender As System.Object, ByVal e As System.EventArgs) Handles MyBase.Load
    Try
      'point to help file
      hlpAuthors.HelpNamespace = Application.StartupPath + "\books.chm"
      'connect to books database
      BooksConnection = New SqlConnection("Data Source=.\SQLEXPRESS; AttachDbFilename=" + Application.StartupPath + "\SQLBooksDB.mdf; Integrated Security=True; Connect Timeout=30; User Instance=True")
      BooksConnection.Open()
      .
      .
  End Sub
```

7. Save and run the application (Access version saved in the **Example 8-1** folder in **VBDB\Access\Class 8** folder; SQL Server version saved in the **Example 8-1** folder in **VBDB\SQL Server\Class 8** folder) one last time. When the **Titles** form appears, click the **Authors** button and make sure the database file opens properly. Stop the application. Operation should remain the same as before. The only difference is the books database is now assumed to be in the projects' startup folder. We have removed the 'hard-wired' directory structure used in program development.

Database File Location with OpenFile Dialog Control

An alternate to placing the database file in the application directory is to allow the user to tell us where the database is. We actually do this a lot. An example was referred to way back in Chapter 5, where we first looked at the **open file dialog control**. The example we used was a schoolteacher using a database application to keep track of grades. The teacher would have database files for each class. When the application starts, the teacher needs to specify which database file is to be opened and where it is located. The Visual Basic open file dialog control is perfect for this use.

We need to open the database file before generating any other data objects and the associated data bound controls. Hence, the best place to use the open file dialog control is in the application's form **Load** procedure. The user chooses the database file at this point. This selected file is then used to establish the connection object used by the other data objects.

Here is a code segment that displays an open file dialog control (**dlgOpen**). If the user clicks **OK**, the connection object (**MyConnection**) is created using the selected file. If the user clicks **Cancel**, nothing happens. In this case, you would need code to decide what to do (continue, try again, abort):

Access Database:

```
    If dlgOpen.ShowDialog = Windows.Forms.DialogResult.OK Then
        MyConnection = New OleDbConnection("Provider=Microsoft.ACE.OLEDB.12.0; Data Source = " + dlgOpen.FileName)
    Else
        ' do something if user clicks Cancel
    End If
```

SQL Server Database:

```
    If dlgOpen.ShowDialog = Windows.Forms.DialogResult.OK Then
        MyConnection = New SqlConnection("Data Source=SQLInstance; AttachDbFilename=" + dlgOpen.FileName +"; Integrated Security=True; Connect Timeout=30; User Instance=True")
    Else
      ' do something if user clicks Cancel
    End If
```

One other thing to consider. What if our application requires a database with the structure of the books database, but the user selects some other database that our application can't use? This is a place where error trapping code (using a **Try/End Try** block) will come in handy. When we try to open the database and create the data tables, errors will fly! Based on error codes, we relay this information to the user and give them another chance.

Example 8-2

Opening Database Files with OpenFile Dialog Control

We build a little example, to illustrate the use of the open file dialog control to open a database file. We will open the books database file and display the **Titles** table.

1. Start a new application. Add a data grid view and an open file dialog control. Set these properties:

Form1:
<pre>
    Name   frmTitles
    FormBorderStyle   FixedSingle
    StartPosition   CenterScreen
    Text   Titles Table
</pre>

DataGridView1:
<pre>
    Name   grdTitles
</pre>

Access Database:

OpenFileDialog1:
<pre>
    Name   dlgOpen
    FileName   [blank]
    Filter   Access Databases (*.accdb)|*.accdb
</pre>

SQL Server Database:

OpenFileDialog1:
<pre>
    Name   dlgOpen
    FileName   [blank]
    Filter   SQL Server Databases (*.mdf)|*.mdf
</pre>

8-14   Visual Basic and Databases

The finished form looks like this:

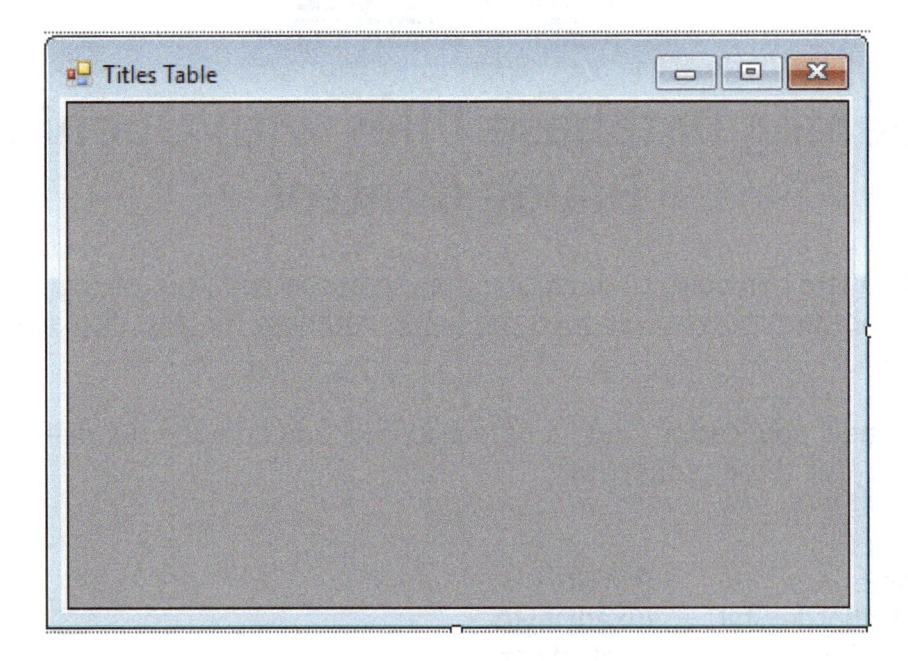

Below the form is:

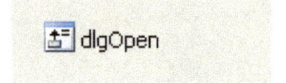

dlgOpen

2. Add these lines at the top of the code window:

Access Database:

```
Imports System.Data
Imports System.Data.OleDb
```

SQL Server Database:

```
Imports System.Data
Imports System.Data.SqlClient
```

3. Add these form level declarations to declare data objects:

Access Database:

```
Dim BooksConnection As OleDbConnection
Dim TitlesCommand As OleDbCommand
Dim TitlesAdapter As OleDbDataAdapter
Dim TitlesTable As DataTable
```

SQL Server Database:

```
Dim BooksConnection As SqlConnection
Dim TitlesCommand As SqlCommand
Dim TitlesAdapter As SqlDataAdapter
Dim TitlesTable As DataTable
```

4. Dispose of these objects in the **frmTitles FormClosing** procedure:

```
Private Sub FrmTitles_FormClosing(ByVal sender As Object,
ByVal e As System.Windows.Forms.FormClosingEventArgs)
Handles Me.FormClosing
    BooksConnection.Dispose()
    TitlesCommand.Dispose()
    TitlesAdapter.Dispose()
    TitlesTable.Dispose()
End Sub
```

5. The crucial code is in the **frmTitles Load** event procedure:

Access Database:

```
  Private Sub FrmTitles_Load(ByVal sender As System.Object, ByVal e As System.EventArgs) Handles MyBase.Load
    If dlgOpen.ShowDialog = Windows.Forms.DialogResult.OK Then
      Try
        'connect to books database
        BooksConnection = New OleDbConnection("Provider=Microsoft.ACE.OLEDB.12.0; Data Source = " + dlgOpen.FileName)
        BooksConnection.Open()
        'establish command object
        TitlesCommand = New OleDbCommand("Select * from Titles ORDER BY Title", BooksConnection)
        'establish data adapter/data table
        TitlesAdapter = New OleDbDataAdapter()
        TitlesAdapter.SelectCommand = TitlesCommand
        TitlesTable = New DataTable()
        TitlesAdapter.Fill(TitlesTable)
        'bind grid to data table
        grdTitles.DataSource = TitlesTable
      Catch ex As Exception
        MessageBox.Show(ex.Message, "Error establishing Titles table.", MessageBoxButtons.OK, MessageBoxIcon.Error)
        Exit Sub
      End Try
    Else
      MessageBox.Show("No file selected", "Program stopping", MessageBoxButtons.OK, MessageBoxIcon.Information)
      Me.Close()
    End If
  End Sub
```

Distributing a Database Application 8-17

SQL Server Database:

```vbnet
  Private Sub FrmTitles_Load(ByVal sender As System.Object, ByVal e As System.EventArgs) Handles MyBase.Load
    If dlgOpen.ShowDialog = Windows.Forms.DialogResult.OK Then
      Try
        'connect to books database
        BooksConnection = New SqlConnection("Data Source=.\SQLEXPRESS; AttachDbFilename=" + dlgOpen.FileName + "; Integrated Security=True; Connect Timeout=30; User Instance=True")
        BooksConnection.Open()
        'establish command object
        TitlesCommand = New SqlCommand("Select * from Titles ORDER BY Title", BooksConnection)
        'establish data adapter/data table
        TitlesAdapter = New SqlDataAdapter()
        TitlesAdapter.SelectCommand = TitlesCommand
        TitlesTable = New DataTable()
        TitlesAdapter.Fill(TitlesTable)
        'bind grid to data table
        grdTitles.DataSource = TitlesTable
      Catch ex As Exception
        MessageBox.Show(ex.Message, "Error establishing Titles table.", MessageBoxButtons.OK, MessageBoxIcon.Error)
        Exit Sub
      End Try
    Else
      MessageBox.Show("No file selected", "Program stopping", MessageBoxButtons.OK, MessageBoxIcon.Information)
      Me.Close()
    End If
  End Sub
```

In this code, we obtain the database filename, create the needed data objects and bind the grid to the resulting data table object (all fields in the **Titles** table). If the user doesn't select a file, a message box appears. If an error occurs, error trapping prints a message.

8-18　　Visual Basic and Databases

6. Save (Access version saved in the **Example 8-2** folder in **VBDB\Access\Class 8** folder; SQL Server version saved in the **Example 8-2** folder in **VBDB\SQL Server\Class 8** folder) and run the application. The open file dialog box will appear (Access version):

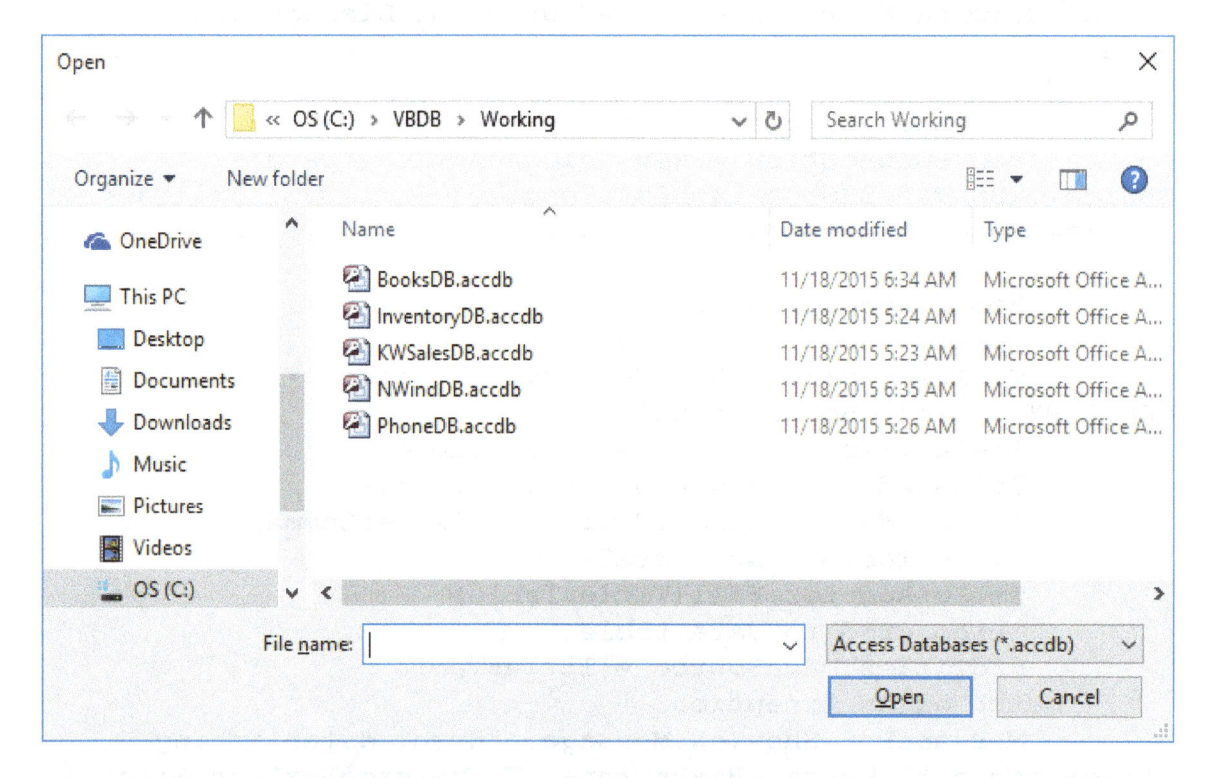

Note the **Filter** property is set so only Access databases (**accdb** files) can be opened. Find your working copy of **BooksDB.accdb** and click **Open**. The file is opened and the data grid filled with the **Titles** table:

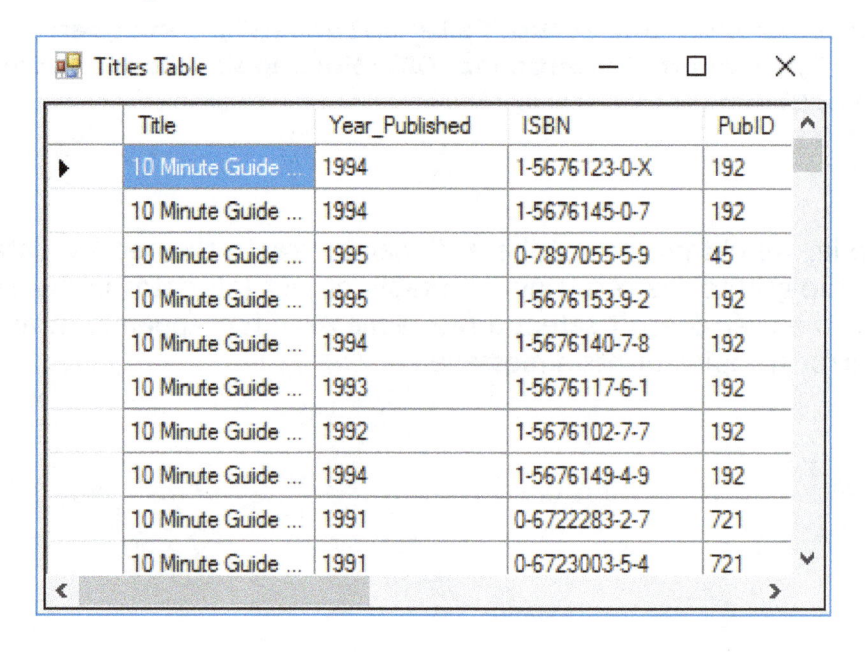

Distributing a Database Application   8-19

7. Stop the application and run it again. When the open file dialog box appears, click **Cancel** and you will see:

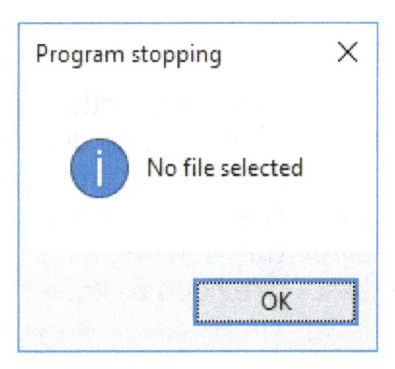

   Program stopping — No file selected — OK

This is one option if a file is not selected – just stop the program. You may want to give the user another chance.

8. Re-run the application, but this time select some other database file (not a books database, for example the **NWindDB.accdb** file). Click **Open** and you should see (a similar message will appear if working with SQL Server databases):

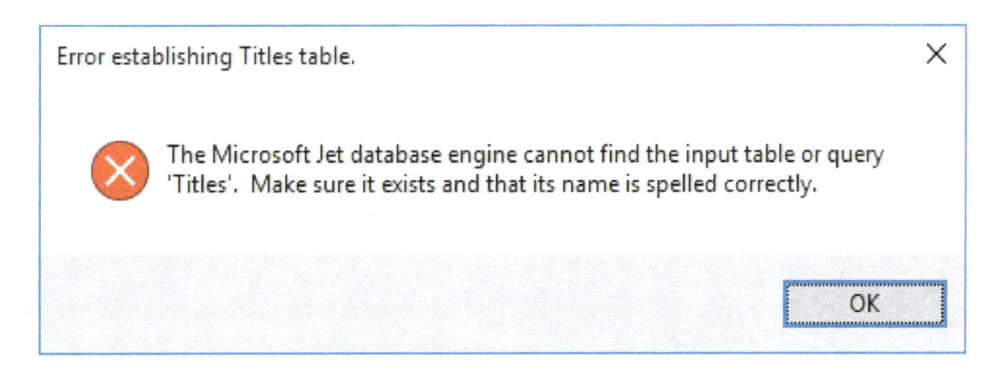

   Error establishing Titles table. — The Microsoft Jet database engine cannot find the input table or query 'Titles'. Make sure it exists and that its name is spelled correctly. — OK

The **Titles** table cannot be located. With this error, we would give the user another try at locating a proper database file.

Distribution of a Visual Basic Database Application

I bet you're ready to show your friends and colleagues some of the database applications you have built using Visual Basic. Just give them a copy of all your project files and databases, ask them to buy and install Visual Basic and learn how to open and run a project. Then, have them open your project and run the application. I think you'll agree this is asking a lot of your friends, colleagues, and, ultimately, your user base. We need to know how to run an application **without** Visual Basic.

To run an application without Visual Basic, you need to create an **executable** version of the application. So, how is an executable created? A little secret ... Visual Basic builds an executable version of an application every time we run the application! The executable file is in the **Bin\Debug** folder (**Bin\x86\Debug** for **Access**). Open the **Bin\Debug** folder for any project you have built and you'll see a file with your project name of type **Application**. For example, using Windows Explorer to open the **Bin\x86\Debug** folder for the Access version of **Example 8-1** shows:

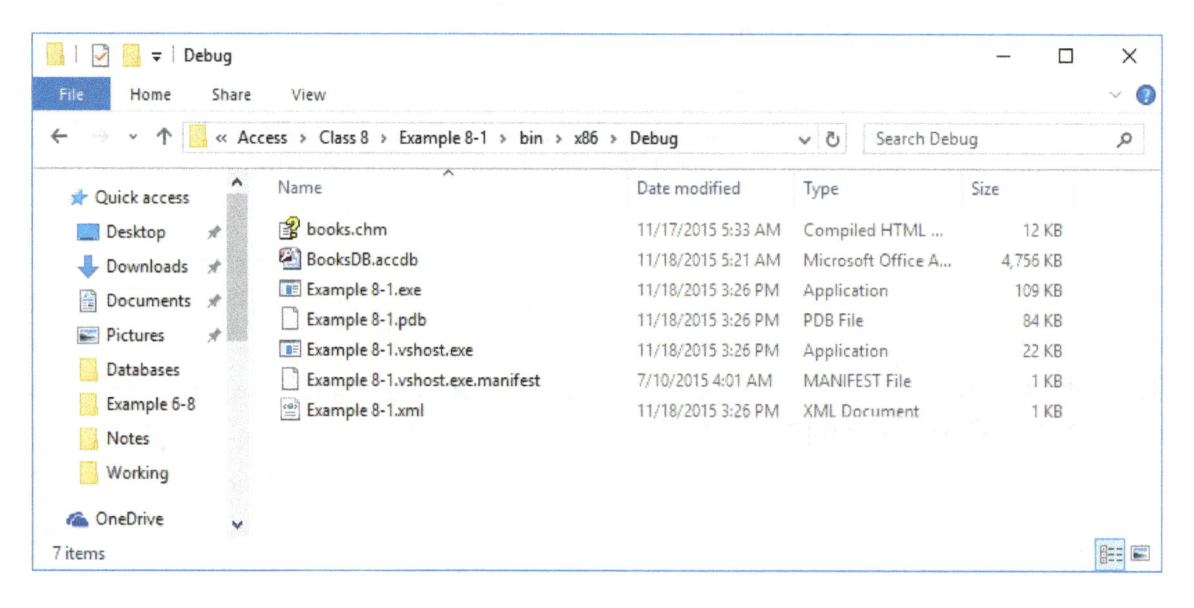

Notice the database file (**BooksDB.accdb**) is there.

Distributing a Database Application 8-21

The file named **Example 8-1.exe** (the **Application** file) is the executable version of the application. If I make sure Visual Basic is not running and double-click this file, the following appears:

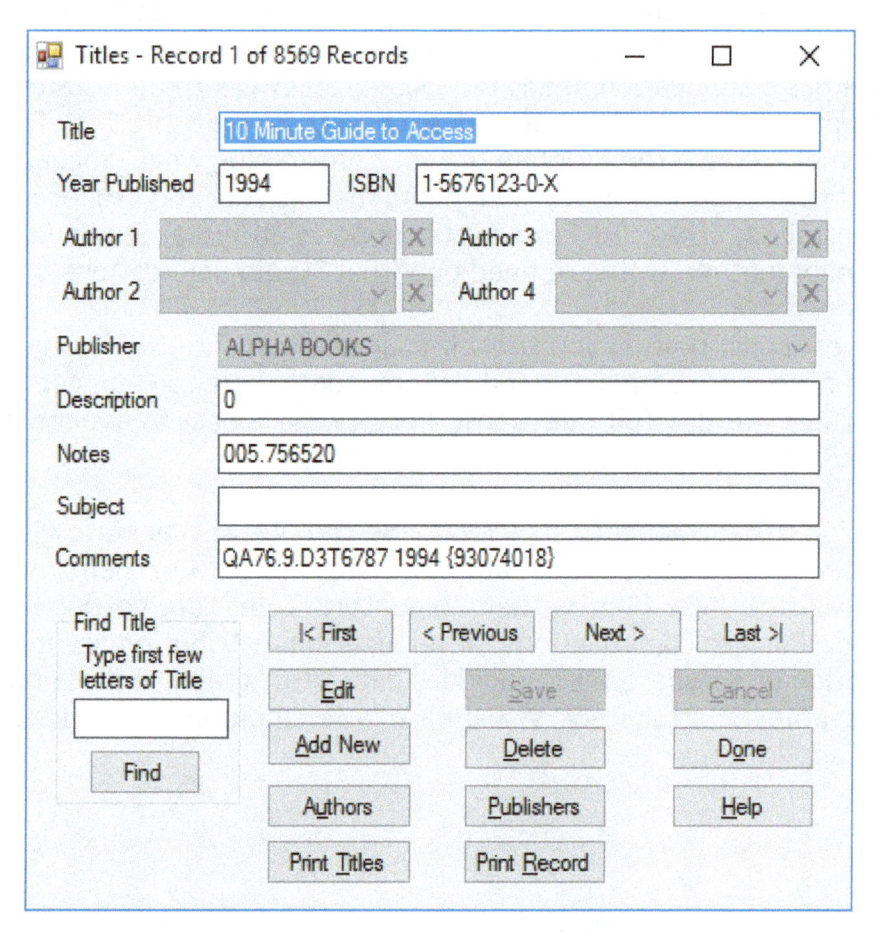

Voila! The Books DBMS application is running outside of the Visual Basic IDE!

So distributing a Visual Basic database application is as simple as giving your user a copy of the executable file, having them place it in a folder on their computer and double-clicking the file to run it? Maybe. This worked on my computer (and will work on yours) because I have a very important set of files known as the **.NET Framework** installed (they are installed when Visual Basic is installed). Every Visual Basic application needs the .NET Framework to be installed on the hosting computer. The .NET Framework is central to Microsoft's .NET initiative. It is an attempt to solve the problem of first determining what language (and version) an application was developed in and making sure the proper run-time files were installed. The .NET Framework supports all Visual Studio languages, so it is the only runtime software need by Visual Studio applications.

The next question is: how do you know if your user has the .NET Framework installed on his or her computer? And, if they don't, how can you get it installed? These are difficult questions. For now, it is best to assume your user does not have the .NET Framework on their computer.

So, in addition to our application's executable file, we also need to give a potential user the Microsoft .NET Framework files and inform them how to install and register these files on their computer. Things are getting complicated. Further complications for application distribution are inclusion and installation of database files, ancillary data files, graphics files and configuration files. Fortunately, Visual Basic offers help in distributing, or **deploying**, applications.

Distributing a Database Application

Visual Basic uses **Setup Wizard** for deploying applications. **Setup Wizard** will identify all files needed by your application and bundle these files into a **Setup** program. You distribute this program to your user base (usually on a CD-ROM). Your user then runs the resulting **Setup** program. This program will:

➢ Install the application (and all needed files) on the user's computer.
➢ Add an entry to the user's **Start/Programs** menu to allow execution of your application.
➢ Add an icon to the user's desktop to allow execution of your application.

We'll soon look at use of **Setup Wizard** to build a deployment package for a Visual Basic application. First, let's quickly look at the topic of icons.

Application Icons

Notice there is an icon file that looks like a little, blank Windows form associated with the application executable. And, notice that whenever you design a form in the Visual Basic IDE (and run it), a small icon appears in the upper left hand corner of the form. Here's the **Titles** form from our DBMS:

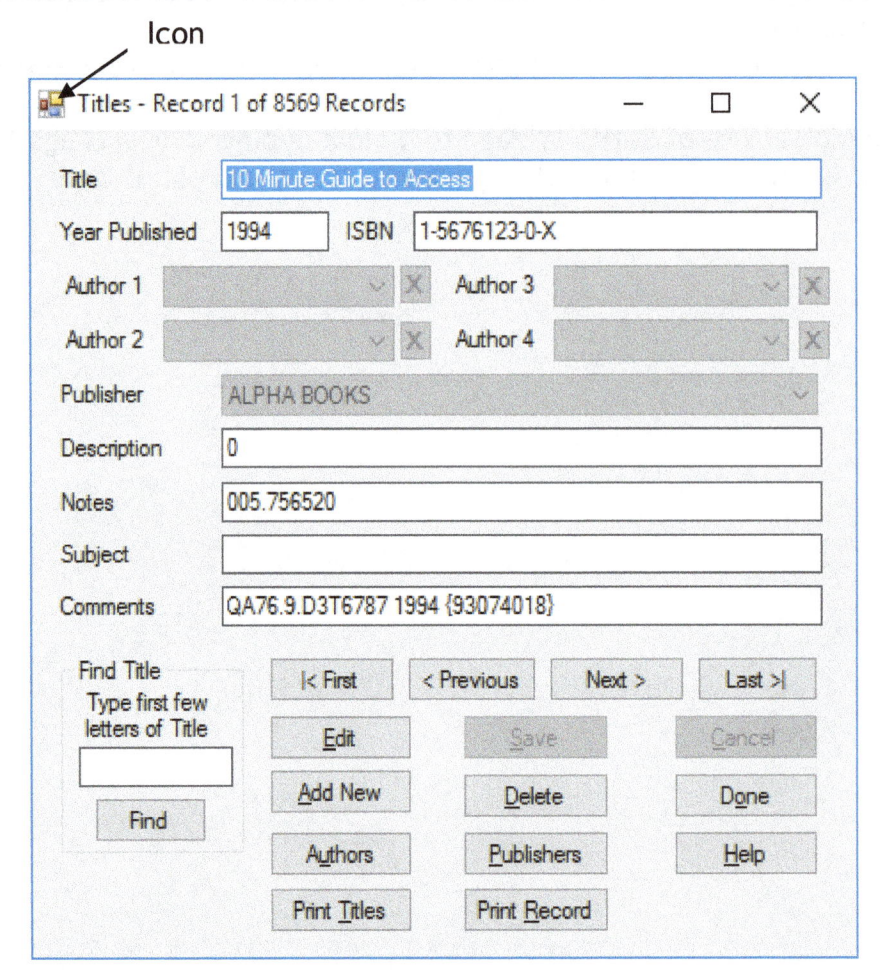

Icons are used in several places in Visual Basic applications: to represent files in Windows Explorer, to represent programs in the Programs menu, to represent programs on the desktop and to identify an application removal tool. Icons are used throughout applications. The default icons are ugly! We need the capability to change them.

Distributing a Database Application   8-25

Changing the icon connected to a form is simple. The idea is to assign a unique icon to indicate the form's function. To assign an icon, click on the form's **Icon** property in the properties window. Click on the ellipsis (...) and a window that allows selection of icon files will appear. The icon file you load must have the **.ico** filename extension and format.

A different icon can be assigned to the application. This will be the icon that appears next to the executable file's name in Windows Explorer, in the Programs menu and on the desktop. To choose this icon, first make sure the project file is highlighted in the **Solution Explorer** window of the IDE. Choose the **View** menu item and select **Property Pages**. Select the **Application** page and this window will appear:

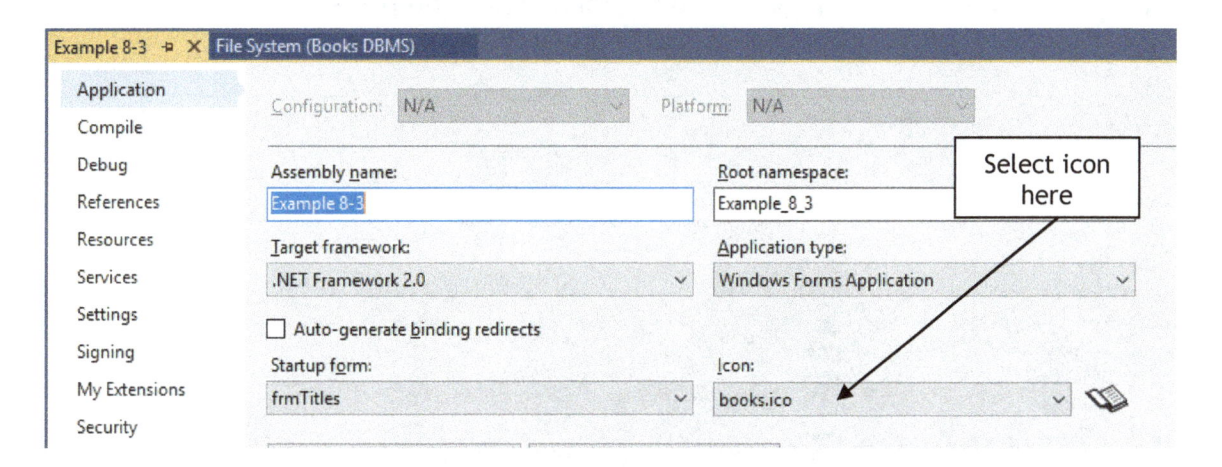

The icon is selected in the **Icon** drop-down box. You can either choose an icon already listed or click the ellipsis (...) that allows you to select an icon using a dialog box. Once you choose an icon, two things will happen. The icon will appear on the property pages and the icon file will be added to your project's folder. This will be seen in the Solution Explorer window.

The Internet and other sources offer a wealth of icon files from which you can choose an icon to assign to your form(s) and applications. But, it's also fun to design your own icon to add that personal touch.

Custom Icons

An icon is a special type of graphics file with an **ico** extension. It is a picture with a specific size of 32 by 32 pixels. The internet has a wealth of free icons you can download to your computer and use. Do a search on 'free 32 x 32 ico files'. You will see a multitude of choices. One site we suggest is:

http://www.softicons.com/toolbar-icons/32x32-free-design-icons-by-aha-soft/

At such a site, you simply download the ico file to your computer and save it.

It is possible to create your own icon using Visual Studio. To create an icon for a particular project, in **Solution Explorer**, right-click the project name, choose **Add**, then **New Item**. This window will appear:

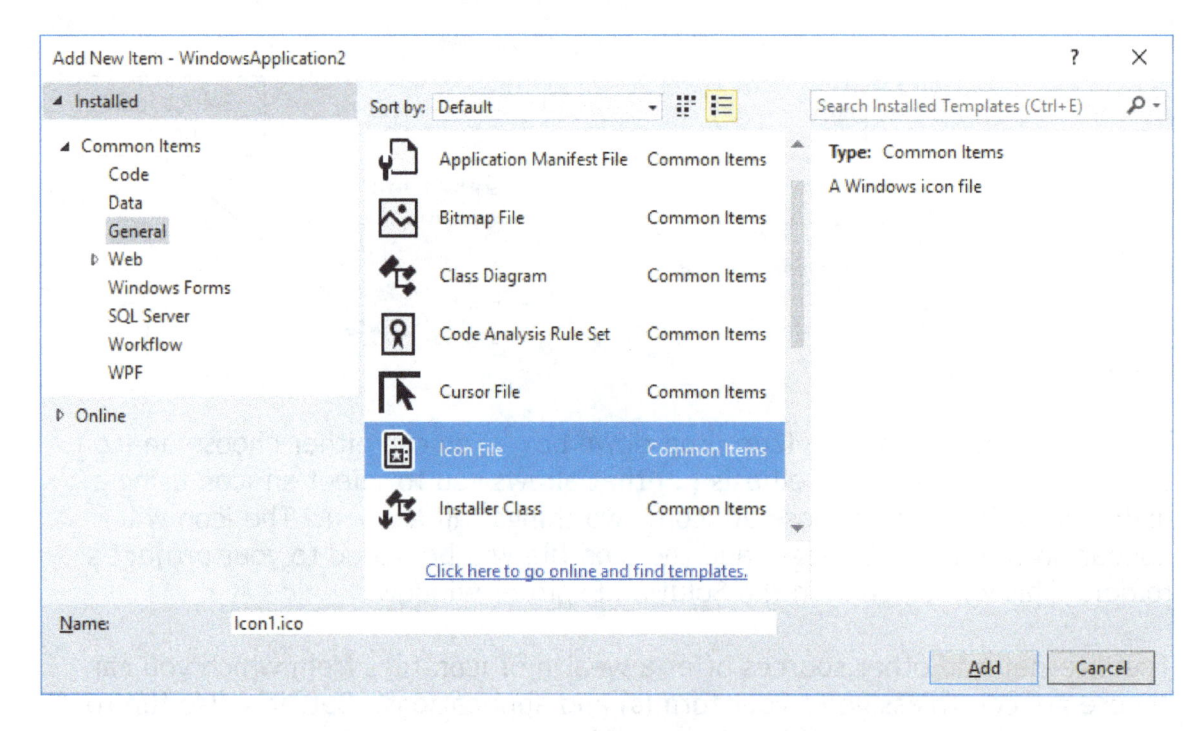

As shown, expand **Common Items** and choose **General**. Then, pick **Icon File**. Name your icon and click **Add**.

Distributing a Database Application 8-27

A generic icon will open:

The icon is very large. Let's make a few changes to make it visible and editable. First, resize the image to 32 x 32 pixels. Then, use the magnifying tool to make the image as large as possible. Finally, add a grid to the graphic. When done, I see:

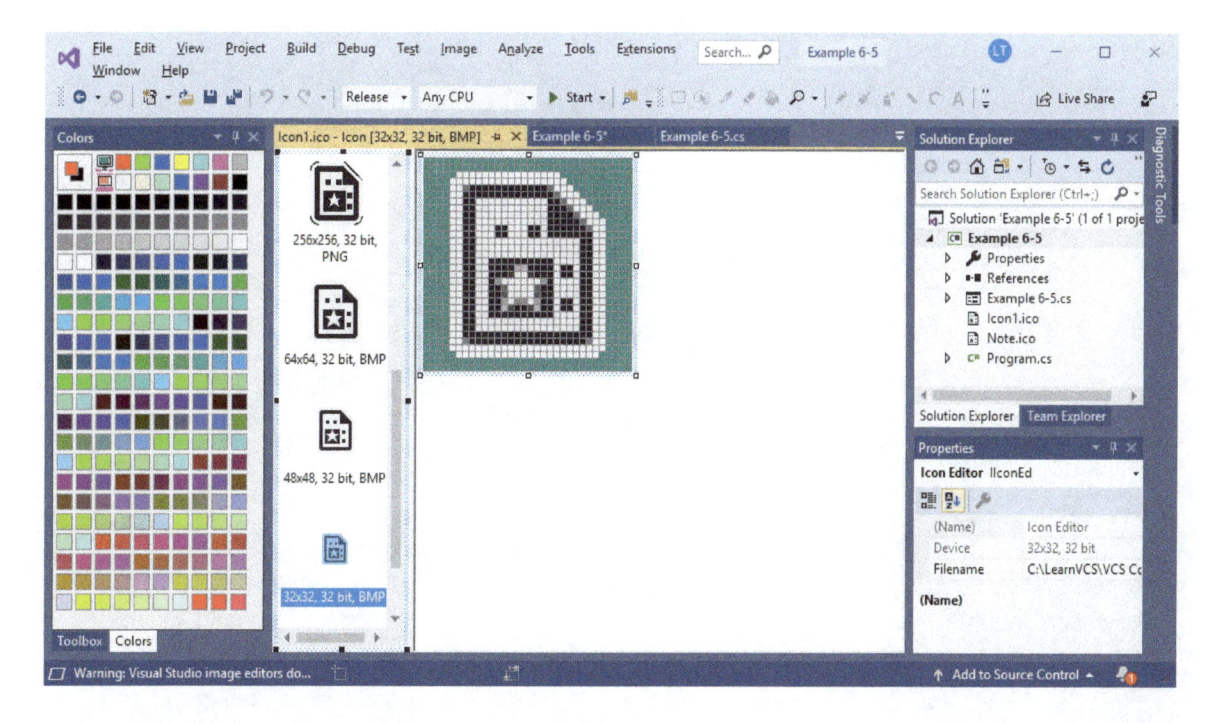

At this point, we can add any detail we need by setting pixels to particular colors. Consult on-line help for the exact steps needed. Once done, the icon will be saved in your project file and can be used by your project. The icon file (**Icon1.ico** in this case) is also listed in **Solution Explorer:**

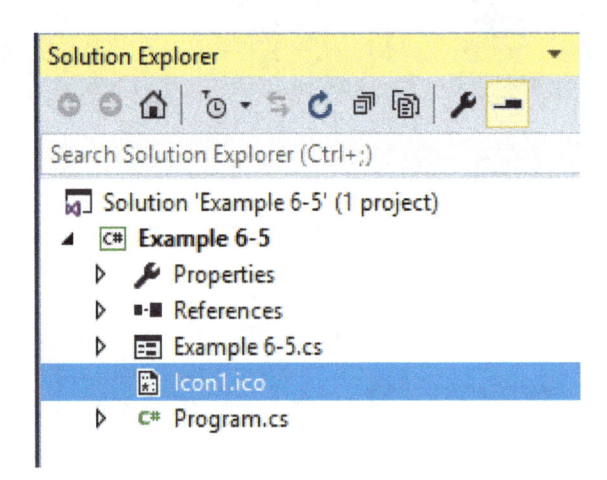

Example 8-3

Visual Basic Setup Wizard

As mentioned earlier, to allow someone else to install and run your Visual Basic database application requires more than just a simple transfer of the executable file. Visual Basic provides **Setup Wizard** that simplifies this task of application **deployment**.

Note: **Setup Wizard** must be a part of your Visual Studio installation. To download and install **Setup Wizard**, use the following link:

Download Setup Wizard

Setup Wizard will build a **Setup** program that lets the user install the application (and other needed files) on their computer. At the same time, **Program** menu entries, desktop icons and application removal programs are placed on the user's computer.

The best way to illustrate use of **Setup Wizard** is through an example. In these notes, we will build a Setup program for our Books DBMS example. Follow the example closely to see all steps involved. All results of this example for an Access database will be found in the **Example 8-3** and **Books DBMS** folders of the **VBDB\Access\Class 8** folder. The same example for a SQL Server database is in the **Example 8-3** and **Books DBMS** folders of the **VBDB\SQL Server\Class 8** folder. Let's start.

Open the **Books DBMS** project (**Example 8-1**). Attach an icon to the **Titles** form (one possible icon, **BOOKS.ICO**, is included in the project folder). The form should look like this with its new icon:

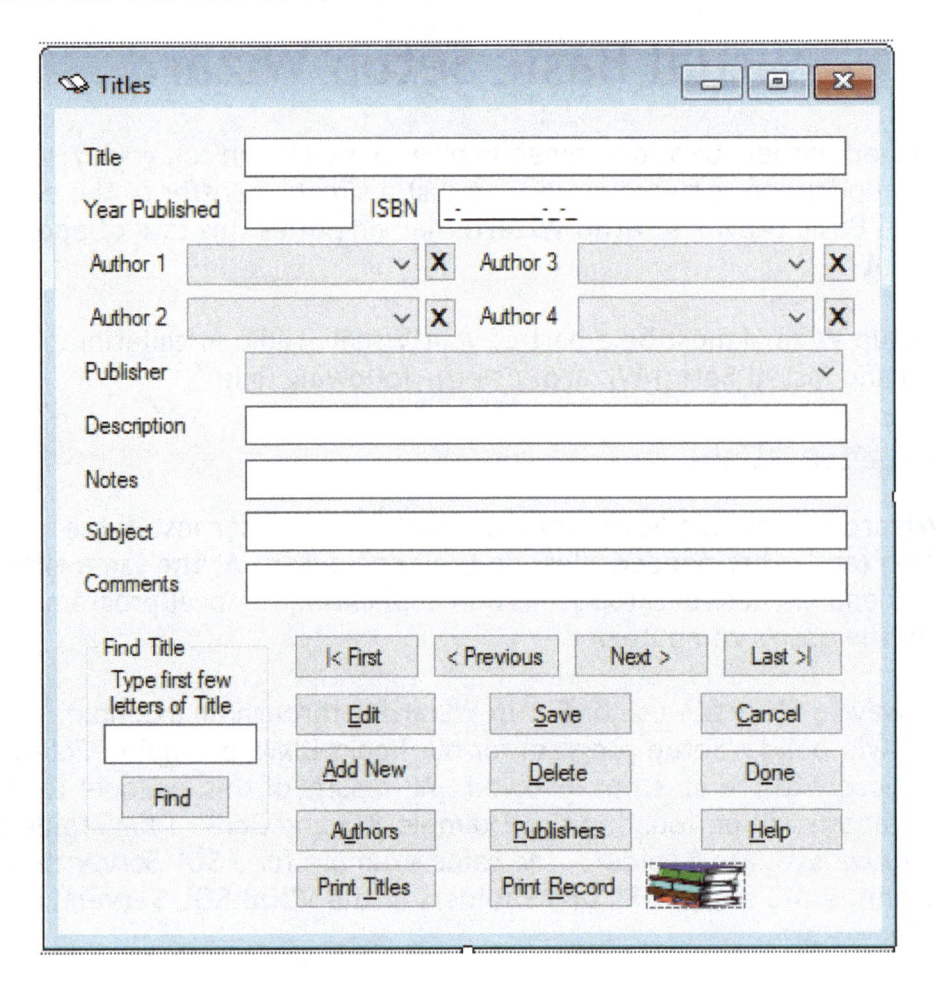

Assign this same icon to the application using the steps mentioned earlier:

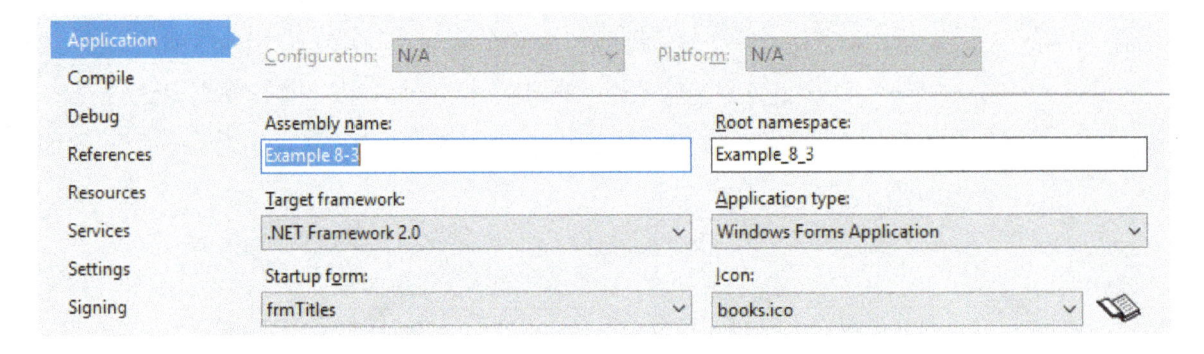

Distributing a Database Application 8-31

Setup Wizard is a separate project you add to your application solution. Choose the **File** menu option, then **New** then **Project**. In the window that appears, select **Setup Wizard** and click **Next**:

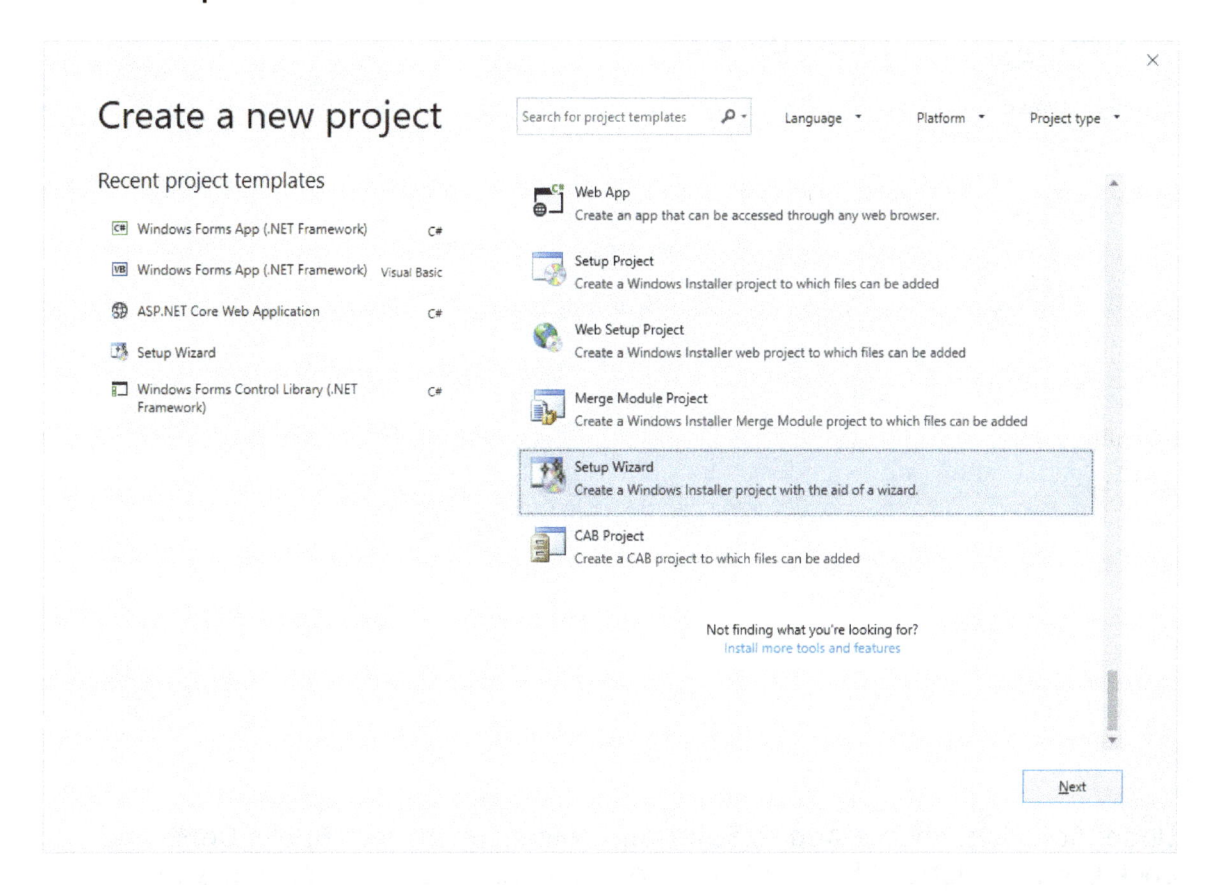

Create a new project

Recent project templates

- Windows Forms App (.NET Framework) C#
- Windows Forms App (.NET Framework) Visual Basic
- ASP.NET Core Web Application C#
- Setup Wizard
- Windows Forms Control Library (.NET Framework) C#

Web App
Create an app that can be accessed through any web browser.

Setup Project
Create a Windows Installer project to which files can be added

Web Setup Project
Create a Windows Installer web project to which files can be added

Merge Module Project
Create a Windows Installer Merge Module project to which files can be added

Setup Wizard
Create a Windows Installer project with the aid of a wizard.

CAB Project
Create a CAB project to which files can be added

Not finding what you're looking for?
Install more tools and features

[Next]

8-32   **Visual Basic and Databases**

This window appears:

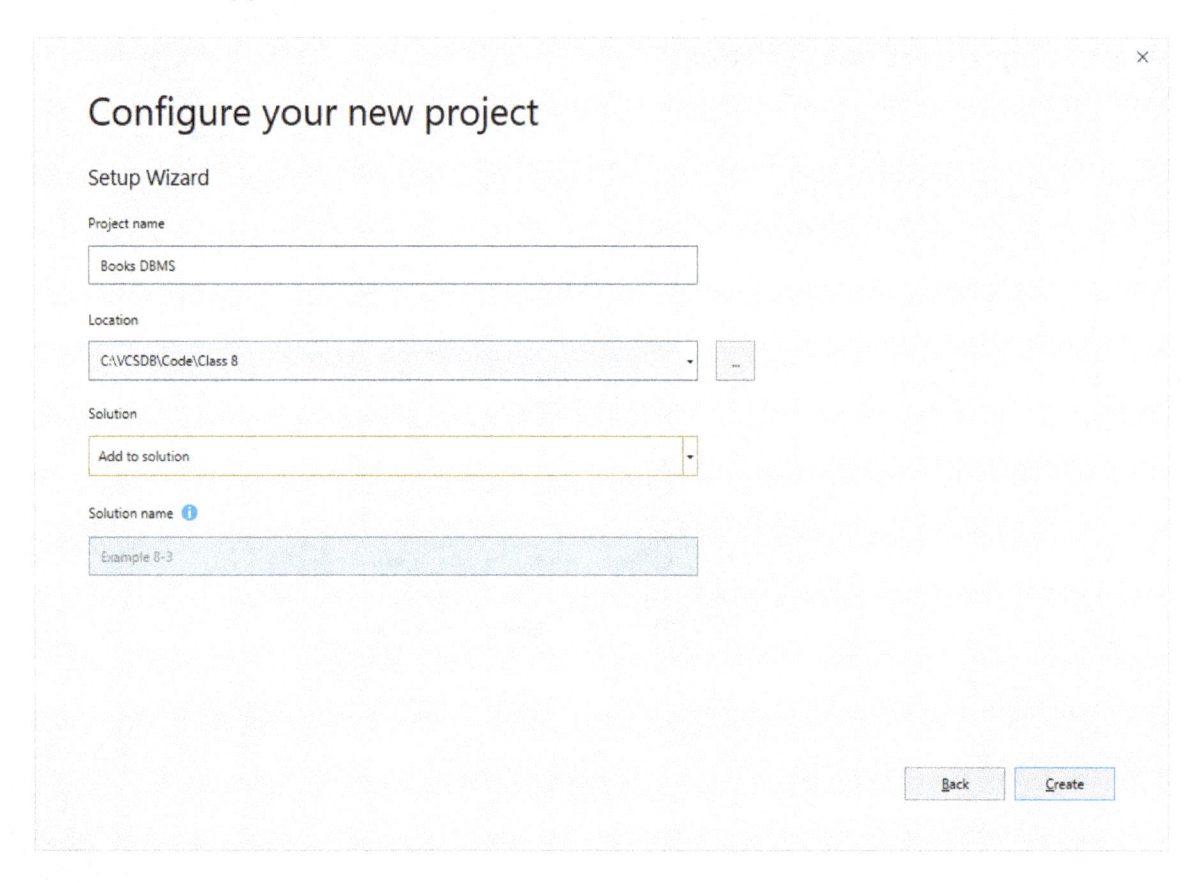

Configure your new project

Setup Wizard

Project name

Books DBMS

Location

C:\VCSDB\Code\Class 8

Solution

Add to solution

Solution name

Example 8-3

[Back] [Create]

Under **Solution**, choose **Add to Solution**. **Name** the project **Books DBMS** and click **Create**. Notice I have put the project folder in the **VBDB\Access\Class 8** folder (for a SQL Server database, you might choose **VBDB\SQL Server\Class 8**).

Distributing a Database Application 8-33

The **Setup Wizard** will begin with Step 1 of 5.

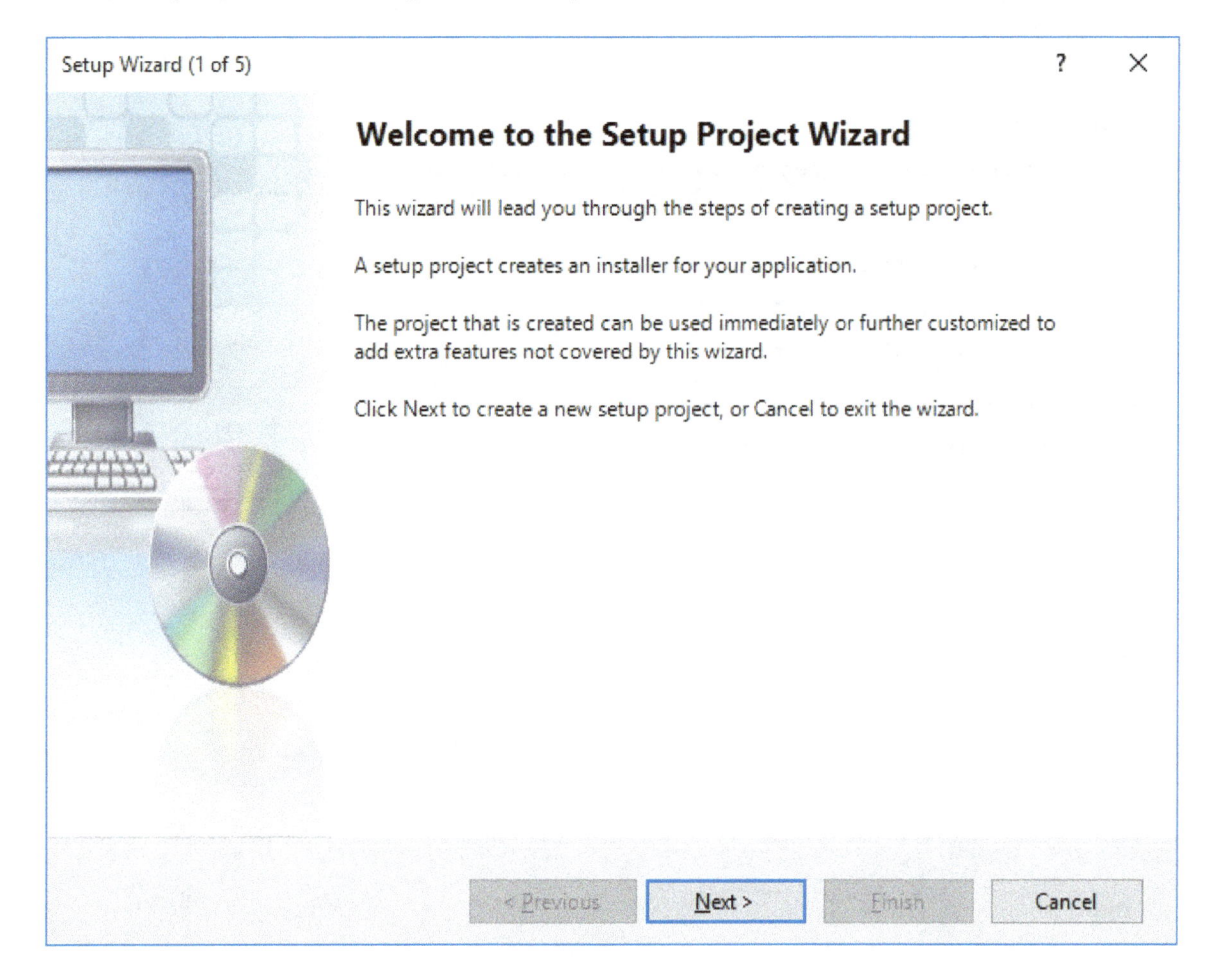

Continue from step to step, providing the requested information. Here, just click **Next**.

Step 2.

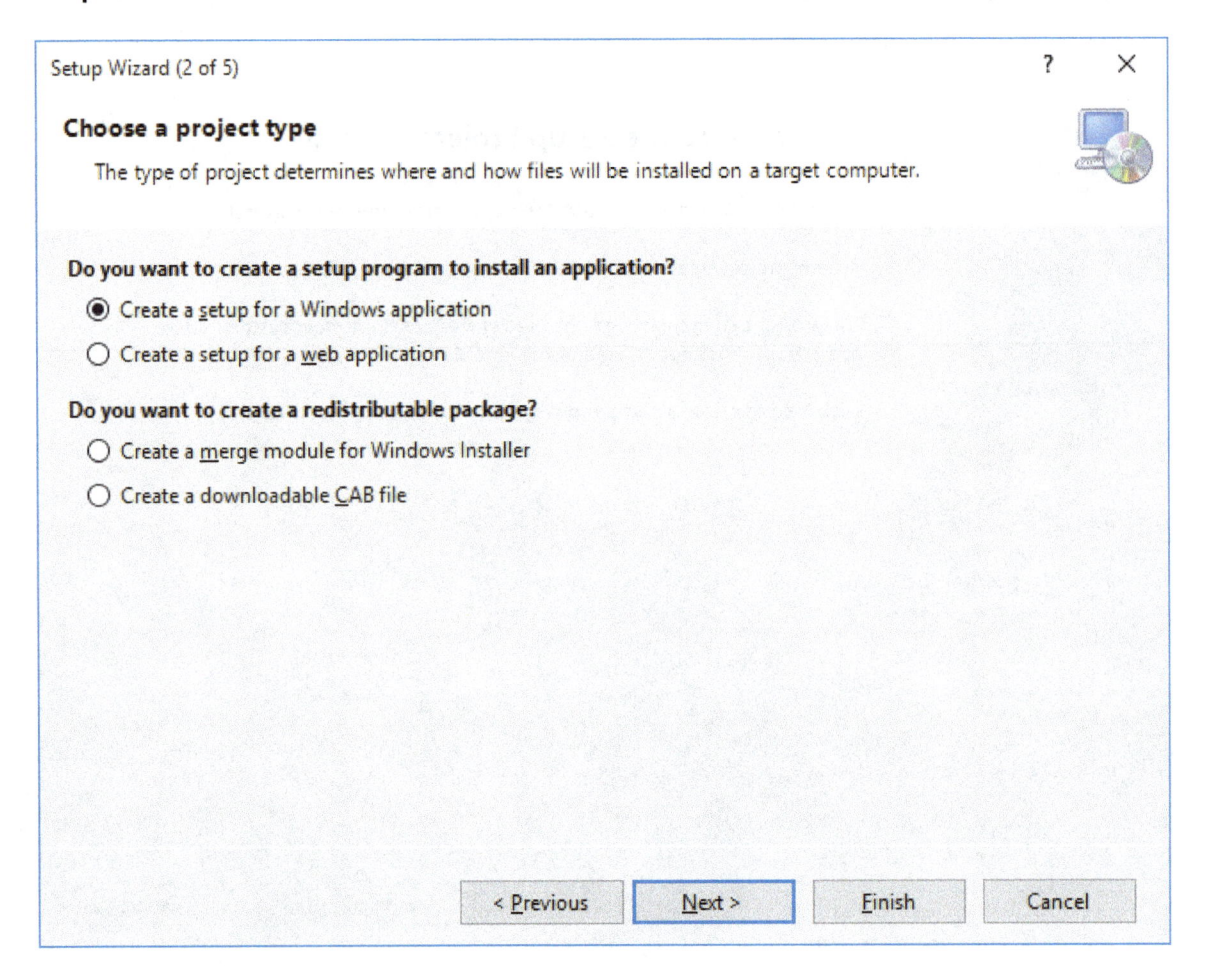

Setup Wizard (2 of 5)

Choose a project type
The type of project determines where and how files will be installed on a target computer.

Do you want to create a setup program to install an application?
- ◉ Create a **s**etup for a Windows application
- ○ Create a setup for a **w**eb application

Do you want to create a redistributable package?
- ○ Create a **m**erge module for Windows Installer
- ○ Create a downloadable **C**AB file

[< Previous] [Next >] [Finish] [Cancel]

Choose **Create a setup for a Windows application**. Click **Next**.

Step 3.

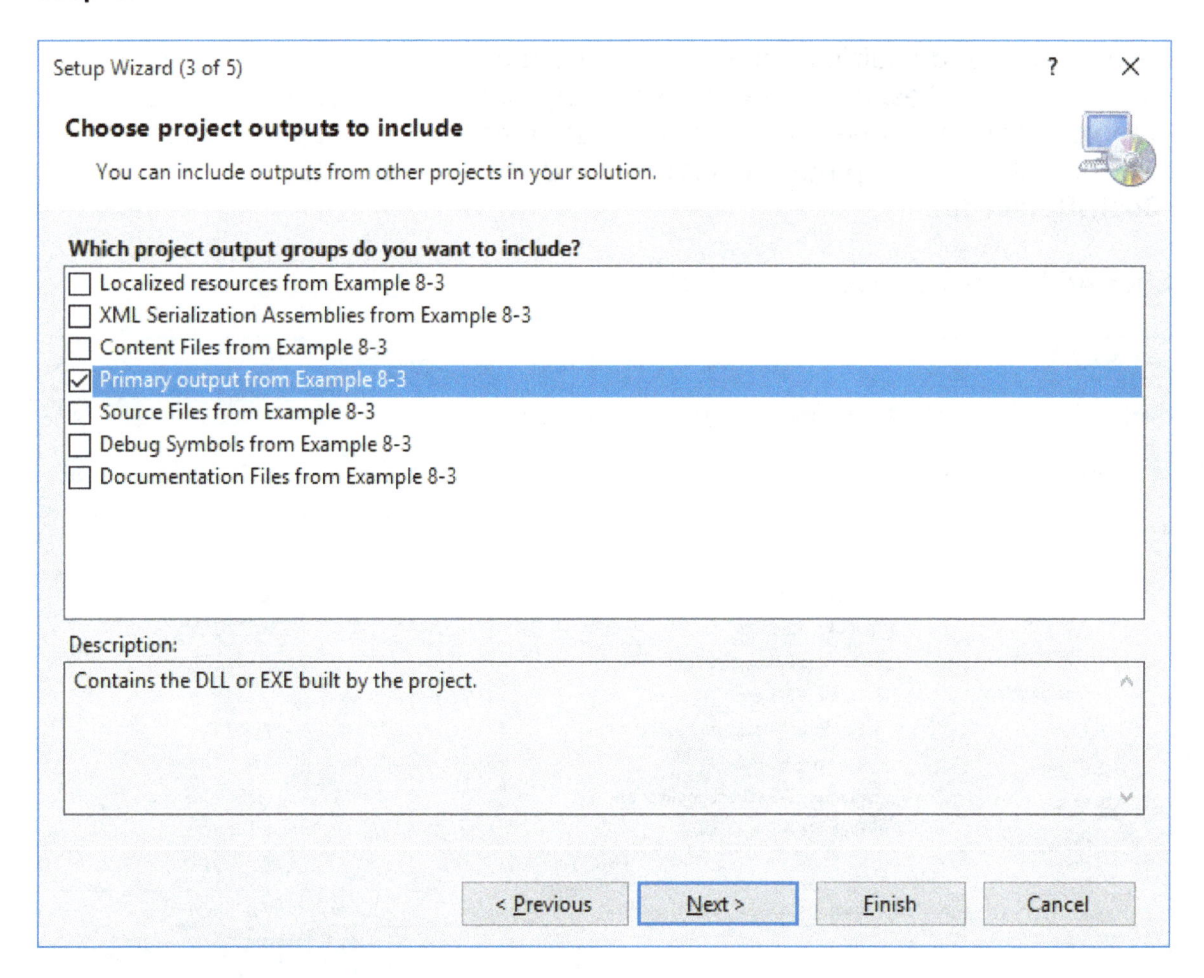

[Setup Wizard (3 of 5) dialog box — "Choose project outputs to include". Options listed: Localized resources from Example 8-3, XML Serialization Assemblies from Example 8-3, Content Files from Example 8-3, ☑ Primary output from Example 8-3 (highlighted), Source Files from Example 8-3, Debug Symbols from Example 8-3, Documentation Files from Example 8-3. Description: "Contains the DLL or EXE built by the project." Buttons: < Previous, Next >, Finish, Cancel.]

Here you choose the files to install. The main one is the executable file (known here as the **primary output file**). Place a check next to **Primary ouput from Example 8-3** and click **Next**.

8-36　　　　　　　　Visual Basic and Databases

Step 4.

Here you can add additional files with your deployment package. You could specify ReadMe files, configuration files, help files, data files, sound files, graphic files or any other files your application needs. Our application needs two such files: the help file (**books.chm**) and the database file (**BooksDB.accdb**).

Click **Add**. A dialog box will appear:

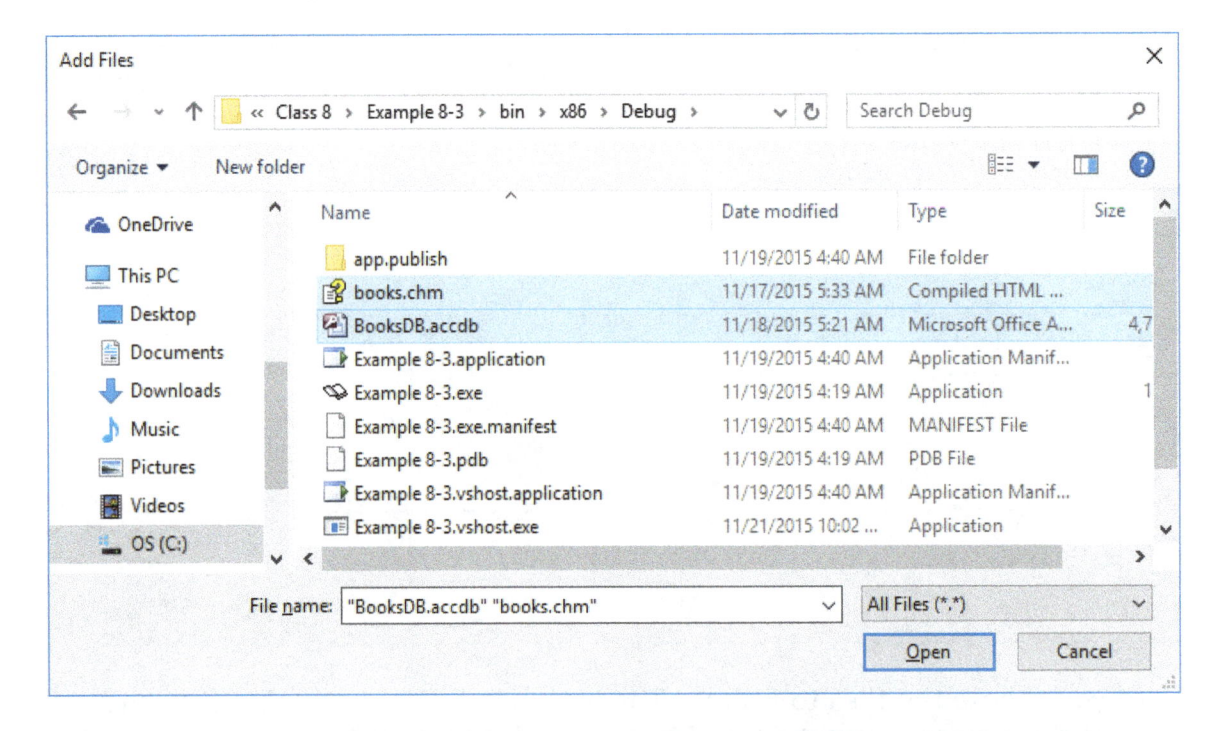

Navigate to the project's **Bin\Debug** folder (**Bin\x86\Debug** for **Access**) and select the two files as shown. For SQL Server, you would choose that SQL Server version of the database (**SQLBooksDB.mdf**).

Click **Open**. The two files should now appear in the window:

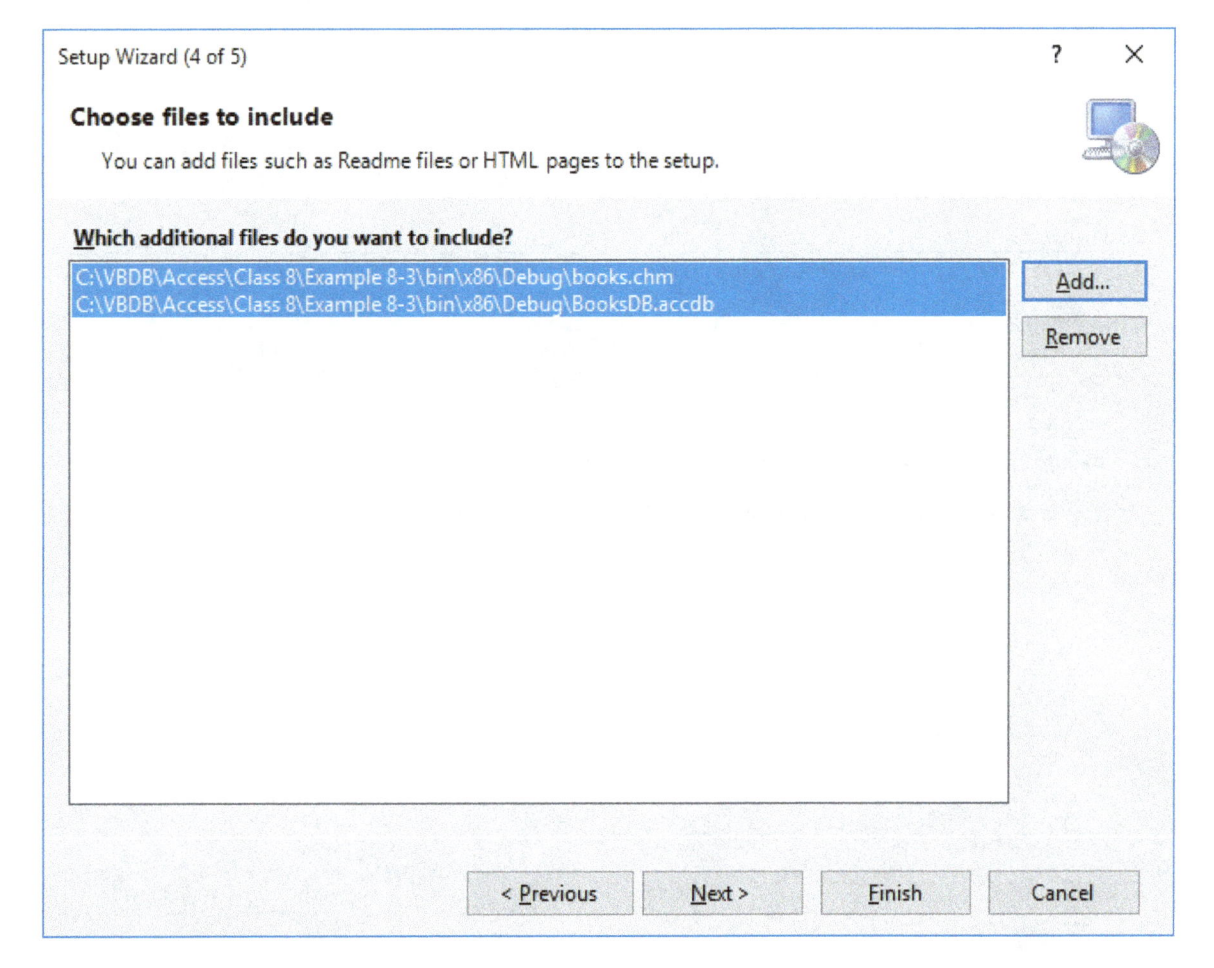

Move to the next step (click **Next**).

Step 5.

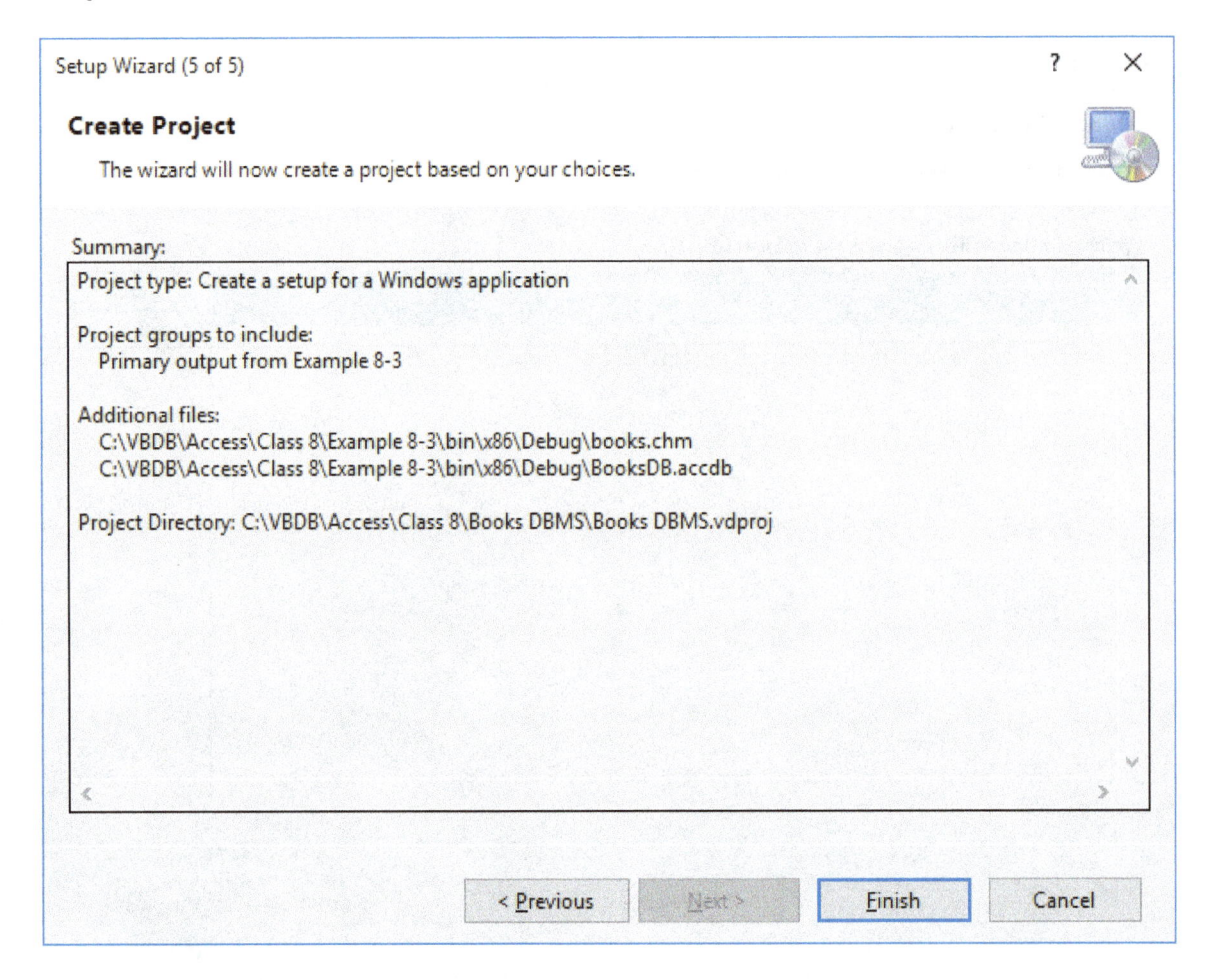

Setup Wizard (5 of 5)

Create Project

The wizard will now create a project based on your choices.

Summary:

Project type: Create a setup for a Windows application

Project groups to include:
   Primary output from Example 8-3

Additional files:
   C:\VBDB\Access\Class 8\Example 8-3\bin\x86\Debug\books.chm
   C:\VBDB\Access\Class 8\Example 8-3\bin\x86\Debug\BooksDB.accdb

Project Directory: C:\VBDB\Access\Class 8\Books DBMS\Books DBMS.vdproj

[< Previous] [Next >] [**Finish**] [Cancel]

Click **Finish** to see the resulting **File System**:

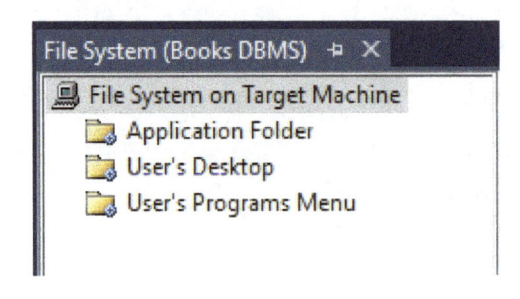

File System (Books DBMS)
- File System on Target Machine
  - Application Folder
  - User's Desktop
  - User's Programs Menu

Distributing a Database Application   8-39

We also want shortcuts to start the program both on the **Desktop** and the **Programs Menu.** First, we do the **Desktop** shortcut. To do this, open the **Application Folder** to see:

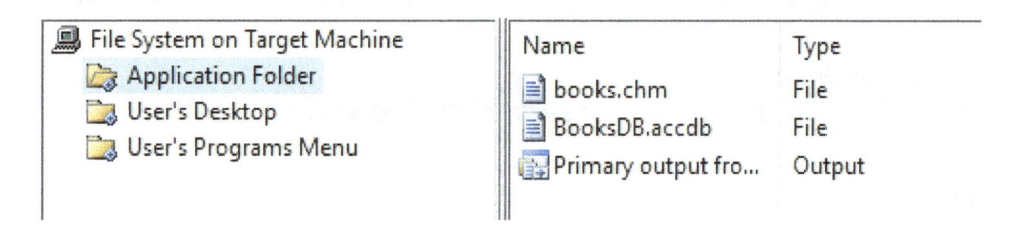

```
File System on Target Machine      Name                Type
    Application Folder              books.chm           File
    User's Desktop                  BooksDB.accdb       File
    User's Programs Menu            Primary output fro… Output
```

Right-click **Primary output from ...** and choose **Create Shortcut to Primary output ....** Cut the resulting shortcut from the **Application Folder** and paste it into the **User's Desktop** folder:

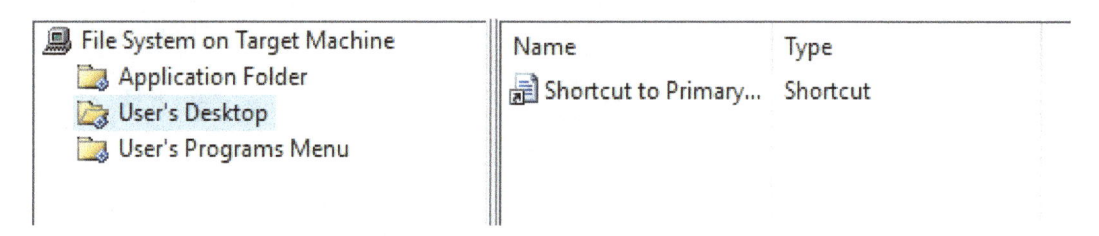

```
File System on Target Machine      Name                   Type
    Application Folder              Shortcut to Primary…   Shortcut
    User's Desktop
    User's Programs Menu
```

Rename the shortcut **Books DBMS** to yield

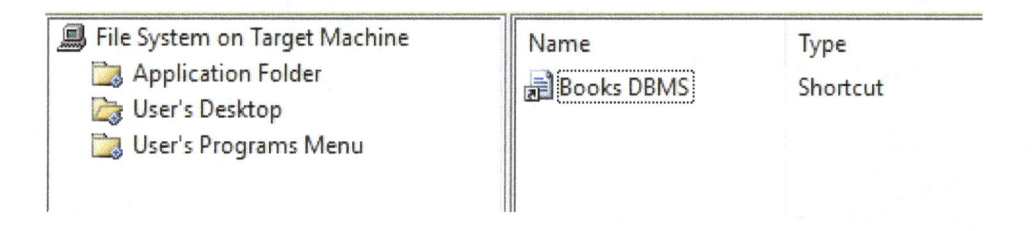

```
File System on Target Machine      Name          Type
    Application Folder              Books DBMS    Shortcut
    User's Desktop
    User's Programs Menu
```

Lastly, we want to change the icon associated with the shortcut. This is a little tricky. The steps are:

> Highlight the shortcut and choose the **Icon** property in the Properties window
> Choose **Browse**.
> When the **Icon** dialog box appears, click **Browse**. You will see

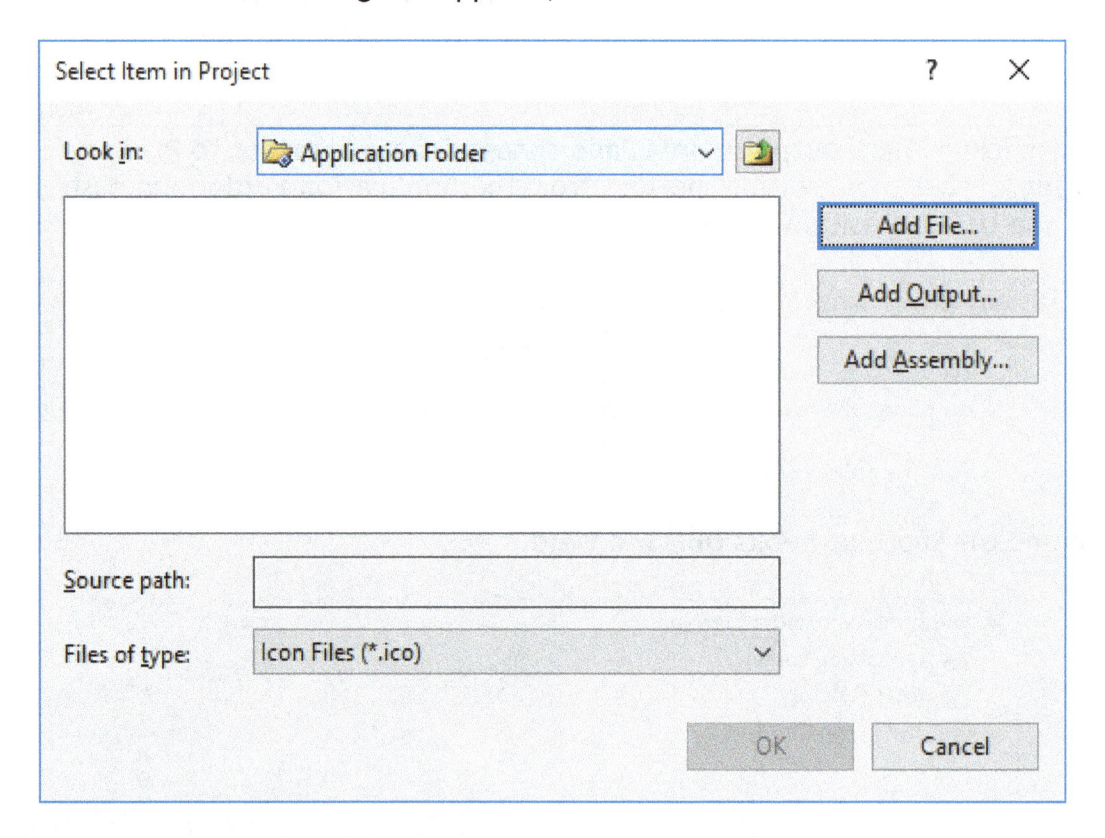

As shown, look in the **Application Folder** and click **Add File**.

Distributing a Database Application 8-41

Locate and select the icon file (there is one in the **VBDB\Access\Class 8\Example 8-3** folder), then click **OK**. The **Icon** window will appear:

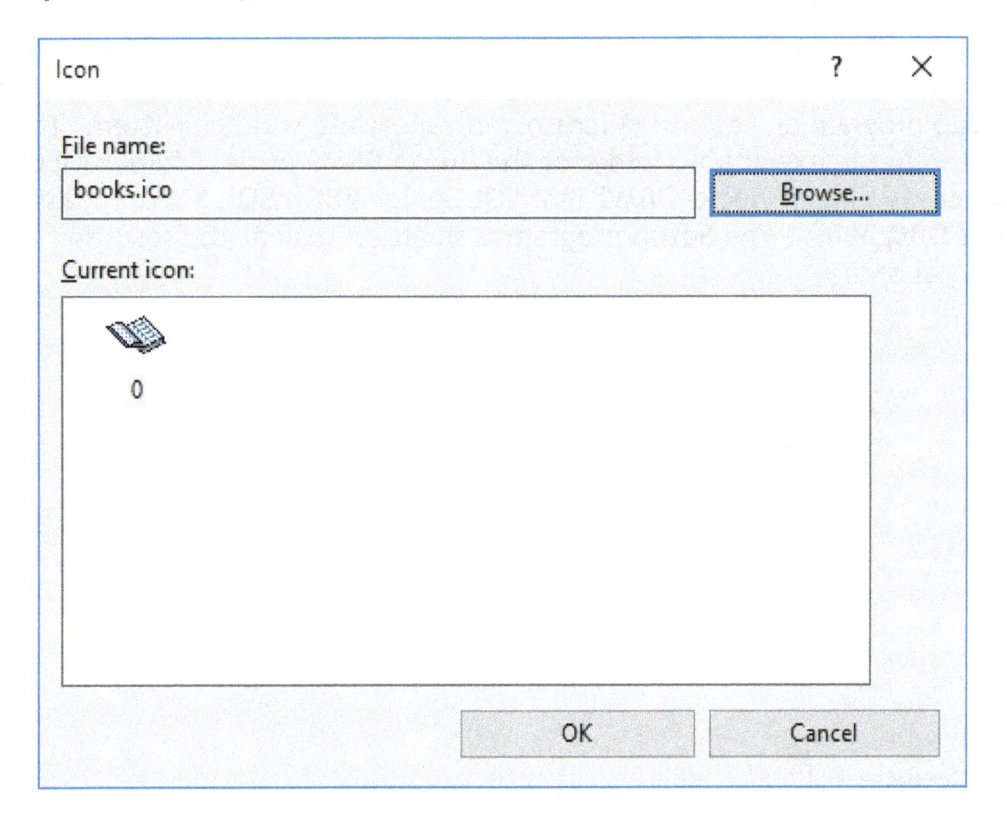

Select the desired icon and click **OK**.

Next, follow nearly identical steps to put a shortcut in the **User's Programs Menu** folder. The **Setup Wizard** has completed its job.

Building the Setup Program

Now, let's build the **Setup** program. In the Solution Explorer window, right-click the **Books DBMS** project and choose **Build** from the menu. After a short time, the **Setup** program and an msi (Microsoft Installer) file will be written. They will be located in the executable folder of the **Books DBMS** project folder (Access - **VBDB\Access\Class 8\Books DBMS\Bin**; SQL Server **VBDB\SQL Server\Class 8\Books DBMS\Bin**). The **Setup** program is small. A look at the resulting directory shows:

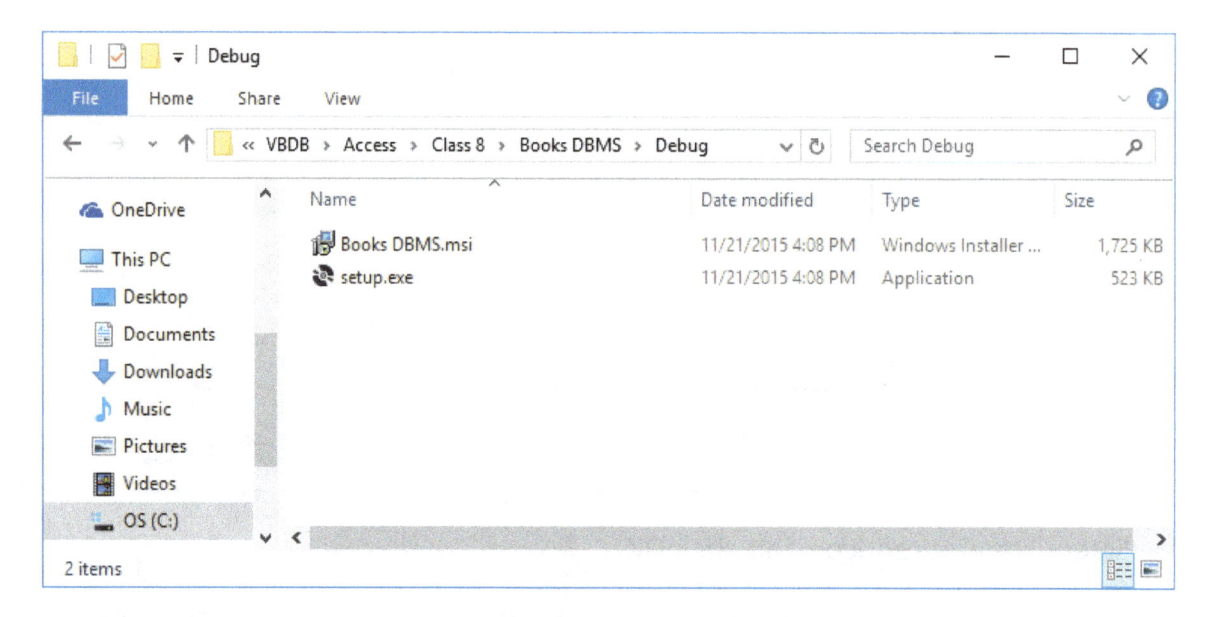

Use some media (zip disk, CD-ROM or downloaded files) to distribute these files your user base. Provide the user with the simple instruction to run the **Setup.exe** program and installation will occur.

Installing a Visual Basic Application

To install the program, simply run the **Setup.exe** program. These are the same brief instructions you need to provide a user. Users have become very familiar with installing software and running Setup type programs. Let's try the example just created and see what a nice installation interface is provided. Double-click the **Setup.exe** program from Example 8-3 and this introduction window should appear:

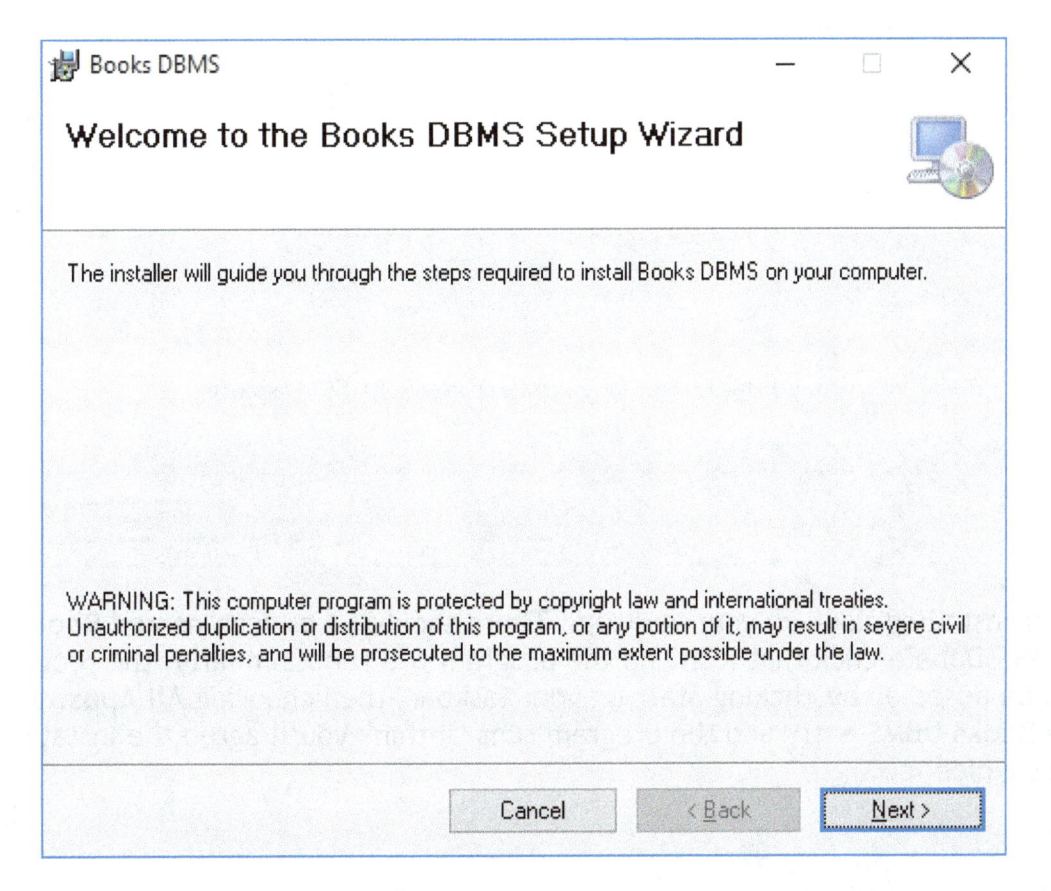

Click **Next** and you will be asked where you want the application installed.

8-44　　　　　　　　　Visual Basic and Databases

After a few clicks, installation is complete and you will see:

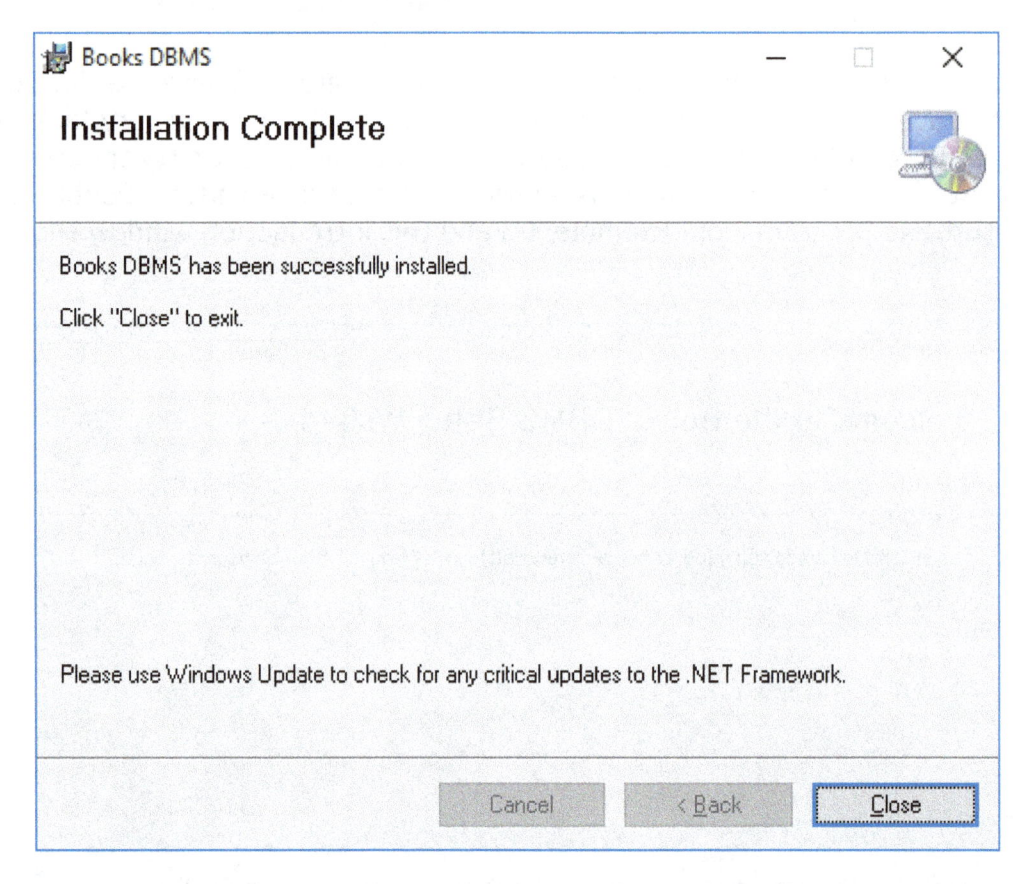

After installing, look on your desktop. There should be an icon named **Books DBMS**. Double-click that icon and the program will run. Similarly, the program can be accessed by clicking **Start** on your taskbar, then choosing **All Apps**. Click the **Books DBMS** entry and the program runs. I think you'll agree the installer does a nice job.

Summary

In this chapter, we gained the skills needed to be able to run a database application outside the Visual Basic design environment. Steps needed to open a database file were outlined. Creation of an executable version of an application was discussed, as was attaching a unique icon to each form.

The Visual Basic **Setup Wizard** was introduced. The steps required to create an application distribution package using the wizard were illustrated.

9
Database Design Considerations

Review and Preview

All work done in this course so far has involved using existing databases. I'm sure you are intimately familiar with the books database by now! Many times, as a database programmer, this may be the only task you are involved in – building database management systems for so-called legacy systems.

If, however, you embark on a new database project, suggested by others or developed by yourself, you will need to design the database structure and contents. In this chapter, we address some of the considerations you must make in designing a database from scratch. We also look at available tools for building databases.

Database Design

A key step in developing a **database** is proper **design**. If you take the time to design your database properly, you will save yourself many headaches in developing and maintaining the associated database management system. We will follow several steps in database design:

1. Database modeling
2. Information requirements
3. Table requirements
4. Field requirements
5. Database implementation
6. Database testing
7. Design refinements

It is difficult to discuss database design philosophy in general. As we discuss each of these steps, we will use, as an example, a modified version of the database used by our company to track its product sales. This sample database (named **KWSALES**) design should help guide you in any designs you take on. And, yes, KIDware's database management system is written entirely in Visual Basic – what else would we use? This brings up an interesting point. For a while, we searched for a product to handle our sales invoicing, but couldn't find a product that did what we wanted at a price we wanted to pay. The solution was to use our Visual Basic skills to build the exact product we wanted. You may find your Visual Basic skills will help you out in a similar, future, dilemma.

Database Modeling

Database modeling is the task of determining just what you want your database to do. Is it a mailing list to contact clients, a complete sales tracking system, a room reservation process or a school membership list? Create some functional specifications for your database. It is best to write all this information down to have a list to work from. And, such a list helps in drawing up a schedule for task development.

A good place to start in modeling your database could be the existing process for maintaining the same data. Many times, a database is developed to replace a 'less automatic' procedure for data management. For example, perhaps a small company has always tracked its sales using a three-ring binder with columns to store all the data. This is just a 'paper and pencil' version of a database table. Replacing an existing data management process with a new automatic database is sometimes a straightforward task. You simply model the existing process.

If you are creating a database for others to use, go talk to those people. Ask them how they would like things to work. After all, these are the people who have to be happy with your work, so including them early on helps maximize those chances of happiness. See if they have a system to replace or particular reports they need to produce. Ask lots of questions to understand your user's objectives.

In the **KWSALES** example we will use here, the database must contain all information about each sale that comes into the company. We want to know "who bought what and when they bought it." We want to track customer information and each order a particular customer makes. We want to know what each customer bought. And, we would like to know which products in our inventory are the most popular. Each of these functional specifications determines what information is needed in the database.

Information Requirements

After modeling your database requirements, you can begin to determine what **information** is needed in the database. The end-result is a shopping list of all information you want to store and have access to.

This may seem like a trivial step, but it's one of the most important. You have seen in your studies that a database is highly structured. This structure is what allows us to efficiently process SQL queries and to find information within the database. Once a database structure (tables, fields) is defined, it is difficult to change. Hence, if you omit an important piece of information from your database design, many times you have to throw out all your work and start over to include the new information. Such rework and modifications can be costly.

So, take lots of time in planning your information requirements. Check with those who will use the database to make sure you haven't forgotten anything. Is there an existing **information model**? With new databases, I will sometimes allow for a few 'empty fields' that can be used for account for possible omissions. Yes, I know this is a waste of storage space if they are never used, but they have also saved me lots of headaches.

For the **KWSALES** database, we had a model to work with - our previous sales tracking system written in Microsoft QuickBasic, a Visual Basic predecessor. The basic information needed in this database is:

- Customer Name
- Customer Mailing Address
- Customer Phone
- Order Date
- Product(s) Ordered

Database Design Considerations

Realize that your first set of information requirements may lead to additional requirements as you continue your database design. That is, your information list will grow. As an example, in the **KWSALES** database, when database fields are specified, the Customer Name will be separated into two pieces of information – a first name and a last name. The Customer Address will be broken into City, State, and Zip. When the database design is complete, the information list should also be complete and separated into its smallest components. So this first set of requirements can be general, but it must be complete. If, at a later time, we decide we also need the customer's e-mail address, a redesign would be necessary.

Table Requirements

At this point in the database design process, we know what we want the database to do and what general information is to be in the database. Now, we begin the detailed design of deciding what tables and fields will be available in the database. In this section, we address the problem of separating the information into **tables**.

Recall a **table** is a collection of information related to a particular topic. Databases use multiple tables to minimize and, hopefully eliminate, redundant data. The books database (**BooksDB.accDB**) we have been using is a good example of the separation of information into tables. The topics used by **BooksDB.accdb** for separation are: **Titles**, **Authors**, and **Publishers**. These are very logical groupings. And, most of the time, a grouping of information into tables is very logical. You just have to realize what the logic is!

The process of separating database information into individual tables is known as **database normalization**. The ultimate goal of proper normalization is to try to make sure each piece of information in the database appears just once. This is just a goal, not a requirement. Such complete elimination of redundancies is not always practical or desirable. Let's see how normalization works with the **KWSALES** database.

In **KWSALES**, for each sale, we need information about the buyer and details on what the buyer purchased. If we put all this information in a single table (a flat database), there would be a lot of repeated data. For example, if a particular buyer had ordered with our company ten times, that buyer's contact information would be repeated 10 times. If a particular product were purchased 1,000 times, that product's detailed description information would be repeated 1,000 times!

Repeated, or redundant, data presents two problems. The first is wasted space. The second is a problem of accuracy and maintenance. If a product's price changed, we would have to make sure we changed this pricing information everywhere it is listed in the single table. This presents a real potential for error – it would be easy to miss several entries. The solution to the redundancy problem is to place like information in like tables.

Database Design Considerations

For **KWSALES**, a logical grouping would be to put all the customer information in a unique table. We'll call that table **Customers**. Here, each record in the table will have information about a single KIDware customer. This way, if a customer's phone number changes, we only need to change it in one location. A second table will be named **Orders**. Each record in this table will represent a single KIDware order. And, a third logical grouping is **Products**. This table contains information describing each product in our inventory. At this point, our database design is:

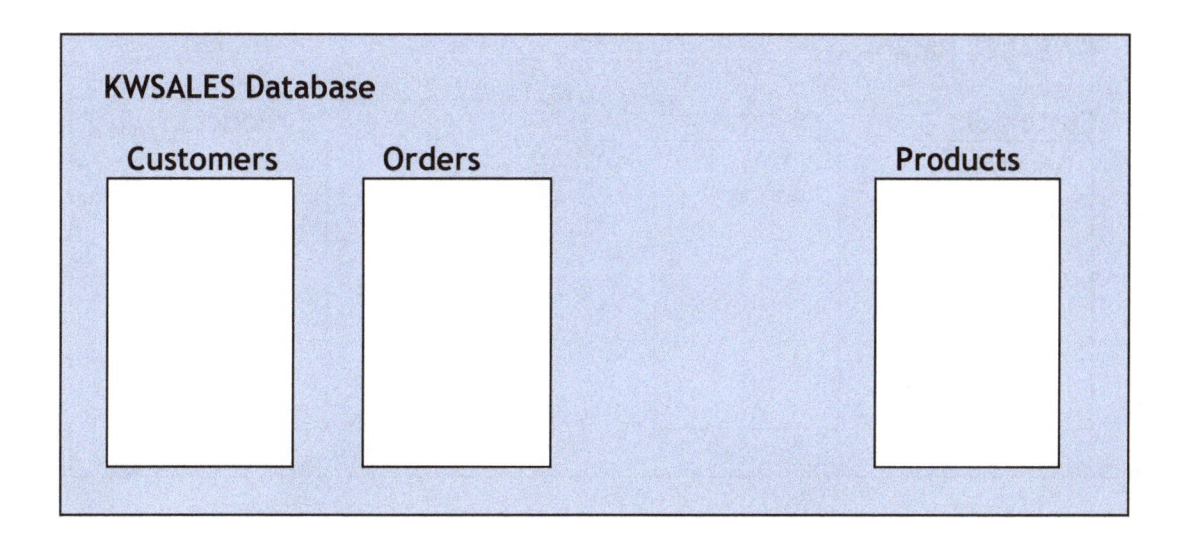

KWSALES Database

Customers   Orders   Products

A couple of words on naming conventions. In our database experience, we have found that it is best to have no embedded spaces in table or field names. They only cause problems. If you like the readability of multi-word names, use the underscore character (_) to separate the words, rather than spaces. Recall such characters were used for table and field names in the books database.

Also table and field names cannot duplicate reserved words in Visual Basic, ADO .NET, SQL or Access. Try to use unique sounding names. Names I've used and encountered problems with (because they are reserved) are: **Number**, **Date**, **Size**. Don't use such simple names!

Once database information is separated into tables, we need a way to relate one table to another. Data keys provide these relationships. Each entry (or record) in a table will usually have a unique identification value (a primary key). And then, foreign keys in other tables can reference primary keys. In the **Customers** table, we will have a **CustomerID** field, in the **Orders** table, an **OrderID** field, and in the **Products** table, a **ProductID** field. The **Orders** table will also have a **CustomerID** field (a foreign key) so we can associate an order with a customer.

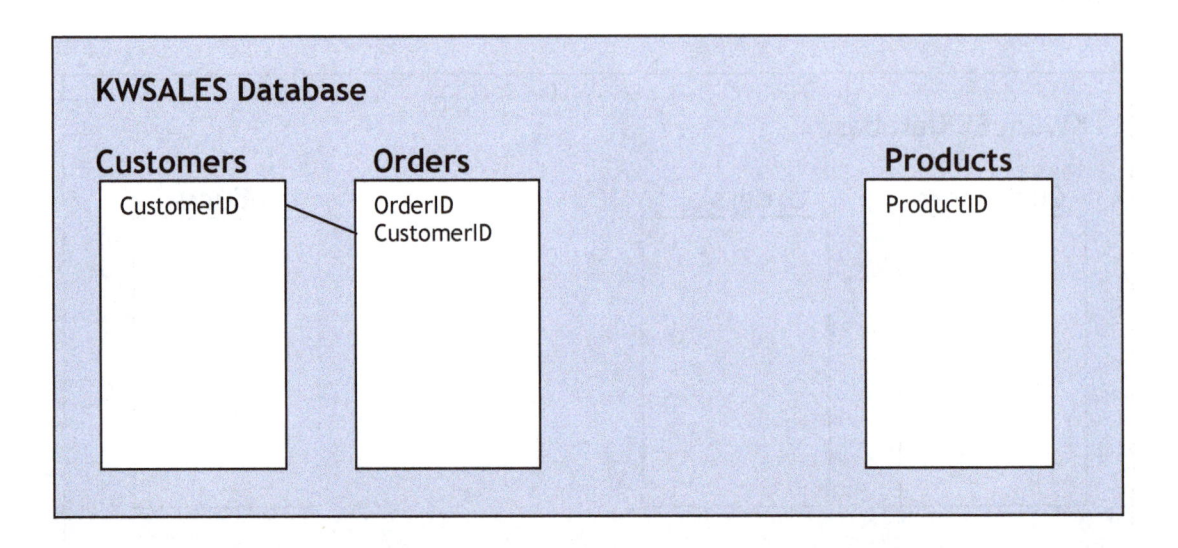

KWSALES Database

Customers
CustomerID

Orders
OrderID
CustomerID

Products
ProductID

In database terminology, we call the **Orders** table a **child table** and the **Customers** table a **parent table**. A child table shares common information that is stored in the parent table. Parent table information is specified once. Then, the child table can refer to a particular parent table record as many times as necessary, saving storage.

Database Design Considerations 9-9

Another table used in database normalization is a **lookup table**. An example of a lookup table would be a list of zip codes related to the corresponding city and state. In such a case, once the user entered a valid zip code, the city and state would appear on the data input form, saving the user typing steps, and saving you validation steps. Lookup tables are also used as **bridges** between database tables, relating foreign keys. Remember the **Title_Author** table in **BooksDB.accdb**. It is a lookup table. It relates ISBN values (corresponding to a book title) to a particular author (Au_ID). This table acts as a bridge between the **Titles** table and the **Authors** table. We will use a lookup table in **KWSALES** to bridge the **Orders** and **Products** table. This table will be called **Purchases**. This table will relate each order with the products purchased. The completed table structure for **KWSALES** is then:

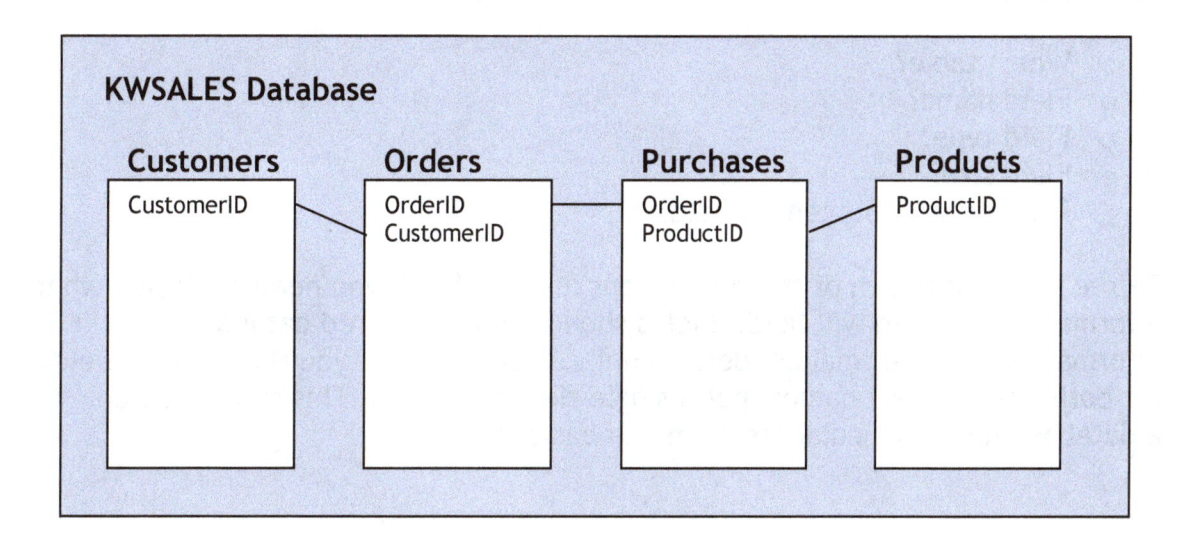

KWSALES Database

Customers	Orders	Purchases	Products
CustomerID	OrderID CustomerID	OrderID ProductID	ProductID

Notice table relationships are complete. We can move from one table to another via the identified keys.

The next step in database design gets down to the details of deciding what each data field should be.

Field Requirements

At this point in the database design process, we have specified, in general terms, what information is to be stored in the database and have developed the table structure. To relate the tables, we have defined the initial fields – primary and foreign keys. Now, we need to determine what additional **fields** are needed in the database so that all the required information is available. Each field added to the database requires some thought. Spending some time in properly defining the database fields will save you lots of time and trouble when you design the database management system.

Several questions should be answered in choosing fields for your database:

- Which table?
- Field name?
- Field type?
- Field size?
- Fixed or variable length field?

Before answering each of these questions about a field, you need to decide what information the field will hold. Fields should break required database information into the smallest desired units. For example, you should have fields for both first and last names, not a single field for name. This makes searching a database for a particular last name an easier task.

Database Design Considerations 9-11

Let's specify the fields for our **KWSALES** example and place them in tables. The **Customers** table holds information on each particular customer. In addition to the **CustomerID** field, the fields will be: **FirstName**, **LastName**, **Address**, **City**, **State**, and **Zip**. The **Orders** table will have one additional field, **OrderDate**. The **Purchases** table will have one additional field, **Quantity**. Finally, the **Products** table will add a **Description** field, a **Price** field, and a **NumberSold** field. The completed table and field structure is:

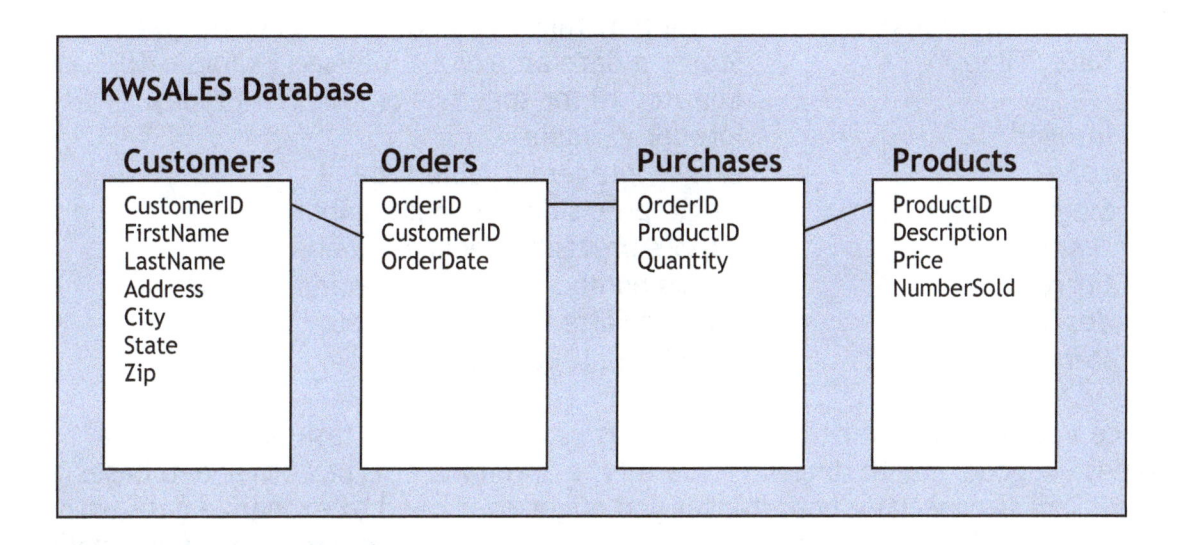

KWSALES Database

Customers	Orders	Purchases	Products
CustomerID	OrderID	OrderID	ProductID
FirstName	CustomerID	ProductID	Description
LastName	OrderDate	Quantity	Price
Address			NumberSold
City			
State			
Zip			

We now address the other questions for each field.

Field Types

Each field in a database must have a defined type. This is similar to typing variables in a Visual Basic application. The **field types** are:

Field Type	Description
Variable length text	String that takes up as much space as needed.
Fixed length text	String that takes up defined amount of space.
Date/Time	Stores a date and/or a time (see Example 10-2 in Chapter 10 for specifics on this field type).
Integer	Integer variable
Long	Larger integer variable type
Single	Single precision decimal number
Double	Double precision decimal number
Currency	Stores numbers with two decimal points
Yes/No	True or False Boolean variable type
Memo	Very large text field

Once your fields have been defined, it is usually a simple task to assign data types. A good way to determine data type is to look at types other databases use. This is especially important if you might ever need to exchange data with another database. In these cases, you need to make sure data types (especially string lengths) match.

There are some other considerations you should keep in mind when defining fields. In particular, pay attention to which fields are **primary keys** and **foreign keys**. We need to make sure primary keys have unique values for proper multi-table relations. Another thing to remember is that for quick and efficient searching of databases, **indexes** must be assigned when defining the database. Knowing which fields will be searched on will determine what indexes must be assigned.

Database Design Considerations 9-13

Now, for our example database - **KWSALES**. These are the types used for the fields in each table:

Table	Field	Type
Customers	CustomerID	Long
	FirstName	Text (40 Characters)
	LastName	Text (40 Characters)
	Address	Text (40 Characters)
	City	Text (40 Characters)
	State	Text (20 Characters)
	Zip	Text (10 Characters)
Orders	OrderID	Text (10 Characters)
	CustomerID	Long
	OrderDate	Date/Time
Purchases	OrderID	Text (10 Characters)
	ProductID	Text (10 Characters)
	Quantity	Integer
Products	ProductID	Text (10 Characters)
	Description	Text (40 Characters)
	Price	Currency
	NumberSold	Integer

In this database, we recognize **CustomerID**, **OrderID**, and **ProductID** will be **primary** keys and searchable fields. In addition, we will search on the customer's **LastName**, a common query.

Null Values

Related to the concept of Field types is the idea of a **Null** value. Whenever a database is designed, the empty database is filled with Null values (unless you assign a default value or specify Null values are not allowed). We looked at Null values briefly way back in Chapter 4 when we studied the use of SQL with databases.

Just what is a **Null** value? It means a particular database field's value is unknown. A numeric field with a zero value is not Null. A blank string field is not Null. An empty string is not Null. Null means Null!

As you progress in your database programming skills, you need to know how to work with Null values. Why? A major reason is that if you attempt to modify a field that does not allow Null values, the database engine will reject the modification. We need techniques to identify Null values and to establish Null values. The Visual Basic function **IsDBNull(Argument)** will tell us if the Argument is a Null value. And, the Visual Basic constant **DBNull.Value** can be used to set a variable to a Null value.

Primary key fields can never be Null. This is obvious. Any mathematical functions performed on your data using SQL aggregate functions will ignore Null values. For example, if you are averaging a column of numbers, any Nulls will not be included. If you want to include the Null values in the average, they must be replaced by zeroes.

In the **Weather Monitor** example in Chapter 10, we will examine ways of working with Null values in a database.

Database Design Implementation

Once your database design is complete (or at least the preliminary design is complete), you need to create the database. The method used to create the database depends on the type of database you are building. In this course, we have worked with Microsoft **Access** (ACE type) databases and **SQL Server** databases. There are different ways to create such databases.

For an **Access** database, you can:

- Use Microsoft Access
- Use Visual Basic ADOX data objects
- Use a third-party product (requiring purchase of that product)

Microsoft Access is the most widely used tool for creating ACE databases. It has many powerful features, including drag and drop interfaces. But, you need to purchase or own Access to use it. Fortunately, most users of products like Visual Basic also have Access. We will look at how to create the **KWSALES** database using Access. It is also possible to create an Access database using just **Visual Basic** and extended ADO .NET (**ADOX**) objects. We will show you how to use such objects to create the **KWSALES** database.

For a **SQL Server** database, you can:

- Use Microsoft Visual Studio's Server Explorer
- Use Visual Basic and SQL
- Use a third-party product (requiring purchase of that product)

Notice you already have the tools needed to build a SQL Server database since you have Visual Studio. We will create a SQL Server version of the **KWSALES** database using **Server Explorer**. And, we'll outline the steps needed to create the same database using just **Visual Basic** and **SQL**.

It is also possible to populate a database (add actual field values) at the same time you design the database. We will not do that here – we only create an empty database. It will be populated using a Visual Basic application in Chapter 10.

Building Databases with Microsoft Access

To build a database using **Microsoft Access**, you obviously need to have Access installed on your computer. This product is part of the Microsoft Office Suite. If you don't have Access or don't want to use Access, skip ahead to the notes on creating a database using Visual Basic.

As with many programs, the use of **Access** is best illustrated with an example. Here, we use Access to build our **KWSALES** database. The file will be named **KWSalesDB.accdb**. The process is straightforward. You define a table and then the fields within each table.

Example 9-1

KWSALES Database with Microsoft Access

In this example, we go through all the steps necessary to build the 4-table **KWSALES** database using **Microsoft Access**. We will build each table and add the associated data fields (along with any necessary keys and indexes) individually. For reference, the table and field structure is:

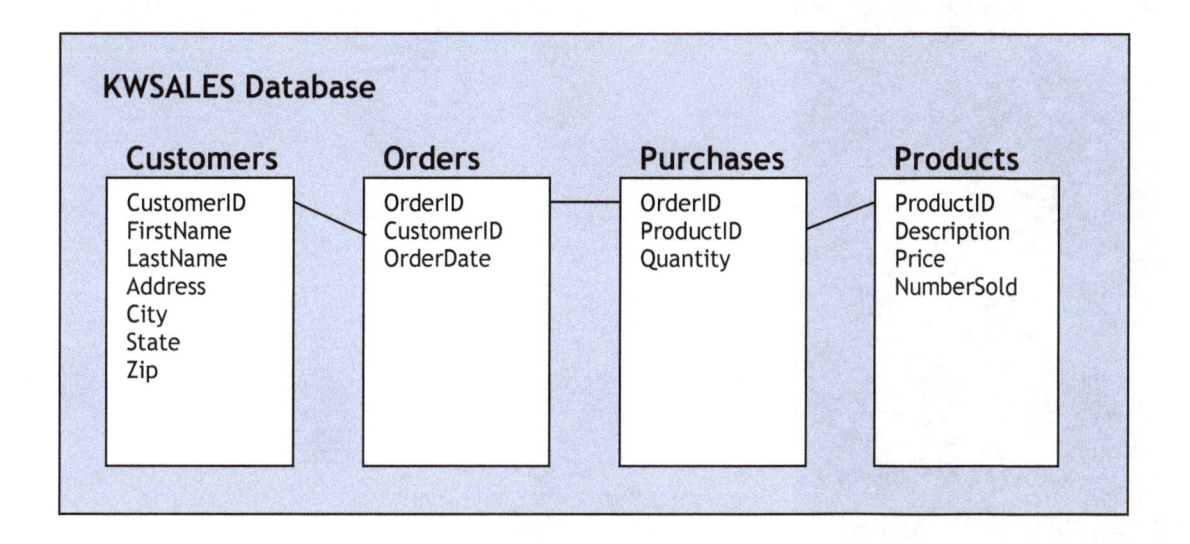

KWSALES Database

Customers	Orders	Purchases	Products
CustomerID FirstName LastName Address City State Zip	OrderID CustomerID OrderDate	OrderID ProductID Quantity	ProductID Description Price NumberSold

In this example, we use **Access** from **Office 365**.

9-18   Visual Basic and Databases

Getting Started

Start **Access**. A screen with entries like this should appear:

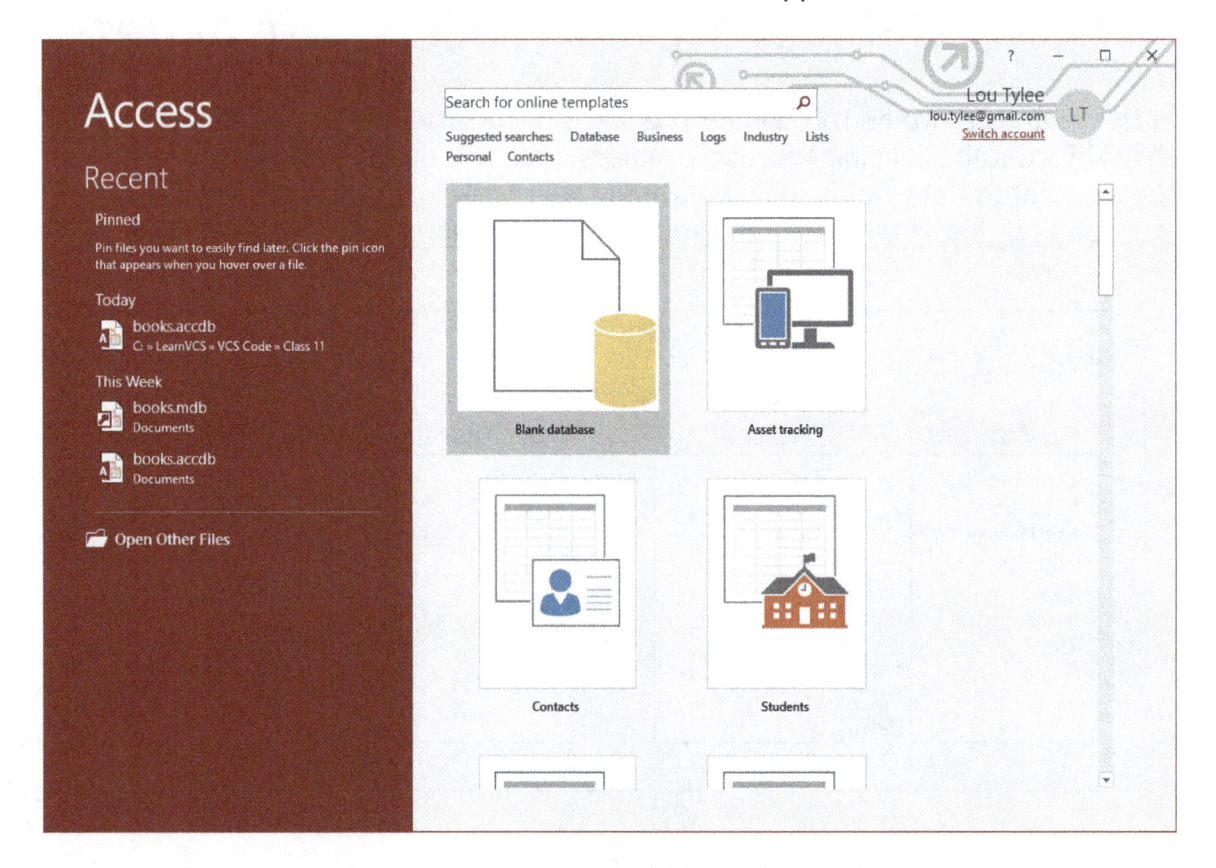

Choose **Blank Database**. Choose the desired directory, name your database **KWSALES** and click **Create**.

Database Design Considerations 9-19

This window will appear, allowing us to design our **KWSALES** database tables:

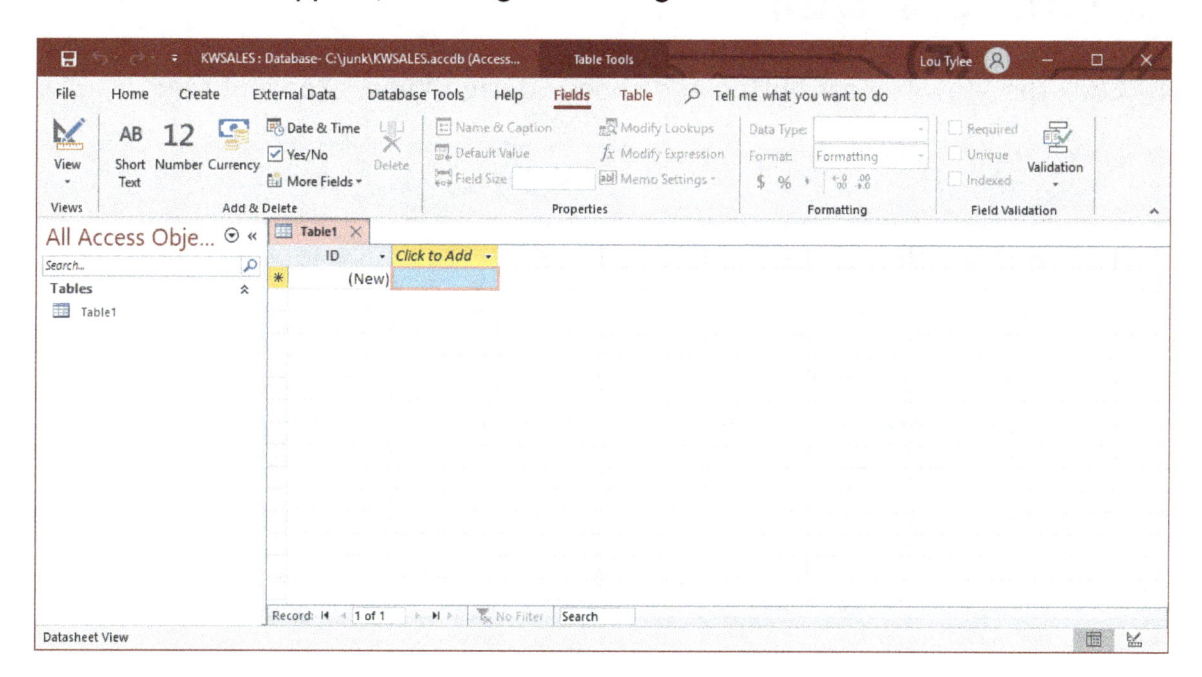

We follow the same steps for each table.

Customers Table

1. Click the **View** toolbar button and choose **Design View**. You will see:

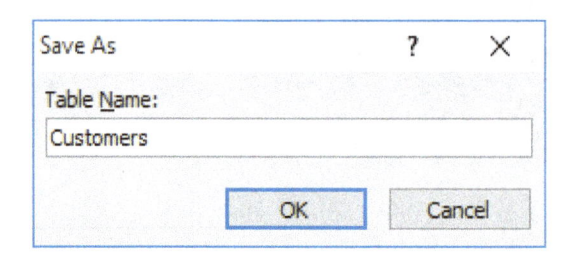

Name the table **Customers** as shown. You will then be taken to design view:

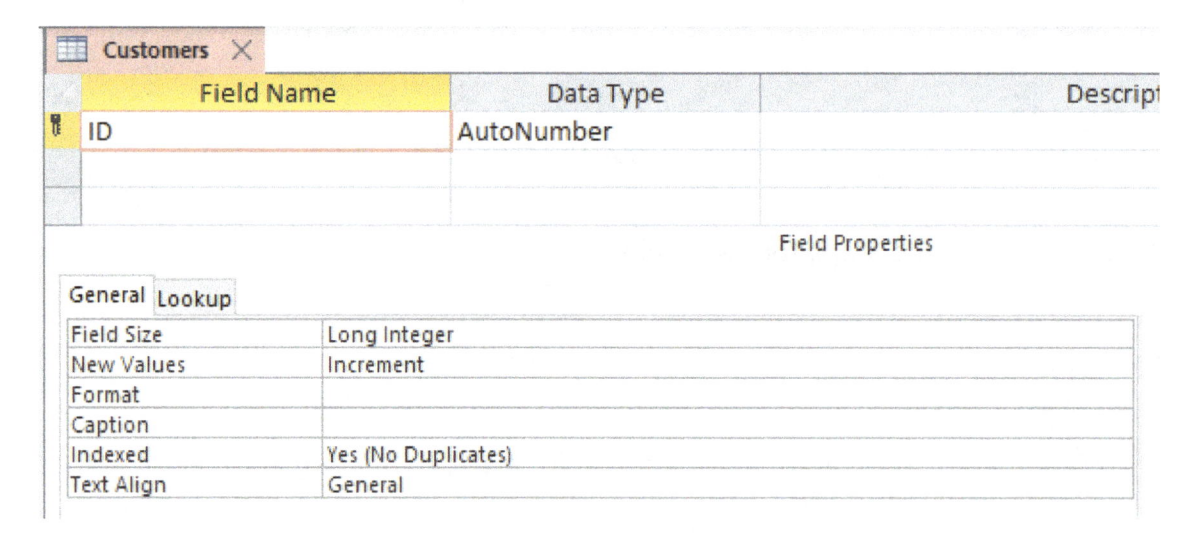

This is the grid used to define each field, so let's look at all that's here. You supply a **Field Name** for the field and define its **Data Type**. A special Data Type is **AutoNumber**. This is used for primary keys to insure unique values. Other options (appear on the **General** tab) include **AllowZeroLength** to allow an empty field and **Required** to make sure a particular field has a value. Each of these options is directly related to your database design.

Database Design Considerations 9-21

2. The first field in the **Customers** table is **CustomerID**. Enter that for a **Field Name** and select **AutoNumber** for **Data Type**. Continue adding the other fields using these choices:

Name	DataType	FieldSize
FirstName	Short Text	40
LastName	Short Text	40
Address	Short Text	40
City	Short Text	40
State	Short Text	20
Zip	Short Text	10

   Make all of the fields **Required** (we want to make sure we have a complete address).

   At this point, the design grid should look like this:

Customers	
Field Name	Data Type
CustomerID	AutoNumber
FirstName	Short Text
LastName	Short Text
Address	Short Text
City	Short Text
State	Short Text
Zip	Short Text

Now, we define the primary key and any indexes to allow quick searching. **CustomerID** is a primary field. If a little key doesn't appear next to the **CustomerID** row, we need to put one there. Right-click the **CustomerID** row and choose **Primary Key**. A small key now appears next to that entry indicating it is a primary key. We want **LastName** to be an index. Select the **LastName** row. On the **General** tab, set the **Indexed** property to **Yes (Duplicates OK)**. Here is the final table structure:

Field Name	Data Type
CustomerID	AutoNumber
FirstName	Short Text
LastName	Short Text
Address	Short Text
City	Short Text
State	Short Text
Zip	Short Text

Database Design Considerations   9-23

3. The table definition is now complete. Click the close button (**X**) in the upper right corner of the window. You will be asked to save the table:

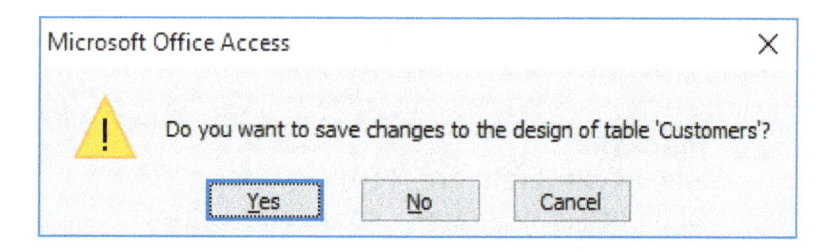

    > **Microsoft Office Access**
    >
    > ⚠ Do you want to save changes to the design of table 'Customers'?
    >
    > [Yes]   [No]   [Cancel]

   Click **Yes**. You will be returned to the **Access** design window where you will see the table has been added to the database:

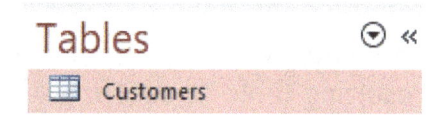

   > **Tables**
   >   Customers

   You can now add the next table.

Orders Table

1. Click the **Create** tab then select the **Table Design** toolbar button. This lets us create a new table in design view. Add the following fields:

Name	DataType
OrderID	Short Text (FieldSize = 10)
CustomerID	Number (Long Integer, no default value)
OrderDate	Date/Time

   We will use Visual Basic code to make sure **OrderID** is a unique value for each order (in Chapter 10). Make all fields **Required**.

2. Make the **OrderID** a primary key. Make the other two fields indexes (allow repeating values). The resulting table structure is:

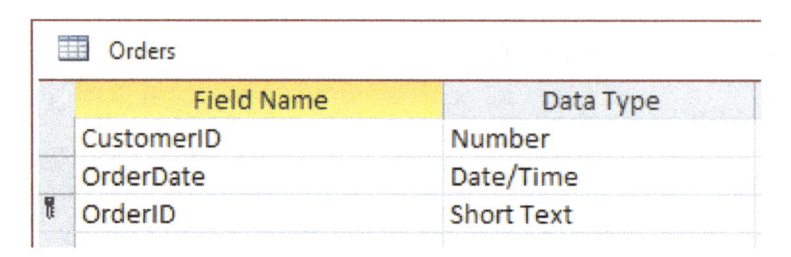

Field Name	Data Type
CustomerID	Number
OrderDate	Date/Time
OrderID	Short Text

3. Close the design window and save the table as **Orders**. There are now two tables in the database:

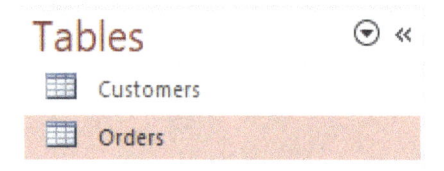

   Tables
   - Customers
   - Orders

Purchases Table

1. Create another table in design view. Add the following fields:

Name	DataType
OrderID	Short Text (FieldSize = 10)
ProductID	Short Text (FieldSize = 10)
Quantity	Number (Integer, no default value)

   Make only **OrderID** a **Required** field (we won't make someone order something!).

2. Add two indexes to the table, one for **OrderID** and one for **ProductID**. Here is the resulting table:

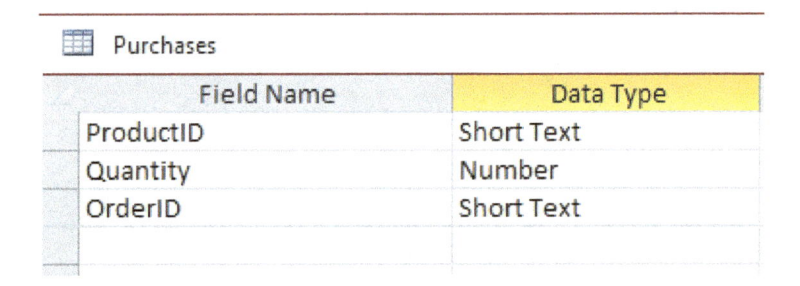

Field Name	Data Type
ProductID	Short Text
Quantity	Number
OrderID	Short Text

3. Close the window. Save the table as **Purchases**. You will see this message asking if you want to define a product key:

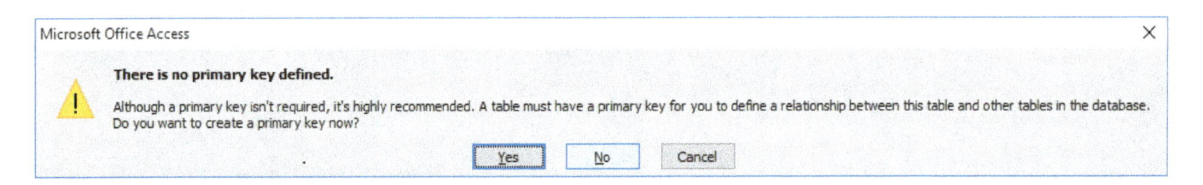

   Microsoft Office Access

   There is no primary key defined.

   Although a primary key isn't required, it's highly recommended. A table must have a primary key for you to define a relationship between this table and other tables in the database. Do you want to create a primary key now?

   [Yes] [No] [Cancel]

We don't need a primary key in this table since it acts as a lookup table. Click **No**.

There are now three tables in the **KWSALES** database:

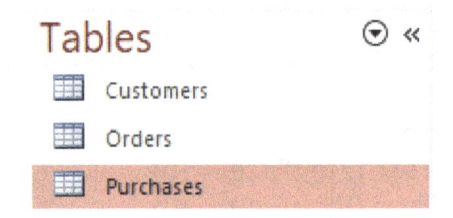

Tables
- Customers
- Orders
- **Purchases**

Products Table

1. Create the final table in design view. Add the following fields:

Name	DataType
ProductID	Short Text (FieldSize = 10)
Description	Short Text (FieldSize = 40)
Price	Currency
NumberSold	Number (Integer, no default value)

   ProductID is our product SKU (and, I forget what SKU stands for), a unique manufacturer serial number for each product. Make all fields **Required**.

2. Make **ProductID** a primary key. Here is the resulting structure:

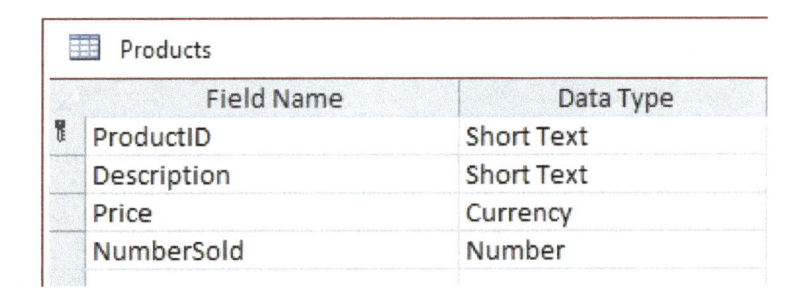

Field Name	Data Type
ProductID	Short Text
Description	Short Text
Price	Currency
NumberSold	Number

Close the window, saving the table as **Products**.

We now have all four tables needed by the **KWSALES** database:

- Customers
- Orders
- Products
- Purchases

Define Relationships

We have the four tables in the **KWSALES** database, but they are independent entities. A last step is to define the relationships between primary and/or foreign keys. Be aware you can only define relationships between two fields if they are the same data type.

1. Select the **Database Tools** tab from the **Access** main menu, then choose **Relationships**. The **Show Table** dialog will appear:

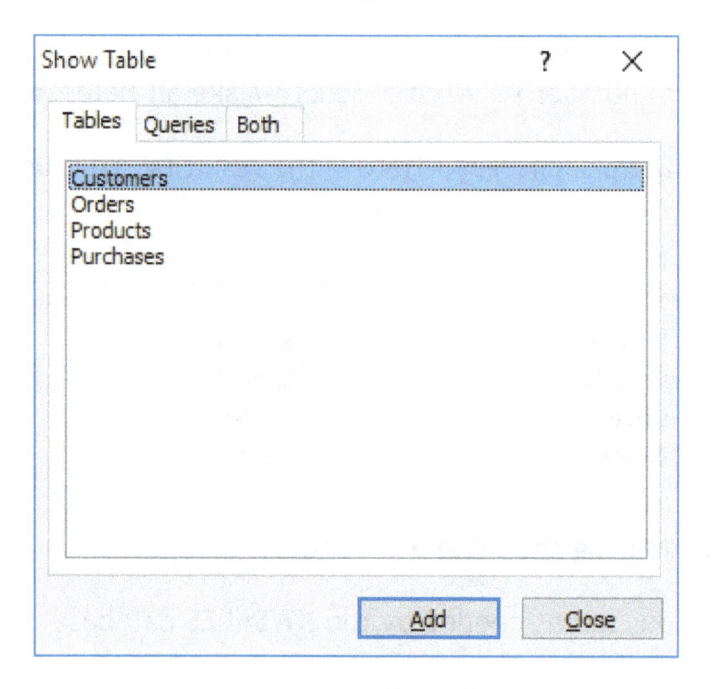

Select all the tables listed and click **Add**. Then close this dialog. The four tables will appear in the **Relationships** window (the primary keys are shown with little keys):

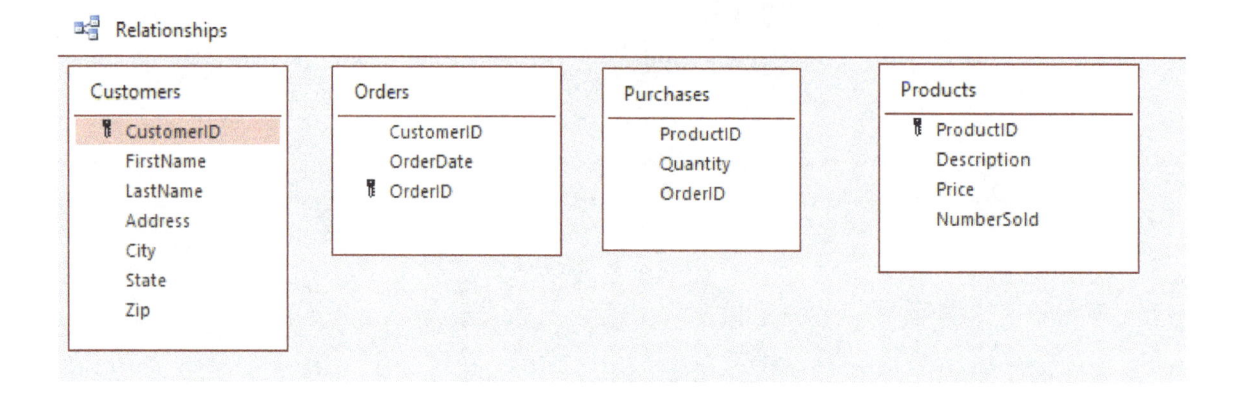

Database Design Considerations

2. To relate a key from one table to the next, simply drag that key from one table to the corresponding key in another table. For example, drag the **CustomerID** (primary key) from the **Customers** table to **CustomerID** (foreign key) in the **Orders** table. You will see:

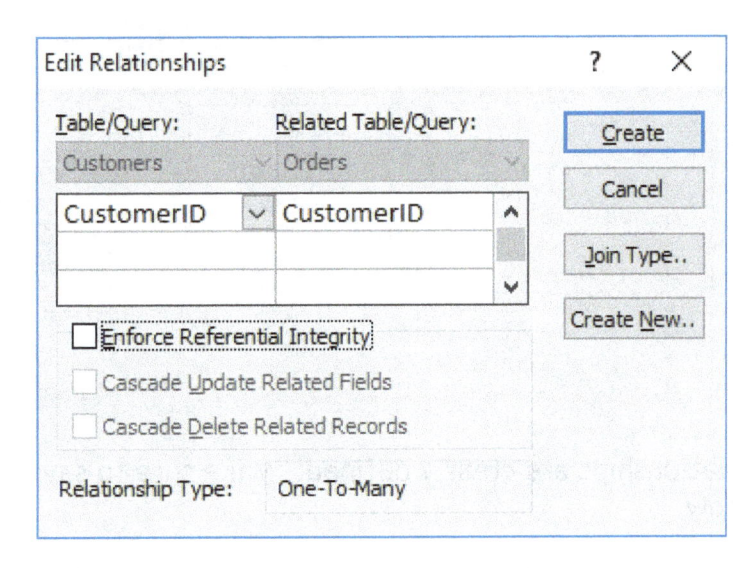

Click **Create** and the link is formed:

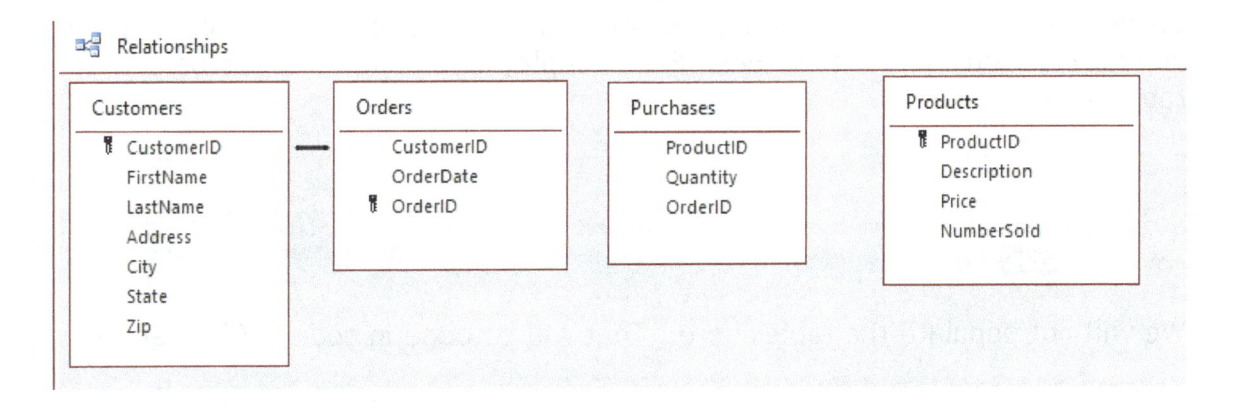

3. Create two more links. Link **OrderID** (primary key) in the **Orders** table to **OrderID** (foreign key) in the **Purchases** table. And, link **ProductID** (foreign key) in the **Purchases** table to **ProductID** (primary key) in the **Products** table. The **Relationships** window should now show:

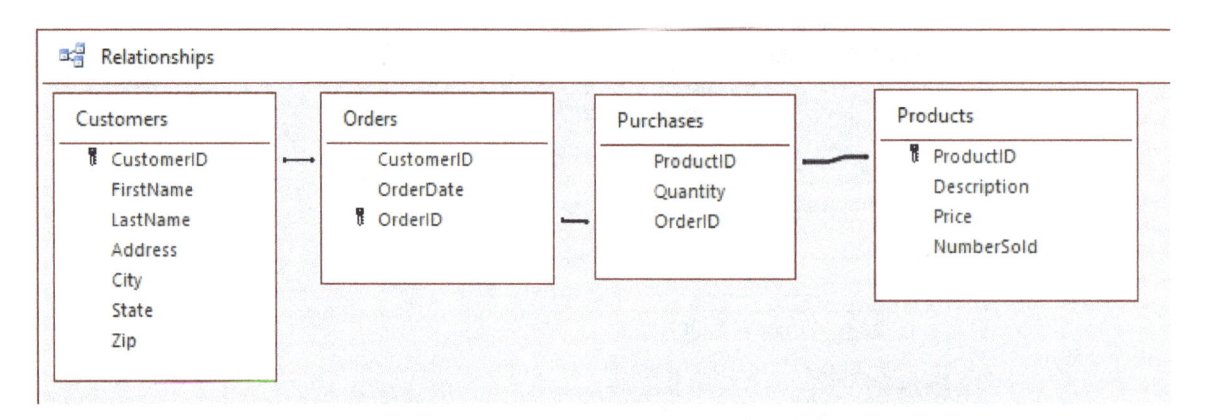

Relationships

Customers	Orders	Purchases	Products
CustomerID	CustomerID	ProductID	ProductID
FirstName	OrderDate	Quantity	Description
LastName	OrderID	OrderID	Price
Address			NumberSold
City			
State			
Zip			

All of the key relationships are clearly defined. Make sure to save these when closing the window.

The definition of the **KWSALES** database is now complete. This version of the database is saved as **KWSalesDB.accdb** in the **VBDB\Databases** folder. It is possible to add values to the tables at this point, if desired. Simply open a table and fill the result grid with values. For example, if you open the **Customers** table, you will see:

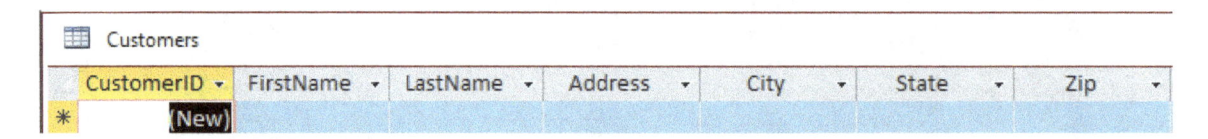

CustomerID	FirstName	LastName	Address	City	State	Zip
(New)						

We will not populate the tables here. That will be done in code in Chapter 10.

Building SQL Server Databases with Server Explorer

Microsoft **Visual Studio** can be used to build a **SQL Server** database. The **Server Explorer** tool aids in this construction.

Like the Access version of KWSALES, building a SQL Server version (named **SQLKWSalesDB.mdf**) is best illustrated with an example. Here, we use **Visual Studio** to build our **KWSALES** database. You will notice Server Explorer uses a different vocabulary for building a database. For example, **fields** are called **columns** and many of the data types have different names (**varchar** is used for a **Text** field). These differences should be easy to follow.

Example 9-2

KWSALES Database with Server Explorer

In this example, we go through all the steps necessary to build a SQL Server version (**SQLKWSalesDB.mdf**) of the 4-table **KWSALES** database using **Microsoft Visual Studio**. We will build each table and add the associated data fields (along with any necessary keys and indexes) individually. For reference, the table and field structure is:

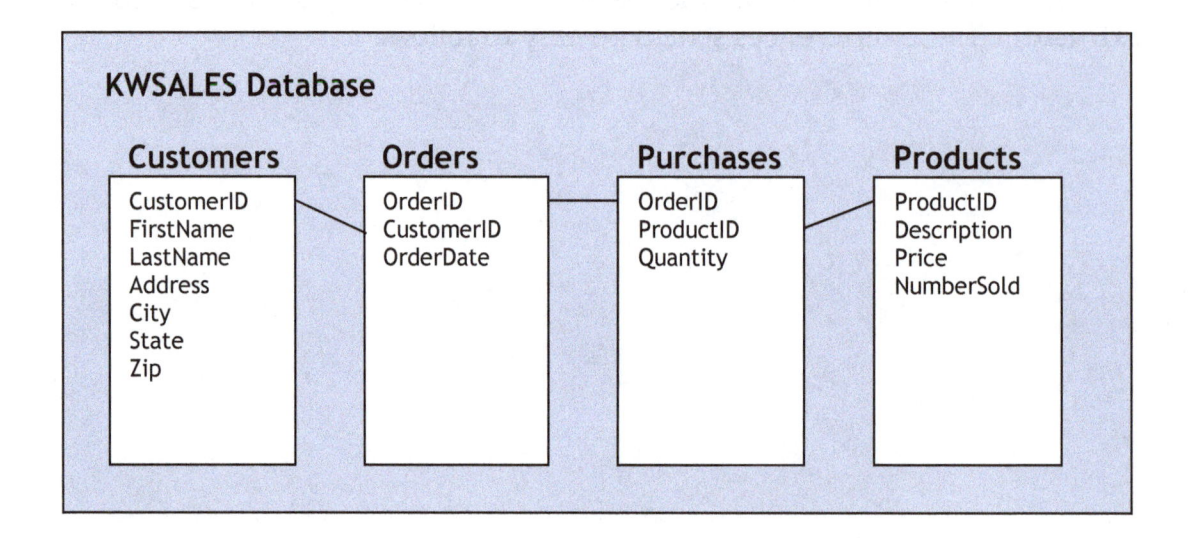

KWSALES Database

Customers
CustomerID
FirstName
LastName
Address
City
State
Zip

Orders
OrderID
CustomerID
OrderDate

Purchases
OrderID
ProductID
Quantity

Products
ProductID
Description
Price
NumberSold

Database Design Considerations 9-33

Getting Started

1. Start **Visual Studio**. Bring up **Server Explorer** by choosing the **View** menu option and selecting **Server Explorer**. Find this window:

   ```
   Server Explorer
   ▷  Azure
      Data Connections
   ▲  Servers
      ▷  LOULAPTOP
   ```

   Right-click **Data Connections** and choose **Create New SQL Server Database**. This window appears:

   ```
   Create New SQL Server Database

   Enter information to connect to a SQL Server, then specify the
   name of a database to create.

   Server name:
   DESKTOP-SGLR6T0\SQLEXPRESS        [Refresh]

   Log on to the server
   ● Use Windows Authentication
   ○ Use SQL Server Authentication
        User name:
        Password:
        □ Save my password

   New database name:
   SQLKWSalesDB

                            [OK]   [Cancel]
   ```

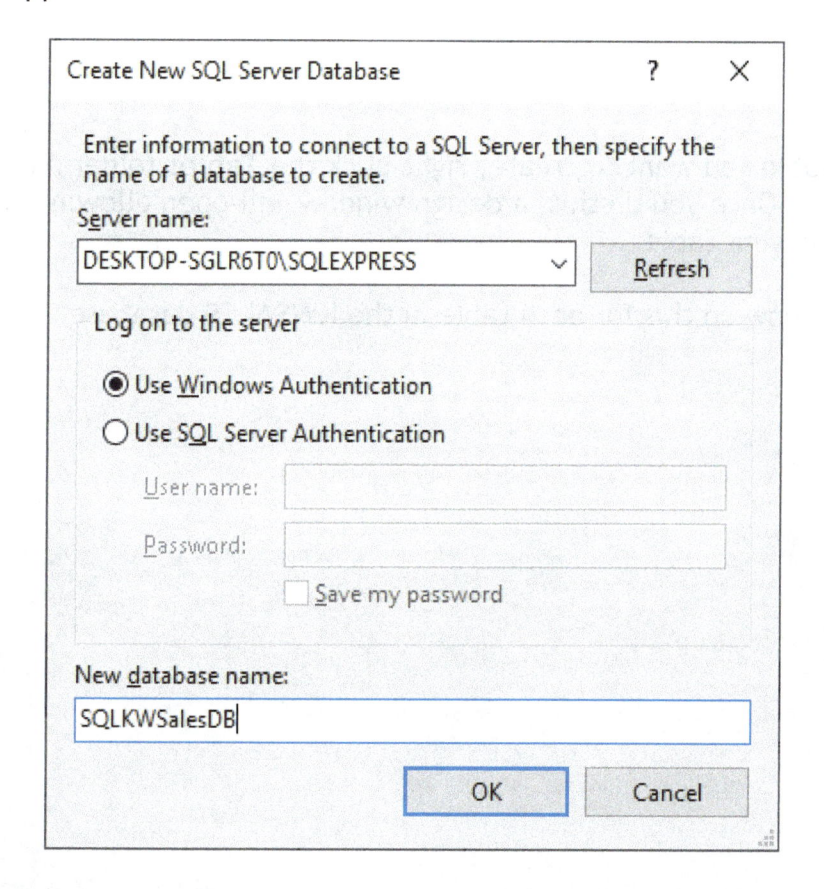

   Enter your **Server name** (your computer name followed by a backslash and **SQLEXPRESS**). Enter **SQLKWSalesDB** for the **New database name** and click **OK**.

2. The new database (I've expanded the connection to show included folders) will appear in the **Server Explorer** window under **Data Connections**:

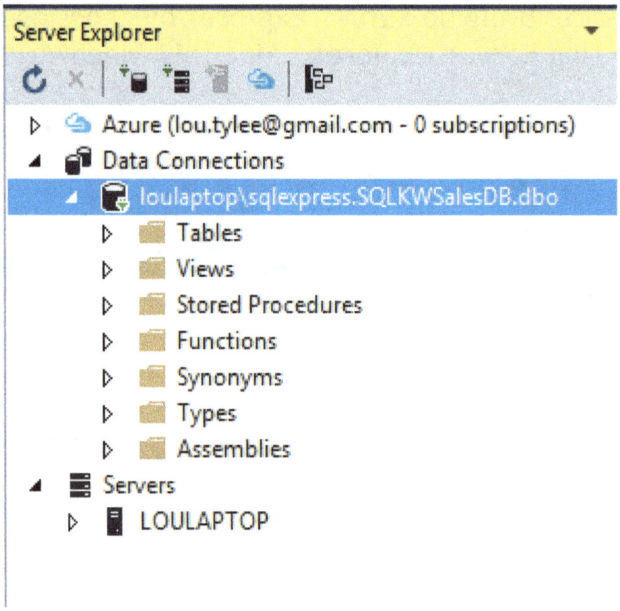
Server Explorer
Azure (lou.tylee@gmail.com - 0 subscriptions)
Data Connections
loulaptop\sqlexpress.SQLKWSalesDB.dbo
Tables
Views
Stored Procedures
Functions
Synonyms
Types
Assemblies
Servers
LOULAPTOP

For each table you want to create, right-click the **Tables** folder and choose **Add New Table**. Once you do this, a design window will open allowing you to enter the fields in your table.

3. We will now do this for each table in the **KWSALES** database.

Customers Table

1. Create a new table in design view. You will see:

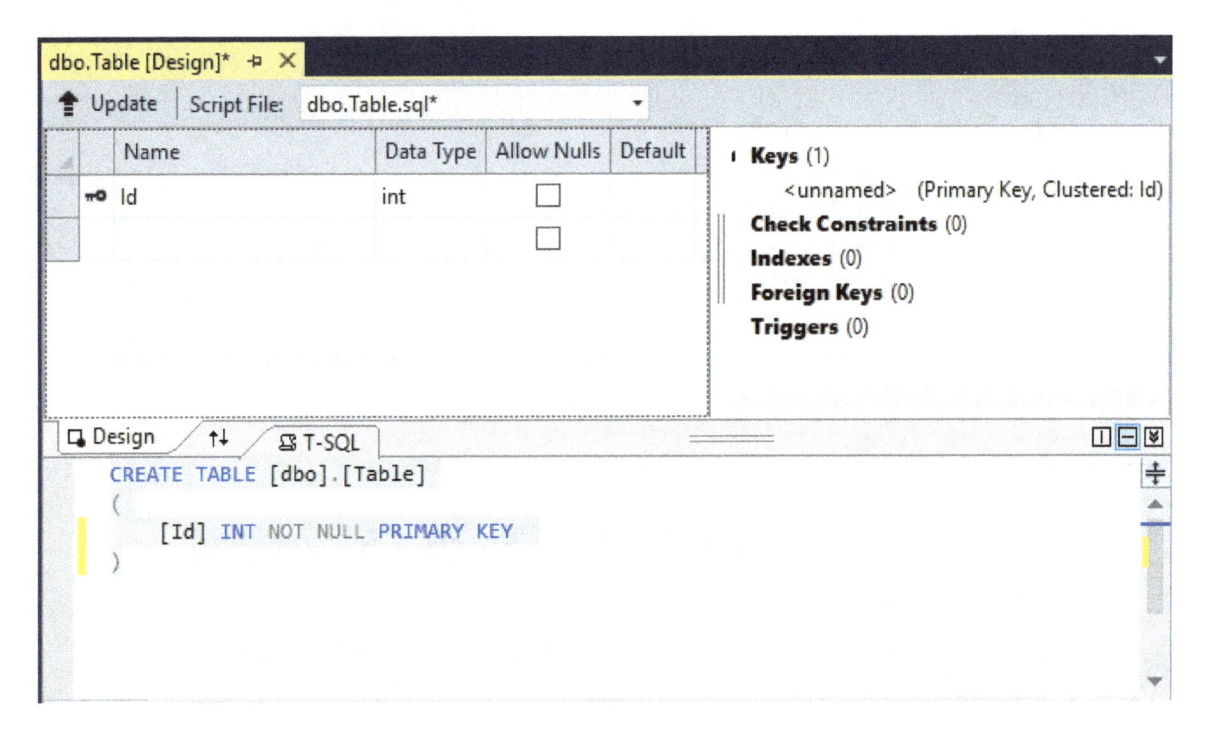

```
dbo.Table [Design]*
Update   Script File:  dbo.Table.sql*

 Name              Data Type   Allow Nulls   Default
 Id                int              □
                                    □

Keys (1)
    <unnamed>    (Primary Key, Clustered: Id)
Check Constraints (0)
Indexes (0)
Foreign Keys (0)
Triggers (0)

Design   T-SQL
CREATE TABLE [dbo].[Table]
(
    [Id] INT NOT NULL PRIMARY KEY
)
```

There is a grid to define each field (referred to as a column here). You supply a **Column Name** for the field and define its **Data Type**. You also decide if the field can be null. For each field, you set field (column) properties using the **Properties Window**. A special property is **Identity Specification**. This is used for primary keys to insure unique values (set **Is Identity** to **True**). To the right of the grid is where keys and indexes are defined. Below the grid is a **Design** window where the actual script language to create the table is written. Name the **Customers** table by changing the first line in the script pane to:

CREATE TABLE [dbo].[Customers]

2. The first field in the **Customers** table is **CustomerID**. Enter that for a **Column Name**, use a **bigint Data Type** and set the **Is Identity** property to **True**. Continue adding the other fields using these choices (the dimension indicates the length of the field):

Name	DataType
FirstName	varchar(40)
LastName	varchar(40)
Address	varchar(40)
City	varchar(40)
State	varchar(20)
Zip	varchar(10)

Make sure all of the fields do not allow **Null** values (we want to make sure we have a complete address).

At this point, the design grid should look like this:

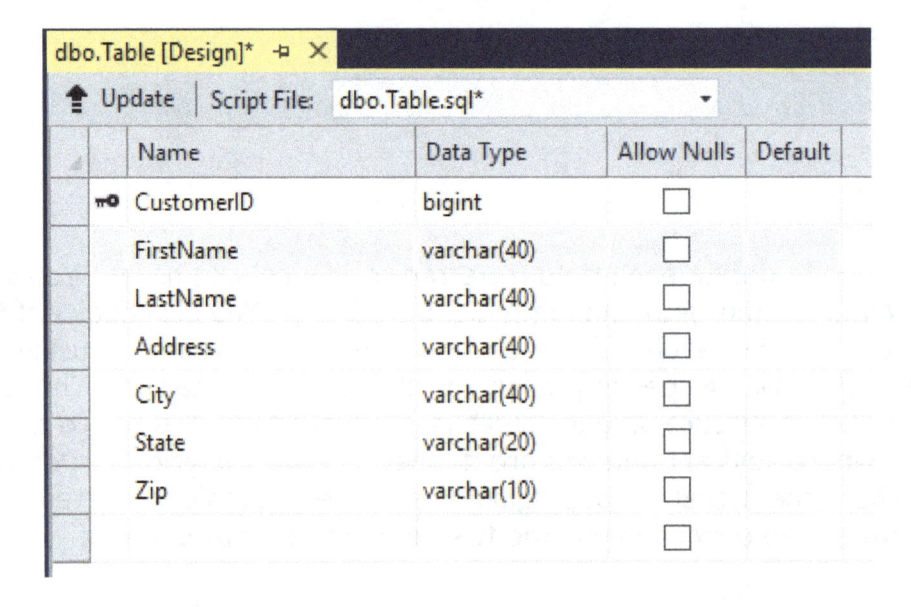

Name	Data Type	Allow Nulls	Default
CustomerID (PK)	bigint	☐	
FirstName	varchar(40)	☐	
LastName	varchar(40)	☐	
Address	varchar(40)	☐	
City	varchar(40)	☐	
State	varchar(20)	☐	
Zip	varchar(10)	☐	
		☐	

Now, we define the primary key and any indexes to allow quick searching. **CustomerID** is a primary field. If a small key does not appear next to that field, we need to put one there. Right-click the **CustomerID** row and choose **Set Primary Key**. A small key now appears next to that entry indicating it is a primary key.

We want **LastName** to be an index. Look for this pane:

▲ **Keys** (1)
    <unnamed>   (Primary Key, Clustered: CustomerID)
Check Constraints (0)
Indexes (0)
Foreign Keys (0)
Triggers (0)

Right-click **Indexes** and choose **Add New**, then **Index**. You will see an added index (**IX_Customers_Column**)

▲ **Keys** (1)
    <unnamed>   (Primary Key, Clustered: CustomerID)
Check Constraints (0)
▲ **Indexes** (1)
    IX_Customers_Column   (Column)
Foreign Keys (0)
Triggers (0)

Highlight the index that appears and go to the **Properties Window**. Choose the **Columns** property and click the ellipsis to see (I have expanded the column selections)

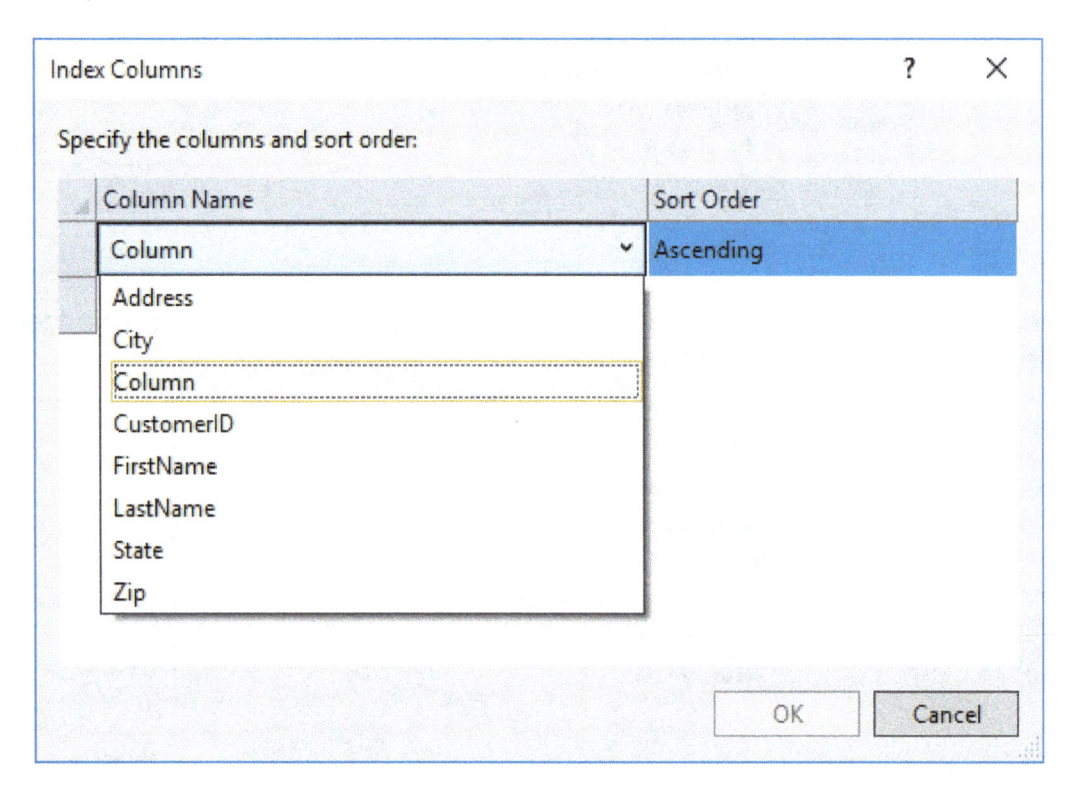

Choose the **LastName** column and have **Ascending Sort Order**

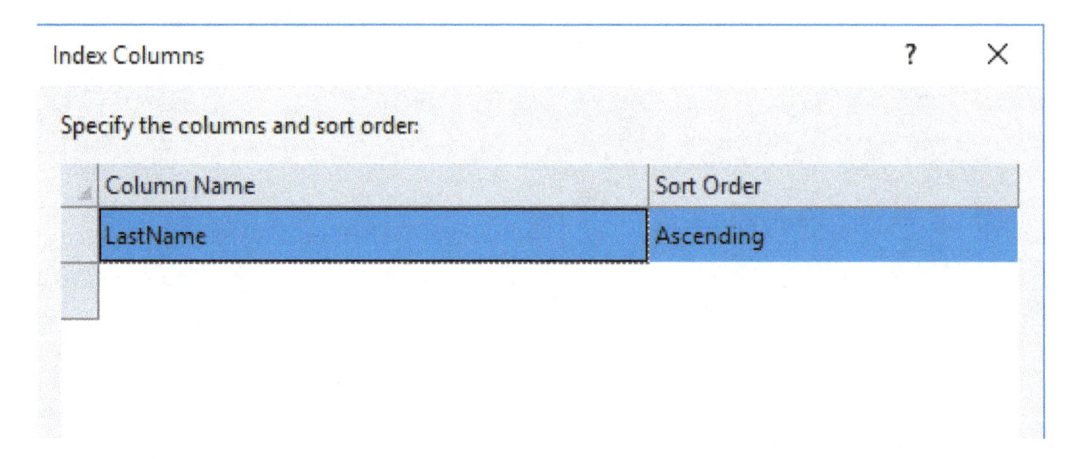

Click **OK**.

Database Design Considerations 9-39

Here is the final table design pane:

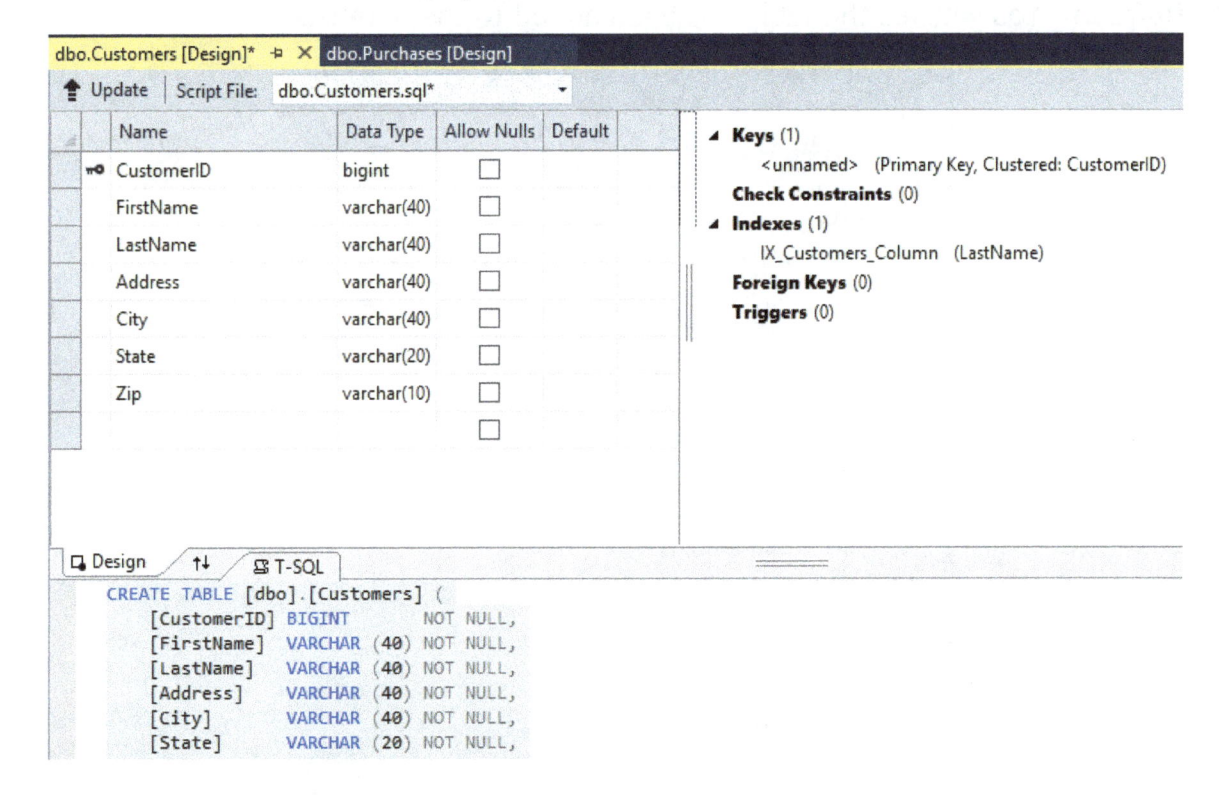

```
dbo.Customers [Design]*    dbo.Purchases [Design]
Update  Script File: dbo.Customers.sql*

   Name            Data Type     Allow Nulls  Default      ▲ Keys (1)
🔑 CustomerID      bigint        ☐                             <unnamed>  (Primary Key, Clustered: CustomerID)
   FirstName       varchar(40)   ☐                          Check Constraints (0)
   LastName        varchar(40)   ☐                          ▲ Indexes (1)
   Address         varchar(40)   ☐                             IX_Customers_Column  (LastName)
   City            varchar(40)   ☐                          Foreign Keys (0)
   State           varchar(20)   ☐                          Triggers (0)
   Zip             varchar(10)   ☐
                                 ☐

Design    ↑↓    T-SQL
   CREATE TABLE [dbo].[Customers] (
       [CustomerID] BIGINT        NOT NULL,
       [FirstName]  VARCHAR (40)  NOT NULL,
       [LastName]   VARCHAR (40)  NOT NULL,
       [Address]    VARCHAR (40)  NOT NULL,
       [City]       VARCHAR (40)  NOT NULL,
       [State]      VARCHAR (20)  NOT NULL,
```

The table definition is now complete. In the upper-left corner of the **Table Designer**, choose the **Update** button. In the **Preview Database Updates** dialog box, choose the **Update Database** button. Your changes are saved to the local database file.

Return to the **Server Explorer** window. Right-click the window and choose **Refresh**. You will see the table has been added to the database:

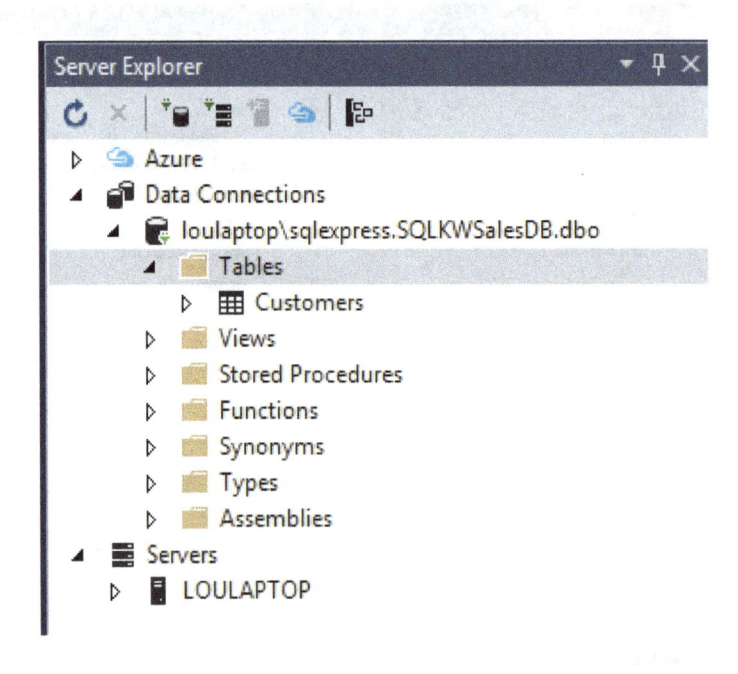

You can now add the next table.

Orders Table

1. Create a new table in the **Server Explorer** window. Follow the same steps we did for the Customers table to create this **Orders** table. Add the following fields:

Name	DataType
OrderID	varchar(10)
CustomerID	bigint
OrderDate	datetime

   We will use Visual Basic code to make sure **OrderID** is a unique value for each order (in Chapter 10). Make sure none of the fields allow nulls.

2. Make the **OrderID** a primary key. Make the other two fields indexes. The resulting design pane is (don't forget to modify the first line in the design script to save the table as **Orders**).

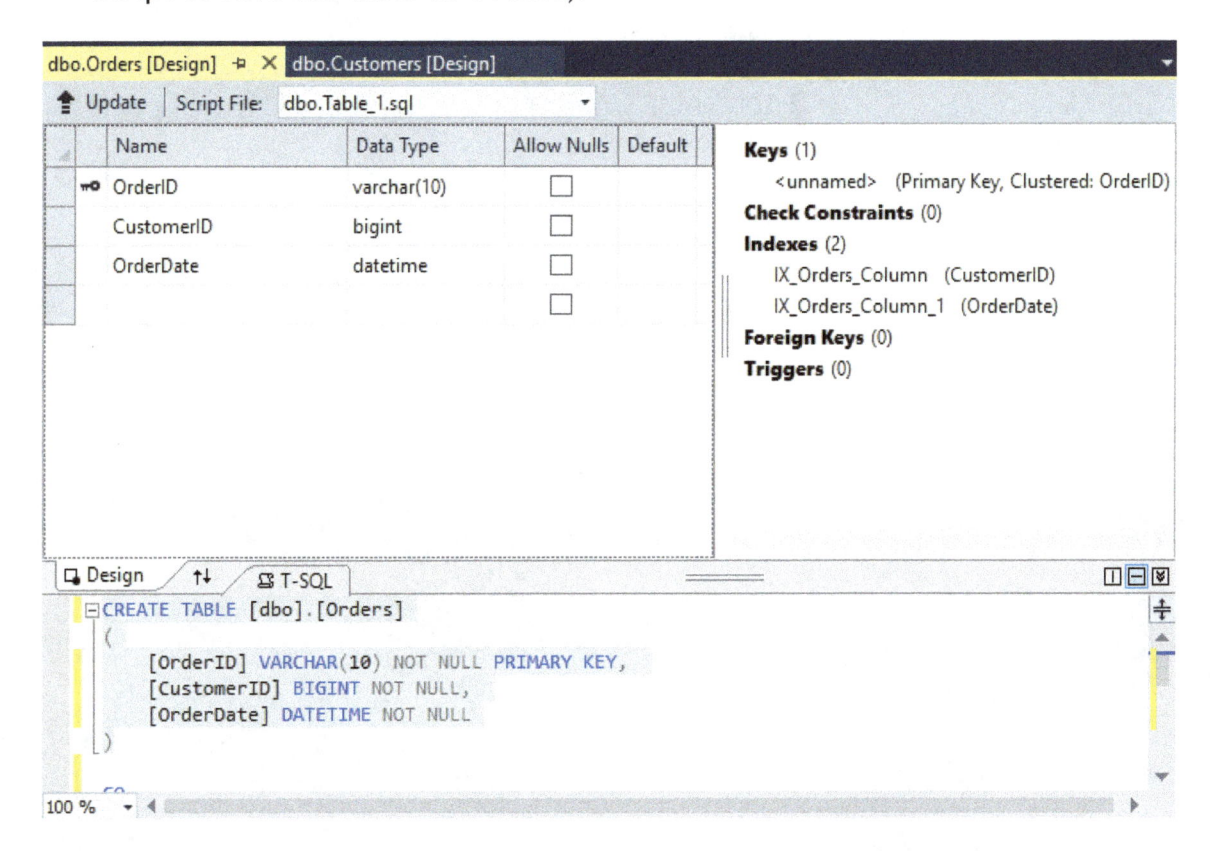

```
CREATE TABLE [dbo].[Orders]
(
    [OrderID] VARCHAR(10) NOT NULL PRIMARY KEY,
    [CustomerID] BIGINT NOT NULL,
    [OrderDate] DATETIME NOT NULL
)
```

Visual Basic and Databases

3. In the upper-left corner of the **Table Designer**, choose the **Update** button. In the **Preview Database Updates** dialog box, choose the **Update Database** button. Your changes are saved to the local database file (after refreshing the Server Explorer window).

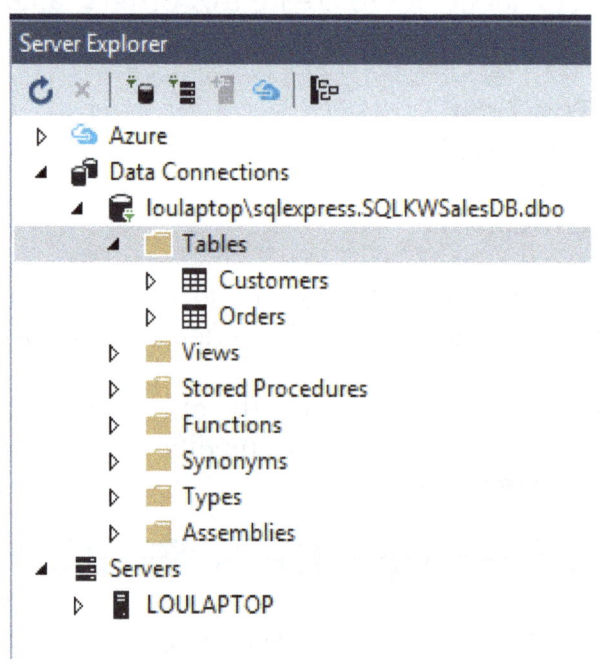

Purchases Table

1. Create another table in design view. Add the following fields:

Name	DataType
OrderID	varchar(10)
ProductID	varchar(10)
Quantity	int

   Set **Allow Nulls** to **Yes** for **ProductID** and **Quantity** (we won't make someone order something!).

2. We don't need a primary key in this table since it acts as a lookup table. Add two indexes to the table, one for **OrderID** and one for **ProductID**. Here is the resulting design pane:

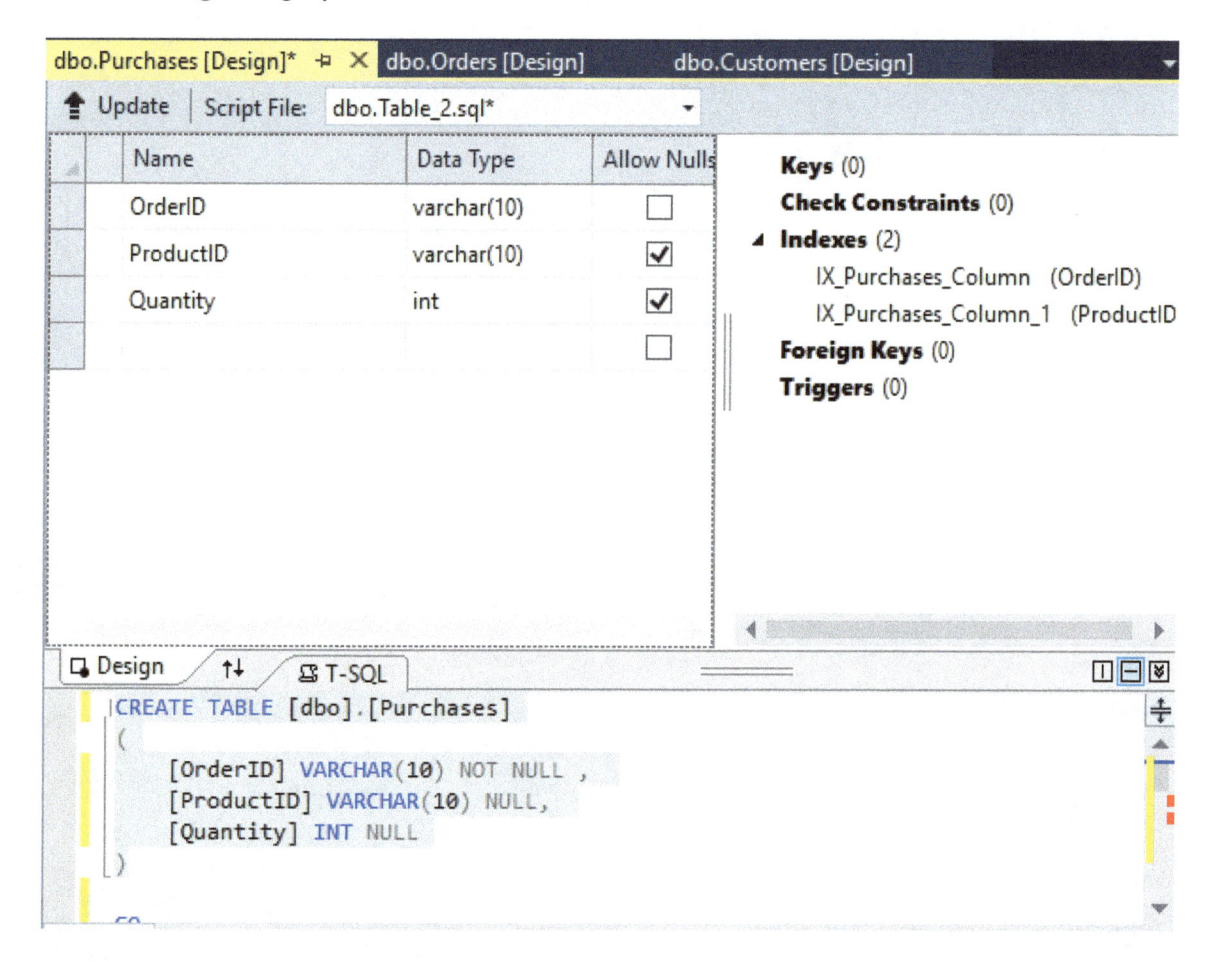

```
CREATE TABLE [dbo].[Purchases]
(
    [OrderID] VARCHAR(10) NOT NULL ,
    [ProductID] VARCHAR(10) NULL,
    [Quantity] INT NULL
)
```

Note the table is saved as **Purchases**.

In the upper-left corner of the **Table Designer**, choose the **Update** button. In the **Preview Database Updates** dialog box, choose the **Update Database** button. There are now three tables in the **KWSALES** database:

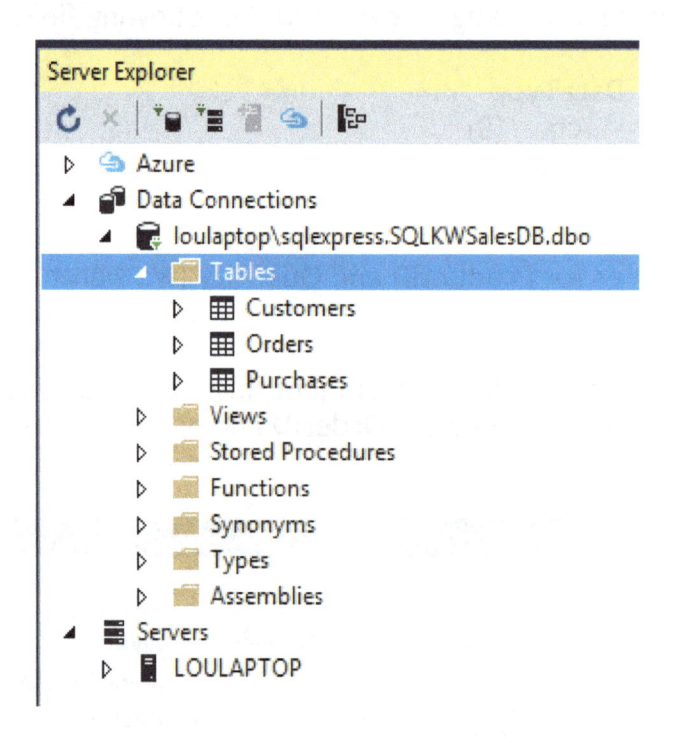

Products Table

1. Create the final table in design view. Add the following fields:

Name	DataType
ProductID	varchar(10)
Description	varchar(40)
Price	money
NumberSold	int

   ProductID is our product SKU (and, I forget what SKU stands for), a unique manufacturer serial number for each product. Do not allow any fields to accept a Null value.

2. Make **ProductID** a primary key. Here is the design pane (table saved as Products):

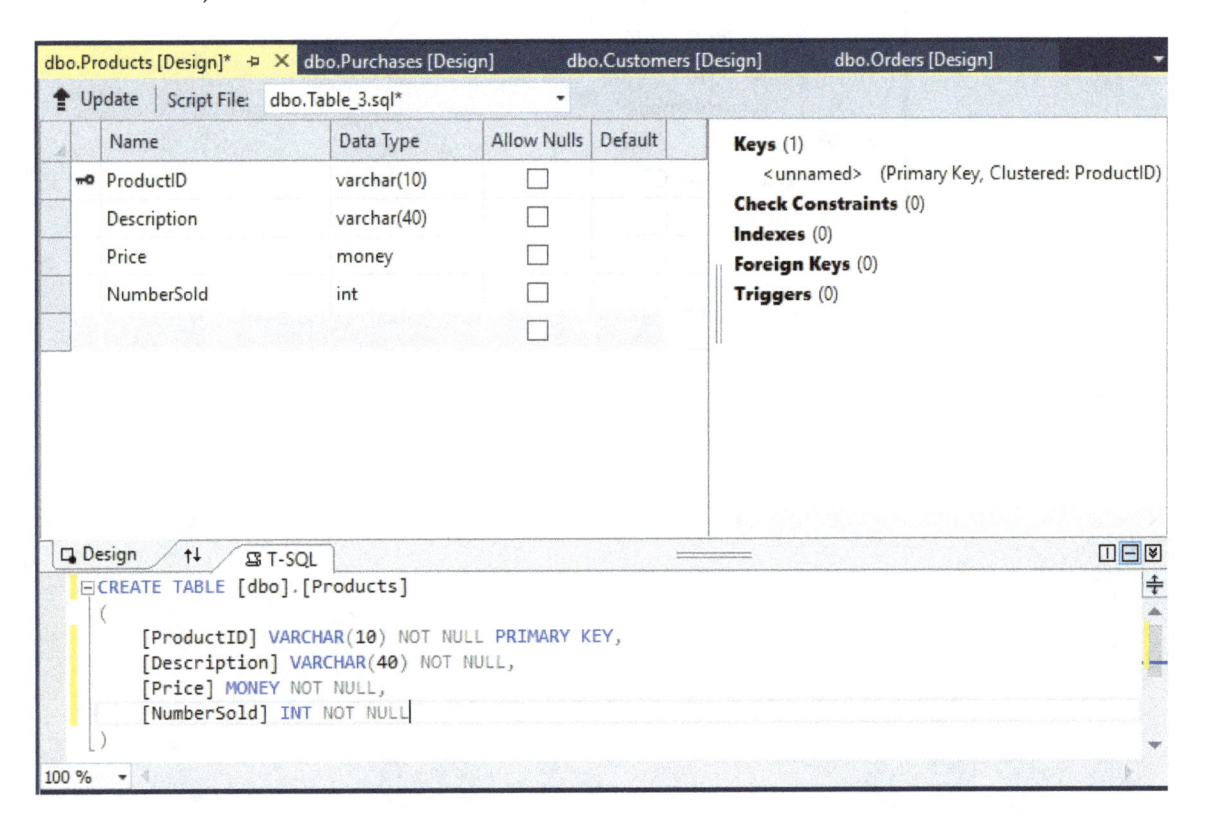

```sql
CREATE TABLE [dbo].[Products]
(
    [ProductID] VARCHAR(10) NOT NULL PRIMARY KEY,
    [Description] VARCHAR(40) NOT NULL,
    [Price] MONEY NOT NULL,
    [NumberSold] INT NOT NULL
)
```

In the upper-left corner of the **Table Designer**, choose the **Update** button. In the **Preview Database Updates** dialog box, choose the **Update Database** button. We now have all four tables needed by the **KWSALES** database:

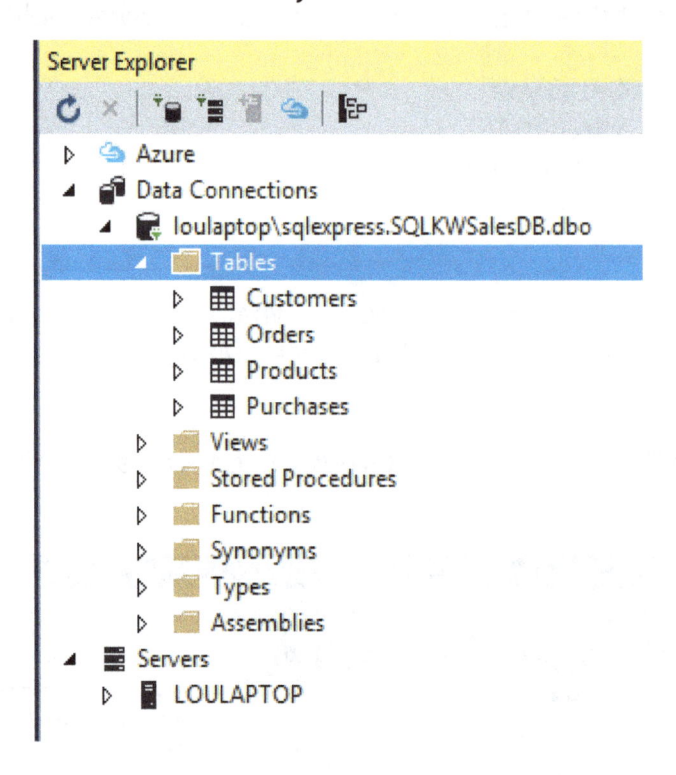

Database Design Considerations 9-47

Define Relationships

We have the four tables in the **KWSALES** database, but they are independent entities. A last step is to define the relationships between primary and/or foreign keys. Be aware you can only define relationships between two fields if they are the same data type.

Here is a graphic depiction of the relationships we want to define

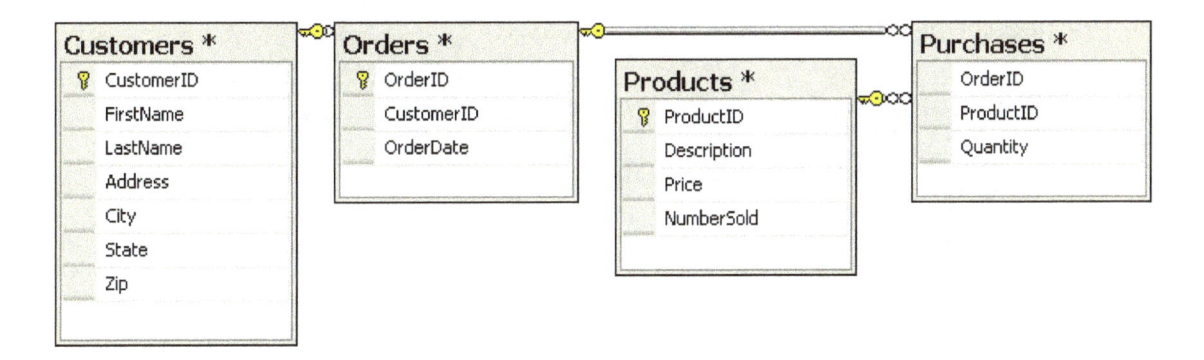

```
Customers *              Orders *                                    Purchases *
  CustomerID               OrderID          Products *                 OrderID
  FirstName                CustomerID         ProductID                ProductID
  LastName                 OrderDate          Description              Quantity
  Address                                     Price
  City                                        NumberSold
  State
  Zip
```

To define these, we need to modify script code in the table designers.

1. To relate a foreign key from one table with a primary key in another table, right-click the table holding the foreign key and choose **Open Table Definition**. As an example, we want to relate the **CustomerID** field (foreign key) in **Orders** with the **CustomerID** (primary key) in **Customers**. To do this, right-click the **Orders** table in Server Explorer and choose **Open Table Definition**. In the right-side of the design pane, right-click **Foreign Keys** then choose **Add New Foreign Key**. A default key will be formed - You will see:

   ▲ **Keys** (1)
        <unnamed>   (Primary Key, Clustered: Ord(
      Check Constraints (0)
   ▲ **Indexes** (2)
        IX_Orders_Column   (CustomerID)
        IX_Orders_Column_1   (OrderDate)
   ▲ **Foreign Keys** (1)
        FK_Orders_ToTable   (ToTableColumn)
      Triggers (0)

Click the script pane (**Design** tab) under the table definition, and replace the default definition of the foreign key reference with the following:

CONSTRAINT [FK_Orders_CustomerID] FOREIGN KEY ([CustomerID]) REFERENCES [dbo].[Customers] ([CustomerID])

This says we have a constraint (relationship) named **FK_Orders_CustomerID** that relates the **CustomerID** field in the **Orders** table with the **CustomerID** field in the **Customers** table.

The finished script pane for **Orders** appears as:

```
CREATE TABLE [dbo].[Orders] (
    [OrderID]    VARCHAR (10)  NOT NULL,
    [CustomerID] BIGINT        NOT NULL,
    [OrderDate]  DATETIME      NOT NULL,
    PRIMARY KEY CLUSTERED ([OrderID] ASC),
    CONSTRAINT [FK_Orders_CustomerID] FOREIGN KEY ([CustomerID]) REFERENCES [dbo].[Customers]
```

We need two more relationships using foreign keys in the **Purchases** table. We follow the same steps.

2. We want to relate the **OrderID** field (foreign key) in **Purchases** with the **OrderID** (primary key) in **Orders**. To do this, right-click the **Purchases** table in Server Explorer and choose **Open Table Definition**. In the right-side of the design pane, right-click **Foreign Keys** then choose **Add New Foreign Key**. A default key will be formed.

Click the script pane (**Design** tab) under the table definition, and replace the default definition of the foreign key reference with the following:

CONSTRAINT [FK_Purchases_OrderID] FOREIGN KEY ([OrderID]) REFERENCES [dbo].[Orders] ([OrderID]),

Database Design Considerations

3. Lastly, we want to relate the **ProductID** field (foreign key) in **Purchases** with the **ProductID** (primary key) in **Products**. The Purchases table should still be displayed. In the right-side of the design pane, right-click **Foreign Keys** then choose **Add New Foreign Key.** A default key will be formed.

Click the script pane (**Design** tab) under the table definition, and replace the default definition of the foreign key reference with the following:

CONSTRAINT [FK_Purchases_ProductID] FOREIGN KEY ([ProductID]) REFERENCES [dbo].[Products] ([ProductID]),

The finished script pane for **Purchases** appears as:

```sql
CREATE TABLE [dbo].[Purchases] (
    [OrderID]   VARCHAR (10) NOT NULL,
    [ProductID] VARCHAR (10) NULL,
    [Quantity]  INT          NULL,
    CONSTRAINT [FK_Purchases_OrderID] FOREIGN KEY ([OrderID]) REFERENCES [dbo].[Orders] ([OrderID]),
    CONSTRAINT [FK_Purchases_ProductID] FOREIGN KEY ([ProductID]) REFERENCES [dbo].[Products] ([ProductID])
);
```

All of the key relationships are clearly defined. Click **Update**, then choose **Update Database.**

The definition of the **KWSALES** database is now complete. This SQL Server version of the database is saved as **SQLKWSalesDB.mdf** in the **VBDB\Databases** folder. It is possible to populate the database using Server Explorer, if desired. To do this, right-click a table and choose **Show Table Data**. A window will open allowing you to add values to a grid. For example, if you choose the **Customers** table, you will see:

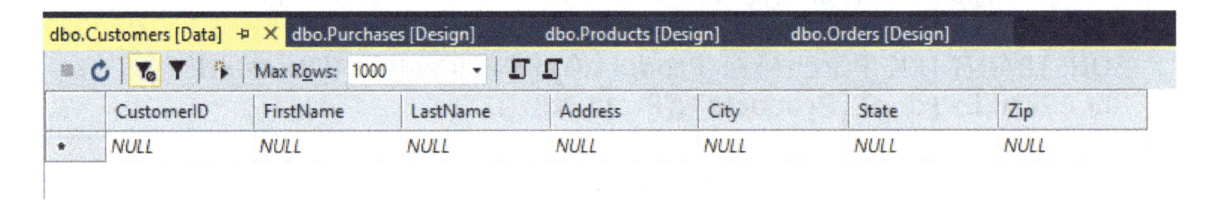

CustomerID	FirstName	LastName	Address	City	State	Zip
NULL	NULL	NULL	NULL	NULL	NULL	NULL

We will not populate the tables here. That will be done in code in Chapter 10.

You may wonder where SQL Server stores this database on your computer. If you used default settings, it will be in a folder something like this:

C:\Program Files\Microsoft SQL Server\MSSQL14.SQLEXPRESS\MSSQL\DATA

Building Access Databases with ADOX Objects

If you don't have Access or don't want to use Access to create an Access database, don't despair. An Access type database can be created and populated using Visual Basic programming. To do this, we use something called the ADO Extensions (**ADOX**) library. ADOX is related to a predecessor to ADO .NET technology, but it is very useful for the task at hand.

Actually there are times when you need or want to use Visual Basic to create your database. An example would be an application where a user chooses what fields he/she would want included in a particular table. In such a case, the database table structure is not known until run-time necessitating the use of Visual Basic to build the database. Or maybe your application requires a blank database to start. In such a case, if the user wanted to start a new file, we would need to copy a saved database file into a new file. When we build the distribution package for such an application, we need to remember to include that empty file or problems will result. Rather than trust our memory, we could just build the empty file in Visual Basic using the ADOX.

The steps followed are nearly identical to those followed using Access:

1. Create the database
2. Create the table(s)
3. Add fields to the table(s)
4. Define primary key for the table(s)
5. Define indexes for the table(s)
6. Once all tables are created, define relationships between tables

Each of the above steps will be discussed as we work through the example of building an Access version of the **KWSALES** database using Visual Basic. As you build a database file in code, you should check the structure as it is built. In the example to follow, we use Access to check the structure. We suggest you do the same. If you don't have Access, there are several free products available on the Internet that allows viewing of Access-type database files.

Example 9-3

KWSALES Access Database with ADOX

In this example, we go through all the steps necessary to build the 4-table **KWSALES** Access database using **Visual Basic** and **ADOX**. We will build each table and add the associated data fields (along with any necessary keys and indexes) individually. For reference, the table and field structure is:

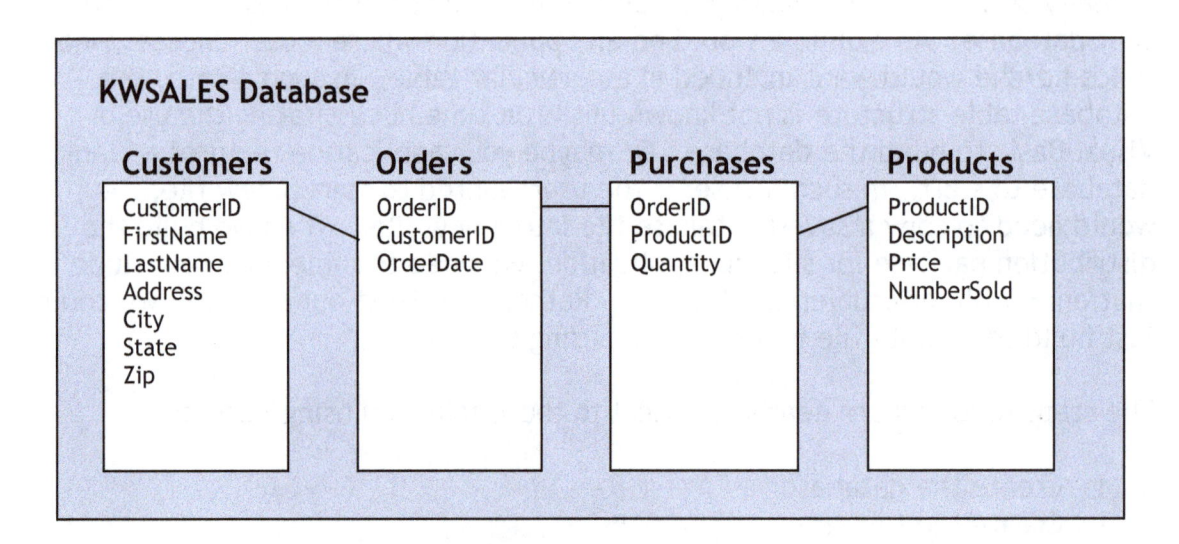

KWSALES Database

Customers	Orders	Purchases	Products
CustomerID	OrderID	OrderID	ProductID
FirstName	CustomerID	ProductID	Description
LastName	OrderDate	Quantity	Price
Address			NumberSold
City			
State			
Zip			

Add Reference to ADOX Library

1. Start a new project in Visual Basic. This project will have a single button (**Name** property **btnCreate**, **Text** property **Create Database**). We will simply write code in the **BtnCreate_Click** event procedure to build the database. My form looks like this:

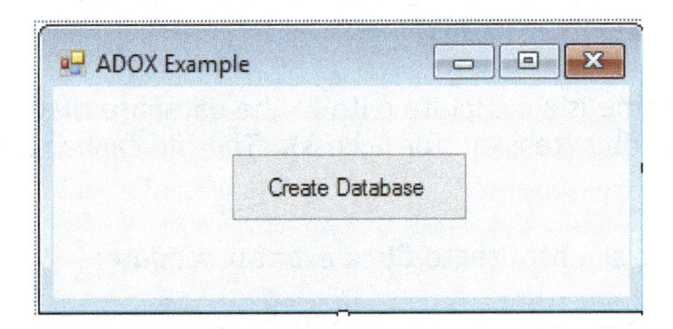

2. To use **ADOX**, we must add a reference to the component. Go to the **Solution Explorer** window for your new project. Right-click the project name and choose **Add**, then **Reference**. The **Add Reference** window will appear:

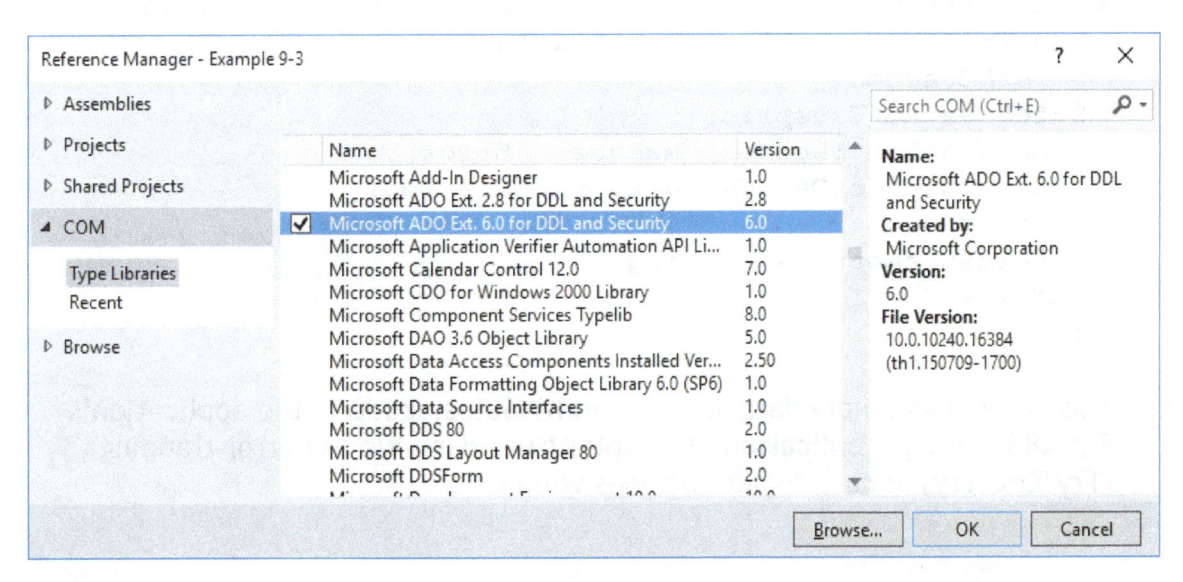

   As shown, select the **COM** tab and select the latest version (here **6.0**) of the **Microsoft ADO Ext. 6.0** library. Click **OK**. This step makes the **ADOX** library available to our project.

3. Go to your project code window and add a single line to the top of code window:

   ```
   Imports ADOX
   ```

Create a Database

A first step is to create the empty database. This uses the ADOX **Catalog** object and its **Create** method. The code syntax for an Access database is:

```
Dim MyDatabase As New Catalog
MyDatabase.Create("Provider=Microsoft.ACE.OLEDB.12.0;Data Source = " + DatabaseName)
```

where **DatabaseName** is a complete path to the database filename. This name should have an **accdb** extension (for Access). The file cannot already exist or an error will occur.

1. Add this code to the **btnCreate Click** event procedure:

```
Private Sub BtnCreate_Click(ByVal sender As System.Object, ByVal e As System.EventArgs) Handles btnCreate.Click
   Dim SalesDatabase As New Catalog
   Try
      SalesDatabase.Create("Provider=Microsoft.ACE.OLEDB.12.0;Data Source = " + Application.StartupPath + "\KWSalesDB.accdb")
   Catch ex As Exception
      MessageBox.Show(ex.Message, "Error", MessageBoxButtons.OK, MessageBoxIcon.Error)
   Finally
      SalesDatabase = Nothing
   End Try
End Sub
```

This creates an empty database named **KWSales.accdb** in the application's **Bin\x86\Debug** (**Application.StartupPath**) folder. We use error trapping (**Try/End Try**) in case something goes wrong.

Database Design Considerations   9-55

2. Save (saved in **Example 9-3** folder of **VBDB\Access\Example 9-3** folder) the application and run it. Click **Create Database**. Go to the **Bin\x86\Debug** folder for your project and you should see a copy of the database you just created. Here is mine:

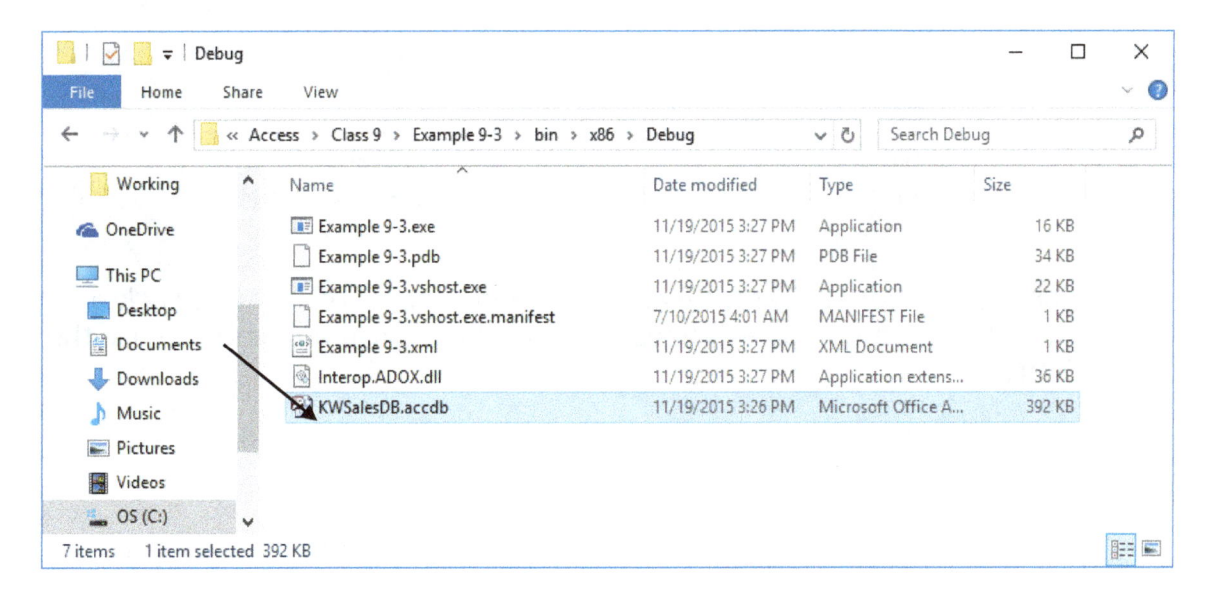

[File Explorer screenshot showing Debug folder contents: Example 9-3.exe, Example 9-3.pdb, Example 9-3.vshost.exe, Example 9-3.vshost.exe.manifest, Example 9-3.xml, Interop.ADOX.dll, KWSalesDB.accdb (highlighted)]

You may see this error when you try to run this example:

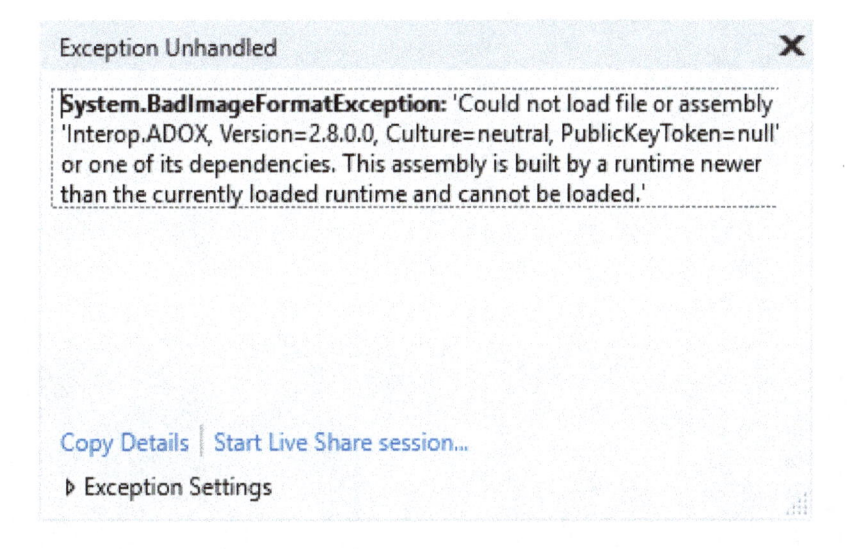

[Exception Unhandled dialog: **System.BadImageFormatException:** 'Could not load file or assembly 'Interop.ADOX, Version=2.8.0.0, Culture=neutral, PublicKeyToken=null' or one of its dependencies. This assembly is built by a runtime newer than the currently loaded runtime and cannot be loaded.']

The ADOX library was built with .NET Framework 4.0 and it's likely your project is using .NET Framework 2.0. It's easy to change.

Select the project in **Solution Explorer** and choose **Properties**:

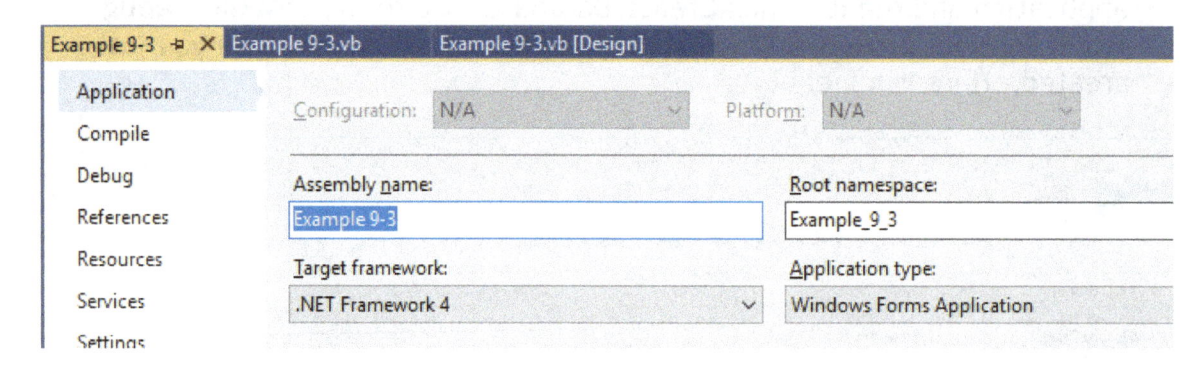

Use the drop-down box for **Target framework** and choose **.NET Framework 4**. Things should now work. You will need to make this change anytime you use the ADOX library.

Create a Table

A table is created using the ADOX **Table** object. You must provide a **Name** (a **String** type) for the table. The code to create a table object (**MyTable**) with **Name MyTableName** and add it to an existing catalog object (**MyDatabase**) is:

```
Dim MyTable As Table
MyTable = New Table
MyTable.Name = MyTableName
MyDatabase.Tables.Append(MyTable)
```

Let's create the **Customers** table.

1. Return to your project. Add the shaded code to the **btnCreate Click** procedure:

```
Private Sub BtnCreate_Click(ByVal sender As System.Object, ByVal e As System.EventArgs) Handles btnCreate.Click
    Dim SalesDatabase As New Catalog
    Dim DatabaseTable As Table
    Try
        SalesDatabase.Create("Provider=Microsoft.ACE.OLEDB.12.0; Data Source = " + Application.StartupPath + "\KWSalesDB.accdb")
        'Create Customers table
        DatabaseTable = New Table
        DatabaseTable.Name = "Customers"
        SalesDatabase.Tables.Append(DatabaseTable)
    Catch ex As Exception
        MessageBox.Show(ex.Message, "Error", MessageBoxButtons.OK, MessageBoxIcon.Error)
    Finally
        SalesDatabase = Nothing
    End Try
End Sub
```

2. Save and run the application. Click **Create Database**. You should see:

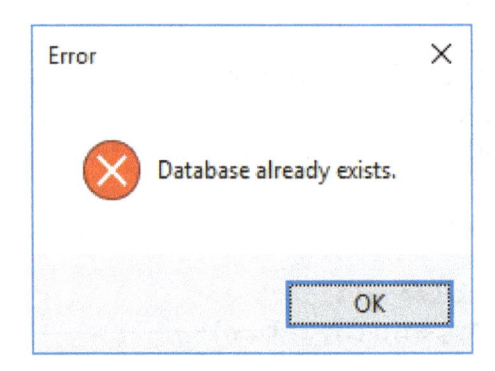

Recall you cannot create a database with ADOX if the name selected already exists. We already have a database named **KWSalesDB.accdb**, so we can't create it again. This is a continuous problem as you design a new database. You must always remember to delete the old version before trying some change. Fortunately, you can do this at run-time. Just find the file and delete it, then continue running your program. Try it. Delete **KWSalesDB.accdb** from your project's **Bin\x86\Debug** folder, then click **Create Database** again. The file will reappear in the folder (now with the added, albeit empty, **Customers** table).

3. If you have **Access**, open the created file. You should see that there really is a **Customers** table:

Add Fields to Table

Once a table is created, we need to add fields to the table. Fields are referred to as columns. For each field added, we need to know the field name (**MyFieldName**) and the data type (**MyFieldType**). To add this field (column) to a table object (**MyTable**), there are two possible syntaxes. If the data type is of variable width, use:

`MyTable.Columns.Append(MyFieldName, MyFieldType)`

If you need to specify width (**MyFieldWidth**), use:

`MyTable.Columns.Append(MyFieldName, MyFieldType, MyFieldWidth)`

Field types we use in our work are:

FieldType	Description
`DataTypeEnum.adSmallInt`	Variable length Integer
`DataTypeEnum.adInteger`	Variable length Long integer
`DataTypeEnum.adCurrency`	Currency type (two decimal places)
`DataTypeEnum.adDate`	Variable width date
`DataTypeEnum.adSingle`	Variable width single precision decimal numbers
`DataTypeEnum.adDouble`	Variable width double precision decimal numbers
`DataTypeEnum.adWChar`	Fixed width string
`DataTypeEnum.adVarWChar`	Variable width string

By default, added fields are **required** entries. For our sales database, that is desired. In many cases, it is not. To remove this restriction from a field, use:

`MyTable.Columns(MyFieldName).Attributes = ColumnAttributesEnum.adColNullable`

Let's add fields to the **Customers** table. Recall the field specifications are (all required fields):

Name	DataType	FieldSize
CustomerID	Long	Variable
FirstName	Short Text	40
LastName	Short Text	40
Address	Short Text	40
City	Short Text	40
State	Short Text	20
Zip	Short Text	10

1. Return to your project. Add the shaded code to the **btnCreate_Click** event procedure:

```
Private Sub btnCreate_Click(ByVal sender As System.Object, ByVal e As System.EventArgs) Handles btnCreate.Click
    Dim SalesDatabase As New Catalog
    Dim DatabaseTable As Table
    Try
        SalesDatabase.Create("Provider=Microsoft.ACE.OLEDB.12.0; Data Source = " + Application.StartupPath + "\KWSalesDB.accdb")
        ' Create Customers table
        DatabaseTable = New Table
        DatabaseTable.Name = "Customers"
        ' Add fields
        DatabaseTable.Columns.Append("CustomerID", DataTypeEnum.adInteger)
        DatabaseTable.Columns.Append("FirstName", DataTypeEnum.adWChar, 40)
        DatabaseTable.Columns.Append("LastName", DataTypeEnum.adWChar, 40)
        DatabaseTable.Columns.Append("Address", DataTypeEnum.adWChar, 40)
        DatabaseTable.Columns.Append("City", DataTypeEnum.adWChar, 40)
        DatabaseTable.Columns.Append("State", DataTypeEnum.adWChar, 20)
        DatabaseTable.Columns.Append("Zip", DataTypeEnum.adWChar, 10)
        SalesDatabase.Tables.Append(DatabaseTable)
    Catch ex As Exception
        MessageBox.Show(ex.Message, "Error", MessageBoxButtons.OK, MessageBoxIcon.Error)
    Finally
```

```
        SalesDatabase = Nothing
    End Try
End Sub
```

2. Save and run the application. Click **Create Database**. The **Customers** table will now have fields. If I open my file in Access and view the **Customers** table in **Design View**, I see:

Field Name	Data Type
CustomerID	Number
FirstName	Short Text
LastName	Short Text
Address	Short Text
City	Short Text
State	Short Text
Zip	Short Text

Recall that the **CustomerID** needs to be an '**autonumber**' field meaning it is automatically generated. Let's make that change.

3. After the line of code creating and appending the **CustomerID** field, add this code:

   ```
   DatabaseTable.Columns("CustomerID").ParentCatalog = SalesDatabase
   DatabaseTable.Columns("CustomerID").Properties("Autoincrement").Value = True
   ```

   Now, if you rerun the application and view the table in Access, you see the field is the proper type:

Field Name	Data Type
CustomerID	AutoNumber
FirstName	Short Text
LastName	Short Text
Address	Short Text
City	Short Text
State	Short Text
Zip	Short Text

Define Table Primary Key

We want to be able to define a primary key for a table. To do this, we use the **Keys** collection of a ADOX **Table** object. The syntax for a table object named **MyTable** is:

```
MyTable.Keys.Append(MyKeyName, KeyTypeEnum.adKeyPrimary, MyFieldName)
```

where **MyKeyName** is a named assigned to the key and **MyFieldName** is the field designated as a primary key.

Our **Customers** table has a single primary key, **CustomerID**. Let's define that key.

1. Return to the project. Add the shaded line of code to the **btnCreate Click** event procedure:

```
Private Sub BtnCreate_Click(ByVal sender As System.Object, ByVal e As System.EventArgs) Handles btnCreate.Click
    Dim SalesDatabase As New Catalog
    Dim DatabaseTable As Table
    Try
        SalesDatabase.Create("Provider=Microsoft.ACE.OLEDB.12.0;Data Source = " + Application.StartupPath + "\KWSalesDB.accdb")
        ' Create Customers Table
        DatabaseTable = New Table
        DatabaseTable.Name = "Customers"
        ' Add fields
        DatabaseTable.Columns.Append("CustomerID", DataTypeEnum.adInteger)
        DatabaseTable.Columns("CustomerID").ParentCatalog = SalesDatabase

        DatabaseTable.Columns("CustomerID").Properties("Autoincrement").Value = True
        DatabaseTable.Columns.Append("FirstName", DataTypeEnum.adWChar, 40)
        DatabaseTable.Columns.Append("LastName", DataTypeEnum.adWChar, 40)
        DatabaseTable.Columns.Append("Address", DataTypeEnum.adWChar, 40)
        DatabaseTable.Columns.Append("City", DataTypeEnum.adWChar, 40)
```

```
              DatabaseTable.Columns.Append("State",
DataTypeEnum.adWChar, 20)
              DatabaseTable.Columns.Append("Zip",
DataTypeEnum.adWChar, 10)
              SalesDatabase.Tables.Append(DatabaseTable)
              ' Add keys
              DatabaseTable.Keys.Append("PK_Customers",
KeyTypeEnum.adKeyPrimary, "CustomerID")
          Catch ex As Exception
              MessageBox.Show(ex.Message, "Error",
MessageBoxButtons.OK, MessageBoxIcon.Error)
          Finally
              SalesDatabase = Nothing
          End Try
      End Sub
```

2. Resave and run the application. Click **Create Database**. Examining the **Customers** table now shows **CustomerID** as a primary key (note the key icon in the first column):

Field Name	Data Type
CustomerID	AutoNumber
FirstName	Short Text
LastName	Short Text
Address	Short Text
City	Short Text
State	Short Text
Zip	Short Text

Define Table Indexes

Lastly, we want to be able to define indexes for tables. To do this, we use the **Indexes** collection of a ADOX **Table** object. The syntax for a table object named **MyTable** is:

`MyTable.Indexes.Append(MyIndexName, MyFieldName)`

where **MyIndexName** is a named assigned to the index and **MyFieldName** is the field designated as an index. These two names can have the same value.

Our **Customers** table has two indexed fields, **CustomerID** and **LastName**. Let's define them.

1. Return to the project. Add the shaded code to the **btnCreate Click** event procedure:

```
  Private Sub BtnCreate_Click(ByVal sender As System.Object,
ByVal e As System.EventArgs) Handles btnCreate.Click
    Dim SalesDatabase As New Catalog
    Dim DatabaseTable As Table
    Try

SalesDatabase.Create("Provider=Microsoft.ACE.OLEDB.12.0;
Data Source = " + Application.StartupPath +
"\KWSalesDB.accdb")
      ' Create Customers table
    DatabaseTable = New Table
    DatabaseTable.Name = "Customers"
      ' Add fields
    DatabaseTable.Columns.Append("CustomerID",
DataTypeEnum.adInteger)
    DatabaseTable.Columns("CustomerID").ParentCatalog =
SalesDatabase

DatabaseTable.Columns("CustomerID").Properties("Autoincrement").Value = True
    DatabaseTable.Columns.Append("FirstName",
DataTypeEnum.adWChar, 40)
    DatabaseTable.Columns.Append("LastName",
DataTypeEnum.adWChar, 40)
    DatabaseTable.Columns.Append("Address",
DataTypeEnum.adWChar, 40)
    DatabaseTable.Columns.Append("City",
DataTypeEnum.adWChar, 40)
```

```
      DatabaseTable.Columns.Append("State",
DataTypeEnum.adWChar, 20)
      DatabaseTable.Columns.Append("Zip",
DataTypeEnum.adWChar, 10)
      ' Add keys
      DatabaseTable.Keys.Append("PK_Customers",
KeyTypeEnum.adKeyPrimary, "CustomerID")
      ' Add indexes
      DatabaseTable.Indexes.Append("CustomerID",
"CustomerID")
      DatabaseTable.Indexes.Append("LastName", "LastName")
      SalesDatabase.Tables.Append(DatabaseTable)
    Catch ex As Exception
      MessageBox.Show(ex.Message, "Error",
MessageBoxButtons.OK, MessageBoxIcon.Error)
    Finally
      SalesDatabase = Nothing
    End Try
  End Sub
```

2. Resave and run the application. Click **Create Database**. If you examine the **CustomerID** and **LastName** fields in the **Customers** table (using Access), you will see that they are indexes. The **Customers** table is now complete. Let's create the other three tables.

3. The **Orders** table has three fields:

Name	DataType
OrderID	Short Text (FieldSize = 10)
CustomerID	Number (Long Integer, no default value)
OrderDate	Date/Time

The primary key is **OrderID**. All three fields are indexed fields. The code that creates this table structure is:

```
' Create Orders table
DatabaseTable = New Table
DatabaseTable.Name = "Orders"
' Add fields
DatabaseTable.Columns.Append("OrderID",
DataTypeEnum.adWChar, 10)
DatabaseTable.Columns.Append("CustomerID",
DataTypeEnum.adInteger)
DatabaseTable.Columns.Append("OrderDate",
DataTypeEnum.adDate)
' Add keys
DatabaseTable.Keys.Append("PK_OrderID",
KeyTypeEnum.adKeyPrimary, "OrderID")
' Add indexes
DatabaseTable.Indexes.Append("OrderID", "OrderID")
DatabaseTable.Indexes.Append("CustomerID", "CustomerID")
DatabaseTable.Indexes.Append("OrderDate", "OrderDate")
SalesDatabase.Tables.Append(DatabaseTable)
```

Add this code to the **btnCreate Click** procedure following creation of the **Customers** table. Save the application once again and run it. Click **Create Database**. Viewing the **Orders** table in Access shows the fields are correct and the primary index is identified:

Field Name	Data Type
OrderID	Text
CustomerID	Number
OrderDate	Date/Time

4. The **Purchases** table has three fields:

Name	DataType
OrderID	ShortText (FieldSize = 10)
ProductID	ShortText (FieldSize = 10)
Quantity	Number (Integer, no default value)

   There is no primary key. **OrderID** and **ProductID** are indexed fields. The code that creates this table structure is:

   ```
   ' Create Purchases table
   DatabaseTable = New Table
   DatabaseTable.Name = "Purchases"
   ' Add fields
   DatabaseTable.Columns.Append("OrderID", DataTypeEnum.adWChar, 10)
   DatabaseTable.Columns.Append("ProductID", DataTypeEnum.adWChar, 10)
   DatabaseTable.Columns.Append("Quantity", DataTypeEnum.adSmallInt)
   ' Add indexes
   DatabaseTable.Indexes.Append("OrderID", "OrderID")
   DatabaseTable.Indexes.Append("ProductID", "ProductID")
   SalesDatabase.Tables.Append(DatabaseTable)
   ```

   Add this code to the **btnCreate Click** procedure following creation of the **Orders** table. Save the application once again and run it. Click **Create Database**. Viewing the **Purchases** table in Access shows the fields are correct:

Field Name	Data Type
OrderID	Text
ProductID	Text
Quantity	Number

Database Design Considerations 9-69

5. And, lastly, the **Products** table has four fields:

Name	DataType
ProductID	ShortText (FieldSize = 10)
Description	ShortText (FieldSize = 40)
Price	Currency
NumberSold	Number (Integer, no default value)

ProductID is a primary key. There are no indexes. The code that creates this table structure is:

```
' Create Products table
DatabaseTable = New Table
DatabaseTable.Name = "Products"
' Add fields
DatabaseTable.Columns.Append("ProductID",
DataTypeEnum.adWChar, 10)
DatabaseTable.Columns.Append("Description",
DataTypeEnum.adWChar, 40)
DatabaseTable.Columns.Append("Price",
DataTypeEnum.adCurrency)
DatabaseTable.Columns.Append("NumberSold",
DataTypeEnum.adSmallInt)
' Add keys
DatabaseTable.Keys.Append("PK_ProductID",
KeyTypeEnum.adKeyPrimary, "ProductID")
SalesDatabase.Tables.Append(DatabaseTable)
```

Add this code to the **btnCreate Click** procedure following creation of the **Purchases** table. Save the application once again and run it. Click **Create Database**. Viewing the **Products** table in Access shows the fields are correct and the primary index is identified:

Field Name	Data Type
ProductID	Text
Description	Text
Price	Currency
NumberSold	Number

We now have all four tables in the **KWSALES** database.

Define Table Relationships

The last step in creating a database using Visual Basic is to define the relationships between keys in the various tables. The process involves first creating needed foreign keys. Each foreign key is then related to the corresponding primary key in another table.

Say we have **Field1** in **Table1** that is a primary key. Now, say **Field2** in **Table2** is a foreign key object (named **MyForeignKey**) related to that primary key. The steps to create such a relationship are (assuming both tables are part of an ADOX catalog **MyCatalog**):

```
Dim MyForeignKey As New Key
MyForeignKey.Name = MyForeignKeyName
MyForeignKey.Type = KeyTypeEnum.adKeyForeign
MyForeignKey.Columns.Append(Field2)
MyForeignKey.RelatedTable = Table1
MyForeignKey.Columns(Field2).RelatedColumn = Field1
MyCatalog.Tables(Table2).Keys.Append(MyForeignKey)
```

where **MyForeignKeyName** is a named assign to the key. This code adds **Field2** to the foreign key, then relates it to **Field1** in **Table1**. The key is then appended to **Table2**.

There are three foreign keys in the **KWSALES** database. Let's define each one.

Database Design Considerations

1. Return to the project. The first foreign key (name is **FK_CustomerID**) is **CustomerID** in the **Orders** table. It is related to the **CustomerID** (primary key) in the **Customers** table. The code to make this relation is:

```
' Define relationships
Dim ForeignKey As Key
' Relate CustomerID field in Customers to CustomerID in
Orders (Foreign key)
ForeignKey = New Key
ForeignKey.Name = "FK_CustomerID"
ForeignKey.Type = KeyTypeEnum.adKeyForeign
ForeignKey.Columns.Append("CustomerID")
ForeignKey.RelatedTable = "Customers"
ForeignKey.Columns("CustomerID").RelatedColumn =
"CustomerID"
SalesDatabase.Tables("Orders").Keys.Append(ForeignKey)
```

Place this code in the **btnCreate Click** procedure after creation of the **Products** table.

2. The second foreign key (name is **FK_OrderID**) is **OrderID** in the **Purchases** table. It is related to the **OrderID** (primary key) in the **Orders** table. The code to create this relation is:

```
' Relate OrderID field in Orders to OrderID in Purchases
(Foreign key)
ForeignKey = New Key
ForeignKey.Name = "FK_OrderID"
ForeignKey.Type = KeyTypeEnum.adKeyForeign
ForeignKey.Columns.Append("OrderID")
ForeignKey.RelatedTable = "Orders"
ForeignKey.Columns("OrderID").RelatedColumn = "OrderID"
SalesDatabase.Tables("Purchases").Keys.Append(ForeignKey)
```

Place this code in the **btnCreate Click** procedure after creation of the **CustomerID** foreign key.

3. The final foreign key (name is **FK_ProductID**) is **ProductID** in the **Purchases** table. It is related to the **ProductID** (primary key) in the **Products** table. The code to create this relation is:

```
' Relate ProductID field in Products to ProductID in
Purchases (Foreign key)
ForeignKey = New Key
ForeignKey.Name = "FK_ProductID"
ForeignKey.Type = KeyTypeEnum.adKeyForeign
ForeignKey.Columns.Append("ProductID")
ForeignKey.RelatedTable = "Products"
ForeignKey.Columns("ProductID").RelatedColumn = "ProductID"
SalesDatabase.Tables("Purchases").Keys.Append(ForeignKey)
```

Place this code in the **btnCreate Click** procedure after creation of the **OrderID** foreign key.

4. Save the application one last time (saved in **Example 9-3** folder of **VBDB\Access\Example 9-3** folder). Run it. Click **Create Database**. The database and all relationships should now be created. If you open the database in Access and view the relationships (click **Tools**, then **Relationships**) you see:

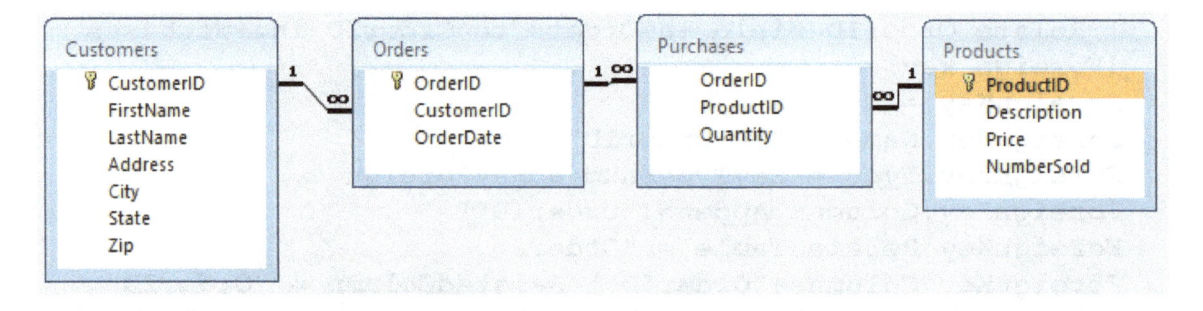

All of the key relationships are clearly defined.

Like the earlier Access example, it is possible to add values to the tables at this point, if desired. You would use the data objects discussed in previous chapters. Once the objects are created, you could programmatically add rows to tables and update the database. We will not populate the tables here. It will be done in the examples in Chapter 10.

Example 9-4

SQL Server Databases with Visual Basic

It is also possible to create SQL Server databases using Visual Basic. The process involves executing SQL statements to perform each step in the development:

- Create the database
- Create the table(s)
- Add fields to the table(s)
- Define primary key for the table(s)
- Define indexes for the table(s)
- Define relationships between tables

In this example, we will perform just the first step – create a SQL server database. The remaining steps involve using some fairly complicated SQL statements which are beyond the scope of this course. We direct the reader to SQL references (and the Internet) for further information.

1. Start a new project in Visual Basic. This project will have a single button (**Name** property **btnCreate**, **Text** property **Create Database**). We will simply write code in the **btnCreate Click** event procedure to create the database. My form looks like this:

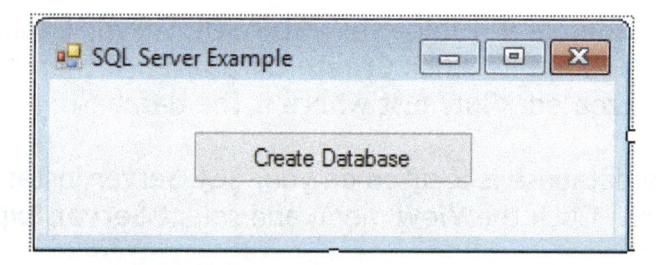

2. Go to your project code window and add the usual lines at the top of the code window:

```
Imports System.Data
Imports System.Data.SqlClient
```

3. Add this code to the **btnCreate Click** event procedure:

```
 Private Sub BtnCreate_Click(ByVal sender As System.Object, ByVal e As System.EventArgs) Handles btnCreate.Click
    Dim MyConnection As SqlConnection = New SqlConnection("Server=.\SQLEXPRESS; Trusted_Connection=Yes")
    Dim MyCommand As SqlCommand = New SqlCommand("CREATE DATABASE SQLDatabase", MyConnection)
    MyConnection.Open()
    MyCommand.ExecuteNonQuery()
    MyConnection.Close()
  End Sub
```

This creates an empty database named **SQLDatabase.mdf** on your SQL Server instance (named **.\SQLEXPRESS** on my computer). The database is created by executing the SQL command:

CREATE DATABASE SQLDatabase

against the open connection object **MyConnection**.

4. Save (saved in **Example 9-4** folder of **VBDB\SQL Server\Example 9-4** folder) the application and run it. Click **Create Database**. If there are no errors, the database is created. But, just where is the database?

The newly created database is located on your SQL Server instance. Start a new Visual Basic project. Click the **View** menu and select **Server Explorer**. You should see:

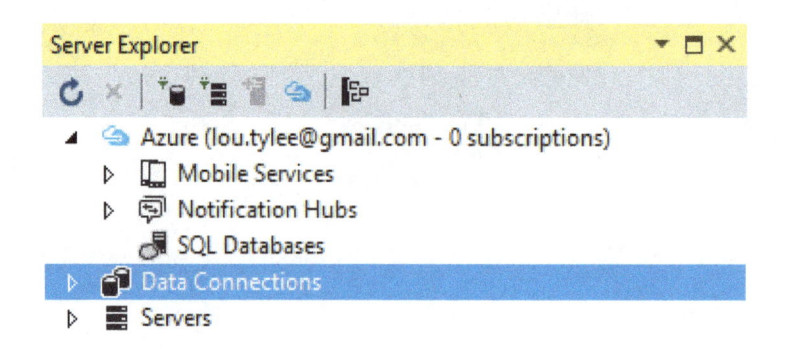

Database Design Considerations 9-75

Right-click **Data Connections** and choose **Add Connection**. This form appears:

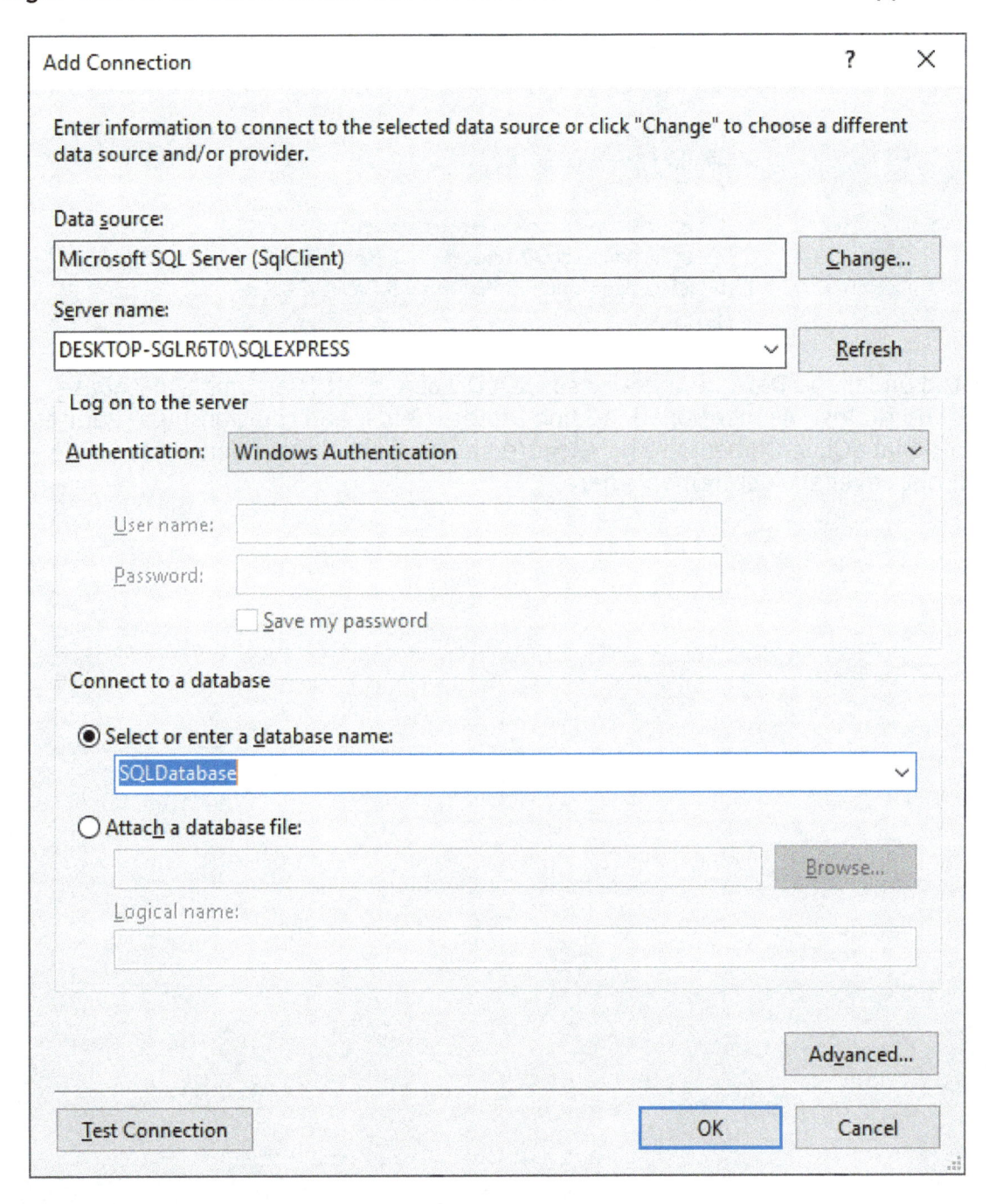

Make the shown entries (user your server name) and click **OK**.

In the Server Explorer, you will now see:

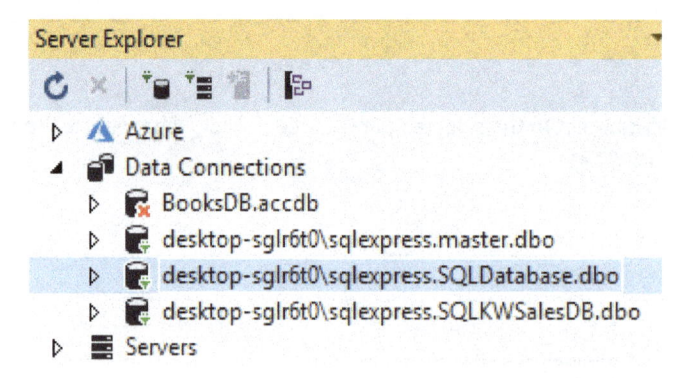

Listed under the **Data Connections** is **SQLDatabase**. It is an empty database with no tables. As mentioned, adding tables, fields, and relationships requires additional SQL statements to be executed against the connection object. We will not cover such statements here.

Database Design Considerations 9-77

If you do continue development of a SQL Server database with Visual Basic, be aware when you run your application again, you will probably get an error message like this:

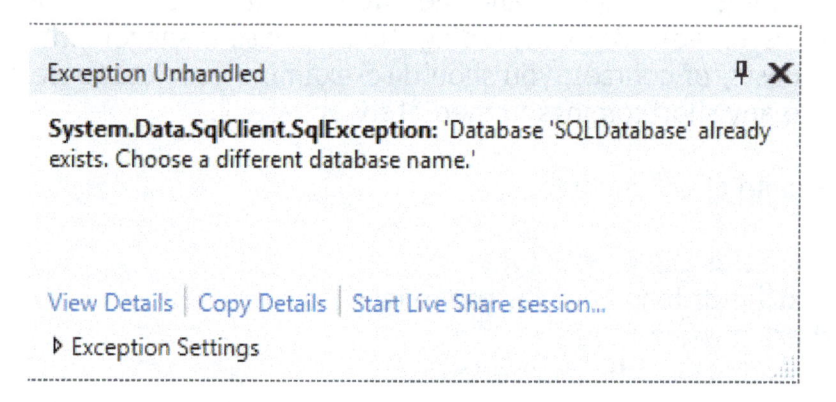

> **Exception Unhandled**
>
> **System.Data.SqlClient.SqlException:** 'Database 'SQLDatabase' already exists. Choose a different database name.'
>
> View Details | Copy Details | Start Live Share session...
> ▷ Exception Settings

You cannot create a database if the name selected already exists. We already have a database named **SQLDatabase**, so we can't create it again. This is a continuous problem as you design a new database. You must always remember to delete the old version before trying some change. This deletion is done by right-clicking the database in the **Server Management** tool and choosing **Delete**.

Database Design Refinement

The database design is complete and the database has been built (using one of the methods discussed). Before building the database management system (using Visual Basic, of course), you should re-examine your database design. This will make any shortcomings immediately apparent.

Things you should check include:

- Are the fields the proper type?
- Are text fields long enough, too long?
- Are there missing fields?
- Are any additional fields needed?

You may find you need to redesign your database. And, yes, you may need to start over. A database structure is usually permanent and cannot be easily changed. But, modifying your database now, before you build a complete management system to work with it, is much easier than changing things further down the development road.

Summary

In this chapter, we discussed several steps for developing a well-designed database for use in a database management system (like the one built in Chapter 6 and modified in Chapter 7). The major considerations in designing a database are to be complete, thorough, and accurate. Later modification of a database project can be a major undertaking.

The use of the Access and the Visual Basic ADOX library to build an Access database were examined. Building a SQL Server database using Server Explorer was also covered. The empty database built can be connected to a Visual Basic front-end interface to form a complete database management system. In the next chapter, we look at three case studies that do just that.

10

Sample Database Projects

Review and Preview

We have completed our introduction (a long introduction) into database programming with Visual Basic. We have learned about database structure, proper interface design, database management techniques, database reports, and how to create a database.

In this chapter, we put all our skills to work and look at some sample projects. These projects are typical database applications. The applications studied are a program using the **KWSALES** database just built in Chapter 9, a home inventory tracking system, and a weather monitor.

Overview of Database Projects

We will build three projects in this chapter. The first is a sales order form for the **KWSALES** database built in the previous chapter. The second application allows a user to keep track of items in their homes or other locations, for possible insurance claim use. And, the final application is a weather-monitoring program that records and plots temperatures and precipitation over time.

Each project will be built in stages. And, the steps followed in each stage are explained in detail. This will give you an idea of how to use Visual Basic to build a database management system. Visual Basic is an ideal environment for building applications in this way. Suggestions for improving each application are also provided.

One other suggestion – when building your applications, make a copy of your database before starting. Many errors can occur when developing a project and you wouldn't want any of these errors to destroy needed data. So, always build with a working copy of your database. When you are sure the project is working correctly, you can use a 'clean' copy.

Example 10-1

Sales Order Form Project

In Chapter 9, we built a database similar to the one we use here at our company (KIDware) to track orders and sales. In this application, we build a Visual Basic interface for that database. The interface will be used to enter new orders into the database.

The order form should allow entry of the following information into the database:

> Order ID
> Order Date
> Customer ID
> Customer first and last name
> Customer address information
> Product(s) ordered information

The form should have the ability to add new orders, find past customers, and add new customers. Completed order invoices should be available as printed reports. Before starting this project, we suggest a quick review of Chapter 9 to get reacquainted with the structure of the **KWSALES** database.

Preliminaries

Start a new project in Visual Basic.

Access Database:

Copy **KWSalesDB.accdb** into your project's **Bin\x86\Debug** folder (you may have to create it first). One option is to use the blank database from Chapter 9 in the **VBDB\Databases** folder. To use this, you would first need to add some entries in the **Products** table (using **Access**). Or, you might like to use the copy included with this example's course code (in **Example 10-1** folder of the **VBDB\Access\Class 10** folder). Product information is included in this database and there are a few customers and orders you can look at. We use the latter in this example.

SQL Server Database:

Copy **SQLKWSalesDB.mdf** into your project's **Bin\Debug** folder (you may have to create it first). One option is to use the blank database from Chapter 9 in the **VBDB\Databases** folder. To use this, you would first need to add some entries in the **Products** table. Or, you might like to use the copy included with this example's course code (in **Example 10-1** folder of the **VBDB\SQL Server\Class 10** folder). Product information is included in this database and there are a few customers and orders you can look at. We use the latter in this example.

Order Information

We'll begin this project by developing the ability to submit an order or exit the program. The order submission capability will not be coded now, but the interface for access will be begun.

1. Near the top of the displayed form, place a group box, two buttons, and four label controls. The top of the form should look something like this:

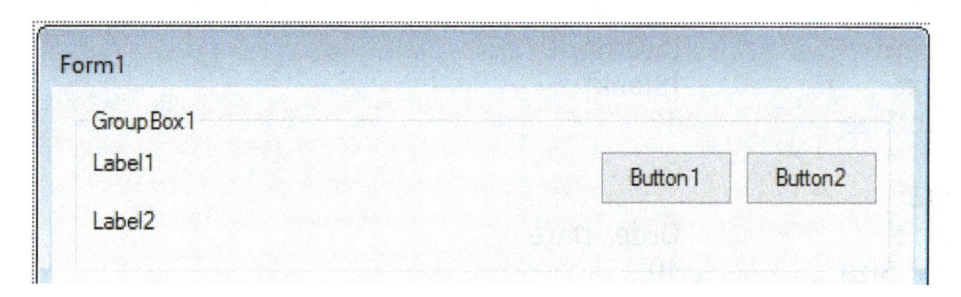

2. Set these properties:

   Form1:
       Name   frmKWSales
       ControlBox   False
       FormBorderStyle   Fixed Single
       StartPosition   CenterScreen
       Text   KWSales Order Form

   GroupBox1:
       Name   grpOrder
       Text   Order
       FontSize   10
       FontBold   True

   Button1:
       Name   btnSubmitOrder
       Text   Submit
       FontSize   10

Button2:
    Name   btnExit
    Text   Exit
    FontSize   10

Label1:
    Text   KIDware Order
    FontSize   10

Label2:
    Name   lblOrderID
    Text   [Blank]
    FontSize   10

Label3:
    Text   Order Date
    FontSize   10

Label4:
    Name   lblDate
    Text   [Blank]
    FontSize   10

The top of my finished form looks like this:

Sample Database Projects

When the application begins, the form will be in a mode to accept a new order. In this mode, we want a new order number and the current date. (Later, we will ensure the customer information is also blank.)

1. Place these two lines at the top of the code window to allow use of data objects:

   Access Database:

   ```
   Imports System.Data
   Imports System.Data.OleDb
   ```

   SQL Server Database:

   ```
   Imports System.Data
   Imports System.Data.SqlClient
   ```

2. Place this code in the form level declarations:

   Access Database:

   ```
   Dim OrderNumber As Integer
   Dim KWSalesConnection As OleDbConnection
   Dim OrdersCommand As OleDbCommand
   Dim OrdersAdapter As OleDbDataAdapter
   Dim OrdersTable As DataTable
   ```

   SQL Server Database:

   ```
   Dim OrderNumber As Integer
   Dim KWSalesConnection As SqlConnection
   Dim OrdersCommand As SqlCommand
   Dim OrdersAdapter As SqlDataAdapter
   Dim OrdersTable As DataTable
   ```

The variable **OrderNumber** tells us how many orders have been entered on a particular day. The remaining declarations are the data objects needed to look at the **Orders** table in the database.

10-8　　　　　　　　Visual Basic and Databases

3. Place this code in the **frmKWSales Load** event procedure:

   Access Database:

```
  Private Sub FrmKWSales_Load(ByVal sender As System.Object, ByVal e As System.EventArgs) Handles MyBase.Load
    'connect to sales database
    KWSalesConnection = New OleDbConnection("Provider=Microsoft.ACE.OLEDB.12.0; Data Source = " + Application.StartupPath + "\KWSalesDB.accdb")
    KWSalesConnection.Open()
    'establish Orders command object
    OrdersCommand = New OleDbCommand("SELECT * FROM Orders ORDER BY OrderID", KWSalesConnection)
    'establish Orders data adapter/data table
    OrdersAdapter = New OleDbDataAdapter()
    OrdersAdapter.SelectCommand = OrdersCommand
    OrdersTable = New DataTable()
    OrdersAdapter.Fill(OrdersTable)
    OrderNumber = 0
    Call NewOrder()
  End Sub
```

   SQL Sales Database:

```
  Private Sub FrmKWSales_Load(ByVal sender As System.Object, ByVal e As System.EventArgs) Handles MyBase.Load
    'connect to sales database
    KWSalesConnection = New SqlConnection("Data Source=.\SQLEXPRESS; AttachDbFilename=" + Application.StartupPath + "\SQLKWSalesDB.mdf; Integrated Security=True; Connect Timeout=30; User Instance=True")
    KWSalesConnection.Open()
    'establish Orders command object
    OrdersCommand = New SqlCommand("SELECT * FROM Orders ORDER BY OrderID", KWSalesConnection)
    'establish Orders data adapter/data table
    OrdersAdapter = New SqlDataAdapter()
    OrdersAdapter.SelectCommand = OrdersCommand
    OrdersTable = New DataTable()
    OrdersAdapter.Fill(OrdersTable)
    OrderNumber = 0
    Call NewOrder()
  End Sub
```

This code connects to the **KWSALES** database (in the application folder) and creates the data objects needed to view the **Orders** table. It initializes the **OrderNumber** and starts a new order (**NewOrder** procedure will be seen soon).

4. Place this code in the **frmKWSales FormClosing** event procedure to clean up objects:

```
Private Sub FrmKWSales_FormClosing(ByVal sender As
System.Object, ByVal e As
System.Windows.Forms.FormClosingEventArgs) Handles
MyBase.FormClosing
  'close the connection
  KWSalesConnection.Close()
  'dispose of the objects
  OrdersCommand.Dispose()
  OrdersAdapter.Dispose()
  OrdersTable.Dispose()
End Sub
```

5. Add a general procedure named **NewOrder** and use this code:

```
Private Sub NewOrder()
  Dim IDString As String
  Dim ThisDay As Date = Now
  lblDate.Text = Format(ThisDay, "d")
  'Build order ID as string
  OrderNumber += 1
  IDString = Mid(ThisDay.Year.ToString, 3, 2)
  IDString += Format(ThisDay.Month, "00")
  IDString += Format(ThisDay.Day, "00")
  IDString += Format(OrderNumber, "000")
  lblOrderID.Text = IDString
End Sub
```

This code places today's date in the **lblDate** control, and generates a new **OrderID** value. In our work, we establish our own format for **OrderID**. It has nine characters: the first two are the last two numbers in the year, the next two the month, the next two the day, and the final three unique digits incremented with each order. For example, if this is the third order on October 8, 2006, the **OrderID** is: **061008003**.

6. Place this code in the **btnExit Click** event:

```
Private Sub BtnExit_Click(ByVal sender As System.Object, ByVal e As System.EventArgs) Handles btnExit.Click
    Me.Close()
End Sub
```

7. Save the application (Access version saved in **Example 10-1** folder in **VBDB\Access\Class 10** folder; SQL Server version saved in **Example 10-1** folder in **VBDB\SQL Server\Class 10** folder) and run it. You should see this (assuming it's June 13, 2019 today!) at the top of the form:

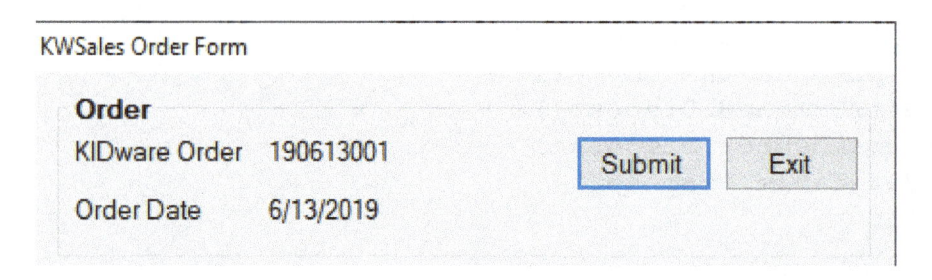

Next we look at adding customer information. We have not coded the **Submit Order** button yet – this is intentional.

Existing Customer Information

We now add the ability to find an existing customer in our database and display the corresponding information on our order form. We want to display the customer name and address information.

1. Add another group box, a combo box control, 6 labels and 6 text box controls to the form under the **Order** group box. The form should look like this:

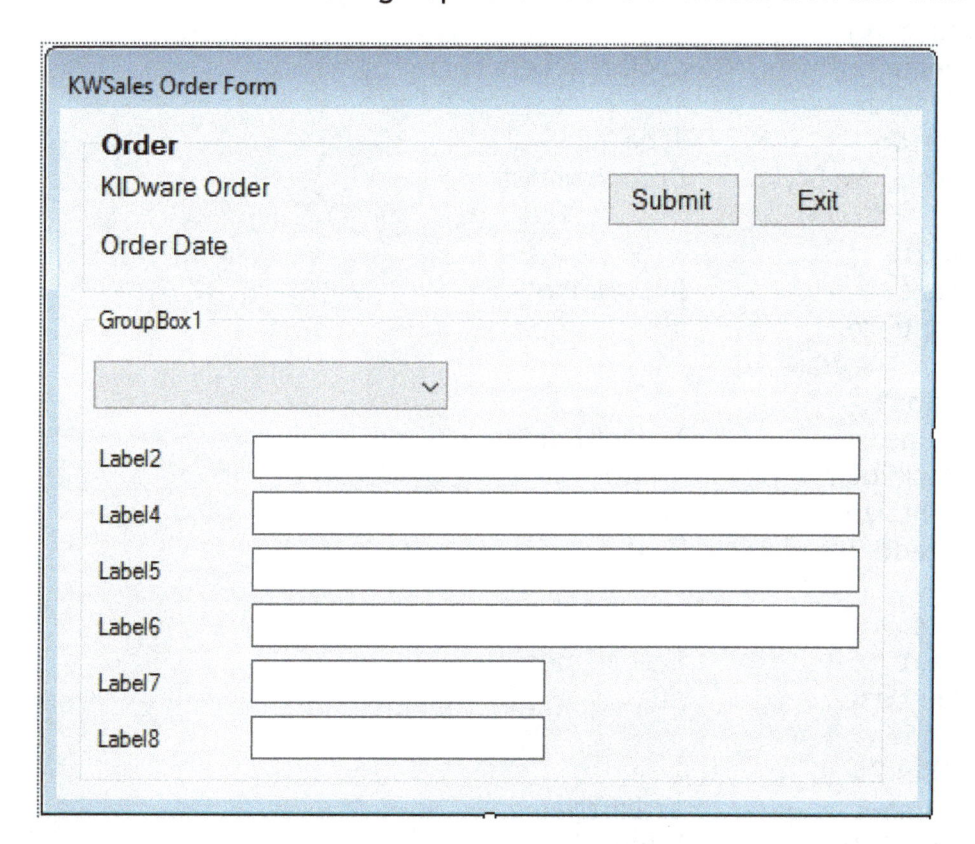

2. Use these properties (note the default names may differ depending on where you placed controls):

GroupBox1:
Name	grpCustomer
Text	Customer
FontSize	10
FontBold	True

ComboBox1:
Name	cboCustomers
FontSize	10
Sorted	True
DropDownStyle	DropdownList

Label2:
Text	First Name:
FontSize	10

TextBox1:
Name	txtFirstName
BackColor	White
FontSize	10
ReadOnly	True

Label4:
Text	Last Name:
FontSize	10

TextBox2:
Name	txtLastName
BackColor	White
FontSize	10
ReadOnly	True

Label5:
   Text   Address:
   FontSize   10

TextBox3:
   Name   txtAddress
   BackColor   White
   FontSize   10
   ReadOnly   True

Label6:
   Text   City:
   FontSize   10

TextBox4:
   Name   txtCity
   BackColor   White
   FontSize   10
   ReadOnly   True

Label7:
   Text   State:
   FontSize   10

TextBox5:
   Name   txtState
   BackColor   White
   FontSize   10
   ReadOnly   True

Label8:
   Text   Zip:
   FontSize   10

TextBox6:
   Name   txtZip
   BackColor   White
   FontSize   10
   ReadOnly   True

The form should now look like this:

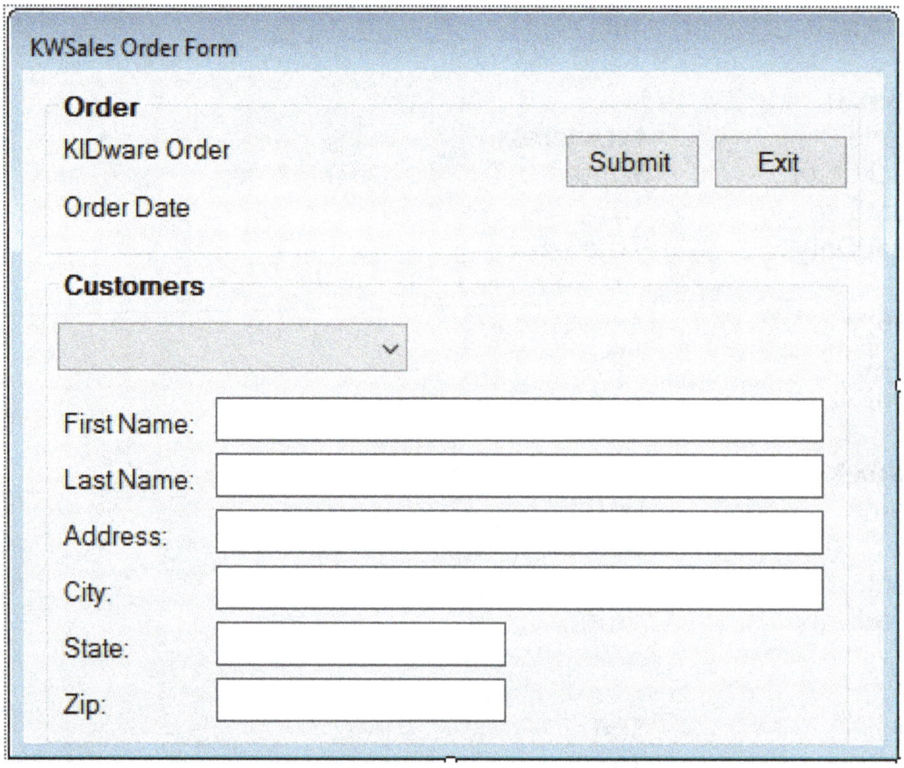
KWSales Order Form
Order
KIDware Order
Order Date
Submit
Exit
Customers
First Name:
Last Name:
Address:
City:
State:
Zip:

Sample Database Projects   10-15

3. We add another set of data objects that connect to the **Customers** table in the database. Add these form level declarations:

   Access Database:

   ```
   Dim CustomersCommand As OleDbCommand
   Dim CustomersAdapter As OleDbDataAdapter
   Dim CustomersTable As DataTable
   Dim CustomersManager As CurrencyManager
   ```

   SQL Server Database:

   ```
   Dim CustomersCommand As SqlCommand
   Dim CustomersAdapter As SqlDataAdapter
   Dim CustomersTable As DataTable
   Dim CustomersManager As CurrencyManager
   ```

4. Add the shaded code to the **frmKWSales Load** event procedure to create the new objects and bind the label controls:

   Access Database:

   ```
   Private Sub FrmKWSales_Load(ByVal sender As System.Object, ByVal e As System.EventArgs) Handles MyBase.Load
       'connect to sales database
       KWSalesConnection = New OleDbConnection("Provider=Microsoft.ACE.OLEDB.12.0; Data Source = " + Application.StartupPath + "\KWSalesDB.accdb")
       KWSalesConnection.Open()
       'establish Orders command object
       OrdersCommand = New OleDbCommand("SELECT * FROM Orders ORDER BY OrderID", KWSalesConnection)
       'establish Orders data adapter/data table
       OrdersAdapter = New OleDbDataAdapter()
       OrdersAdapter.SelectCommand = OrdersCommand
       OrdersTable = New DataTable()
       OrdersAdapter.Fill(OrdersTable)
       'establish Customers command object
       CustomersCommand = New OleDbCommand("SELECT * FROM Customers", KWSalesConnection)
       'establish Customers data adapter/data table
       CustomersAdapter = New OleDbDataAdapter()
       CustomersAdapter.SelectCommand = CustomersCommand
       CustomersTable = New DataTable()
       CustomersAdapter.Fill(CustomersTable)
       'bind controls to data table
   ```

```vb
    txtFirstName.DataBindings.Add("Text", CustomersTable, "FirstName")
    txtLastName.DataBindings.Add("Text", CustomersTable, "LastName")
    txtAddress.DataBindings.Add("Text", CustomersTable, "Address")
    txtCity.DataBindings.Add("Text", CustomersTable, "City")
    txtState.DataBindings.Add("Text", CustomersTable, "State")
    txtZip.DataBindings.Add("Text", CustomersTable, "Zip")
    'establish currency manager
    CustomersManager = DirectCast(Me.BindingContext(CustomersTable), CurrencyManager)
    OrderNumber = 0
    Call NewOrder()
  End Sub
```

SQL Server Database:

```vb
  Private Sub FrmKWSales_Load(ByVal sender As System.Object, ByVal e As System.EventArgs) Handles MyBase.Load
    'connect to sales database
    KWSalesConnection = New SqlConnection("Data Source=.\SQLEXPRESS; AttachDbFilename=" + Application.StartupPath + "\SQLKWSalesDB.mdf; Integrated Security=True; Connect Timeout=30; User Instance=True")
    KWSalesConnection.Open()
    'establish Orders command object
    OrdersCommand = New SqlCommand("SELECT * FROM Orders ORDER BY OrderID", KWSalesConnection)
    'establish Orders data adapter/data table
    OrdersAdapter = New SqlDataAdapter()
    OrdersAdapter.SelectCommand = OrdersCommand
    OrdersTable = New DataTable()
    OrdersAdapter.Fill(OrdersTable)
    'establish Customers command object
    CustomersCommand = New SqlCommand("SELECT * FROM Customers", KWSalesConnection)
    'establish Customers data adapter/data table
    CustomersAdapter = New SqlDataAdapter()
    CustomersAdapter.SelectCommand = CustomersCommand
    CustomersTable = New DataTable()
    CustomersAdapter.Fill(CustomersTable)
    'bind controls to data table
    txtFirstName.DataBindings.Add("Text", CustomersTable, "FirstName")
```

Sample Database Projects 10-17

```
        txtLastName.DataBindings.Add("Text", CustomersTable,
"LastName")
        txtAddress.DataBindings.Add("Text", CustomersTable,
"Address")
        txtCity.DataBindings.Add("Text", CustomersTable, "City")
        txtState.DataBindings.Add("Text", CustomersTable,
"State")
        txtZip.DataBindings.Add("Text", CustomersTable, "Zip")
        'establish currency manager
        CustomersManager =
DirectCast(Me.BindingContext(CustomersTable),
CurrencyManager)
        OrderNumber = 0
        Call NewOrder()
    End Sub
```

5. Add the shaded code to the **frmKWSales FormClosing** procedure:

```
    Private Sub FrmKWSales_FormClosing(ByVal sender As
System.Object, ByVal e As
System.Windows.Forms.FormClosingEventArgs) Handles
MyBase.FormClosing
        'close the connection
        KWSalesConnection.Close()
        'dispose of the objects
        OrdersCommand.Dispose()
        OrdersAdapter.Dispose()
        OrdersTable.Dispose()
        CustomersCommand.Dispose()
        CustomersAdapter.Dispose()
        CustomersTable.Dispose()
    End Sub
```

6. We will use the combo box to list existing customers in the following format:

   LastName, FirstName (CustomerID)

This will let us easily locate an existing customer based on unique **CustomerID**. When a user selects a name, the name and address fields will be filled in. Add this general procedure (**FillCustomers**) to the project (this code initializes the listings in the combo box):

```
Private Sub FillCustomers()
  Dim NRec As Integer
  cboCustomers.Items.Clear()
  If CustomersTable.Rows.Count <> 0 Then
    For NRec = 0 To CustomersTable.Rows.Count - 1

cboCustomers.Items.Add(CustomerListing(CustomersTable.Rows(NRec).Item("LastName").ToString, CustomersTable.Rows(NRec).Item("FirstName").ToString, CustomersTable.Rows(NRec).Item("CustomerID").ToString))
      Next NRec
    End If
End Sub
```

This uses a little function (**CustomerListing**) to generate the proper format:

```
Private Function CustomerListing(ByVal LastName As String, ByVal FirstName As String, ByVal ID As String) As String
    Return (LastName + ", " + FirstName + " (" + ID + ")")
End Function
```

Now add this to the **frmKWSales Load** event procedure right after the code establishing the **Customers** table data objects (before the **OrderNumber = 0** line:

```
'Fill customers combo box
Call FillCustomers()
```

Sample Database Projects 10-19

7. Place this code in the **cboCustomers SelectedIndexChanged** event (this code fills the customer address information based on the selected customer):

```
Private Sub CboCustomers_SelectedIndexChanged(ByVal sender
As System.Object, ByVal e As System.EventArgs) Handles
cboCustomers.SelectedIndexChanged
    Dim ID As String, PL As Integer
    Try
      PL = InStr(cboCustomers.SelectedItem.ToString, "(")
      If PL = 0 Then Exit Sub
      'extract ID from selected item
      ID = Mid(cboCustomers.SelectedItem.ToString, PL + 1,
Len(cboCustomers.SelectedItem.ToString) - PL - 1)
      CustomersTable.DefaultView.Sort = "CustomerID"
      CustomersManager.Position =
CustomersTable.DefaultView.Find(ID)
    Catch ex As Exception
      MessageBox.Show("Could not find customer", "Search
Error", MessageBoxButtons.OK, MessageBoxIcon.Information)
    End Try
  End Sub
```

8. Place this code at the bottom of the **NewOrder** procedure to initialize customer information:

```
If cboCustomers.Items.Count <> 0 Then
  cboCustomers.SelectedIndex = 0
End If
```

9. Save and run the application. Choose a customer (assuming there are some in your database – the sample has a few). Here's what I get when I choose myself:

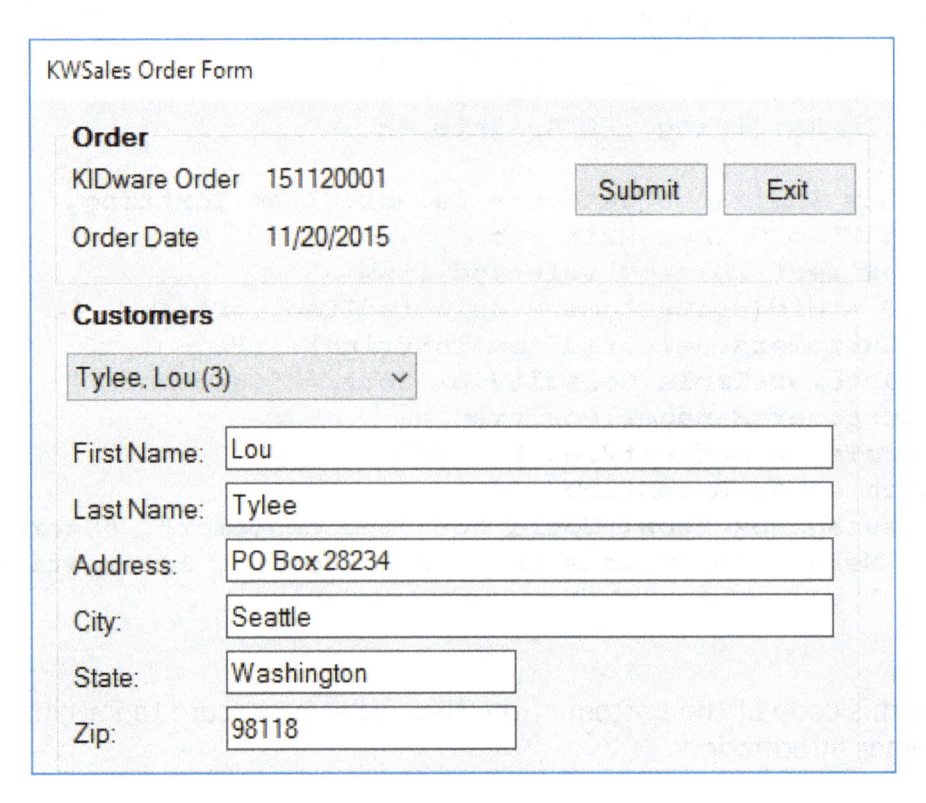

KWSales Order Form

Order

KIDware Order   151120001

Order Date   11/20/2015

Submit   Exit

Customers

Tylee, Lou (3)

First Name: Lou

Last Name: Tylee

Address: PO Box 28234

City: Seattle

State: Washington

Zip: 98118

Adding a New Customer

What if the customer placing an order is new and has no information on file? We need to modify the project to account for this possibility. The coding is a little tricky. Recall from our work with the books database that autonumber fields (like the **CustomerID** field) are not generated by ADO .NET until the database is written back to file. We need the **CustomerID** for any new customers we add to our database. Hence, when names are added, we need to close, then reopen the database to retrieve the **CustomerID** value. See the **btnSave_Click** event procedure for details.

1. Add three buttons to the right of the combo box in the **Customer** area of the **KWSales** form:

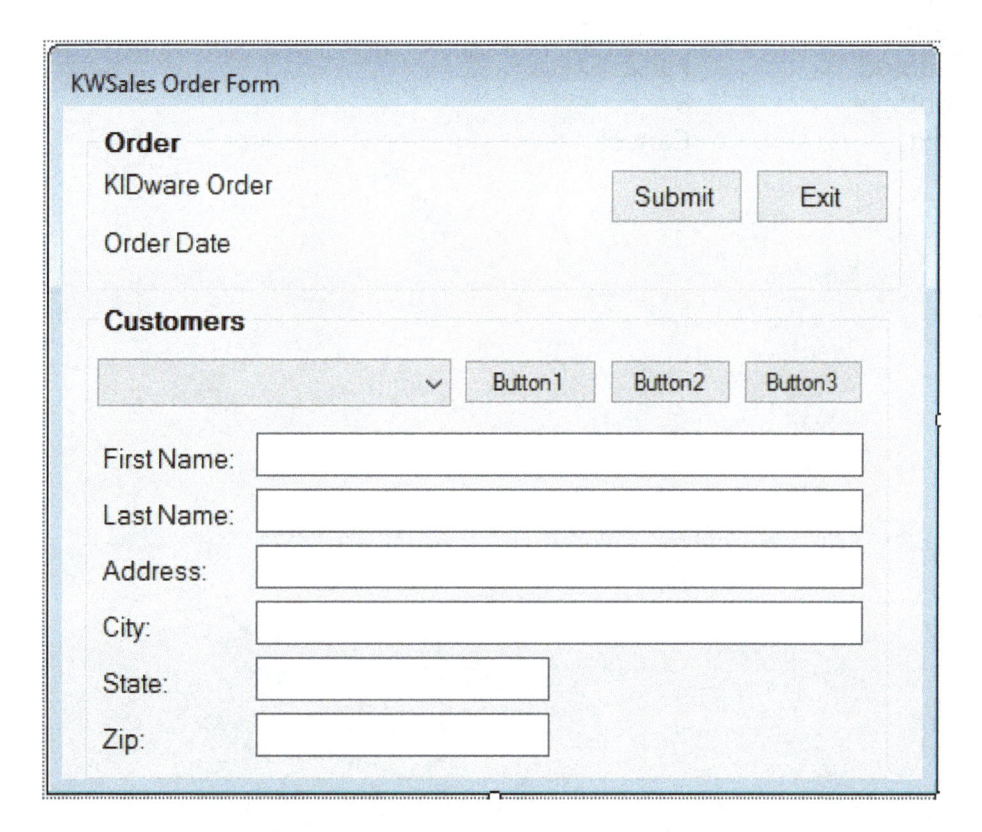

2. Use these properties:

   Button1:
Name	btnNew
FontSize	8
Text	New

   Button2:
Name	btnSave
Enabled	False
FontSize	8
Text	Save

   Button3:
Name	btnCancel
Enabled	False
FontSize	8
Text	Cancel

When the **New** button is clicked, the user can type in new customer information. This can then be saved in the database. The form now looks like this:

3. Add two variables in the form level declarations:

```
Dim NewCustomer As Boolean = False, SavedIndex As Integer
```

NewCustomer is used to indicate if we are adding a customer. **SavedIndex** is used to return to the currently displayed customer if adding a new customer is cancelled.

4. Add this code to the **btnNew Click** event procedure:

```
Private Sub BtnNew_Click(ByVal sender As System.Object, ByVal e As System.EventArgs) Handles btnNew.Click
    'enable text boxes for editing and add row
    NewCustomer = True
    txtFirstName.ReadOnly = False
    txtLastName.ReadOnly = False
    txtAddress.ReadOnly = False
    txtCity.ReadOnly = False
    txtState.ReadOnly = False
    txtZip.ReadOnly = False
    btnNew.Enabled = False
    btnSave.Enabled = True
    btnCancel.Enabled = True
    SavedIndex = cboCustomers.SelectedIndex
    cboCustomers.SelectedIndex = -1
    cboCustomers.Enabled = False
    CustomersManager.AddNew()
    txtFirstName.Focus()
End Sub
```

This sets the form in proper state and adds an empty record to the customer list.

5. Add this single line at the top of the **cboCustomers SelectedIndexChanged** event procedure (to keep the search from occurring while entering a new customer):

```
If NewCustomer Then Exit Sub
```

Sample Database Projects 10-25

6. Code the **KeyPress** event for each text box to let the **<Enter>** key change focus:

```
Private Sub TxtFirstName_KeyPress(ByVal sender As
System.Object, ByVal e As
System.Windows.Forms.KeyPressEventArgs) Handles
txtFirstName.KeyPress
    If e.KeyChar = ControlChars.Cr Then txtLastName.Focus()
End Sub

Private Sub TxtLastName_KeyPress(ByVal sender As
System.Object, ByVal e As
System.Windows.Forms.KeyPressEventArgs) Handles
txtLastName.KeyPress
    If e.KeyChar = ControlChars.Cr Then txtAddress.Focus()
End Sub

Private Sub TxtAddress_KeyPress(ByVal sender As
System.Object, ByVal e As
System.Windows.Forms.KeyPressEventArgs) Handles
txtAddress.KeyPress
    If e.KeyChar = ControlChars.Cr Then txtCity.Focus()
End Sub

Private Sub TxtCity_KeyPress(ByVal sender As
System.Object, ByVal e As
System.Windows.Forms.KeyPressEventArgs) Handles
txtCity.KeyPress
    If e.KeyChar = ControlChars.Cr Then txtState.Focus()
End Sub

Private Sub TxtState_KeyPress(ByVal sender As
System.Object, ByVal e As
System.Windows.Forms.KeyPressEventArgs) Handles
txtState.KeyPress
    If e.KeyChar = ControlChars.Cr Then txtZip.Focus()
End Sub

Private Sub TxtZip_KeyPress(ByVal sender As System.Object,
ByVal e As System.Windows.Forms.KeyPressEventArgs) Handles
txtZip.KeyPress
    If e.KeyChar = ControlChars.Cr Then btnSave.Focus()
End Sub
```

7. Add this code to the **btnCancel Click** event procedure (this returns the screen to the previous customer without changing anything):

```
Private Sub BtnCancel_Click(ByVal sender As System.Object, ByVal e As System.EventArgs) Handles btnCancel.Click
    'return to previous customer
    NewCustomer = False
    txtFirstName.ReadOnly = True
    txtLastName.ReadOnly = True
    txtAddress.ReadOnly = True
    txtCity.ReadOnly = True
    txtState.ReadOnly = True
    txtZip.ReadOnly = True
    btnNew.Enabled = True
    btnSave.Enabled = False
    btnCancel.Enabled = False
    CustomersManager.CancelCurrentEdit()
    cboCustomers.Enabled = True
    cboCustomers.SelectedIndex = SavedIndex
End Sub
```

8. Use this code in the **btnSave Click** event procedure:

Access Database:

```
Private Sub BtnSave_Click(ByVal sender As System.Object, ByVal e As System.EventArgs) Handles btnSave.Click
    Dim AllOK As Boolean = True
    'make sure there are entries
    If txtFirstName.Text = "" Then AllOK = False
    If txtLastName.Text = "" Then AllOK = False
    If txtAddress.Text = "" Then AllOK = False
    If txtCity.Text = "" Then AllOK = False
    If txtState.Text = "" Then AllOK = False
    If txtZip.Text = "" Then AllOK = False
    If Not (AllOK) Then
       MessageBox.Show("All text boxes require an entry.", "Information Missing", MessageBoxButtons.OK, MessageBoxIcon.Information)
       txtFirstName.Focus()
       Exit Sub
    End If
    CustomersManager.EndCurrentEdit()
    'save to database then reopen to retrieve assigned CustomerID
    Dim SavedFirstName As String = txtFirstName.Text
    Dim SavedLastName As String = txtLastName.Text
```

```vb
        Dim CustomersAdapterCommands As New OleDbCommandBuilder(CustomersAdapter)
        CustomersAdapter.Update(CustomersTable)
        KWSalesConnection.Close()
        'reconnect to sales database
        KWSalesConnection = New OleDbConnection("Provider=Microsoft.ACE.OLEDB.12.0; Data Source = " + Application.StartupPath + "\KWSalesDB.accb")
        KWSalesConnection.Open()
        CustomersCommand = New OleDbCommand("SELECT * FROM Customers", KWSalesConnection)
        CustomersAdapter = New OleDbDataAdapter()
        CustomersAdapter.SelectCommand = CustomersCommand
        CustomersTable = New DataTable()
        CustomersAdapter.Fill(CustomersTable)
        'rebind controls to data table
        txtFirstName.DataBindings.Clear()
        txtLastName.DataBindings.Clear()
        txtLastName.DataBindings.Clear()
        txtAddress.DataBindings.Clear()
        txtCity.DataBindings.Clear()
        txtState.DataBindings.Clear()
        txtZip.DataBindings.Clear()
        txtFirstName.DataBindings.Add("Text", CustomersTable, "FirstName")
        txtLastName.DataBindings.Add("Text", CustomersTable, "LastName")
        txtAddress.DataBindings.Add("Text", CustomersTable, "Address")
        txtCity.DataBindings.Add("Text", CustomersTable, "City")
        txtState.DataBindings.Add("Text", CustomersTable, "State")
        txtZip.DataBindings.Add("Text", CustomersTable, "Zip")
        CustomersManager = DirectCast(Me.BindingContext(CustomersTable), CurrencyManager)
        'find added customer
        Dim I As Integer, ID As String = ""
        For I = 0 To CustomersTable.Rows.Count - 1
          If CustomersTable.Rows(I).Item("FirstName").ToString = SavedFirstName And CustomersTable.Rows(I).Item("LastName").ToString = SavedLastName Then
            ID = CustomersTable.Rows(I).Item("CustomerID").ToString
            Exit For
          End If
        Next
```

```
        cboCustomers.Enabled = True
        'refill customers combo box
        Call FillCustomers()
        'display new customer
        NewCustomer = False
        txtFirstName.ReadOnly = True
        txtLastName.ReadOnly = True
        txtAddress.ReadOnly = True
        txtCity.ReadOnly = True
        txtState.ReadOnly = True
        txtZip.ReadOnly = True
        btnNew.Enabled = True
        btnSave.Enabled = False
        btnCancel.Enabled = False
        cboCustomers.SelectedItem =
CustomerListing(SavedLastName, SavedFirstName, ID)
    End Sub
```

SQL Server Database:

```
    Private Sub BtnSave_Click(ByVal sender As System.Object,
ByVal e As System.EventArgs) Handles btnSave.Click
        Dim AllOK As Boolean = True
        'make sure there are entries
        If txtFirstName.Text = "" Then AllOK = False
        If txtLastName.Text = "" Then AllOK = False
        If txtAddress.Text = "" Then AllOK = False
        If txtCity.Text = "" Then AllOK = False
        If txtState.Text = "" Then AllOK = False
        If txtZip.Text = "" Then AllOK = False
        If Not (AllOK) Then
            MessageBox.Show("All text boxes require an entry.",
"Information Missing", MessageBoxButtons.OK,
MessageBoxIcon.Information)
            txtFirstName.Focus()
            Exit Sub
        End If
        CustomersManager.EndCurrentEdit()
        'save to database then reopen to retrieve assigned
CustomerID
        Dim SavedFirstName As String = txtFirstName.Text
        Dim SavedLastName As String = txtLastName.Text
        Dim CustomersAdapterCommands As New
SqlCommandBuilder(CustomersAdapter)
        CustomersAdapter.Update(CustomersTable)
        KWSalesConnection.Close()
        'reconnect to sales database
```

```vb
        KWSalesConnection = New SqlConnection("Data
Source=.\SQLEXPRESS; AttachDbFilename=" +
Application.StartupPath + "\SQLKWSalesDB.mdf; Integrated
Security=True; Connect Timeout=30; User Instance=True")
        KWSalesConnection.Open()
        CustomersCommand = New SqlCommand("SELECT * FROM
Customers", KWSalesConnection)
        CustomersAdapter = New SqlDataAdapter()
        CustomersAdapter.SelectCommand = CustomersCommand
        CustomersTable = New DataTable()
        CustomersAdapter.Fill(CustomersTable)
        'rebind controls to data table
        txtFirstName.DataBindings.Clear()
        txtLastName.DataBindings.Clear()
        txtLastName.DataBindings.Clear()
        txtAddress.DataBindings.Clear()
        txtCity.DataBindings.Clear()
        txtState.DataBindings.Clear()
        txtZip.DataBindings.Clear()
        txtFirstName.DataBindings.Add("Text", CustomersTable,
"FirstName")
        txtLastName.DataBindings.Add("Text", CustomersTable,
"LastName")
        txtAddress.DataBindings.Add("Text", CustomersTable,
"Address")
        txtCity.DataBindings.Add("Text", CustomersTable, "City")
        txtState.DataBindings.Add("Text", CustomersTable,
"State")
        txtZip.DataBindings.Add("Text", CustomersTable, "Zip")
        CustomersManager =
DirectCast(Me.BindingContext(CustomersTable),
CurrencyManager)
        'find added customer
        Dim I As Integer, ID As String = ""
        For I = 0 To CustomersTable.Rows.Count - 1
           If CustomersTable.Rows(I).Item("FirstName").ToString =
SavedFirstName And
CustomersTable.Rows(I).Item("LastName").ToString =
SavedLastName Then
              ID =
CustomersTable.Rows(I).Item("CustomerID").ToString
              Exit For
           End If
        Next
        cboCustomers.Enabled = True
        'refill table
        Call FillCustomers()
        'display new customer
```

```
    NewCustomer = False
    txtFirstName.ReadOnly = True
    txtLastName.ReadOnly = True
    txtAddress.ReadOnly = True
    txtCity.ReadOnly = True
    txtState.ReadOnly = True
    txtZip.ReadOnly = True
    btnNew.Enabled = True
    btnSave.Enabled = False
    btnCancel.Enabled = False
    cboCustomers.SelectedItem = CustomerListing(SavedLastName, SavedFirstName, ID)
  End Sub
```

This is a lot of code, but actually pretty easy to follow. This code first checks to make sure all text boxes are filled. It then ends the edit and saves the changes to the database. This allows us to retrieve the needed **CustomerID** field (an autonumber field not available until the database is saved). We then reopen the database file, recreate the Customers data objects, rebind the controls and add the new customer. A lot of work, but necessary.

Sample Database Projects 10-31

9. Add the shaded code to the **frmKWSales FormClosing** event procedure. This code saves any changes made back to the database file.

Access Database:

```
Private Sub FrmKWSales_FormClosing(ByVal sender As
System.Object, ByVal e As
System.Windows.Forms.FormClosingEventArgs) Handles
MyBase.FormClosing
    If NewCustomer Then
        MessageBox.Show("You must finish the current edit
before stopping.", "", MessageBoxButtons.OK,
MessageBoxIcon.Information)
        e.Cancel = True
    Else
      Try
        'save the tables to the database file
        Dim OrdersAdapterCommands As New
OleDbCommandBuilder(OrdersAdapter)
        OrdersAdapter.Update(OrdersTable)
        Dim CustomersAdapterCommands As New
OleDbCommandBuilder(CustomersAdapter)
        CustomersAdapter.Update(CustomersTable)
      Catch ex As Exception
        MessageBox.Show("Error saving database", "Save
Error", MessageBoxButtons.OK, MessageBoxIcon.Error)
      End Try
        'close the connection
        KWSalesConnection.Close()
        'dispose of the objects
        OrdersCommand.Dispose()
        OrdersAdapter.Dispose()
        OrdersTable.Dispose()
        CustomersCommand.Dispose()
        CustomersAdapter.Dispose()
        CustomersTable.Dispose()
    End If
End Sub
```

SQL Server Database:

```vb
    Private Sub FrmKWSales_FormClosing(ByVal sender As System.Object, ByVal e As System.Windows.Forms.FormClosingEventArgs) Handles MyBase.FormClosing
        If NewCustomer Then
            MessageBox.Show("You must finish the current edit before stopping.", "", MessageBoxButtons.OK, MessageBoxIcon.Information)
            e.Cancel = True
        Else
            Try
                'save the tables to the database file
                Dim OrdersAdapterCommands As New SqlCommandBuilder(OrdersAdapter)
                OrdersAdapter.Update(OrdersTable)
                Dim CustomersAdapterCommands As New SqlCommandBuilder(CustomersAdapter)
                CustomersAdapter.Update(CustomersTable)
            Catch ex As Exception
                MessageBox.Show("Error saving database", "Save Error", MessageBoxButtons.OK, MessageBoxIcon.Error)
            End Try
            'close the connection
            KWSalesConnection.Close()
            'dispose of the objects
            OrdersCommand.Dispose()
            OrdersAdapter.Dispose()
            OrdersTable.Dispose()
            CustomersCommand.Dispose()
            CustomersAdapter.Dispose()
            CustomersTable.Dispose()
        End If
    End Sub
```

10. Save and run the application. Make sure you can add new customers and make sure they appear in the combo box for selection after addition. Check to insure they are saved to database after closing the application. Make sure the **Cancel** button works correctly. Here's an entry I added:

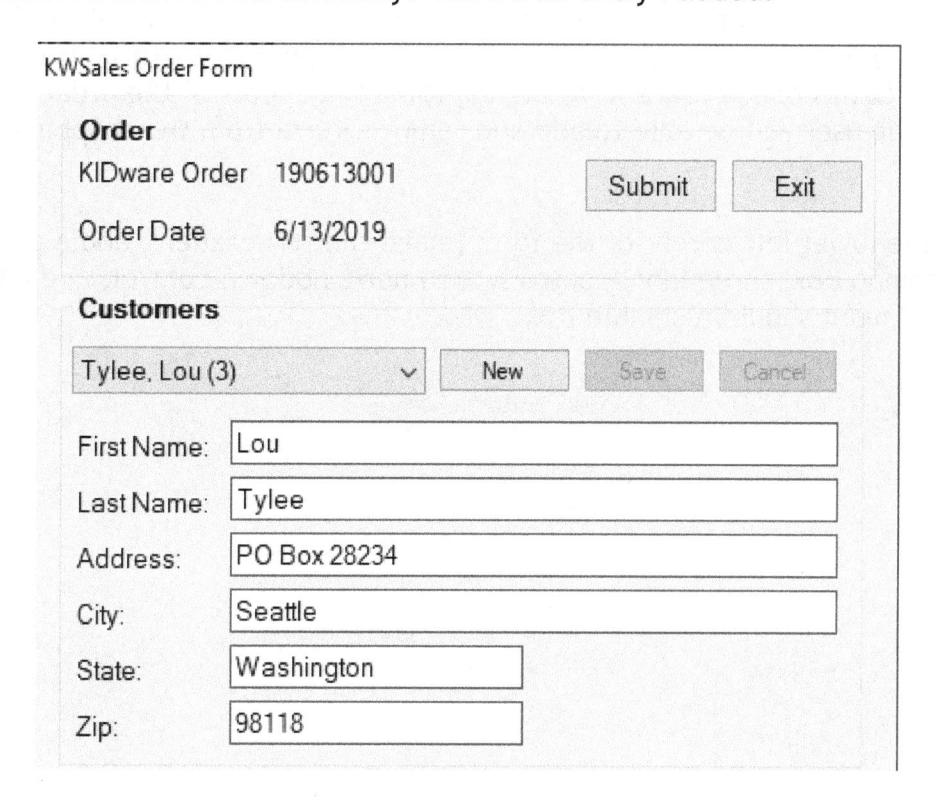

```
KWSales Order Form

Order
  KIDware Order   190613001              Submit      Exit
  Order Date      6/13/2019

Customers
  [Tylee, Lou (3)        v]   [New]  [Save]  [Cancel]

  First Name:  [Lou            ]
  Last Name:   [Tylee          ]
  Address:     [PO Box 28234   ]
  City:        [Seattle        ]
  State:       [Washington     ]
  Zip:         [98118          ]
```

Product Selection

Now, we're ready to add the ability to select products for ordering. We'll use the popular 'shopping cart' approach. A user will select the quantity of product(s) desired. These will be added to a shopping cart (list box) so it is clear what has been ordered. A running total of the cost of the order will be kept. The user will be able to add and remove items from the shopping cart at will.

1. In the lower left corner of the form (make the form taller), add a group box, a combo box, three label controls, a numeric updown control, and a button. The layout should resemble this:

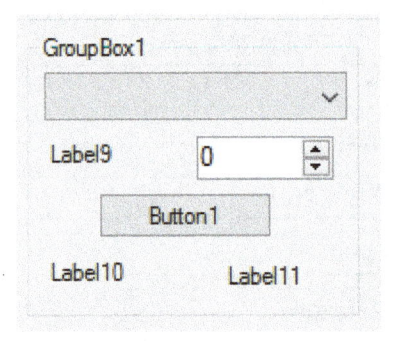

2. Set these properties:

   GroupBox1:
Name	grpProducts
Text	Products
FontSize	10
FontBold	True

   ComboBox1:
Name	cboProducts
DropdownStyle	DropdownList

   Label9:
Text	Quantity
FontSize	10

   Label10:
Text	Total:
FontSize	10

   Label11:
Name	lblTotal
AutoSize	False
BackColor	White
BorderStyle	Fixed3D
Text	0.00
TextAlign	MiddleCenter
FontSize	10

   NumericUpDown1:
Name	nudQuantity
Minimum	1
Maximum	99
TextAlign	Center
Value	1

   Button1:
Name	btnAdd
FontSize	8
Text	Add to Cart

At this point, the new group box appears like:

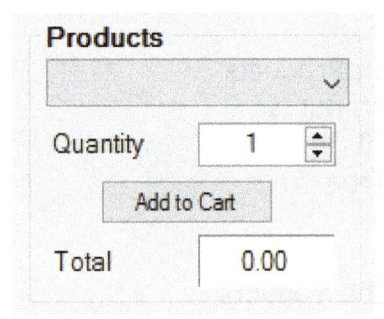

This will work as follows: the user selects a product using the combo box and sets the quantity using the numeric updown control. The purchase is added to the shopping cart by clicking **Add to Cart**. The **Total** box will indicate the current cost of the order. Let's build the shopping cart, and then do the coding.

1. Add a group box next to the **Products** group box. Place a list box and a button in the group box. The additions should resemble this:

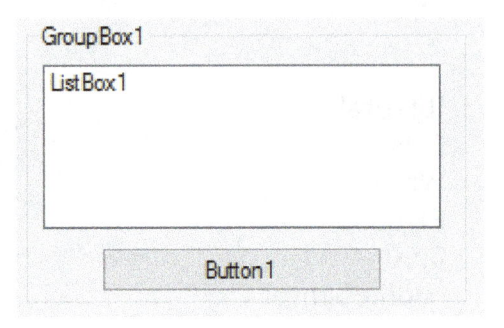

2. Set these properties:

    GroupBox1:
        Name   grpCart
        Text   Shopping Cart
        FontSize   10
        FontBold   True

    ListBox1:
        Name   lstCart
        FontSize   8
        Sorted   True

Button1:
    Name   btnRemove
    FontSize   8
    Text   Remove from Cart

The completed **Order Form** with the added Products and Shopping Cart group boxes now looks like this:

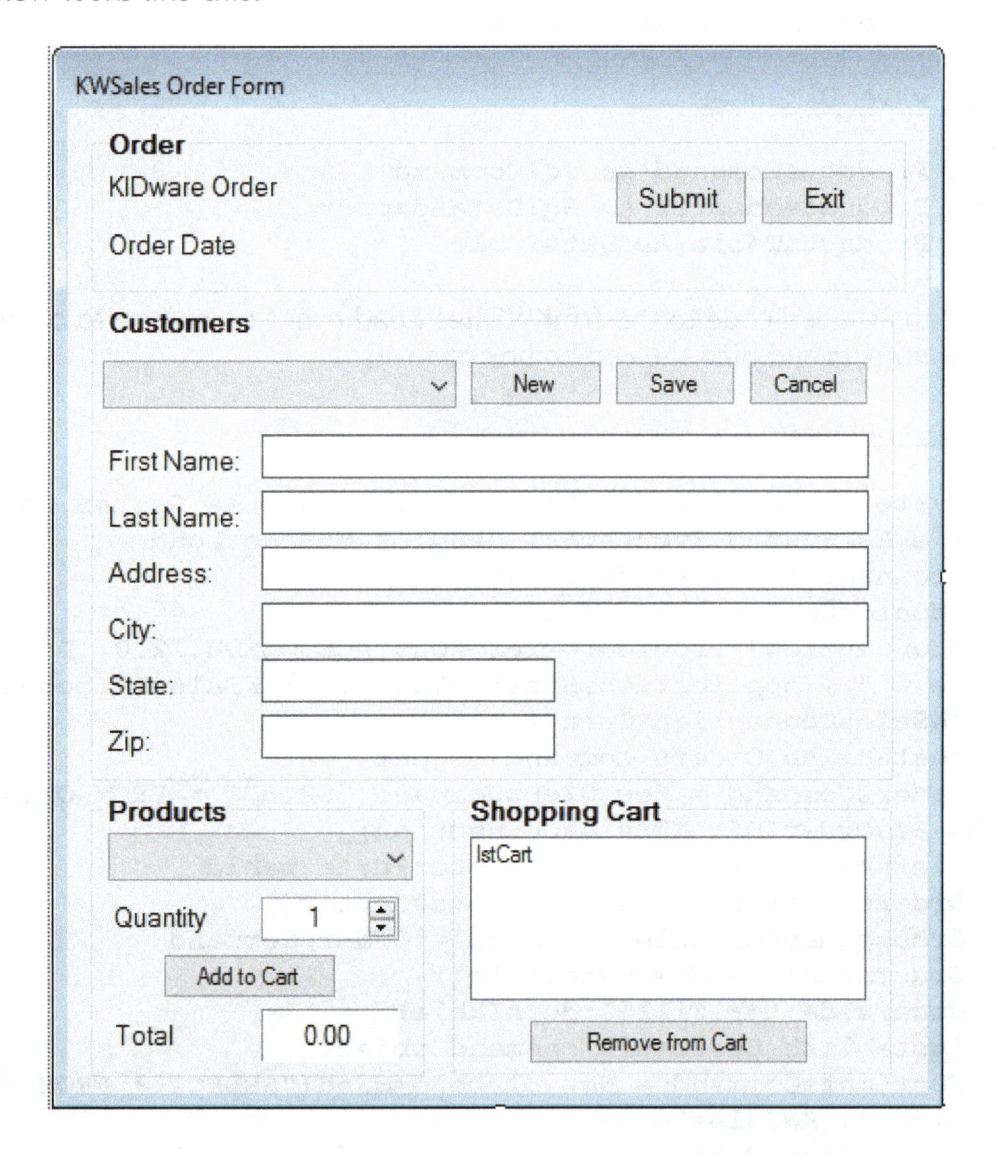

3. We add another set of data objects that connect to the **Products** table in the database. Add these form level declarations:

Access Database:

```
Dim ProductsCommand As OleDbCommand
Dim ProductsAdapter As OleDbDataAdapter
Dim ProductsTable As DataTable
```

SQL Server Database:

```
Dim ProductsCommand As SqlCommand
Dim ProductsAdapter As SqlDataAdapter
Dim ProductsTable As DataTable
```

4. Add the shaded code to the **frmKWSales Load** event procedure to create the new objects and bind the combo box control:

Access Database:

```
Private Sub FrmKWSales_Load(ByVal sender As System.Object, ByVal e As System.EventArgs) Handles MyBase.Load
    'connect to sales database
    KWSalesConnection = New OleDbConnection("Provider=Microsoft.ACE.OLEDB.12.0; Data Source = " + Application.StartupPath + "\KWSalesDB.accdb")
    KWSalesConnection.Open()
    'establish Orders command object
    OrdersCommand = New OleDbCommand("SELECT * FROM Orders ORDER BY OrderID", KWSalesConnection)
    'establish Orders data adapter/data table
    OrdersAdapter = New OleDbDataAdapter()
    OrdersAdapter.SelectCommand = OrdersCommand
    OrdersTable = New DataTable()
    OrdersAdapter.Fill(OrdersTable)
    'establish Customers command object
    CustomersCommand = New OleDbCommand("SELECT * FROM Customers", KWSalesConnection)
    'establish Customers data adapter/data table
    CustomersAdapter = New OleDbDataAdapter()
    CustomersAdapter.SelectCommand = CustomersCommand
    CustomersTable = New DataTable()
    CustomersAdapter.Fill(CustomersTable)
    'bind controls to data table
    txtFirstName.DataBindings.Add("Text", CustomersTable, "FirstName")
```

Sample Database Projects   10-39

```vb
    txtLastName.DataBindings.Add("Text", CustomersTable, "LastName")
    txtAddress.DataBindings.Add("Text", CustomersTable, "Address")
    txtCity.DataBindings.Add("Text", CustomersTable, "City")
    txtState.DataBindings.Add("Text", CustomersTable, "State")
    txtZip.DataBindings.Add("Text", CustomersTable, "Zip")
    'establish currency manager
    CustomersManager = DirectCast(Me.BindingContext(CustomersTable), CurrencyManager)
    'establish Products command object
    ProductsCommand = New OleDbCommand("SELECT * FROM Products ORDER BY Description", KWSalesConnection)
    'establish Products data adapter/data table
    ProductsAdapter = New OleDbDataAdapter()
    ProductsAdapter.SelectCommand = ProductsCommand
    ProductsTable = New DataTable()
    ProductsAdapter.Fill(ProductsTable)
    'bind combobox to data table
    cboProducts.DataSource = ProductsTable
    cboProducts.DisplayMember = "Description"
    cboProducts.ValueMember = "ProductID"
    'Fill customers combo box
    Call FillCustomers()
    OrderNumber = 0
    Call NewOrder()
  End Sub
```

<u>SQL Server Database:</u>

```vb
  Private Sub FrmKWSales_Load(ByVal sender As System.Object, ByVal e As System.EventArgs) Handles MyBase.Load
    'connect to sales database
    KWSalesConnection = New SqlConnection("Data Source=.\SQLEXPRESS; AttachDbFilename=" + Application.StartupPath + "\SQLKWSalesDB.mdf; Integrated Security=True; Connect Timeout=30; User Instance=True")
    KWSalesConnection.Open()
    'establish Orders command object
    OrdersCommand = New SqlCommand("SELECT * FROM Orders ORDER BY OrderID", KWSalesConnection)
    'establish Orders data adapter/data table
    OrdersAdapter = New SqlDataAdapter()
    OrdersAdapter.SelectCommand = OrdersCommand
    OrdersTable = New DataTable()
    OrdersAdapter.Fill(OrdersTable)
```

```vb
    'establish Customers command object
    CustomersCommand = New SqlCommand("SELECT * FROM Customers", KWSalesConnection)
    'establish Customers data adapter/data table
    CustomersAdapter = New SqlDataAdapter()
    CustomersAdapter.SelectCommand = CustomersCommand
    CustomersTable = New DataTable()
    CustomersAdapter.Fill(CustomersTable)
    'bind controls to data table
    txtFirstName.DataBindings.Add("Text", CustomersTable, "FirstName")
    txtLastName.DataBindings.Add("Text", CustomersTable, "LastName")
    txtAddress.DataBindings.Add("Text", CustomersTable, "Address")
    txtCity.DataBindings.Add("Text", CustomersTable, "City")
    txtState.DataBindings.Add("Text", CustomersTable, "State")
    txtZip.DataBindings.Add("Text", CustomersTable, "Zip")
    'establish currency manager
    CustomersManager = DirectCast(Me.BindingContext(CustomersTable), CurrencyManager)
    'establish Products command object
    ProductsCommand = New SqlCommand("SELECT * FROM Products ORDER BY Description", KWSalesConnection)
    'establish Products data adapter/data table
    ProductsAdapter = New SqlDataAdapter()
    ProductsAdapter.SelectCommand = ProductsCommand
    ProductsTable = New DataTable()
    ProductsAdapter.Fill(ProductsTable)
    'bind combobox to data table
    cboProducts.DataSource = ProductsTable
    cboProducts.DisplayMember = "Description"
    cboProducts.ValueMember = "ProductID"
    'Fill customers combo box
    Call FillCustomers()
    OrderNumber = 0
    Call NewOrder()
End Sub
```

5. Add these three lines near the bottom of the **frmKWSales FormClosing** procedure (where the other objects are disposed):

```
ProductsCommand.Dispose()
ProductsAdapter.Dispose()
ProductsTable.Dispose()
```

6. Put this code at the bottom of the **NewOrder** procedure (this will initialize the **Purchases** and **Shopping Cart** group boxes):

```
'Clear purchase information
cboProducts.SelectedIndex = -1
nudQuantity.Value = 1
lblTotal.Text = "0.00"
lstCart.Items.Clear()
```

7. Put this code in the **btnAdd_Click** procedure:

```
Private Sub BtnAdd_Click(ByVal sender As System.Object, ByVal e As System.EventArgs) Handles btnAdd.Click
    Dim UnitPrice As Single
    If cboProducts.SelectedIndex = -1 Then
       MessageBox.Show("You must select a product.", "Purchase Error", MessageBoxButtons.OK, MessageBoxIcon.Information)
       Exit Sub
    End If
    'Find unit price of selected product
    Dim NRec As Integer
    For NRec = 0 To ProductsTable.Rows.Count - 1
      If ProductsTable.Rows(NRec).Item("Description").ToString = cboProducts.Text.ToString Then
        UnitPrice = CSng(ProductsTable.Rows(NRec).Item("Price"))
        Exit For
      End If
    Next
    lstCart.Items.Add(Format(nudQuantity.Value, "##") + " " + cboProducts.SelectedValue.ToString + "-" + cboProducts.Text.ToString + " " + Format(UnitPrice, "$0.00"))
    'Adjust total price
    lblTotal.Text = Format(Val(lblTotal.Text) + nudQuantity.Value * UnitPrice, "0.00")
  End Sub
```

This code finds the price and description of the selected product and adds the item to the **Shopping Cart** list box. The format of the listing is:

Quantity ProductID-Description Price

The code also adjusts the displayed total price.

8. Add this code to the **btnRemove Click** event procedure (this removes a selected object and adjusts the displayed price):

```
Private Sub BtnRemove_Click(ByVal sender As System.Object, ByVal e As System.EventArgs) Handles btnRemove.Click
    Dim Q As Integer, P As Single, I As Integer
    If lstCart.SelectedIndex <> -1 Then
      'Adjust total before removing
      'find Q (quantity) and P (price)
      I = InStr(lstCart.Text, " ")
      Q = CInt(Mid(lstCart.Text, 1, I - 1))
      I = InStr(lstCart.Text, "$")
      P = CSng(Mid(lstCart.Text, I + 1, Len(lstCart.Text) - I))
      lblTotal.Text = Format(Val(lblTotal.Text) - Q * P, "0.00")
      lstCart.Items.RemoveAt(lstCart.SelectedIndex)
    End If
  End Sub
```

3. Save and run the application. Try selecting and adding items to the shopping cart. Try removing items. Make sure everything works as it should. Here's what the form looks like after selecting a customer and a few items:

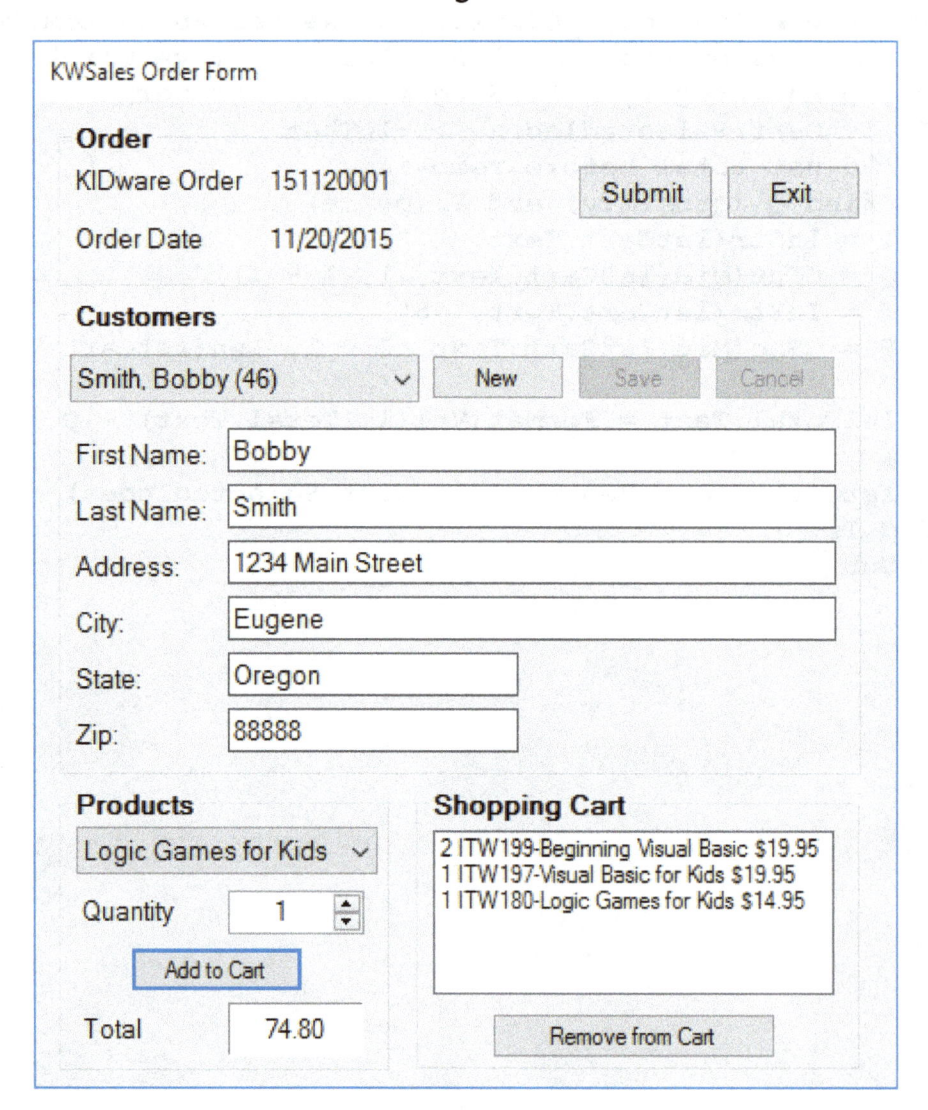

Submitting an Order

We now have the ability to specify what to order. A final step is to commit all order information to the database. The procedure is a bit complicated but straightforward. When the user clicks the **Submit** button, the following will occur:

Cycle through each item in the shopping cart. For each:

- Add a new row to **OrdersTable**. Set values for **OrderID**, **CustomerID**, **OrderDate** fields.
- Add a new row to **PurchasesTable** (not created yet; the data table representing the Purchases table).
- Parse the shopping cart listing to obtain quantity purchased and product identification.
- Update **PurchasesTable** with **OrderID**, **Quantity** and **ProductID** fields.
- Update **NumberSold** field in **ProductsTable** (use **Quantity** and **ProductID** for reference).

Start a new order.

Let's implement these steps.

1. We add a final set of data objects that connect to the **Purchases** table in the database and a variable to store the Customer ID. Add these form level declarations:

   Access Database:

   ```
   Dim PurchasesCommand As OleDbCommand
   Dim PurchasesAdapter As OleDbDataAdapter
   Dim PurchasesTable As DataTable
   Dim CustomerID As Long
   ```

   SQL Server Database:

   ```
   Dim PurchasesCommand As SqlCommand
   Dim PurchasesAdapter As SqlDataAdapter
   Dim PurchasesTable As DataTable
   Dim CustomerID As Long
   ```

2. Add the shaded code to the **frmKWSales Load** event procedure to create the new objects:

Access Database:

```
Private Sub FrmKWSales_Load(ByVal sender As System.Object, ByVal e As System.EventArgs) Handles MyBase.Load
    'connect to sales database
    KWSalesConnection = New OleDbConnection("Provider=Microsoft.ACE.OLEDB.12.0; Data Source = " + Application.StartupPath + "\KWSalesDB.accdb")
    KWSalesConnection.Open()
    'establish Orders command object
    OrdersCommand = New OleDbCommand("SELECT * FROM Orders ORDER BY OrderID", KWSalesConnection)
    'establish Orders data adapter/data table
    OrdersAdapter = New OleDbDataAdapter()
    OrdersAdapter.SelectCommand = OrdersCommand
    OrdersTable = New DataTable()
    OrdersAdapter.Fill(OrdersTable)
    'establish Customers command object
    CustomersCommand = New OleDbCommand("SELECT * FROM Customers", KWSalesConnection)
    'establish Customers data adapter/data table
    CustomersAdapter = New OleDbDataAdapter()
    CustomersAdapter.SelectCommand = CustomersCommand
    CustomersTable = New DataTable()
    CustomersAdapter.Fill(CustomersTable)
    'bind controls to data table
    txtFirstName.DataBindings.Add("Text", CustomersTable, "FirstName")
    txtLastName.DataBindings.Add("Text", CustomersTable, "LastName")
    txtAddress.DataBindings.Add("Text", CustomersTable, "Address")
    txtCity.DataBindings.Add("Text", CustomersTable, "City")
    txtState.DataBindings.Add("Text", CustomersTable, "State")
    txtZip.DataBindings.Add("Text", CustomersTable, "Zip")
    'establish currency manager
    CustomersManager = DirectCast(Me.BindingContext(CustomersTable), CurrencyManager)
    'establish Products command object
    ProductsCommand = New OleDbCommand("SELECT * FROM Products ORDER BY Description", KWSalesConnection)
    'establish Products data adapter/data table
    ProductsAdapter = New OleDbDataAdapter()
```

```vb
        ProductsAdapter.SelectCommand = ProductsCommand
        ProductsTable = New DataTable()
        ProductsAdapter.Fill(ProductsTable)
        'bind combobox to data table
        cboProducts.DataSource = ProductsTable
        cboProducts.DisplayMember = "Description"
        cboProducts.ValueMember = "ProductID"
        'establish Purchases command object
        PurchasesCommand = New OleDbCommand("SELECT * FROM
Purchases ORDER BY OrderID", KWSalesConnection)
        'establish Purchases data adapter/data table
        PurchasesAdapter = New OleDbDataAdapter()
        PurchasesAdapter.SelectCommand = PurchasesCommand
        PurchasesTable = New DataTable()
        PurchasesAdapter.Fill(PurchasesTable)
        'Fill customers combo box
        Call FillCustomers()
        OrderNumber = 0
        Call NewOrder()
    End Sub
```

SQL Server Database:

```vb
    Private Sub FrmKWSales_Load(ByVal sender As System.Object,
ByVal e As System.EventArgs) Handles MyBase.Load
        'connect to sales database
        KWSalesConnection = New SqlConnection("Data
Source=.\SQLEXPRESS; AttachDbFilename=" +
Application.StartupPath + "\SQLKWSalesDB.mdf; Integrated
Security=True; Connect Timeout=30; User Instance=True")
        KWSalesConnection.Open()
        'establish Orders command object
        OrdersCommand = New SqlCommand("SELECT * FROM Orders
ORDER BY OrderID", KWSalesConnection)
        'establish Orders data adapter/data table
        OrdersAdapter = New SqlDataAdapter()
        OrdersAdapter.SelectCommand = OrdersCommand
        OrdersTable = New DataTable()
        OrdersAdapter.Fill(OrdersTable)
        'establish Customers command object
        CustomersCommand = New SqlCommand("SELECT * FROM
Customers", KWSalesConnection)
        'establish Customers data adapter/data table
        CustomersAdapter = New SqlDataAdapter()
        CustomersAdapter.SelectCommand = CustomersCommand
        CustomersTable = New DataTable()
        CustomersAdapter.Fill(CustomersTable)
        'bind controls to data table
```

```vb
    txtFirstName.DataBindings.Add("Text", CustomersTable, "FirstName")
    txtLastName.DataBindings.Add("Text", CustomersTable, "LastName")
    txtAddress.DataBindings.Add("Text", CustomersTable, "Address")
    txtCity.DataBindings.Add("Text", CustomersTable, "City")
    txtState.DataBindings.Add("Text", CustomersTable, "State")
    txtZip.DataBindings.Add("Text", CustomersTable, "Zip")
    'establish currency manager
    CustomersManager = DirectCast(Me.BindingContext(CustomersTable), CurrencyManager)
    'establish Products command object
    ProductsCommand = New SqlCommand("SELECT * FROM Products ORDER BY Description", KWSalesConnection)
    'establish Products data adapter/data table
    ProductsAdapter = New SqlDataAdapter()
    ProductsAdapter.SelectCommand = ProductsCommand
    ProductsTable = New DataTable()
    ProductsAdapter.Fill(ProductsTable)
    'bind combobox to data table
    cboProducts.DataSource = ProductsTable
    cboProducts.DisplayMember = "Description"
    cboProducts.ValueMember = "ProductID"
    'establish Purchases command object
    PurchasesCommand = New SqlCommand("SELECT * FROM Purchases ORDER BY OrderID", KWSalesConnection)
    'establish Purchases data adapter/data table
    PurchasesAdapter = New SqlDataAdapter()
    PurchasesAdapter.SelectCommand = PurchasesCommand
    PurchasesTable = New DataTable()
    PurchasesAdapter.Fill(PurchasesTable)
    'Fill customers combo box
    Call FillCustomers()
    OrderNumber = 0
    Call NewOrder()
  End Sub
```

Sample Database Projects 10-49

3. Add the shaded code to the **frmKWSales FormClosing** procedure to save the remaining data tables and dispose of the newly added objects:

Access Database:

```
Private Sub FrmKWSales_FormClosing(ByVal sender As
System.Object, ByVal e As
System.Windows.Forms.FormClosingEventArgs) Handles
MyBase.FormClosing
    If NewCustomer Then
      MessageBox.Show("You must finish the current edit
before stopping.", "", MessageBoxButtons.OK,
MessageBoxIcon.Information)
      e.Cancel = True
    Else
      Try
        'save the tables to the database file
        Dim OrdersAdapterCommands As New
OleDbCommandBuilder(OrdersAdapter)
        OrdersAdapter.Update(OrdersTable)
        Dim CustomersAdapterCommands As New
OleDbCommandBuilder(CustomersAdapter)
        CustomersAdapter.Update(CustomersTable)
        Dim ProductsAdapterCommands As New
OleDbCommandBuilder(ProductsAdapter)
        ProductsAdapter.Update(ProductsTable)
        Dim PurchasesAdapterCommands As New
OleDbCommandBuilder(PurchasesAdapter)
        PurchasesAdapter.Update(PurchasesTable)
      Catch ex As Exception
        MessageBox.Show("Error saving database", "Save
Error", MessageBoxButtons.OK, MessageBoxIcon.Error)
      End Try
      'close the connection
      KWSalesConnection.Close()
      'dispose of the objects
      OrdersCommand.Dispose()
      OrdersAdapter.Dispose()
      OrdersTable.Dispose()
      CustomersCommand.Dispose()
      CustomersAdapter.Dispose()
      CustomersTable.Dispose()
      ProductsCommand.Dispose()
      ProductsAdapter.Dispose()
      ProductsTable.Dispose()
      PurchasesCommand.Dispose()
      PurchasesAdapter.Dispose()
      PurchasesTable.Dispose()
```

```vb
        End If
    End Sub

SQL Server Database:

    Private Sub FrmKWSales_FormClosing(ByVal sender As System.Object, ByVal e As System.Windows.Forms.FormClosingEventArgs) Handles MyBase.FormClosing
        If NewCustomer Then
            MessageBox.Show("You must finish the current edit before stopping.", "", MessageBoxButtons.OK, MessageBoxIcon.Information)
            e.Cancel = True
        Else
          Try
            'save the tables to the database file
            Dim OrdersAdapterCommands As New SqlCommandBuilder(OrdersAdapter)
            OrdersAdapter.Update(OrdersTable)
            Dim CustomersAdapterCommands As New SqlCommandBuilder(CustomersAdapter)
            CustomersAdapter.Update(CustomersTable)
            Dim ProductsAdapterCommands As New SqlCommandBuilder(ProductsAdapter)
            ProductsAdapter.Update(ProductsTable)
            Dim PurchasesAdapterCommands As New SqlCommandBuilder(PurchasesAdapter)
            PurchasesAdapter.Update(PurchasesTable)
          Catch ex As Exception
            MessageBox.Show("Error saving database", "Save Error", MessageBoxButtons.OK, MessageBoxIcon.Error)
          End Try
          'close the connection
          KWSalesConnection.Close()
          'dispose of the objects
          OrdersCommand.Dispose()
          OrdersAdapter.Dispose()
          OrdersTable.Dispose()
          CustomersCommand.Dispose()
          CustomersAdapter.Dispose()
          CustomersTable.Dispose()
          ProductsCommand.Dispose()
          ProductsAdapter.Dispose()
          ProductsTable.Dispose()
          PurchasesCommand.Dispose()
          PurchasesAdapter.Dispose()
          PurchasesTable.Dispose()
```

```
        End If
    End Sub
```

4. Add the single shaded line to the **cboCustomers SelectedIndexChanged** procedure to establish the **CustomerID** variable:

```
Private Sub CboCustomers_SelectedIndexChanged(ByVal sender As System.Object, ByVal e As System.EventArgs) Handles cboCustomers.SelectedIndexChanged
    If NewCustomer Then Exit Sub
    Dim ID As String, PL As Integer
    Try
      PL = InStr(cboCustomers.SelectedItem.ToString, "(")
      If PL = 0 Then Exit Sub
      'extract ID from selected item
      ID = Mid(cboCustomers.SelectedItem.ToString, PL + 1, Len(cboCustomers.SelectedItem.ToString) - PL - 1)
      CustomersTable.DefaultView.Sort = "CustomerID"
      CustomersManager.Position = CustomersTable.DefaultView.Find(ID)
      CustomerID = CLng(ID)
    Catch ex As Exception
      MessageBox.Show("Could not find customer", "Search Error", MessageBoxButtons.OK, MessageBoxIcon.Information)
    End Try
  End Sub
```

10-52   Visual Basic and Databases

5. Place this code in the **btnSubmitOrder Click** event procedure:

```
    Private Sub BtnSubmitOrder_Click(ByVal sender As System.Object, ByVal e As System.EventArgs) Handles btnSubmitOrder.Click
      Dim I As Integer, J As Integer
      Dim Q As Integer, ID As String
      'Make sure there is customer information
      If cboCustomers.SelectedIndex = -1 Then
         MessageBox.Show("You need to select a customer.", "Submit Error", MessageBoxButtons.OK, MessageBoxIcon.Information)
         Exit Sub
      End If
      If lstCart.Items.Count = 0 Then
         MessageBox.Show("You need to select some items.", "Submit Error", MessageBoxButtons.OK, MessageBoxIcon.Information)
         Exit Sub
      End If
      'Submit purchases to database
      Dim NewRow As DataRow
      NewRow = OrdersTable.NewRow
      NewRow.Item("OrderID") = lblOrderID.Text
      NewRow.Item("CustomerID") = CustomerID
      NewRow.Item("OrderDate") = lblDate.Text
      OrdersTable.Rows.Add(NewRow)
      For I = 0 To lstCart.Items.Count - 1
        NewRow = PurchasesTable.NewRow
        J = InStr(lstCart.Items.Item(I).ToString, " ")
        Q = CInt(Mid(lstCart.Items.Item(I).ToString, 1, J - 1))
        ID = Mid(lstCart.Items.Item(I).ToString, J + 1, 6)
        NewRow.Item("OrderID") = lblOrderID.Text
        NewRow.Item("ProductID") = ID
        NewRow.Item("Quantity") = Q
        PurchasesTable.Rows.Add(NewRow)
        'Update number sold
        'find row with correct productid
        Dim PR As Integer
        For PR = 0 To ProductsTable.Rows.Count - 1
           If ProductsTable.Rows(PR).Item("ProductID").ToString = ID Then
             Exit For
           End If
        Next
        ProductsTable.Rows(PR).Item("NumberSold") = CInt(ProductsTable.Rows(PR).Item("NumberSold")) + Q
```

```
    Next I
    Call NewOrder()
End Sub
```

Notice how this code implements the previously specified steps.

6. Save and run the application. You now have complete order taking and saving capabilities. When running this application for a second time in the same day, you will probably receive this error message when you stop the application:

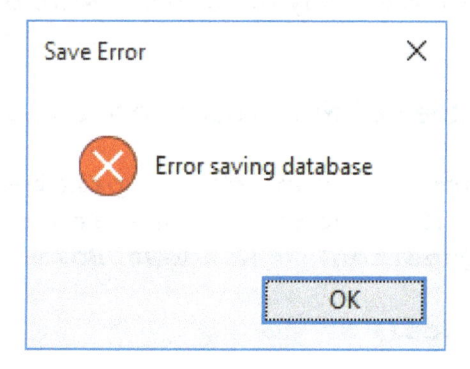

Save Error: Error saving database

The **OrderID** field is based on the date. The second time you run the application in the same day, duplicate **OrderID** values will be generated. To avoid this, you can do one of two things. In **FrmKWSales_Load**, change the **OrderNumber** variable to the last order number used (remember to change it back to zero, eventually, though). Or, start each running of the application with a new copy of the database. I know this is a headache, but it is one of the typical headache's programmers must endure in testing their applications.

Printing an Invoice

As a last step, let's add the ability to print an invoice for each order. We will make this an option. And, we will use the Visual Basic **PrintDocument** object to create this database report. Pay close attention to the printing code in the **PrintInvoicePage** procedure - it's long, but straightforward. It just goes through the form and pulls out the information it needs. The complicated part is parsing the list box contents to obtain quantities, product identification, description, and price information. Make sure you know what all the string manipulation functions are doing. The easiest way to do this is write out a string on paper and try the functions.

1. Add this code before the **Call NewOrder** line in **btnSubmitOrder Click**:

```
If MessageBox.Show("Do you want a printed invoice?",
"Print Inquiry", MessageBoxButtons.YesNo,
MessageBoxIcon.Question) = Windows.Forms.DialogResult.Yes
Then
   Call PrintInvoice()
End If
```

2. Add a procedure named **PrintInvoice**. This creates the **PrintDocument** object which prints the invoice using the **PrintInvoicePage** procedure:

```
Private Sub PrintInvoice()
   'Declare the document
   Dim RecordDocument As Drawing.Printing.PrintDocument
   'Create the document and name it
   RecordDocument = New Drawing.Printing.PrintDocument()
   RecordDocument.DocumentName = "KWSales Invoice"
   'Add code handler
   AddHandler RecordDocument.PrintPage, AddressOf Me.PrintInvoicePage
   'Print document
   RecordDocument.Print()
   'Dispose of document when done printing
   RecordDocument.Dispose()
End Sub
```

Sample Database Projects

3. Add this code to the **PrintInvoicePage** procedure:

```
Private Sub PrintInvoicePage(ByVal sender As Object, ByVal e As Drawing.Printing.PrintPageEventArgs)
    Dim Y As Integer = 100
    Dim S As String
    Dim I As Integer
    Dim J As Integer
    Dim TI As String
    Dim Q As String, ID As String, Desc As String, Unit As String, T As String
    Dim MyFont As Font = New Font("Courier New", 14, FontStyle.Bold)
    'Print Heading
    e.Graphics.DrawString("KIDware Order " + lblOrderID.Text, MyFont, Brushes.Black, 100, Y)
    Y += CInt(MyFont.GetHeight)
    e.Graphics.DrawString("Order Date " + lblDate.Text, MyFont, Brushes.Black, 100, Y)
    Y += 2 * CInt(MyFont.GetHeight)
    'Print buyer address
    MyFont = New Font("Courier New", 12, FontStyle.Regular)
    e.Graphics.DrawString(txtFirstName.Text + " " + txtLastName.Text, MyFont, Brushes.Black, 100, Y)
    Y += CInt(MyFont.GetHeight)
    e.Graphics.DrawString(txtAddress.Text, MyFont, Brushes.Black, 100, Y)
    Y += CInt(MyFont.GetHeight)
    e.Graphics.DrawString(txtCity.Text + ", " + txtState.Text + " " + txtZip.Text, MyFont, Brushes.Black, 100, Y)
    Y += 2 * CInt(MyFont.GetHeight)
    'Print items purchased and totals
    e.Graphics.DrawString("Qty   ProductID  Description           Unit    Total", MyFont, Brushes.Black, 100, Y)
    Y += CInt(MyFont.GetHeight)
    e.Graphics.DrawString("-------------------------------------------------------", MyFont, Brushes.Black, 100, Y)
    Y += CInt(MyFont.GetHeight)
    'Parse the shopping cart listings
    For I = 0 To lstCart.Items.Count - 1
      TI = lstCart.Items.Item(I).ToString
      J = InStr(TI, " ")
      Q = Mid(TI, 1, J - 1)
      ID = Mid(TI, J + 1, 6)
      Desc = Mid(TI, J + 8, Len(TI) - (J + 7))
      J = InStr(Desc, "$")
```

```
            Unit = Mid(Desc, J + 1, Len(Desc) - J)
            Desc = Mid(Desc, 1, J - 2)
            If Len(Desc) > 25 Then Desc = Mid(Desc, 1, 25)
            S = Space(56)
            Mid(S, 4 - Len(Q), Len(Q)) = Q
            Mid(S, 8, 6) = ID
            Mid(S, 16, Len(Desc)) = Desc
            Mid(S, 48 - Len(Unit), Len(Unit)) = Unit
            T = Format(Val(Q) * Val(Unit), "0.00")
            Mid(S, 57 - Len(T), Len(T)) = T
            e.Graphics.DrawString(S, MyFont, Brushes.Black, 100, Y)
            Y += CInt(MyFont.GetHeight)
        Next I
        e.Graphics.DrawString("-----------------------------------------------------------", MyFont, Brushes.Black, 100, Y)
        Y += CInt(MyFont.GetHeight)
        S = Space(56)
        Mid(S, 42, 5) = "Total"
        Mid(S, 57 - Len(lblTotal.Text) - 1, Len(lblTotal.Text) + 1) = "$" + lblTotal.Text
        e.Graphics.DrawString(S, MyFont, Brushes.Black, 100, Y)
        e.HasMorePages = False
    End Sub
```

4. Save and run the application (you may need a clean copy of the database to do this). Enter orders and print them. Here's the top of a printed invoice:

KIDware Order 151120001
Order Date 11/20/2015

Bobby Smith
1234 Main Street
Eugene, Oregon 88888

```
Qty    ProductID      Description              Unit       Total
-----------------------------------------------------------------
  2    ITW199     Beginning Visual Basic       19.95      39.90
  1    ITW197     Visual Basic for Kids        19.95      19.95
  1    ITW180     Logic Games for Kids         14.95      14.95
-----------------------------------------------------------------
                                                Total     $74.80
```

The application is now complete.

Suggested Improvements

Even though the **Sales Order Form Project** is complete (the final Access version is saved in **Example 10-1** folder in **VBDB\Access\Class 10** folder; the final SQL Server version is saved in **Example 10-1** folder in **VBDB\SQL Server\Class 10** folder), there is always room for improvement. We'll give you some of our ideas. I'm sure you have some ideas too.

When running the application for the second time in a day, we noted problems with generated duplicate **OrderID** values. This would not be a problem if we start the application early in the day and leave it running all day. If we need to stop the application and restart it, we need some way of knowing what the last assigned **OrderNumber** was. The best way to do this is to establish a simple configuration file that reads the last **OrderNumber** when the application begins and writes it back to disk when the application ends. Try adding this ability to the application. You will also need logic to recognize a new day to allow restarting the counter at zero.

As written, the application can only take orders. This is suitable for a strictly ordering environment. A more complete system would allow the review of past orders (and perhaps the editing of past orders). Try adding the ability to find and display old orders. This should be a straightforward modification – you just need some way to indicate what order you are looking for. Do you want to search by order number, order date, customer name, or some combination? Your SQL skills will come in handy here.

For practice, try creating a distribution package for this application. Design an icon to represent the application. Make sure you include a clean copy of the database with your package.

Example 10-2

Home Inventory Project

In this project, we build a database management system that lets you store information about valuables around your home. The database will have seven fields:

Item (description of item)
Location (where item is located)
Store (where item was purchased)
Date Purchased (when item was purchased)
Purchase Cost (how much we paid)
Serial Number (item serial number)
Photo File (path to photo of item)
Engraved (indicates whether item is engraved with identifying information)

Development of the **Home Inventory Project** will proceed in the usual, logical sequence. We first create the database. Next, the interface is built which allows the user to view, edit, add, or delete records from the database. Lastly, we add some code to create a printable list of information in the database.

Home Inventory Database

In this application, the user enters specific information about each item in the database. A single table will be used to hold the data. We will give the steps to create the inventory database (refer to Chapter 9 for further details).

Access Database:

We will use Microsoft Access to create a database named **InventoryDB.accdb**. If you don't have Access, you can try to create the database using ADOX as described in the previous chapter. Or, you can just use the copy of **InventoryDB.accdb** found in the **VBDB\Databases** folder.

1. Start a new database (**InventoryDB.accdb**) in Access. Add a table in design view. Add seven fields to the database. The information needed to build the database is:

Field Name	**Field Type**
Item	Short Text (50 characters)
Location	Short Text (50 characters)
Store	Short Text (50 characters)
DatePurchased	Date/Time
PurchaseCost	Currency
SerialNumber	Short Text (50 characters)
PhotoFile	Short Text (200 characters)
Engraved	Yes/No (Boolean)

   Only the **Item** field is required.

2. Make the **Item** field a **Primary** key.

When done, the **Table Structure** appears as:

Field Name	Data Type
Item (primary key)	Short Text
Location	Short Text
Store	Short Text
DatePurchased	Date/Time
PurchaseCost	Currency
SerialNumber	Short Text
PhotoFile	Short Text
Engraved	Yes/No

3. Close the table design view and name the database table **InventoryDB.accdb**. Close **Access** to complete the database design.

<u>SQL Server Database:</u>

We will use Server Explorer to create a database named **SQLInventoryDB.mdf**. Or, you can just use the copy of **SQLInventoryDB.mdf** found in the **VBDB\Databases** folder.

1. Start Server Explorer in Visual Studio. Create a new SQL Server database (**SQLInventoryDB.mdf**). Add a new table. Add eight fields (columns) to the database. The information needed to build the database is:

Column Name	Field Type
Item	varchar(50)
Location	varchar(50)
Store	varchar(50)
DatePurchased	datetime
PurchaseCost	money
SerialNumber	varchar(50)
PhotoFile	varchar(200)
Engraved	bit (Boolean)

   Only the **Item** field cannot allow a null.

2. Make the **Item** field a **Primary** key.

Sample Database Projects 10-61

When done, the **Table Structure** appears as:

Name	Data Type	Allow Nulls
Item	varchar(50)	☐
Location	varchar(50)	☑
Store	varchar(50)	☑
DatePurchased	datetime	☑
PurchaseCost	money	☑
SerialNumber	varchar(50)	☑
PhotoFile	varchar(200)	☑
Engraved	bit	☑

3. Close the table design view and name the database table **Inventory**. Close **Server Explorer** to complete the database design. If you installed SQL Server using default settings, the finished file will be found in (or a very similar directory):

C:\Program Files\Microsoft SQL Server\MSSQL14.SQLEXPRESS\MSSQL\DATA

Preliminaries

<u>Access Database:</u>

Start a new project in Visual Basic. Copy **InventoryDB.accdb** into your project's **Bin\x86\Debug** folder (you may have to create it first). Use either the one just created in Access or the one found in the **VBDB\Databases** folder. Or, you might like to use the copy included with this example's course code (in **Example 10-2** folder of the **VBDB\Access\Class 10** folder). Some inventory information is included in this database to give you some things to look at. We use the latter in this example.

<u>SQL Server Database:</u>

Start a new project in Visual Basic. Copy **SQLInventoryDB.mdf** into your project's **Bin\Debug** folder (you may have to create it first). Use either the one just created in with Server Explorer or the one found in the **VBDB\Databases** folder. Or, you might like to use the copy included with this example's course code (in **Example 10-2** folder of the **VBDB\SQL Server\Class 10** folder). Some inventory information is included in this database to give you some things to look at. We use the latter in this example.

Home Inventory Interface

The home inventory interface will let the user view, edit, delete, or add records to the database. Each field will be displayed on the interface form.

1. Place six labels, five text box controls, a check box and a date time picker (used to select purchase date) on the form. Also, add a picture box control with a label and button under it. The form should look something like this:

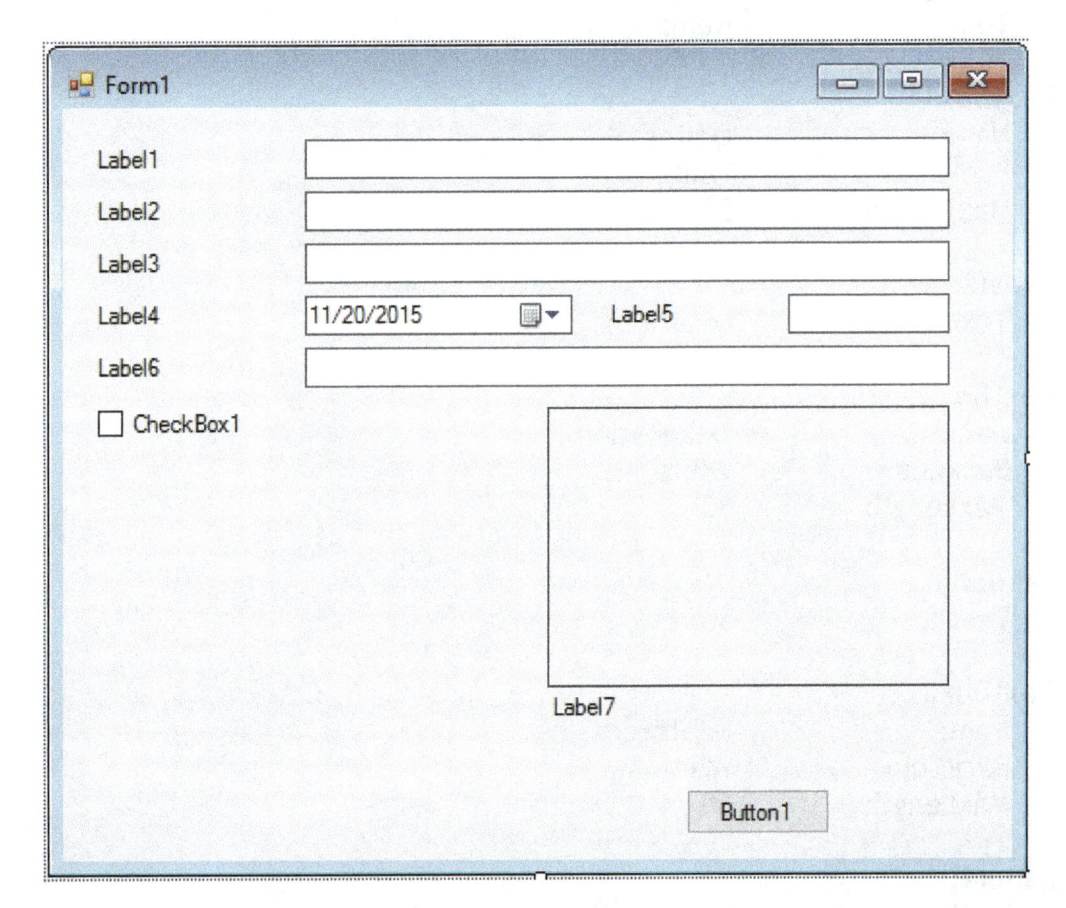

2. Set these properties:

   Form1:
      Name   frmInventory
      FormBorderStyle Fixed Single
      StartPosition   CenterScreen
      Text   Home Inventory

   Label1:
      Text   Item:

   TextBox1:
      Name   txtItem
      BackColor   White
      MaxLength   50

   Label2:
      Text   Location:

   TextBox2:
      Name   txtLocation
      BackColor   White
      MaxLength   50

   Label3:
      Text   Store:

   TextBox3:
      Name   txtStore
      BackColor   White
      MaxLength   50

   Label4:
      Text   Date Purchased:

   DateTimePicker1:
      Name   dtpDatePurchased
      Format   Short

Label5:
   Text   Purchase Cost:

TextBox4:
   Name   txtPurchaseCost
   BackColor   White

Label6:
   Text   Serial Number:

TextBox5:
   Name   txtSerialNumber
   BackColor   White
   MaxLength   50

CheckBox1:
   Name   chkEngraved
   Text   Engraved

PictureBox1:
   Name   picItem
   BorderStyle   FixedSingle
   SizeMode   Zoom

Label7:
   Name   lblPhotoFile
   AutoSize   False
   BackColor   LightYellow
   BorderStyle   Fixed3D
   Text   [Blank]

Button1:
   Name   btnLoadPhoto
   Text   Load Photo

My finished form looks like this:

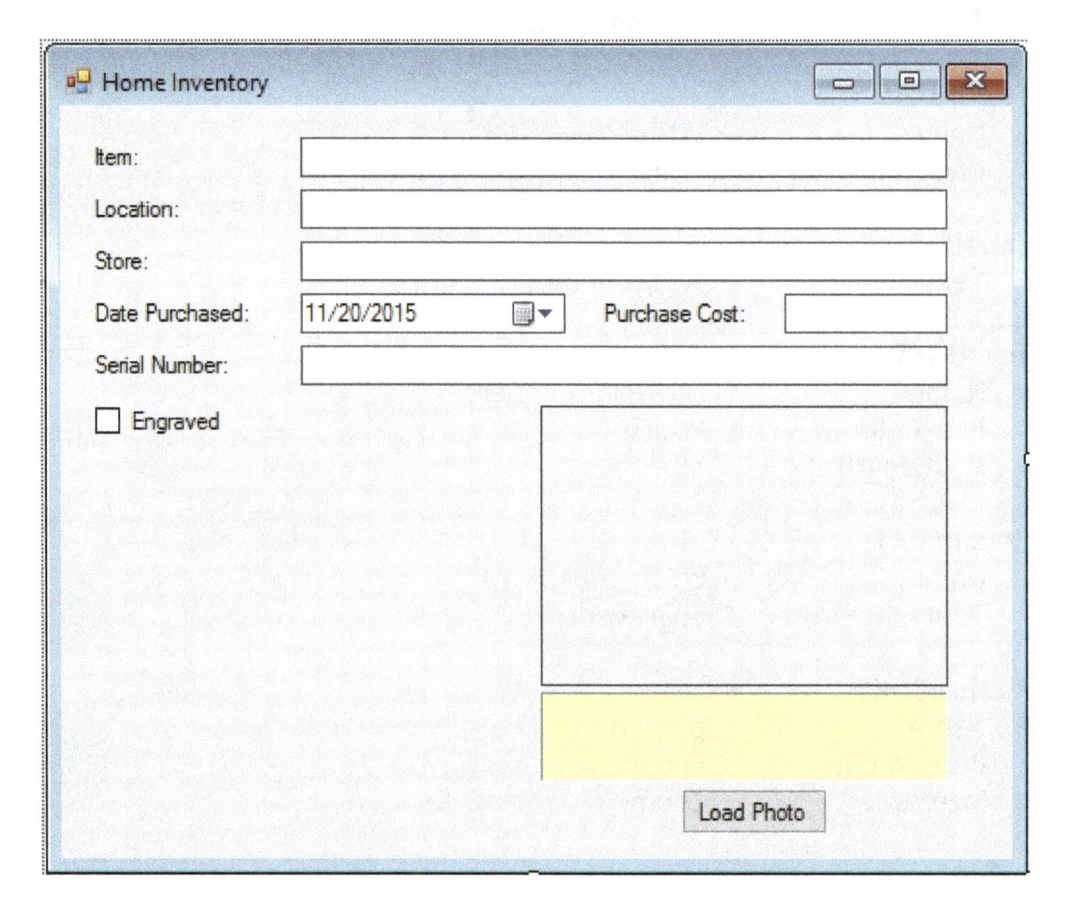

We'll add more controls as we continue.

Database Connection

We need to open the inventory database and bind the controls to the corresponding fields.

1. Place these two lines at the top of the code window to allow use of data objects:

   Access Database:

   ```
   Imports System.Data
   Imports System.Data.OleDb
   ```

   SQL Server Database:

   ```
   Imports System.Data
   Imports System.Data.SqlClient
   ```

2. Place this code in the form level declarations to create the needed data objects:

   Access Database:

   ```
   Dim InventoryConnection As OleDbConnection
   Dim InventoryCommand As OleDbCommand
   Dim InventoryAdapter As OleDbDataAdapter
   Dim InventoryTable As DataTable
   Dim InventoryManager As CurrencyManager
   ```

   SQL Server Database:

   ```
   Dim InventoryConnection As SqlConnection
   Dim InventoryCommand As SqlCommand
   Dim InventoryAdapter As SqlDataAdapter
   Dim InventoryTable As DataTable
   Dim InventoryManager As CurrencyManager
   ```

Visual Basic and Databases

3. Place this code in the **frmInventory Load** event procedure:

Access Database:

```vb
Private Sub FrmInventory_Load(ByVal sender As System.Object, ByVal e As System.EventArgs) Handles MyBase.Load
    'connect to database
    InventoryConnection = New OleDbConnection("Provider=Microsoft.ACE.OLEDB.12.0; Data Source = " + Application.StartupPath + "\InventoryDB.accdb")
    InventoryConnection.Open()
    'establish Inventory command object
    InventoryCommand = New OleDbCommand("SELECT * FROM Inventory ORDER BY Item", InventoryConnection)
    'establish Inventory data adapter/data table
    InventoryAdapter = New OleDbDataAdapter()
    InventoryAdapter.SelectCommand = InventoryCommand
    InventoryTable = New DataTable()
    InventoryAdapter.Fill(InventoryTable)
    'bind controls
    txtItem.DataBindings.Add("Text", InventoryTable, "Item")
    txtLocation.DataBindings.Add("Text", InventoryTable, "Location")
    txtStore.DataBindings.Add("Text", InventoryTable, "Store")
    dtpDatePurchased.DataBindings.Add("Text", InventoryTable, "DatePurchased")
    txtPurchaseCost.DataBindings.Add("Text", InventoryTable, "PurchaseCost")
    txtSerialNumber.DataBindings.Add("Text", InventoryTable, "SerialNumber")
    chkEngraved.DataBindings.Add("Checked", InventoryTable, "Engraved")
    lblPhotoFile.DataBindings.Add("Text", InventoryTable, "PhotoFile")
    'establish currency manager
    InventoryManager = DirectCast(Me.BindingContext(InventoryTable), CurrencyManager)
End Sub
```

Sample Database Projects 10-69

SQL Server Database:

```vb
Private Sub FrmInventory_Load(ByVal sender As System.Object, ByVal e As System.EventArgs) Handles MyBase.Load
    'connect to database
    InventoryConnection = New SqlConnection("Data Source=.\SQLEXPRESS; AttachDbFilename=" + Application.StartupPath + "\SQLInventoryDB.mdf; Integrated Security=True; Connect Timeout=30; User Instance=True")
    InventoryConnection.Open()
    'establish Inventory command object
    InventoryCommand = New SqlCommand("SELECT * FROM Inventory ORDER BY Item", InventoryConnection)
    'establish Inventory data adapter/data table
    InventoryAdapter = New SqlDataAdapter()
    InventoryAdapter.SelectCommand = InventoryCommand
    InventoryTable = New DataTable()
    InventoryAdapter.Fill(InventoryTable)
    'bind controls
    txtItem.DataBindings.Add("Text", InventoryTable, "Item")
    txtLocation.DataBindings.Add("Text", InventoryTable, "Location")
    txtStore.DataBindings.Add("Text", InventoryTable, "Store")
    dtpDatePurchased.DataBindings.Add("Text", InventoryTable, "DatePurchased")
    txtPurchaseCost.DataBindings.Add("Text", InventoryTable, "PurchaseCost")
    txtSerialNumber.DataBindings.Add("Text", InventoryTable, "SerialNumber")
    chkEngraved.DataBindings.Add("Checked", InventoryTable, "Engraved")
    lblPhotoFile.DataBindings.Add("Text", InventoryTable, "PhotoFile")
    'establish currency manager
    InventoryManager = DirectCast(Me.BindingContext(InventoryTable), CurrencyManager)
End Sub
```

This code connects to the inventory database file (in the application folder) and creates the data objects needed to view the **Inventory** table. It also binds the controls to the fields. Note in particular binding of the date time picker and check box controls.

4. Place this code in the **frmInventory FormClosing** event procedure to save any changes back to the database and to clean up objects:

Access Database:

```
Private Sub FrmInventory_FormClosing(ByVal sender As Object, ByVal e As System.Windows.Forms.FormClosingEventArgs) Handles Me.FormClosing
    Try
      'save the update Inventory table
      Dim InventoryAdapterCommands As New OleDbCommandBuilder(InventoryAdapter)
        InventoryAdapter.Update(InventoryTable)
    Catch ex As Exception
        MessageBox.Show(ex.Message, "Error Saving Database", MessageBoxButtons.OK, MessageBoxIcon.Error)
    End Try
    'close the connection
    InventoryConnection.Close()
    'dispose of the objects
    InventoryCommand.Dispose()
    InventoryAdapter.Dispose()
    InventoryTable.Dispose()
  End Sub
```

SQL Server Database:

```
Private Sub FrmInventory_FormClosing(ByVal sender As Object, ByVal e As System.Windows.Forms.FormClosingEventArgs) Handles Me.FormClosing
    Try
      'save the update Inventory table
      Dim InventoryAdapterCommands As New SqlCommandBuilder(InventoryAdapter)
        InventoryAdapter.Update(InventoryTable)
    Catch ex As Exception
        MessageBox.Show(ex.Message, "Error Saving Database", MessageBoxButtons.OK, MessageBoxIcon.Error)
    End Try
    'close the connection
    InventoryConnection.Close()
    'dispose of the objects
    InventoryCommand.Dispose()
    InventoryAdapter.Dispose()
    InventoryTable.Dispose()
  End Sub
```

Sample Database Projects   10-71

4. Save the application (Access version saved in **Example 10-2** folder in **VBDB\Access\Class 10** folder; SQL Server version saved in **Example 10-2** folder in **VBDB\SQL Server\Class 10** folder) and run it. If you used the example database included with the notes, you should see (if you used the empty database, you'll see nothing but blanks):

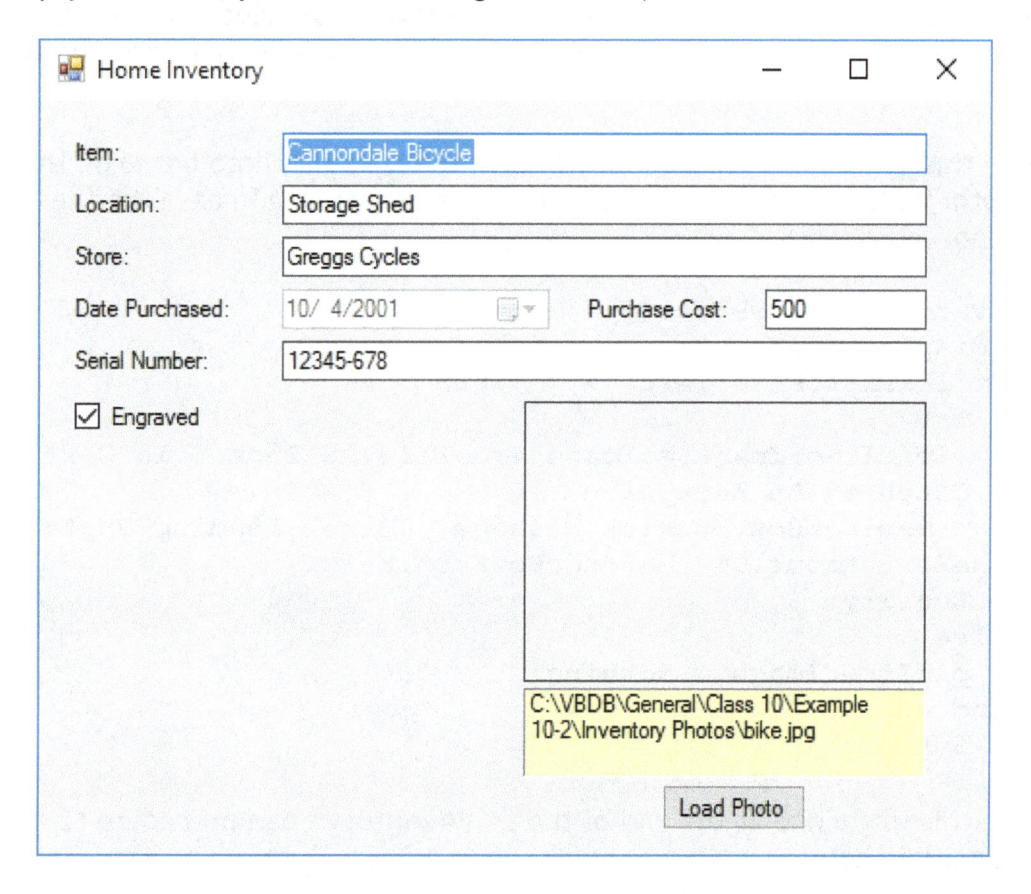

```
┌─────────────────────────────────────────────────────────────┐
│ 🖳 Home Inventory                          —    □    ×      │
├─────────────────────────────────────────────────────────────┤
│                                                             │
│  Item:          │Cannondale Bicycle                       │ │
│                                                             │
│  Location:      │Storage Shed                             │ │
│                                                             │
│  Store:         │Greggs Cycles                            │ │
│                                                             │
│  Date Purchased: │10/ 4/2001    │▼│  Purchase Cost: │500 │ │
│                                                             │
│  Serial Number: │12345-678                                │ │
│                                                             │
│  ☑ Engraved           ┌──────────────────────────────┐     │
│                       │                              │     │
│                       │                              │     │
│                       │                              │     │
│                       │                              │     │
│                       │                              │     │
│                       │                              │     │
│                       └──────────────────────────────┘     │
│                       ┌──────────────────────────────┐     │
│                       │C:\VBDB\General\Class 10\Example│   │
│                       │10-2\Inventory Photos\bike.jpg │   │
│                       └──────────────────────────────┘     │
│                              [ Load Photo ]                │
│                                                             │
└─────────────────────────────────────────────────────────────┘
```

This is the first record in the sample database listing all the fields. The photo doesn't display. We need some code for this – we'll do that now.

Display Photo

The database doesn't store the actual photos of items in the inventory, but a path to the file with the photo. In this example, all photos are stored in the **VBDB\General\Class 10\Example 10-2\InventoryPhotos** folder. As we continue with the interface, we will add the ability for a user to specify where photos are located.

1. Add this general procedure (**ShowPhoto**) to display a photo based on the **PhotoFile** field in the database. We use error trapping in case the file cannot be opened:

```
Private Sub ShowPhoto()
  'display photo
  If lblPhotoFile.Text <> "" Then
    Try
      picItem.Image = Image.FromFile(lblPhotoFile.Text)
    Catch ex As Exception
      MessageBox.Show(ex.Message, "Error Loading Photo", MessageBoxButtons.OK, MessageBoxIcon.Error)
    End Try
  Else
    picItem.Image = Nothing
  End If
End Sub
```

2. Add this single line at the end of the **frmInventory Load** procedure to display the initial photo:

```
Call ShowPhoto()
```

Sample Database Projects   10-73

3. Resave and rerun the application. The photo of the bicycle should now appear:

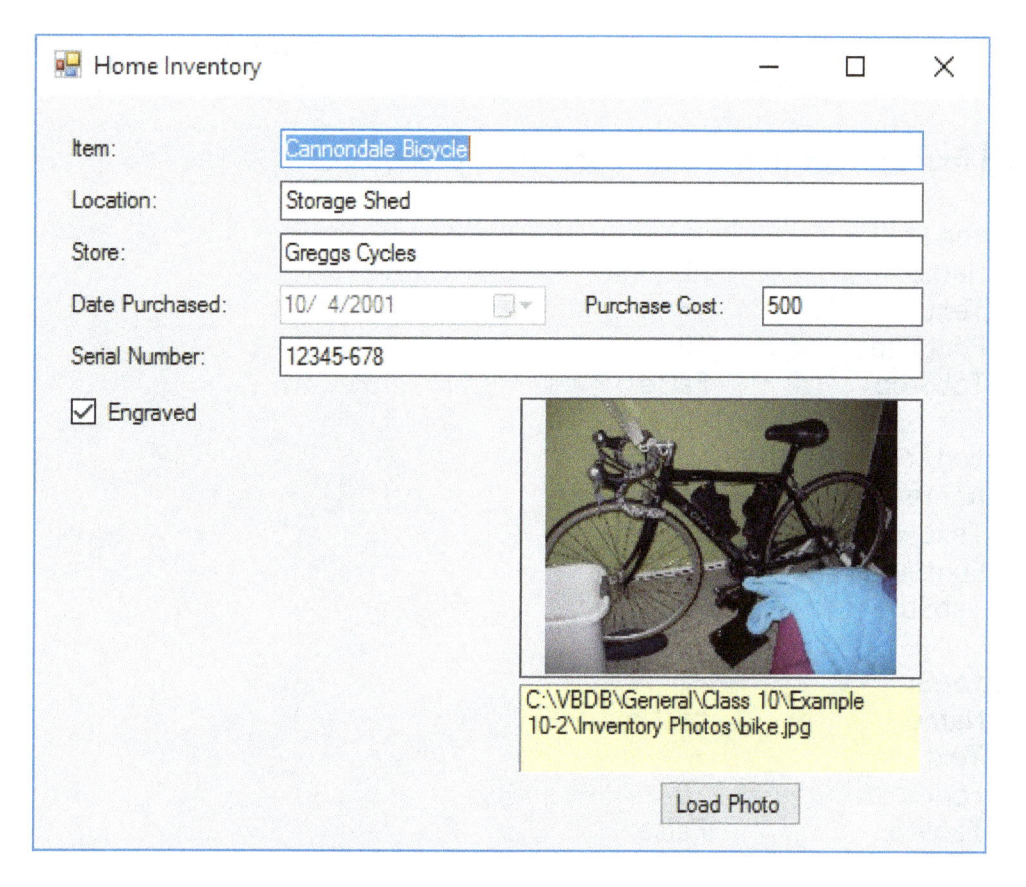

At this point, we are able to display all the fields in our database. The interface still needs work, but it's a beginning. We need to add navigational abilities, editing capability, and the ability to add and delete records.

Database Navigation

As a first step, we need the ability to move from one record to another in the home inventory database. This is something we've done many times before.

1. Add four buttons to the form. Set these properties:

   Button1:
Name	btnFirst
Text	|<
FontSize	10
TabStop	False

   Button2:
Name	btnPrevious
Text	<
FontSize	10
TabStop	False

   Button3:
Name	btnNext
Text	>
FontSize	10
TabStop	False

   Button4:
Name	btnLast
Text	>|
FontSize	10
TabStop	False

Sample Database Projects

The form looks like this:

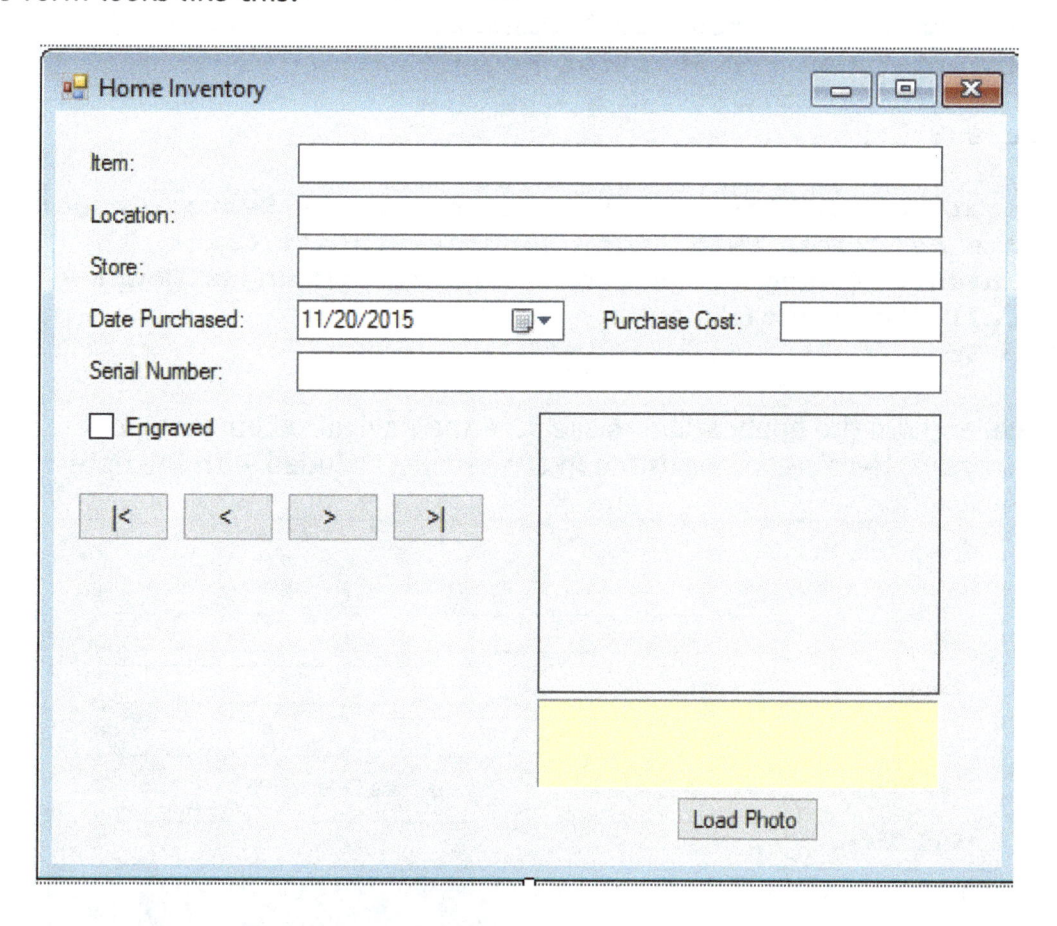

2. Add this code to the **Click** event procedures for each of the new buttons (notice that anytime a new record is displayed, we need to reload the photo):

```
Private Sub BtnFirst_Click(ByVal sender As System.Object, ByVal e As System.EventArgs) Handles btnFirst.Click
    InventoryManager.Position = 0
    Call ShowPhoto()
End Sub

Private Sub BtnPrevious_Click(ByVal sender As System.Object, ByVal e As System.EventArgs) Handles btnPrevious.Click
    InventoryManager.Position -= 1
    Call ShowPhoto()
End Sub
```

```
Private Sub BtnNext_Click(ByVal sender As System.Object, _
ByVal e As System.EventArgs) Handles btnNext.Click
    InventoryManager.Position += 1
    Call ShowPhoto()
End Sub

Private Sub BtnLast_Click(ByVal sender As System.Object, _
ByVal e As System.EventArgs) Handles btnLast.Click
    InventoryManager.Position = InventoryManager.Count - 1
    Call ShowPhoto()
End Sub
```

3. Save and run the application. Make sure the navigation buttons work correctly. Here's another listing in the sample included with the notes:

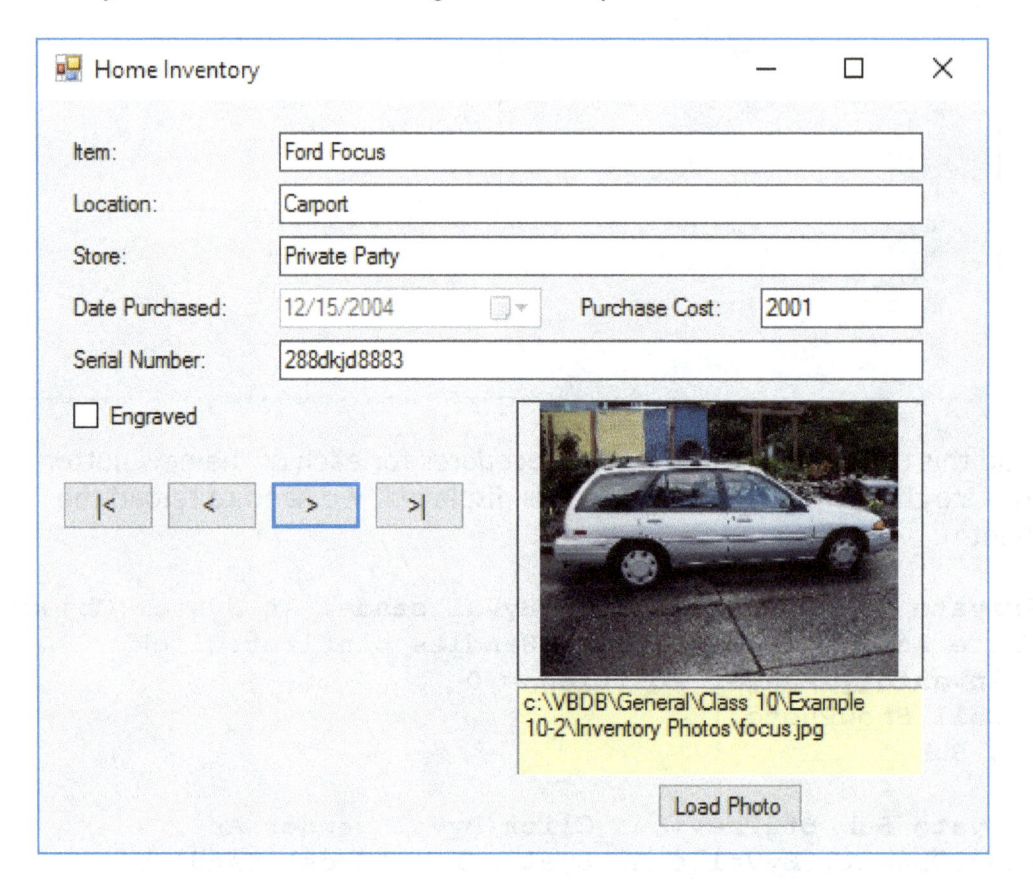

Editing Records

We now add the ability to edit records in the home inventory database.

1. Lock all text boxes (**ReadOnly** = **True**) on the form (we will decide when editing is allowed). Also disable the date time picker and the button to load photos (**Enabled** = **False**).

2. Add three buttons to the form. Use these properties:

   Button1:
Name	btnEdit
Text	Edit
TabStop	False

   Button2:
Name	btnSave
Text	Save
Enabled	False
TabStop	False

   Button3:
Name	btnCancel
Text	Cancel
Enabled	False
TabStop	False

The form now looks like this:

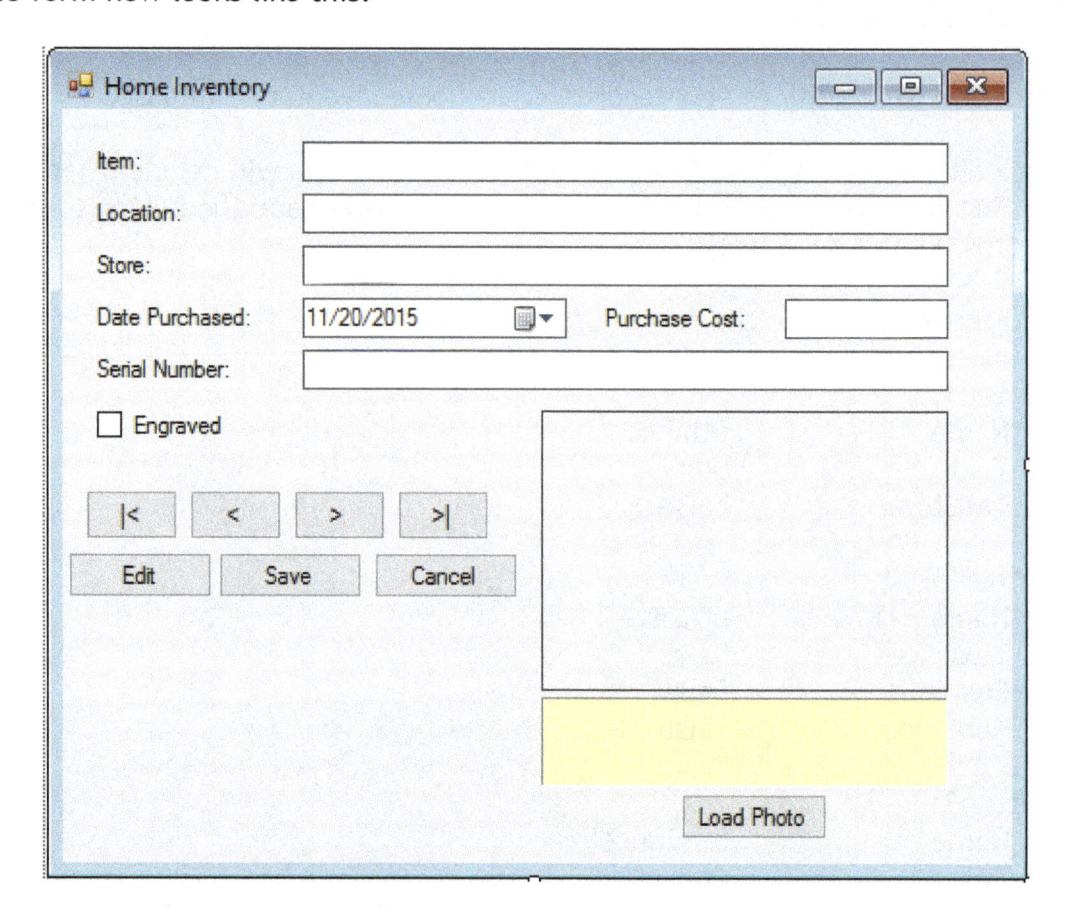

3. Add a variable to the form level declarations to track system state:

   ```
   Dim MyState As String
   ```

Sample Database Projects

4. Add a procedure named **SetState** to establish the application state. Use this code:

```
Private Sub SetState(ByVal AppState As String)
  MyState = AppState
  Select Case AppState
    Case "View"
      btnFirst.Enabled = True
      btnPrevious.Enabled = True
      btnNext.Enabled = True
      btnLast.Enabled = True
      btnEdit.Enabled = True
      btnSave.Enabled = False
      btnCancel.Enabled = False
      txtItem.ReadOnly = True
      txtLocation.ReadOnly = True
      txtStore.ReadOnly = True
      dtpDatePurchased.Enabled = False
      txtPurchaseCost.ReadOnly = True
      txtSerialNumber.ReadOnly = True
      chkEngraved.Enabled = False
      btnLoadPhoto.Enabled = False
    Case "Edit"
      btnFirst.Enabled = False
      btnPrevious.Enabled = False
      btnNext.Enabled = False
      btnLast.Enabled = False
      btnEdit.Enabled = False
      btnSave.Enabled = True
      btnCancel.Enabled = True
      txtItem.ReadOnly = False
      txtLocation.ReadOnly = False
      txtStore.ReadOnly = False
      dtpDatePurchased.Enabled = True
      txtPurchaseCost.ReadOnly = False
      txtSerialNumber.ReadOnly = False
      chkEngraved.Enabled = True
      btnLoadPhoto.Enabled = True
  End Select
  txtItem.Focus()
End Sub
```

This procedure has two modes: **View** and **Edit**. In View mode (default when the form loads), we can just look at the data. In Edit mode, data can be changed, and then saved (or the edit operation canceled).

5. Place this line of code at the end of the **frmInventory Load** event procedure:

```
Call SetState("View")
```

This puts the form in **View** mode initially.

6. Place this code in the **btnEdit Click** event procedure:

```
Private Sub BtnEdit_Click(ByVal sender As System.Object, ByVal e As System.EventArgs) Handles btnEdit.Click
    Call SetState("Edit")
End Sub
```

This places the form in **Edit** mode and allows the data table to be edited.

7. Place this code in the **btnSave Click** event procedure:

```
Private Sub BtnSave_Click(ByVal sender As System.Object, ByVal e As System.EventArgs) Handles btnSave.Click
    Dim SavedItem As String = txtItem.Text
    Dim SavedRow As Integer
    InventoryManager.EndCurrentEdit()
    InventoryTable.DefaultView.Sort = "Item"
    SavedRow = InventoryTable.DefaultView.Find(SavedItem)
    InventoryManager.Position = SavedRow
    Call SetState("View")
End Sub
```

This code saves any changes and returns to **View** mode. It sets the currency manager position to the saved record when done.

8. Place this code in the **btnCancel Click** procedure:

```
Private Sub BtnCancel_Click(ByVal sender As System.Object, ByVal e As System.EventArgs) Handles btnCancel.Click
    InventoryManager.CancelCurrentEdit()
    Call ShowPhoto()
    Call SetState("View")
End Sub
```

This code cancels the edit operation, displays the correct photo and resets the application state to **View** mode.

9. Save and run the application. Make sure the **Edit** function works, as it should. Also, test the **Save** and **Cancel** functions. Here's the form in **Edit** mode:

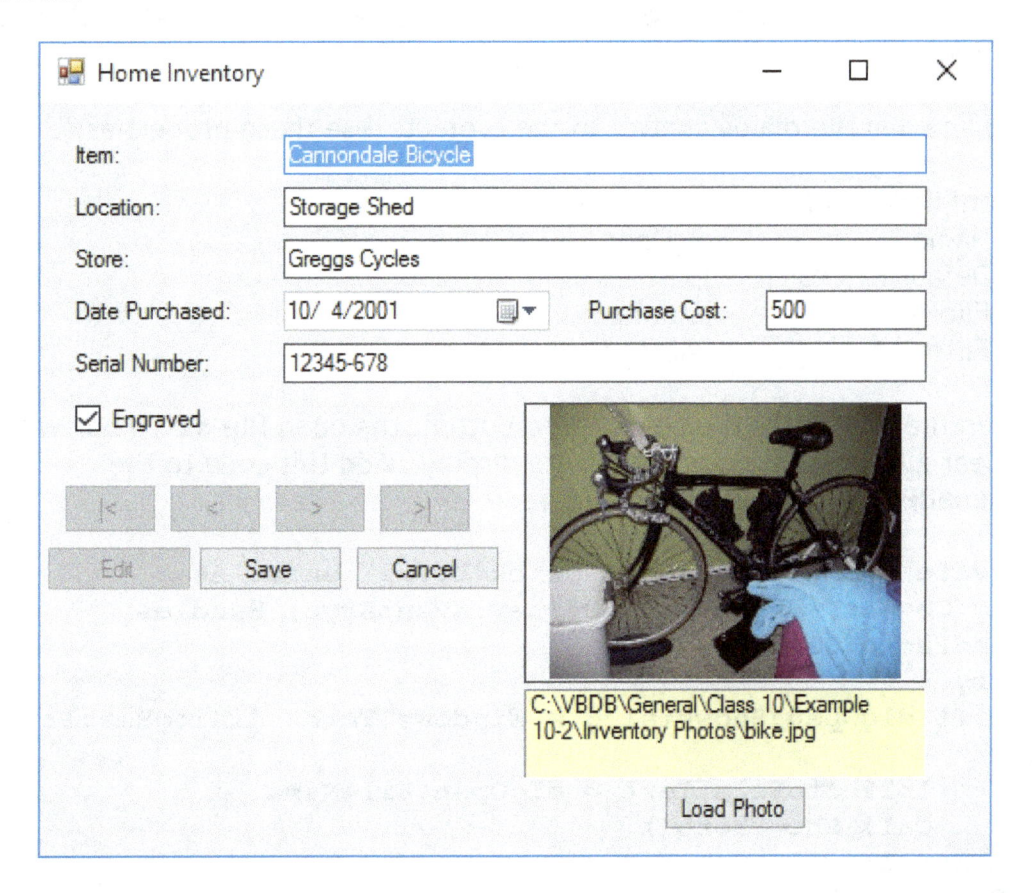

Try changing and saving information. Notice how the date time picker control works.

Load Photo

We can edit any fields on the form except the displayed photo. Let's add that capability.

1. Add an open file dialog control to the project. Use these properties:

   OpenFileDialog1:
      Name   dlgOpen
      DefaultExtension   jpg
      FileName   [blank]
      Filter   Photos (*.jpg)|*.jpg

2. When the user clicks the **Load Photo** button, the open file dialog box will appear allowing choice of a photo to display. Add this code to the **btnLoadPhoto Click** event procedure:

```
Private Sub BtnLoadPhoto_Click(ByVal sender As System.Object, ByVal e As System.EventArgs) Handles btnLoadPhoto.Click
    Try
      If dlgOpen.ShowDialog = Windows.Forms.DialogResult.OK Then
        lblPhotoFile.Text = dlgOpen.FileName
        Call ShowPhoto()
      End If
    Catch ex As Exception
      MessageBox.Show(ex.Message, "Error Opening Photo", MessageBoxButtons.OK, MessageBoxIcon.Error)
    End Try
  End Sub
```

Sample Database Projects   10-83

3. Save and run the application. Click **Edit**. Then, click **Load Photo**. Navigate to the folder holding the photos; this dialog appears:

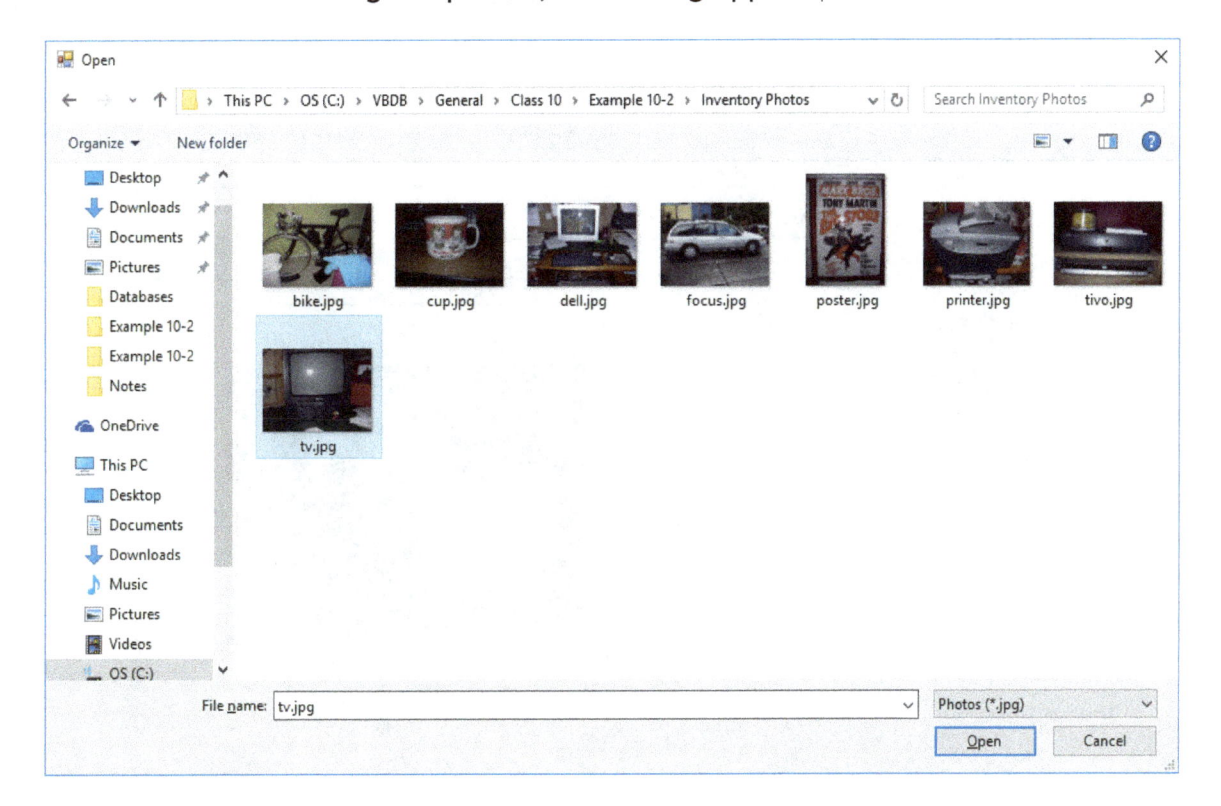

Select a photo and click **Open**.

10-84 **Visual Basic and Databases**

Here I changed the bike to a television:

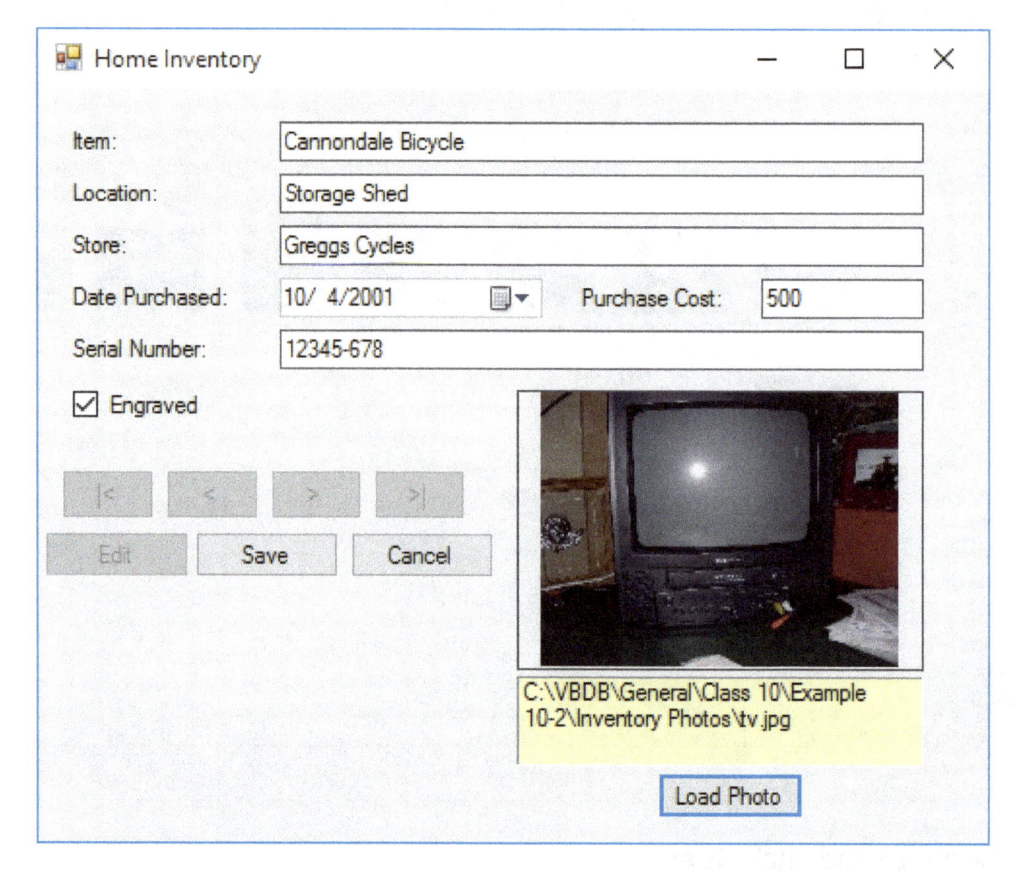

When I click **Cancel**, it returns to the bike.

Adding Records

Now, we add the capability of adding new records to the home inventory database.

1. Add a button to the form under the **Edit** button. Use these properties:

Name	btnAdd
Text	Add
TabStop	False

    The form will look like this:

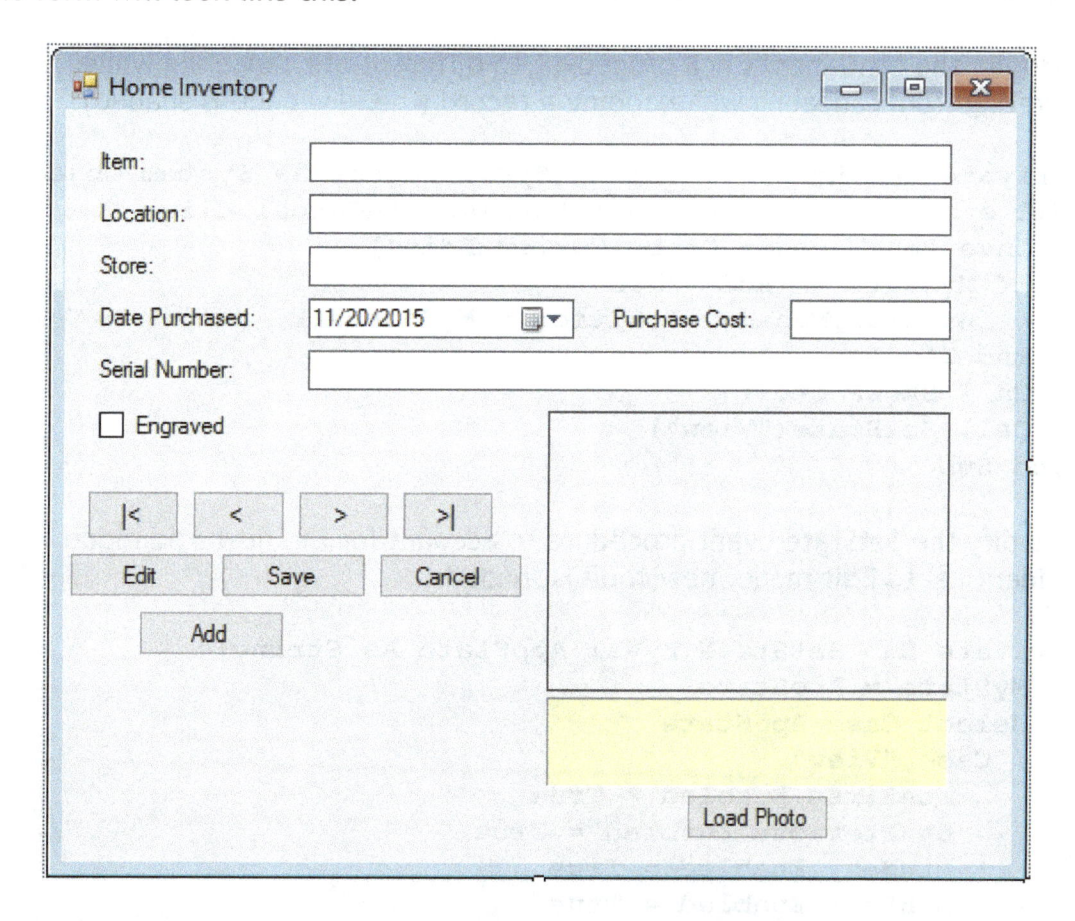

2. Add this line to the form level declarations to save the current record (in case the **Add** operation is cancelled):

    ```
    Dim MyBookmark As Integer
    ```

3. Place this code in the **btnAdd Click** event procedure:

```
Private Sub BtnAdd_Click(ByVal sender As System.Object,
ByVal e As System.EventArgs) Handles btnAdd.Click
    MyBookmark = InventoryManager.Position
    'clear picture
    picItem.Image = Nothing
    Call SetState("Add")
    InventoryManager.AddNew()
End Sub
```

The code first saves the bookmark. It then clears the picture, places the application in **Add** mode and adds a record.

4. Modify the **btnCancel Click** procedure to differentiate canceling while editing from canceling while adding a record (the new code is shaded):

```
Private Sub BtnCancel_Click(ByVal sender As System.Object,
ByVal e As System.EventArgs) Handles btnCancel.Click
    InventoryManager.CancelCurrentEdit()
    If MyState = "Add" Then
      InventoryManager.Position = MyBookmark
    End If
    Call ShowPhoto()
    Call SetState("View")
End Sub
```

5. Modify the **SetState** event procedure to account for the new **Add** mode (identical to **Edit** mode, new code is shaded):

```
Private Sub SetState(ByVal AppState As String)
  MyState = AppState
  Select Case AppState
    Case "View"
      btnFirst.Enabled = True
      btnPrevious.Enabled = True
      btnNext.Enabled = True
      btnLast.Enabled = True
      btnEdit.Enabled = True
      btnSave.Enabled = False
      btnCancel.Enabled = False
      btnAdd.Enabled = True
      txtItem.ReadOnly = True
      txtLocation.ReadOnly = True
      txtStore.ReadOnly = True
      dtpDatePurchased.Enabled = False
      txtPurchaseCost.ReadOnly = True
```

```
            txtSerialNumber.ReadOnly = True
            chkEngraved.Enabled = False
            btnLoadPhoto.Enabled = False
        Case "Edit", "Add"
            btnFirst.Enabled = False
            btnPrevious.Enabled = False
            btnNext.Enabled = False
            btnLast.Enabled = False
            btnEdit.Enabled = False
            btnSave.Enabled = True
            btnCancel.Enabled = True
            btnAdd.Enabled = False
            txtItem.ReadOnly = False
            txtLocation.ReadOnly = False
            txtStore.ReadOnly = False
            dtpDatePurchased.Enabled = True
            txtPurchaseCost.ReadOnly = False
            txtSerialNumber.ReadOnly = False
            chkEngraved.Enabled = True
            btnLoadPhoto.Enabled = True
    End Select
    txtItem.Focus()
End Sub
```

6. Save the application and run it. Click **Add**. You will see this:

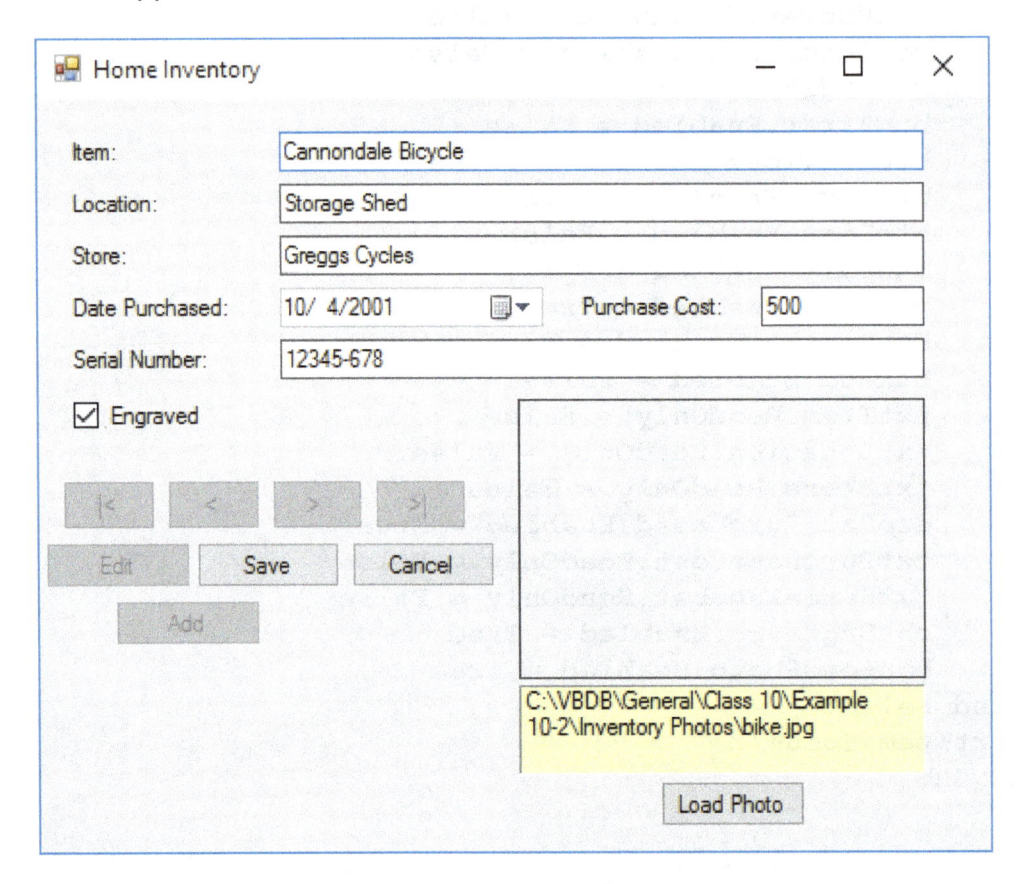

Notice the fields are <u>not cleared</u> as they should be when adding a new record to the database. What's wrong? This is a documented bug in Visual Basic. It occurs when binding a check box to a currency manager. We need to work our way around this bug. This is something we must often do in programming –find ways around bugs and problems. Since the problem lies with the binding of the check box, we will remove this binding when adding a record, then rebind after the addition is saved. Stop the application.

Sample Database Projects   10-89

7. Add the shaded code to the **btnAdd Click** event procedure (removes the binding from the check box and removes any check mark):

```
Private Sub BtnAdd_Click(ByVal sender As System.Object, ByVal e As System.EventArgs) Handles btnAdd.Click
    MyBookmark = InventoryManager.Position
    'clear picture
    picItem.Image = Nothing
    'remove binding from checkbox
    chkEngraved.DataBindings.Clear()
    chkEngraved.Checked = False
    Call SetState("Add")
    InventoryManager.AddNew()
End Sub
```

Add this shaded code to the **btnSave Click** event procedure (manually sets database field and re-establishes data binding):

```
Private Sub BtnSave_Click(ByVal sender As System.Object, ByVal e As System.EventArgs) Handles btnSave.Click
    Dim SavedItem As String = txtItem.Text
    Dim SavedRow As Integer
    InventoryManager.EndCurrentEdit()
    If MyState = "Add" Then
       InventoryTable.Rows(InventoryManager.Count - 1).Item("Engraved") = chkEngraved.Checked
       chkEngraved.DataBindings.Add("Checked", InventoryTable, "Engraved")
    End If
    InventoryTable.DefaultView.Sort = "Item"
    SavedRow = InventoryTable.DefaultView.Find(SavedItem)
    InventoryManager.Position = SavedRow
    Call SetState("View")
End Sub
```

Lastly, add this shaded code to the **btnCancel Click** event procedure (re-establishes data bindings if cancelled while adding a record):

```
Private Sub BtnCancel_Click(ByVal sender As System.Object, ByVal e As System.EventArgs) Handles btnCancel.Click
    InventoryManager.CancelCurrentEdit()
    If MyState = "Add" Then
        InventoryManager.Position = MyBookmark
        chkEngraved.DataBindings.Add("Checked", InventoryTable, "Engraved")
    End If
    Call ShowPhoto()
    Call SetState("View")
End Sub
```

8. Save and run the application again. The fields will now be blank as desired. Type in new values (make sure you type a valid cost or you'll receive an error message). Click **Save**. The new record will appear. I've added my TIVO unit to the inventory:

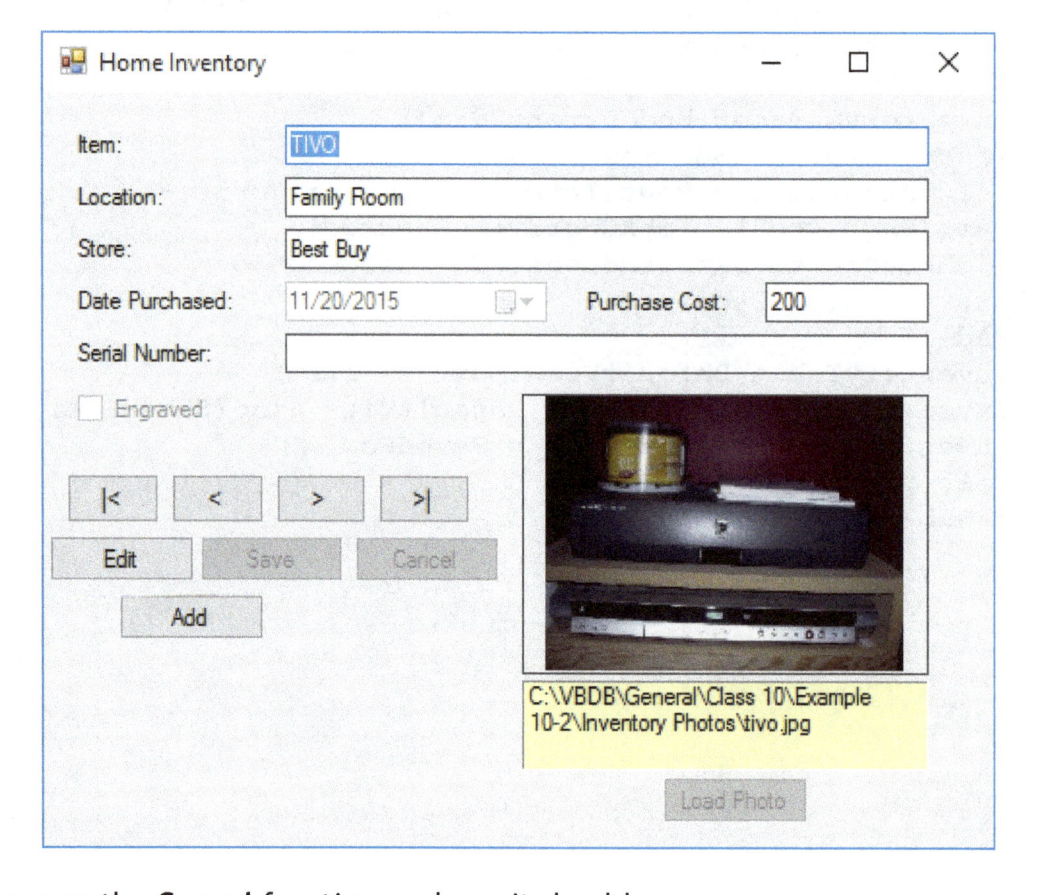

Make sure the **Cancel** function works as it should.

Deleting Records

The final management function needed is the ability to delete records from the home inventory database.

1. Add a button to the form next to the **Add** button. Use these properties:

Name	btnDelete
Text	Delete
TabStop	False

The form will look like this:

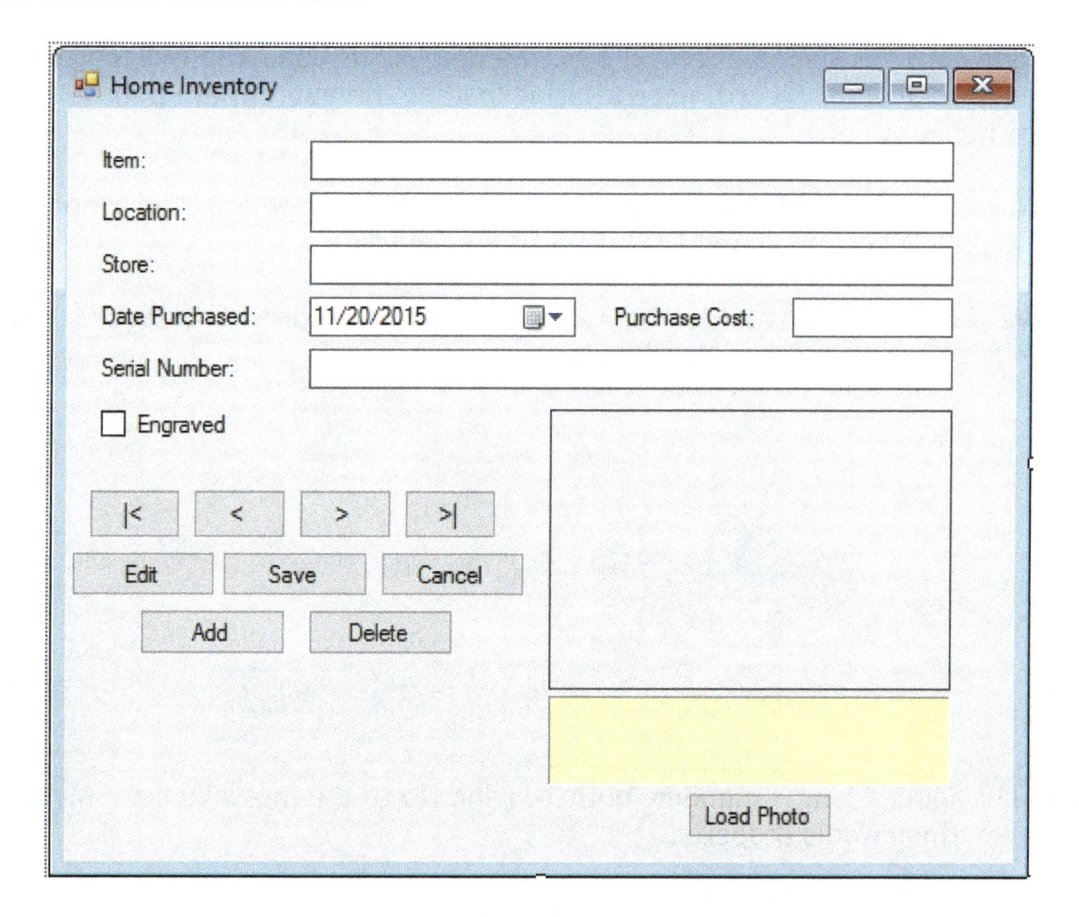

2. Add this code to the **btnDelete Click** event procedure:

```
Private Sub BtnDelete_Click(ByVal sender As System.Object, ByVal e As System.EventArgs) Handles btnDelete.Click
    If MessageBox.Show("Are you sure you want to delete this record?", "Delete", MessageBoxButtons.YesNo, MessageBoxIcon.Question, MessageBoxDefaultButton.Button2) = Windows.Forms.DialogResult.Yes Then
        InventoryManager.RemoveAt(InventoryManager.Position)
        Call ShowPhoto()
    End If
    Call SetState("View")
End Sub
```

This code confirms the deletion. If **Yes**, the deletion is done and the controls are bound to another record, necessitating loading the appropriate photo. If **No**, nothing happens.

3. Add code to the **SetState** procedure to set the **btnDelete Enabled** property to **True** in **View** mode and **False** in **Add/Edit** mode.

4. Save the application and run it. Click **Add**. Add a record. Click **Save**. Now try deleting the record. You should see:

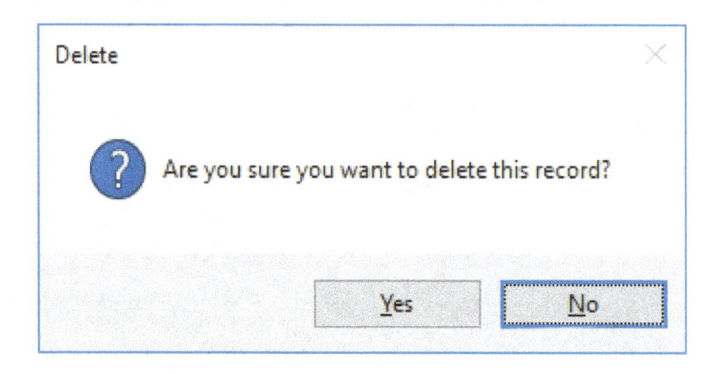

Test your application, responding both **Yes** and **No** to the message box. Make sure everything works properly.

Entry Validation

Recall entry validation checks for proper characters in the data fields. In this database, most of the fields can contain any characters. There is only one exceptions **PurchaseCost** field can only contain numeric characters and a decimal point. Here we implement this restriction. And, we'll also implement the ability to allow pressing **<Enter>** to move us from one field to the next. We'll start at the top and work our way down.

1. Add this code to the **txtItem KeyPress** event:

```
Private Sub TxtItem_KeyPress(ByVal sender As
System.Object, ByVal e As
System.Windows.Forms.KeyPressEventArgs) Handles
txtItem.KeyPress
   If e.KeyChar = ControlChars.Cr Then
      txtLocation.Focus()
   End If
End Sub
```

When the user presses **<Enter>**, focus is set on the next text box control (**txtLocation**).

2. Add this code to the **txtLocation KeyPress** event:

```
Private Sub TxtLocation_KeyPress(ByVal sender As
System.Object, ByVal e As
System.Windows.Forms.KeyPressEventArgs) Handles
txtLocation.KeyPress
   If e.KeyChar = ControlChars.Cr Then
      txtStore.Focus()
   End If
End Sub
```

When the user presses **<Enter>**, focus is set on the next text box control (**txtStore**).

3. Add this code to the **txtStore KeyPress** event:

```
Private Sub TxtStore_KeyPress(ByVal sender As
System.Object, ByVal e As
System.Windows.Forms.KeyPressEventArgs) Handles
txtStore.KeyPress
    If e.KeyChar = ControlChars.Cr Then
      If dtpDatePurchased.Enabled Then
        dtpDatePurchased.Focus()
      Else
        txtPurchaseCost.Focus()
      End If
    End If
End Sub
```

When the user presses **<Enter>**, focus is set on the date time picker (**dtpDatePurchased**), if it is enabled. Otherwise, focus is set on the next text box control (**txtPurchaseCost**).

4. Add this code to the **dtpDatePurchased KeyPress** event:

```
Private Sub DtpDatePurchased_KeyPress(ByVal sender As
System.Object, ByVal e As
System.Windows.Forms.KeyPressEventArgs) Handles
dtpDatePurchased.KeyPress
    If e.KeyChar = ControlChars.Cr Then
      txtPurchaseCost.Focus()
    End If
End Sub
```

When the user presses **<Enter>**, focus is set on the next text box control (**txtPurchaseCost**).

5. Add this code to the **txtPurchaseCost KeyPress** event:

```
  Private Sub TxtPurchaseCost_KeyPress(ByVal sender As System.Object, ByVal e As System.Windows.Forms.KeyPressEventArgs) Handles txtPurchaseCost.KeyPress
    'only allow numbers, a single decimal point, backspace or enter
    Select Case e.KeyChar
      Case CChar("0") To CChar("9"), ControlChars.Back
        e.Handled = False
      Case ControlChars.Cr
        txtSerialNumber.Focus()
        e.Handled = False
      Case CChar(".")
        If InStr(txtPurchaseCost.Text, ".") = 0 Then
          e.Handled = False
        Else
          e.Handled = True
        End If
      Case Else
        e.Handled = True
    End Select
  End Sub
```

When the user presses **<Enter>**, focus is set on the next text box control (**txtSerialNumber**). It also restricts inputs to numbers, the backspace and a single decimal point.

6. Add this code to the **txtSerialNumber KeyPress** event:

```
Private Sub TxtSerialNumber_KeyPress(ByVal sender As
System.Object, ByVal e As
System.Windows.Forms.KeyPressEventArgs) Handles
txtSerialNumber.KeyPress
    If e.KeyChar = ControlChars.Cr Then
      If btnLoadPhoto.Enabled Then
        btnLoadPhoto.Focus()
      Else
        txtItem.Focus()
      End If
    End If
End Sub
```

When the user presses **<Enter>**, focus is set on the **Load Photo** button (**btnLoadPhoto**) is it is enabled. If the button is not enabled, focus returns to the top control (**txtItem**).

7. Save and run the application. Try moving from field to field with the **<Enter>** key in both **View** and **Edit** modes. Test the key trapping implemented in the **Purchase Cost** field.

Input Validation

There is only one validation rule: the **Item** field cannot be empty since it is a primary key.

1. Add the shaded lines of code to the **btnSave Click** procedure to check that a value for **Item** has been entered:

```
Private Sub BtnSave_Click(ByVal sender As System.Object, ByVal e As System.EventArgs) Handles btnSave.Click
    'Check for Item
    If txtItem.Text.Trim = "" Then
      MessageBox.Show("You must enter an Item description.", "Input Error", MessageBoxButtons.OK, MessageBoxIcon.Information)
      txtItem.Focus()
      Exit Sub
    End If
    Dim SavedItem As String = txtItem.Text
    Dim SavedRow As Integer
    InventoryManager.EndCurrentEdit()
    If MyState = "Add" Then
      InventoryTable.Rows(InventoryManager.Count - 1).Item("Engraved") = chkEngraved.Checked
      chkEngraved.DataBindings.Add("Checked", InventoryTable, "Engraved")
    End If
    InventoryTable.DefaultView.Sort = "Item"
    SavedRow = InventoryTable.DefaultView.Find(SavedItem)
    InventoryManager.Position = SavedRow
    Call SetState("View")
  End Sub
```

If the **Item** field is blank, the user is given a message to that effect.

2. Save and run the application. Click **Add New**. Click **Save**. A message box saying the **Item** field is blank should appear:

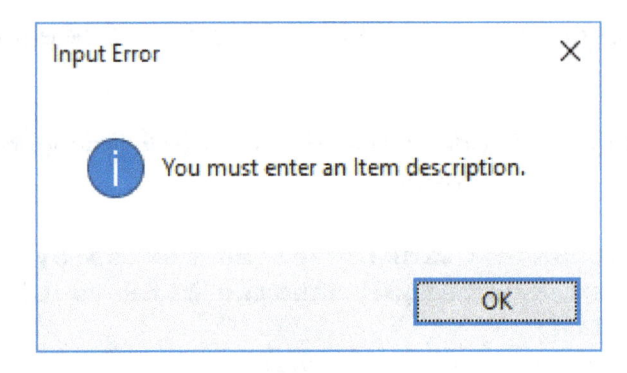

> **Input Error**
>
> ⓘ You must enter an Item description.
>
> [OK]

Type an item description. Click **Save** again. The entry should be accepted.

Inventory Report

We have a great interface to get data into our home inventory database. Now, let's add the ability to get data out of the database. We need a database report. The report will be simple. For each record, a listing of all fields will be displayed. The listing can be previewed before printing.

1. Open the home inventory application and add a button and a print preview dialog control to the project. Set these properties.

   Button1:
Name	btnPrint
Text	Print
TabStop	False

   PrintPreviewDialog1:
Name	dlgPreview

The form will look like this:

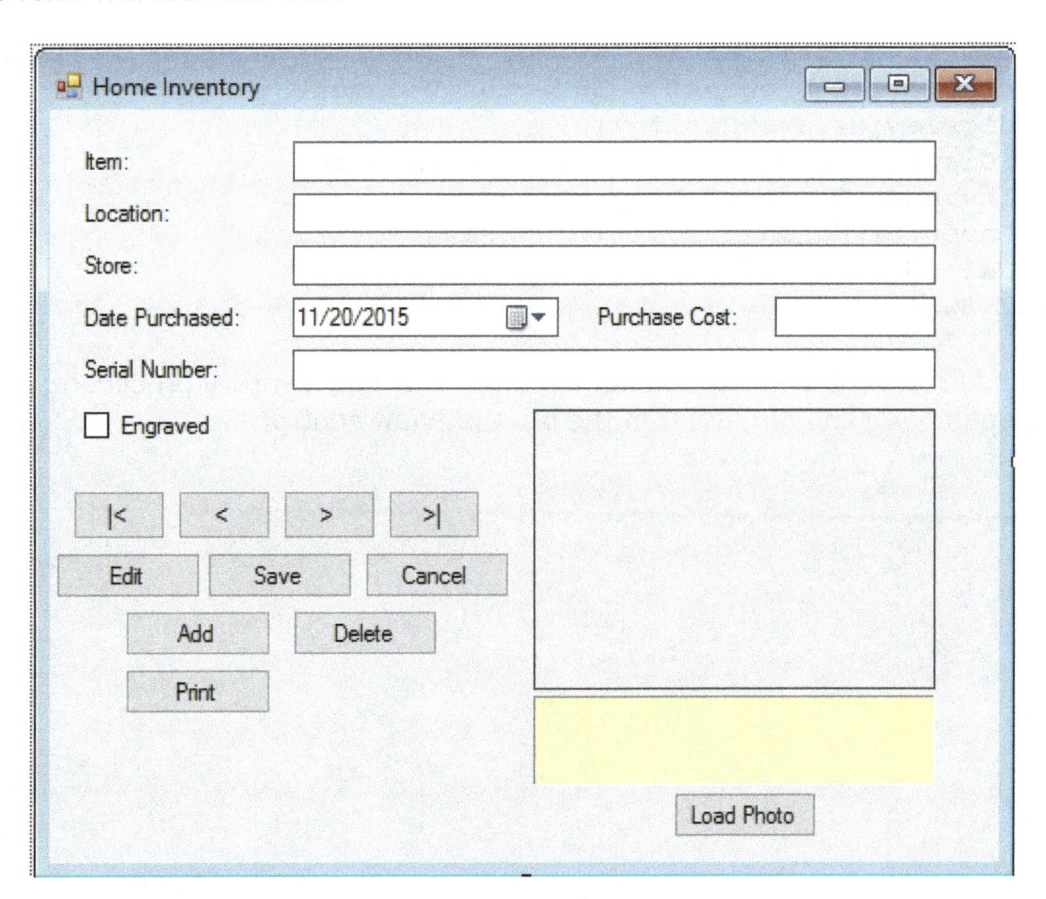

Visual Basic and Databases

2. Add the **PageNumber** variable to the form level declarations:

   ```
   Dim PageNumber As Integer
   ```

3. Add code to the **SetState** procedure to set the **btnPrint Enabled** property to **True** in **View** mode and **False** in **Add/Edit** mode.

4. Add this code to the **btnPrint Click** event procedure:

   ```
   Private Sub BtnPrint_Click(ByVal sender As System.Object, ByVal e As System.EventArgs) Handles btnPrint.Click
       'Declare the document
       Dim InventoryDocument As Drawing.Printing.PrintDocument
       'Create the document and name it
       InventoryDocument = New Drawing.Printing.PrintDocument()
       InventoryDocument.DocumentName = "Home Inventory"
       'Add code handler
       AddHandler InventoryDocument.PrintPage, AddressOf Me.PrintInventory
       'Print document in preview control
       PageNumber = 1
       Dim SavedPosition As Integer = InventoryManager.Position
       dlgPreview.Document = InventoryDocument
       dlgPreview.ShowDialog()
       'Dispose of document when done printing
       InventoryDocument.Dispose()
       InventoryManager.Position = SavedPosition
       Call ShowPhoto()
   End Sub
   ```

This code sets up the **PrintDocument** (using the **PrintInventory** procedure; developed next) and displays it in the print preview control.

5. Add this code to the **PrintInventory** procedure:

```
Private Sub PrintInventory(ByVal sender As Object, ByVal e As Drawing.Printing.PrintPageEventArgs)
    'move through records, printing each one
    InventoryManager.Position = PageNumber - 1
    Call ShowPhoto()
    'print header
    Dim MyFont As Font = New Font("Arial", 14, FontStyle.Bold)
    Dim Y As Integer = e.MarginBounds.Top + 50
    e.Graphics.DrawString("Home Inventory (" + Format(Now, "d") + ") - Page" + Str(PageNumber), MyFont, Brushes.Black, e.MarginBounds.Left, Y)
    Y += 2 * CInt(MyFont.GetHeight())
    'print text information
    MyFont = New Font("Arial", 12, FontStyle.Regular)
    e.Graphics.DrawString("Item:", MyFont, Brushes.Black, e.MarginBounds.X, Y)
    e.Graphics.DrawString(txtItem.Text, MyFont, Brushes.Black, e.MarginBounds.X + 150, Y)
    Y += CInt(MyFont.GetHeight())
    e.Graphics.DrawString("Location:", MyFont, Brushes.Black, e.MarginBounds.X, Y)
    e.Graphics.DrawString(txtLocation.Text, MyFont, Brushes.Black, e.MarginBounds.X + 150, Y)
    Y += CInt(MyFont.GetHeight())
    e.Graphics.DrawString("Store:", MyFont, Brushes.Black, e.MarginBounds.X, Y)
    e.Graphics.DrawString(txtStore.Text, MyFont, Brushes.Black, e.MarginBounds.X + 150, Y)
    Y += CInt(MyFont.GetHeight())
    e.Graphics.DrawString("Date Purchased:", MyFont, Brushes.Black, e.MarginBounds.X, Y)
    e.Graphics.DrawString(dtpDatePurchased.Text, MyFont, Brushes.Black, e.MarginBounds.X + 150, Y)
    Y += CInt(MyFont.GetHeight())
    e.Graphics.DrawString("Purchase Cost:", MyFont, Brushes.Black, e.MarginBounds.X, Y)
    e.Graphics.DrawString(Format(CSng(txtPurchaseCost.Text), "$0.00"), MyFont, Brushes.Black, e.MarginBounds.X + 150, Y)
    Y += CInt(MyFont.GetHeight())
    e.Graphics.DrawString("Serial Number:", MyFont, Brushes.Black, e.MarginBounds.X, Y)
    e.Graphics.DrawString(txtSerialNumber.Text, MyFont, Brushes.Black, e.MarginBounds.X + 150, Y)
    Y += 50
```

```
    'print picture (4 inches wide, height based on
height/width ratio of image)
    Dim H As Integer = CInt(400 * picItem.Image.Height / picItem.Image.Width)
    e.Graphics.DrawImage(picItem.Image, e.MarginBounds.X, Y, 400, H)
    PageNumber += 1
    If PageNumber <= InventoryManager.Count Then
      e.HasMorePages = True
    Else
      e.HasMorePages = False
      PageNumber = 1
    End If
  End Sub
```

On each page, a header is printed along with a listing of the fields and the item picture.

6. Save and run the application. Click **Print**. The print preview control will appear with all pages of the inventory:

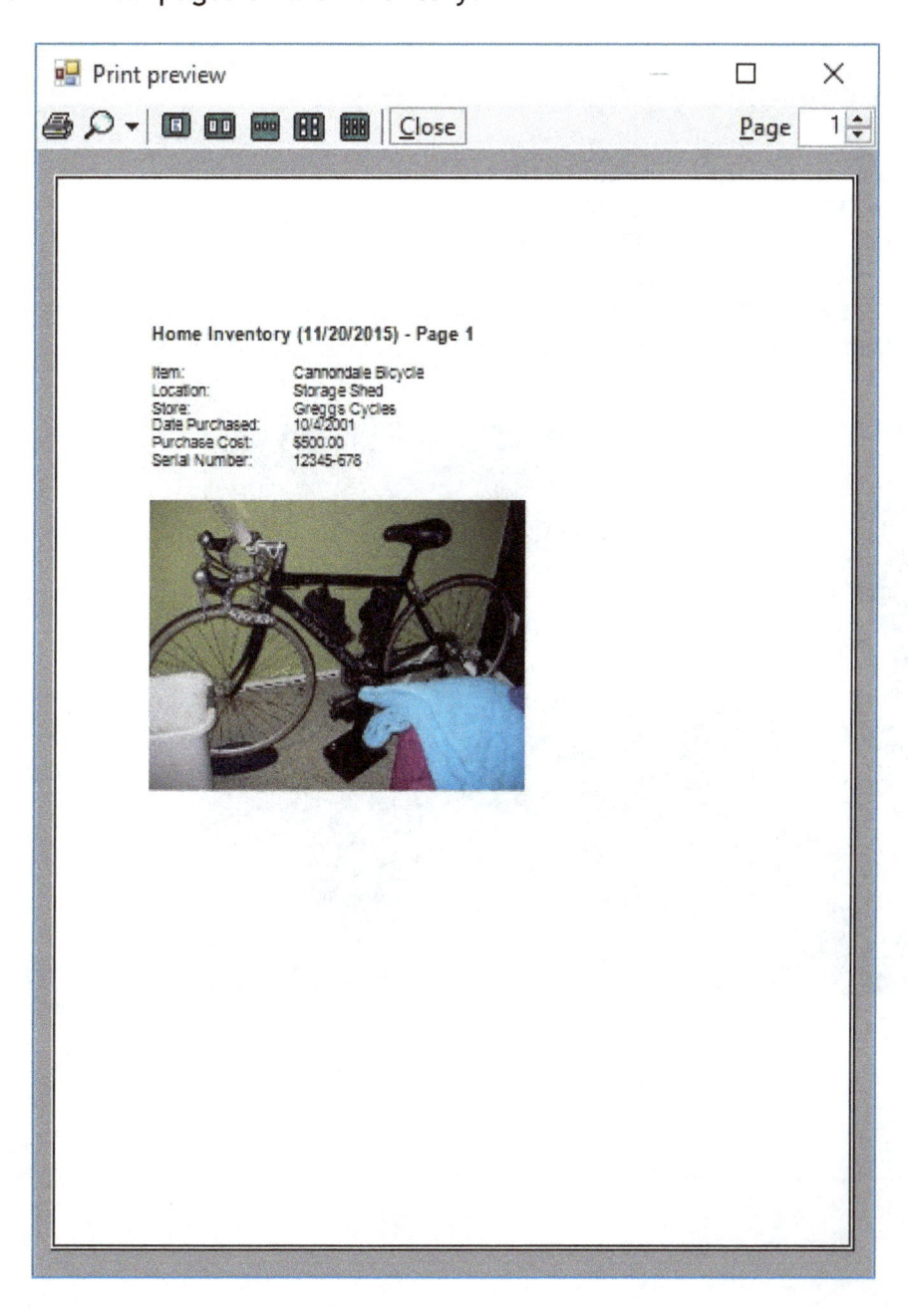

10-104 Visual Basic and Databases

At this point, the user can choose to obtain a hard copy of the report if desired. Here's the top of the Ford Focus page:

Home Inventory (11/20/2015) - Page 3

Item:	Ford Focus
Location:	Carport
Store:	Private Party
Date Purchased:	12/15/2004
Purchase Cost:	$2001.00
Serial Number:	288dkjd8883

Stopping the Application

Lastly, we add controls and code to allow us to elegantly exit from the home inventory application.

1. Add a button to the form next to the **Print** button. Use these properties:

Name	btnExit
Text	Exit
TabStop	False

   The form will look like this:

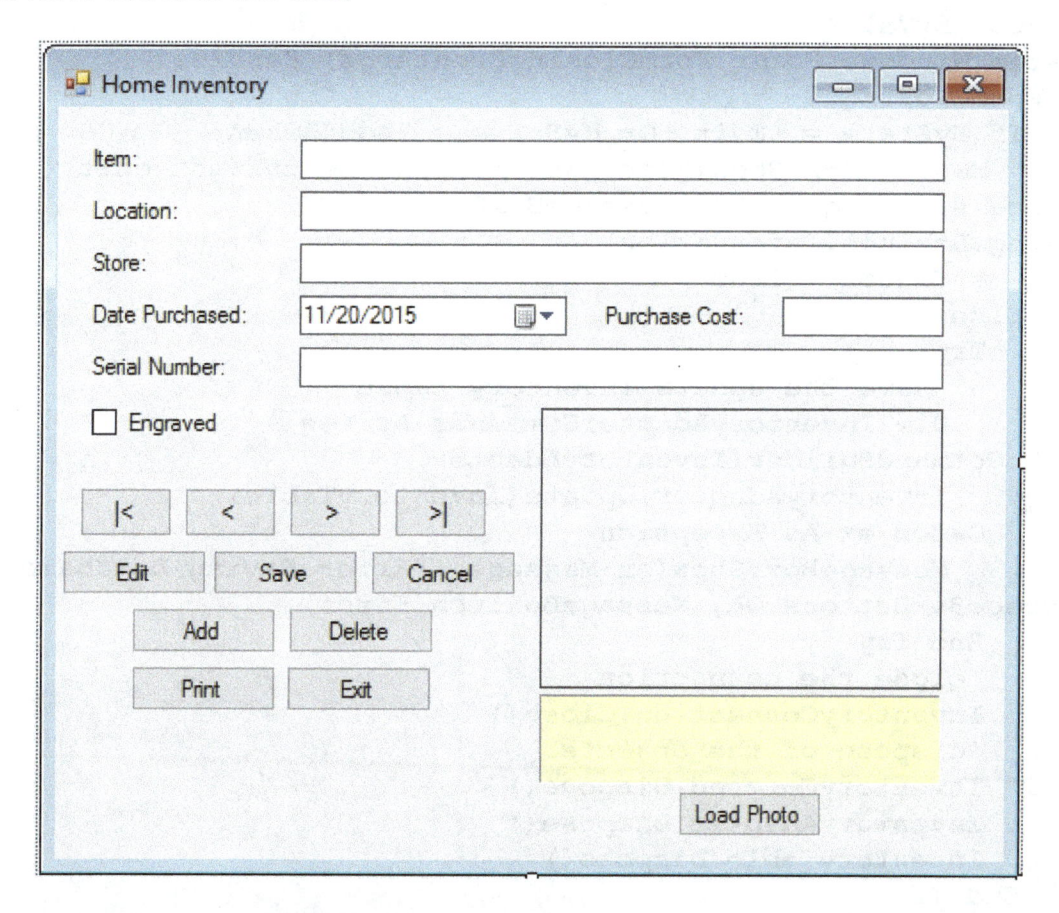

2. Add code to the **SetState** procedure to set the **btnExit Enabled** property to **True** in **View** mode and **False** in **Add/Edit** mode.

3. Add this code to the **btnExit Click** event procedure:

```vb
Private Sub BtnExit_Click(ByVal sender As System.Object, ByVal e As System.EventArgs) Handles btnExit.Click
    Me.Close()
End Sub
```

4. Add the shaded code to the **frmInventory FormClosing** event procedure (we won't stop the application if editing a record):

Access Database:

```vb
Private Sub FrmInventory_FormClosing(ByVal sender As Object, ByVal e As System.Windows.Forms.FormClosingEventArgs) Handles Me.FormClosing
    If MyState = "Edit" Or MyState = "Add" Then
      MessageBox.Show("You must finish the current edit before stopping.", "", MessageBoxButtons.OK, MessageBoxIcon.Information)
      e.Cancel = True
    Else
      Try
        'save the update Inventory table
        Dim InventoryAdapterCommands As New OleDbCommandBuilder(InventoryAdapter)
        InventoryAdapter.Update(InventoryTable)
      Catch ex As Exception
        MessageBox.Show(ex.Message, "Error Saving Database", MessageBoxButtons.OK, MessageBoxIcon.Error)
      End Try
      'close the connection
      InventoryConnection.Close()
      'dispose of the objects
      InventoryCommand.Dispose()
      InventoryAdapter.Dispose()
      InventoryTable.Dispose()
    End If
End Sub
```

SQL Server Database:

```vb
Private Sub FrmInventory_FormClosing(ByVal sender As Object, ByVal e As
System.Windows.Forms.FormClosingEventArgs) Handles Me.FormClosing
    If MyState = "Edit" Or MyState = "Add" Then
       MessageBox.Show("You must finish the current edit before stopping.", "", MessageBoxButtons.OK, MessageBoxIcon.Information)
       e.Cancel = True
    Else
      Try
        'save the update Inventory table
        Dim InventoryAdapterCommands As New SqlCommandBuilder(InventoryAdapter)
        InventoryAdapter.Update(InventoryTable)
      Catch ex As Exception
        MessageBox.Show(ex.Message, "Error Saving Database", MessageBoxButtons.OK, MessageBoxIcon.Error)
      End Try
      'close the connection
      InventoryConnection.Close()
      'dispose of the objects
      InventoryCommand.Dispose()
      InventoryAdapter.Dispose()
      InventoryTable.Dispose()
    End If
  End Sub
```

5. Save and run the application. Try exiting (click the **X** in the upper right corner of the form) the application while editing a record. This should appear:

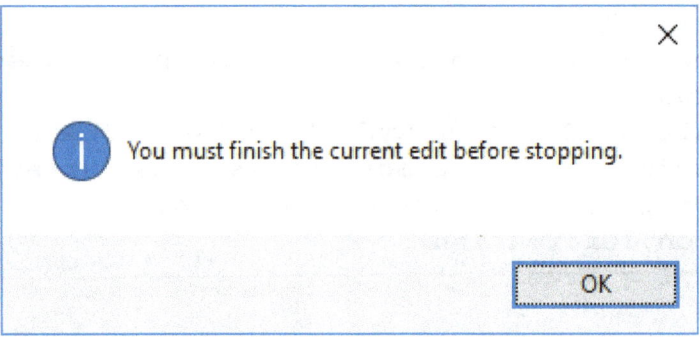

> You must finish the current edit before stopping.
>
> OK

Make sure the **Exit** button works too.

Suggested Improvements

The Home Inventory Project is now complete (the final Access version is saved in **Example 10-2** folder in **VBDB\Access\Class 10** folder; the final SQL Server version is saved in **Example 10-2** folder in **VBDB\SQL Server\Class 10** folder). It was fun and easy to build. And, there is still room for improvement. Some of our ideas follow.

The database file is built into the application. Users might like to have separate inventory files for separate locations. Perhaps they have rental properties they would like to keep track of. You could modify the application to allow the user to specify the database file they want to work with. We do this in the **Weather Monitor** application (Example 10-3). The steps would be the same here.

Add some search capabilities to the application. For very large inventories, it might be helpful to search for particular items or serial numbers. You have the ability to add this feature.

For very small databases, there's a chance the user might accidentally delete the last remaining record in the database. We have nothing in our code to prevent such an occurrence and if a user tries it, an error message will appear. Can you modify the application to handle deletion of all records?

Add an icon to the form, develop on-line help, create a distribution package and pass the program out to your friends and neighbors. Everyone could use a home inventory program. Their feedback could help you improve the application into a commercially viable program.

Example 10-3

Weather Monitor Project

In this last sample project, we build an application that lets you track daily high and low temperatures and precipitation amounts (if any). We will follow many steps in building the application, from development of the database to creation of a distribution package. The steps followed are similar to those you would use to develop a commercial database application.

The steps followed to build the **Weather Monitor** are:

1. Building and testing of the Visual Basic interface
2. Creation of an empty database
3. Database reports
4. Development of a help system
5. Designing a project icon
6. Creation of a distribution package

The interface will allow the user to enter high and low temperatures and precipitation for any dates they choose within a particular year. This information will be saved in the database. Plotted results will be available, as will summary information regarding maximum, minimum, and average values.

Weather Monitor Interface

In this application, for each day in a single year, the user enters a high temperature, a low temperature, a precipitation amount, and any comment. The database manager will automatically provide the date. For the Access version of the project, when the user starts a new weather monitoring file, we will build the new empty database file using Visual Basic code and ADOX technology (like in Chapter 9). For the SQL Server version, a provided empty database will be used. We will use a tab control as the major component of the Weather Monitor interface. The control will have three tabs: one to view and edit the weather data, one to view a temperature data graph, and one to view a precipitation data graph. Each tab in this control operates like the Visual Basic panel control. Each tab's control must be drawn in the appropriate tab region.

1. Start a new application. Add a tab control to the form. Set these properties:

   Form1:
Name	frmWeather
FormBorderStyle	FixedSingle
StartPosition	CenterScreen
Text	Weather Monitor

   TabControl1:
Name	tabWeather
Dock	Fill
FontSize	10

   TabPage1:
Name	tabPageData
Text	Record Weather Data

   TabPage2:
Name	tabPageTemp
Text	View Temperature Data

   TabPage3:
Name	tabPagePrecip
Text	View Precipitation Data

2. Save the application (Access version saved in **Example 10-3** folder in **VBDB\Access\Class 10** folder; SQL Server version saved in **Example 10-3** folder in **VBDB\SQL Server\Class 10** folder) – you can run it to see how the tab switching works. The form looks like this when running (to give you an idea of how large it should be):

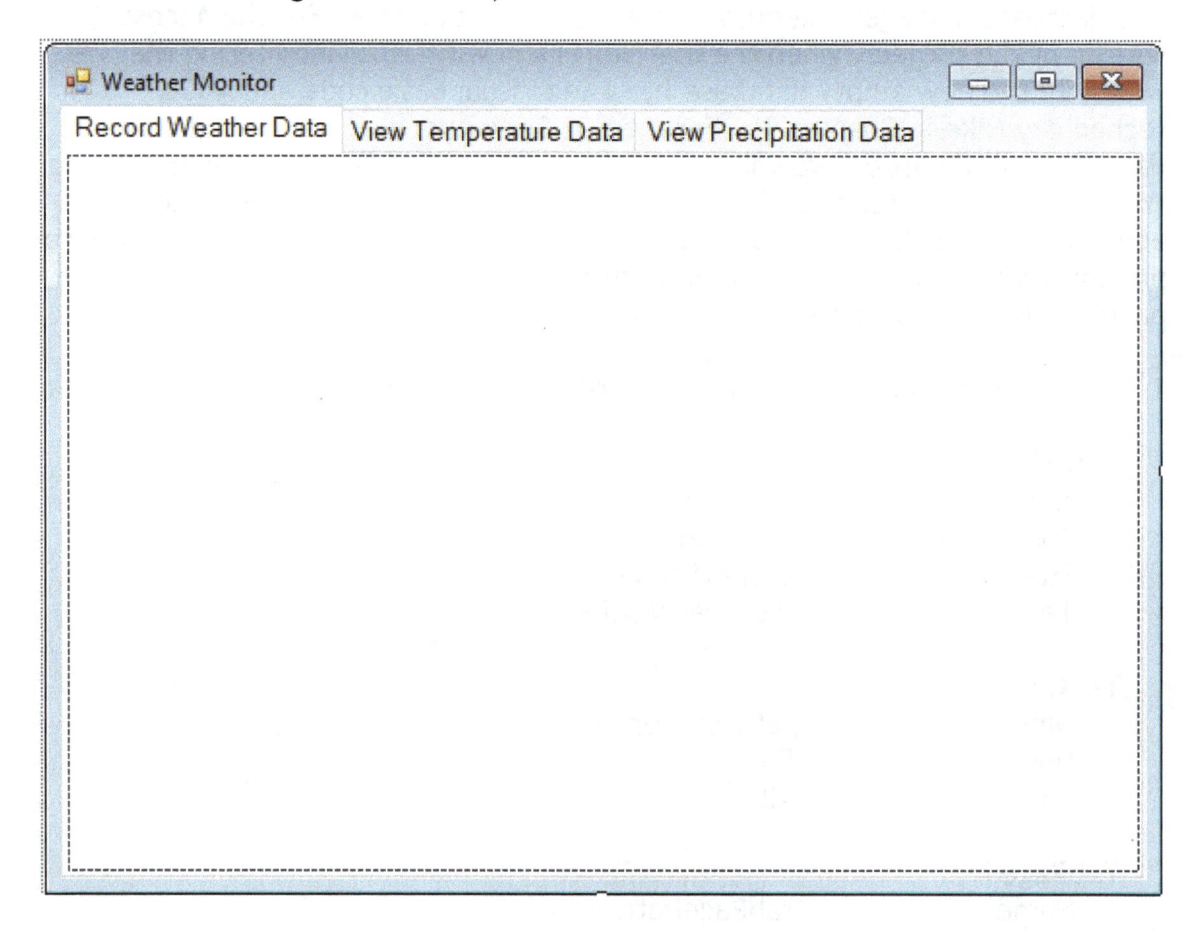

Sample Database Projects 10-113

Record Weather Data Tab

On this tab, we will have the ability to start a new file or open an existing file. The data will be displayed in a grid control for viewing and editing. Here's what the finished tab will look like (this should guide you while placing controls and setting properties):

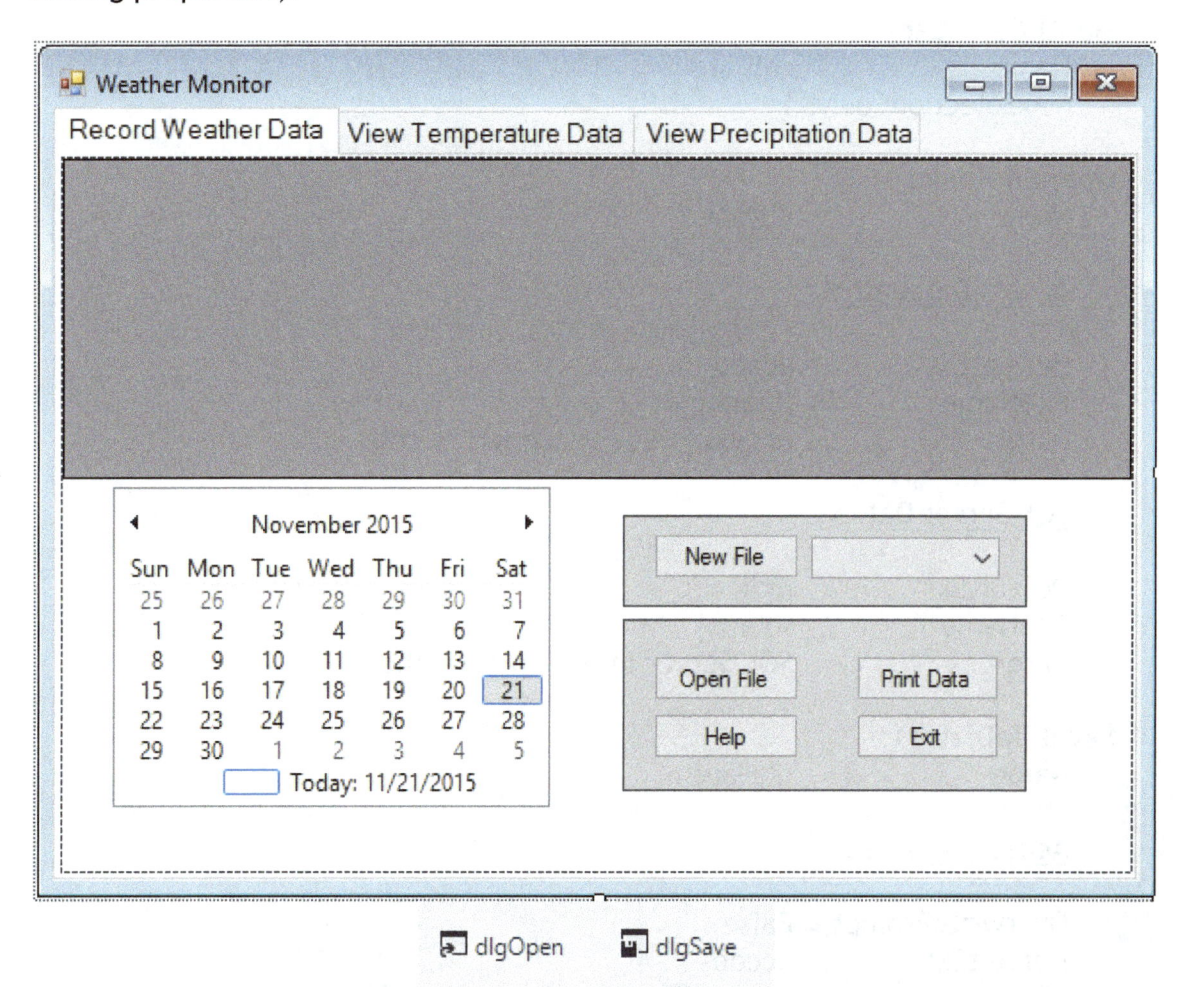

Visual Basic and Databases

1. Make sure the **Record Weather Data** tab is active. Add a data grid view, a month calendar control, an open file dialog control, a save file dialog control and two panel controls. Set these properties:

   DataGridView1:
      Name   grdWeather

   MonthCalendar1:
      Name   calDate
      MaxSelectionCount 1

   OpenFileDialog1:
      Name   dlgOpen

   Access Database:

      DefaultExt   accdb
      FileName   [blank]
      Filter   Access Files (*.accdb)|*.accdb

   SQL Server Database:

      DefaultExt   mdf
      FileName   [blank]
      Filter   SQL Server Files (*.mdf)|*.mdf

   SaveFileDialog1:
      Name   dlgSave

   Access Database:

      OverwritePrompt False
      DefaultExt   accdb
      Filter   Access Files (*.accdb)|*.accdb

   SQL Server Database:

      OverwritePrompt True
      DefaultExt   mdf
      Filter   SQL Server Files (*.mdf)|*.mdf

Panel1:
    Name   pnlNew
    BackColor   Light Gray
    BorderStyle   FixedSingle

Panel2:
    Name   pnlFiles
    BackColor   Light Gray
    BorderStyle   FixedSingle

2. In the **pnlNew** panel, add a button and a combo box. Set these properties:

Button1:
    Name   btnNew
    FontSize   8
    Text   New File

ComboBox1:
    Name   cboYear
    FontSize   8
    FontBold   True
    DropdownStyle DropdownList

10-116 Visual Basic and Databases

3. In the **pnlFiles** panel, add four buttons. Set these properties:

   Button1:
Name	btnOpen
FontSize	8
Text	Open File

   Button2:
Name	btnPrintData
FontSize	8
Text	Print Data

   Button3:
Name	btnHelpData
FontSize	8
Text	Help

   Button4:
Name	btnExitData
FontSize	8
Text	Exit

4. Save and run the application. Make sure all controls are on first tab and not just floating around somewhere on the form.

Let's explain how this will all work. The grid will display the weather data and the calendar control will provide a visual representation of the current date. The user will be able to start a new weather file or open an existing file. If starting a new file (click **New File**), the user selects the year using the displayed combo box control. The user then chooses a name for that file using the save file dialog. An empty database with that name will be created. How it is created depends on whether you are using an Access or SQL Server database.

If using Access, we will build the empty database in code using ADOX technology (make sure your project uses .NET Framework 4). We could do something similar for SQL Server databases (using advanced SQL statements) but that is beyond the scope of this particular course. For SQL Server databases, we will copy a provided empty database to the database named by the user.

Weather Monitor Database (Access)

For Access databases, an empty Access database with a selected name will be built in code. Let's write that code using ADOX technology.

1. Referring back to Example 9-2, add a reference to the ADOX library. Add this line at the top of the code window to allow use of this library:

   ```
   Imports ADOX
   ```

2. Add this code to the **btnNew Click** event procedure:

```
  Private Sub BtnNew_Click(ByVal sender As System.Object, ByVal e As System.EventArgs) Handles btnNew.Click
     Dim WeatherDatabase As New Catalog
     Dim DatabaseTable As Table
     Try
       'get filename
       If dlgSave.ShowDialog = Windows.Forms.DialogResult.OK Then
         WeatherDatabase.Create("Provider=Microsoft.ACE.OLEDB.12.0; Data Source = " + dlgSave.FileName)
         'create table
         DatabaseTable = New Table
         DatabaseTable.Name = "Weather"
         WeatherDatabase.Tables.Append(DatabaseTable)
       End If
     Catch ex As Exception
       MessageBox.Show(ex.Message, "Error Creating Database", MessageBoxButtons.OK, MessageBoxIcon.Error)
     Finally
       WeatherDatabase = Nothing
     End Try
  End Sub
```

This code creates an empty database (user selected name) with a table named **Weather**.

3. Save and run the project. Click **New File** – the save file dialog appears:

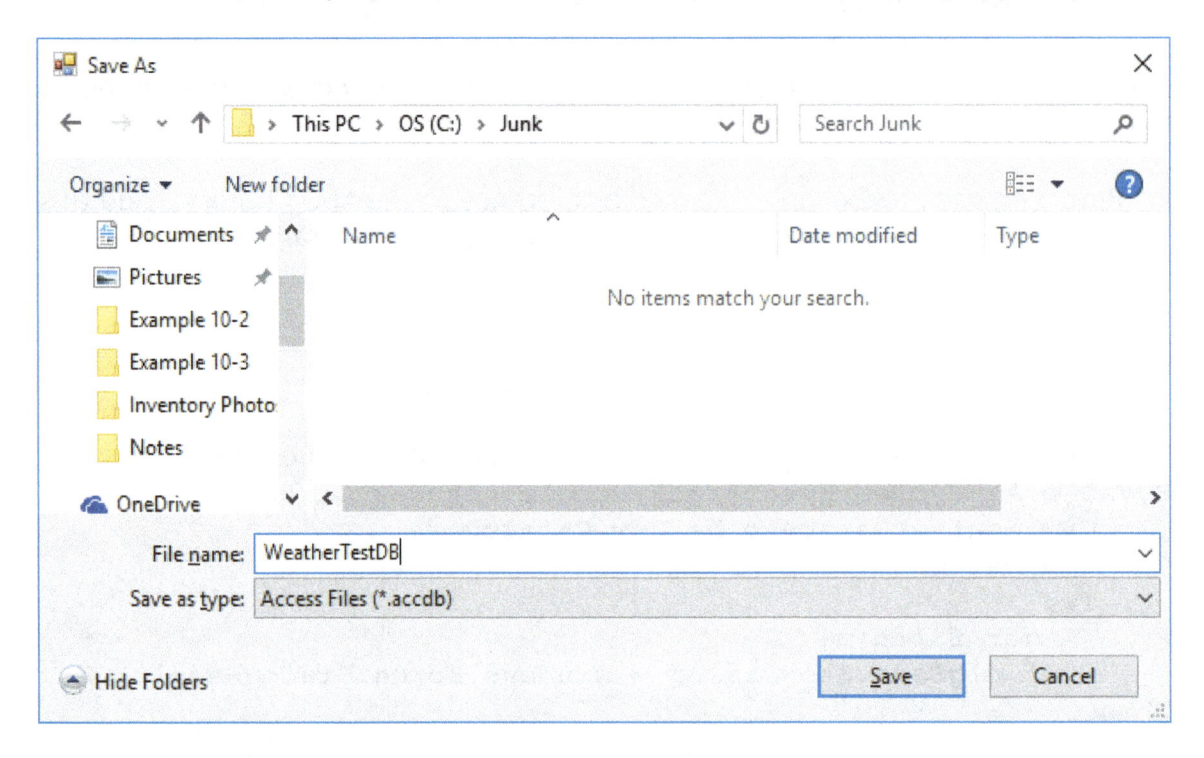

Choose a location and name (it can't be a name already used for a database). I chose **WeatherTestDB** in my **c:\junk** folder. Click **Save**. Stop the application. Go to the directory you selected and your new database should be there. Here's mine:

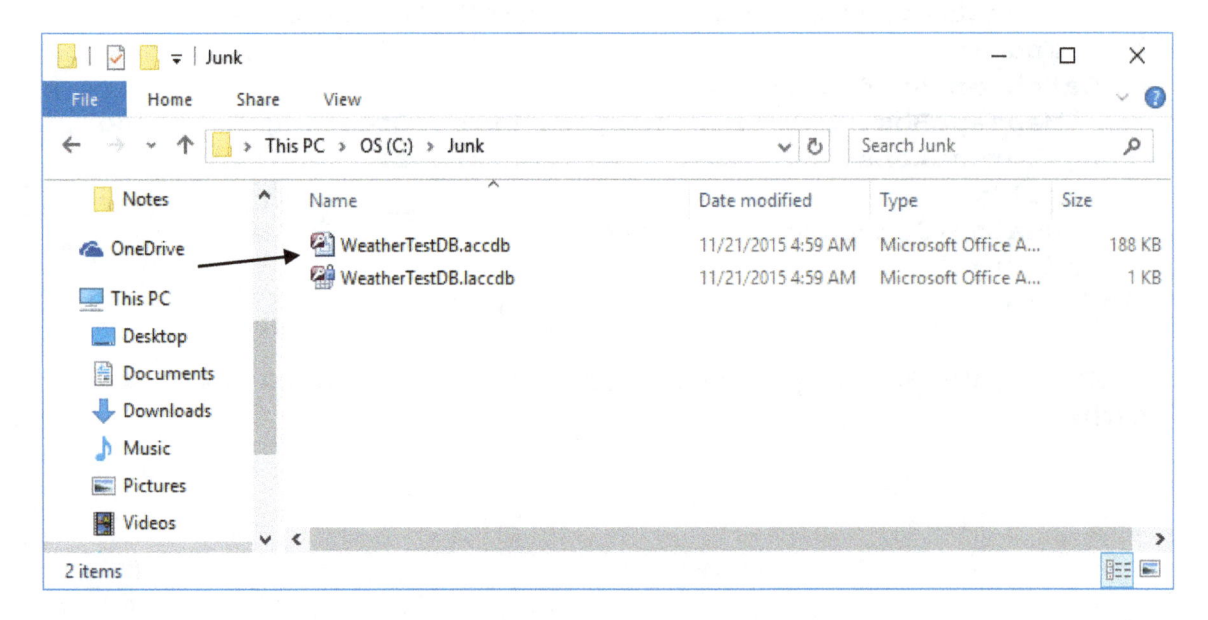

This is an empty database. We'll use our programming skills to add information – defining the fields and pre-populating the date information.

Sample Database Projects

Let's add the fields. There are five fields in the database. They are:

Field Name	Field Type
WeatherDate	Date/Time
HighTemp	Single
LowTemp	Single
Precip	Single
Comment	Short Text (50 characters)

Only the **WeatherDate** field is required (it is the primary key).

1. Add the shaded code to the **btnNew Click** event procedure. This code adds each field, removes the requirement field from all but the **WeatherDate** field, then defines the primary key and index.

```
Private Sub BtnNew_Click(ByVal sender As System.Object, ByVal e As System.EventArgs) Handles btnNew.Click
    Dim WeatherDatabase As New Catalog
    Dim DatabaseTable As Table
    Try
      'get filename
      If dlgSave.ShowDialog = Windows.Forms.DialogResult.OK Then
        WeatherDatabase.Create("Provider=Microsoft.ACE.OLEDB.12.0; Data Source = " + dlgSave.FileName)
        'create table
        DatabaseTable = New Table
        DatabaseTable.Name = "Weather"
        'add fields
        DatabaseTable.Columns.Append("WeatherDate", DataTypeEnum.adDate)
        DatabaseTable.Columns.Append("HighTemp", DataTypeEnum.adSingle)
        DatabaseTable.Columns.Append("LowTemp", DataTypeEnum.adSingle)
        DatabaseTable.Columns.Append("Precip", DataTypeEnum.adSingle)
        DatabaseTable.Columns.Append("Comment", DataTypeEnum.adWChar, 50)
        DatabaseTable.Columns("HighTemp").Attributes = ColumnAttributesEnum.adColNullable
        DatabaseTable.Columns("LowTemp").Attributes = ColumnAttributesEnum.adColNullable
        DatabaseTable.Columns("Precip").Attributes = ColumnAttributesEnum.adColNullable
```

```
            DatabaseTable.Columns("Comment").Attributes =
ColumnAttributesEnum.adColNullable
            'primary key
            DatabaseTable.Keys.Append("PK_Weather",
KeyTypeEnum.adKeyPrimary, "WeatherDate")
            DatabaseTable.Indexes.Append("WeatherDate",
"WeatherDate")
            WeatherDatabase.Tables.Append(DatabaseTable)
        End If
    Catch ex As Exception
        MessageBox.Show(ex.Message, "Error Creating Database",
MessageBoxButtons.OK, MessageBoxIcon.Error)
    Finally
        WeatherDatabase = Nothing
    End Try
End Sub
```

2. Save and run the application. Create a new database. You must choose a unique name. If you don't you will see:

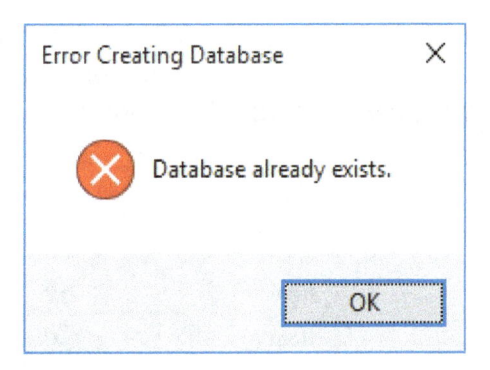

> **Error Creating Database**
>
> Database already exists.
>
> OK

Each time you create a database, you have to use a different name – this is a protective mechanism to keep you from completely wiping out any previously created database. If I open a newly created weather database in Access (using design view), I see all the fields of the **Weather** table have been correctly defined:

Field Name	Data Type
WeatherDate	Date/Time
HighTemp	Number
LowTemp	Number
Precip	Number
Comment	Short Text

We now have a complete Access database we can use with our weather monitoring project. To use this database, we open it and manage it using the same ADO .NET objects we've used throughout these notes. We begin by pre-populating the date field with fixed values.

Weather Monitor Database (SQL Server)

In the **VBDB/Databases** folder is an empty weather database named **SQLWeatherDBBlankDB**. This was created using Server Explorer. It has a single table (**Weather**) with the following fields (Columns):

Name	Data Type	Allow Nulls	Default
WeatherDate	datetime	☐	
HighTemp	float	☑	
LowTemp	float	☑	
Precip	float	☑	
Comment	varchar(50)	☑	
		☐	

Copy this file to your application's **Bin\Debug** folder (you may have to create it). When a user selects **New File**, we will copy this database file to the name selected by the user with the save dialog control.

1. Add this code to the **btnNew Click** event procedure:

```
Private Sub BtnNew_Click(ByVal sender As System.Object, ByVal e As System.EventArgs) Handles btnNew.Click
    Try
        'get filename
        If dlgSave.ShowDialog = Windows.Forms.DialogResult.OK Then
            'copy blank database file
            FileCopy(Application.StartupPath + "\SQLWeatherDBBlank.mdf", dlgSave.FileName)
    Catch ex As Exception
        MessageBox.Show(ex.Message, "Error Creating Database", MessageBoxButtons.OK, MessageBoxIcon.Error)
    End Try
End Sub
```

This code creates an empty weather database using the selected name, **dlgSave.FileName**. Note this code assumes the empty file (**SQLWeatherDBBlank.mdf**) is in the application startup directory.

Sample Database Projects 10-123

2. Save and run the project. Click **New File** – the save file dialog appears:

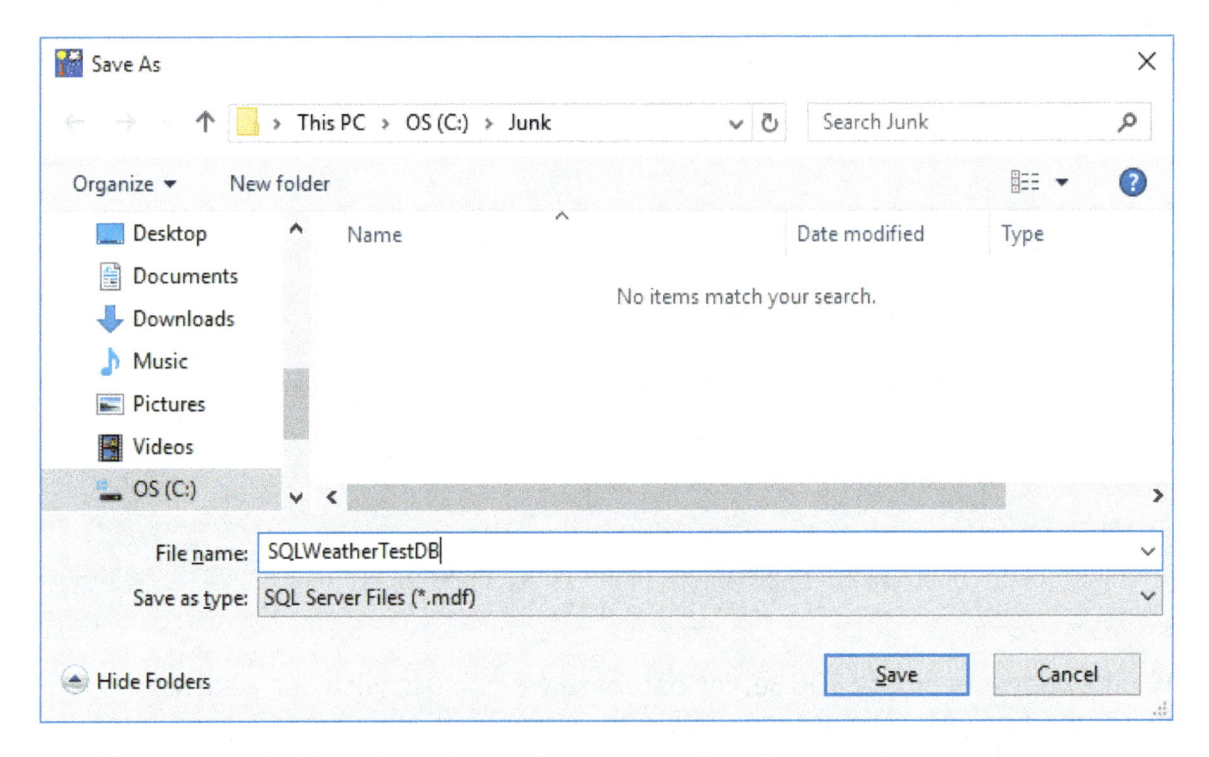

Choose a location and name (it can't be a name already used for a database). I chose **SQLWeatherTestDB** in my **c:\junk** folder. Click **Save**. Stop the application.

Go to the directory you selected and your new database should be there. Here's mine:

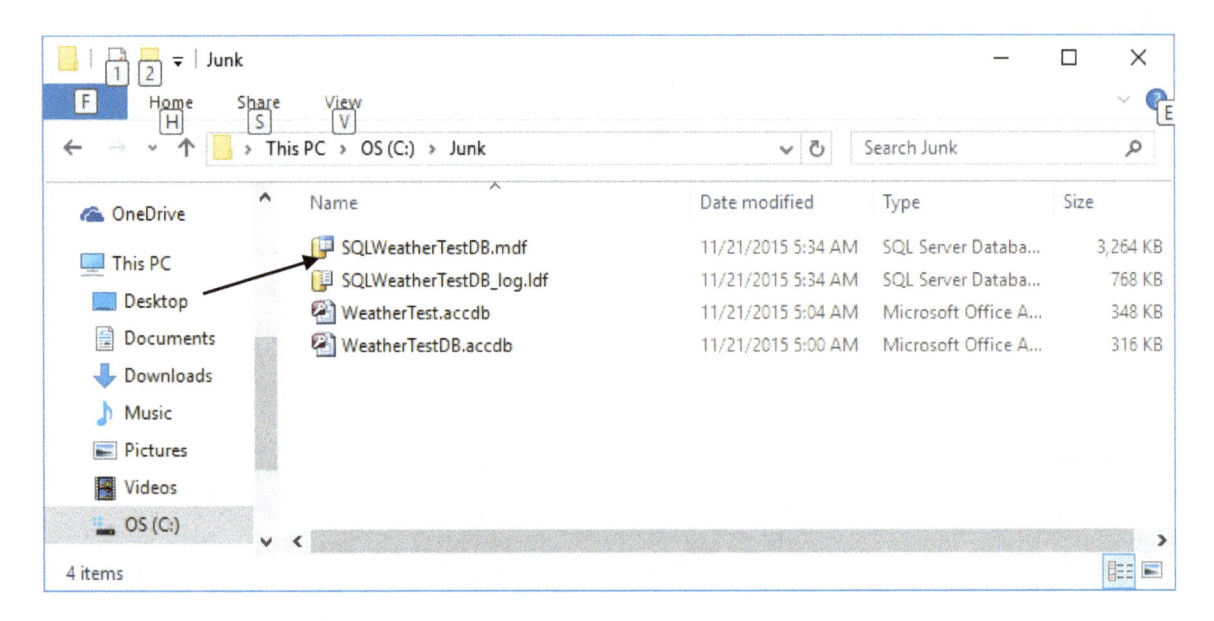

[File Explorer screenshot showing Junk folder with files: SQLWeatherTestDB.mdf (3,264 KB), SQLWeatherTestDB_log.ldf (768 KB), WeatherTest.accdb (348 KB), WeatherTestDB.accdb (316 KB)]

We now have an empty SQL Server database we can use with our weather monitoring project. To use this database, we open it and manage it using the same ADO .NET objects we've used throughout these notes. We begin by pre-populating the date field with fixed values.

Adding Date Values and Editing Features

We continue our database design by pre-populating the date field using the year selected in the combo box control. We use the familiar ADO .NET data objects to accomplish this task. We also add editing features incorporating key trapping in the data grid view.

1. Place this code in the **frmWeather_Load** event procedure:

```
Private Sub frmWeather_Load(ByVal sender As Object, ByVal e As System.EventArgs) Handles Me.Load
  Dim Y As Integer
  For Y = 1900 To 2100
    cboYear.Items.Add(Y.ToString)
  Next Y
  cboYear.Text = calDate.SelectionStart.Year.ToString
  tabWeather.SelectedTab = tabPageData
  grdWeather.AutoSizeColumnsMode = DataGridViewAutoSizeColumnsMode.Fill
  grdWeather.AllowUserToAddRows = False
End Sub
```

This places years we need in the combo box control and displays the first tab. We also set some grid control properties.

2. Add the usual two lines to the top of the code window:

Access Database:

```
Imports System.Data
Imports System.Data.OleDb
```

SQL Server Database:

```
Imports System.Data
Imports System.Data.SqlClient
```

3. Add these general declarations for the needed data objects:

   Access Database:

   ```
   Dim WeatherConnection As OleDbConnection
   Dim WeatherCommand As OleDbCommand
   Dim WeatherAdapter As OleDbDataAdapter
   Dim WeatherTable As DataTable
   ```

   SQL Server Database:

   ```
   Dim WeatherConnection As SqlConnection
   Dim WeatherCommand As SqlCommand
   Dim WeatherAdapter As SqlDataAdapter
   Dim WeatherTable As DataTable
   ```

4. Add the shaded code to the **btnNew Click** event procedure to fill in the **Date** column with each day of the selected year:

   Access Database:

   ```
   Private Sub BtnNew_Click(ByVal sender As System.Object, ByVal e As System.EventArgs) Handles btnNew.Click
       Dim WeatherDatabase As New Catalog
       Dim DatabaseTable As Table
       'close any open database
       Call CloseConnection()
       Try
         'get filename
         If dlgSave.ShowDialog = Windows.Forms.DialogResult.OK Then
   WeatherDatabase.Create("Provider=Microsoft.ACE.OLEDB.12.0; Data Source = " + dlgSave.FileName)
           'create table
           DatabaseTable = New Table
           DatabaseTable.Name = "Weather"
           'add fields
           DatabaseTable.Columns.Append("WeatherDate", DataTypeEnum.adDate)
           DatabaseTable.Columns.Append("HighTemp", DataTypeEnum.adSingle)
           DatabaseTable.Columns.Append("LowTemp", DataTypeEnum.adSingle)
           DatabaseTable.Columns.Append("Precip", DataTypeEnum.adSingle)
   ```

```vb
            DatabaseTable.Columns.Append("Comment",
DataTypeEnum.adWChar, 50)
            DatabaseTable.Columns("HighTemp").Attributes =
ColumnAttributesEnum.adColNullable
            DatabaseTable.Columns("LowTemp").Attributes =
ColumnAttributesEnum.adColNullable
            DatabaseTable.Columns("Precip").Attributes =
ColumnAttributesEnum.adColNullable
            DatabaseTable.Columns("Comment").Attributes =
ColumnAttributesEnum.adColNullable
            'primary key
            DatabaseTable.Keys.Append("PK_Weather",
KeyTypeEnum.adKeyPrimary, "WeatherDate")
            DatabaseTable.Indexes.Append("WeatherDate",
"WeatherDate")
            WeatherDatabase.Tables.Append(DatabaseTable)
            'connect to database
            Call OpenConnection(dlgSave.FileName)
            'fill dates
            Dim TableDate As Date = New Date(CInt(cboYear.Text),
1, 1)
            Dim NDays As Integer =
CInt(DateDiff(DateInterval.Day, TableDate, New
Date(CInt(cboYear.Text) + 1, 1, 1)))
            Dim NewRow As DataRow
            Dim N As Integer
            For N = 1 To NDays
                NewRow = WeatherTable.NewRow
                NewRow.Item("WeatherDate") = TableDate
                WeatherTable.Rows.Add(NewRow)
                TableDate = DateAdd(DateInterval.Day, 1,
TableDate)
            Next
        End If
    Catch ex As Exception
        MessageBox.Show(ex.Message, "Error Creating Database",
MessageBoxButtons.OK, MessageBoxIcon.Error)
    Finally
        WeatherDatabase = Nothing
    End Try
End Sub
```

SQL Server Database:

```
Private Sub BtnNew_Click(ByVal sender As System.Object, ByVal e As System.EventArgs) Handles btnNew.Click
    'close any open database
    Call CloseConnection()
    Try
      'get filename
      If dlgSave.ShowDialog = Windows.Forms.DialogResult.OK Then
        'copy blank database file
        FileCopy(Application.StartupPath + "\SQLWeatherDBBlank.mdf", dlgSave.FileName)
        'connect to database
        Call OpenConnection(dlgSave.FileName)
        'fill dates
        Dim TableDate As Date = New Date(CInt(cboYear.Text), 1, 1)
        Dim NDays As Integer = CInt(DateDiff(DateInterval.Day, TableDate, New Date(CInt(cboYear.Text) + 1, 1, 1)))
        Dim NewRow As DataRow
        Dim N As Integer
        For N = 0 To NDays - 1
          NewRow = WeatherTable.NewRow
          NewRow.Item(0) = DateAdd(DateInterval.Day, N, TableDate)
          WeatherTable.Rows.Add(NewRow)
        Next
      End If
    Catch ex As Exception
      MessageBox.Show(ex.Message, "Error Creating Database", MessageBoxButtons.OK, MessageBoxIcon.Error)
    End Try
  End Sub
```

The new code first disconnects from any current database (using **CloseConnection**). The code then connects to the newly created database and forms all the data objects (**OpenConnection**). Rows are added to the **WeatherTable** object filling in the **WeatherDate** field. After each row is added, the corresponding adapter is updated to save the new row to the database.

5. Add the general procedure **CloseConnection** that closes the any open database and saves changes prior to creating another database:

Access Database:

```
Private Sub CloseConnection()
  Try
    If Not (WeatherConnection Is Nothing) Then
      If WeatherConnection.State = ConnectionState.Open Then
        Dim WeatherAdapterCommand As New OleDbCommandBuilder(WeatherAdapter)
        WeatherAdapter.Update(WeatherTable)
        WeatherConnection.Close()
        WeatherConnection.Dispose()
        WeatherCommand.Dispose()
        WeatherAdapter.Dispose()
        WeatherTable.Dispose()
        WeatherAdapterCommand.Dispose()
      End If
    End If
  Catch ex As Exception
    MessageBox.Show(ex.Message, "Error Saving Database", MessageBoxButtons.OK, MessageBoxIcon.Error)
  End Try
End Sub
```

SQL Server Database:

```
Private Sub CloseConnection()
    Try
        If Not (WeatherConnection Is Nothing) Then
            If WeatherConnection.State = ConnectionState.Open Then
                Dim WeatherAdapterCommand As New SqlCommandBuilder(WeatherAdapter)
                WeatherAdapter.Update(WeatherTable)
                WeatherConnection.Close()
                WeatherConnection.Dispose()
                WeatherCommand.Dispose()
                WeatherAdapter.Dispose()
                WeatherTable.Dispose()
                WeatherAdapterCommand.Dispose()
            End If
        End If
    Catch ex As Exception
        MessageBox.Show(ex.Message, "Error Saving Database", MessageBoxButtons.OK, MessageBoxIcon.Error)
    End Try
End Sub
```

6. Add the general procedure **OpenConnection** that connects to the database, creates the data objects and binds the data grid control (**grdWeather**) to the table object.

Access Database:

```
  Private Sub OpenConnection(ByVal FName As String)
    Try
      WeatherConnection = New
OleDbConnection("Provider=Microsoft.ACE.OLEDB.12.0; Data
Source = " + FName)
      WeatherConnection.Open()
      'establish command object
      WeatherCommand = New OleDbCommand("SELECT * FROM
Weather ORDER BY WeatherDate", WeatherConnection)
      'establish data adapter/data table
      WeatherAdapter = New OleDbDataAdapter()
      WeatherAdapter.SelectCommand = WeatherCommand
      WeatherTable = New DataTable()
      WeatherAdapter.Fill(WeatherTable)
      grdWeather.DataSource = WeatherTable
      grdWeather.Columns(0).ReadOnly = True
    Catch ex As Exception
      MessageBox.Show(ex.Message, "Error Opening Database",
MessageBoxButtons.OK, MessageBoxIcon.Error)
    End Try
  End Sub
```

SQL Server Database:

```vb
Private Sub OpenConnection(ByVal FName As String)
  Try
    WeatherConnection = New SqlConnection("Data Source=.\SQLEXPRESS; AttachDbFilename=" + FName + "; Integrated Security=True; Connect Timeout=30; User Instance=True")
    WeatherConnection.Open()
    'establish command object
    WeatherCommand = New SqlCommand("SELECT * FROM Weather ORDER BY WeatherDate", WeatherConnection)
    'establish data adapter/data table
    WeatherAdapter = New SqlDataAdapter()
    WeatherAdapter.SelectCommand = WeatherCommand
    WeatherTable = New DataTable()
    WeatherAdapter.Fill(WeatherTable)
    grdWeather.DataSource = WeatherTable
    grdWeather.Columns(0).ReadOnly = True
  Catch ex As Exception
    MessageBox.Show(ex.Message, "Error Opening Database", MessageBoxButtons.OK, MessageBoxIcon.Error)
  End Try
End Sub
```

7. Add this code to the **frmWeather FormClosing** event procedure to save an open database when exiting the program:

```vb
Private Sub FrmWeather_FormClosing(ByVal sender As Object, ByVal e As System.Windows.Forms.FormClosingEventArgs) Handles Me.FormClosing
   'close connection
   Call CloseConnection()
End Sub
```

Sample Database Projects 10-133

8. Handling key trapping with the data grid view control is a little tricky. First, add this code to the **grdWeather EditingControlShowing** event procedure:

```
Private Sub GrdWeather_EditingControlShowing(ByVal sender As Object, ByVal e As System.Windows.Forms.DataGridViewEditingControlShowingEventArgs) Handles grdWeather.EditingControlShowing
    RemoveHandler grdWeather.EditingControl.KeyPress, AddressOf Me.grdWeather_KeyPress
    AddHandler grdWeather.EditingControl.KeyPress, AddressOf Me.grdWeather_KeyPress
  End Sub
```

This code attaches the current cell to a **KeyPress** procedure (named **grdWeather_KeyPress**).

9. Add this code to the **grdWeather_KeyPress** event:

```
Private Sub grdWeather_KeyPress(ByVal sender As Object, ByVal e As System.Windows.Forms.KeyPressEventArgs)
    'numeric entries only in first three columns
    Dim CurrentColumn As Integer = grdWeather.CurrentCell.ColumnIndex
    If CurrentColumn > 0 And CurrentColumn < 4 Then
      Select Case e.KeyChar
        Case CChar("0") To CChar("9"), CChar("-"), CChar("."), ControlChars.Back
          e.Handled = False
        Case Else
          e.Handled = True
      End Select
    End If
  End Sub
```

This insures only numbers, a decimal point, or a minus sign can be entered into the temperature and precipitation fields (columns 1 through 3).

10. Save and run the application. Start a **New File**. You should see the grid now appears with the date values filled in:

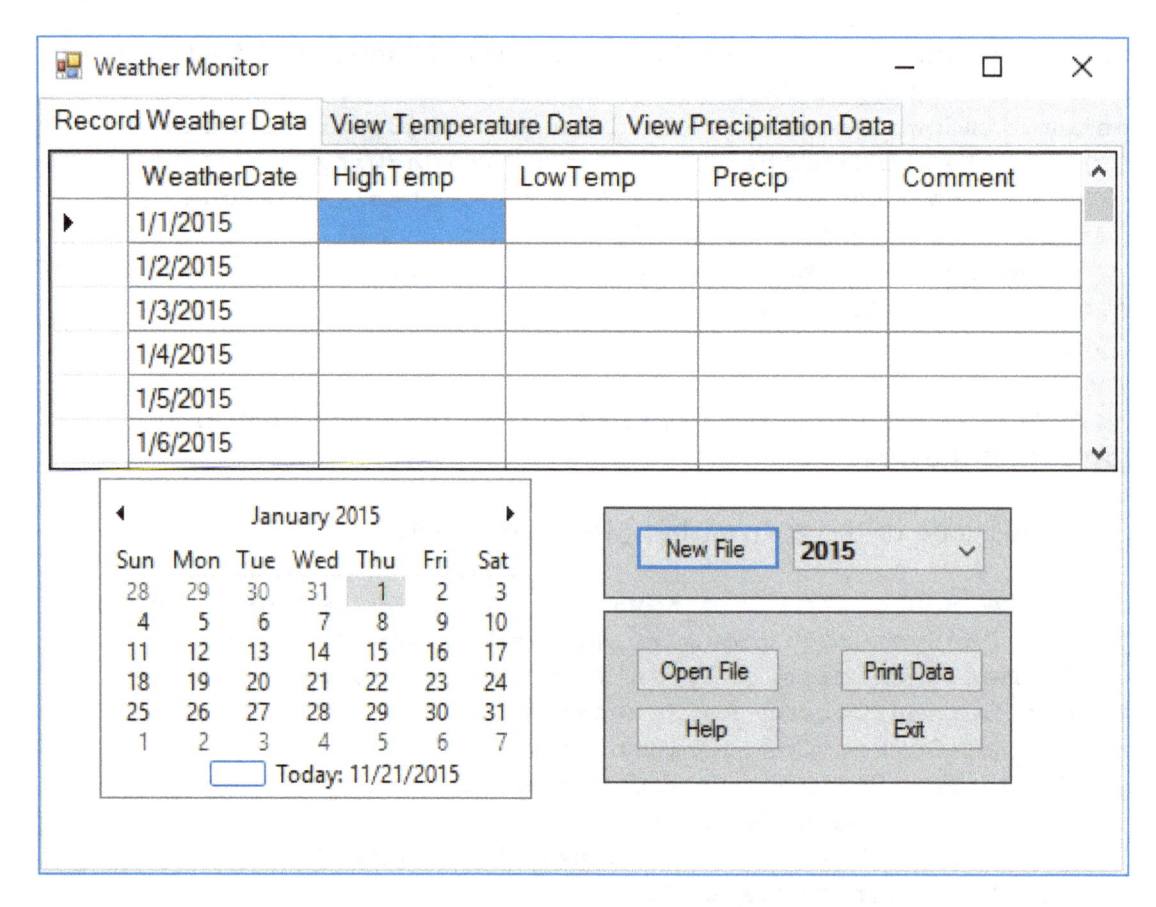

Try inputting some values. Check out the key trapping code. Notice how the grid navigation works. Once you exit the program, your changes will be saved to the newly formed database. Now, of course, you need some way to open the saved file.

Opening Database Files

1. Place the code to open an existing database file in the **btnOpen Click** event procedure:

```
Private Sub BtnOpen_Click(ByVal sender As System.Object, ByVal e As System.EventArgs) Handles btnOpen.Click
    Try
       'close connection if open
       Call CloseConnection()
       'get filename
       If dlgOpen.ShowDialog = Windows.Forms.DialogResult.OK Then
          'connect to database
          Call OpenConnection(dlgOpen.FileName)
       End If
    Catch ex As Exception
       MessageBox.Show(ex.Message, "Error Opening File", MessageBoxButtons.OK, MessageBoxIcon.Error)
    End Try
End Sub
```

Here, we close a connection if it exists. Then, we retrieve a filename from the user and open the selected file.

2. Save and run the application. Try to open a file. There are two example Access databases in the **VBDB\Access\Class 10\Example 10-3** folder. The files are **Sea02DB.accdb** and **Sea03DB.accdb** and contain weather for my hometown of Seattle for the years 2002 and 2003. The corresponding SQL Server databases (**SQLSea02DB.mdf** and **SQLSea03.mdf**) are in the **VBDB\SQL Server\Class 10\Example 10-3** folder. Opening the 2002 database file (**Sea02DB.accdb** or **SQLSea02DB.mdf**) reveals:

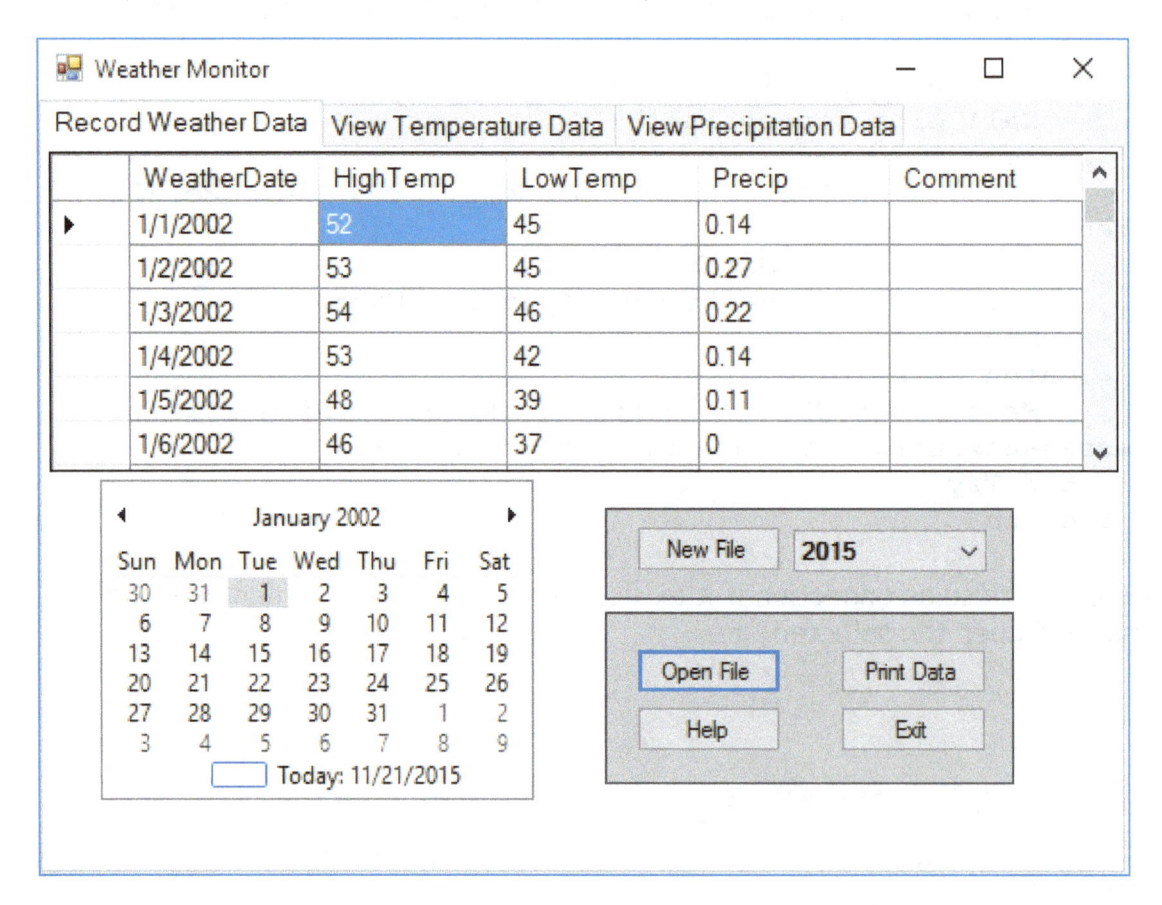

We're almost done with this tab - one more change is needed. It would be nice to be able to select a date on the calendar and have the corresponding entry appear in the data grid. Likewise, if we select a grid row, that date should be displayed on the calendar. That is, we want the date displays to be coordinated with each other.

Date Display Coordination

1. Place this code in the **calDate DateChanged** event procedure:

```
   Private Sub CalDate_DateChanged(ByVal sender As
System.Object, ByVal e As
System.Windows.Forms.DateRangeEventArgs) Handles
calDate.DateChanged
     'match selected date to grid (if possible)
     If Not (WeatherConnection Is Nothing) Then
       WeatherTable.DefaultView.Sort = "WeatherDate"
       Dim DateRow As Integer =
WeatherTable.DefaultView.Find(calDate.SelectionStart)
       If DateRow <> -1 Then
         grdWeather.CurrentCell = grdWeather(1, DateRow)
       End If
     End If
   End Sub
```

When the date changes on the calendar control, the corresponding grid row will be displayed (assuming there is a grid and the date is in the grid).

2. Use this code in the **grdWeather CellClick** event procedure:

```
   Private Sub GrdWeather_CellClick(ByVal sender As Object,
ByVal e As System.Windows.Forms.DataGridViewCellEventArgs)
Handles grdWeather.CellClick
      calDate.SelectionStart = CDate(grdWeather(0,
grdWeather.CurrentCell.RowIndex).Value)
   End Sub
```

This code coordinates the date shown in a selected row in the grid with the calendar control.

3. We need to make sure the dates are coordinated initially. Place this line of code:

```
   Call GrdWeather_CellClick(nothing, nothing)
```

in two places: (1) after the **Call OpenConnection** line in the **btnOpen Click** event procedure, (2) after the For/Next loop adding dates in the **btnNew Click** event procedure.

10-138   Visual Basic and Databases

3. Save and run the application. Open an existing database or one of the samples. Notice how the date displayed in the grid matches the calendar. Here's what I see when I load 2003 database file (**Sea03DB.accdb** or **SQLSea03.mdf**) and scroll down the grid a bit:

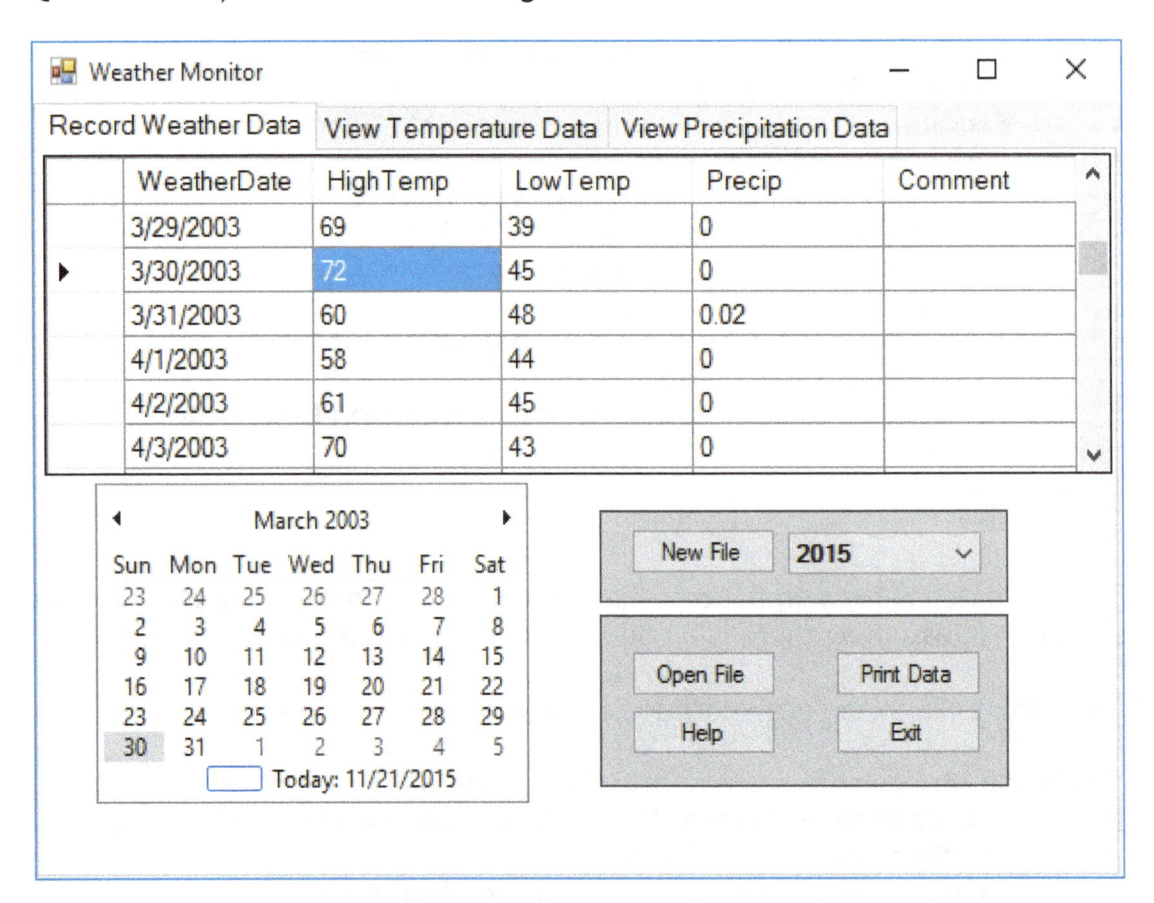

We have not coded the **Print Data**, **Help** or **Exit** buttons. This will be done later. Let's now look at the other two tabs in the project.

View Temperature Data Tab

When this tab is clicked, we will provide a plot of the high and low temperatures and some summary statistics. You can choose what season of the year to plot temperatures for. Here's the finished tab layout to assist you in building the interface:

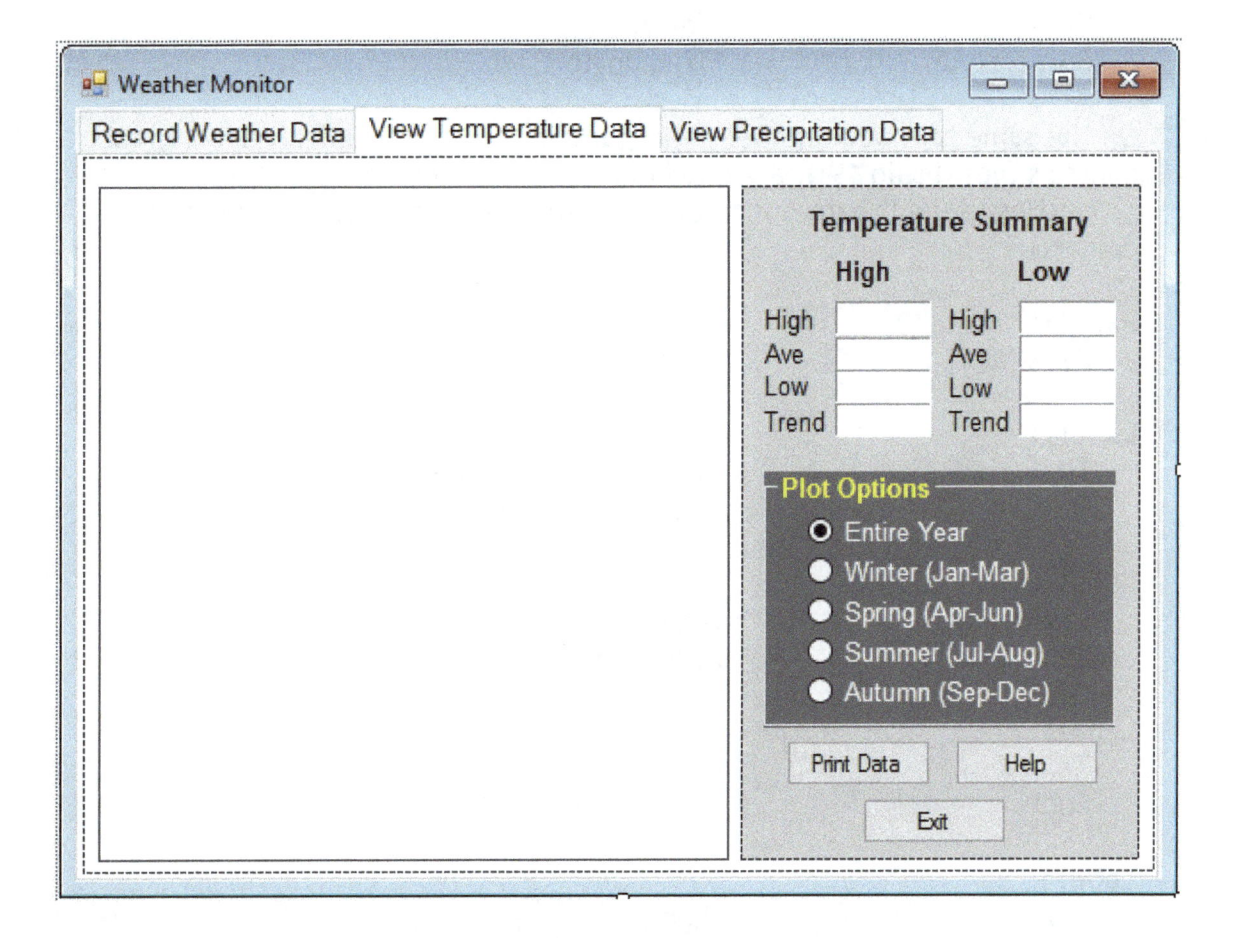

1. In design mode, select the **View Temperature Data** tab. Place a panel control on the form. It will be used to hold a plot of temperature data – it should take up a little more than one-half the width of the tab. Set these properties:

   Panel1:
      Name   pnlTempPlot
      BackColor   White
      BorderStyle   FixedSingle

2. On the same tab, add another panel, and in the panel control, add 19 label controls (yes, I said 19!), a group box, and three buttons. Set these properties (default names may differ – refer to the finished form for each control)

   Panel1:
      BackColor   Light Gray

   Label1:
      Text   Temperature Summary
      Font   Arial, Bold, Size 10

   Label2:
      Text   High
      Font   Arial, Bold, Size 10

   Label3:
      Text   Low
      Font   Arial, Bold, Size 10

   Label4:
      Text   High
      Font   Arial, Size 10

Label5:
    Name   lblTHH
    AutoSize   False
    BorderStyle   Fixed3D
    BackColor   White
    ForeColor   Blue
    Font   Arial, Size 10
    Text   [Blank]
    TextAlign   MiddleCenter

Label6:
    Text   Ave
    Font   Arial, Size 10

Label7:
    Name   lblTHA
    AutoSize   False
    BorderStyle   Fixed3D
    BackColor   White
    ForeColor   Blue
    Font   Arial, Size 10
    Text   [Blank]
    TextAlign   MiddleCenter

Label8:
    Text   Low
    Font   Arial, Size 10

Label9:
    Name   lblTHL
    AutoSize   False
    BorderStyle   Fixed3D
    BackColor   White
    ForeColor   Blue
    Font   Arial, Size 10
    Text   [Blank]
    TextAlign   MiddleCenter

Label10:
   Text   Trend
   Font   Arial, Size 10

Label11:
   Name   lblTHT
   AutoSize   False
   BorderStyle   Fixed3D
   BackColor   White
   ForeColor   Blue
   Font   Arial, Size 10
   Text   [Blank]
   TextAlign   MiddleCenter

Label12:
   Text   High
   Font   Arial, Size 10

Label13:
   Name   lblTLH
   AutoSize   False
   BorderStyle   Fixed3D
   BackColor   White
   ForeColor   Blue
   Font   Arial, Size 10
   Text   [Blank]
   TextAlign   MiddleCenter

Label14:
   Text   Ave
   Font   Arial, Size 10

Label15:
   Name   lblTLA
   AutoSize   False
   BorderStyle   Fixed3D
   BackColor   White
   ForeColor   Blue
   Font   Arial, Size 10
   Text   [Blank]
   TextAlign   MiddleCenter

Label16:
   Text   Low
   Font   Arial, Size 10

Label17:
   Name   lblTLL
   AutoSize   False
   BorderStyle   Fixed3D
   BackColor   White
   ForeColor   Blue
   Font   Arial, Size 10
   Text   [Blank]
   TextAlign   MiddleCenter

Label18:
   Text   Trend
   Font   Arial, Size 10

Label19:
   Name   lblTLT
   AutoSize   False
   BorderStyle   Fixed3D
   BackColor   White
   ForeColor   Blue
   Font   Arial, Size 10
   Text   [Blank]
   TextAlign   MiddleCenter

Button1:
   Name   btnPrintTemp
   FontSize   8
   Text   Print Data

Button2:
   Name   btnHelpTemp
   FontSize   8
   Text   Help

Button3:
   Name   btnExitTemp
   FontSize   8
   Text   Exit

GroupBox1:
    Text   Plot Options
    BackColor   Dark Gray
    Font   Arial, Bold, Size 10
    ForeColor   Yellow

3. In the group box, place five radio buttons. Use these properties:

RadioButton1:
    Name   rdoTempYear
    Text   Entire Year
    Checked   True
    Font   Arial, Size 10
    ForeColor   White

RadioButton2:
    Name   rdoTempWinter
    Text   Winter (Jan-Mar)
    Font   Arial, Size 10
    ForeColor   White

RadioButton3:
    Name   rdoTempSpring
    Text   Spring (Apr-Jun)
    Font   Arial, Size 10
    ForeColor   White

RadioButton4:
    Name   rdoTempSummer
    Text   Summer (Jul-Sep)
    Font   Arial, Size 10
    ForeColor   White

RadioButton5:
    Name   rdoTempAutumn
    Text   Autumn (Oct-Dec)
    Font   Arial, Size 10
    ForeColor   White

The tab layout is complete. Time for coding! When the tab is selected, we will form the required plot and compute the needed summary statistics. We will do the summaries first.

Temperature Summary Statistics

1. Add a general procedure **TemperatureData** to the project and use this code:

```
Private Sub TemperatureData()
  'make sure there is a data table
  If (WeatherConnection Is Nothing) Then
    Exit Sub
  End If
  Dim Temp As Single
  Dim X As Integer
  Dim XStart As Integer, XEnd As Integer, NDays As Integer, IsLeap As Integer
  Dim TempHH As Single, TempHL As Single
  Dim TempLH As Single, TempLL As Single
  Dim SumH As Single, SumL As Single
  Dim NH As Integer, NL As Integer
  Dim SXH As Double, SX2H As Double
  Dim SXYH As Double
  Dim SXL As Double, SX2L As Double
  Dim SXYL As Double
  Dim A1H As Single, A1L As Single
  Dim NoData As Boolean
  Dim HighTemp(366) As Single
  Dim LowTemp(366) As Single
  If WeatherTable.Rows.Count = 365 Then
    IsLeap = 0
  Else
    IsLeap = 1
  End If
  Select Case TempPlot
    Case 0
      XStart = 1
      XEnd = 365 + IsLeap
    Case 1
      XStart = 1
      XEnd = 90 + IsLeap
    Case 2
      XStart = 91 + IsLeap
      XEnd = 181 + IsLeap
    Case 3
      XStart = 182 + IsLeap
      XEnd = 273 + IsLeap
    Case 4
      XStart = 274 + IsLeap
      XEnd = 365 + IsLeap
  End Select
```

```
      NDays = XEnd - XStart + 1
      'Temperature data
      TempHH = -1000 : TempHL = 1000
      TempLH = -1000 : TempLL = 1000
      SumH = 0 : NH = 0
      SumL = 0 : NL = 0
      SXH = 0 : SX2H = 0 : SXYH = 0
      SXL = 0 : SX2L = 0 : SXYL = 0
      For X = XStart To XEnd
        If Not (IsDBNull(WeatherTable.Rows(X - 1).Item("HighTemp"))) Then
          Temp = CSng(WeatherTable.Rows(X - 1).Item("HighTemp"))
          HighTemp(X - XStart + 1) = Temp
          If Temp > TempHH Then TempHH = Temp
          If Temp < TempHL Then TempHL = Temp
          SumH += Temp
          NH += +1
          SXH += X
          SX2H += X * X
          SXYH += X * Temp
        Else
          HighTemp(X - XStart + 1) = -1000.0
        End If
        If Not (IsDBNull(WeatherTable.Rows(X - 1).Item("LowTemp"))) Then
          Temp = CSng(WeatherTable.Rows(X - 1).Item("LowTemp"))
          LowTemp(X - XStart + 1) = Temp
          If Temp > TempLH Then TempLH = Temp
          If Temp < TempLL Then TempLL = Temp
          SumL = SumL + Temp
          NL += 1
          SXL += X
          SX2L += X * X
          SXYL += X * Temp
        Else
          LowTemp(X - XStart + 1) = -1000.0
        End If
      Next X
      If TempLL >= TempHH Then
        NoData = True
      Else
        NoData = False
      End If
      If Not (NoData) Then
        lblTHH.Text = Format(TempHH, "0.0")
        lblTHL.Text = Format(TempHL, "0.0")
```

```
      lblTLH.Text = Format(TempLH, "0.0")
      lblTLL.Text = Format(TempLL, "0.0")
      If NH > 1 Then
         A1H = CSng((NH * SXYH - SXH * SumH) / (NH * SX2H - SXH ^ 2))
         If A1H >= 0 Then
            lblTHT.Text = "+" + Format((NDays - 1) * A1H, "0.0")
         Else
            lblTHT.Text = Format((NDays - 1) * A1H, "0.0")
         End If
      End If
      If NL > 1 Then
         A1L = CSng((NL * SXYL - SXL * SumL) / (NL * SX2L - SXL ^ 2))
         If A1L >= 0 Then
            lblTLT.Text = "+" + Format((NDays - 1) * A1L, "0.0")
         Else
            lblTLT.Text = Format((NDays - 1) * A1L, "0.0")
         End If
      End If
      lblTHA.Text = Format(SumH / NH, "0.0")
      lblTLA.Text = Format(SumL / NL, "0.0")
   Else
      lblTHH.Text = "---"
      lblTLH.Text = "---"
      lblTHL.Text = "---"
      lblTLL.Text = "---"
      lblTHA.Text = "---"
      lblTLA.Text = "---"
      lblTHT.Text = "---"
      lblTLT.Text = "---"
   End If
End Sub
```

This code goes through every record in the database table and stores temperature values for plotting in the **HighTemp** and **LowTemp** arrays. The code computes summary information (highs, lows, averages). Notice how the **IsDBNull** function is used to only include records with actual numeric values. If there is no value, the plot value is set to -1000.0 as a flag for the plotting code. Don't worry about the equations for the 'trend' value (the **A1H** and **A1L** values). If you want to impress your friends, you can tell them it uses a linear least squares computation to determine the slope of the values.

2. To bring up this screen, add this code to the **tabWeather SelectedIndexChanged** event procedure:

```
Private Sub TabWeather_SelectedIndexChanged(ByVal sender As Object, ByVal e As System.EventArgs) Handles tabWeather.SelectedIndexChanged
    Select Case tabWeather.SelectedIndex
      Case 1
        Call TemperatureData()
    End Select
End Sub
```

3. Add this variable to the form level declarations (it tells us which plot option is selected):

```
Dim TempPlot As Integer = 0
```

4. Place this code in the **rdoTempPlot CheckedChanged** event procedure (handles clicks on all radio buttons):

```
Private Sub RdoTempPlot_CheckedChanged(ByVal sender As
System.Object, ByVal e As System.EventArgs) Handles
rdoTempYear.CheckedChanged, rdoTempWinter.CheckedChanged,
rdoTempSummer.CheckedChanged, rdoTempSpring.CheckedChanged,
rdoTempAutumn.CheckedChanged
    Dim WhichButton As RadioButton = CType(sender,
RadioButton)
    Select Case WhichButton.Name
      Case "rdoTempYear"
        TempPlot = 0
      Case "rdoTempWinter"
        TempPlot = 1
      Case "rdoTempSpring"
        TempPlot = 2
      Case "rdoTempSummer"
        TempPlot = 3
      Case "rdoTempAutumn"
        TempPlot = 4
    End Select
    Call TemperatureData()
  End Sub
```

5. Save the application. Run it. Try entering some data to plot. When I load the 2003 database (**Sea03DB.accdb** or **SQLSea03DB.mdf**) and choose the **Entire Year** option, here's what I get:

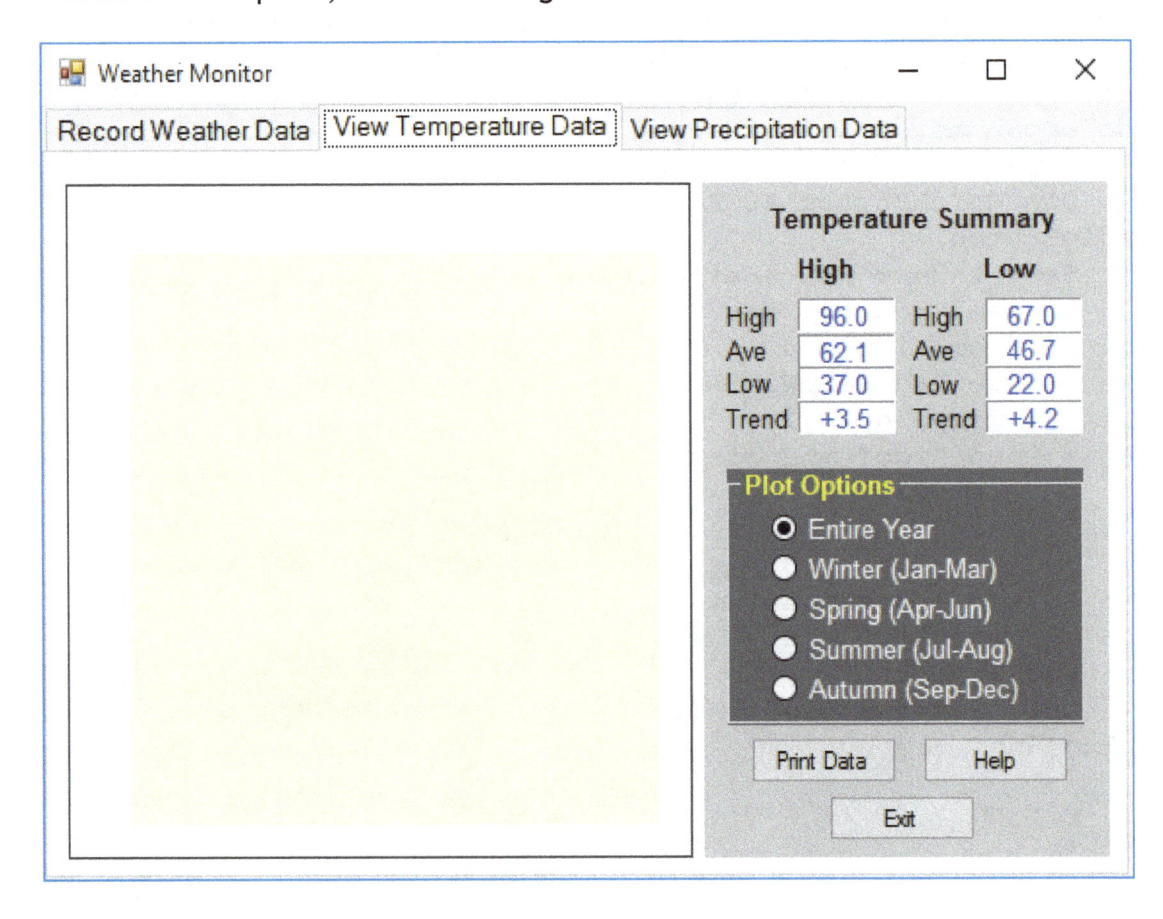

Now, let's tackle the missing data plot.

Temperature Plot

Older versions of Visual Basic had a control called the **Chart Control**. It allowed plotting of data in several formats. This control is no longer included with Visual Basic. There are third party tools available for plotting, but cost money. So, how do we get a plot of the temperature values in our project? We'll write the code ourselves! Well, actually, I'll give you the code.

Included in the **VBDB\General\Class 10\Example 10-3** is a file (a Visual Basic class) named **TempPlot.vb**. This file contains the code to do our plotting task using a **TempPlot** object. The TempPlot object will draw line charts of the high and low temperatures in the blank panel on the **View Temperature Data** tab. It uses several Visual Basic graphics methods to draw the plot and save it to a bitmap to allow printing. We won't go into the details of the routine – you can look through the code if you'd like. Just use it like any other object we've used in this course. The techniques used to develop the code are taught in a course named **Learn Visual Basic** which is available on our website (http:\\www.kidwaresoftware.com).

1. Add the **TempPlot.vb** class to your project. To do this, right-click the weather monitor project name in the Solution Explorer window. Select **Add**, then **Existing Item**. Navigate to the **TempPlot.vb** file and click **Add**. The file will now appear in your project's Solution Explorer window.

2. Add these four lines of code at the bottom of the **TemperatureData** general procedure:

    ```
    Dim TemperaturePlot As New TempPlot(pnlTempPlot)
    If Not(NoData) Then
       TemperaturePlot.Draw(NDays, HighTemp, LowTemp)
    End If
    ```

These lines first create a **TempPlot** object named **TemperaturePlot** using the panel control **pnlTempPlot**. If there is data, it is then plotted (using the **HighTemp** and **LowTemp** arrays) with the **Draw** method. It's that simple!

10-152 **Visual Basic and Databases**

3. Save and run the application. Create a file and enter some data or open an existing file. Click the **View Temperature Data** tab. Here's the plotted data for the 2003 data file (**Sea03DB.accdb** or **SQLSea03.mdf**):

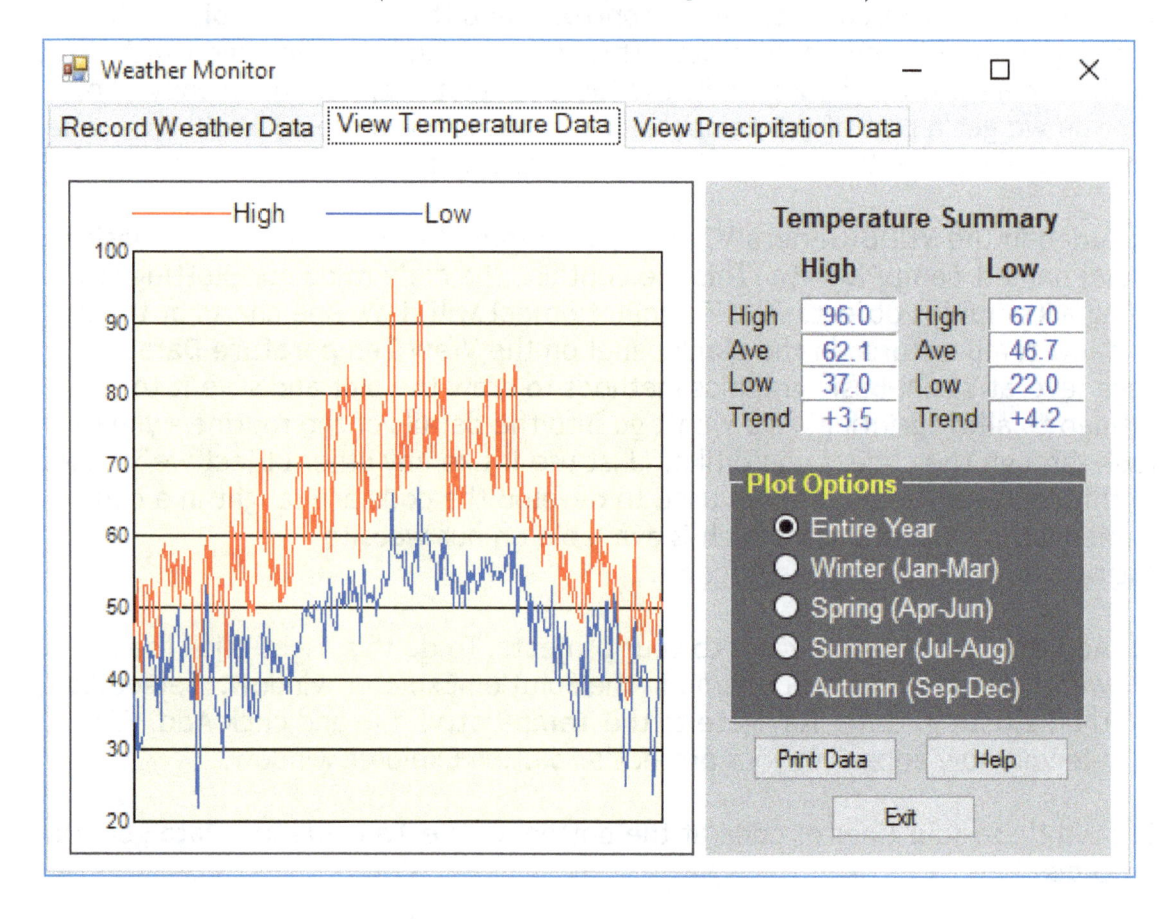

Now, let's create a very similar tab for the precipitation data.

View Precipitation Data Tab

When this tab is clicked, we will provide a plot of precipitation amounts and some summary statistics. You can choose what season of the year to plot precipitation for. Here's the finished tab layout to assist you in building the interface:

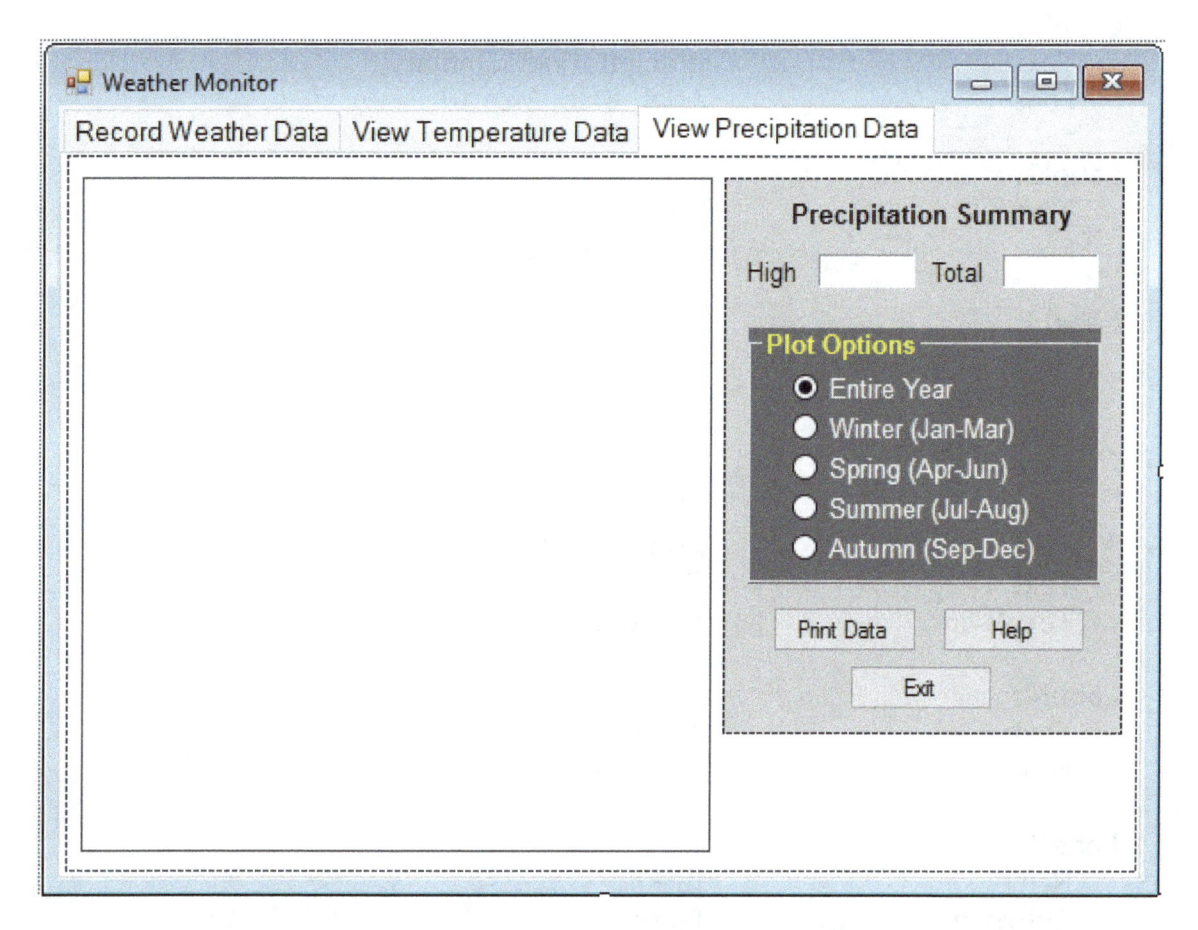

1. In design mode, select the **View Precipitation** tab. Like we did for the temperature tab, place a panel control on the form for the plot. It should take up a little more than one-half the tab width. Set these properties:

   Panel1:
       Name   pnlPrecipPlot
       BackColor   White
       BorderStyle   FixedSingle

10-154 Visual Basic and Databases

2. On the same tab, add another panel, and in the panel control, add five label controls, a group box, and three buttons. Set these properties (default names may differ – refer to the finished form for each control)

Panel1:
   BackColor   Light Gray

Label1:
   Text   Precipitation Summary
   Font   Arial, Bold, Size 10

Label2:
   Text   High
   Font   Arial, Size 10

Label3:
   Name   lblPH
   AutoSize   False
   BorderStyle   Fixed3D
   BackColor   White
   ForeColor   Blue
   Font   Arial, Size 10
   Text   [Blank]
   TextAlign   MiddleCenter

Label4:
   Text   Total
   Font   Arial, Size 10

Label5:
   Name   lblPT
   AutoSize   False
   BorderStyle   Fixed3D
   BackColor   White
   ForeColor   Blue
   Font   Arial, Size 10
   Text   [Blank]
   TextAlign   MiddleCenter

Button1:
   Name   btnPrintPrecip
   FontSize   8
   Text   Print Data

Button2:
   Name   btnHelpPrecip
   FontSize   8
   Text   Help

Button3:
   Name   btnExitPrecip
   FontSize   8
   Text   Exit

GroupBox1:
   Text   Plot Options
   BackColor   Dark Gray
   Font   Arial, Bold, Size 10
   ForeColor   Yellow

4. In the group box, place five radio buttons. Use these properties:

RadioButton1:
Name	rdoPrecipYear
Text	Entire Year
Checked	True
Font	Arial, Size 10
ForeColor	White

RadioButton2:
Name	rdoPrecipWinter
Text	Winter (Jan-Mar)
Font	Arial, Size 10
ForeColor	White

RadioButton3:
Name	rdoPrecipSpring
Text	Spring (Apr-Jun)
Font	Arial, Size 10
ForeColor	White

RadioButton4:
Name	rdoPrecipSummer
Text	Summer (Jul-Sep)
Font	Arial, Size 10
ForeColor	White

RadioButton5:
Name	rdoPrecipAutumn
Text	Autumn (Oct-Dec)
Font	Arial, Size 10
ForeColor	White

The tab layout is complete. When the tab is selected, we will form the required plot and compute the needed summary statistics. We will do the summaries first.

Precipitation Summary Statistics

1. Add a general procedure named **PrecipitationData** to the project and use this code:

```
Private Sub PrecipitationData()
   'make sure there is a data table
   If (WeatherConnection Is Nothing) Then
     Exit Sub
   End If
   Dim Prec As Single
   Dim X As Integer
   Dim XStart As Integer, XEnd As Integer, NDays As Integer, IsLeap As Integer
   Dim PrecH As Single, PrecT As Single
   Dim NoData As Boolean
   Dim Precip(366) As Single
   If WeatherTable.Rows.Count = 365 Then
     IsLeap = 0
   Else
     IsLeap = 1
   End If
   Select Case PrecipPlot
     Case 0
       XStart = 1
       XEnd = 365 + IsLeap
     Case 1
       XStart = 1
       XEnd = 90 + IsLeap
     Case 2
       XStart = 91 + IsLeap
       XEnd = 181 + IsLeap
     Case 3
       XStart = 182 + IsLeap
       XEnd = 273 + IsLeap
     Case 4
       XStart = 274 + IsLeap
       XEnd = 365 + IsLeap
   End Select
   NDays = XEnd - XStart + 1
   'precipitation data
   PrecH = -1000 : PrecT = 0
   NoData = True
   For X = XStart To XEnd
     If Not (IsDBNull(WeatherTable.Rows(X - 1).Item("Precip"))) Then
       Prec = CSng(WeatherTable.Rows(X - 1).Item("Precip"))
```

```
          NoData = False
      Else
        Prec = 0.0
      End If
      Precip(X - XStart + 1) = Prec
      If Prec > PrecH Then PrecH = Prec
      PrecT += Prec
    Next X
    If Not (NoData) Then
      lblPH.Text = Format(PrecH, "0.00")
      lblPT.Text = Format(PrecT, "0.0")
    Else
      lblPH.Text = "---"
      lblPT.Text = "---"
    End If
  End Sub
```

Similar to the temperature plot, this code simply goes through every record in the database and stores points for plotting in the **Precip** array. Any null value is assigned a value of zero. It also computes summary information.

Sample Database Projects 10-159

2. To bring up the information on this tab, modify the **tabWeather SelectedIndexChanged** event procedure (new code is shaded):

```
Private Sub TabWeather_SelectedIndexChanged(ByVal sender
As Object, ByVal e As System.EventArgs) Handles
tabWeather.SelectedIndexChanged
    Select Case tabWeather.SelectedIndex
      Case 1
        Call TemperatureData()
      Case 2
        Call PrecipitationData()
    End Select
End Sub
```

3. Add this variable to the form level declarations (it tells us which plot option is selected):

```
Dim PrecipPlot As Integer = 0
```

4. Place this code in the **rdoPrecipPlot CheckedChanged** event procedure (handles click on all precipitation radio buttons):

```
Private Sub RdoPrecipPlot_CheckedChanged(ByVal sender As
System.Object, ByVal e As System.EventArgs) Handles
rdoPrecipYear.CheckedChanged,
rdoPrecipWinter.CheckedChanged,
rdoPrecipSummer.CheckedChanged,
rdoPrecipSpring.CheckedChanged,
rdoPrecipAutumn.CheckedChanged
    Dim WhichButton As RadioButton = CType(sender,
RadioButton)
    Select Case WhichButton.Name
      Case "rdoPrecipYear"
        PrecipPlot = 0
      Case "rdoPrecipWinter"
        PrecipPlot = 1
      Case "rdoPrecipSpring"
        PrecipPlot = 2
      Case "rdoPrecipSummer"
        PrecipPlot = 3
      Case "rdoPrecipAutumn"
        PrecipPlot = 4
    End Select
    Call PrecipitationData()
End Sub
```

10-160　　　　　　　　　　**Visual Basic and Databases**

5. Save the application. Run it. Try entering some data to plot. When I load **Sea03DB.accdb** or **SQLSea03DB.mdf**, here's what I get for a year's worth of precipitation:

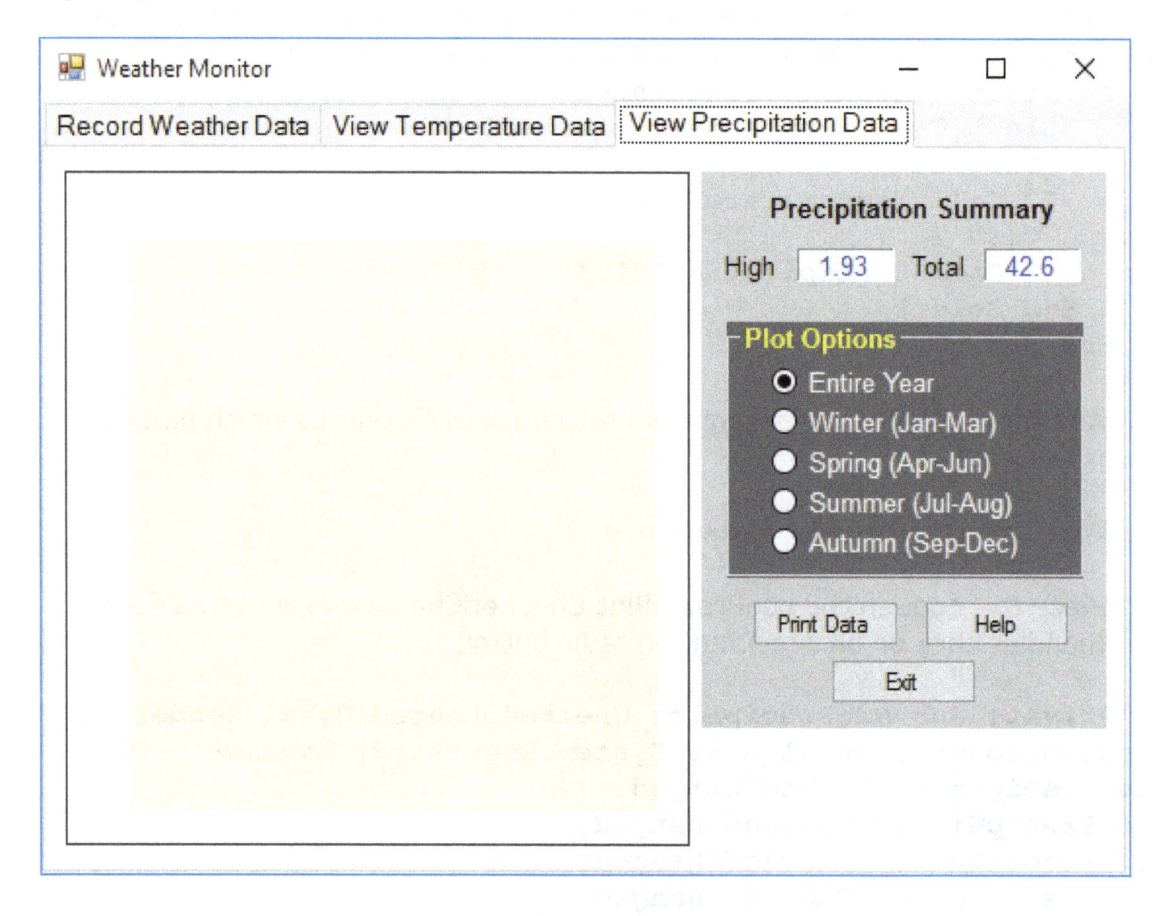

We complete the tab by adding a bar chart of the precipitation.

Precipitation Plot

Like the Temperature Plot, we'll give you the code to draw the **Precipitation Plot**. Included in the **VBDB\General\Class 10\Example 10-3** is a file (a Visual Basic class) named **PrecipPlot.vb**. This file contains the code to do our plotting task using a **PrecipPlot** object. The PrecipPlot object will draw a bar chart of the precipitation data in the blank panel on the **View Precipitation Data** tab

1. Add the **PrecipPlot.vb** class to your project. To do this, right-click the project name in the Solution Explorer window. Select **Add**, then **Existing Item**. Navigate to the **PrecipPlot.vb** file and click **Add**. The file will now appear in your project's Solution Explorer window.

2. Add these two lines of code at the bottom of the **PrecipitationData** general procedure:

```
Dim PrecipitationPlot As New PrecipPlot(pnlPrecipPlot)
If Not (NoData) Then
   PrecipitationPlot.Draw(NDays, Precip)
End If
```

These lines first create a **PrecipPlot** object named **PrecipitationPlot** using the panel control **pnlPrecipPlot**. If there is data to plot, it is done (using the **Precip** array) with the **Draw** method.

Visual Basic and Databases

3. Save and run the application. Create a file and enter some data or open an existing file. Click the **View Precipitation Data** tab. Here's the plotted data for the **Sea03DB.accdb** or **SQLSea03DB.mdf** file:

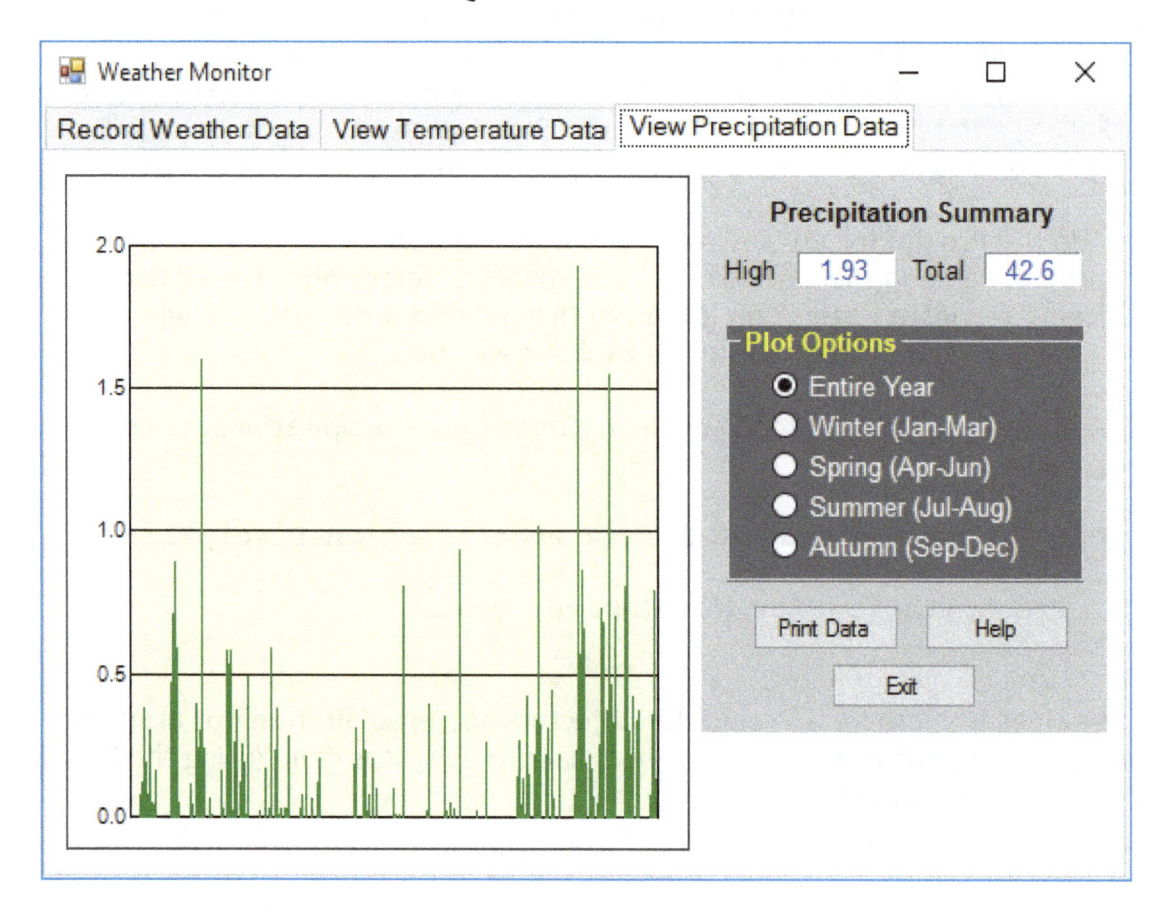

Weather Monitor Printed Reports

Each of the tabs in the Weather Monitor application has a **Print Data** tab. On the first tab, we want a printed listing of all temperatures, precipitation, and any comment. On the other tabs, we want a copy of the displayed plot and summary information. Here, we develop those reports, doing the data listing report first. But first, let's build some boilerplate.

1. Add a print preview dialog control. Name it **dlgPreview**.

2. Add a variable to the form level declarations to keep track of page number:

```
Dim PageNumber As Integer
```

10-164   Visual Basic and Databases

3. Add this code to the **btnPrint Click** event procedure (handles clicking on all three print buttons):

```
Private Sub BtnPrint_Click(ByVal sender As System.Object, ByVal e As System.EventArgs) Handles btnPrintData.Click, btnPrintTemp.Click, btnPrintPrecip.Click
   'make sure there is a data table
    If (WeatherConnection Is Nothing) Then
      Exit Sub
    End If
    'Declare the document
    Dim RecordDocument As Drawing.Printing.PrintDocument
    'Create the document and name it
    RecordDocument = New Drawing.Printing.PrintDocument()
    RecordDocument.DocumentName = "Weather Data"
    'Add code handler based on button pressed
    Dim WhichButton As Button = CType(sender, Button)
    Select Case WhichButton.Name
       Case "btnPrintData"
         AddHandler RecordDocument.PrintPage, AddressOf Me.PrintDataReport
       Case "btnPrintTemp"
         AddHandler RecordDocument.PrintPage, AddressOf Me.PrintTemperatureReport
       Case "btnPrintPrecip"
         AddHandler RecordDocument.PrintPage, AddressOf Me.PrintPrecipitationReport
    End Select
    'Preview document
    pageNumber = 1;
    dlgPreview.Document = RecordDocument
    dlgPreview.ShowDialog()
    'Dispose of document when done printing
    RecordDocument.Dispose()
  End Sub
```

Depending on which button is clicked, the corresponding print document is formed and attached to the proper procedure for printing (**PrintDataReport**, **PrintTemperatureReport**, or **PrintPrecipitationReport**).

Weather Data Report

In this report, we will print a multiple page listing of all the data in the database in a tabulated form.

1. Add this code to the **PrintDataReport** procedure:

```
Private Sub PrintDataReport(ByVal sender As Object, ByVal e As Drawing.Printing.PrintPageEventArgs)
    Dim MyFont As Font
    Dim Y As Integer
    Const DaysPerPage As Integer = 40
    MyFont = New Font("Courier New", 14, FontStyle.Bold)
    Y = e.MarginBounds.Top + 50
    'Print header
    e.Graphics.DrawString("Weather Data - Page" + Str(PageNumber), MyFont, Brushes.Black, e.MarginBounds.Left, Y)
    Y += 2 * CInt(MyFont.GetHeight(e.Graphics))
    MyFont = New Font("Courier New", 12, FontStyle.Bold Or FontStyle.Underline)
    e.Graphics.DrawString("Date", MyFont, Brushes.Black, e.MarginBounds.Left, Y)
    e.Graphics.DrawString("HighTemp", MyFont, Brushes.Black, e.MarginBounds.Left + 125, Y)
    e.Graphics.DrawString("LowTemp", MyFont, Brushes.Black, e.MarginBounds.Left + 225, Y)
    e.Graphics.DrawString("Precip", MyFont, Brushes.Black, e.MarginBounds.Left + 325, Y)
    e.Graphics.DrawString("Comment", MyFont, Brushes.Black, e.MarginBounds.Left + 425, Y)
    MyFont = New Font("Courier New", 12, FontStyle.Regular)
    Y += CInt(MyFont.GetHeight(e.Graphics))
    Dim N As Integer
    Dim N1 As Integer = 1 + (PageNumber - 1) * DaysPerPage
    Dim N2 As Integer = N1 + DaysPerPage - 1
    If N2 > WeatherTable.Rows.Count Then
      N2 = WeatherTable.Rows.Count
    End If
    Dim S As String
    For N = N1 To N2
       e.Graphics.DrawString(Format(WeatherTable.Rows(N - 1).Item("WeatherDate"), "d"), MyFont, Brushes.Black, e.MarginBounds.X, Y)
        If Not IsDBNull(WeatherTable.Rows(N - 1).Item("HighTemp")) Then
```

```
          S = Format(WeatherTable.Rows(N -
1).Item("HighTemp"), "0.0")
        Else
          S = ""
        End If
        e.Graphics.DrawString(S, MyFont, Brushes.Black,
e.MarginBounds.X + 200 - e.Graphics.MeasureString(S,
MyFont).Width, Y)
        If Not IsDBNull(WeatherTable.Rows(N -
1).Item("LowTemp")) Then
          S = Format(WeatherTable.Rows(N - 1).Item("LowTemp"),
"0.0")
        Else
          S = ""
        End If
        e.Graphics.DrawString(S, MyFont, Brushes.Black,
e.MarginBounds.X + 300 - e.Graphics.MeasureString(S,
MyFont).Width, Y)
        If Not IsDBNull(WeatherTable.Rows(N -
1).Item("Precip")) Then
          S = Format(WeatherTable.Rows(N - 1).Item("Precip"),
"0.0")
        Else
          S = ""
        End If
        e.Graphics.DrawString(S, MyFont, Brushes.Black,
e.MarginBounds.X + 375 - e.Graphics.MeasureString(S,
MyFont).Width, Y)
        S = WeatherTable.Rows(N - 1).Item("Comment").ToString
        'limit length of comment to 20 characters
        S = Mid(S, 1, 20)
        e.Graphics.DrawString(S, MyFont, Brushes.Black,
e.MarginBounds.X + 425, Y)
        Y += CInt(MyFont.GetHeight(e.Graphics))
      Next N
      If N2 <> WeatherTable.Rows.Count Then
        PageNumber += 1
        e.HasMorePages = True
      Else
        e.HasMorePages = False
        PageNumber = 1
      End If
    End Sub
```

This goes through each record in the database table and formats a single line listing. Blanks are inserted if fields are null. The report is over 10 pages for a full year of data.

Sample Database Projects 10-167

2. Save and run the application. Click **Print Data** on the **Record Weather Data** tab. Here's the first page of a report for the 2003 sample database (**Sea03DB.accdb** or **SQLSea03DB.mdf**) shown in the print preview dialog control:

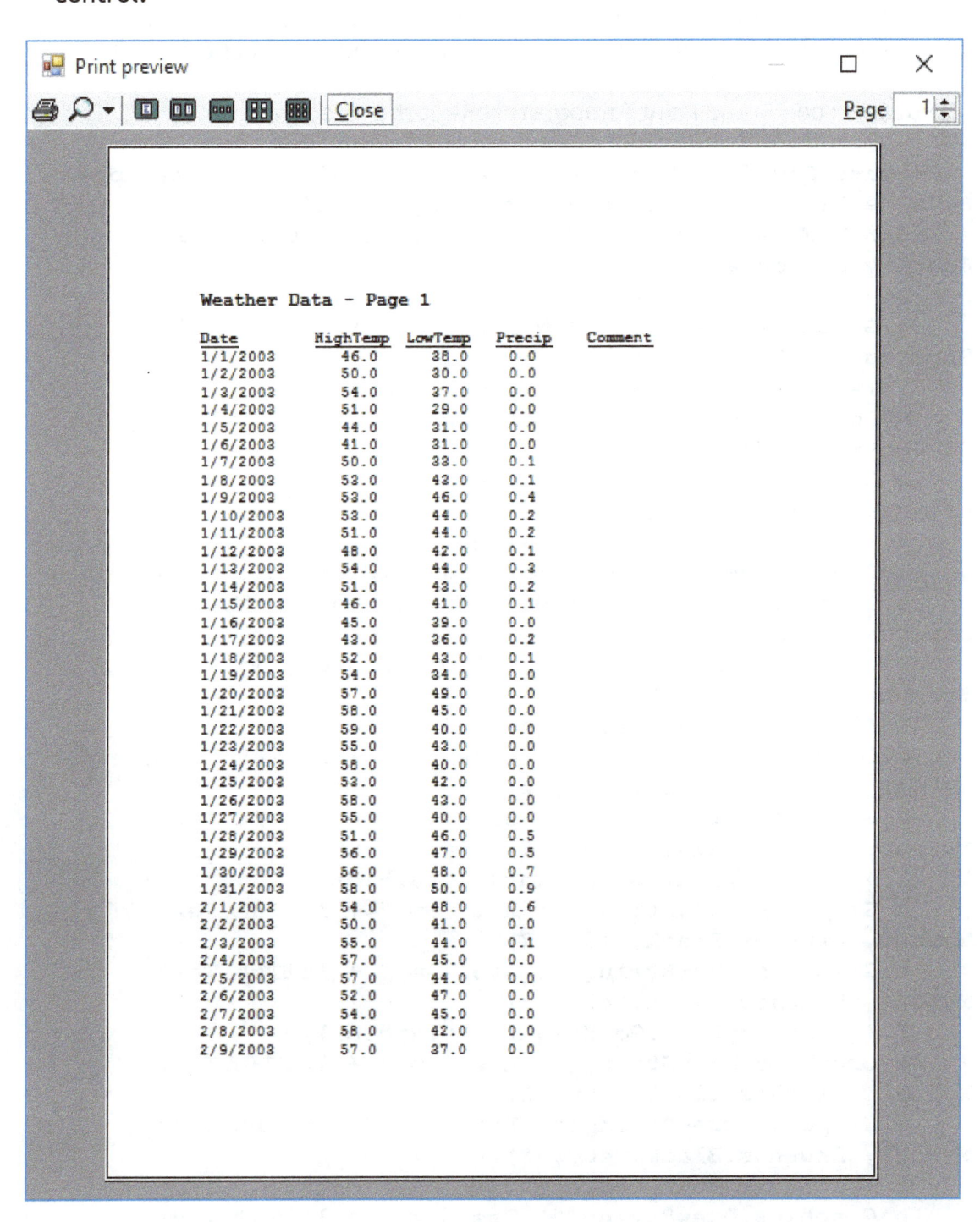

```
Weather Data - Page 1

Date        HighTemp  LowTemp  Precip  Comment
1/1/2003      46.0     38.0     0.0
1/2/2003      50.0     30.0     0.0
1/3/2003      54.0     37.0     0.0
1/4/2003      51.0     29.0     0.0
1/5/2003      44.0     31.0     0.0
1/6/2003      41.0     31.0     0.0
1/7/2003      50.0     33.0     0.1
1/8/2003      53.0     43.0     0.1
1/9/2003      53.0     46.0     0.4
1/10/2003     53.0     44.0     0.2
1/11/2003     51.0     44.0     0.2
1/12/2003     48.0     42.0     0.1
1/13/2003     54.0     44.0     0.3
1/14/2003     51.0     43.0     0.2
1/15/2003     46.0     41.0     0.1
1/16/2003     45.0     39.0     0.0
1/17/2003     43.0     36.0     0.2
1/18/2003     52.0     43.0     0.1
1/19/2003     54.0     34.0     0.0
1/20/2003     57.0     49.0     0.0
1/21/2003     58.0     45.0     0.0
1/22/2003     59.0     40.0     0.0
1/23/2003     55.0     43.0     0.0
1/24/2003     58.0     40.0     0.0
1/25/2003     53.0     42.0     0.0
1/26/2003     58.0     43.0     0.0
1/27/2003     55.0     40.0     0.0
1/28/2003     51.0     46.0     0.5
1/29/2003     56.0     47.0     0.5
1/30/2003     56.0     48.0     0.7
1/31/2003     58.0     50.0     0.9
2/1/2003      54.0     48.0     0.6
2/2/2003      50.0     41.0     0.0
2/3/2003      55.0     44.0     0.1
2/4/2003      57.0     45.0     0.0
2/5/2003      57.0     44.0     0.0
2/6/2003      52.0     47.0     0.0
2/7/2003      54.0     45.0     0.0
2/8/2003      58.0     42.0     0.0
2/9/2003      57.0     37.0     0.0
```

Temperature Data Report

Here, we want to obtain a printed copy of the information displayed in the **View Temperature Data** tab. The information we want to print is: the summary information on all temperatures and the graphs in the panel control.

1. Put this code in the **PrintTemperatureReport** procedure:

```
  Private Sub PrintTemperatureReport(ByVal sender As Object, ByVal e As Drawing.Printing.PrintPageEventArgs)
    Dim MyFont As Font = New Font("Courier New", 12, FontStyle.Regular)
    Dim Y As Integer = 125
    e.Graphics.DrawString("Weather Monitor", MyFont, Brushes.Black, e.MarginBounds.X, Y)
    Y += CInt(2 * MyFont.GetHeight(e.Graphics))
    MyFont = New Font("Courier New", 12, FontStyle.Regular Or FontStyle.Underline)
    e.Graphics.DrawString("Temperatures:", MyFont, Brushes.Black, e.MarginBounds.X, Y)
    Y += CInt(2 * MyFont.GetHeight(e.Graphics))
    MyFont = New Font("Courier New", 12, FontStyle.Regular)
    e.Graphics.DrawString("High Temperature", MyFont, Brushes.Black, 150, Y)
    e.Graphics.DrawString("Low Temperature", MyFont, Brushes.Black, 400, Y)
    Y += CInt(MyFont.GetHeight(e.Graphics))
    e.Graphics.DrawString("  High  = " + lblTHH.Text, MyFont, Brushes.Black, 150, Y)
    e.Graphics.DrawString("  High  = " + lblTLH.Text, MyFont, Brushes.Black, 400, Y)
    Y += CInt(MyFont.GetHeight(e.Graphics))
    e.Graphics.DrawString("  Ave   = " + lblTHA.Text, MyFont, Brushes.Black, 150, Y)
    e.Graphics.DrawString("  Ave   = " + lblTLA.Text, MyFont, Brushes.Black, 400, Y)
    Y += CInt(MyFont.GetHeight(e.Graphics))
    e.Graphics.DrawString("  Low   = " + lblTHL.Text, MyFont, Brushes.Black, 150, Y)
    e.Graphics.DrawString("  Low   = " + lblTLL.Text, MyFont, Brushes.Black, 400, Y)
    Y += CInt(MyFont.GetHeight(e.Graphics))
    e.Graphics.DrawString("  Trend = " + lblTHT.Text, MyFont, Brushes.Black, 150, Y)
    e.Graphics.DrawString("  Trend = " + lblTLT.Text, MyFont, Brushes.Black, 400, Y)
    If Not (pnlTempPlot.BackgroundImage Is Nothing) Then
```

Sample Database Projects   10-169

```
        e.Graphics.DrawImage(pnlTempPlot.BackgroundImage, 150,
300, 500, CInt(500 * pnlTempPlot.ClientSize.Height /
pnlTempPlot.ClientSize.Height))
      End If
      e.HasMorePages = False
   End Sub
```

The summary information is printed first. Then the **DrawImage** method is used to print the graph (the height to width ratio is maintained).

2. Save and run the application. Load a database. Go to the **View Temperature Data** tab. Click **Print Data**. The report for 2003 database (**Sea03DB.accdb** or **SQLSea03DB.mdf**) looks like this (full year of data):

```
Weather Monitor

Temperatures:

    High Temperature          Low Temperature
      High  = 96.0               High  = 67.0
      Ave   = 62.1               Ave   = 46.7
      Low   = 37.0               Low   = 22.0
      Trend = +3.5               Trend = +4.2
```

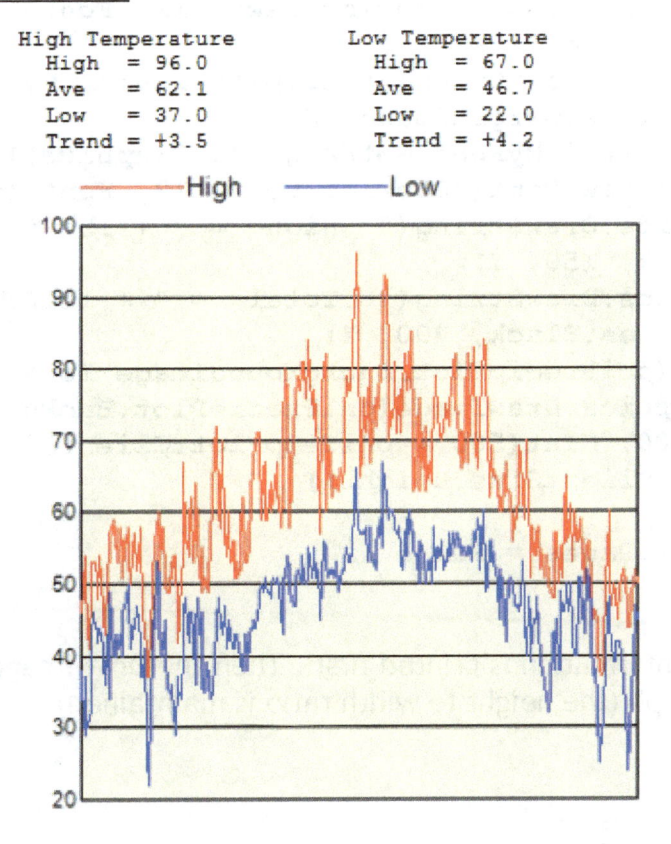

Precipitation Data Report

Lastly, we need to obtain a printed copy of the information displayed in the **View Precipitation Data** tab. The information we want to print is: the summary information on precipitation and the graph in the panel control.

1. Put this code in the **PrintPrecipitationReport** procedure:

```
Private Sub PrintPrecipitationReport(ByVal sender As Object, ByVal e As Drawing.Printing.PrintPageEventArgs)
    Dim MyFont As Font = New Font("Courier New", 12, FontStyle.Regular)
    Dim Y As Integer = 125
    e.Graphics.DrawString("Weather Monitor", MyFont, Brushes.Black, e.MarginBounds.X, Y)
    Y += CInt(2 * MyFont.GetHeight(e.Graphics))
    MyFont = New Font("Courier New", 12, FontStyle.Regular Or FontStyle.Underline)
    e.Graphics.DrawString("Precipitation:", MyFont, Brushes.Black, e.MarginBounds.X, Y)
    Y += CInt(2 * MyFont.GetHeight(e.Graphics))
    MyFont = New Font("Courier New", 12, FontStyle.Regular)
    e.Graphics.DrawString("  High  = " + lblPH.Text, MyFont, Brushes.Black, 150, Y)
    e.Graphics.DrawString("  Total  = " + lblPT.Text, MyFont, Brushes.Black, 400, Y)
    If Not (pnlPrecipPlot.BackgroundImage Is Nothing) Then
       e.Graphics.DrawImage(pnlPrecipPlot.BackgroundImage, 150, 250, 500, CInt(500 * pnlTempPlot.ClientSize.Height / pnlTempPlot.ClientSize.Height))
    End If
    e.HasMorePages = False
End Sub
```

The summary information is printed first. Then the **DrawImage** method is used to print the graph (the height to width ratio is maintained).

2. Save and run the application. Load a database. Go to the **View Precipitation Data** tab. Click **Print Data**. The report (**Sea03DB.accdb** or **SQLSea03DB.mdf**) looks like this (full year of data):

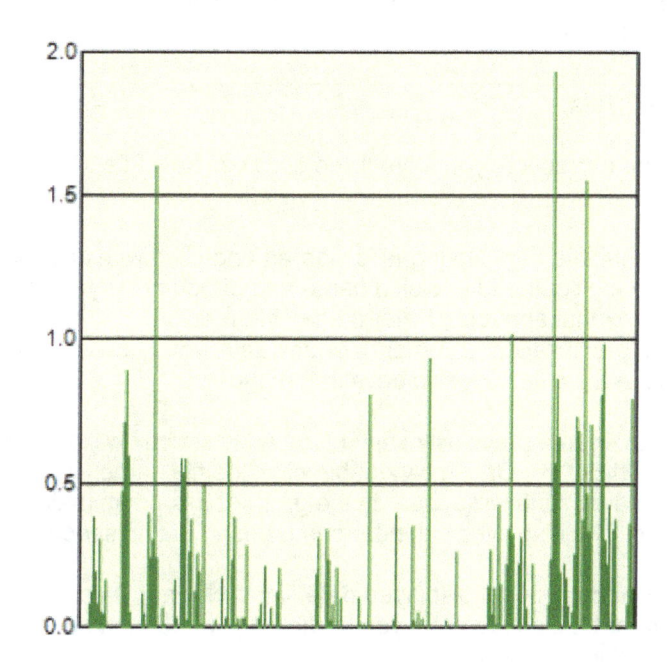

```
Weather Monitor

Precipitation:

    High  = 1.93          Total  = 42.6
```

Weather Monitor Help System

The last thing left to code in the Weather Monitor application is the **Help** button. We will develop a simple help system for our application and write the code necessary to access it. We will use the **HTML Help Workshop** discussed in Chapter 5. Review that material if needed.

1. Create a help topic file using FrontPage or similar product (saved as **weather.htm** in the **VBDB\General\Class 10\Example 10-3\HelpFile** folder). The file I developed is:

> **Record Weather Data**
>
> When you choose this option, you have three choices: New File, Open File, and Print Data.
>
> If you click New File, the data input grid is cleared and filled with days for the corresponding year. You need to pick a name and directory for your new file using the common dialog box that appears. Enter data in the resulting grid (high temperature, low temperature, precipitation, comment) for any days you choose. The displayed calendar can be used to find specific days in the grid.
>
> Click Open File to open a previously saved file. A file list box will appear - click on the desired file, then click OK. Or, simply double-click the file name. The file will be opened and the saved data will appear in the grid. At this point, make any changes or additions needed. The displayed calendar can be used to find specific days in the grid.
>
> To obtain a printed copy of the displayed data file, click Print Data. This printed copy can contain data or be blank to allow you to record your data on paper, occasionally transferring the values to the computer.
>
> **View Temperature Data**
>
> Choose this option to obtain a graphical view of the temperature data entered under Record Weather Data. Also see summaries of the data. The line plot shows the high and low temperatures. Also shown on the form are various data summaries. You are given the high, average, and low values for both the high and low temperatures and their trend values. You can obtain a printed copy of these summary values and the plots by clicking on Print Data.
>
> **View Precipitation Data**
>
> Choose this option to obtain a graphical view of the precipitation data entered under Record Weather Data. Also see summaries of the data. The bar plot shows the daily precipitation. Also shown on the form are various data summaries. You are given the high and total measured precipitation. You can obtain a printed copy of these summary values and the plot by clicking on Print Data.

2. In the HTML Help Workshop, prepare a project file (**weather.hhp**) including the topic file just created. Compile the help file (**weather.chm**). All these files are saved in the **VBDB\General\Class 10\Example 10-3\HelpFile** folder. Copy **weather.chm** to the Weather Monitor projects' **Bin\Debug** folder (**Bin\x86\Debug** for **Access**).

3. Load the Weather Monitor application. Add a help provider control. **Name** it **hlpWeather**. Set the **HelpNavigator** property of **frmWeather** to **TableofContents**.

4. Add the shaded code to the **frmWeather Load** procedure. This points to the help file:

```
Private Sub FrmWeather_Load(ByVal sender As Object, ByVal e As System.EventArgs) Handles Me.Load
    'point to help file
    hlpWeather.HelpNamespace = Application.StartupPath + "\weather.chm"
    Dim Y As Integer
    For Y = 1900 To 2100
      cboYear.Items.Add(Y.ToString)
    Next Y
    cboYear.Text = calDate.SelectionStart.Year.ToString
    tabWeather.SelectedTab = tabPageData
    grdWeather.AutoSizeColumnsMode = DataGridViewAutoSizeColumnsMode.Fill
    grdWeather.AllowUserToAddRows = False
End Sub
```

5. Use this code in the **btnHelp Click** event procedure. All three help buttons are handled by this procedure:

```
Private Sub BtnHelp_Click(ByVal sender As System.Object, ByVal e As System.EventArgs) Handles btnHelpData.Click, btnHelpTemp.Click, btnHelpPrecip.Click
    Help.ShowHelp(Me, hlpWeather.HelpNamespace)
End Sub
```

6. Lastly, add this code to the **btnExit Click** event procedure, which handles the Click event for any of the three help buttons:

```
  Private Sub BtnExit_Click(ByVal sender As System.Object,
ByVal e As System.EventArgs) Handles btnExitData.Click,
btnExitTemp.Click, btnExitPrecip.Click
    Me.Close()
  End Sub
```

7. Save and run the application. Make sure the **Help** button works in all three tabs of the tab control. Make sure <**F1**> brings up help. Here's what you should see:

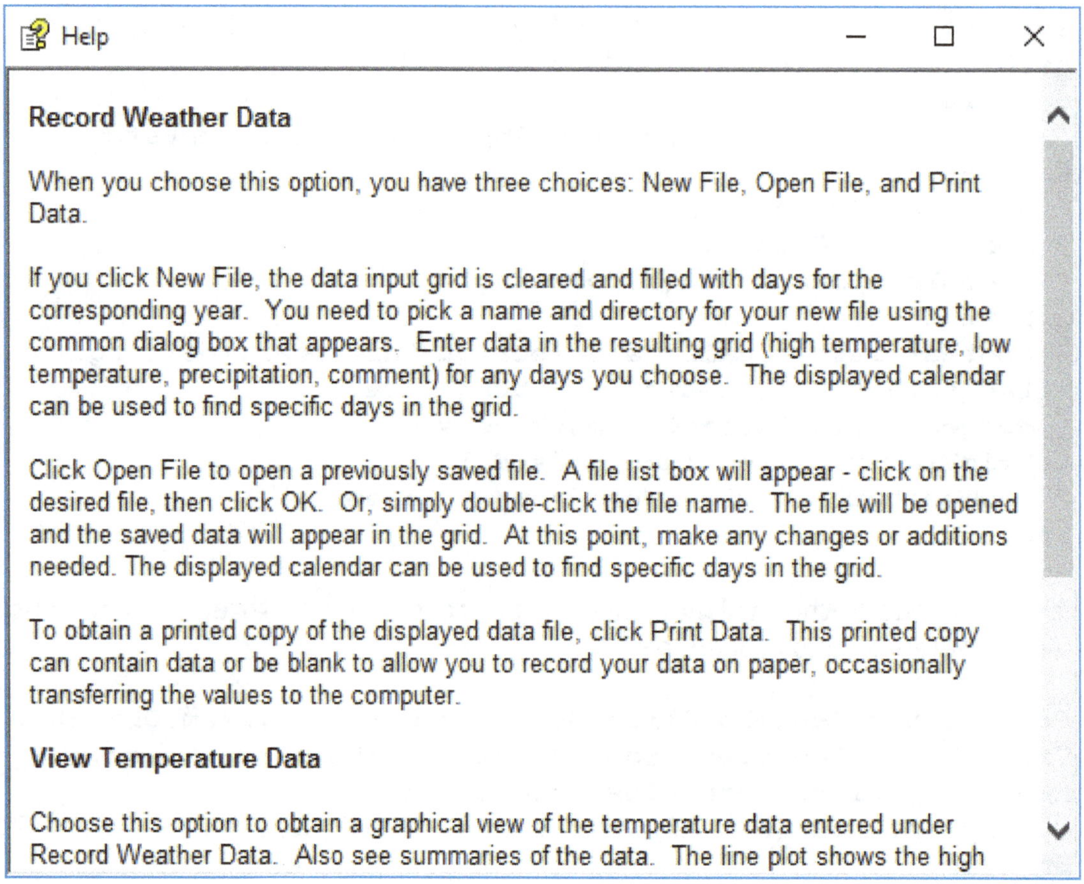

Make sure all the **Exit** buttons work too.

Weather Monitor Icon

The coding for the Weather Monitor application is now complete. A goal is to distribute this application to other users for their comments. Before doing that, let's get rid of the rather ugly Visual Basic icon stuck on our form.

Find an icon on the internet or design your own using the Microsoft Paint program. We include one you might like. It is saved as **weather.ico** in the **VBDB\General\Class 10\Example 10-3** folder.

Go to Visual Basic and load your application. Go to the **Properties** window and click the form's **Icon** property. Select your new icon. The icon should now appear in the upper left hand corner of your form when you run the program. It's much nicer than the default icon, don't you agree?

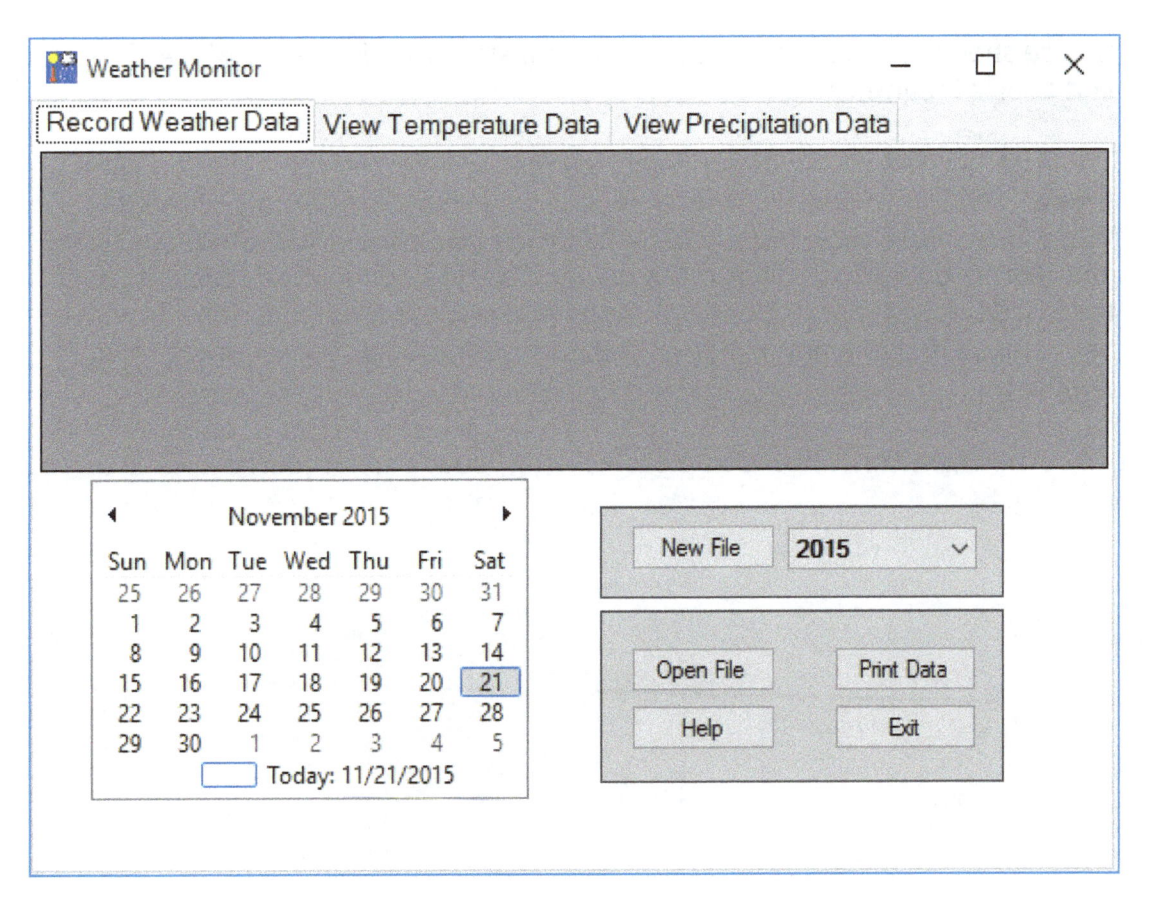

Weather Monitor Distribution Package

We're now ready to send our Weather Monitor program out into the world. But, first we need to build a distribution package. We will use the Visual Studio **Setup Wizard** discussed in Chapter 8. You may like to review this material before proceeding.

1. Add a **Setup Wizard** project to the **Weather Monitor** solution. The Access version of the project developed here is **Weather Monitor** in the **VBDB\Access\Class 10** folder. The SQL Server version is **Weather Monitor** in the **VBDB\SQL Server\Class 10** folder. Follow the wizard steps. It is important to remember to add the **weather.chm** file in Step 4 where you are asked what additional files to include. For the SQL Server version, also add the **SQLWeatherDBBlank.mdf** file (the empty database).

2. Create shortcuts and associated icons for installation in the User's Desktop and User's Program Menu.

3. Try installing the application on your computer. Better yet, take the files (use a CD-ROM) to another Windows-based machine, preferably without Visual Basic installed. Install the application using the distribution package and test its operation. To run the newly installed application, click **Start** on the Windows task bar. Choose **All Apps** and click your application. It will begin executing like any Windows program! If desired, try removing your application.

The **Weather Monitor** is now complete - a long, educational journey.

Suggested Improvements

Even though the **Weather Monitor Project** is complete (the final Access version is saved in **Example 10-3** folder in **VBDB\Access\Class 10** folder; the final SQL Server version is saved in **Example 10-3** folder in **VBDB\SQL Server\Class 10** folder), there are some possible changes we could make. We'll give you some of our ideas. I'm sure you have some ideas too.

➢ We make sure the user can only type numbers, decimal points, or the negative sign in the temperature and precipitation fields. But, there is no way to prevent the user from typing multiple decimal points and negative signs. Can you think of a way to modify the entry validation code to limit each field to (at most) one decimal point and one negative sign.

➢ In its current implementation, we plot temperature and precipitation data from a single file. It would be interesting to be able to plot another file on the same grids. This would allow a user to compare one year with another or compare weather files from two different locations. You would need additional data objects for each file you wanted to add. Editing of multiple files could also get tricky.

➢ The plotted data is static – no user interaction is possible. It would be nice to have the ability to 'zoom' in on certain plot areas. See if this is possible with the panel we use.

➢ Add more labels to plots and printed reports. For example, the printed plots do not indicate any time period. Add this information by indicating which radio button is clicked.

➢ Add other fields to the database and modify the application. Perhaps add barometric pressure. Performing such a modification will point out the importance of thinking through your database design correctly the first time. Adding a field, though increasing the usability of your application, also causes many headaches in later modifications.

➢ Add the ability to automatically convert external data files to a format usable by the application. For example, the US Weather Service makes temperature and precipitation files available for download on the Internet. Can you adapt this application to read those files and load the data into an Access database file? We'll look at one way to do this in Chapter 11.

Summary

In this chapter, we developed three different database applications. Each application addressed some typical concerns you may encounter in developing your own applications.

At this point in your studies, you should have a good understanding of the Visual Basic data objects. You are fluent in the development of well-designed Visual Basic database interfaces. And, you know how to create databases and database reports. In the final course chapter, we address a few final topics that can serve as springboards into making you an advanced database programmer.

11

Other Database Topics

Review and Preview

You have essentially completed the **Visual Basic and Databases** course. At this point, you have a good intermediate understanding of using Visual Basic with Access and SQL Server databases. There is still much to learn.

In this last chapter, we look at several unrelated topics. This information is provided to help you progress in your skills as a Visual Basic database programmer. We discuss exporting and importing database data, working with other database types, multi-user considerations, and web applications. The examples in this chapter use Access databases. If using SQL Server, you should, by now, have the skills necessary to modify the examples to work with SQL Server databases.

Exporting Database Data

A common task in any application, and not just database applications, is to have the ability to move information from one application to another. In this section, we discuss **exporting** data from a database. And, in the next, we will cover the related **importing** problem. Data can be transferred in a variety of formats. Here, we only discuss how to transfer data via **sequential disk files**. An increasingly popular format is XML files for Internet use – this is something you might like to investigate if you will be using your applications on the Internet.

A sequential file is a line-by-line list of data. You can view a sequential file with any text editor. We will use a particular type of a sequential file – a **comma-delimited** file. This file has a Windows extension of **csv** (comma separated variables) and is the most common format for exporting and importing data between applications. When working with a database, we simply go through our data table and, for each record, write the desired field values on a single line of the file, separating them by commas.

The procedure followed to export data from a database to a sequential file is:

1. Open the database and establish the database table using the ADO .NET data objects.
2. Open the desired output sequential file (use a **csv** extension with its name).
3. For each record in the data table, write the desired fields (separated by commas) to the output file.
4. Close and save the sequential file.

We know how to establish the data table. Let's look at the other steps.

Opening a Sequential File for Output

The Visual Basic syntax to open a sequential file for output is:

```
Dim OutputFile As System.IO.StreamWriter
OutputFile = New System.IO.StreamWriter(MyFile)
```

where **MyFile** is the name (a **String**) of the file to open and **OutputFile** is the returned **StreamWriter** object used to write information to disk. Make sure **MyFile** has an extension of **csv**. Be aware if the file being opened already exists, the first thing the Windows operating system does is erase the existing file! So, put in any protections you might want to avoid wiping out a needed file. Once the file is opened, it is ready for writing data to it.

If the data export feature is to be an integral part of your database application, an open file dialog box should be used to obtain the path to the sequential file. Use a **DefaultExt** of **csv** and check for overwrite permissions. If you are using files for just a quick export job, we suggest putting the sequential file in your application directory. Recall the **Application.StartupPath** property provides this path. As an example, to open **test.csv** in our application directory as **OutputFile**, we would use:

```
OutputFile = New
System.IO.StreamWriter(Application.StartupPath +
"\test.csv")
```

Writing Data to a Sequential File

Once opened, writing data to the file is a simple task. Information (variables or text) is written to a sequential file in an appended fashion. Separate Visual Basic statements are required for each appending.

For a file opened as **OutputFile**, the syntax is to save a variable named **MyVariable** is:

```
OutputFile.Write(MyVariable)
```

This statement will append the specified variable (a field from our database) to the current line in the sequential file. With **Write** for output, everything will be written in one very long line. For **csv** files, we append a comma to the line after each piece of information.

Example for three fields **Field1**, **Field2**, **Field3**:

```
Dim OutputFile As System.IO.StreamWriter
OutputFile = New System.IO.StreamWriter("c:\junk\TestOut.csv")
OutputFile.Write(Field1)
OutputFile.Write(",")
OutputFile.Write(Field2)
OutputFile.Write(",")
OutputFile.Write(Field3)
```

After this code runs, the file **c:\junk\TestOut.txt** will have a single line with all three fields separated by commas.

To move to a new line once a line is complete, use:

```
OutputFile.Write(OutputFile.NewLine)
```

You should know that we are not restricted to only exporting data in comma-delimited format. With Visual Basic, we can write data to files in any format we want. In fact, there are instances where applications may require a file that is not comma-delimited. We won't do that here, however.

Saving a Sequential File

When done writing to the file, it is closed using the **Close** method. For our example, the syntax is:

```
OutputFile.Close()
```

Once a file is closed, it is saved on the disk under the path and filename used to open the file.

Example 11-1

Exporting Database Data

In this example, we will export the customer data from the **KWSalesDB.accdb** database (copy it to your working directory) studied in Chapters 9 and 10 to a comma-delimited file. We will then load the resulting **csv** file into Microsoft Excel for viewing. This is typical of export tasks. Recall the customers table has seven fields: **CustomerID**, **FirstName**, **LastName**, **Address**, **City**, **State** and **Zip**.

1. Start a new application. Place a button on the form. Set these properties:

   Form1:
Name	frmExport
FormBorderStyle	FixedSingle
StartPosition	CenterScreen
Text	Export Data

   Button1:
Name	btnExport
Text	Export

   My little form looks like this:

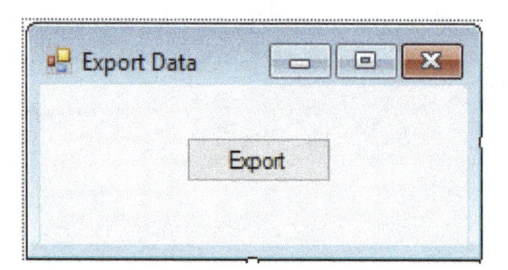

2. Copy **KWSalesDB.accdb** from the **VBDB\Access\Class 10\Example 10-1** folder to your working directory. This copy has some customers to look at.

3. Add these lines at the top of the code window:

   ```
   Imports System.Data
   Imports System.Data.OleDb
   ```

Other Database Topics   11-7

4. Form level declarations to create data objects:

```
Dim KWSalesConnection As OleDbConnection
Dim CustomersCommand As OleDbCommand
Dim CustomersAdapter As OleDbDataAdapter
Dim CustomersTable As DataTable
```

5. Add this code to the **frmExport Load** event procedure (creates data objects assuming the **KWSALES.MDB** database is in your working directory):

```
Private Sub FrmExport_Load(ByVal sender As System.Object, ByVal e As System.EventArgs) Handles MyBase.Load
    'connect to  database
    KWSalesConnection = New OleDbConnection("Provider=Microsoft.ACE.OLEDB.12.0; Data Source = c:\VBDB\Working\KWSalesDB.accdb")
    KWSalesConnection.Open()
    'establish command object
    CustomersCommand = New OleDbCommand("Select * from Customers", KWSalesConnection)
    'establish data adapter/data table
    CustomersAdapter = New OleDbDataAdapter()
    CustomersAdapter.SelectCommand = CustomersCommand
    CustomersTable = New DataTable()
    CustomersAdapter.Fill(CustomersTable)
End Sub
```

6. Add this code to the **frmExport FormClosing** event procedure to dispose of objects:

```
Private Sub FrmExport_FormClosing(ByVal sender As Object, ByVal e As System.Windows.Forms.FormClosingEventArgs) Handles Me.FormClosing
    'close the connection
    KWSalesConnection.Close()
    'dispose of the objects
    KWSalesConnection.Dispose()
    CustomersCommand.Dispose()
    CustomersAdapter.Dispose()
    CustomersTable.Dispose()
End Sub
```

7. Place this code in the **btnExport Click** event procedure:

```
Private Sub BtnExport_Click(ByVal sender As System.Object, ByVal e As System.EventArgs) Handles btnExport.Click
    Dim N As Integer
    Dim OutputFile As System.IO.StreamWriter
    OutputFile = New System.IO.StreamWriter(Application.StartupPath + "\customer.csv")
    'write headers
    For N = 0 To CustomersTable.Columns.Count - 1
      OutputFile.Write(CustomersTable.Columns(N))
      If N < CustomersTable.Columns.Count - 1 Then
        OutputFile.Write(",")
      End If
    Next
    OutputFile.Write(OutputFile.NewLine)
    'write all fields
    Dim MyRow As DataRow
    For Each MyRow In CustomersTable.Rows
      For N = 0 To CustomersTable.Columns.Count - 1
        If Not IsDBNull(MyRow(N)) Then
          OutputFile.Write(MyRow.Item(N).ToString)
        End If
        If N < CustomersTable.Columns.Count - 1 Then
          OutputFile.Write(",")
        End If
      Next
      OutputFile.Write(OutputFile.NewLine)
    Next
    OutputFile.Close()
End Sub
```

In this code, we first open the sequential file **customer.csv**. We write the column headers to the file. We then cycle through each row in the data table. For each record, we write the seven fields to the file. When done the file is closed (and saved).

8. Save (saved in **Example 11-1** folder in the **VBDB\Access\Class 11** folder) and run the application. Click **Export**. Stop the application. Go to Windows Explorer and you should see **customer.csv** saved in your application directory (the project's **Bin\x86\Debug** folder). Double-click the file. **Excel** will probably fire up and you'll see:

	A	B	C	D	E	F	G
1	CustomerID	FirstName	LastName	Address	City	State	Zip
2	3	Lou	Tylee	PO Box 28	Seattle	Washingto	98118
3	4	Bob	Johnson	1111 First	Bellevue	Washingto	98008
4	7	Joe	Johnson	1234 Brow	Minneapo	Minnesota	83333
5	8	Marcy	Jones	84784 Tree	Port Mary	Oregon	83838
6	9	Frank	Robertson	2397943 S	Johnson	Tennessee	98383
7	18	Wally	Cleaver	112 Pine S	Mayfield	Who Knov	12345
8	23	Bobby	Thompson	48848 Doc	New York	New York	11111
9	24	Dillon	Pikachu	234 Poken	MyCity	His State	ZIP
10	45	Lou	Tylee	5821 Oakh	Seattle	WA	98118

The data has been moved out of the database into Excel. We could now use this (in conjunction with Microsoft Word) to generate mailing labels. The **csv** file can also be opened using **Notepad**. Do this and you'll see the comma-delimited nature of the file:

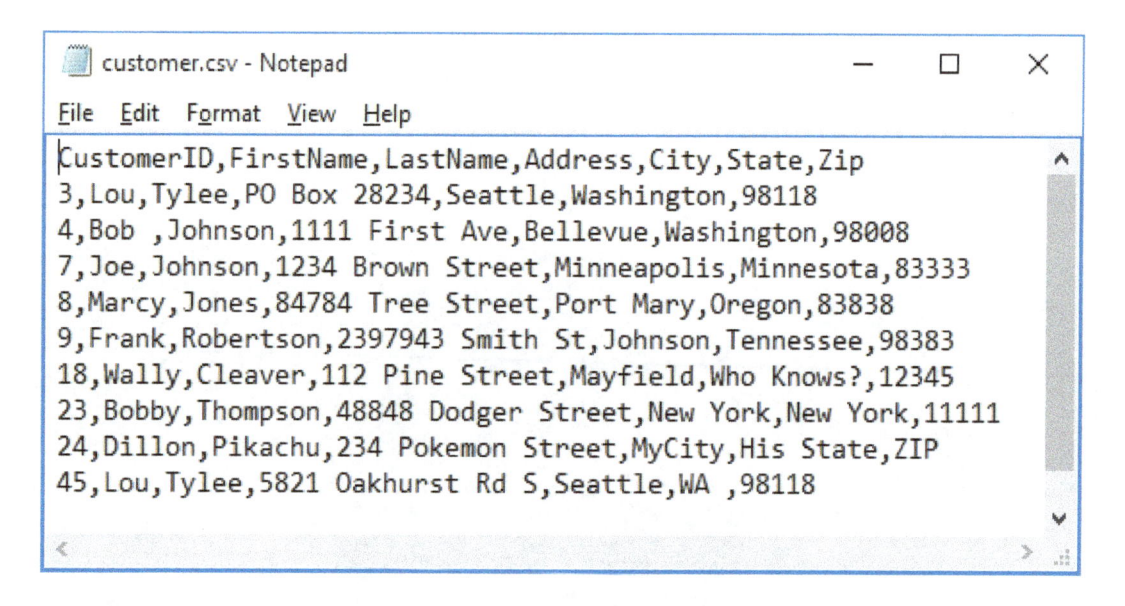

```
CustomerID,FirstName,LastName,Address,City,State,Zip
3,Lou,Tylee,PO Box 28234,Seattle,Washington,98118
4,Bob ,Johnson,1111 First Ave,Bellevue,Washington,98008
7,Joe,Johnson,1234 Brown Street,Minneapolis,Minnesota,83333
8,Marcy,Jones,84784 Tree Street,Port Mary,Oregon,83838
9,Frank,Robertson,2397943 Smith St,Johnson,Tennessee,98383
18,Wally,Cleaver,112 Pine Street,Mayfield,Who Knows?,12345
23,Bobby,Thompson,48848 Dodger Street,New York,New York,11111
24,Dillon,Pikachu,234 Pokemon Street,MyCity,His State,ZIP
45,Lou,Tylee,5821 Oakhurst Rd S,Seattle,WA ,98118
```

Importing Database Data

Another common task is to take data from some other source and put it in a database. This is the data **import** problem. We assume that the data is available in a sequential file of some kind. It is not necessary that the file be comma-delimited. As long as we know what the file looks like, we can write the Visual Basic code to read it. Here, however, we will assume a comma-delimited file.

The procedure followed to import data from a sequential file to a database is:

1. Establish the empty database data table using Access or ADOX code.
2. Open the desired input sequential file (will have a **csv** extension).
3. For each desired record in the data table, read the needed fields (separated by commas) from the input file and commit them to the database.
4. Close the sequential file.

Again, we know how (or should know how) to do the required database tasks. Let's look at the other steps.

Opening a Sequential File for Input

The Visual Basic syntax to open a sequential file for input is:

```
Dim InputFile As System.IO.StreamReader
InputFile = New System.IO.StreamReader(MyFile)
```

where **MyFile** is a complete path (drive, directory, file name) to the file being opened and **InputFile** is the returned **StreamReader** object used to read information from disk. **MyFile** may or may not have an extension of **csv** - it depends on how the file was created.

If the data import feature is to be an integral part of your database application, an open file dialog box should be used to obtain the path to the sequential file. If you are using files for just a quick export job, we suggest putting the sequential file in your application directory. Recall the **Application.StartupPath** property provides this path. To open **test.csv** in our application path, write:

```
InputFile = New
System.IO.StreamReader(Application.StartupPath +
"\test.csv")
```

Reading Data from a Sequential File

Once opened, data is read from the sequential file one line at a time. Each line of input requires a separate statement. A line of data (**MyLine**) is read from the file using:

```
MyLine = InputFile.ReadLine()
```

For a **csv** file, **MyLine** is a list of variables, separated by commas. To determine the individual variables, this line is 'parsed' using commas as delimiters.

Once the variables are parsed (read), they can be committed to the database by simply equating the database fields to their corresponding value from the sequential file. Sometimes, we may have to generate the field based on some function of the file variables. This is easy to do in code. For example, if the variables include first and last name, but the database wants a full name, we could concatenate the name variables before committing them to the database.

Once we have the line (**MyLine**) to parse, what we do with it depends on what we know. The basic idea is to determine the bounding character positions of each variable within the line. Character location is zero-based, hence the first character in a string is character 0. If the first position is **FP** and the last position is **LP**, the substring representation of this variable (**VariableString**) can be found using the Visual Basic **Substring** method:

```
VariableString = MyLine.Substring(FP, LP - FP + 1)
```

This says return the **Substring** in **MyLine** that starts at position **FP** and is **LP - FP + 1** characters long. Once we have extracted **VariableString**, we convert it to the proper data type.

So, how do you determine the starting and ending positions for a variable in a line? For a **csv** file, you search for commas using then **IndexOf** method. For example,

```
MyLine.IndexOf(",")
```

returns the position of the first comma encountered in **MyLine**.

As variables are extracted from the input data line, we shorten the line (excluding the extracted substring) before looking for the next variable. To do this, we use again use the **Substring** method. If **LP** was the last position of the substring removed from left side of **MyLine**, we shorten this line using:

```
MyLine = MyLine.Substring(LP + 1, MyLine.Length - LP - 1).Trim()
```

This removes the first **LP** characters from the left side of **MyLine**. The **Trim** method removes any leading and/or trailing spaces and **MyLine** is replaced by the shortened line. Notice by shortening the string in this manner, the first position for finding each extracted substring will always be 0 (**FP** = 0). Parsing may seem confusing, but it's really not. Look at the example.

Closing a Sequential File

When all values have been read from the sequential file, it is closed using the **Close** method. For our example, use:

```
InputFile.Close()
```

Example 11-2

Importing Database Data

Look back at Example 10-1, our **Weather Monitor** example. Note we included two weather databases with this example. These files, **Sea02DB.accdb** and **Sea03DB.accdb**, include weather information recorded in Seattle, Washington, in 2002 and 2003, respectively. We did not type this information into the database table. It was imported from a file supplied by the National Weather Service. In this example, we show how we took the Weather Service sequential file and loaded it into an Access database.

1. First, let's look at the sequential file. Open **Sea02.txt**, included in the **VBDB\Access\Class 11\Example 11-2 folder**. Using **Notepad**, this file appears as:

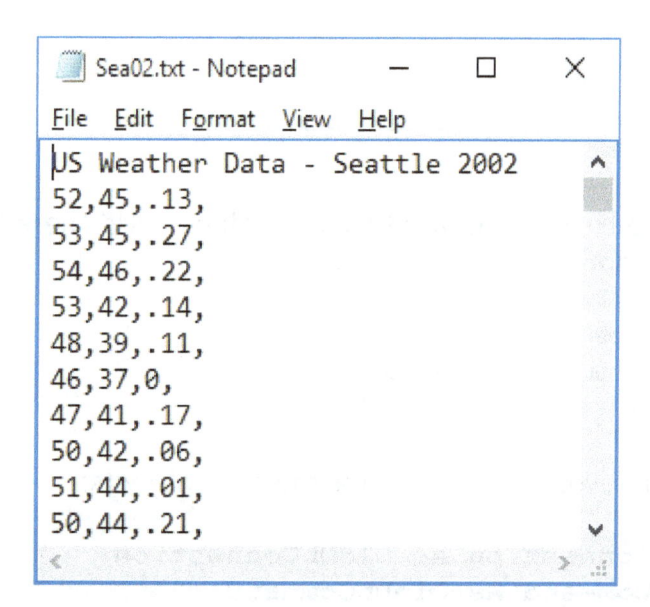

```
US Weather Data - Seattle 2002
52,45,.13,
53,45,.27,
54,46,.22,
53,42,.14,
48,39,.11,
46,37,0,
47,41,.17,
50,42,.06,
51,44,.01,
50,44,.21,
```

Note the file has a single line of header information (we'll skip this line). Then, each line after this has the high temperature, the low temperature, precipitation amount, and any comment that might be added. These <u>four</u> values will be loaded into the corresponding database fields. Recall the database has <u>five</u> fields are: **WeatherDate**, **HighTemp**, **LowTemp**, **Precip**, and **Comment**. Obviously, we'll have to generate the **WeatherDate** field in code (not a tough job, given we know the year is 2002).

2. Start a new application. Place a button on the form. Set these properties:

   Form1:
Name	frmImport
FormBorderStyle	FixedSingle
StartPosition	CenterScreen
Text	Import Data

   Button1:
Name	btnImport
Text	Import

   My little form looks like this:

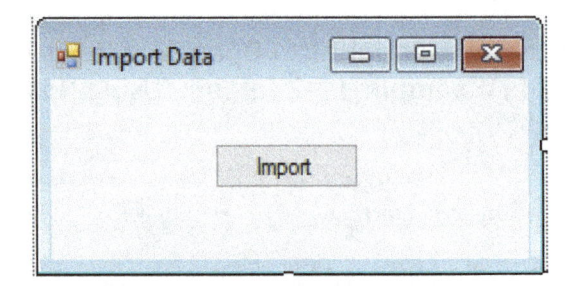

3. Add a reference to ADOX library to your project. Add these lines at the top of the code window:

   ```
   Imports System.Data
   Imports System.Data.OleDb
   Imports ADOX
   ```

4. Add these form level declarations for the data objects:

   ```
   Dim WeatherConnection As OleDbConnection
   Dim WeatherCommand As OleDbCommand
   Dim WeatherAdapter As OleDbDataAdapter
   Dim WeatherTable As DataTable
   ```

5. Place this code in the **btnImport Click** event procedure:

```
Private Sub BtnImport_Click(ByVal sender As System.Object, ByVal e As System.EventArgs) Handles btnImport.Click
    Dim WeatherDatabase As New Catalog
    Dim DatabaseTable As Table
    Dim DatabaseFile As String = Application.StartupPath + "\Sea02DB.accdb"
    Dim DataFile As String = Application.StartupPath + "\Sea02.txt"
    'create empty database
    Try
        WeatherDatabase.Create("Provider=Microsoft.ACE.OLEDB.12.0; Data Source = " + DatabaseFile)
        'create table
        DatabaseTable = New Table
        DatabaseTable.Name = "Weather"
        'add fields
        DatabaseTable.Columns.Append("WeatherDate", DataTypeEnum.adDate)
        DatabaseTable.Columns.Append("HighTemp", DataTypeEnum.adSingle)
        DatabaseTable.Columns.Append("LowTemp", DataTypeEnum.adSingle)
        DatabaseTable.Columns.Append("Precip", DataTypeEnum.adSingle)
        DatabaseTable.Columns.Append("Comment", DataTypeEnum.adWChar, 50)
        DatabaseTable.Columns("HighTemp").Attributes = ColumnAttributesEnum.adColNullable
        DatabaseTable.Columns("LowTemp").Attributes = ColumnAttributesEnum.adColNullable
        DatabaseTable.Columns("Precip").Attributes = ColumnAttributesEnum.adColNullable
        DatabaseTable.Columns("Comment").Attributes = ColumnAttributesEnum.adColNullable
        'primary key
        DatabaseTable.Keys.Append("PK_Weather", KeyTypeEnum.adKeyPrimary, "WeatherDate")
        DatabaseTable.Indexes.Append("WeatherDate", "WeatherDate")
        WeatherDatabase.Tables.Append(DatabaseTable)
    Catch ex As Exception
        MessageBox.Show(ex.Message, "Error Creating Database", MessageBoxButtons.OK, MessageBoxIcon.Error)
    Finally
        WeatherDatabase = Nothing
```

```vb
      End Try
      'open data file and add fields
      WeatherConnection = New
OleDbConnection("Provider=Microsoft.ACE.OLEDB.12.0; Data
Source = " + DatabaseFile)
      WeatherConnection.Open()
      WeatherCommand = New OleDbCommand("SELECT * FROM Weather
ORDER BY WeatherDate", WeatherConnection)
      WeatherAdapter = New OleDbDataAdapter()
      WeatherAdapter.SelectCommand = WeatherCommand
      WeatherTable = New DataTable()
      WeatherAdapter.Fill(WeatherTable)
      'fill dates and other fields
      Dim InputFile As System.IO.StreamReader
      InputFile = New System.IO.StreamReader(DataFile)
      'skip first line
      InputFile.ReadLine()
      Dim TableDate As Date = New Date(2002, 1, 1)
      Dim NDays As Integer = CInt(DateDiff(DateInterval.Day,
TableDate, New Date(2003, 1, 1)))
      Dim NewRow As DataRow
      Dim N As Integer
      Dim MyLine As String, MyVariable As String, CL As
Integer
      For N = 1 To NDays
        NewRow = WeatherTable.NewRow
        NewRow.Item("WeatherDate") = TableDate
        'read data line and parse out four fields
        MyLine = InputFile.ReadLine
        'high temperature
        CL = MyLine.IndexOf(",")
        MyVariable = MyLine.Substring(0, CL)
        NewRow.Item("HighTemp") = CSng(MyVariable)
        MyLine = MyLine.Substring(CL + 1, MyLine.Length - CL -
1).Trim()
        'low temperature
        CL = MyLine.IndexOf(",")
        MyVariable = MyLine.Substring(0, CL)
        NewRow.Item("LowTemp") = CSng(MyVariable)
        MyLine = MyLine.Substring(CL + 1, MyLine.Length - CL -
1).Trim()
        'precip
        CL = MyLine.IndexOf(",")
        MyVariable = MyLine.Substring(0, CL)
        If MyVariable <> "" Then
          NewRow.Item("Precip") = CSng(MyVariable)
        Else
          NewRow.Item("Precip") = 0.0
```

```
        End If
        MyLine = MyLine.Substring(CL + 1, MyLine.Length - CL - 1).Trim()
        'comment
        NewRow.Item("Comment") = MyLine
        WeatherTable.Rows.Add(NewRow)
        TableDate = DateAdd(DateInterval.Day, 1, TableDate)
    Next
    InputFile.Close()
    'save database and dispose of objects
    Dim WeatherAdapterCommand As New OleDbCommandBuilder(WeatherAdapter)
    WeatherAdapter.Update(WeatherTable)
    WeatherConnection.Close()
    WeatherConnection.Dispose()
    WeatherCommand.Dispose()
    WeatherAdapter.Dispose()
    WeatherTable.Dispose()
    WeatherAdapterCommand.Dispose()
  End Sub
```

Most of this code was borrowed from Example 10-3 (the Weather Monitor project). We use ADOX to create the empty **Sea02DB.accdb** database and create the fields (make sure your project uses .NET Framework 4). We then create the data objects needed to add rows to the database.

Next, the data file (**Sea02.txt**) is opened and the date is initialized. Note we skip the header line. Each data line in the file has four values. As each line is read, a new record is added and the proper values (after parsing using comma positions) are placed in the five database fields. Once done, the sequential file is closed and the data table is saved to the database.

6. Save (saved in **Example 11-2** folder in the **VBDB\Access\Class 11** folder) and run the application. Make sure **Sea02.txt** is in your project's **Bin\x86\Debug** folder (you may have to create it first). If no errors occur, the database file was successfully written and will be in your project's **Bin\x86\Debug** folder. Here's the **Weather** table from the newly created **Sea02DB.accdb** file opened in Access:

WeatherDat	HighTemp	LowTemp	Precip	Comment
1/2/2002	53	45	0.27	
1/3/2002	54	46	0.22	
1/4/2002	53	42	0.14	
1/5/2002	48	39	0.11	
1/6/2002	46	37	0	
1/7/2002	47	41	0.17	
1/8/2002	50	42	0.06	
1/9/2002	51	44	0.01	
1/10/2002	50	44	0.21	
1/11/2002	50	46	0	
1/12/2002	50	47	0.11	
1/13/2002	55	46	0.01	
1/14/2002	48	39	0	
1/15/2002	50	44	0	
1/16/2002	50	43	0	
1/17/2002	50	38	0	

Notice all the data is in the proper places. If you change the **DatabaseFile** and **DataFile** names in the code, you can also create the **Sea03DB.accdb** database.

Other Database Types

Every example we have built in this course has used the Microsoft **Access** database format (**OLE DB** data model). Visual Basic also supports other database formats including: **ODBC** (Open Database Connectivity) and **Oracle**.

Fortunately, since all databases use the same concept of records (rows) and fields (columns), all the techniques discussed in this course for editing, adding, and deleting records apply no matter what type of database you are working with. The only change you need to make is to use the ADO .NET data objects associated with your particular database type. The website:

http://msdn.microsoft.com/en-us/library/32c5dh3b(v=vs.71).aspx

provides links to pages to explain connections to various database types.

As you study other database types, you will see that the various data objects are similar, but there are differences. We suggest you check other references to see if particular properties, methods, or events are supported by your particular database.

One other note: the **OLE DB** technology we've used in these notes can also be used to connect to ODBC, SQL Server, and Oracle databases. You just need a database specific connection string. This makes any application built with OLE DB **database-independent**. If however, you want to use database-specific data objects, we provide a brief overview.

ODBC Data Objects

ODBC is a technology that predates OLE DB (the technology used by Access). As such, it is used by many older databases. ODBC data objects are contained within the **System.Data.Odbc** namespace.

The data connection object is **OdbcConnection**.

The data adapter object is **OdbcDataAdapter**.

The command object is **OdbcCommand**.

Oracle Data Objects

Oracle is perhaps the most widely used large scale database management tool. It is produced by the Oracle Corporation. The ADO .NET data objects for Oracle databases provide the most efficient access. These objects can be used with Oracle Version 8.1.7 and later. If you are using an older version, use the ODBC data objects. Oracle data objects are contained within the **System.Data.OracleClient** namespace.

The data connection object is **OracleConnection**.

The data adapter object is **OracleDataAdapter**.

The command object is **OracleCommand.**

Multi-User Considerations

Every example we've studied in this course has assumed a single user will be accessing the database at any one time. This is appropriate for many Visual Basic applications. But, eventually, you will encounter an application that is constructed for use in a **networked** environment. The database file will be on a file server and shared by many users. This allows centralized data collection and querying.

Supporting **multiple users** with simultaneous access to a single database requires special consideration. Fortunately, Visual Basic provides us with several tools to handle multiple users. The ADO .NET database engine works well in a multiple-user environment. To use a database in such environment, you need to:

- Place the database file in a shared directory.
- Make sure the file server is configured so each user has read and write access to the directory containing the database file.
- Configure all data sources in your application so it points to the shared database file.

Multiple users can cause problems when trying to access the same data. Typical problems include:

- Two users try to update the same record.
- One user updates a record while the other is viewing it, making the visible data out of date.
- One user deletes a record while the other is using it.

The concept of **locking** is used to try to mitigate these, and other, problems. And, lots of error trapping is required in multiple user environments, but these are skills you have.

Database Web Applications

We all know the Internet has become part of everyday life. A great new feature of Visual Basic is the idea of web forms. With web forms, we can build applications that run on the Internet – **web applications**. Web applications differ from the Windows applications we have been building. A user (**client**) makes a request of a **server** computer. The server generates a web page (in HTML) and returns it to the client computer so it can be viewed with browser software.

Web applications are built in Visual Basic using something called **ASP .NET** (**Active Server Pages .NET**). ASP .NET is an improved version of previous technologies used to build web applications. In the past, to build a dynamic web application, you needed to use a mishmash of programming technologies. Web pages were generated with HTML (yes, the same HTML we used to write help files) and programming was done with ASP (Active Server Pages) and VB Script (a Visual Basic scripting language).

With ASP .NET, the process for building **web applications** is the same process used to build Windows applications. To build a web application, we start with a form, add web controls and write code for web control events. There is a visual project component that shows the controls and a code component with event procedures and general procedures and functions.

In these notes, we introduce the idea of web applications with databases. You can use your new programming skills to delve into more advanced references on ASP .NET and web applications. Here, we cover a few web applications topics:

> Address the approaches used to build web applications using **web forms**.
> Discuss the **web form controls** and how they differ from their Windows counterparts.
> Demonstrate the process of building web applications with a simple database example.

Starting a New Web Application

To start the process of building a web application, you select the **File** menu option in Visual Basic. Then, click **New**, then **Project**. This window appears:

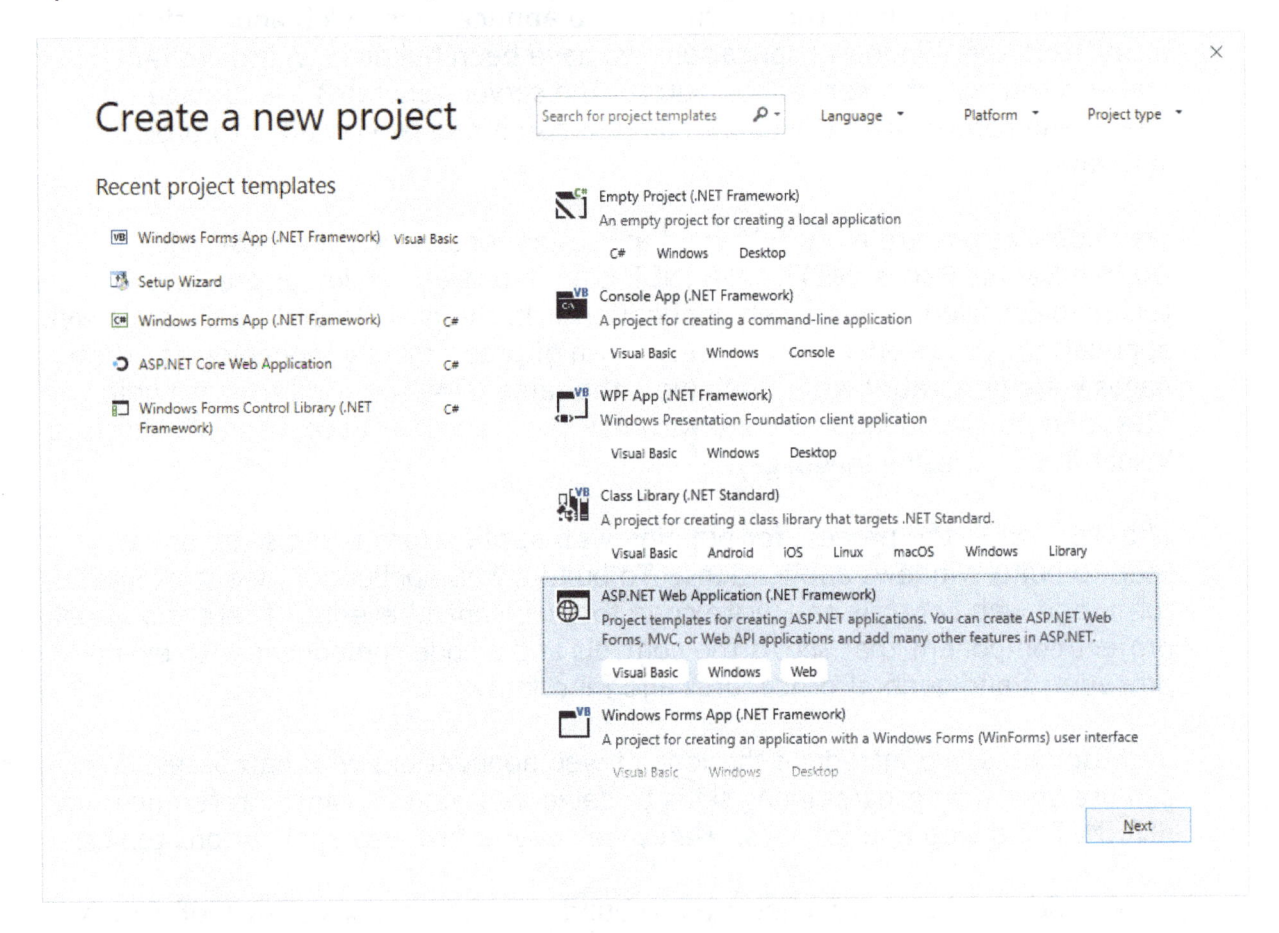

Select **ASP .NET Web Application**. Click **Next**.

This window appears:

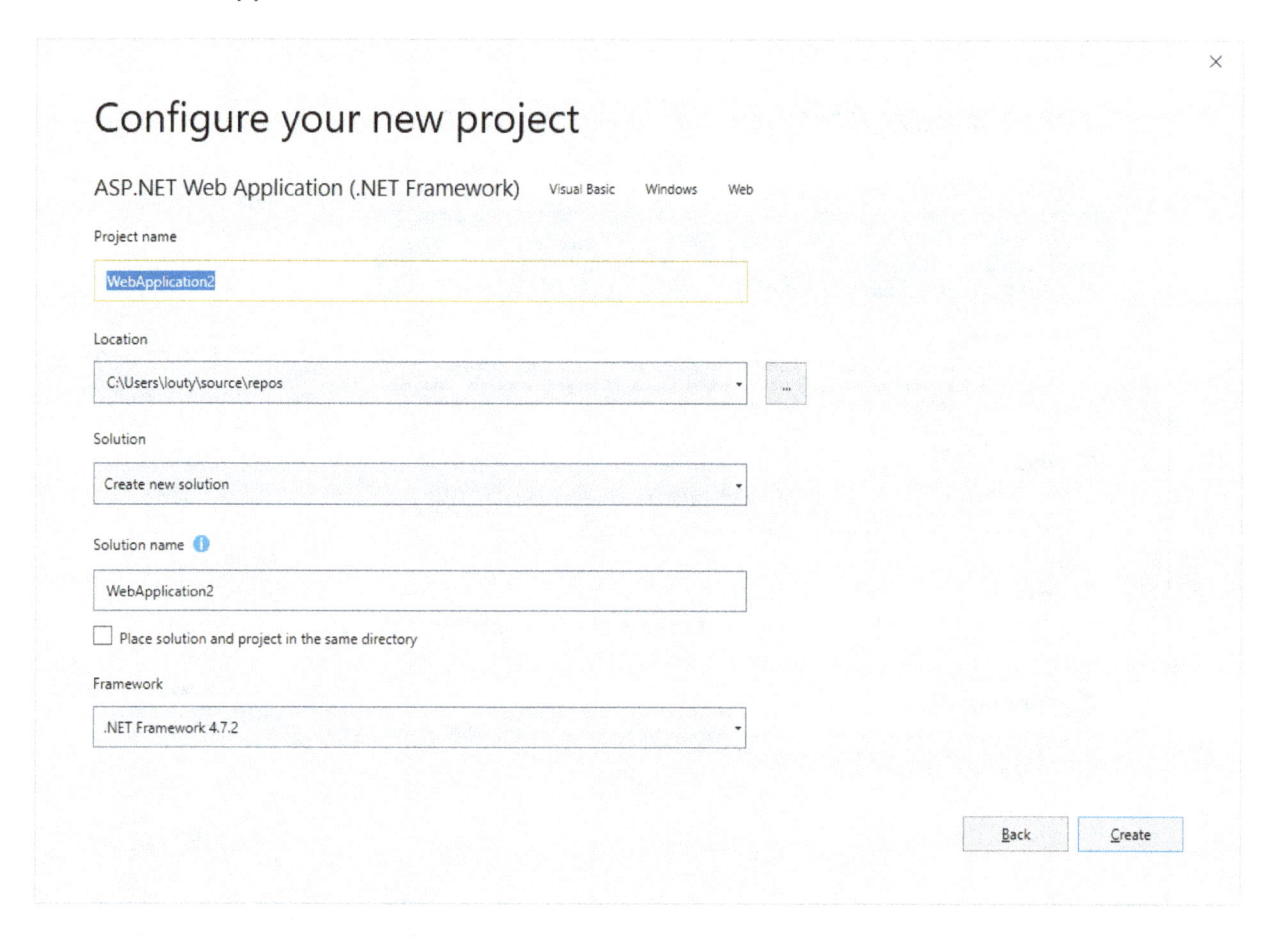

Configure your new project

ASP.NET Web Application (.NET Framework)   Visual Basic   Windows   Web

Project name

WebApplication2

Location

C:\Users\louty\source\repos

Solution

Create new solution

Solution name

WebApplication2

☐ Place solution and project in the same directory

Framework

.NET Framework 4.7.2

Back   Create

In the drop-down box to the left of the **Browse** button, either select or type the name of a folder to hold your new web site. Make sure the selected **Language** is **Visual Basic**. Click **Create** to create the application.

This window appears:

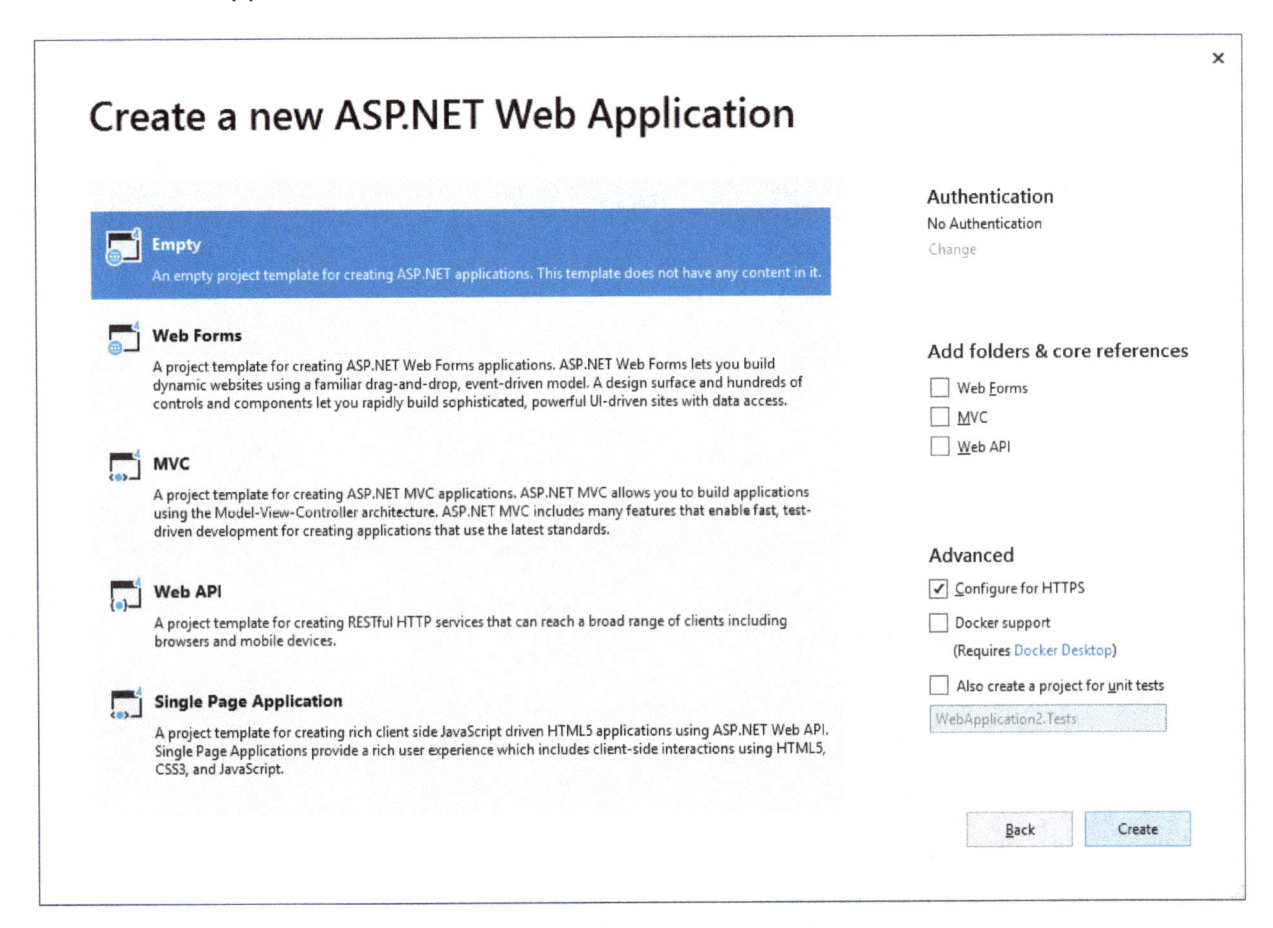

Create a new ASP.NET Web Application

Empty
An empty project template for creating ASP.NET applications. This template does not have any content in it.

Web Forms
A project template for creating ASP.NET Web Forms applications. ASP.NET Web Forms lets you build dynamic websites using a familiar drag-and-drop, event-driven model. A design surface and hundreds of controls and components let you rapidly build sophisticated, powerful UI-driven sites with data access.

MVC
A project template for creating ASP.NET MVC applications. ASP.NET MVC allows you to build applications using the Model-View-Controller architecture. ASP.NET MVC includes many features that enable fast, test-driven development for creating applications that use the latest standards.

Web API
A project template for creating RESTful HTTP services that can reach a broad range of clients including browsers and mobile devices.

Single Page Application
A project template for creating rich client side JavaScript driven HTML5 applications using ASP.NET Web API. Single Page Applications provide a rich user experience which includes client-side interactions using HTML5, CSS3, and JavaScript.

Authentication
No Authentication
Change

Add folders & core references
☐ Web Forms
☐ MVC
☐ Web API

Advanced
☑ Configure for HTTPS
☐ Docker support
(Requires Docker Desktop)
☐ Also create a project for unit tests
WebApplication2.Tests

[Back] [Create]

Choose **Empty** and click **Create**.

Other Database Topics 11-29

Once created, right-click the web application name in the **Solution Explorer** window and select **Add**, then **New Item**. Choose **Web**, then **Web Forms** and choose **Web Form**. Click **OK**.

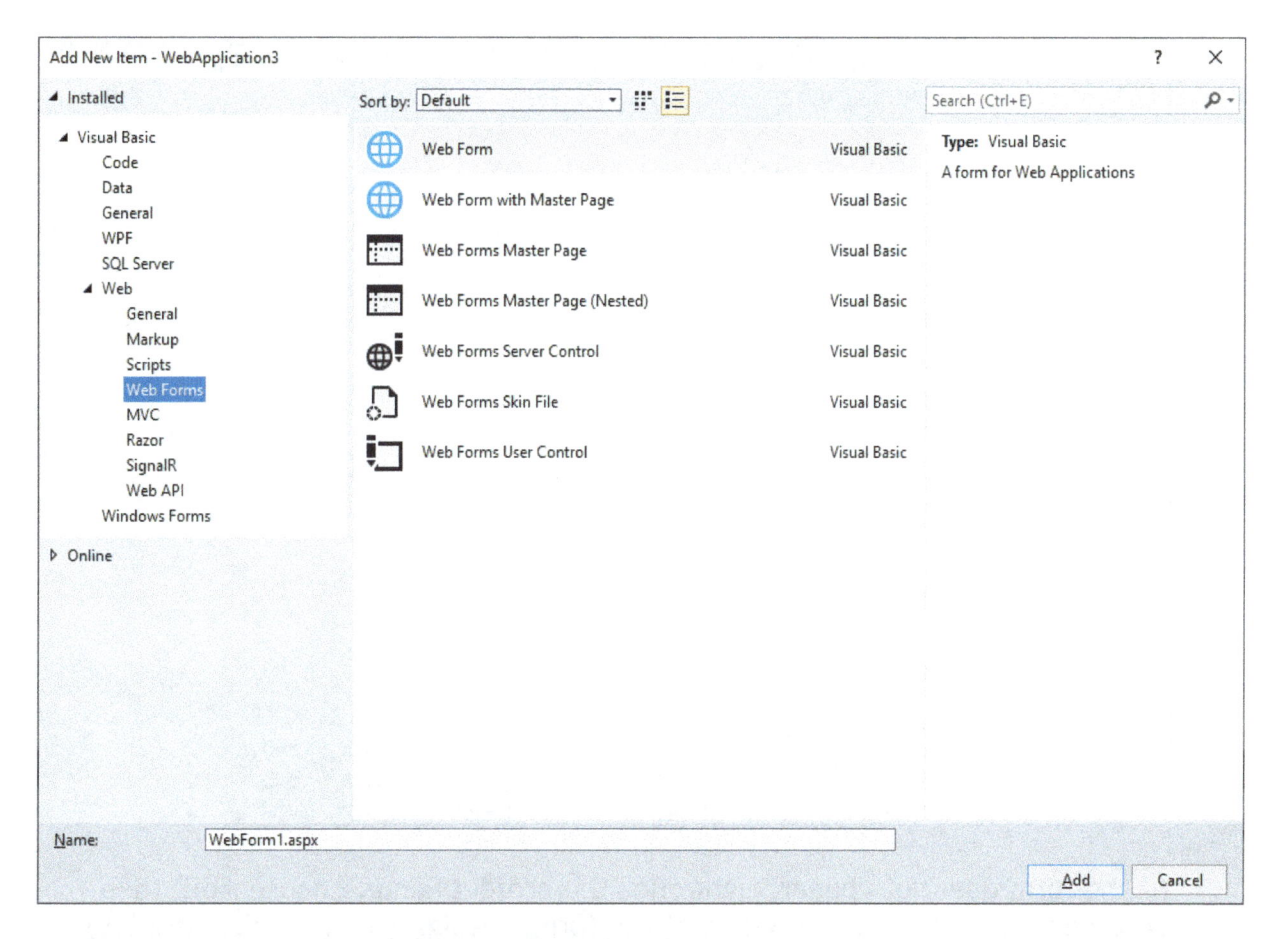

A blank web form appears (with extension **aspx**).

At this point, we can start building our first web application by placing controls on the web form and writing code for various events. A blank form will appear in the design window:

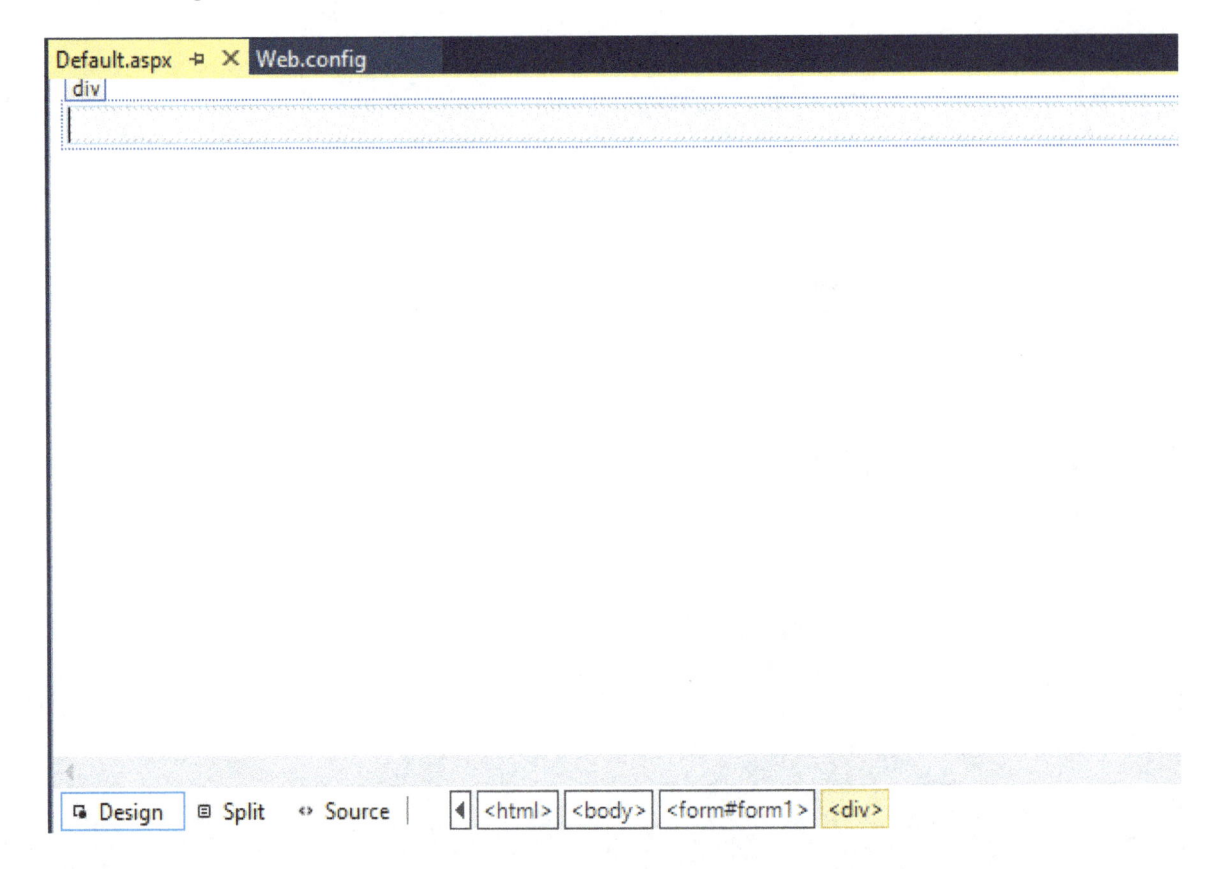

(If the form does not appear, right click the project name, choose **Add**, then **Web Form**). There are two views of the form: **Design** (the graphical display) and **Source** (the HTML code behind the form).

Let's look at the controls available and how to place them on the form.

Web Form Controls

When a web form is being edited, the controls available for placing on a web form are found in the Visual Basic toolbox. A view showing some of the resulting controls is:

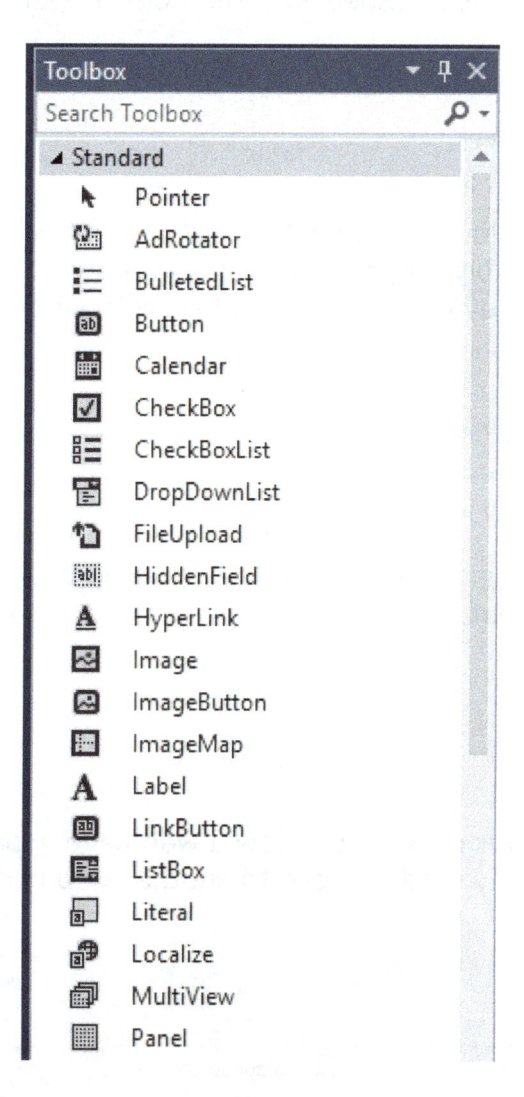

```
Toolbox
Search Toolbox
▲ Standard
    Pointer
    AdRotator
    BulletedList
    Button
    Calendar
    CheckBox
    CheckBoxList
    DropDownList
    FileUpload
    HiddenField
    HyperLink
    Image
    ImageButton
    ImageMap
    Label
    LinkButton
    ListBox
    Literal
    Localize
    MultiView
    Panel
```

The names in this menu should be familiar. The controls are similar to the Windows form controls we've used throughout this course. There are differences, however. The major differences are in the names of some properties (for example, the **ID** property is used in place of a **Name** property) and web form controls usually have far fewer events than their Windows counterparts. Let's look at some of the controls – feel free to study other controls for your particular needs.

Label Control:

A Label

The label control allows placement of formatted text information on a form (**Text** property). Font is established with the **Font** property.

TextBox Control:

abl TextBox

The text box controls allows placement of text information on a form (**Text** property). This is probably the most commonly used web form control. There is no **KeyPress** event for key trapping. Validation with web controls can be done using **validator** controls.

Button Control:

ab Button

The button control is nearly identical to the Windows counterpart. Code is written in the **Click** event.

LinkButton Control:

ab LinkButton

The link button control is clicked to follow a web page hyperlink (set with **Text** property). This is usually used to move to another web page. Code is added to the **Click** event.

ImageButton Control:

ImageButton

This control works like a button control - the user clicks it and code in the **Click** event is executed. The difference is the button displays an image (**ImageURL** property) rather than text.

Other Database Topics 11-33

HyperLink Control:

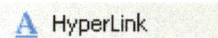

A HyperLink

The control works like the link button control except there is no Click event. Clicking this control moves the user to the link in the **Text** property.

DropDownList Control:

DropDownList

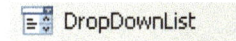

Drop down list controls are very common in web applications. Users can choose from a list of items (states, countries, product). The listed items are established using an **Items** collection and code is usually written in the **SelectedIndexChanged** event (like the Windows counterpart).

ListBox Control:

ListBox

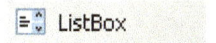

A list box control is like a drop down list with the list portion always visible. Multiple selections can be made with a list box control.

GridView Control:

GridView

The grid view control is used to list a table of data (whether a data set from a database or data generated in your web application).

CheckBox Control:

CheckBox

The check box control is used to provide a yes or no answer to a question. The **Checked** property indicates its state. Code is usually added to the **CheckedChanged** event.

CheckBoxList Control:

CheckBoxList

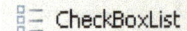

The check box list control contains a series of independent check box controls. It is a useful control for quickly adding a number of check boxes to a form. It can be used in place of a list box control for a small (less than 10) number of items. The individual controls are defined in an **Items** collection (**Text** property specifies the caption, **Selected** specifies its status).

RadioButton Control:

RadioButton

The radio button control is identical to the Windows radio button control. It is used to select from a mutually exclusive group of options. The **Checked** property indicates its state. Code is usually added to the **CheckedChanged** event.

RadioButtonList Control:

RadioButtonList

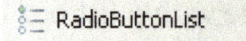

The radio button list control provides an easy way to place a group of dependent radio buttons in a web application. The individual controls are defined in an **Items** collection (**Text** property specifies the caption, **Selected** specifies its status).

Image Control:

Image

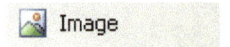

Images are useful in web applications. They give your application a polished look. The image control holds graphics. The image (set with **ImageURL** property) is usually a gif or jpg file.

By default, web controls are placed on the form in **flow mode**. This means each element is placed to the right of the previous element. This is different than the technique used in building Windows forms. We want to mimic the Windows forms behavior. To do this, choose the **Tools** menu option in the development environment and choose **Options**.

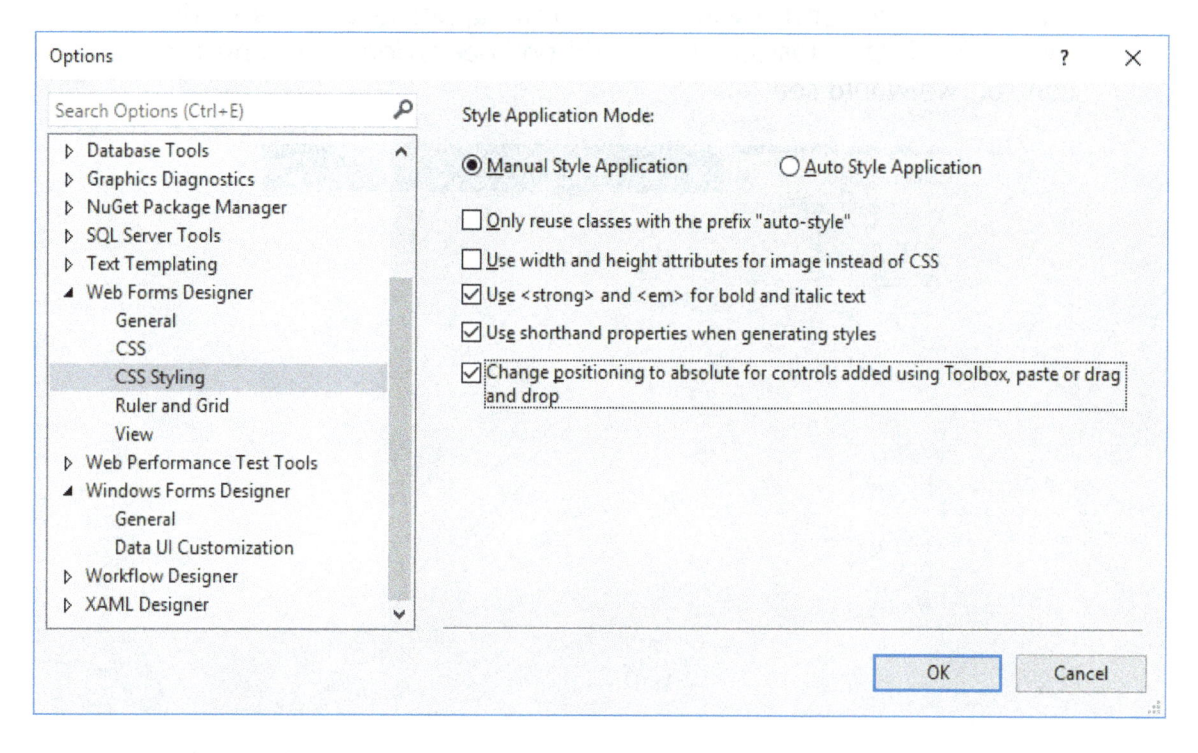

Choose the **Web Forms Designer** and **CSS Styling**. Place check next to **"Change position to absolute for controls ..."**. Then click **OK**.

With this change, there are two ways to move a web control from the toolbox to the web form:

1. Click the tool in the toolbox and hold the mouse button down. Drag the selected tool over the form. When the mouse button is released, the default size control will appear in the upper left corner of the form. This is the classic "drag and drop" operation. For a button control, we would see:

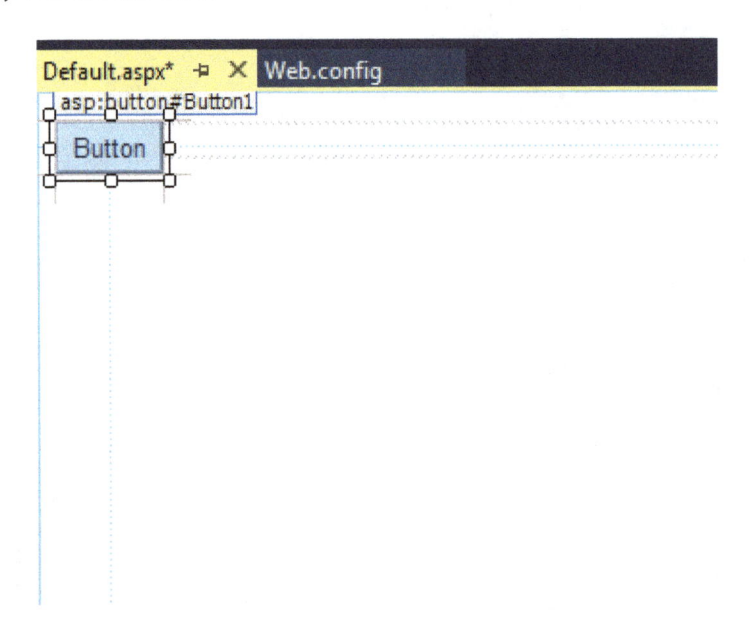

2. Double-click the tool in the toolbox and it is created with a default size on the form. It will be in the upper left corner of the form. You can then move it or resize it. Here is a button control placed on the form using this method:

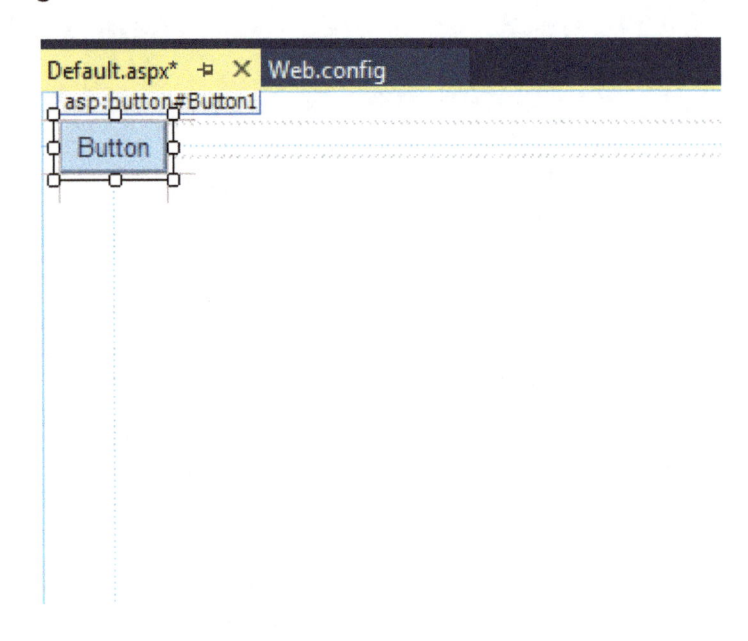

Other Database Topics   11-37

To **move** a control you have drawn, click the object in the form (a cross with arrows will appear). Now, drag the control to the new location. Release the mouse button.

To **resize** a control, click the control so that it is selected (active) and sizing handles appear. Use these handles to resize the object.

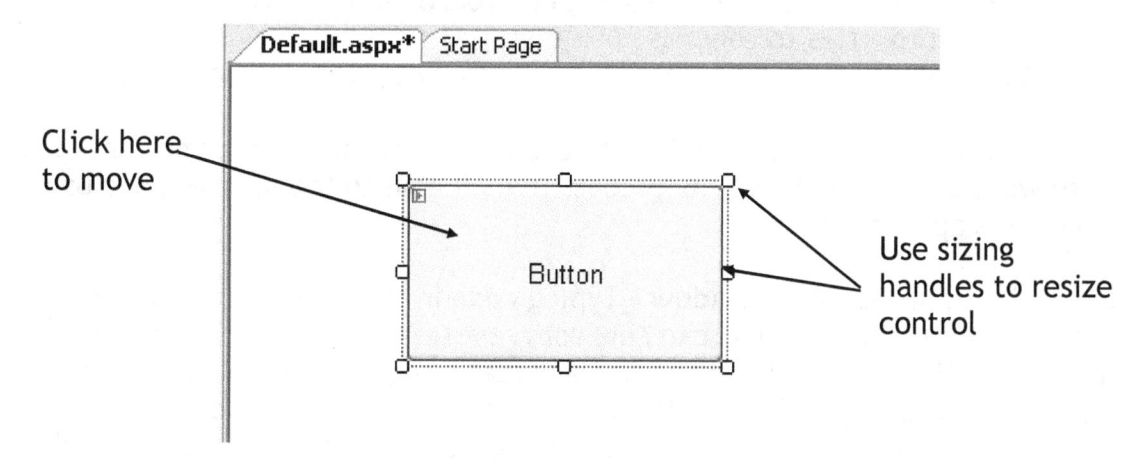

Click here to move

Use sizing handles to resize control

To delete a control, select that control so it is active (sizing handles will appear). Then, press **<Delete>** on the keyboard. Or, right-click the control. A menu will appear. Choose the **Delete** option. You can change your mind immediately after deleting a control by choosing the **Undo** option under the **Edit** menu.

Building a Web Application

To build a web application, we follow the same three steps used in building a Windows application:

1. **Draw** the user **interface** by placing controls on a web form
2. **Assign properties** to controls
3. **Write code** for control events (and perhaps write other procedures)

We've seen the web controls and how to place them on the web form. Let's see how to write code. You'll see the process is analogous to the approach we use for Windows applications.

Code is placed in the **Code Window**. Typing code in the code window is just like using any word processor. You can cut, copy, paste and delete text (use the **Edit** menu or the toolbar). You access the code window using the menu (**View**), toolbar, or by pressing <**F7**> (and there are still other ways – try double clicking a control) while the form is active. Here is the Code window for a 'blank' web application:

```
Partial Class _Default
    Inherits System.Web.UI.Page

End Class
```

The header begins with **Partial Class**. Any web form scope level declarations are placed after this line. There is a **Page_Load** event. This is similar to the Windows form **Load** event where any needed initializations are placed.

Other Database Topics 11-39

At the top of the code window are two boxes, the **object** (or control) **list** on the left and the **procedure list** on the right. Select an object and the corresponding event procedure. A blank procedure will appear in the window where you write BASIC code. Again, this is just like we do for Windows applications. That's the beauty of web forms – there is nothing new to learn about building an application.

Once your controls are in place and code is written, you can run your web application. Before running, it is a good idea to make sure your browser is up and running. Click the **Start** button in the Visual Basic toolbar and your browser should display your application (the **aspx** file). You may see this window once started:

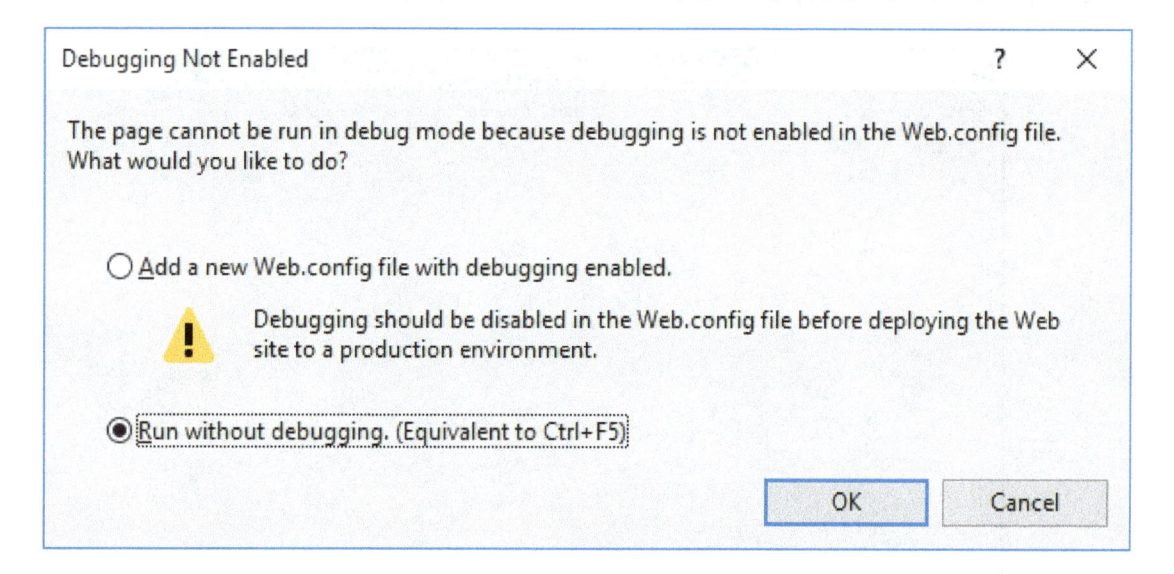

Special steps need to be taken to use the debugger with web applications. We will not take these steps. So, if this window appears, just select **Run without debugging** and click **OK**. Once running in the browser, select the **View** menu and choose **View Source** to see the actual HTML code used to produce the displayed web page.

We conclude this brief examination of web applications with a simple database example.

Example 11-3

Viewing Weather Data

We will build a simple web application that displays the **Sea02.accdb** data in a grid view control. A copy of this database is saved in the **VBDB\Access\Class 11\Example 11-3** folder. The entire example is built without writing any code.

1. Start a new web application. Place a single label control on the form. Set its **Text** property to **Seattle Weather 2002**. It should look like this:

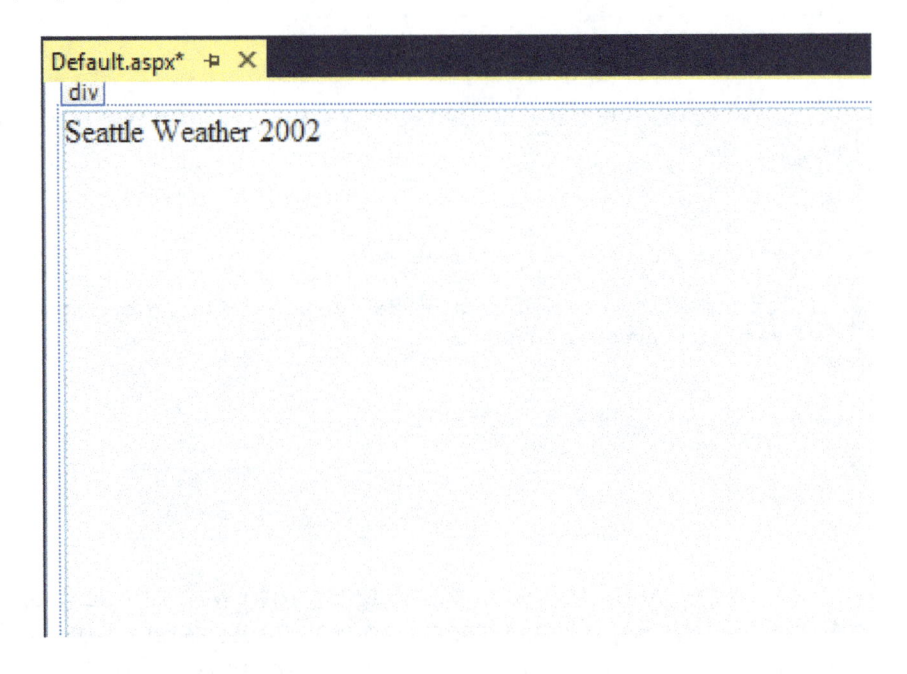

Other Database Topics   11-41

2. We will create a data source using the database file, then use a drag and drop feature to create a data grid that will display the **Weather** table in the database. Display the **Server Explorer** window (click the **View** menu item, then select **Server Explorer**). Right-click the **Data Connections** item and select **Add Connection**. This window should appear:

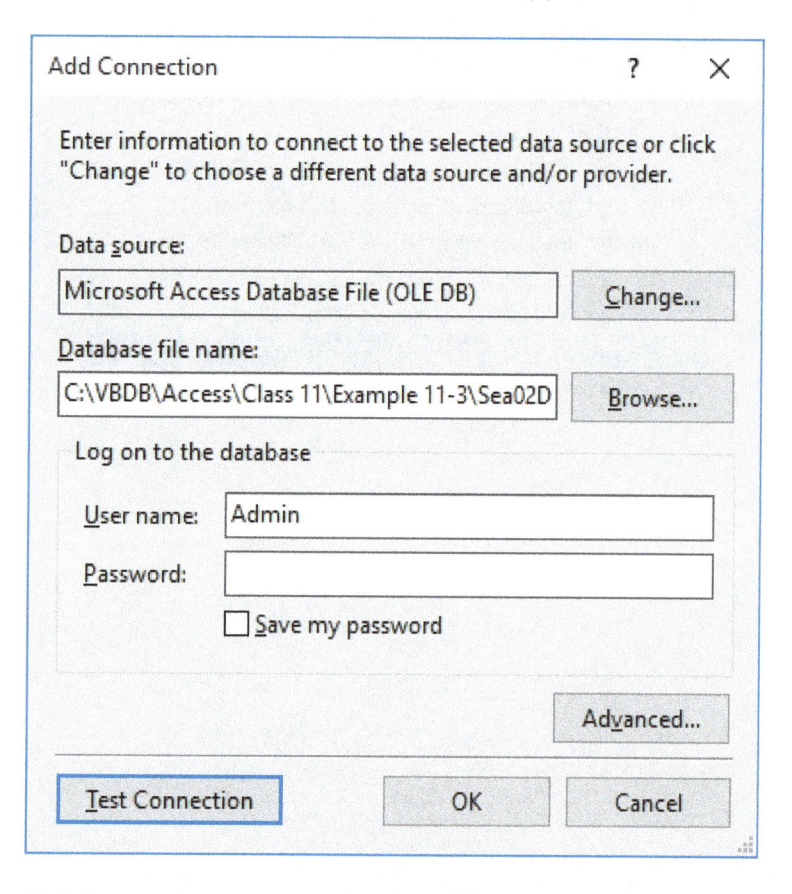

```
Add Connection                                    ?    ×

Enter information to connect to the selected data source or click
"Change" to choose a different data source and/or provider.

Data source:
┌─────────────────────────────────────────────┐  ┌──────────┐
│ Microsoft Access Database File (OLE DB)     │  │ Change...│
└─────────────────────────────────────────────┘  └──────────┘
Database file name:
┌─────────────────────────────────────────────┐  ┌──────────┐
│ C:\VBDB\Access\Class 11\Example 11-3\Sea02D │  │ Browse...│
└─────────────────────────────────────────────┘  └──────────┘
 ┌─ Log on to the database ──────────────────────────────────┐
 │                                                            │
 │  User name:  ┌────────────────────────────────────────┐   │
 │              │ Admin                                  │   │
 │              └────────────────────────────────────────┘   │
 │  Password:   ┌────────────────────────────────────────┐   │
 │              │                                        │   │
 │              └────────────────────────────────────────┘   │
 │              ☐ Save my password                           │
 └────────────────────────────────────────────────────────────┘
                                              ┌──────────┐
                                              │ Advanced.│
                                              └──────────┘
┌────────────────┐        ┌──────────┐   ┌──────────┐
│Test Connection │        │    OK    │   │  Cancel  │
└────────────────┘        └──────────┘   └──────────┘
```

Browse to **Sea02DB.accdb** and click **OK.**

3. The data connection (I've expanded it a bit) is now shown in the Server Explorer window:

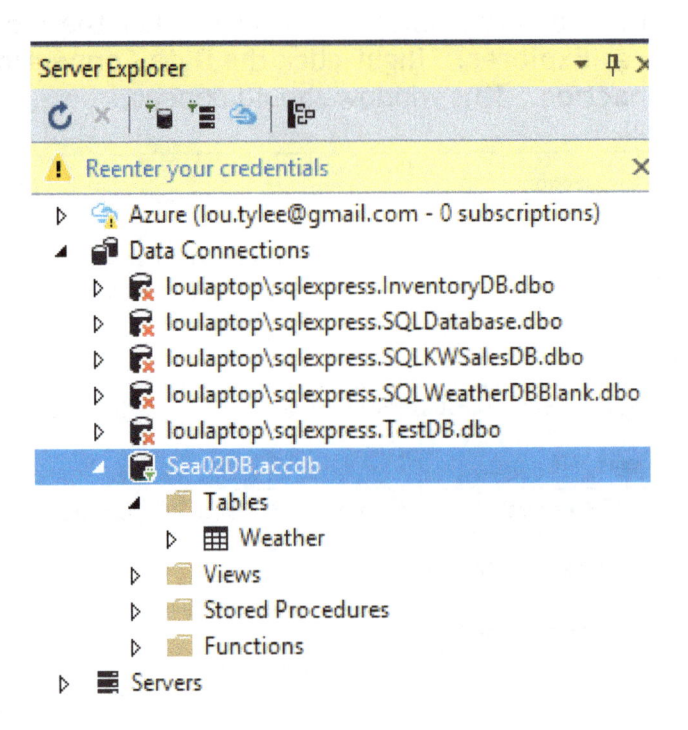

Other Database Topics   11-43

4. Drag and drop the **Weather** table from the Server Explorer window to the web form. Two things will happen. A data source will be added, as will a data grid. My web form looks like this (I've moved the grid down):

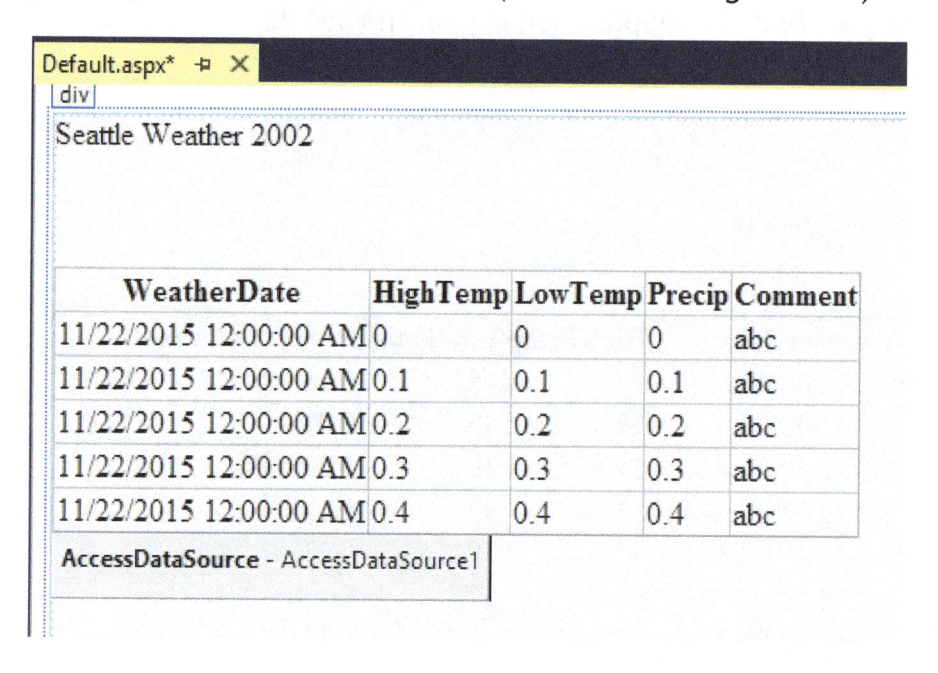

Seattle Weather 2002

WeatherDate	HighTemp	LowTemp	Precip	Comment
11/22/2015 12:00:00 AM	0	0	0	abc
11/22/2015 12:00:00 AM	0.1	0.1	0.1	abc
11/22/2015 12:00:00 AM	0.2	0.2	0.2	abc
11/22/2015 12:00:00 AM	0.3	0.3	0.3	abc
11/22/2015 12:00:00 AM	0.4	0.4	0.4	abc

AccessDataSource - AccessDataSource1

5. Save your web application. (This application is saved in the **Example 11-3** folder in the **VBDB\Access\Class 11** folder.) At this point, if things all work well, you can click the **Start** button (remember to run without debugging) and see your first web application appear in your default browser:

Seattle Weather 2002

WeatherDate	HighTemp	LowTemp	Precip	Comment
1/1/2002 12:00:00 AM	52	45	0.14	
1/2/2002 12:00:00 AM	53	45	0.27	
1/3/2002 12:00:00 AM	54	46	0.22	
1/4/2002 12:00:00 AM	53	42	0.14	
1/5/2002 12:00:00 AM	48	39	0.11	
1/6/2002 12:00:00 AM	46	37	0	
1/7/2002 12:00:00 AM	47	41	0.17	
1/8/2002 12:00:00 AM	50	42	0.06	
1/9/2002 12:00:00 AM	51	44	0.01	
1/10/2002 12:00:00 AM	50	44	0.21	
1/11/2002 12:00:00 AM	50	46	0	
1/12/2002 12:00:00 AM	50	47	0.11	
1/13/2002 12:00:00 AM	55	46	0.01	
1/14/2002 12:00:00 AM	48	39	0	
1/15/2002 12:00:00 AM	50	44	0	

We did this all with no code!

Obviously, this is a very brief introduction to web applications with databases, but it should give you some idea of the power of such applications.

Summary

The Visual Basic and Databases course is complete. At this point, you have significant programming skills for using Visual Basic with desktop (single-user) applications. Yet, even after over 700 pages, we've only just begun to look at all the capabilities of Visual Basic in working with databases.

Good programmers never stop learning. Study the material in this course until you are comfortable with it. Throughout this course, suggestions were given for extending your knowledge base. Do it! Extend your knowledge to multiple-user, networked environments. The new world out there is the Internet. Study how to deploy database applications on the Internet. There are lots of good advanced books available addressing these topics and more. And, perhaps, some day we'll have another course delving deeper into the world of database programming with Visual Basic.

Example 11-4

The Last Database Project

We end all of our courses with this same general project. Design a database management application in Visual Basic that everyone on the planet wants to buy. Build a world-class interface. Thoroughly debug and test your application. Create a distribution package. Find a distributor or distribute it yourself through your newly created 'dot-com' company. Become fabulously wealthy. Remember those who made it all possible by rewarding them with jobs and stock options.

More Self-Study or Instructor-Led Computer Programming Tutorials by Kidware Software

ORACLE JAVA PROGRAMMING TUTORIALS

Java™ For Kids is a beginning programming tutorial consisting of 10 chapters explaining (in simple, easy-to-follow terms) how to build a Java application. Students learn about project design, object-oriented programming, console applications, graphics applications and many elements of the Java language. Numerous examples are used to demonstrate every step in the building process. The projects include a number guessing game, a card game, an allowance calculator, a state capitals game, Tic-Tac-Toe, a simple drawing program, and even a basic video game. Designed for kids ages 12 and up.

Beginning Java™ is a semester long "beginning" programming tutorial consisting of 10 chapters explaining (in simple, easy-to-follow terms) how to build a Java application. The tutorial includes several detailed computer projects for students to build and try. These projects include a number guessing game, card game, allowance calculator, drawing program, state capitals game, and a couple of video games like Pong. We also include several college prep bonus projects including a loan calculator, portfolio manager, and checkbook balancer. Designed for students age 15 and up.

Learn Java™ GUI Applications is a 9 lesson Tutorial covering object-oriented programming concepts, using an integrated development environment to create and test Java projects, building and distributing GUI applications, understanding and using the Swing control library, exception handling, sequential file access, graphics, multimedia, advanced topics such as printing, and help system authoring. Our Beginning Java or Java For Kids tutorial is a pre-requisite for this tutorial

Programming Games with Java™ is a semester long "intermediate" programming tutorial consisting of 10 chapters explaining (in simple, easy-to-follow terms) how to build a Visual C# Video Games. The games built are non-violent, family-friendly and teach logical thinking skills. Students will learn how to program the following Visual C# video games: Safecracker, Tic Tac Toe, Match Game, Pizza Delivery, and Moon Landing. This intermediate level self-paced tutorial can be used at home or school. The tutorial is simple enough for kids yet engaging enough for beginning adults. Our Learn Java GUI Applications tutorial is a required pre-requisite for this tutorial.

Java™ Homework Projects is a Java GUI Swing tutorial covering object-oriented programming concepts. It explains (in simple, easy-to-follow terms) how to build Java GUI project to use around the home. Students learn about project design, the Java Swing controls, many elements of the Java language, and how to distribute finished projects. The projects built include a Dual-Mode Stopwatch, Flash Card Math Quiz, Multiple Choice Exam, Blackjack Card Game, Weight Monitor, Home Inventory Manager and a Snowball Toss Game. Our Learn Java GUI Applications tutorial is a pre-requisite for this tutorial

MICROSOFT SMALL BASIC PROGRAMMING TUTORIALS

Small Basic For Kids is an illustrated introduction to computer programming that provides an interactive, self-paced tutorial to the new Small Basic programming environment. The book consists of 30 short lessons that explain how to create and run a Small Basic program. Elementary students learn about program design and many elements of the Small Basic language. Numerous examples are used to demonstrate every step in the building process. The tutorial also includes two complete games (Hangman and Pizza Zapper) for students to build and try. Designed for kids ages 8+.

The Beginning Microsoft Small Basic Programming Tutorial is a self-study first semester "beginner" programming tutorial consisting of 11 chapters explaining (in simple, easy-to-follow terms) how to write Microsoft Small Basic programs. Numerous examples are used to demonstrate every step in the building process. The last chapter of this tutorial shows you how four different Small Basic games could port to Visual Basic, Visual C# and Java. This beginning level self-paced tutorial can be used at home or at school. The tutorial is simple enough for kids ages 10+ yet engaging enough for adults.

Basic Computer Games - Small Basic Edition is a re-make of the classic BASIC COMPUTER GAMES book originally edited by David H. Ahl. It contains 100 of the original text based BASIC games that inspired a whole generation of programmers. Now these classic BASIC games have been re-written in Microsoft Small Basic for a new generation to enjoy! The new Small Basic games look and act like the original text based games. The book includes all the original spaghetti code and GOTO commands!

Programming Home Projects with Microsoft Small Basic is a self-paced programming tutorial explains (in simple, easy-to-follow terms) how to build Small Basic Windows applications. Students learn about program design, Small Basic objects, many elements of the Small Basic language, and how to debug and distribute finished programs. Sequential file input and output is also introduced. The projects built include a Dual-Mode Stopwatch, Flash Card Math Quiz, Multiple Choice Exam, Blackjack Card Game, Weight Monitor, Home Inventory Manager and a Snowball Toss Game.

The Developer's Reference Guide to Microsoft Small Basic While developing all the different Microsoft Small Basic tutorials we found it necessary to write The Developer's Reference Guide to Microsoft Small Basic. The Developer's Reference Guide to Microsoft Small Basic is over 500 pages long and includes over 100 Small Basic programming examples for you to learn from and include in your own Microsoft Small Basic programs. It is a detailed reference guide for new developers.

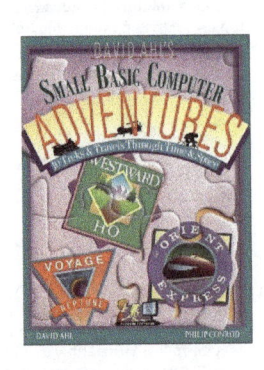

David Ahl's Small Basic Computer Adventures is a Microsoft Small Basic re-make of the classic *Basic Computer Games* programming *book* originally written by David H. Ahl. This new book includes the following classic adventure simulations; Marco Polo, Westward Ho!, The Longest Automobile Race, The Orient Express, Amelia Earhart: Around the World Flight, Tour de France, Subway Scavenger, Hong Kong Hustle, and Voyage to Neptune. Learn how to program these classic computer simulations in Microsoft Small Basic.

MICROSOFT VISUAL BASIC & VISUAL C# PROGRAMMING TUTORIALS

LEARN VISUAL BASIC is a comprehensive college level programming tutorial covering object-oriented programming, the Visual Basic integrated development environment, building and distributing Windows applications using the Windows Installer, exception handling, sequential file access, graphics, multimedia, advanced topics such as web access, printing, and HTML help system authoring. The tutorial also introduces database applications (using ADO .NET) and web applications (using ASP.NET).

VISUAL BASIC AND DATABASES is a tutorial that provides a detailed introduction to using Visual Basic for accessing and maintaining databases for desktop applications. Topics covered include: database structure, database design, Visual Basic project building, ADO .NET data objects (connection, data adapter, command, data table), data bound controls, proper interface design, structured query language (SQL), creating databases using Access, SQL Server and ADOX, and database reports. Actual projects developed include a book tracking system, a sales invoicing program, a home inventory system and a daily weather monitor.

LEARN VISUAL C# is a comprehensive college level computer programming tutorial covering object-oriented programming, the Visual C# integrated development environment and toolbox, building and distributing Windows applications (using the Windows Installer), exception handling, sequential file input and output, graphics, multimedia effects (animation and sounds), advanced topics such as web access, printing, and HTML help system authoring. The tutorial also introduces database applications (using ADO .NET) and web applications (using ASP.NET).

VISUAL C# AND DATABASES is a tutorial that provides a detailed introduction to using Visual C# for accessing and maintaining databases for desktop applications. Topics covered include: database structure, database design, Visual C# project building, ADO .NET data objects (connection, data adapter, command, data table), data bound controls, proper interface design, structured query language (SQL), creating databases using Access, SQL Server and ADOX, and database reports. Actual projects developed include a book tracking system, a sales invoicing program, a home inventory system and a daily weather monitor.

CPSIA information can be obtained
at www.ICGtesting.com
Printed in the USA
LVHW062334030620
657291LV00007B/180